Australia

BUG Australia

Fourth edition – October 2008

Produced by **BUG Travel Publishing Pty Ltd** for **Explore Australia Publishing Pty Ltd**
2 Coastal Rise, Kilcunda, VIC 3995, Australia
www.bug.co.uk

85 High Street, Prahran, VIC 3181, Australia
www.hardiegrant.com.au/explore_aus/

Printed in China by C & C Offset Printing Co. Ltd

ISBN 978 1 74117 263 8

Cover photos
Front cover photo: Road sign, Nullarbor Plain, SA
Front cover credit: © iStockphoto/Linda & Colin McKie *(**website** www.istockphoto.com)*

Back cover photos: Backpackers 4WDing on Fraser Island, QLD © iStockphoto/bamse009; Oodnadatta Track, SA © iStockphoto/iTobi; Kangaroo road sign, NSW © iStockphoto/Karen Moller; Eastern grey kangaroo © iStockphoto/Jeremy Edwards; Surfers at Bondi Beach, Sydney, NSW © iStockphoto/pxlar8

Map credits
Maps are created by BUG Travel Publishing Pty Ltd using data and base maps supplied by the following organisations: Department of Lands (NSW); Department of Infrastructure, Planning and Environment (NT); Department of Natural Resources & Water (QLD); Openstreetmap.org (ACT, NSW, QLD, TAS & WA); RAA (SA & NT) and TUMAS (VIC). Full map acknowlegements are on page 439.

Disclaimer
This book is current at the time of writing and information may change after the publication date. Every effort has been made to make this book as complete and accurate as possible. However, there may be mistakes, both typographical and in content.

The reviews in this book are the opinion of the BUG researcher at the time of reviewing. This information is to be used as a general guide and readers should be aware that prices, opening hours, facilities and standards may change over time.

There are many factors that may cause prices to change and establishments reviewed and listed in this book to close down or alter the services that they offer. Many hostels may also change their prices throughout the year to take advantage of variations in seasonal demand.

This book is not intended to be used as a sole source of information, but rather to complement existing sources of information such as word of mouth, travel brochures, timetables, travel magazines and other guidebooks. You are urged to read all the available material and talk to hostel staff and other travellers to learn as much as you can about your travel options.

Like anything in life, travel entails certain risks. BUG Travel Publishing Pty Ltd, Explore Australia Publishing Pty Ltd and the authors shall have neither liability nor responsibility to any person or entity with respect to any loss or damage caused, or alleged to have been caused, directly or indirectly, by the information contained within this book.

BUG provides honest and independent travel advice. BUG Travel Publishing Pty Ltd does not receive any payment in exchange for listing any establishment and BUG's researchers never accept free accommodation in exchange for favourable reviews.

Contents

Map Contents

Australia

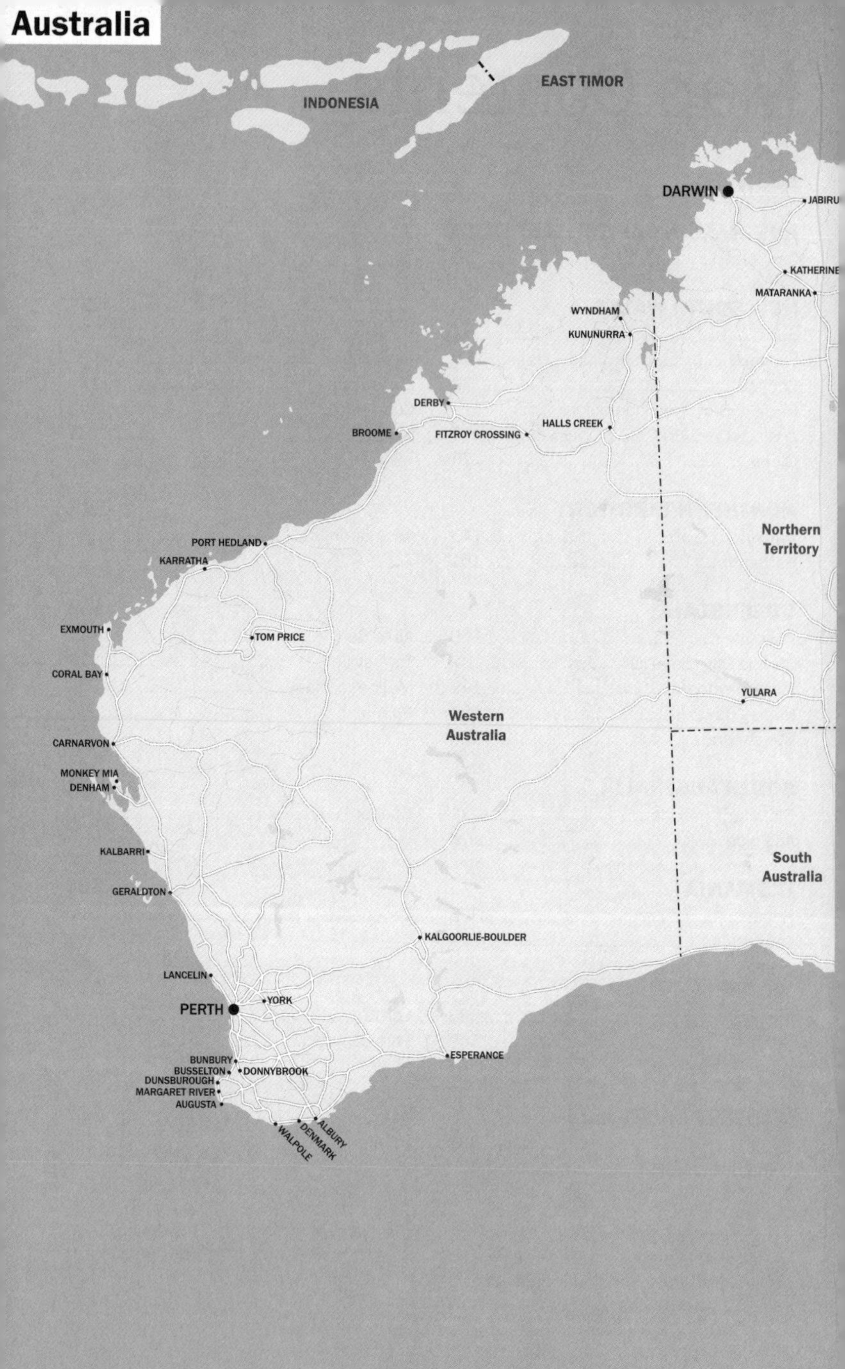

INDONESIA
EAST TIMOR
DARWIN
JABIRU
KATHERINE
MATARANKA
WYNDHAM
KUNUNURRA
DERBY
BROOME
FITZROY CROSSING
HALLS CREEK
PORT HEDLAND
KARRATHA
Northern Territory
EXMOUTH
TOM PRICE
CORAL BAY
YULARA
Western Australia
CARNARVON
MONKEY MIA
DENHAM
KALBARRI
South Australia
GERALDTON
KALGOORLIE-BOULDER
LANCELIN
YORK
PERTH
ESPERANCE
BUNBURY
BUSSELTON
DONNYBROOK
DUNSBUROUGH
MARGARET RIVER
AUGUSTA
WALPOLE
DENMARK
ALBURY

PAPUA NEW GUINEA
COOKTOWN
PORT DOUGLAS
CAIRNS
KARUMBA
NORMANTON
INNISFAIL
TULLY
MISSION BEACH
CARDWELL
TENNANT CREEK
Queensland
TOWNSVILLE
AYR
CHARTERS TOWERS
MT ISA
JULIA CREEK
RICHMOND
BOWEN
AIRLIE BEACH
PROSERPINE
HUGHENDEN
MACKAY
WINTON
ALICE SPRINGS
LONGREACH
YEPPOON
ROCKHAMPTON
GLADSTONE
BUNDABERG
HERVEY BAY
MARYBOROUGH
CHARLEVILLE
ROMA
RAINBOW BEACH
OODNADATTA
NOOSA
MAROOCHYDORE
CALOUNDRA
TOWOOMBA
BRISBANE
COOBER PEDY
WILLIAM CREEK
GOLD COAST
COOLANGATTA
MURWILLUMBAH
MARREE
LISMORE
BYRON BAY
BALLINA
BOURKE
GLEN INNES
ROXBY DOWNS
GRAFTON
WOOMERA
PARACHILNA
ARMIDALE
COFFS HARBOUR
CEDUNA
HAWKER
BROKEN HILL
TAMWORTH
QUORN
PORT AUGUSTA
PORT MACQUARIE
New South Wales
DUBBO
SCONE
WYHALLA
TAREE
FORSTER
PORT STEPHENS
ORANGE
BATHURST
NEWCASTLE
RENMARK
MILDURA
BERRI
COWRA
PORT LINCOLN
ADELAIDE
HAY
GRIFFITH
SYDNEY
GOULBURN
WOLLONGONG
VICTOR HARBOR
WAGGA WAGGA
KIAMA
NOWRA
SWAN HILL
CANBERRA
ULLADULLA
ALBURY
ACT
ECHUCA
BATEMANS BAY
NARRACOORTE
HORSHAM
BENDIGO
ROBE
BRIGHT
ARARAT
BEGA
MERIMBULA
BALLARAT
EDEN
MOUNT GAMBIER
MELBOURNE
PORTLAND
GEELONG
PORT FAIRY
ANGLESEA
LAKES ENTRANCE
WARRNAMBOOL
FOSTER
Victoria
APOLLO BAY
STANLEY
BURNIE
DEVONPORT
GEORGE TOWN
BRIDPORT
LAUNCESTON
ST HELENS
QUEENSTOWN
STRAHAN
BICHENO
Tasmania
TRIABUNNA
HOBART
PORT ARTHUR

About the authors

Isak Ladegård

Isak was born in Oslo and stayed in Norway until he discovered the joys of travelling as an 18 year old, bumming around Europe with a rail pass. The following years were dominated by travels in South America, the Middle-East, Asia and Australia. He works as a freelance-journalist and has written plenty of travel articles. This is his first book for BUG.

Isak researched the top end of the Northern Territory, southern South Australia and Western Australia.

Thomas Maresca

Thomas Maresca is from New York City, where he worked for several years as a freelance writer for television, magazines and newspapers. He left the US to travel in February 2007, and has spent time in 10 countries since. He's currently living and writing in Ho Chi Minh City but thinks fondly of meat pies, beaches and clean air, and daydreams about going back down under soon.

Thomas wrote about Melbourne's hostels.

Tiffany Miller

Tiffany is a freelance travel writer living on the Big Island of Hawaii. She began travelling on surf trips in the South Pacific, and soon found herself backpacking around the world. Although her writing career began while living in Europe, the Pacific always calls her home, and updating BUG Australia was a very rewarding challenge. The best parts of her east coast road trip were the warm water, laid-back lifestyle, and the fertile rainforests of far north Queensland.

Tiffany researched the coastal areas of New South Wales and Queensland.

Tim Uden

Tim is BUG's managing editor. He first started backpacking in 1989 when he travelled around Europe with a rail pass and he has made numerous around the world trips since then. He got hooked on travel writing while on a working holiday in the UK where he edited a travel magazine. After returning home to Australia he worked for a few years before setting off on his own to start BUG. Tim lives in the seaside village of Kilcunda, Australia with his wife and two cats, and travels as much as he can.

Tim researched outback Northern Territory and South Australia, the Australian Capital Territory, southern New South Wales, Victoria and Tasmania.

Welcome

Welcome to BUG

BUG is the Backpackers' Ultimate Guide and we believe this is the best guidebook available for anyone backpacking around Australia. We set out to publish a guidebook dedicated solely for backpackers (independent budget travellers). You won't find any information about fancy hotels in this book and because of this we can better concentrate on giving you honest and detailed information about hostels and budget travel options across Australia. Compare us with other guides, you'll find that we have more details on more hostels for any given destination.

This is the fourth edition of BUG Australia. Over time BUG will grow to fill a major niche in the guidebook market, but we don't plan on emulating other guidebook publishers and bringing out hundreds of different titles. Instead we will stick to a small number of guidebooks and fill them with accurate and honest information.

How to use this book

We've travelled extensively and know what should be in a guidebook and what you can find out for yourself. We've kept this in mind when putting this book together to ensure that it's packed with loads of useful information and not weighed down with stuff you don't need.

The book won't bore you with trivial details such as history or politics, which often turn out to be just a soapbox for the author to air his or her views. Instead of making you lug around an extra 100 or more pages we jump straight into the useful stuff.

The Essentials chapter has information on passports and visas, discount cards, money and keeping in touch. Boring, but important things that you need to know before you arrive.

The next chapter is Getting Around – we don't tell you how to get to Australia because that's what travel agents are for. The Getting Around chapter has the low-down on transport options in Australia including details on bus and train passes, hitchhiking, flying and driving. Read this before you go to buy your ticket so you know whether you're getting a good deal when the travel agent tries to sell you a travel pass.

After these introductory chapters it's straight into the destination chapters. There's a chapter for each state, which is organised geographically.

When you arrive in a new destination you generally want to find a place to stay, take your backpack off and start exploring. We have put details on local transport and accommodation at the start of each destination guide, so you can choose where you want to stay and find your way there.

Once you've checked into a hostel you'll find that the staff behind the front desk are experts on the local area and will be able to help you with any little questions such as where to do your laundry, check your email or grab a bite to eat. For this reason we cut out the crap such as restaurant reviews and shopping information to make room for much more comprehensive accommodation reviews, although we will still point you in the right direction if you're hungry.

We have organised the information on accommodation and attractions so that every listing is followed by the address, a list of which bus or tram routes stop nearby, telephone number, website address, prices and opening hours (reception hours for accommodation listings).

A lot of hostels give discounts to holders of Nomads, VIP or HI/YHA hostel cards. When we list accommodation prices the discounted price is shown after the full price as follows: Dorm bed $25 ($23 HI/YHA, VIP). Just because a hostel offers a discount to someone holding a card from a particular hostel organisation is no indication that that hostel is affiliated with it. Where a price range is specified, for example: (Dorm bed $22-28), the low price is often the cheapest bed off-season and the high price the most expensive in the peak season. In a lot of hostels the cheapest beds are in the largest dormitories and the more expensive ones in the small dorms.

In BUG, we define a dormitory bed (or dorm bed) as any bed in a room that you share with other people who you are not travelling with. In Australia most dorms have four to six beds. We quote the price per person for a dorm bed and the price per room for single, double and twin rooms.

We classify a double room as a private room with one double, queen or king-size bed in it. A twin room is a private room with two single beds.

Some small hostels don't keep regular reception hours, in this case we don't list any hours. If the reception is unattended there is usually a phone number to call to speak with the manager who usually isn't far away. If you're arriving late it's a good idea to call in advance to arrange a bed for the night, in some cases you may be able to check in after reception hours if this is arranged in advance.

Each hostel review includes symbols indicating that hostel's facilities. These symbols are:

- Off street parking
- Secure off-street parking
- Wheelchair access
- Lockers for each dormitory bed
- TV lounge
- Kitchen
- Laundry
- Bar
- Swimming pool
- Tennis court
- Free use of bicycles
- Women only hostel (no male guests allowed)
- No alcohol allowed
- All indoor areas smoke-free
- Not all dormitories can be locked

BUG's hostel ratings

We wanted to provide the most comprehensive resource that could quickly describe a hostel while also providing more in depth information on hostels than any other guidebook. To achieve this we set about creating our own star rating system that highlighted the maintenance and cleanliness, facilities, atmosphere and character and security of each hostel while also providing an overall rating.

BUG's hostel reviewers fill out a two page form that collects information about various features, which are then rated to calculate that hostel's star rating. In addition to determining an objective star rating, the BUG hostel reviewer also writes a more subjective review of each hostel.

The individual ratings for particular characteristics are a handy way for travellers to choose a hostel based on what is important to them. For instance if a place with a great atmosphere is more important to you than cleanliness and maintenance, then you can just look at the atmosphere & character star rating rather than the other ratings.

When we set about creating our hostel rating system, we used what we believe are the best hostels as a benchmark for being awarded five stars. For instance we looked at the hostel we thought offered the most facilities to calculate our scoring system for this category. We did the same for security, cleanliness and atmosphere. It is very rare to find a hostel that excels in each area and because of this we have yet to award a full five stars to any hostel but any place with an overall score of four stars or higher can be considered outstanding.

The 'cleanliness and maintenance' rating shows how clean and well maintained the hostel is. A brand new purpose built place should score five stars and recently renovated hostels shouldn't be too far behind. The 'facilities' rating indicates the extent, but not necessarily the quality, of the facilities and amenities. The 'atmosphere and character' rating combines the charm of the building with the fun factor of staying at the hostel. The 'security' rating indicates the degree of security precautions that the hostel has taken.

The overall rating is calculated by averaging the other four ratings, but this is weighted to give priority to the more important aspects of the hostel

There are other rating systems out there. AAA Tourism, an independent rating agency that is affiliated with the Australian state motoring organisations, also produces a star rating system for hostels. The AAA star rating focuses mostly on the hostel's facilities but very little emphasis is placed on the hostel's atmosphere or character. The main differences are that we developed our rating system from the ground up as a hostel rating (rather than an adaptation of a hotel or motel rating), we rate every hostel and the BUG score is broken into categories so you can see how the overall score is awarded. Unlike the AAA Tourism score, hostels don't choose to be rated and we certainly don't charge them for a rating or give advance warning that we are coming so they can make their hostel look nice for us.

We use the same criteria to rate hostels regardless of where they are in the world. No other hostel rating system has the same international consistency and you can be confident that a 3½ star hostel in Barcelona will offer a similar standard of accommodation as a hostel in Brisbane that has the same BUG rating.

Help keep us up-to-date

Although everything in this guidebook is current at the time of publication, it is impossible to keep everything current for the entire life of this guide.

If you find something wrong please let us know so we can keep everyone up-to-date; you can email us at tim@bug.co.uk or fax us at +61 3 5678 7033 (or (03) 5678 7033 from within Australia). If you think one our hostel reviews is way off track, you can write your own review on our website (www.bug.co.uk).

We update our website with the correct details as soon as we know them. Check our website (www.bugaustralia.com or www.bug.co.uk) for up-to-date facts.

Visit us on the Web

BUG started out in 1997 with a small website about budget travel in Europe and we have grown to become an extensive network of websites that can be accessed from our homepage (www.bug.co.uk). This guide is online (www.bugaustralia.com) and features interactive hostel reviews where you can write your own reviews of hostels all over Australia (and throughout the world). There are also forums where you can share travel tips with other travellers.

If you're also planning on visiting New Zealand and other Pacific islands such as Fiji or Hawaii; then take a look at BUG Pacific (www.bugpacific.com). BUG America (www.bugamerica.com) is handy if you're visiting the Americas and BUG Europe (www.bugeurope.com) is useful if you're planning to travel in Europe.

Travel Essentials

Information Centres

The Australian Tourism Commission *(**website** www.australia.com)* promotes Australian tourism internationally and operates a network of information centres around the world.

Frankfurt
Neue Mainzerstraße 22, D 60311 Frankfurt/Main
☎ *(069) 274 00622*

London
Australia Centre, Australia House, 6th Floor, Melbourne Place/Strand, London WC2B 4LG
☎ *(020) 7438 4601*

Los Angeles
6100 Center Drive, Suite 1150, Los Angeles CA 90045
☎ *(310) 695 3200*

Each state and territory also maintains its own department promoting tourism, each with its own network of tourist information centres. The main information centres are listed below:

Australian Capital Territory (Canberra Tourism)
330 Northbourne Avenue, Dickson
30, 31, 32, 33, 51, 52, 56, 251, 252, 256
☎ *(02) 6205 0044 or 1300 554 114*
Website *www.canberratourism.com.au*
Open *Mon-Fri 9am-5pm, Sat-Sun 9am-4pm*

New South Wales (Tourism NSW)
Palm Grove, Darling Harbour, Sydney
Convention *Town Hall*
☎ *(02) 9281 0788*
Website *www.visitnsw.com*
Open *10am-6pm daily*

Northern Territory (NT Tourism Commission)
43 Mitchell Street, Darwin
4, 5, 6, 8, 10
☎ *13 61 10*
Website *www.ntholidays.com*
Open *Mon-Fri 8.30am-5pm, Sat 9am-3pm, Sun 10am-3pm*

Queensland (Tourism Queensland)
30 Makerston Street, Brisbane
Roma Street
☎ *13 88 30*
Website *www.queensland-holidays.com.au*
Open *Mon-Fri 7.30am-7.30pm, Sat 8am-4pm, Sun 9am-5pm*

South Australia (SA Tourism Commission)
18 King William Street, Adelaide
☎ *1300 764 227 or (08) 8303 2220*
Website *www.southaustralia.com*
Open *Mon-Fri 8.30am-5pm, Sat-Sun 9am-2pm*

Tasmania (Tourism Tasmania)
20 Davey Street, Hobart
☎ *(03) 6230 8233*
Website *www.discovertasmania.com.au*
Open *Mon-Fri 8.30am-5pm*

Victoria (Tourism Victoria)
Federation Square, corner Finders Street & St Kilda Road, Melbourne
1, 3, 5, 6, 8, 16, 19, 22, 25, 48, 57, 59, 64, 67, 68, 72, 75, city circle
Flinders Street
☎ *13 28 42 or (03) 9658 9658*
Website *www.visitvictoria.com*
Open *9am-6pm daily*

Western Australia (WA Tourism Commission)
Forrest Place (corner Wellington Street), Perth
☎ *1300 361 351 or (08) 9483 1111*
Website *www.westernaustralia.net*
Open *Jan-Apr Mon-Thu 8.30am-6pm, Fri 8.30am-7pm, Sat 9.30am-4.30pm, Sun noon-4.30pm; May-Aug Mon-Thu 8.30am-5.30pm, Fri 8.30am-6pm, Sat 9.30am-4.30pm, Sun noon-4.30pm; Sep-Dec Mon-Thu 8.30am-6pm, Fri 8.30am-7pm, Sat 9.30am-4.30pm, Sun noon-4.30pm*

Entry Requirements

Everyone visiting Australia needs a valid passport and all travellers except New Zealanders require a visa.

Passports

It is essential that your passport does not expire within six months of entering Australia or you will not be allowed into the country – even if you're only planning on staying a few days.

You should allow plenty of time to apply for a new passport, although some passport agencies will rush your application for an additional cost.

Most travellers apply for a passport at the passport agency in their home country, but people living outside their country of citizenship should apply through their nearest embassy or consulate.

Canada

To obtain a passport you will need the following: two identical passport photos; at least one document, such as a drivers' licence, to prove your identity; proof of Canadian citizenship; any previous Canadian passport, certificate of identity or refugee travel document issued to you in the last five years; a completed application form and the application fee. A Canadian passport costs CDN$87-92 and is usually issued within two weeks if you apply in person and up to a month if you apply by mail or through an agent.

You can either apply at your local passport office or by sending your application forms to the main passport office in Gatineau, Québec.

Passport Canada, 22 de Varennes Building, 22 rue de Varennes, Gatineau Québec J8T 8R1, Canada
☎ *1 800 567 6868 or (819) 997 8338*
Website *www.ppt.gc.ca*
Open *Mon-Fri 8.30am-4.30pm*

Ireland

Passport application forms are available from all Garda stations and from Post Offices that provide the Passport Express service. Completed application forms should be sent to the passport office in Cork (if you live in the counties of Clare, Cork, Kerry, Limerick, Tipperary or Waterford) or Dublin (if you live elsewhere in Ireland, including Northern Ireland). Passports should be issued within 10 working days.

A passport application should include two passport photos (which have been signed and certified) as well as proof of citizenship and the application fee. An Irish passport is valid for 10 years and costs €75 for a 32-page passport and €100 for a 48-page passport.

Dublin
Passport Office Dublin, Setanta Centre, Molesworth Street, Dublin 2
St Stephens Green *11, 11A, 11B, 14, 14A, 15C, 15X, 20B, 27C, 33X, 39B, 41X, 46B, 46C, 46D, 46E, 46X, 51X, 58C, 58X, 66D, 74, 74A, 84X, 116, 117, 118, 127, 142, 145, 746*
☎ *(01) 671 1633*
Website *http://foreignaffairs.gov.ie/home/index.aspx?id=253*
Open *Mon-Fri 9.30am-4.30pm*

Cork
Passport Office Cork, 1a South Mall, Cork
☎ *(021) 494 4700*
Open *Mon-Fri 9.30am-4.30pm*

New Zealand

New Zealand passport application forms can be downloaded from the passport office website and are also available from most travel agencies. Completed application forms should be sent to the passport office in Wellington along with two passport photos and the NZ$150 application fee. If you were not born in New Zealand you may also need to send proof of citizenship and identity along with your passport application. In most cases passport applications are processed within 10 working days. New Zealand passports are valid for 10 years.

Level 3, Boulcott House, 47 Boulcott Street, Wellington 6011
☎ *0800 22 50 50 or (04) 474 8100*

Website *www.passports.govt.nz*
Open *Mon-Wed 8.30am-5pm, Thu 9am-5pm, Fri 8.30am-5pm*

South Africa

Passport application forms are available at all Department of Home Affairs offices in South Africa and South African consulates and embassies abroad. South African passports are valid for 10 years and cost R 165. Allow six weeks for the application to be processed.
Department of Home Affairs, Civitas Building, 242 Struben Street, Pretoria
☎ *(012) 314 8911*
Website *www.home-affairs.gov.za/services_citizens.asp?topic=travel*

United Kingdom

British citizens can apply for a passport at offices of the UK Identity & Passport Service *(☎ 0870 521 0410;* ***website*** *www.ips.gov.uk/passport/)* in Belfast, Durham, Glasgow, Liverpool, London, Newport and Peterborough or at one of 76 interview offices. British passports cost £72 for a 32-page passport and £85 for a 48-page passport. Expedited passport renewal applications lodged in person at a Passport Office cost £97 for a one-week service or £114 for same day service. British passports are valid for 10 years.

Passport renewals take around three weeks but if this is your first passport you will need to allow around six weeks as you may need to attend an interview.
London Passport Office, Globe House, 89 Eccleston Square, London SW1V 1PN
Victoria *Victoria*
☎ *0870 521 0410*
Website *www.ips.gov.uk/passport/*
Open *Mon-Fri 7.45am-7pm, Sat 9.15am-3.15pm*

British citizens living outside the UK should apply through the Foreign & Commonwealth Office *(FCO;* ***website*** *www.fco.gov.uk).*

United States of America

US citizens can apply for a passport at over 9,000 public places that accept passport applications, which include courthouses, and many post offices. Applications take around four weeks to be processed but applications lodged at one of 13 regional passport agencies (Aurora CO, Boston MA, Chicago IL, Honolulu HI, Houston TX, Los Angeles CA, Miami FL, New Orleans LA, New York NY, Norwalk CT, Philadelphia PA, San Francisco CA, Seattle WA and Washington DC) are processed within two weeks. Passports cost US$100 ($75 application fee plus a $25 execution fee).

For more information, contact the US Passport office *(☎ (202) 647 0518;* ***website*** *http://travel.state.gov/).*

Tourist Visas

All nationalities apart from New Zealanders require a visa to visit Australia.

There are two types of tourist visa issued to visitors to Australia. Most visitors are issued with an Electronic Travel Authority (ETA), however citizens of some countries must apply for an old fashioned stamp in their passport that is valid for visits of either three or six months and costs $75.

See the Working in Australia section later in this chapter for information on work visas.

Electronic Travel Authority (ETA)

If you are planning on visiting Australia on a three-month tourist visa you may be given an electronic visa known as an Electronic Travel Authority (ETA). The majority of tourist visas issued to visitors to Australia are ETAs. An ETA is similar to a visa, however there is no stamp in your passport and you do not need to visit an Australian embassy, consulate or high commission to get your ETA.

ETAs are issued to citizens of the following countries: Andorra, Austria, Belgium, Brunei, Canada, Denmark, Finland, France, Germany, Greece, Hong Kong (SAR), Iceland, Ireland, Italy, Japan, Liechtenstein, Luxembourg, Malaysia, Malta, Monaco, The Netherlands, Norway, Portugal, San Marino, Singapore,

South Korea, Spain, Sweden, Switzerland, Taiwan, United Kingdom, United States of America and Vatican City.

Most applications for ETAs are submitted through travel agents or airlines but you can also apply for them online at the Australian Department of Immigration and Multicultural Affairs' website *(www.eta.immi.gov.au)* for $20, which is charged even if your application is unsuccessful. Alternatively you can apply for an ETA through the Australian Visas website *(www.australiavisas.com)*, which costs US$18.

ETAs are issued within a few seconds from making an application, either online or through a travel agent, however in rare cases you may be asked to provide additional information before an ETA is issued.

Australian Embassies, Consulates & High Commissions

Austria

Mattiellistrasse 2-4, 1040 Vienna
U Karlsplatz D 4A, N71, N75
☎ (01) 506 740
Website *www.australian-embassy.at*
Open *Mon-Fri 8.30am-4.30pm*

Canada

Suite 710, 50 O'Connor Street, Ottawa, Ontario K1P 6L2
☎ (613) 236 0841
Website *www.ahc-ottawa.org*
Open *Mon-Thu 8.30am-5pm, Fri 8.30am-4.30pm*

France

4, rue Jean Rey, 75724 Paris Cedex 15
M Bir-Hakeim RER Champ de Mars-Tour Eiffel
☎ (01) 40 59 33 00
Website *www.france.embassy.gov.au*
Open *Mon-Fri 9am-5pm*

Germany

Wallstraße 76-79, 10179 Berlin
U Markisches Museum
☎ (030) 88 00 88 0
Website *www.germany.embassy.gov.au*
Open *Mon-Thu 8.30am-5pm, Fri 8.30am-4.15pm*

Ireland

7th Floor, Fitzwilton House, Wilton Terrace, Dublin 2
☎ (01) 664 5300
Website *www.ireland.embassy.gov.au*
Open *Mon-Fri 8.30am-4.30pm*

Irish residents who are not able to apply for an ETA through their travel agent will need to make visa applications through the Australian High Commission in London.

Malta

Ta' Xbiex Terrace, Ta' Xbiex XBX 1034
☎ 2133 8201
Website *www.malta.embassy.gov.au*
Open *Mon-Fri 8am-4pm*

The Netherlands

Carnegielaan 4, 2517 KH The Hague
☎ (070) 310 8200
Website *www.netherlands.embassy.gov.au*
Open *Mon-Fri 8.30am-5pm*

Residents of the Netherlands who are not able to apply for an ETA through their travel agent will need to make visa applications through the Australian Embassy in Berlin.

New Zealand

72-76 Hobson Street, Thorndon, Wellington
☎ (04) 473 6411
Website *www.newzealand.embassy.gov.au*
Open *Mon-Fri 8.30am-5pm*

Singapore

25 Napier Road, Singapore
M Orchard
☎ 6836 4100
Website *www.singapore.embassy.gov.au*
Open *Mon-Fri 8.30am-4.50pm*

South Africa

292 Orient Street, Arcadia, Pretoria
☎ *12 423 6000*
Website *www.southafrica.embassy.gov.au*
Open *Mon-Fri 8am-4.10pm*

Sweden

Sergels Torg 12, 11th Floor, Stockholm
☎ *(08) 613 2900*
Website *www.sweden.embassy.gov.au*
Open *Mon-Fri 8.30am-4.30pm*

United Kingdom

Australia House, Strand, London WC2
⊖ *Temple* 🚆 *Charing Cross*
☎ *(020) 7379 4334*
Website *www.uk.embassy.gov.au*
Open *Mon-Fri 9am-5pm*

United States of America

Washington DC

Australian Embassy
1601 Massachusetts Ave, NW Washington DC 20036
Ⓜ *Dupont Circle, Farragut North*
☎ *(202) 797 3000*
Website *www.usa.embassy.gov.au*
Open *Mon-Fri 8.30am-5pm*

Atlanta

Australian Consulate-General
Atlanta Financial Center, Suite 1140, 3353 Peachtree Road NE, Atlanta GA
Ⓜ *Buckhead*
☎ *(404) 760 3400*
Website *www.usa.embassy.gov.au*
Open *Mon-Fri 8.30am-5pm*

Chicago

Australian Consulate-General
123 North Wacker Drive, Suite 1330, Chicago IL 60606
Ⓜ *Washington/Wells* 🚆 *(Metra) Ogilvie Transportation Center*
☎ *(312) 419 1480*
Website *www.usa.embassy.gov.au*
Open *Mon-Fri 8.40am-4.00pm*

Honolulu

Australian Consulate-General
1000 Bishop Street, Penthouse, Honolulu HI 96813
☎ *(808) 529 8100*
Website *www.usa.embassy.gov.au*
Open *Mon-Fri 8am-4pm*

Los Angeles

Australian Consulate-General
2029 Century Park East, Suite 3150, Los Angeles CA 90067
☎ *(310) 229 4800*
Website *www.usa.embassy.gov.au*
Open *Mon-Fri 9am-5pm*

The Los Angeles Consulate-General does not have a visa section. Call 1 888 990 8888 for visa enquiries.

New York

Australian Consulate-General
150 East 42nd Street, 34th Floor, New York
Ⓜ *Grand Central (7), Grand Central-42nd St (4, 5, 6, S)* 🚆 *(Metro North) Grand Central Terminal*
☎ *(212) 351 6500*
Website *www.australianyc.org*
Open *Mon-Fri 9am-5pm*

The New York Consulate-General does not have a visa section. Call 1 888 990 8888 for visa enquiries.

San Francisco

Australian Consulate-General
575 Market Street, Suite 1800, San Francisco, CA 94105
Ⓜ *Montgomery Street*
☎ *(415) 536 1970*
Website *www.usa.embassy.gov.au*
Open *Mon-Fri 8.30am-5pm*

The San Francisco Consulate-General does not have a visa section. Call 1 888 990 8888 for visa enquiries.

Customs & Quarantine

Australia's customs regulations are similar to those of other countries but it has some of the toughest quarantine policies in the world.

Customs

Visitors aged over 18 are allowed to bring 2250ml of alcohol and 250 cigarettes or 250 grams of tobacco into Australia without paying import duties. You are also allowed to import up to A$900 of other goods such as cameras, electronic goods etc which have been purchased duty free. The duty free limit for travellers aged under 18 is $450.

Like many other countries, you are not allowed to bring weapons, steroids or many drugs into Australia.

Visit the Australian Customs Service website *(www.customs.gov.au)* for more information.

Quarantine

Because Australia is free of many pests and diseases that plague other countries, the Australian Quarantine and Inspection Service *(**website** www.daffa.gov.au/aqis)* are extremely vigilant about keeping these out of Australia.

You will have to declare any food and animal or plant products that you have with you and most unpackaged food will not be allowed into the country. Quarantine officers will also check for dirty boots or shoes as well as camping equipment that may contain dirt that may introduce pests and diseases into Australia. You will also be questioned if you have visited a farm or engaged in any outdoor activity or if you have visited certain African or South American countries within the past week.

Working in Australia

Because of the common language and availability of working holiday permits, Australia is a popular spot for travellers to find work.

Work Visas

The Working Holiday and Work and Holiday visas are very similar programmes although the Working Holiday Visa is more flexible and usually easier to get.

The Work and Holiday visa is available only to people who have completed a university or other teritiary qualification, while there is no minimum educational qualification for the Working Holiday Visa. Also it is possible to apply for a second Working Holiday Visa if you have done seasonal work (such as picking fruit) in regional Australia.

Working Holiday Visa

Citizens of Belgium, Canada, Cyprus, Denmark, Estonia, Finland, France, Germany, Hong Kong, Ireland, Italy, Japan, Malta, Netherlands, Norway, South Korea, Sweden, Taiwan and United Kingdom aged between 18 and 30 are eligible to apply for a Working Holiday Visa.

This visa lets you work for up to 12 months in Australia to supplement the cost of your holiday.

The Working Holiday Visa allows you to enter Australia within 12 months being granted the visa, stay in Australia for up to 12 months, leave and re-enter Australia any number of times while the visa is valid, work in Australia for up to 6 months with each employer and study for up to 4 months.

The application fee for the Working Holiday Visa is $190.

Citizens of Chile, Thailand, Turkey and the United States are not eligible to apply for the Working Holiday Visa, but they can apply for the similar Work and Holiday Visa.

Applying for a second Working Holiday Visa

If you have worked as a seasonal worker in regional Australia for a minimum of three months while on your first Working Holiday visa, you may be eligible to apply for a second Working Holiday visa.

There is no requirement to do further seasonal work on the second visa and you may return to work for a further six months for an employer with whom you worked on your first visa.

Work & Holiday Visa

Tertiary educated people aged between 19 and 30 from Chile, Thailand, Turkey and the United States can apply for the Work and Holiday Visa, which is a similar programme to the Working Holiday Visa.

This visa lets you take up temporary and casual employment for up to 12 months to supplement your travel costs. Most countries that participate in this visa programme have an annual limit of 100 Work and Holiday visas per year.

If your application for the Work and Holiday visa is successful you can enter Australia at any time within three months of the visa grant date, stay for up to 12 months in Australia, leave and re-enter Australia any number of times in the 12 months from the date of first entry, undertake temporary employment in Australia and study for up to 4 months.

The application fee for the Work and Holiday Visa is $180.

Citizens of Belgium, Canada, Cyprus, Denmark, Estonia, Finland, France, Germany, Hong Kong, Ireland, Italy, Japan, Malta, Netherlands, Norway, South Korea, Sweden, Taiwan and United Kingdom are not eligible to apply for the Work and Holiday Visa, but they can apply for the similar Working Holiday Visa.

Tax

If you're working in Australia, you will have to pay tax on your income there.

In most cases a traveller on a Working Holiday visa is treated as a non-resident, which means that you will be taxed at a higher rate than an Australian resident and have to pay tax on every dollar you earn (as opposed to Australian residents who are entitled to a $6000 tax-free threshold).

As a non-resident you will be taxed at a rate of 29% on the first $30,000 you earn, with the tax rate rising to a maximum of 45% once you earn over $150,000.

Even though most travellers on a Working Holiday visa are taxed as non-residents there are some cases where you may be classed as a resident, which can save you thousands of dollars a year in tax. If you spend most of your time in one location and establish ties with Australia (such as renting a flat and having your name on the lease, getting an Australian drivers licence and joining local clubs and generally living a lifestyle that is closer to a regular Australian resident rather than a traveller), then you may be able to be taxed as a resident. Being classed as a resident by the Australian Taxation Office can mean that you pay around half as much tax as a non-resident. If you think your travel and work patterns in Australia allow you to be classed as a resident then it is a good idea to see a good tax accountant when you need to submit your tax return.

Residents don't pay tax on the first $6000 they earn and they only pay 15% on what they earn between $6001 and $30,000. This means that if you earn $30,000 in one year you would pay $8700 tax if you are classed as a non-resident but only $3,600 if you are classed as a resident. See www.ato.gov.au/individuals/content.asp?doc=/content/64131.htm and www.ato.gov.au/individuals/content.asp?doc=/content/36280.htm for more information about what is required to be taxed as a resident.

You will need to get a Tax File Number to avoid paying a higher tax rate than you need to. You'll need to quote this number when applying for work. If you have a Working Holiday Visa and an Australian address you can apply for a Tax File Number online at the Australian Taxation Office's website *(www.ato.gov.au)*.

At the end of the Australian tax year (30 June) and before you return home, you will need to complete a tax return. In Australia this is much more complex than in the UK and many travellers get an accountant or tax agent to do this for them. An accountant will charge around $120 for this service, but they are familiar with Australian tax law and will often be able to get you a better refund than you could get yourself.

Superannuation

If you are earning over $450 per month (before tax), you employer will pay a minimum of 9% of your earnings into a superannuation fund (retirement savings fund).

Normally you cannot access this money until you reach 55, but temporary residents and visitors on a Working Holiday visa can reclaim their money when they leave Australia. Money in your super fund is subject to withholding tax.

Contact the Australian Taxation Office *(☎ 13 10 20; **website** www.ato.gov.au/super/)* for further information on superannuation.

Finding Work in Australia

Your best option for work is to register at temporary employment agencies. This fits within the scope of your working holiday permit and also lines you up for reasonably well paying work.

There are also several good employment websites that are a good starting point. These include CareerOne *(www.careerone.com.au)*, MyCareer *(www.mycareer.com.au)* and Seek *(www.seek.com.au)*. Also try Hippo *(www.hippo.com.au)*, which has more of a focus on casual and part time work.

To get a good idea about the availability of work, long-term accommodation and costs of living, check the classified ads in the main Australian newspapers. The Saturday editions of the *Age* (Melbourne), the *Courier Mail* (Brisbane) and the *Sydney Morning Herald* are particularly good places to look for work.

Fruit picking is a popular backpackers' job in Australia. It is hard work, but it's a good way to keep fit and get a tan and picking fruit for three months may make you eligible for a second Working Holiday visa. This sort of work is usually in small rural towns that you wouldn't otherwise want to visit, however there is work available in most parts of Australia. Most hostels in fruit-picking destinations will find work for you and a quick phone call to the hostel before arriving can give you a quick rundown on the work situation.

The National Harvest Labour Information Service *(NHLIS; ☎ 1800 062 332; **website** www.jobsearch.gov.au/harvesttrail)* is a good place to look for fruit picking work as they have a regularly updated database on where harvest work is available. It's a good idea to contact them before leaving for the area where you want to work as conditions can quickly change.

Health Cover

Finland, Ireland, Italy, Malta, the Netherlands, New Zealand, Norway, Sweden and the UK have reciprocal health agreements with Australia. If you are from one of these countries you may be entitled to free emergency health care although this sometimes limited if you are on a Working Holiday Visa.

Visitors from Ireland and New Zealand are entitled to subsidised medicine under the Pharmaceutical Benefits Scheme and free treatment at public hospitals. Irish and New Zealand travellers do not have access to Medicare benefits for non-hospital care and are not issued with a Medicare card. You simply show your passport at the hospital or pharmacy.

Residents of Finland, Italy, Malta, the Netherlands, Norway, Sweden and the UK who visit Australia are entitled to subsidised medicine under the Pharmaceutical Benefits Scheme, free treatment at public hospitals and Medicare benefits for treatment by doctors in private surgeries.

The reciprocal health care agreements don't cover other medical expenses such as dental and chiropractic services, glasses and contact lenses, elective surgery or hospital treatment that is not considered necessary before returning home.

Travellers from countries covered by this scheme, except visitors from Italy and Malta, are covered for the duration of their permitted stay. Visitors from Italy and Malta are covered for six months from the date of arrival in Australia.

Contact Medicare *(☎ 13 20 11; **website** www.medicareaustralia.gov.au/public/migrants/visitors/)* for more information on the reciprocal health scheme.

If you are not covered by a reciprocal health agreement you may want to take out comprehensive travel insurance or sign up with an Australian private health insurer. Australian Unity *(☎ 13 29 39; **website** www.australianunity.com.au)* has a private health insurance policy for international visitors called Healthy Travel, which you may want to consider; although some travel insurance policies offer better value.

Money

Australia is a fairly cheap country to travel around, particularly when taking into account the quality of hostel accommodation. However prices can come as a shock if you've arrived here after a couple of months on the road in Asia.

Work out your daily budget by tripling your accommodation cost. Multiply this by the number of days you're planning on travelling, and add the cost of your airfare and bus/travel passes and you should get a pretty good idea of the costs of travelling around Australia.

You should be able to save some money by cooking all your own meals and not drinking alcohol, however there are lots of easy ways to blow through a wad of cash such as a few big nights out on the town or adventure activities such as scuba diving, bungee jumping or white water rafting.

Travellers' Cheques

Travellers' cheques used to be the best way to carry travel money, but they're not as common now that ATMs and credit cards are so widespread.

It is worthwhile taking some of your money as travellers' cheques since it is a great backup if you lose your wallet with all your credit cards or if you arrive to discover that your cash card won't work in the ATM.

The beauty of travellers' cheques is that they can be replaced if they're lost or stolen. It helps if you keep a record of your travellers' cheque numbers in a safe place, preferably a copy with you (but not with your cheques) and another copy at home (or somewhere where someone can fax them to you if you need to make a claim for lost cheques).

Many travellers buy travellers cheques in British pounds, euros or US dollars, which is fine if you're travelling through lots of different countries. However travellers' cheques in Australian dollars have the advantage of being able to be used as an alternative to cash as long as you can find someone willing to accept them.

If you bring travellers' cheques with you, make sure that you sign them when you buy them, but do not countersign them until you are ready to cash them. You may also need to have identification such as your passport with you when you cash your cheques.

The most widely accepted brands of travellers' cheques are American Express, Thomas Cook and Visa. Don't travel with anything else as many people will not recognise or accept them.

ATMs, Credit Cards & EFTPOS

Plastic is the preferred way to access your cash while you're on the road and most cards are widely accepted throughout Australia.

There are several types of cards, each with their advantages. Most travellers have at least one credit card, and also a card to draw cash from an ATM (either from an account at home or from an Australian bank account).

Credit Cards

Credit cards are great for getting out of trouble and are often tied to a frequent flyer programme. One of the main advantages of credit cards is the favourable currency exchange rate as well the freedom to spend more money than you have. Of course this spending can get out of hand and you'll end up paying for it later on.

The most useful cards in Australia are MasterCard and Visa, followed by American Express and Diners Club. In tourist areas you may find some places that accept JCB and – occasionally – UnionPay cards, but Discover card is not accepted in Australia.

Most credit cards can be replaced quickly if they are lost or stolen. Call one of the following numbers if you need a new card:

American Express
☎ *1300 132 639*
Website *www.americanexpress.com*

Diners Club
☎ *1300 360 060*
Website *www.dinersclub.com*

MasterCard
☎ *1800 120 113*
Website *www.mastercard.com*

Visa
☎ *1800 450 346*
Website *www.visa.com*

ATM & EFTPOS Cards

ATM cards are a popular way to access your cash, particularly if your card is part of an international network allowing you to use Australian Automatic Teller Machines (ATMs). If the bank that issued your card is part of the Plus, Cirrus or Visa networks you should find plenty of ATMs in Australia where you can withdraw money.

Despite the favourable exchange rate and the ease of drawing your money from a cash dispenser, there are sometimes problems using your cash card abroad. Before leaving home you should check with your bank whether it is possible to use your card in Australia. In some cases you may need to change your PIN or even have a new card issued.

Cards issued by Australian banks are a lot more useful, working in virtually all ATMs and also at EFTPOS terminals in most shops, hotels, service stations and pubs.

Electronic Funds Transfer at Point of Sale (EFTPOS) terminals at cash registers at most Australian shops allow you to use an Australian issued ATM card to pay for goods and withdraw cash from your account. The combination of ATMs and EFTPOS terminals everywhere makes getting an Aussie bank account essential if you're planning on staying in the country for more than a few months.

Australian Bank Accounts

If you're planning on spending a lot of time in Australia, your own bank account will make things a lot easier, particularly if you're planning on finding work.

The four biggest banks in Australia are ANZ *(**website** www.anz.com)*, Commonwealth Bank *(**website** www.commbank.com.au)*, NAB *(National Australia Bank; **website** www.nab.com.au)* and Westpac *(**website** www.westpac.com.au)*. Smaller banks like BankWest *(**website** www.bankwest.com.au)*, Bendigo Bank *(**website** www.bendigobank.com.au)* and St George *(**website** www.stgeorge.com.au)* may give you better service and lower fees but you won't always be able to find a branch when you're on the road, so you may be charged higher fees to withdraw cash from another bank's ATM, which makes it a good idea to open an account with one of the bigger banks as they have branches everywhere.

If you've just arrived in the country you can open an Australian bank account by presenting your passport as identification, but you may be asked for additional identification if you try to open an account after spending more than six weeks in the country.

GST & the Tourist Refund Scheme

Australia has a 10% Goods and Services Tax on most retail purchases, but there is a scheme where travellers can reclaim the GST on some purchases.

The Tourist Refund Scheme (TRS) enables you to claim a refund of the Goods and Services Tax (GST) and Wine Equalisation Tax (WET) that you pay on goods you buy in Australia. The refund only applies to goods you take with you as hand luggage or wear onto the plane when you leave the country. It does not apply to services or goods consumed or partly consumed in Australia. Unlike other tourist shopping schemes, such as duty free shopping, you can use the goods before leaving Australia.

To qualify for the scheme you need to: spend $300 or more on a single item that you want to claim a refund for; purchase the goods no more than 30 days before leaving Australia; get a tax invoice from the shop you bought the goods from; take the goods with you as carry on luggage (except liquids, which can't be taken as carry on luggage because of security regulations).

It is essential that you get a tax invoice when you buy the goods you want to claim a refund on and take this with you to the airport. There are TRS booths at the departure areas of Sydney, Brisbane, Melbourne, Perth, Cairns, Adelaide, Darwin and Coolangatta airports where you need to show the goods you want to claim the refund on, the tax invoice, your passport and boarding pass. If you're leaving from an international airport that doesn't have a TRS booth, such as Broome or Newcastle you will need to contact a Customs office *(Broome ☎ (08) 9193 6999; Newcastle ☎ (02) 4926 0411)* to make a claim before leaving the country.

Contact the Customs Service *(☎ 1300 363 263; **website** www.customs.gov.au)* for more information on the scheme.

Tipping & Bribery

Bribery in exchange for good service isn't as widely practised in Australia as in other countries although tipping is starting to catch on, particularly in fancy restaurants in trendy inner-city neighbourhoods.

Ten or 15 years ago it would be rare to find an Australian who would regularly tip, but now there are many people who regularly tip 10% in restaurants and who even self-righteously promote this custom. However, despite the increasing number of people tipping, the average Aussie doesn't tip and even in more expensive restaurants it is quite normal to pay the exact change for your meal. You never tip in a pub or bar, which also means that pub meals are tip-free. Don't feel you need to tip in a café either, even if there is a tip jar on the counter.

When paying taxi fares it is commonplace to round up the fare, such as paying $10 for a $9.60 fare; but it is not uncommon for a taxi driver to round a $10.20 fare down to an even $10.

Discount Cards

If you're travelling on a budget you're crazy to pay full price if there is a cheaper option. Armed with a wallet full of discount cards you should be able to drastically cut the cost of travel.

Discount cards come in two varieties – hostel cards and student/youth cards. Both types of cards are worth taking, particularly if you're travelling for a while. Student cards are generally best for getting cut-price admission to museums and other attractions and often allow for cut-price transport; with hostel cards, the emphasis is on cheaper accommodation although these also give you excellent discounts on bus and train fares.

Student & Youth Cards

It's worth bringing along several student cards if you're a student, if you're not a student but are aged under 26 you can get a youth discount card that gives you similar discounts.

Most sightseeing attractions including museums, wildlife parks and zoos allow substantial discounts for students. Many attractions throughout Australia refer to the discounted price as the concession rate. Some hostels will also extend the HI/YHA or VIP discount to you if you have a student card. In many cases just flashing the card issued by your university will get you these discounts; however some attractions require an internationally recognised card such as the ISIC or ISE card. This is a good reason why you should have at least two student cards.

Both ISIC and ISE publish a list of available discounts, however virtually all establishments that offer discounts will grant the discount for either card even if it that establishment is not listed in the card's discount guide.

The concession rate on the public transport networks in most Australian cities is not available with these cards and in most cases it is restricted to students enrolled in local schools.

ISE

The International Student Exchange (ISE) card is a good option with loads of discounts. Although this card is not as established as the ISIC, many establishments that give discounts to the ISIC will also provide the same discounts to ISE cardholders. The ISE card costs US$25 and you can order it online. See the ISE website *(www.isecards.com)* for more information.

ISIC, IYTC & ITIC

The International Student Travel Confederation *(ISTC; **website** www.isiccard.com)* produces three discount cards that give discounts to students; teachers and travellers aged under 26. Some of these cards include basic travel insurance although this is dependent on where the card is issued. ISIC, IYTC and ITIC cards each cost US$22 or £9.

The International Student Identity Card (ISIC) is the most widely accepted of the student cards. Many travellers buy fake ISIC cards while they're travelling through Asia which means non-students can sometimes pick one up; because of this the cards aren't quite as good for big discounts as they used to be and you may sometimes be asked for a secondary identification such as your student ID from your university at home. This is a good reason why you should have a couple of student ID cards.

The International Youth Travel Card (IYTC) is an alternative for travellers aged under 26 who do not qualify for an ISIC. There is a wide range of discounts, but it isn't as good as a student card.

The International Teacher Identity Card (ITIC) is a good alternative if you are a full-time teacher. Like the IYTC this isn't quite as good as a student card but it's worthwhile if you don't qualify for anything else.

Hostel Cards

Cards issued by the different hostelling organisations offer excellent discounts, particularly for transport and accommodation. Many travellers take along two cards, a YHA or Hostelling International card and one issued by an independent hostelling organisation such as VIP Backpackers Resorts or Nomads. There is more information about hostel cards in the following hostel section.

In our accommodation listings we list the price without a hostel card followed by the price charged if you have a card. Just because a hostel offers a discount to someone with a card from a particular hostel network does not mean that that hostel is part of the network.

Keeping in Touch

It is increasingly easy to keep in touch with the world. Mobile phones, voicemail and VOIP services such as Skype make it easy for people to call you and most hostels offer internet access, which is supplemented by internet cafes and wireless hotspots.

Telephone

The phone is still the easiest way to keep in touch and having your own number means that people can call you (which will save you a fortune in phone calls). Your own local phone number is also essential if you're looking for work.

Mobile phones

Virtually every backpacker travels with a mobile phone. If your mobile phone works with the GSM system (most European phones do) and is unlocked (not locked into your home network) then you can simply buy an Australian SIM card and stick it in your phone. If you don't already have a compatible phone, then you will need to buy a prepaid starter pack including a phone and SIM card for around $70-100.

Most Australian mobile phone companies charge a connection fee of 20-30c on each call and their advertised call charges are usually quoted per 30 seconds (not per minute as you would expect).

There are four mobile phone network operators in Australia, plus lots of virtual network operators (companies that sell their own branded mobile phone service using someone else's network) so there is plenty of choice and enough competition to keep prices reasonable.

The main networks are Optus *(**website** www.optus.com.au)*, Telstra *(**website** www.telstra.com.au)*, Three *(**website** www.three.com.au)* and Vodafone *(**website** www.vodafone.com.au)*. With the exception of Virgin Mobile, most of the virtual network operators are small little-known companies, but they are usually much cheaper than the big guys.

While the bigger phone companies offer some very good deals for customers on long term contracts, their prepaid deals aren't so great, but the smaller virtual networks offer some good value prepaid deals:

Prices and mobile phone deals change all the time so we haven't listed prices here but you can get a good idea of the strengths and weaknesses of each network and then check their websites to see which one is best for you.

OPTUS

Australia's second largest mobile network has excellent coverage in most parts of Australia, especially along the east coast; but there are some gaping holes where their network doesn't work such as Kununurra, WA and both the east and west coasts of Tasmania. All in all, Optus is good value and a good compromise between coverage and price.

TELSTRA

Telstra is Australia's most expensive mobile network but it also has the best coverage and there is almost nowhere their service doesn't work. Sure it may be nice to get access on a dirt track in the middle of the outback, but it shouldn't have to cost as much as it does.

THREE

Three is good value and they have some great extra services (like the ability to make free Skype calls from your mobile and free calls to other Three customers) but their network is limited to just a handful of the bigger Australian cities. Fortunately Australian Three customers can roam onto Telstra's GSM network when they are outside Three's own network.

Three is a good option if you are are going to spend most of your time in Melbourne, Sydney or Brisbane; but if you're planning on picking fruit or spending months travelling up the coast then you'd better look at one of the other networks.

The '3 Like Home' promotion means that Three customers in Ireland, the UK and some European countries can use their mobile in Australia without roaming charges, but this only applies when you are on the network that Three operates in Australia and not the Telstra network that Three's Australian customers have access to.

VODAFONE

Vodafone is one of the more popular mobile networks for many backpackers even though their coverage is pretty limited compared with Optus and Telstra. Vodafone SIM cards only cost $2, so it is cheap to get set up and they have some of the better value pre-paid plans.

VIRTUAL MOBILE PHONE NETWORKS

There are several other mobile companies in Australia that offer their own branded service using the network infrastructure of one of the larger companies. They are generally the cheapest for prepaid services.

Dodo

Dodo *(**website** www.dodo.com.au)* are a cheap mobile service that includes free calls to Vodafone and other Dodo customers.

Just Mobile

Just Prepaid Mobile *(**website** www.justmobile.com.au)* is the only Australian mobile phone company we could find that has no connection charge. No connection charge makes their rates easy to understand and coupled with low call rates makes Just Mobile a good deal if you make lots of short calls. Just Mobile use the Vodafone network.

Revolution Telecom

Revolution Telecom *(**website** www.revtel.com.au)* have cheap call rates and use the Vodafone network.

Savvytel

Savvytel *(**website** www.savvytel.com.au)* is one of the best value mobile phone companies in Australia with capped pre-paid plans, credits that never expire and cheap call rates. At the time of writing they were the cheapest pre-paid mobile deal in Australia. Savvytel uses the Vodafone network.

Virgin Mobile

Virgin *(**website** www.virginmobile.com.au)* is one of the biggest of the virtual networks with good value call rates. Virgin use the Optus network, which gives you better coverage than Just Mobile or Savvytel (unless you're going to spend all your time in Kununurra).

BUYING A SIM CARD BEFORE YOU TRAVEL

There are several companies that sell SIM cards over the internet. Buying an Australian SIM card over the internet from a company in the US or the UK is a complete rip-off! You can pay US$49 or £29 for a SIM card online, but if you wait till you get to Australia you can buy a Vodafone SIM for just $2 (other SIM cards don't cost that much more). Wait until you get to Australia unless you absolutely need to know your phone number before you travel.

ALTERNATIVES TO ROAMING

Roaming (leaving your home SIM card in your phone when you travel abroad) is the most expensive way to make calls. Not only are you charged exorbitant rates for your calls but you are also charged for an international call every time you answer your phone. Usually roaming is something you use in isolated cases, such as a one-day stopover when it doesn't make sense to buy a local SIM card.

Roaming does give you the advantage of having a single number (usually in your home country) that people can contact you on regardless of what country you are travelling in. There are many cases when you need to offer a single point of contact so you can receive important calls, this is especially the case if you do freelance work and you don't want your clients to know that you are travelling down under.

One of the easiest and cheapest options is to use a SkypeIn number (or another VoIP service) that is diverted to your mobile in Australia. You still have to pay for the incoming call but it is a lot cheaper than roaming and you don't need to update everyone with your new number every time you visit a new country. To save on call costs give your Australian mobile number to people who call you frequently so they can call you directly.

Another option is to use an international SIM. This is a SIM from a small country (they usually come from Estonia, Liechtenstein, Iceland or the Isle of Man). It is free to receive calls in most countries (Australia is almost always on the list countries with free incoming calls) and making a call is also reasonably priced. However the quality is dire and many travellers give up on the service (or lack thereof) after they realise that it is almost impossible for people to contact them.

The best option is to simply buy a local SIM in every country where you spend a week or longer and combine this with a SkypeIn number so you don't miss those really important calls.

Calling cards

Despite the popularity of mobile phones, calling cards are still the cheapest way to call home. Virtually every service station, newsagent and corner store sell a huge range of calling cards.

Rates are generally cheapest if you call a local access number rather than the toll-free number on the back of the card but this means that you may have to pay for a local call on a payphone in addition to the calling card rate.

Skype & other VoIP services

VoIP (Voice over Internet Protocol) is one of the cheapest ways to make a phone call but the quality isn't so great if you have a bad internet connection. Generally VoIP lets you call other customers of the same VoIP service for free, which gives the biggest VoIP services the advantage of more people you can talk to for nothing.

Skype *(**website** www.skype.com)* is the biggest of the internet-based phone services and Skype software (and webcams for video calling) is installed in most internet cafes and in many hostels, which makes choosing Skype a no-brainer even though many of Skype's competitors are cheaper.

Although many travellers just sign up for the free Skype account so they can talk to other Skype users for free, it is worth the money to go for a fully fledged account with a SkypeIn number (a proper number that anyone with a phone can call) and even opt for the €3.95 monthly subscription that gives you free calls to landlines either at home or in Australia.

Of course you still have to pay to use the computers at the internet cafe so it's a better deal if you're staying at a hostel with free internet access or if you have your own notebook computer and a free Wi-Fi connection.

Internet

It's easy to get online virtually everywhere you travel in Australia, but it is cheaper in the bigger cities and more popular tourist destinations.

Internet cafés

It is easy to find internet cafés in big cities like Melbourne, Sydney and Brisbane and popular tourist destinations like Airlie Beach, Byron Bay and Cairns. You can get online cheaply – as little as $2 an hour – in Sydney but more remote places – like Uluṟu – are a lot more expensive and in small towns and less touristy areas you may have to use slow and expensive coin-operated terminals.

Many internet cafés, including big chains like Global Gossip *(**website** www.globalgossip.com)*, are now fitted with webcams and headsets to make Skype calls and many also let you download photos from your digital camera.

We list internet cafés in the Practical Information section at the beginning of each destination guide.

Using your own computer

An increasing number of travellers are choosing to travel with their own notebook computer.

Wi-Fi hotspot access

Australia isn't as well set up with wireless hotspots as you would expect and when you do find them they tend to be expensive. However free hotspots are slowly starting to catch on.

Most backpackers use the Global Gossip Connect hotspots that are in many backpackers' hostels around Australia (and in New Zealand). They're not cheap but they are an affordable option if you can't find a free hotspot and you can use any remaining credit at other Global Gossip Connect hotspots.

If you're really desperate to get online and can't find anywhere to connect you can use the expensive Telstra hotspots at McDonalds and Starbucks.

Fortunately free hotspots are starting to catch on, although they are still a bit thin on the ground in some parts of the country. Adelaide and Melbourne are the most connected cities although there are a few free hotspots around Brisbane and Sydney. Check the Free Wireless Internet directory *(**website** www.freewifi.com.au)* to find free Wi-Fi hotspots around Australia.

We list free Wi-Fi hotspots in the Practical Information section at the beginning of each destination guide.

Mobile HSDPA & WiMAX broadband access

All Australia's mobile phone networks operate their own wireless broadband service using HSDPA technology, which gives you internet access wherever there is mobile phone coverage. This isn't such a popular option with backpackers but it is an affordable option with medium to high usage plans for around $40 a month. It is worth considering if you're on a working holiday and will be travelling for a while.

Basically your options are Optus *(**website** www.optus.com.au)*, Telstra *(**website** www.telstra.com.au)*, Three *(**website** www.three.com.au)* and Vodafone *(**website** www.vodafone.com.au)*.

Optus have good prices and coverage with broadband speed across their entire network; Telstra have the widest coverage but are the most expensive; Three are the cheapest but only have coverage in the major cities (useless if you're travelling in North Queensland) and Vodafone have coverage across their whole network but broadband speeds are only available in the big cities.

If you have a Three mobile phone you may also be able to use your phone as a modem and use the bandwidth allowance from an X-Series plan to connect your computer to the net.

At the time of writing both Telstra and Vodafone only offered their mobile broadband service with a long contract, effectively ruling it out as a viable option for travellers; but Optus and Three will let you use their service without signing a contract (although they may want you to pay full price for an HSDPA modem, which you would otherwise get for free if you go with a 24-month contract).

Another option is wireless broadband using WiMAX technology with Unwired *(**website** www.unwired.com.au)*; which are limited mostly to the bigger cities but are a reliable connection that is worth it if you're spending most of your time the bigger cities.

Hostels

Hostels are a great cheap accommodation option; however they are much more than just a cheap bed. A good backpackers' hostel is also a place to party, meet new friends from around the world and get information on other cool places to go.

Hostels provide dormitory accommodation, along with shared shower and kitchen facilities. Generally there are four to six people sharing a room and there is somewhere like a TV room or bar where you can meet other travellers. Often the people running the hostel are backpackers themselves, and are a mine of information about places to see, things to do and transport and accommodation options elsewhere in Australia.

Australia has some of the world's best hostels and they often include facilities that you would seldom find in hostels in Europe or North America such as spas, swimming pools and courtesy buses. The Australian backpacking industry is very competitive and this keeps the standard of accommodation relatively high.

The best hostels are usually either small hostels in historic buildings that are full of character or newer purpose-built places with first-class facilities. Hostels in popular destinations such as Airlie Beach, Byron Bay, Mission Beach, Noosa and Port Douglas tend to be excellent as the competition between hostels in these places drives up the standard of accommodation. However hostels in bigger cities and less visited regional centres aren't as predictable.

A good hostel should provide a way for travellers to meet each other with common areas and a design that is conducive to meeting other people. This is one of the main features that distinguish hostels from hotels and motels, which are designed to offer their guests privacy. For this reason, many hostels with self-contained facilities (usually those that are former motels or apartment complexes) don't have as much atmosphere as your average backpackers' hostel.

Hostels that are located above pubs are often among the worst. In many of these places the bar downstairs is the main business and a lot less attention is paid to the accommodation.

Hostels catering to working holidaymakers are usually not that great either, existing solely to provide accommodation to backpackers picking fruit and they do little for travellers that happen to be passing through town and only staying a night or two. However the management of workers' hostels do have a lot of employment contacts and sometimes also provide transport to and from work. These hostels work for the employers as much as the backpackers and they have more rules than your standard hostel. Often there are restrictions on alcohol consumption in workers' hostels as local farms rely on them to provide a reliable, hard-working and sober workforce. Despite the overall lower standard of workers' hostels, there are a handful that stand out from the crowd.

Although the hostel reviews in BUG guidebooks are more comprehensive than any other travel guide, the reviews on BUG's website *(www.bug.co.uk)* are even more detailed and allow you to write your own hostel reviews and read reviews submitted by other travellers. A lot of the hostels reviewed on our website also allow online booking; where this is possible there will be a booking engine on the hostel's review page.

Hostel Chains

There are three major hostel chains in Australia. Each offers its own discount/membership card that gives discounts on accommodation and transport.

Nomads

Nomads *(**website** www.nomadsworld.com)* started out by setting up hostels above pubs and the overall quality of their hostels wasn't all that great. However they seem to be really cleaning up their act and have recently opened some excellent hostels. Nomads is the smallest of the three hostel chains.

The Nomads travel card offers over 600 discounts in Australia including around $1 off Nomads hostels. Transport discounts include 10% off Greyhound buses, 5% off Oz Experience and the Wayward bus and discounts on trains operated by Great Southern Railway. The Nomads card costs $34 and is available from Nomads hostels.

VIP

VIP Backpackers Resorts *(**website** www.vipbackpackers.com)* is a group of independently run hostels that vary enormously as far as facilities are concerned.

Don't let the bed bugs bite

Bed bugs are a serious problem encountered by travellers throughout the world. They can be found on buses, on trains, in cinemas, in hostels and even in five-star hotels.

Although they are blood-sucking parasites, bed bugs do not transmit any disease and for most people the bites are no more irritating than a flea, mosquito or sand fly bite. However some people do have serious reactions to bed bug bites.

There is quite a stigma surrounding bed bugs and travellers that have been bitten often feel dirty and are ashamed to tell people about them, or they assume that it is the hostel's fault and tell other travellers to avoid the hostel. However bed bugs can prefer cleaner environments and an isolated case of bed bugs is no indication of a bad hostel.

It is impossible for hostels to completely eliminate bed bugs but they can take steps to prevent bed bugs from becoming a serious problem. These include not having carpet, wallpaper and wooden furniture where bed bugs can hide and prohibiting guests from using their own sleeping bags. However one of the best things that hostel owners can do is to admit the problem exists and react quickly whenever they discover a case of bed bugs. Hostel managers who claim to never have bed bugs are deluded and inevitably will be slow to act when bed bugs are found in their hostel.

There are a lot of misconceptions about bed bugs. A lot of people think that they are so tiny that they are virtually invisible; however they are brown flat oval insects that are around 5mm across and quite easy to spot on your bed.

It is quite easy to quickly inspect your room for bed bugs by checking for small dots of blood on the bed slats and around the seams of mattresses, but blood spots could merely indicate a previous infestation that has been cleaned up. Infested rooms may also have an unpleasant almond-like smell.

If you think you have bed bugs you should:

- Tell hostel staff so they can treat your room
- Wash all your clothes and anything else that can be washed on the highest heat setting and dry in a clothes dryer for 20 minutes
- Have a hot shower
- Empty your backpack, clean it with boiling water and (if possible) dry in a clothes dryer for 20 minutes
- Visually check anything that can't be washed for signs of bed bugs

The VIP card is one of the most useful hostel cards and a lot of backpackers buy one. Hundreds of hostels in Australia, New Zealand and other countries give discounts to VIP cardholders. Most of the hostels give a $1 discount per night. The card also has excellent transport discounts such as 10-15% discounts on Greyhound buses, discounts on trains operated by Great Southern Railway and discounts on rental cars. A VIP card costs $37 for one year and is available online and from VIP hostels.

Hostelling International (HI)/ Youth Hostels Association (YHA)

The Youth Hostel Association *(website www.yha.com.au)* is the Australian branch of Hostelling International (HI) and its hostels have a fairly consistent standard. In Australia the YHA's main market is independent travellers as opposed to school groups that fill a lot of European hostels and consequently youth hostels in Australia have a much better atmosphere than the institutional hostels that you find in Europe. The competition between hostels in Australia has also forced the YHA to clean up its act and you won't find any YHA hostels in Australia with chores, a curfew or a lockout. Although YHA hostels in Australia are better than Hostelling International hostels elsewhere, they still have a reputation as a dull and relatively boring place to stay and very few YHA hostels fit the description of 'party hostel'.

Most travellers take along a YHA or Hostelling International card. This hostel card allows the biggest accommodation discounts with savings of at least 10% per night. The card is good at any of the thousands of hostels around the world, including over 140 in Australia, that are part of the Hostelling International organisation. Most YHA youth hostels only give discounts on this card so it is essential if you are planning on staying at a lot of YHA hostels. Many independent backpackers' hostels will also extend the Nomads or VIP discount to YHA members making this a good card to bring along even if you don't stay at that many YHA hostels. HI or YHA cards are available through many student travel agencies as well as at YHA offices and hostels and costs US$28/£15.95/€20 although you can collect stamps towards a membership for every night you stay at a YHA hostel at the non-member rate, which can work out cheaper than buying a card in advance. The YHA card also has good discounts on transport including discounts on car rental, bus and train travel.

Top 10 small hostels

Australia has developed a reputation for top quality "flashpackers" hostels; big flash hostels with top quality facilties like Gilligans in Cairns, Nomads Industry in Melbourne and Wake Up! in Sydney. However sometimes the most memorable hostels are the small ones that are often just as clean as the big hostels but with a warm atmosphere that you can only get in a small place.

The following are our favourite small hostels (with less than 60 beds):

- Bellingen YHA (Bellingen, NSW)
- Black Cockatoo (Nannup, WA)
- Eco-Beach YHA (Apollo Bay, VIC)
- Eumeralla Backpackers (Yambuk, VIC)
- Grampians Eco YHA (Halls Gap, VIC)
- Lakeside Manor YHA (Robe, SA)
- Number 14 (Katoomba, NSW)
- Olembia (Melbourne, VIC)
- On the Wallaby (Yungaburra, QLD)
- Tim's Place (Halls Gap, VIC)

Getting Around

Air Travel

Australia has four major airlines plus a number of smaller regional carriers.

The main airlines are the long-established Qantas and budget airlines JetStar, Tiger Airways and Virgin Blue. Qantas has the most extensive flight network followed by Virgin Blue and Jetstar. Tiger Airways is the new kid on the block having started service in November 2007. All four airlines have relatively young fleets.

Generally JetStar *(☎ 13 15 38; **website** www.jetstar.com.au)* and Tiger *(☎ (03) 9335 3033; **website** www.tigerairways.com.au)* offer the cheapest fares. Virgin Blue *(☎ 13 67 89; **website** www.virginblue.com.au)* started out as a low cost airline then moved more upmarket, but their fares are still competitive. Qantas *(☎ 13 13 13; **website** www.qantas.com.au)* is more expensive but they have good value red e-deals advertised on their website.

Regional Express, also known as Rex Airlines *(☎ 13 17 13; **website** www.rex.com.au)* is Australia's main regional airline. Rex flies to around 35 regional destinations in New South Wales, Queensland, South Australia, Tasmania and Victoria. The main cities that Rex flies to are Adelaide, Canberra, Melbourne and Sydney; the most northern destination on the Rex network is Maryborough (near Hervey Bay) and they also fly to outback towns like Broken Hill, Olympic Dam and Coober Pedy. Rex has introduced two excellent value backpacker travel passes that allow either one month unlimited standby travel for $499 or two months for $949. These passes are only available to international travellers with a HI/YHA, ISIC, IYTC or VIP card and you cannot use this pass to accrue frequent flyer points. Despite the limited reach of the Rex network, this is probably Australia's best value travel pass.

Other regional airlines include Skywest *(☎ 1300 66 00 88; **website** www.skywest.com.au)* and Airnorth *(☎ 1800 627 474; **website** www.airnorth.com.au)*. These two airlines operate flights to smaller cities (mostly in Western Australia and the Northern Territory). They tend to be a bit more expensive than the larger airlines but it is still worth checking their fares as occasionally you can get a good deal.

Frequent Flyer Points

Qantas is part of the One World network along with American Airlines and British Airways. If you're not already a member of a OneWorld airline's frequent flyer programme you can join American Airlines' programme for free and earn points with Qantas flights, rather than paying to join the Qantas frequent flyer programme. You can sign up for the American Airlines frequent flyer programme on their website *(www.aa.com)*.

Bus Travel

Bus travel is the most popular way to get around Australia. Coaches go virtually everywhere and many bus tickets allow you to hop on and off en route to your destination.

There is a fairly comprehensive network of coach routes with lots of competition on the more heavily travelled routes between Adelaide, Melbourne and Sydney and up the east coast to Cairns making it a cheap way to get around.

Once you start to head west from Adelaide, there is less competition between various bus companies and the distances between towns are much longer making it a less cost effective transport option.

Bus travel is split between scheduled coach operators such as Firefly, Premier Motor Services and Greyhound and backpacker buses such as Easyrider, Oz Experience and the Wayward Bus. Scheduled buses are usually cheaper and run more frequently but the specialist backpacker buses often go to out of the way places that you would otherwise miss. Unfortunately some backpacker buses are too organised and feel a lot more like tours, which goes against the whole spirit of backpacking and independent travel.

Scheduled Buses

Scheduled coaches are the cheapest and most common way to get around. This is everyday travel for many Australians and is often a good way to meet the locals. These bus services are operated by loads of small companies covering regional areas but there are a few bigger companies that operate a national network.

CountryLink

CountryLink coaches supplement CountryLink's train network *(☎ 132 232; **website** www.countrylink.info)* in New South Wales. Because they are a supplement to CountryLink's rail system, their routes are not always practical in their own right and are often best combined with a train trip. However CountryLink coaches are one of the only ways to travel between many destinations in inland New South Wales.

Firefly Express

Firefly *(☎ 1800 631 164; **website** www.fireflyexpress.com.au)* operate express coach services in southeastern Australia with the following routes; Adelaide-Melbourne and, Melbourne-Sydney. Firefly buses operate both daytime and nighttime services.

Greyhound Australia

Greyhound Australia *(☎ 1300 GREYHOUND or 1300 473 946; **website** www.greyhound.com.au)* have an extensive route network covering all of mainland Australia, but not Tasmania. Greyhound no longer operate services across the Nullarbor between Perth and Adelaide but Greyhound passes are valid on the *Indian Pacific* train between Adelaide and Perth.

Greyhound Australia sells the following travel passes:

AUSSIE KILOMETRE PASSES

Greyhound's Aussie Kilometre Pass offers more flexibility than the predetermined routes covered by their Aussie Explorer Passes.

Travel is purchased in kilometre blocks starting at 2000km and increasing in blocks of 1000km to a maximum of 20,000km.

This pass allows you to visit any destination on the Greyhound Australia network. Aussie Kilometre Passes are valid for 12 months. The Aussie Kilometre Pass costs the same for everyone, however discount card holders get 15% more kilometres of travel on their pass.

Pass	Price	Full fare kms	Discount kms
500km	$99	500	575
750km	$142	750	1,150
1,000km	$185	1,000	1,150
2,000km	$360	2,000	2,300
3,000km	$509	3,000	3,450
4,000km	$657	4,000	4,600
5,000km	$769	5,000	5,750
6,000km	$875	6,000	6,900
7,000km	$1,002	7,000	8,050
8,000km	$1,124	8,000	9,200
9,000km	$1,240	9,000	10,350
10,000km	$1,352	10,000	11,500
11,000km	$1,457	11,000	12,650
12,000km	$1,558	12,000	13,800
13,000km	$1,654	13,000	14,950
14,000km	$1,745	14,000	16,100
15,000km	$1,832	15,000	17,250
16,000km	$1,916	16,000	18,400
17,000km	$1,995	17,000	19,550
18,000km	$2,070	18,000	20,700
19,000km	$2,141	19,000	21,850
20,000km	$2,209	20,000	23,000

AUSSIE EXPLORER PASSES

Greyhound Aussie Explorer Passes allow you to travel along a pre-set route getting on and off at stops along the way. Some passes allow free tours and transfers to places like Kakadu National Park. Passes are valid from 45 to 365 days.

Fare rules:

- Valid for travel for days shown from the date of the first sector travelled
- The first sector must be travelled within six months of buying the pass
- Backtracking is not allowed

- Aussie Explorer Passes are non-refundable after the first sector has been used

Various Aussie Explorer Passes are listed below. Discounted fares apply to holders of Euro 26, HI/YHA, ISIC, Nomads and VIP cards.

All Australian Pass

Covers the whole country except Tasmania. This pass includes trips to Kakadu National Park and travel between Perth and Adelaide on the *Indian Pacific* train.
Full fare *$2,968*
Discount fare *$2,672*
Travel distance *approx 22,716km*
Validity *365 days*

Aussie Highlights Pass

The Greyhound Australia Aussie Highlights Pass covers the eastern half of the country including Adelaide, Melbourne and Sydney; the east coast as far north as Cairns; Darwin and Kakadu National Park and the outback including Alice Springs.
Full fare *$1,781*
Discount fare *$1,603*
Travel distance *approx 12,860km*
Validity *365 days*

Aussie Coast & Red Centre Pass

The Greyhound Australia Aussie Coast & Red Centre Pass takes you to Darwin and Kakadu National Park and the outback including Alice Springs. It also includes travel to Cairns and Townsville and the east coast to either Sydney, Melbourne or Adelaide.

You can start this pass in Cairns, Brisbane, Sydney or Darwin and travel in either direction.

Ex BRISBANE
Full fare *$1,234*
Discount fare *$1,111*
Travel distance *approx 8,446km*

Ex CAIRNS
Full fare *$991*
Discount fare *$892*
Travel distance *approx 6,204km*

Ex SYDNEY
Full fare *$1,358*
Discount fare *$1,222*
Travel distance *approx 9,564km*
Validity *183 days*

Best of the East Pass

The Greyhound Best of the East Pass covers the eastern half of the country including Adelaide, Melbourne and Sydney; the east coast as far north as Cairns; and the outback including Alice Springs.

You can start travel in Adelaide, Melbourne, Sydney, Brisbane or Cairns and travel in either direction.
Full fare *$1,421*
Discount fare *$1,279*
Travel distance *approx 10,710km*
Validity *365 days*

Best of the Outback Pass

The Greyhound Australia Best of the Outback Pass takes you through the centre of Australia north from Adelaide to Darwin and includes Alice Springs and Kakadu National Park.

You can start this pass in Adelaide, Darwin, Melbourne or Sydney and travel in either direction. Passes starting in Melbourne do not include travel to Sydney and passes starting in Adelaide only allow travel north from Adelaide.

Ex ADELAIDE
Full fare *$825*
Discount fare *$742*
Travel distance *approx 4,840km*

Ex MELBOURNE
Full fare *$918*
Discount fare *$826*
Travel distance *approx 5,580km*

Ex SYDNEY
Full fare *$1,046*
Discount fare *$942*
Travel distance *approx 6,648km*

Validity *183 days*

Best of the West Pass

The Greyhound Best of the West Pass covers the western half of the country including Adelaide, Perth; the west coast north of Perth including Kalbarri, Monkey Mia, Exmouth and Broome; Darwin and Kakadu National Park; and the outback including Alice

Springs. This pass includes train travel between Adelaide and Perth on the *Indian Pacific*.
Full fare *$1,986*
Discount fare *$1,787*
Travel distance *approx 13,626km*
Validity *365 days*

Brisbane Sydney 2 Stop
Travel between Brisbane and Sydney with two stops en route.
Full fare *$95*
Discount fare *$86*
Travel distance *approx 960km*
Validity *14 days*

Canberra Stopover
Melbourne to Sydney with a stop in Canberra
Full fare *$90*
Discount fare *$82*
Travel distance *approx 965km*
Validity *10 days*

Central Coaster Pass
The Central Coaster Pass is good for travel between Brisbane and Sydney including stops in Port Macquarie, Coffs Harbour, Byron Bay and the Gold Coast.
Full fare *$193*
Discount fare *$173*
Travel distance *approx 1,110km*
Validity *183 days*

Cosmopolitan Pass
The Cosmopolitan Pass includes travel to the big cities of South Eastern Australia including Brisbane, the Gold Coast, Byron Bay, Sydney, Canberra, Melbourne and Adelaide. You can start the Cosmopolitan Pass in Brisbane or Adelaide and travel in either direction.
Full fare *$351*
Discount fare *$316*
Travel distance *approx 2,770km*
Validity *30 days*

Exmouth Adventurer Pass
The Exmouth Adventurer Pass gives you a return trip up the west coast between Perth and Exmouth with stops in Kalbarri and Monkey Mia.
Full fare *$469*
Discount fare *$422*
Travel distance *approx 3,796km*
Validity *183 days*

Opal Stopover
Travel between Adelaide and Alice Springs with a stop in Coober Pedy.
Full fare *$210*
Discount fare *$189*
Travel distance *approx 1530km*
Validity *10 days*

Pearl Diver Pass
The Greyhound Australia Pearl Diver Pass lets you travel up the west coast between Perth and Broome with excursions to Kalbarri, Monkey Mia and Exmouth.
Full fare *$535*
Discount fare *$482*
Travel distance *approx 3,886km*
Validity *183 days*

Queenslander Pass
The Queenslander Pass lets you travel between Brisbane and Cairns via Outback Queensland. The route includes Charleville, Longreach and Mt Isa.
Full fare *$443*
Discount fare *$399*
Travel distance *approx 3,150km*
Validity *183 days*

Travellers Pass
The Greyhound Australia Travellers Pass takes you up the east coast to Cairns from either Melbourne, Sydney or Brisbane. It lets you stop off at destinations en route including Airlie Beach, 1770/Agnes Water, Hervey Bay, Byron Bay and Coffs Harbour. You can start this pass in Brisbane, Cairns, Melbourne or Sydney and travel in either direction.

BRISBANE-CAIRNS
Full fare *$326*
Discount fare *$293*
Travel distance *approx 2,330km*

MELBOURNE-CAIRNS
Full fare *$445*
Discount fare *$401*
Travel distance *approx 4,478km*

SYDNEY-CAIRNS
Full fare *$390*
Discount fare *$351*
Travel distance *approx 3,440km*

ADELAIDE-CAIRNS
Full fare *$676*
Discount fare *$608*
Travel distance *approx 4,600km*

Validity *183 days*

Mini Travellers Pass
The Greyhound Australia Travellers Pass takes you up the east coast to Cairns from either Melbourne, Sydney or Brisbane. It lets you stop off at destinations en route including Airlie Beach, 1770/Agnes Water, Hervey Bay, Byron Bay and Coffs Harbour.

This pass is essentially the same as the Travellers Pass, except it is only valid for 45 days, instead of 183. It also comes in shorter versions in case you only want to travel between Brisbane and Airlie Beach or Hervey Bay.

CAIRNS-MELBOURNE
Full fare *$404*
Discount fare *$364*
Travel distance *approx 4,478km*

CAIRNS-BRISBANE
Full fare *$295*
Discount fare *$265*
Travel distance *approx 2,330km*

CAIRNS-SYDNEY
Full fare *$357*
Discount fare *$321*
Travel distance *approx 3,420km*

CAIRNS-BYRON BAY
Full fare *$317*
Discount fare *$285*
Travel distance *approx 2,530km*

HERVEY BAY-BRISBANE
Full fare *$120*
Discount fare *$108*
Travel distance *approx 300km*

HERVEY BAY-CAIRNS
Full fare *$242*
Discount fare *$218*
Travel distance *approx 1,900km*

HERVEY BAY-MELBOURNE
Full fare *$274*
Discount fare *$247*
Travel distance *approx 2,504km*

HERVEY BAY-SYDNEY
Full fare *$217*
Discount fare *$196*
Travel distance *approx 1,450km*

AIRLIE BEACH-BRISBANE
Full fare *$207*
Discount fare *$186*
Travel distance *approx 1,687km*

AIRLIE BEACH-BYRON BAY
Full fare *$237*
Discount fare *$213*
Travel distance *approx 1,887km*

AIRLIE BEACH-SYDNEY
Full fare *$307*
Discount fare *$279*
Travel distance *approx 2,777km*

BRISBANE-MELBOURNE
Full fare *$235*
Discount fare *$212*
Travel distance *approx 2,160km*

BRISBANE-BYRON BAY RETURN
Full fare *$80*
Discount fare *$72*
Travel distance *approx 400km*

BRISBANE-HERVEY BAY RETURN
Full fare *$120*
Discount fare *$108*
Travel distance *approx 700km*

AUSSIE DAY PASSES
Greyhound's Aussie Day Passes are designed for the short-stay visitor who wants to get out of the cities and see the country. They let you go anywhere on the Greyhound Australia network and disjointed travel and backtracking is allowed, but there is a kilometre limit.

The pass validity is for consecutive travel days. In other words it is not a flexi pass (even though Greyhound sometimes market the pass as one of their Oz-Flexi passes) and the number of valid travel days begins on the first day of travel.

Days valid	km limit	Full fare	Discount fare
3 days	1,000km	$133	$119
5 days	1,500km	$201	$181
7 days	2,000km	$267	$240

10 days	3,000km	$360	$324
20 days	6,000km	$725	$653
30 days	10,000km	$1000	$900

Premier Motor Service

Premier (☎ *13 34 10;* ***website*** *www.premierms.com.au)* is the biggest of the small coach operators and has scheduled services along the east coast. They operate coaches on the popular Sydney to Cairns route and also along the coastal route between Melbourne and Sydney. Premier offers several travel passes that allow three months travel along a specified route: these include Melbourne to Cairns, Melbourne to Sydney, Sydney to Cairns and Sydney to Brisbane.

Route	Full fare	Discount fare
Melbourne-Sydney (unltd stops; 3 mths)	$75	$65
Sydney-Brisbane (unltd stops; 3 mths)	$129	$109
Brisbane-Cairns (unltd stops; 2 mths)	$280	$239
Cairns-Sydney (unltd stops; 6 mths)	$340	$289
Melbourne-Cairns (unltd stops; 6 mths)	$350	$320

Premier Stateliner Buses

Premier Stateliner (☎ *(08) 8415 5555;* ***website*** *www.premierstateliner.com.au)* operate bus services in country South Australia.

Most services are centred on Adelaide and they are useful for travelling in south-eastern South Australia (handy for travellers picking fruit along the Murray River) but they run as far west as Ceduna, and they also go as far north as Roxby Downs in the outback.

V/line

V/line (☎ *136 196;* ***website*** *www.vline.com.au)* operate regional bus services in Victoria. V/line bus services are designed to complement V/line's rail network although there are some handy bus routes for independently-minded travellers that want to visit Phillip Island, the Grampians and the Great Ocean Road without taking a tour.

V/line's main hub is the coach terminal at Melbourne's Southern Cross Station.

Backpacker Buses

Australia has a multitude of specialised bus services operated specifically for backpackers. Some of these include very useful services stopping off at hostels and also making detours to attractions that the express coaches miss. However some of these so-called backpacker buses are simply tours, and this runs against the spirit of backpacking and independent travel.

Oz Experience is biggest backpacker bus operator and has routes covering most of the country. It represents a good travel option.

Some smaller companies also offer excellent transport options within a particular region and they often have the benefit of local knowledge.

If you're thinking about buying a pass for one of the smaller backpacker bus companies, first check whether it really caters for independent travellers – allowing you to get on and off as you please – if it doesn't offer this sort of flexibility then it is nothing more than a tour.

Autopia Tours

Autopia Tours (☎ *(03) 9419 8878 or 1800 000 507;* ***website*** *www.autopiatours.com.au)* is a tour company in the same mould as Wildlife Tours and the Wayward Bus that has a good Melbourne-Adelaide trip ($395) and also a Melbourne-Sydney trip ($395) that runs via the Snowy Mountains, Canberra and the Blue Mountains.

Autopia also runs several excellent day trips from Melbourne that are worth considering if you don't have your own car. These include Phillip Island ($109), Great Ocean Road ($105), the Grampians National Park ($99) and the Yarra Valley wineries ($99).

Easyrider Backpacker Tours

Easyrider Adventure Travel (☎ *(08) 9226 0307;* ***website*** *www.easyridertours.*

com.au) operates tours and hop-on hop-off buses in Western Australia.

Easyrider's hop-on hop-off buses are a good travel option if you want to see Western Australia.

They run up the coast from Perth to Exmouth, Broome and Darwin. Their Broometime service goes between Perth and Broome ($799), although you have the option of only travelling Perth-Exmouth ($419) or Exmouth-Broome ($409). Easyrider's Over the Top service runs between Perth and Darwin ($1399) and their Kimberley Krossing ($599) and Territory Trek ($699) services go between Broome and Darwin.

The southwest route ($319) runs a circuit covering southwestern WA, including Albany, Margaret River and Walpole.

Easyrider also have a few shorter trips including one-day tours to Margaret River ($149) and Nambung National Park/the Pinnacles ($159).

Nullarbor Traveller

Nullarbor Traveller *(☎ (08) 8364 0407; **website** www.the-traveller.com.au)* runs nine and 10-day tours between Adelaide and Perth.

Although the Nullabor Traveller is a tour rather than a hop-on hop-off bus there are very few places on the Nullarbor that most travellers would want to stay for longer than a day if they were travelling independently so it is an excellent way of covering this vast distance while seeing all the interesting bits en route.

The westbound route is a day longer than travel in the opposite direction. The reason for this is that the eastbound service travels through Western Australia's central wheat belt to visit Wave Rock and also visits South Australia's Eyre Peninsula, while the westbound service follows Western Australia's coastline.

The Adelaide-Perth tour is a 10-day trip including the Flinders Ranges, the Western Australia coast and the Margaret River region. This trip costs $1450 ($1350 HI/YHA, Nomads, VIP).

The Perth-Adelaide tour is a nine-day trip that visits Wave Rock and Esperance in Western Australia and also has a strong focus on the Eyre Peninsula. This tour includes the opportunity to swim with tuna and at Port Lincoln there is an optional caged swim with Great White Sharks. This tour costs $1295 ($1195 HI/YHA, Nomads, VIP).

Nullarbor Traveller also have a couple of shorter tours including a five-day Adelaide to Eyre Peninsula trip for $840 ($780 HI/YHA, Nomads, VIP) and a five-day Perth to Esperance trip for $840 ($780 HI/YHA, Nomads, VIP).

Oz Experience

Oz Experience *(☎ (02) 8356 1766; **website** www.ozexperience.com)* is the biggest of the backpacker bus operators. They go everywhere except Western Australia and their passes allow you to hop on and off at stops along the way. Most passes are valid for six months although some are valid for 12 months.

Oz Experience includes a lot of extras on its trips such as visits to National Parks and sheep and cattle stations.

Because they offer so many different passes it can be confusing working out which one is best for you.

Oz Experience passes are listed below. Discount fares apply to holders of Euro 26, HI/YHA, ISIC, Nomads and VIP cards.

EAST COAST PASSES (NORTHBOUND)

Bruce (Melbourne-Cairns)
Travel along the east coast from Melbourne to Cairns.
Price *$770*
Recommended minimum trip *26 days*
Plus local payment of $185

Bruce (Sydney-Cairns)
Travel along the east coast from Sydney to Cairns.
Price *$550*
Recommended minimum trip *20 days*
Plus local payment of $110

Matey (Melbourne-Sydney)
Travel from Melbourne to Sydney via Lakes Entrance, the Snowy Mountains and Canberra.
Price *$240*

Recommended minimum trip *3 days*
Plus local payment of $85

Strewth (Brisbane-Cairns)
Brisbane to Cairns via the coast.
Price *$375*
Recommended minimum trip *12 days*
Plus local payment of $60

Strewth (Byron Bay-Cairns)
Byron Bay to Cairns via the coast.
Price *$395*
Recommended minimum trip *16 days*
Plus local payment of $60

Surf (Sydney to Byron Bay or Brisbane)
Sydney to Byron Bay or Brisbane including a surf lesson at Surf Camp.
Price *$250*
Recommended minimum trip *3-5 days*
Plus local payment of $60

Victa Matey (Adelaide-Sydney)
Adelaide to Melbourne via the Grampians and the Great Ocean Road, then up to Sydney via Wilsons Promentory, the Snowy Mountains and Canberra.
Price *$480*
Recommended minimum trip *9 days*
Plus local payment of $165

Victa (Melbourne-Adelaide)
Melbourne to Adelaide via the Great Ocean Road and the Grampians.
Price *$240*
Recommended minimum trip *3 days*
Plus local payment of $85

EAST COAST PASSES (SOUTHBOUND)

Cobber (Cairns-Melbourne)
Travel along the east coast from Cairns to Melbourne.
Price *$745*
Recommended minimum trip *26 days*
Plus local payment of $185

Cobber (Cairns-Sydney)
The east coast from Cairns to Sydney.
Price *$495*
Recommended minimum trip *20 days*
Plus local payment of $110

Matey (Sydney-Melbourne)
Travel from Sydney to Melbourne via Canberra, the Snowy Mountains and Wilsons Promontory.
Price *$240*
Recommended minimum trip *3 days*
Plus local payment of $85

Strewth (Cairns-Brisbane)
Cairns to Brisbane via the east coast.
Price *$375*
Recommended minimum trip *12 days*
Plus local payment of $60

Strewth (Cairns-Byron Bay)
Travel from Cairns to Byron Bay via the east coast.
Price *$395*
Recommended minimum trip *16 days*
Plus local payment of $60

Surf (Brisbane or Byron Bay to Sydney)
Brisbane or Byron Bay to Sydney with a surf lesson at Surf Camp.
Price *$250*
Recommended minimum trip *3-5 days*
Plus local payment of $60

Victa Matey Pass (Sydney-Adelaide)
Sydney to Melbourne via Canberra, the Snowy Mountains and Wilsons Promontory, then to Adelaide via the Great Ocean Road and the Grampians.
Price *$480*
Recommended minimum trip *9 days*
Plus local payment of $165

Victa (Adelaide-Melbourne)
Adelaide to Melbourne via the Grampians and the Great Ocean Road.
Price *$240*
Recommended minimum trip *3 days*
Plus local payment of $85

NATIONAL PASSES

Dazza (Sydney-Cairns plus Uluru)
Travel the East Coast between Sydney and Cairns plus a Uluru safari with transport between Alice Springs to Uluru and Kings Canyon. Dazza is essentially a combination of the Bruce (Sydney-Cairns) and the Big Rock passes. You will need to make your own way to Alice Springs.

Price *$865 (from Sydney)*
Recommended minimum trip *25 days*
Plus local payment of $210

Fair Dinkum
The Fair Dinkum pass covers most of Eastern and Central Australia and the Top End and includes the East Coast between Sydney and Cairns, a Blue Mountains day trip, the Snowy Mountains, Wilsons Promontory, Melbourne, the Great Ocean Road, Grampians National Park, Adelaide, Coober Pedy, Alice Springs, Uluru (Ayers Rock), Katherine, Darwin and Kakadu National Park.

You can start anywhere en route and finish where you started travelling in one direction only.
Price *$2000*
Recommended minimum trip *55 days*
Plus local payment of $560

Fish Hook (Alice Springs-Sydney)
This outback odyssey takes you from Alice Springs to Sydney via Uluru (Ayers Rock), Coober Pedy, the Flinders Ranges, Adelaide, the Grampains National Park, the Great Ocean Road, Melbourne, Wilsons Promontory, Lakes Entrance and the Snowy Mountains.
Price *$1055*
Recommended minimum trip *26 days*
Plus local payment of $340

Fish Hook (Darwin-Melbourne)
This outback odyssey takes you from Darwin to Melbourne via Kakadu National Park, Katherine, Alice Springs, Uluru (Ayers Rock), Coober Pedy, the Flinders Ranges, Adelaide, the Grampains National Park and the Great Ocean Road.
Price *$1160*
Recommended minimum trip *27 days*
Plus local payment of $390

Fish Hook (Darwin-Sydney)
This outback odyssey takes you from Darwin to Sydney via Kakadu National Park, Katherine, Alice Springs, Uluru (Ayers Rock), Coober Pedy, the Flinders Ranges, Adelaide, the Grampains National Park, the Great Ocean Road, Melbourne, Wilsons Promontory, Lakes Entrance and the Snowy Mountains.
Price *$1495*
Recommended minimum trip *32 days*
Plus local payment of $465

Knobs & Bells
The Knobs & Bells covers most of Eastern and Central Australia and includes the East Coast between Sydney and Cairns, a Blue Mountains day trip, the Snowy Mountains, Wilsons Promontory, Melbourne, the Great Ocean Road, Grampians National Park, Adelaide, Coober Pedy, Alice Springs and Uluru (Ayers Rock).

You can start anywhere en route and finish where you started travelling in one direction only.
Price *$1560*
Recommended minimum trip *45 days*
Plus local payment of $435

Shazza (Cairns-Sydney plus Uluru)
Travel the East Coast between Sydney and Cairns plus a Uluru safari with transport between Alice Springs to Uluru and Kings Canyon. Shazza is essentially a combination of the Cobber (Cairns-Sydney) and the Big Rock passes. You will need to make your own way to Alice Springs.
Price *$865*
Recommended minimum trip *25 days*
Plus local payment of $210

Whipper Snapper (Adelaide-Darwin)
The Whipper Snapper pass lets you travel from Adelaide to Darwin via the East Coast. It includes Grampians National Park, the Great Ocean Road, Melbourne, Wilsons Promontory, the Snowy Mountains, Sydney, a Blue Mountains day trip, the East Coast from Sydney to Cairns, Alice Springs, Uluru (Ayers Rock), Katherine and Kakadu National Park.
Price *$1760*
Recommended minimum trip *43 days*
Plus local payment of $460

Whipper Snapper (Melbourne-Darwin)
The Whipper Snapper pass lets you travel from Melbourne to Darwin via

the East Coast. It includes Wilsons Promontory, the Snowy Mountains, Sydney, a Blue Mountains day trip, the East Coast from Sydney to Cairns, Alice Springs, Uluru (Ayers Rock), Katherine and Kakadu National Park.
Price *$1500*
Recommended minimum trip *38 days*
Plus local payment of $375

Whipper Snapper (Sydney-Darwin)
The Whipper Snapper pass lets you travel from Sydney to Darwin via the East Coast. It includes a Blue Mountains day trip, the East Coast from Sydney to Cairns, Alice Springs, Uluru (Ayers Rock), Katherine and Kakadu National Park.
Price *$1300*
Recommended minimum trip *30 days*
Plus local payment of $310

The local payment is an additional charge that covers a food kitty, national park entry fees, some activities and accommodation at compulsory overnight stops.

Wayward Bus

Wayward Bus *(☎ (08) 8410 8833; **website** www.waywardbus.com.au)* is more a tour company than an independent travel option, but they do have some excellent trips that allow you to discover some great out-of-the-way places including the Flinders Ranges, Central Australia and Kangaroo Island. They're also well known for their Great Ocean Road trip in Victoria.

Wayward Bus tours include:

Classic Coast
This three-day Melbourne to Adelaide tour takes in the Great Ocean Road and the Grampians National Park.
Price *$395*

Face the Outback
An eight-day overland trip between Adelaide and Alice Springs through the Outback. This trip includes the Flinders Ranges, travels along the Oodnadatta Track and visits Coober Pedy and Uluru (Ayers Rock).
Price *$995*

Just the Centre
This three-day camping trip from Alice Springs to Uluru is an ideal way to see Uluru (Ayers Rock).
Price *$325*

Kangaroo Island
This two day tour of Kangaroo Island departs from and returns to Adelaide. It seems expensive until you realise how much the return ferry ticket to Kangaroo Island would cost on its own.
Price *$387*

Train Travel

Train travel is the most comfortable way to travel overland, but trains don't run as frequently or go to as many destinations as buses.

Trains go to the most popular destinations along the east coast including the popular Sydney-Cairns route and also along major inter-city lines including Sydney to Adelaide, Canberra and Melbourne and onwards to Perth on the west coast. From Adelaide, there are also trains running north to Darwin.

Great Southern Railway *(GSR; ☎ 13 21 47; **website** www.gsr.com.au)* runs most of Australia's great classic rail journeys, which include the long-distance *Indian-Pacific* between Sydney and Perth and the legendary *Ghan*, running from Adelaide to Darwin. Great Southern Railway offers backpackers discounts when you show your HI/YHA, Nomads or VIP card, which makes the train a cheap alternative to bus travel. Some of the fares with the backpacker discount include Melbourne-Adelaide ($59), Adelaide-Alice Springs ($214), Adelaide-Darwin ($454) and Sydney-Perth ($428). The best deal; however, is Great Southern Railway's Rail Explorer Pass that gives you six months unlimited travel on the *Ghan*, *Indian-Pacific* and *Overland* trains for just $590 (with a backpacker discount card and a non-Australian passport).

Other train services in Australia are operated by independent rail companies in each state. These include CountryLink *(☎ 13 22 32; **website** www.countrylink.*

info), which operate trains in New South Wales; QR *(☎ 13 22 32; **website** www.qr.com.au)*, which run train services in Queensland; V/line *(☎ 13 61 96; **website** www.vline.com.au)*, which runs trains in Victoria. Transwa *(☎ 13 10 53; **website** www.transwa.wa.gov.au)* has limited train services in Western Australia.

There are a number of rail passes available that make train travel a little easier and more affordable. These rail passes are available from student and backpacker travel agents or contact the railway companies listed above for more information.

Australian rail passes include:

Austrail Flexi-Pass

The Austrail Flexi-Pass gives you either 15 or 22 days travel within a six month period on CountryLink, Great Southern Railways or QR train services.

Validity	Price
15 days travel in six months	$950
22 days travel in six months	$1,330

This pass is only available to international (non-Australian) passport holders in possession of a return or onward airline ticket.

Great Southern Railway Rail Explorer Pass

Great Southern Railway's Rail Explorer Pass is one of the best travel deals in Australia. This pass gives you six months unlimited travel on *the Ghan*, *Indian Pacific* and *Overland* trains. It costs $590 if you have a HI/YHA, Nomads or VIP card. This pass is not available to Australian passport holders.

Backtracker Rail Pass

This Backtracker Rail Pass *(☎ 13 22 32; **website** www.countrylink.info/travel_passes/backtracker_rail_pass)* is good for unlimited economy travel on all Countrylink trains and buses in New South Wales and includes travel on Countrylink trains to Brisbane and Melbourne.

This pass is only available to travellers with a valid international passport.

Validity	Price
14 days	$232
1 month	$275
3 months	$298
6 months	$420

East Coast Discovery Pass

The East Coast Discovery Pass is the most economical way to explore the east coast by train. The pass is valid for six months travel in one direction along a predefined route on the CountryLink and QR network between Melbourne and Cairns. This pass is not valid on the *Kuranda Scenic Railway*.

Route	Price
Brisbane to Cairns	$273.90
Sydney to Cairns	$403.90
Melbourne to Brisbane	$220
Melbourne to Gold Coast	$220
Melbourne to Cairns	$500.50
Sydney to Melbourne	$130
Sydney to Brisbane	$130
Sydney to Gold Coast	$130

Driving

Driving is the best way to travel around Australia. Having access to your own set of wheels frees you from the constraints of routes and schedules and allows you to visit places off the beaten track.

Anyone over 18 can drive in Australia with their local licence, providing it is valid and that you've been in the country for less than six months. If you're spending longer in Australia you should bring along an international driving permit or apply for an Australian driver's licence.

Driving in Australia is easy. Traffic drives on the left and roads are generally well-maintained but motorways are usually restricted to the approaches to major cities and heavily travelled routes such as Melbourne-Sydney and Sunshine Coast-Brisbane-Gold Coast. A regular car will take you virtually everywhere in Australia, but a four-wheel-drive is essential for beach driving or if you want to explore Fraser Island and the Cape York Peninsula.

There are some very long and boring stretches of road in Australia and fatigue is a big killer – make plenty of rest stops, drink plenty of coffee or cola and share the driving with someone else. Check noticeboards in hostels to see if another traveller wants a lift. Offering a lift is a good way to split your fuel costs as well as avoiding spending too much time behind the wheel.

Speed limits on most country roads are 100-110km/h, although the top speed limit is 130km/h on highways in the Northern Territory. On motorways the limit is usually 110km/h outside cities and 100km/h in built up areas. Minor roads in towns and cities are 50km/h unless signposted otherwise. It is compulsory to wear seat belts and it's illegal to talk on a mobile phone while driving. You must not park facing oncoming traffic.

Watch out for road trains if you're driving in the outback. These 50-metre-long semi-trailers can't stop as quickly as a regular car so keep out of their way and make sure that you allow plenty of room to overtake one. Also be alert if you're driving in the countryside around dusk – kangaroos are active at this time and are unpredictable – often jumping into the path of an oncoming vehicle.

Motoring organisations

If you're a member of a motoring organisation you can use the facilities of their Australian counterpart. Each state has its own motoring organisation, although they all fall under the umbrella of the Australian Automobile Association (AAA).

If you're not a member of an auto club at home it's worth joining one in Australia if you have your own car; particularly for the peace of mind and the potential savings of the roadside assistance. Roadside assistance can be contacted by calling 13 11 11 in any state.

AANT (Northern Territory)
81 Smith Street, Darwin
☎ *(08) 8981 3837*
Website *www.aant.com.au*

NRMA (New South Wales)
74 -76 King Street, Sydney
🚆 *Martin Place, Wynyard*
☎ *13 21 32*
Website *www.nrma.com.au*

RAA (South Australia)
41 Hindmarsh Square, Adelaide
☎ *(08) 8202 4600*
Website *www.raa.com.au*

RACT (Tasmania)
Corner Murray & Patrick Streets, Hobart
☎ *13 11 11*
Website *www.ract.com.au*

RACQ (Queensland)
300 St Pauls Terrace, Fortitude Valley
🚆 *Brunswick Street*
☎ *(07) 3361 2444*
Website *www.racq.com.au*

RACV (Victoria)
360 Bourke Street, Melbourne
🚋 *19, 57, 59, 68, 86, 96* 🚆 *Flinders Street, Melbourne Central*
☎ *13 19 55*
Website *www.racv.com.au*

RAC of WA (Western Australia)
228 Adelaide Terrace, Perth
☎ *(08) 9421 4444*
Website *www.racwa.com.au*

Renting a Car

Although expensive over a long period, renting a car is a good option if your time is limited and if you want to explore a particular region in depth. Car rental companies with branches nationwide are generally the most expensive although these companies do offer advantages such as airport pick-up and drop-off points, frequent flyer points and long-distance one-way rentals.

The standard insurance cover that comes with most car rental companies requires that you pay an excess of around $2000 before the insurance company pays out. Rental car companies will try and sell you insurance to cover this excess, but at around $20 a day this is overpriced and can substantially increase the cost of your car rental. A much better idea is to take out travel insurance that covers this excess or arrange rental car excess insurance before leaving home. This works out a lot cheaper than paying the excess cover that rental car companies charge.

You will need a credit card to rent a car as it is virtually impossible to rent a car without one.

Car rental companies include:

Avis
220 William Street, Kings Cross
Kings Cross
(02) 9357 2000
***Website** www.avis.com/au/*
***Open** Mon-Thu 7.30am-6pm, Fri 7.30am-7pm, Sat 7.30am-6pm, Sun 7.30am-6pm*

Bayswater Rental Car
180 William Street, Kings Cross
Kings Cross, Museum
(02) 9360 3622
***Website** www.nobirds.com.au*
***Open** Mon-Fri 7am-6.30pm, Sat 8am-3.30pm, Sun 9am-3.30pm*

Budget
93 William Street, East Sydney
Kings Cross, Museum
(02) 8255 9600
***Website** www.budget.com.au*
***Open** Mon-Fri 7.30am-6pm, Sat-Sun 7.30am-6pm*

Europcar
100 William Street, Kings Cross
Kings Cross, Museum
(02) 8255 9050
***Website** www.europcar.com.au*

Hertz
Corner Riley & William Streets, East Sydney
Museum
13 30 39
***Website** www.hertz.com.au*
***Open** 7.30am-6pm daily*

Red Spot Car Rentals
38 College Street, Sydney
Museum
1300 66 88 10 or (02) 8303 2222
***Website** www.redspotcar.com.au*
***Open** Mon-Thu 8am-5pm, Fri 8am-6pm, Sat-Sun 8am-noon*

Thrifty
75 William Street, East Sydney
Museum
1300 367 227
***Website** www.thrifty.com.au*
***Open** 7.30am-6pm daily*

Renting a Campervan

Campervans are a popular alternative to a rental car since they give you somewhere to stay. However they are more expensive than regular car rental and you'll often have to pay to stay in a caravan park so you can have a shower. Also because you spend a lot of time sleeping in your campervan, you generally miss out on being part of the backpacker scene.

Campervan rental companies vary wildly. Large established players like Britz, Kea and Maui rent top quality vans that are professionally fitted out and ideal for a long trip; however cheaper campervan companies like Wicked will rent you a clapped out 15-year-old van with a shoddy campervan conversion. However Wicked are among the cheapest and they may rent you a van without a credit card and your van will have a funky paint job.

Several companies rent fully equipped campervans complete with camping gear and prices are quite reasonable for longer rentals. Campervan rental companies include:

Backpacker Campervans
653 Gardeners Road, Mascot
Mascot
1800 331 454 or (02) 9667 0402
***Website** www.backpackercampervans.com*
***Open** 8am-4.30pm daily*

Britz
653 Gardeners Road, Mascot
Mascot
1800 331 454 or (02) 9667 0402
***Website** www.britz.com.au*
***Open** 8am-4.30pm daily*

Devil Campervans
94 Kennedy Drive, Cambridge TAS
(03) 6248 4493
***Website** www.devilcampervans.com.au*
***Open** 7am-8pm daily*

Hippy Campers
182-196 O'Riordan Street, Botany
🚉 *Mascot*
☎ *1800 777 779*
Website *www.hippiecamper.com*
Open *8am-4.30pm*

Travellers Autobarn
177 William Street, Kings Cross
🚉 *Kings Cross*
☎ *1800 674 374*
Website *www.travellersautobarn.com.au*
Open *Mon-Fri 9am-6pm, Sat 9am-5pm, Sun 10.30am-3pm*

Wicked Campers
79 McLachlan Street, Fortitude Valley, Brisbane
🚉 *Brunswick Street*
☎ *1800 246 869*
Website *www.wickedcampers.com.au*
Open *Mon-Fri 9am-4pm, Sat 9am-noon*

Buying a car

If you're going to be travelling around Australia for several months it may be worth the trouble to buy your own car and sell it before you leave. Cheap reliable cars are generally large cars such as the Ford Falcon and Holden Commodore, which can cost a lot to run but are generally cheap to fix and service.

Ideally it's a good idea to check hostel notice boards and buy your car from another traveller as it may come with camping equipment and you should be able to get a good bargain, considering that other travellers have a flight home to catch and are in a hurry to sell. Other good places to look are the classified ads in Friday's *Sydney Morning Herald* and *Herald Sun* (Melbourne) and Saturday's the *Age* (Melbourne). The *Trading Post (**website** www.tradingpost.com.au)* is also a good spot to find a bargain. Buying a car privately, either from another traveller or through classified advertisements is usually the cheapest option, but it's not always the best choice if your time is limited. Buying from a used car dealer is easier and the dealer will organise the paperwork to get the car transferred into your name. There are loads of used car dealers in the suburbs of the big cities.

Some car dealers that do a lot of business with backpackers offer a buy-back guarantee, where they offer to buy the car back from you at an agreed (lower) price at the end of your trip. You can usually get a much better price selling the car yourself but a buy-back guarantee is handy if you don't want to waste precious time trying to sell the car when you have finished with it. If you buy from a car dealer that offers a buy-back guarantee, read the fine print and make sure that you are not required to pass a roadworthy inspection. Very few vehicles can pass a roadworthy after a trip around Australia and a buy-back guarantee with this condition is virtually worthless. The main car dealer that offers a buy-back guarantee is Travellers Autobarn *(☎ 1800 674 374; **website** www.travellersautobarn.com.au).*

Used cars need a certificate of roadworthiness before they can be sold – don't buy a car without one as you'll need to show it when you transfer the registration. You will also need to get a certificate of roadworthiness before you sell the car at the end of your trip. Many mechanics can assess your car and issue the certificate.

Once you have a roadworthiness certificate, take it along with the receipt, your driver's licence and passport to the local department of transport; this department is known by different names in different states (refer to the list at the end of this paragraph). You will need to pay a fee, which is calculated according to the value of the car. If the annual vehicle registration is due, or if you are buying a car in a different state to which it is registered, this will also need to be paid. The registration (or rego) includes the minimum legal third-party insurance. You can count on these fees running to several hundred dollars. Each state's laws vary, check with the department of transport in the state where you plan on buying or selling your car.

Motor Vehicle Registry (Northern Territory)
18 Goyder Road, Parap
☎ *1300 654 628*
Website *www.nt.gov.au/transport/mvr/*
Open *Mon-Thu 8am-4pm, Fri 8am-5.30pm*

DIER – Transport Division (Tasmania)
Service Tasmania, 134 Macquarie Street, Hobart
☎ *1300 135 513*
Website *www.transport.tas.gov.au*
Open *Mon-Fri 8.15am-5.30pm*

RTA (New South Wales)
Centennial Plaza Motor Registry, Ground Floor, Centennial Plaza, 260 Elizabeth Street, Surry Hills
Central
☎ *13 22 13*
Website *www.rta.nsw.gov.au*
Open *Mon-Fri 8.30am-5pm, Sat 8.30am-noon*

Transport Queensland
229 Elizabeth Street, Brisbane
☎ *13 23 80*
Website *www.transport.qld.gov.au*
Open *Mon-Tue 8.30am-4.30pm, Wed 9.30am-4.30pm, Thu-Fri 8.30am-4.30pm*

Transport Roads & Traffic (Australian Capital Territory)
Dickson Motor Registry, 13-15 Challis Street, Dickson
☎ *13 22 81*
Website *www.canberraconnect.act.gov.au*
Open *Mon 8.30am-5pm, Tue 8.30am-5pm, Wed 8.30am-5pm, Thu 8.30am-5pm, Fri 8.30am-5pm*

Transport SA (South Australia)
Ground Floor, EDS Centre, 108 North Terrace, Adelaide
☎ *13 10 84*
Website *www.transport.sa.gov.au*
Open *Mon-Fri 9am-5pm*

Transport Western Australia
Corner Troode Street & Plaistowe Mews, City West, West Perth
☎ *13 11 56*
Website *www.dpi.wa.gov.au/licensing/566.asp*
Open *Mon-Fri 8.15am-4.30pm*

VicRoads (Victoria)
459 Lygon Street, Carlton
☎ *13 11 71*
Website *www.vicroads.vic.gov.au*
Open *Mon-Thu 8.30am-4.30pm, Fri 8.30am-5pm*

Hitchhiking

Hitchhiking is a great way to travel that allows you to really get to know the locals. Many people prefer hitching to other forms of transport because it you can get dropped off anywhere, allowing you to discover places you may never have dreamt of visiting.

Unfortunately hitchhiking gets a lot of bad press, particularly since the widely publicised hitchhiker murders many years ago. It seems that there are a lot of people who think that you'll get murdered if you hitch. This attitude has two negative effects – people are too frightened to pick you up and a lot of other travellers are scared to hitchhike meaning less hitchers on the road, which ultimately leads to hitchhiking becoming a dying art.

Where to hitch

It is important to choose a good spot to hitchhike. A good spot makes it easier to get a ride and more importantly it is safer for both you and the driver.

If you are leaving a big city it is a good idea to take a bus or train to the outskirts of town to get to a road leading to a motorway and then choose a spot with plenty of room for the driver to safely stop. If possible try and stand in a spot where the traffic isn't too fast. It is much safer and also most drivers want to size you up before they decide whether to give you a lift.

If you've got a lift on a motorway, try and get dropped off at a service area rather than in town. If you're dropped off in town you have to wait hours in local traffic before getting a lift back on to the motorway. If you hitch at a service area you have facilities like a restaurant, shop and toilets; you can chat to truck drivers and ask about getting a lift and you can get a good safe spot to stand where all the traffic is long distance.

Don't hitchhike on motorways, stick to the entrance ramps and service areas.

Not only is hitching on motorways dangerous, it is difficult for cars to safely stop and it is usually illegal.

Signs

A lot of hitchers debate whether to use signs or not. Some argue that drivers won't stop if they don't know where you want to go, while other hitchers say that it is safer to avoid using a sign. If you don't use a sign you can ask the driver where they are going before accepting a lift – the driver won't be able to lie about his destination to get you into the car.

A good compromise is to use a sign indicating the name of the road you want to travel on. This is especially useful if you are on a busy road before a major intersection, without a sign you may get a lift going in the wrong direction.

Tips for getting a ride

You'll find a lot of rides come from regular stoppers – people who've hitchhiked themselves and are repaying the favour and frequent solo travellers, like couriers and truck drivers who want some company. Although you'll find that different people have different reasons for picking you up, there are a number of things you can do to improve your chances of getting a lift.

- Look neat and respectable. Not only should you look non-threatening to any passing driver, but you also help to improve other people's impression of hitchhiking.
- Face the oncoming traffic and smile. It is important that people can see you, so avoid wearing sunglasses.
- Try and look smart and clean.
- When a car stops ask the driver where they are going to. At this point it is easy to decline the lift if you don't like the look of the driver or if they aren't going your way.
- Never smoke in someone else's car.
- Travel light. The lighter your load, the quicker you travel.
- Take an international drivers licence. Many people stop because they want someone to share the driving.

Safety

Although hitchhiking is more hazardous than bus or train travel, it's still safer than other forms of transport such as cycling.

The most dangerous thing about hitchhiking is the possibility of being involved in a car accident or being hit by a car if you stand too close to the side of the road.

There is also a very small danger posed by accepting a lift with a driver that you do not know. The driver could either be a dangerous character or simply a bad driver.

Despite the perceived danger, there are plenty of ways to minimise your risk.

If you're a single female you'll travel quickly, however you'll also attract your fair share of obnoxious drivers. It is a good idea to travel with someone else, preferably a guy. This way you will be perceived as a couple which means that you shouldn't have any sleazy old men trying to come on to you, and if they do at least there is someone to help you out.

Many hitchhikers travel with a mobile phone and only hitch where there is coverage. Being able to call for help makes hitching a safer transport option. For this to work you need to keep your phone charged and in your pocket and you need to know the emergency number (112 is the international emergency number from GSM mobile phones, although the Australian emergency number 000 also works).

Don't let the driver put your backpack in the car boot. Try and keep all your stuff with you, even when you stop for food and fuel.

Don't feel compelled to accept a lift just because someone has stopped for you. If it doesn't feel right, don't get in. Another ride will come along.

Is it legal?

Hitchhiking is illegal in Queensland and Victoria. The law basically says that you cannot stand on a roadway (including the shoulder) where you may obstruct traffic. However this interpretation of the law suggests that it is OK to hitch from a footpath or the grassy area beside the road.

Elsewhere in Australia it is illegal to hitchhike on motorways (where pedestrians are prohibited and where cars are not allowed to stop). Find a safe spot before a motorway entrance and hitch from there.

Australian Capital Territory

While Australia's state capitals owe their existence to convicts, trade, defence or simple geography, Canberra owes its origin to diplomacy and political necessity. It was created because Australia decided, soon after it became a unified nation in 1901, that it needed an independent capital free from political or commercial domination by any one state.

New South Wales and Victoria (always strong rivals) were jockeying at the time for the privilege of housing Federal Parliament. NSW favoured Sydney; Victoria preferred Melbourne. An independently sited capital, surrounded by a neutral buffer zone, was the logical, diplomatic solution. The Australian Capital Territory (ACT) was established in 1911 as an administrative territory to encompass Australia's proposed new capital.

The ACT is surrounded entirely by New South Wales.

Canberra

Canberra is a modern city - there is no old quarter and few historic buildings and many travellers find that feels a little sterile. The city was designed by Chicago architect Walter Burley Griffin, who submitted the design without visiting the site. Burley Griffin planned that his creation should blend with nature rather than imposing itself on the landscape.

Canberra is often overlooked by many backpackers, bypassing the capital in favour of more exciting destinations. Although the city doesn't have much charm or atmosphere, there are a lot of things to see.

In 1988, Canberra's main landmark - Parliament House - opened, replacing an earlier building dating from 1927. Other attractions include the Australian War Memorial, the High Court, National Gallery of Australia, Old Parliament House and the new National Museum of Australia.

Practical Information

INFORMATION CENTRES & USEFUL ADDRESSES

Canberra Tourism
330 Northbourne Avenue, Canberra
30, 31, 32, 39, 50, 80
(02) 6205 0044 or 1300 554 114
Website *www.visitcanberra.com.au*
Open *Mon-Fri 9am-5.30pm, Sat-Sun 9am-4pm*

EMBASSIES, CONSULATES & HIGH COMMISSIONS

British High Commission
Commonwealth Avenue, Yarralumla
29, 31, 32
(02) 6270 6666
Website *www.britaus.net*
Open *Mon-Fri 8.45am-5pm*

Canadian High Commission
Commonwealth Avenue, Yarralumba
29, 31, 32
(02) 6270 4000
Website *http://geo.international.gc.ca/asia/australia/*
Open *Mon-Fri 8.30am-12.30pm & 1pm-4.30pm*

Irish Embassy
20 Arkana Street, Yarralumba
29, 31, 32
(02) 6273 3022
Open *Mon-Fri 9.30am-12.45pm & 2pm-4pm*

New Zealand High Commission
Commonwealth Avenue, Yarralumba
29, 31, 32
(02) 6270 4211
Website *www.nzembassy.com*
Open *Mon-Fri 8.45am-5pm*

South African Embassy
Corner Rhodes Place & State Circle, Yarralumba
29, 31, 32
(02) 6273 2424
Website *www.sahc.org.au*
Open *Mon-Fri 8.30am-1pm & 1.45pm-5pm*

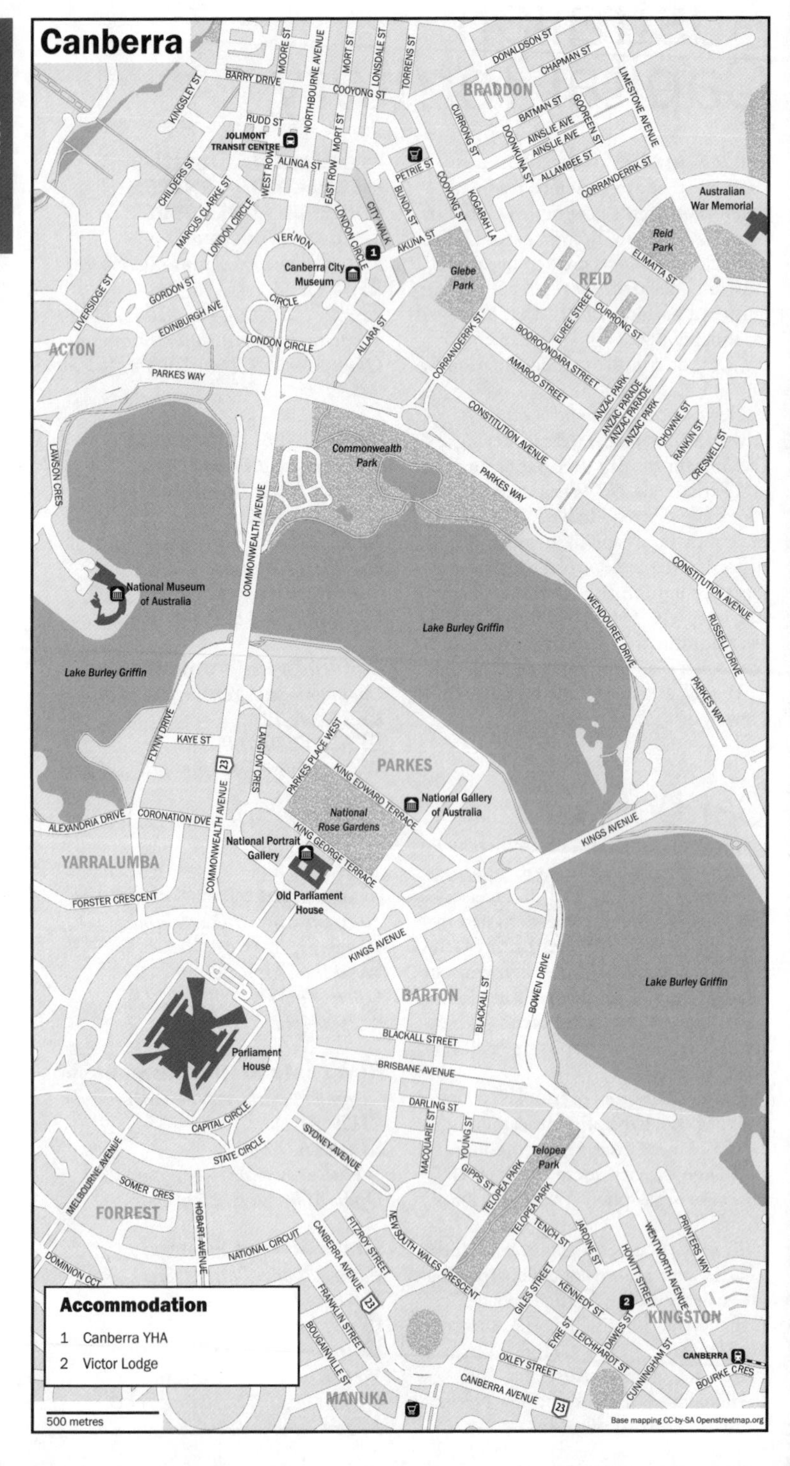
Canberra
Accommodation
1 Canberra YHA
2 Victor Lodge
BRADDON
REID
ACTON
PARKES
YARRALUMBA
BARTON
FORREST
MANUKA
KINGSTON
Jolimont Transit Centre
Canberra City Museum
Australian War Memorial
Reid Park
Glebe Park
Commonwealth Park
National Museum of Australia
Lake Burley Griffin
National Rose Gardens
National Gallery of Australia
National Portrait Gallery
Old Parliament House
Parliament House
Telopea Park
Canberra
Commonwealth Avenue
Northbourne Avenue
Parkes Way
Constitution Avenue
Kings Avenue
Brisbane Avenue
Canberra Avenue
State Circle
Capital Circle
500 metres
Base mapping CC-by-SA Openstreetmap.org

USA Embassy
1 Moonah Place, Yarralumba
29, 31, 32
(02) 6214 5600
***Website** http://canberra.usembassy.gov/*
***Open** Mon-Fri 8am-5pm*

INTERNET ACCESS

The most convenient internet café is at the YHA hostel *(7 Akuna Street, Canberra; (02) 6248 9155; **website** www.yha.com.au; **open** 24 hours)*, but another option is the Barracks *(112-116 Alinga Street, Canberra; (02) 62572008; **website** www.thebarracks.com.au; **open** 9am-midnight; $5 per hour, $20 six hours).*

If you're travelling with your own computer you can use the Global Gossip hotspot at the YHA hostel ($6 per hour). Alternatively there is free Wi-Fi access at the National Library of Australia *(King Edward Terrace, Parkes; (02) 6262 1156; **website** www.nla.gov.au; **open** Mon-Thu 9am-9pm, Fri-Sun 9am-5pm).*

Coming & Going

AIR

Canberra's airport *((02) 6275 2236; **website** www.canberraairport.com.au)* has frequent flights to most major Australian destinations although backpackers rarely use it.

The airport is located 7km east of the city centre and is served by the AirLiner shuttle bus *((02) 6299 3722; **website** www.airliner.com.au)*, which runs every 30 minutes and costs $9 each way.

BUS

There are direct buses to Adelaide, Melbourne, Sydney and country destinations in New South Wales including the ski resorts in the Snowy Mountains.

Murrays Coaches *(13 22 51; **website** www.murrays.com.au)* operate express bus services from Canberra to Sydney; Woollongong; Batemans Bay and Narooma on the South Coast plus Cooma and Jindabyne in the Snowy Mountains.

Greyhound Australia *(1300 GREYHOUND or 1300 473 946; **website** www.greyhound.com.au)* buses go to Adelaide, Melbourne and Sydney.

Must do in the ACT

- Rent a bike and cycle around Lake Burley Griffin
- Visit Parliament House
- Visit the National Museum of Australia

Buses terminate at the Jolimont Transit Centre at 65-57 Northbourne Avenue.

TRAIN

Trains between Canberra and Sydney use the train station on Wentworth Avenue in Kingston. Buses 39, 80, 83 and 84 run between the station and the city centre.

HITCHHIKING

There are a few good hitching spots that are relatively easy to get to by public transport. It is usually not too difficult to get a lift out of Canberra.

Northbourne Avenue runs north from the city centre and splits into the Barton and Federal Highways that join the Hume Freeway, which connects Melbourne and Sydney. Hitching from Canberra is best on one of these two roads.

If you're heading to Melbourne, it's best to get to the Barton Highway, which meets the Hume Freeway near Yass. Buses 51, 52, 56, 251, 252 or 253 take you to where the Barton Highway branches off from Northbourne Avenue.

The Federal Highway is your best bet for a lift to Sydney. This road joins the Hume Highway near Goulburn. Take bus 36 to get to the Federal Highway.

Local Transport

Canberra is a sprawling city and most attractions are spaced too far apart for walking to be a practical option. You're best off with a car or bicycle although Canberra has an extensive bus network.

Canberra's buses, run by ACTION *(13 17 10; **website** www.action.act.gov.au)*, provide a good coverage of the city although the frequency of the services makes it a time consuming way to get around.

A single bus ride costs $3. Ask the driver for a transfer ticket if you need to

ACT

transfer to another bus route; transfer tickets cost no more than regular tickets and allow you to change to other bus routes within a 90-minute period. Ten-ride tickets are available from newsagents for $22 and weekly passes cost $24.60. Day passes are available on board buses or from newsagents for $6.60 or $4.10 for off-peak travel (Mon-Fri 9am-4.30pm & after 6pm, Sat-Sun all day).

Eating & Drinking

Canberra has a reasonably good restaurant scene for such a small city. There are some budget dining options in the city centre including several fast food places, but your best option is to prepare a picnic lunch to eat in one of the city's parks.

Outside the city centre, the two best suburbs for eating and drinking are Kingston and Manuka, both within walking distance of Victor Lodge. The best eating options in these two suburbs are the **Belgian Beer Café** *(29 Jardine Street, Kingston)* for Belgian-style mussels and beer and **Alanya** *(22 Style Arcade, Franklin Street, Manuka)* for Turkish food.

There's a good fresh food market, an Aldi supermarket and a big Supabarn supermarket in the Canberra Centre on Bunda Street and a Coles supermarket on Franklin Street in Manuka.

Accommodation

Canberra City YHA

Canberra City YHA is a big well-appointed and centrally located hostel. It has a lot of facilities including a basic kitchen (no oven), a café with internet access including Wi-Fi ($6 per hour, YHA Connect), an indoor swimming pool, spa pool and a sauna. There are several quiet lounge areas throughout the hostel plus a lounge upstairs with a TV, pool table and table football. There's also a really nice rooftop deck with barbecues, but unfortunately alcohol is only allowed in the kitchen so you won't get a chance to really enjoy the rooftop area. The hostel is clean with not too much atmosphere – just like Canberra – and this isn't helped by the TVs in the dormitories (which keep people away from the common areas).

7 Akuna Street, Canberra
all buses
(02) 6248 9155
***Website** www.yha.com.au*
***Dorm bed** $28-33.50 ($25-30 HI/YHA); **double/twin room** $89 ($80 HI/YHA); **family room** $134 ($120 HI/YHA)*
***Credit cards** MC, Visa*
***Reception open** 24 hours*

Maintenance & cleanliness	★★★★
Facilities	★★★★½
Atmosphere & character	★
Security	★★★★★
Overall rating	★★★½

Victor Lodge

Victor Lodge is a good accommodation option. It is clean with good facilities that include a kitchen, TV lounge and internet access and they provide a good buffet breakfast. The hostel has a quiet location on a residential street between the train station and the new Parliament House. The Kingston shops, which include pubs, cafés and restaurants, are just behind the hostel.

29 Dawes Street, Kingston
38, 39, 80
(02) 6295 7777
***Website** www.victorlodge.com.au*
***Dorm bed** $33; **single room** $69; **double/twin room** $85; prices include breakfast*
***Credit cards** MC, Visa*
***Reception open** 7.30am-9.30pm*

Maintenance & cleanliness	★★★★
Facilities	★½
Atmosphere & character	★★½
Security	★½
Overall rating	★★★

Sights

NORTH OF LAKE BURLEY GRIFFIN

The area north of Lake Burley Griffin is home to the city centre, the War Memorial and the city's main lookouts.

Australian War Memorial

This is the most impressive of Australia's many war memorials. The memorial is home to a small museum

ACT

with exhibits on Australia's military involvement.
Anzac Parade, Reid
🚌 *33, 40*
☎ *(02) 6243 4211*
Website *www.awm.gov.au*
Admission *free*
Open *10am-5pm daily*

Canberra Museum & Gallery
This museum has displays on the city's history and cultural diversity.
Corner Civic Square & London Circuit, Canberra
🚌 *all buses*
☎ *(02) 6207 3968*
Website *www.museumsandgalleries.act.gov.au/cmag/*
Admission *free*
Open *Jan-May Tue-Fri 10am-5pm, Sat-Sun noon-5pm; Jun-Aug Tue-Fri 10am-5pm, Sat-Sun noon-4pm; Sep-Dec Tue-Fri 10am-5pm, Sat-Sun noon-5pm*

CSIRO Discovery
CSIRO Discovery showcases the CSIRO's achievements in science and technology. The complex includes working science laboratories where visitors can view research in progress.
North Science Road at CSIRO Black Mountain laboratories, Clunies Ross Street, Canberra
🚌 *34*
☎ *(02) 6243 4646*
Website *www.csiro.au/places/Discovery.html*
Admission *$6*
Open *Mon-Fri 9am-5pm, Sun 11am-3pm*

Mt Ainslie
This hill behind the War Memorial offers great views of the city. It is accessible via walking tracks from the War Memorial.

National Capital Exhibition
The National Capital Exhibition is a small museum showing the planning, construction and growth of the city. This should be the first thing you see in Canberra as it gives you a good understanding of how the city is laid out.
Regatta Point, Commonwealth Park
🚌 *any Intertown route*
☎ *(02) 6257 1068*
Website *www.nationalcapital.gov.au*
Admission *free*
Open *Mon-Fri 9am-5pm, Sat-Sun 10am-4pm*

National Film & Sound Archive
The National Film and Sound Archive is located on the campus of the Australian National University. Set in a beautiful Art Deco building, it includes much of the nation's film, radio and television history, including recordings of many early programmes.
McCoy Circuit, Acton
🚌 *34*
☎ *(02) 6248 2000*
Website *www.nfsa.afc.gov.au*
Admission *free*
Open *Mon-Fri 9am-5pm, Sat-Sun 10am-5pm*

National Museum of Australia
The new National Museum of Australia features a variety of exhibits on Australian culture with a significant part of the Museum devoted to the history, culture and contemporary issues of Australia's Aboriginal and Torres Strait Islander peoples. The Museum is located on Acton Peninsula with views across Lake Burley Griffin.
Lawson Crescent, Acton Peninsula, Acton
🚌 *34*
☎ *(02) 6208 5000*
Website *www.nma.gov.au*
Admission *free, charge for special exhibits*
Open 9am-5pm daily

National Zoo & Aquarium
Canberra's small zoo has a good selection of Australian and African wildlife including the world's only walk-through puma cave and Australia's only tigons (a cross between a lion and tiger).
Lady Denham Drive, Scrivener Dam
🚌 *81*
☎ *(02) 6287 1211*
Website *www.zooquarium.com.au*
Admission *$26.50 ($21.50 students)*
Open 10am-5pm daily

Telstra Tower (Black Mountain)
The tower at the summit of Black Mountain offers fantastic views of Canberra.

Black Mountain
🚌 *81*
☎ *1800 806 718*
***Admission** $6*
***Open** 9am-10pm daily*

SOUTH OF LAKE BURLEY GRIFFIN

The area immediately south of Lake Burley Griffin is an area known as the Parliamentary Triangle. This area contains many of Canberra's most important buildings including the new and old Parliament Houses as well as the High Court, National Gallery and National Library. Heading further south takes you through Yarralumba, where many of the embassies are located.

High Court of Australia

The High Court of Australia is the pinnacle of Australia's legal system. The building is modern architecture at its most daring. It has been branded an architectural monstrosity, and nicknamed Gar's Mahal after former Chief Justice Sir Garfield Barwick who presided over its opening. A dramatic interior features a public hall that's seven stories high.
King Edward Terrace, Parkes
🚌 *34*
☎ *(02) 6270 6811*
***Website** www.hcourt.gov.au*
***Admission** free*
***Open** Mon-Fri 9.45am-4.30pm*

National Gallery of Australia

Canberra's National Gallery houses Australia's most extensive art collection. The collection is eclectic enough to span Aboriginal masterpieces, Monet's *Water Lilies* and Jackson Pollock's *Blue Poles*.
King Edward Terrace, Parkes
🚌 *30, 34*
☎ *(02) 6240 6411*
***Website** www.nga.gov.au*
***Admission** free*
***Open** 10am-5pm daily*

National Library of Australia

The National Library aims to hold copies of everything published either in or about Australia. The library is adding to its collection at the rate of 500 items every day.
King Edward Terrace, Parkes
🚌 *31, 34, 36, 39*
☎ *(02) 6262 1156*
***Website** www.nla.gov.au*
***Admission** free*
***Open** Mon-Thu 9am-9pm, Fri-Sun 9am-5pm*

Old Parliament House & the National Portrait Gallery

Situated in front of the new Parliament House, is a more traditional building that was originally built as a temporary structure and served as Australia's seat of government from 1927 until 1988. The building now houses the National Portrait Gallery, the Australian Archives Gallery and a museum chronicling Australia's political history.
King George Terrace, Parkes
🚌 *31, 36, 39*
☎ *(02) 6270 8222*
***Website** www.oph.gov.au & www.portrait.gov.au*
***Admission** $2*
***Open** 9am-5pm daily; tours 9.30am, 10.15am, 11am, 11.45am, 12.45pm, 1.30pm, 2.30pm, 3.15pm*

Parliament House

An 81m flag mast that has become the city's major landmark crowns Parliament House. Visitors can join a guided tour, stroll through its public galleries, walk around its striking exterior – or roll down the grassy slopes that are part of its design. You can watch a session of parliament, if it is sitting. This enormous building took half a century to conceive and a decade to build.
Capital Hill, Parkes
🚌 *31, 34, 39*
☎ *(02) 6277 5399*
***Website** www.aph.gov.au*
***Admission** free*
***Open** 9am-5pm daily; tours every ½hr*

Questacon

This excellent hands-on science museum has a lot of exhibits geared towards kids.
King Edward Terrace, Parkes
🚌 *34*
☎ *(02) 6270 2800*
***Website** www.questacon.edu.au*

Admission *$18 ($13 students)*
Open *9am-5pm daily*

Royal Australian Mint
The Royal Australian Mint is where most coins are minted and offers fascinating tours where you can see money being made.

Denison Street, Deakin
🚌 *30, 31, 32*
☎ *(02) 6202 6999*
Website *www.ramint.gov.au*
Admission *free*
Open *Mon-Fri 9am-4pm, Sat-Sun 10am-4pm but you can only see coins being produced on weekday afternoons*

New South Wales

For the first-time visitor to Australia, New South Wales has it all: long stretches of sandy beaches, bustling cities, sprawling outback and snowy mountains. A tour of all this state has to offer could easily fill the itinerary of a fantastic holiday.

To the west are the vast dusty plains of the outback with old mining towns and apocalyptic landscapes. World Heritage-listed subtropical rainforests in the north of New South Wales provide habitat for rare and endangered species. Kosciuszko National Park in the Snowy Mountains contains snowfields and dense forests and along the coast you'll find sun, surf and sand and a strong beach culture.

Sydney

Sydney is one of the world's most spectacular cities with its impressive harbour full of inlets and bays. It is the first port of call for many international travellers and there is a good choice of accommodation, excellent transport connections and plenty to see and do, which ensures that Sydney never fails to impress.

Australia has two internationally recognised urban landmarks (the Harbour Bridge and Opera House) and they're both in Sydney, but there are plenty of other things to see and do ranging from world-class museums and famous beaches to exploring vibrant neighbourhoods like The Rocks, Darlinghurst and Kings Cross.

Harbour cruises, the BridgeClimb and Opera House tours are on top of many visitors' must-do lists, but they are expensive activities and simply walking across the bridge to get a dramatic view of the Opera House is leisurely and free. Likewise a ferry ride from Circular Quay is a much cheaper alternative to a cruise. Jump on a ferry to Manly, it's cheap and a great way to get your bearings.

The Royal Botanic Gardens are a must-see, with their winding pathways and striking harbour views. Just around the corner is the Rocks, one of Sydney's oldest neighbourhoods. With its historic buildings and old world charm, it is worth a look, especially when the market is on.

It is hard to imagine that just over 200 years ago Sydney was little more than a ramshackle convict colony; today it is one of the world's leading innovators in fashion and design, and has a healthy economy to back it up. This is reflected in increased housing prices, causing the impressive suburban sprawl that characterises the city.

Sydney has a reputation as a brash and flamboyant city but despite its ostentatious reputation, many Sydneysiders keep a pretty down-to-earth and fun-loving attitude, which makes Sydney one of the world's more welcoming major cities. Don't be afraid to ask for directions; most people are more than happy to help.

If you're here between Christmas and New Year, watching the annual Sydney

Must do in New South Wales

- Walk over Sydney Harbour Bridge
- Ride a ferry on Sydney Harbour
- Spend a day at Bondi Beach
- See the kangaroos at Pebbly Beach in Murramarang National Park
- Learn to surf at Byron Bay

PHOTO: ANDREW NISBET/ISTOCKPHOTO

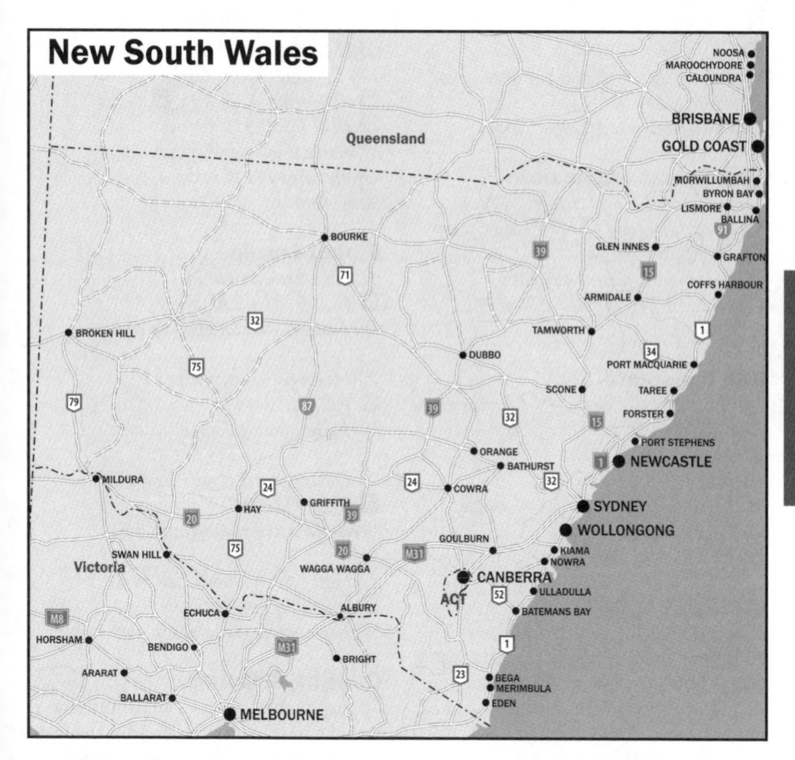

to Hobart yacht race on Boxing Day is a wonderful way to experience the city's love of its harbour. Stay in Sydney a few more days and catch one of the world's best New Year's celebrations. The annual Gay and Lesbian Mardi Gras is held in late February, culminating in a parade when you can see Sydney at its most flamboyant.

Practical Information

INFORMATION CENTRES & USEFUL ADDRESSES

Sydney Visitor Information Centre
Corner Argyle & Playfair Steets, The Rocks
Circular Quay, Wynyard *Circular Quay*
(02) 8255 1788 or 1 800 067 676
Website *www.sydney.com*
Open *9.30am-5.30pm daily*

Darling Harbour Visitor Information Centre
33 Wheat Road, Darling Harbour
Convention, Harbourside *Convention* *Pyrmont Bay*
1800 067 676
Website *www.sydney.com*
Open *9.30am-5.30pm daily*

Manly Visitor Information Centre
The Forecourt, Manly Wharf, Manly
Manly *130, 131, 132, 135, 136, 139, 140, 142, 151, 155, 156, 158, 159, 169, E50, E70*
(02) 9976 1430
Website *www.manlyaustralia.com.au*
Open *Mon-Fri 9am-5pm, Sat-Sun 10am-4pm*

EMBASSIES & CONSULATES

British Consulate-General
Level 16, 1 Macquarie Place, Sydney
all Circular Quay buses *Circular Quay* *Circular Quay*
(02) 9247 7521
Website *www.britaus.net*
Open *Mon-Fri 9am-12.30pm & 1.30pm-5pm*

Canadian Consulate-General
Level 5, 111 Harrington Street, Sydney
Circular Quay *Circular Quay*

(02) 9364 3000
Website *http://geo.international.gc.ca/asia/australia/*
Open *Mon-Fri 8.30am-4.30pm*

New Zealand Consulate
Level 10, 55 Hunter Street, Sydney
Circular Quay *Circular Quay*
(02) 8256 2000
Website *www.nzembassy.com*
Open *Mon-Fri 9am-12.30pm & 1.30pm-5pm*

USA Consulate
Level 59, MLC Centre, 19-29 Martin Place, Sydney
Martin Place
(02) 9373 9200
Website *http://usembassy-australia.state.gov/sydney/*
Open *Mon-Fri 8am-5pm*

INTERNET ACCESS

If you're travelling with your own computer there is free wireless internet access in most areas of the Rocks (the neighbourhood at the southern end of the Harbour Bridge), but you can only log on for 30 minutes at a time.

There are plenty of internet cafés in the city centre, especially in the area between Central Station and Town Hall. Prices are cheap, starting at around $2 an hour.

Central Internet Café
230 Elizabeth Street, Sydney
(02) 9281 9988
Website *www.centralinternetcafe.com.au*
Open *9am-2am daily*

City Hunter Cyber Cafe
Level 1, 374 Sussex Street, Sydney
(02) 9261 0768
Website *www.cityhunter.com.au*
Open *24 hours*

Level 1, 733-735 George Street, Sydney
(02) 9280 2080
Website *www.cityhunter.com.au*
Open *24 hours*

Level 1, 197-199 Oxford Street, Bondi Junction
(02) 9389 0768
Website *www.cityhunter.com.au*

Digi.Kaf
174 St Johns Road. Glebe
431, 432, 433, 434 *Glebe*
(02) 9660 3509
Website *www.digikaf.com.au*
Open *Mon-Fri 8am-5pm, Sat-Sun 9am-4pm*

Global Gossip
415 Pitt Street, Sydney
(02) 9281 6890
Website *www.globalgossip.com*

790 George Street, Sydney
(02) 9212 4444
Website *www.globalgossip.com*

63 Darlinghurst Road, Kings Cross
(02) 9326 9777
Website *www.globalgossip.com*

37 Hall Street, Bondi Beach
(02) 9365 4811
Website *www.globalgossip.com*

Coming & Going

Sydney is the country's main international gateway and has good transport connections to destinations around Australia. The city has a thriving backpacker scene and several travel agents that cater mostly to backpackers who should be able to fix you up with cheap bus or train passes.

AIR

Sydney is a good spot to get a cheap domestic flight up and down the coast with good deals to Brisbane and Melbourne. Check the internet and local papers for the latest specials.

Sydney Airport *((02) 9667 9111; **website** www.sydneyairport.com.au)* is about 8 km south of the city centre and is easily accessible by train from Central Station. The airport is split into domestic and international terminals that are several kilometres apart. The international terminal is all contained in one building, while the domestic terminal is comprised of separate buildings that are used for Jetstar, Qantas, Rex and Virgin Blue flights.

The easiest way to the airport is the new Airport Train line *(**website** www.airportlink.com.au)* that whisks you to the airport in around ten minutes. Trains leave from Central Station and less frequently from other stations on the City Circle line. The one-way fare from the Domestic Terminal to Central Station or Kings Cross is $13.40; one-way fares from the International Terminal are $13.40 to Central Station and $14.20 to Kings Cross.

Bus route 400 connects the airport with Bondi Junction station. This bus costs $4.80, which is the cheapest way to and from the airport and is handy if you're staying at Bondi Beach.

BUS

Sydney has good bus connections to the rest of the country with CountryLink, Firefly Express and Greyhound Australia buses departing from the coach station on Eddy Avenue near Central Station.

TRAIN

Central Station is Sydney's hub for train travel with long-distance services departing upstairs from the bus station in front of the tram stop. The station has all the facilities that you would expect including bars, shops, fast food outlets and lockers.

Countrylink and CityRail both offer intercity train services although CityRail's network extends only as far south as Goulburn and Nowra, west to the Blue Mountains and north to Newcastle and Scone. Countrylink goes further afield within New South Wales and also runs a few interstate services. Really long-distance train journeys are operated by Great Southern Railway and include the *Indian Pacific* to Perth (via Broken Hill and Adelaide) and the *Ghan* to Alice Springs and Darwin (also via Broken Hill and Adelaide).

HITCHHIKING

There are a few good hitching spots that are relatively easy to get to by public transport, but it can take a while to hitch a lift out of town because there is so much local traffic.

There are motorways leaving Sydney to the north, south and west. The southern and eastern approaches go right into the city centre but traffic heading north has to make its way through the suburbs before they get to the motorway. This means travellers heading north can find a good hitchhiking spot right before the motorway entrance with a lot of long-distance traffic. However these roads also carry a lot of local traffic so you'll need a sign indicating that you're looking for a longer ride.

The Sydney-Newcastle Freeway goes to Newcastle and also has a lot of traffic heading further up the coast and towards Queensland. Take the Train to Wahroonga (on the North Shore line), walk down Coonanbarra Road and take the footbridge across the Pacific Highway and wait in front of the Abbotsleigh School for a lift. Use a sign with either your destination or North written on it.

There are a couple of options heading south to Melbourne, although the hitching spots aren't as good as you get for northbound rides. The Hume Highway is the easiest and quickest option while the more scenic coastal route via Wollongong may take you a little longer but there is plenty to see en route.

For the Hume Highway, take a train to Beverly Hills and walk up King Georges Road to the start of the South Western Motorway. This isn't such a good hitching spot as there is a lot of local traffic and most long-distance traffic is already on the motorway.

Because there is less local traffic it may be easier to get a lift on the coastal route to Melbourne, but it will be a longer trip. There are a couple of good hitching spots accessible by train. The cheapest is to take the train to either Heathcote or Waterfall (on the Illawarra line) and try your luck on the Princes Highway before the motorway begins. Alternatively you can take the train further south to Berry and completely bypass Wollongong and all the local traffic between Sydney and Wollongong. This will cost you a bit more than hitching at the northern end of the motorway, but you'll be on a regular road rather than a motorway and will have a better choice of spots to wait for a lift and if you have no luck, at least Berry is a nice town to get stranded in.

If you're heading west, you'll want to get on Parramatta Road before the start of the Western Motorway. Take the Train to Strathfield, walk up Mosely Street and try your luck. You could also try Parramatta Road closer to the city centre although you'll have a longer wait, as there will be more local traffic. In any case you'll need a destination sign to avoid shorter lifts.

Local Transport

Sydney has an extensive transport network comprised of buses, trains, ferries, monorail and a tram. It is pretty easy to get around the city on public transport but it's an expensive system if you don't have a weekly TravelPass.

You can get general information at www.131500.com.au or by calling 13 15 00.

TRAIN

CityRail *(☎ 13 15 00; **website** www.cityrail.info)* is Sydney's comprehensive suburban Train network, which has a good coverage of the western suburbs and the city centre. Most travellers use the Airport, City Circle and Eastern Suburbs lines, which run mostly underground and connect the city centre to Bondi Junction and the airport.

Four stations on the Airport Line *(**website** www.airportlink.com.au)* are not run by CityRail and require either an individual ticket or payment of a GatePass (station access fee). A GatePass costs $10.80 for the Domestic and International airport terminals and $2.20 for Green Square and Mascot stations. It is possible to buy a weekly GatePass or a DayTripper or TravelPass with the GatePass included.

At around $2.60 for a ride in the city centre and increasing to $13.40 for the short hop between the domestic and international airport terminals it can be an expensive way to get around if you don't buy a CityHopper, DayTripper or a weekly TravelPass. See below for more information on fares.

BUS

Sydney's buses *(Transport Infoline ☎ 13 15 00; **website** www.sydneybuses.info)* are a handy way to get to all the spots not covered by the train network, which includes most of Sydney's beaches and some neighbourhoods in the inner west such as Balmain and Glebe. Although traffic can hold buses up, they run frequently and are generally a reliable way to get around.

Bus fares are calculated by distance. The cheapest bus fare is $1.80 and the most expensive is $5.80. Most of the bus routes popular with travellers cost $3.

There are also the Bondi and Sydney Explorer buses that are operated specifically for tourists and run a circuit between the main sights. Forget about these, they're way overpriced at $39 for a day pass – it's cheaper to buy a weekly TravelPass.

FERRY

Sydney's ferries *(**website** www.sydneyferries.info)* are the nicest way to get around and a cheaper alternative to the touristy harbour cruises. All ferries terminate at Circular Quay in the city centre with departures to destinations around the harbour. Most ferries depart at half-hourly intervals.

Ferry fares start at $5.20 for a short hop in the inner harbour and increase to $8.20 for the JetCat to Manly. The most popular ferry route with travellers is the Manly ferry, which costs $6.40 each way.

MONORAIL

The Monorail *(**website** www.metromonorail.com.au)* looks cool and runs right through the city centre, but it is almost completely useless as a way to get around. It runs a circular route in only one direction taking in Pitt Street, Chinatown and Darling Harbour. It is good fun to take a joy ride around the city, but the $4.80 fare is overpriced considering you can walk between Pitt Street and Darling Harbour in about 10 minutes.

The Monorail is not included in any TravelPass ticket but you can buy a day pass for $9.50.

TRAM (METRO LIGHT RAIL)

Sydney's light rail is a tram route designed to complement the monorail. It is a bit like a premetro, running through rail tunnels in Glebe and Pyrmont and then on the streets like a tram when it gets into the city centre. It is a much more useful transport option than the monorail as it actually goes somewhere. The route starts right outside Central Station and trams run through Chinatown, Darling Harbour, Pyrmont, Glebe and Rozelle Bay to Lilyfield. The Glebe and Jubilee Park stops are handy for travellers staying at hostels in the Glebe area.

The tram is quite expensive compared to the bus with fares ranging from $3.20 to $4.20. Day passes cost $9 but the $20 weekly pass is better value. The Metro Light Rail (MLR) tram is not included in any TravelPass ticket.

MULTIPLE TRIP TICKETS

Multiple trip tickets are a good deal if you're staying in Sydney for a while, but don't travel regularly enough on public transport to get value from a weekly TravelPass.

TravelTen

The TravelTen pass is valid for ten bus trips. There is a colour coded range of TravelTen passes based on the number of sections travelled. Prices range from $14.40 for a Blue TravelTen that allows ten short trips of up to two sections to $46.40 for an Orange TravelTen for ten long trips of 16 sections or more. The Brown TravelTen pass is probably the most useful for most travellers and is good for ten rides of three to five sections, which is basically ten trips between Glebe and the city centre. The Brown TravelTen costs $24 whereas ten separate bus tickets would cost you $30.

DAY PASSES

Although these aren't as good value as the weekly tickets, the limited range of day passes is worth considering if you're only in Sydney for a day or two. However if you're going to be in Sydney for more than two days, it is cheaper to buy a weekly Red or Green TravelPass.

The various day passes include:

CityHopper

This ticket is good for one day unlimited train travel between the 11 stations in the central Sydney area that is bounded by Kings Cross, North Sydney and Redfern. The CityHopper costs $7.40 ($5.20 off peak).

DayTripper

The DayTripper allows you to travel all day on buses, trains and ferries for $16. The area covered by this pass corresponds with that of the Purple TravelPass, but you need to pay a GatePass (station access fee) if you want to get off at stations on the Airport line.

A DayTripper is a good deal if you're only in Sydney for a day or two.

SydneyPass

This is the most extensive of the day passes but it is also priced out of reach of most budget travellers. It includes unlimited travel almost everywhere on buses, trains and ferries and includes the Bondi and Sydney Explorer buses and train stations on the Airport line.

A three-day SydneyPass costs a whopping $110, a five-day pass is $145 and a seven-day pass costs $165. It is amazing that people actually buy this ticket when the TravelPass is a much cheaper alternative.

TRAVELPASS TICKETS

There are a number of passes for regular commuters to bring down the otherwise high cost of travelling around Sydney. The TravelPass tickets are available in various configurations including bus only; bus & ferry and train, bus and ferry. The monorail and MLR tram are not covered by the TravelPass.

Most travellers will find the Red and Green TravelPasses the most useful although the bus & ferry and bus only passes offer a slightly cheaper alternative. The various TravelPasses include:

Red TravelPass

This is probably the most handy pass. It allows travel on trains in the central area as far north as Chatswood, west to Croydon, Canterbury and Bardwell Park and south to Rockdale. It also allows travel on Sydney buses in zones 1, 3, 6, & 7 which covers most of the nearby beaches including Bondi and Coogee. Travel on inner harbour ferries is also included, but you cannot take ferries as far afield as Manly or

Parramatta. There is an extra charge for stations on the Airport line. A weekly Red TravelPass is $35.

Green TravelPass

This pass covers a slightly larger area than the red pass and is handy if you're staying in Manly. Train travel on this pass can go as far north as Chatswood or Epping, west to Lidcombe, Regents Park or Kingsgrove and south to Kogarah. You can travel on Sydney Buses in zones 1 to 8 and all ferries except the Manly JetCat. There is an extra charge for stations on the Airport line. A weekly Green TravelPass is $43.

Yellow TravelPass

This pass is similar to the Green TravelPass but you can take the train as far as Parramatta. A weekly Yellow TravelPass is $47.

Pink TravelPass

This pass is the same as the Yellow TravelPass but you can take the train as far as Liverpool, Seven Hills, Hornsby, Holsworthy, Engadine or Carringbah. A weekly Pink TravelPass is $50.

Purple TravelPass

This pass is good for unlimited train travel in the area bounded by Bondi Junction, Cowan, Carlingford, Richmond, Emu Plains, Macarthur, Otford, Cronulla and Olympic Park stations. It is also good for travel on all buses and ferries in zones 1 to 11 (except the Manly Jetcat before 7pm). A weekly Purple TravelPass is $57.

Blue TravelPass

This pass allows travel on buses in zones 1, 3, 6 and 7 and inner harbour ferries. A weekly Blue TravelPass is $32.

Orange TravelPass

This pass allows travel on buses in zones 1 to 8 and all ferries except the Manly JetCat. A weekly Orange TravelPass is $40.

Pittwater TravelPass

This pass allows travel on buses in all zones and all ferries except the Manly JetCat. A weekly Pittwater TravelPass is $55.

Two Zone TravelPass

This pass allows travel on buses in two adjacent zones but is not valid in Zone 1. A weekly Two Zone TravelPass is $32.

Accommodation

BONDI

Bondi is the closest real beach to the city centre and it is a popular spot with travellers. The quickest way to Bondi beach is by train to Bondi Junction, then bus 333 to Bondi Beach.

Beached at Bondi

This hostel is located above a bar, much farther from the beach than the other Bondi hostels. Consequently, it has no real atmosphere. The kitchen is poorly maintained and the common area is one small dusty room crammed with tattered couches and a TV. The bathrooms are also quite a mess.

283 Bondi Road, Bondi
333, 380, 381, 382
(02) 9130 7178 or 1800 216 979
Website *www.beachedatbondi.com.au*
Dorm bed *$24-30;* ***single room*** *$50;* ***double/twin room*** *$60*
Reception open *9am-noon & 5pm-7pm*

Maintenance & cleanliness	★★
Facilities	★
Atmosphere & character	★★★
Security	★
Overall rating	★★

Bondi Backpackers

Steps from the beach, this hostel is spacious and comfortable. It is upstairs from a Peter Pan travel agency and has a good backpacker atmosphere. Dorms are roomy and bright, but could be better maintained although some of them have incredible beachfront views. Showers are average, but the kitchen is sparkling and new. The common room is always full of sun-drenched travellers lounging in front of the television after fun days at the beach. Reception staff here are mostly friendly.

110 Campbell Parade, Bondi Beach
333, 380, 381, 382

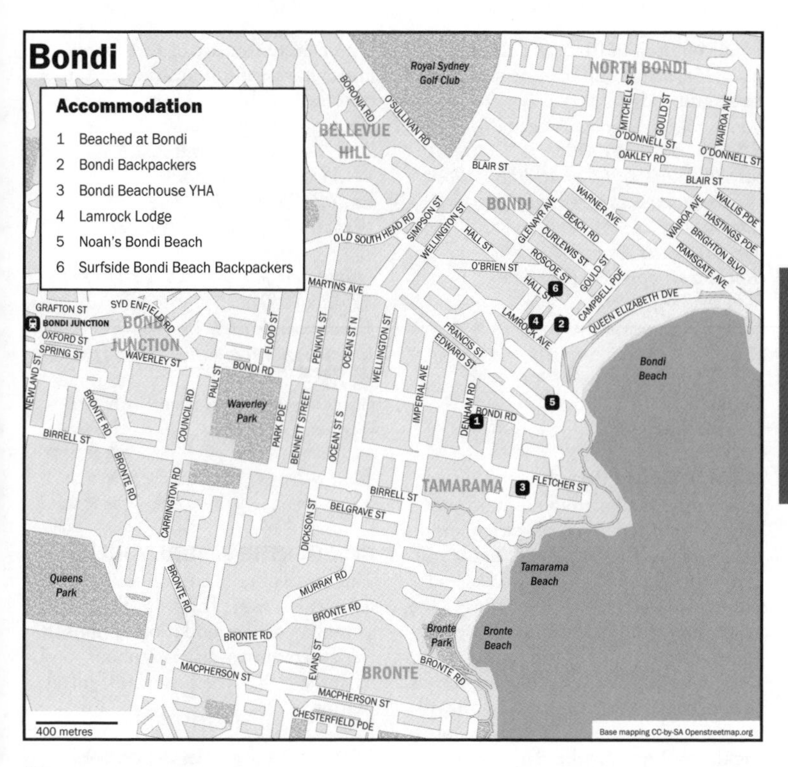

(02) 9130 4660
Website *www.bondibackpackers.com.au*
Dorm bed *$24-30;* ***single room*** *$48-52;* ***double room*** *$60-70; prices include breakfast*
Credit cards *MC, Visa*
Reception open *7.30am-10.30pm*

Maintenance & cleanliness	★★★
Facilities	★½
Atmosphere & character	★★★★
Security	★★★
Overall rating	★★★

Bondi Beachouse YHA

Bondi's YHA is a big art deco building in Tamarama, a short walk south of Bondi Beach. It has a good kitchen (but no oven), several TV lounges (including one with a pool table), internet access plus a courtyard with barbecues and table tennis and a rooftop terrace with panoramic ocean views.
63 Fletcher Street, Tamarama
333, 361, 380, 381, 382
(02) 9365 2088
Website *www.bondibeachouse.com.au*
Dorm bed *$30 ($27 HI/YHA);* ***double room*** *$75-85 ($67.50-76.50 HI/YHA);* ***family room*** *$120-150 ($108-135 HI/YHA)*
Credit cards *Amex, MC, Visa*
Reception open *8am-9pm*

Maintenance & cleanliness	★★½
Facilities	★★½
Atmosphere & character	★★★
Security	★★★★½
Overall rating	★★★

Lamrock Lodge

This hostel just up the street from the beach looks inviting from the outside and has quite a bit of character, but it also shows its age. It has good hardwood floors and a bright purple and green interior. The kitchen is just a small downstairs den with limited appliances, but you can rent cooking kits from reception. Dorms are boring and have a microwave and television which discourages socialising. Bathrooms are kind of grungy too. Internet costs $4 per hour and there is only a

small veranda in front as a common area. Reception staff can be very impatient and rude.
19 Lamrock Avenue, Bondi Beach
333, 380, 381, 382
(02) 9130 5063 or 1800 625 063
***Website** www.lamrocklodge.com*
***Dorm bed** $23-35*
***Credit cards** Amex, MC, Visa*
***Reception open** 8.30am-late*

Maintenance & cleanliness	★★½
Facilities	★
Atmosphere & character	★★
Security	★★
Overall rating	★★

Noah's Bondi Beach

This hostel is a bit rough around the edges, but it has a great location and atmosphere. The Shack restaurant and bar offers cheap food and drinks and a fun crowd gathers in the evenings. The large, breezy common room is a good place to hang out but the rooftop sundeck is better. There are free barbecues on the roof where you have a postcard view of Bondi Beach. Dorms are rather lacklustre but the other facilities make up for it.
2 Campbell Parade, Bondi Beach
333, 361, 380, 381, 382
(02) 9365 7100 or 1800 226 662
***Website** www.noahsbondibeach.com*
***Dorm bed** $22-25; **double room** $55-65; **triple room** $85*
***Credit cards** Amex, MC, Visa; 2% credit card surcharge*
***Reception open** 24 hours*

Maintenance & cleanliness	★★
Facilities	★★½
Atmosphere & character	★★★
Security	★★★★½
Overall rating	★★½

Surfside Bondi Beach Backpackers

This hostel has a cool, laid-back surfer vibe to it. Dorms are spacious but a bit messy and halls are covered in loud graffiti. The kitchen isn't much and despite the otherwise good security there are no lockers; but the hostel has a nice courtyard with barbecues and a TV lounge with a nice ambience. Guests have free use of surfboards. The hostel has a central location and reception staff are hip and fun. It's a great place to meet people.
35A Hall Street, Bondi Beach
333, 380, 381, 382
(02) 9365 4900
***Website** www.surfsidebackpackers.com.au*
***Dorm bed** $28-29 ($27-28 HI/YHA, $25-26 VIP)*
***Credit cards** MC, Visa*
***Reception open** 8am-1pm & 5pm-8pm*

Maintenance & cleanliness	★★★
Facilities	★★½
Atmosphere & character	★★★★
Security	★★★
Overall rating	★★★

CITY CENTRE & SURRY HILLS

The hostels in the city centre are close to all the action. There are also plenty of budget accommodation options in the quieter inner-city neighbourhood of Surry Hills, which is near Central Station.

790 on George Backpackers

This is a brand new hostel in a beautiful green building just across from Central Station. It is very small, but very clean and well-maintained with new furniture and newly renovated bathrooms. It has two plain TV rooms, which are spotlessly clean and the one upstairs has a nice view. The downstairs kitchen is basic. It is in a great location and good value compared to the surrounding hostels. Reception staff are friendly and talkative. Internet access, including Wi-Fi, is $3 per hour.
790 George Street, Sydney NSW 2000
Central
(02) 9080 1155
***Website** www.790ongeorge.com.au*
***Dorm bed** $25-29; **double room** $74-78*
***Credit cards** MC, Visa*
***Reception open** 24 hours*

Maintenance & cleanliness	★★★★½
Facilities	★★
Atmosphere & character	★★★
Security	★★★★★
Overall rating	★★★½

Alfred Park Accommodation

Alfred Park Accommodation is a nice 140-bed hostel with amenities that include a kitchen, TV lounge and laundry plus free internet access (including free Wi-Fi) and a nice covered courtyard. All rooms have a TV and fridge and around half the rooms have en suite facilities. It's located across the road from Prince Alfred Park, about a five-minute walk south of Central Station.

207 Cleveland Street, Strawberry Hills
352, 372, 393, 395 Central, Redfern
(02) 9319 4031
***Website** www.alfredpark.com.au*
***Dorm bed** $25-29; **single room** $55-65; **twin room** $75-95*
***Credit cards** Amex, MC, Visa*
***Reception open** 8am-9pm daily*

Maintenance & cleanliness	★★★
Facilities	★★★½
Atmosphere & character	★★★½
Security	★★★
Overall rating	★★★

Base Backpackers

The lobby of this hostel does not do justice to what is on the upper floors. The travel agency/internet room/TV lounge need a bit of a revamp, but they are planning it soon. The Scary Canary Bar is excellent, opening onto the street, with live music or DJs every night and cheap drinks. The building is Heritage listed, and they are doing renovations, meaning the dorms are modern and beautifully clean, with patches of old brick walls, which gives it a lot of ambiance. Bathrooms are perfectly clean. It also features Sanctuary, a girls-only dorm stocked with hairdryers and bath products. It is one of the most centrally located hostels in Sydney, next to Town Hall Station. The staff are very welcoming and chatty, and it is a good place to meet backpackers.

477 Kent Street, Sydney
441, 442, 443, 501, 506, 507, 515, 518, 520, L20, L88, L90 Town Hall
(02) 9267 7718
***Website** www.basebackpackers.com*
***Dorm bed** $26-34; **single/double room** $89-110*
***Credit cards** MC, Visa*
***Reception open** 24 hours*

Maintenance & cleanliness	★★★★
Facilities	★★★
Atmosphere & character	★★★
Security	★★★★★
Overall rating	★★★½

Big on Elizabeth

This large hostel offers an exceptional standard of accommodation. It has loads of facilities and activities and is a fun place to stay without being a real party hostel. Staff and management are friendly and kind. The TV lounge has a large screen television and fully stocked kitchen. They offer free internet (including Wi-Fi access), a rarity in Sydney. Halls, dorms and toilets are brand new and sparkling clean, with high ceilings and beautiful artwork on the walls. Décor is modern with dark red and grey paint, and there is a really cool rooftop sundeck with a barbecue where you can watch the bats fly over from the park at sunset and get a nice view of the city. Check out is later than most at 11am, and they offer free breakfast. They also have a Peterpans travel agency in the reception. This is definitely one of the best options in Sydney.

212 Elizabeth Street, Sydney
308, 309, 310, 311, 339, 343, 372, 378, 393, 395 Central Central
(02) 9281 6030 or 1800 212 244
***Website** www.bighostel.com*
***Dorm bed** $28-32 ($27-31 VIP); **single room** $75 ($74 VIP); **double room** $96 ($64 VIP); **twin room** $89 ($87 VIP); prices include breakfast*
***Credit cards** MC, Visa*
***Reception open** 24 hours*

Maintenance & cleanliness	★★★★
Facilities	★★★½
Atmosphere & character	★★★½
Security	★★★★½
Overall rating	★★★★

Broadway Inn

Broadway Inn is a neat and tidy hostel just off Broadway, about a 10-minute walk to Central Station or Glebe. The

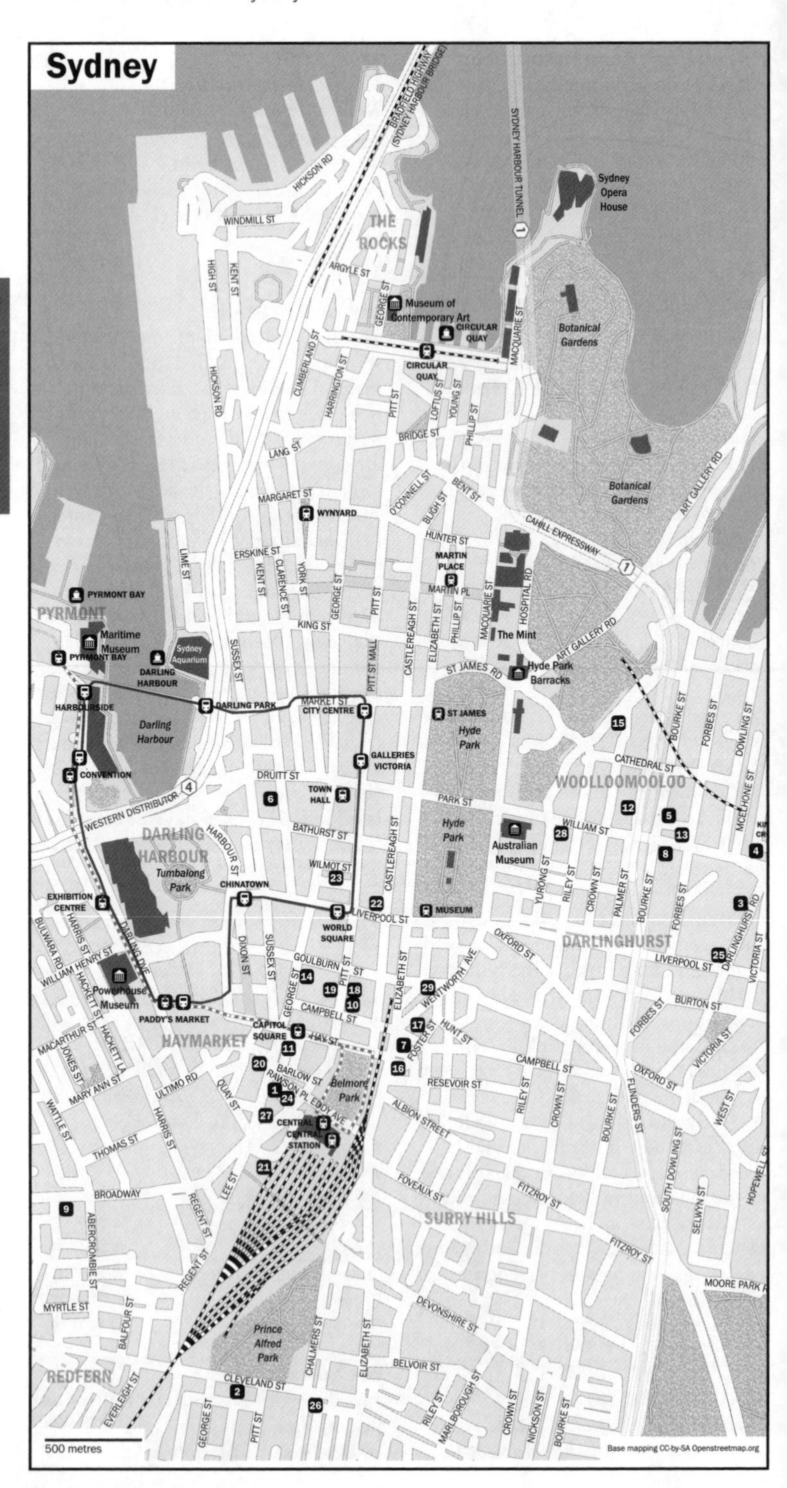
Sydney
THE ROCKS
Sydney Opera House
Museum of Contemporary Art
CIRCULAR QUAY
Botanical Gardens
WYNYARD
MARTIN PLACE
PYRMONT BAY
PYRMONT
Maritime Museum
Sydney Aquarium
DARLING HARBOUR
The Mint
Hyde Park Barracks
HARBOURSIDE
DARLING PARK
CITY CENTRE
ST JAMES
Hyde Park
Darling Harbour
GALLERIES VICTORIA
CONVENTION
TOWN HALL
WOOLLOOMOOLOO
Australian Museum
Tumbalong Park
CHINATOWN
EXHIBITION CENTRE
WORLD SQUARE
MUSEUM
DARLINGHURST
Powerhouse Museum
PADDY'S MARKET
CAPITOL SQUARE
HAYMARKET
Belmore Park
CENTRAL
CENTRAL STATION
SURRY HILLS
Prince Alfred Park
REDFERN
500 metres
Base mapping CC-by-SA Openstreetmap.org

Accommodation

1 790 on George
2 Alfred Park Accommodation
3 Hotel Altamont
4 Asylum Sydney
5 Australian Backpackers
6 Base Backpackers
7 Big on Elizabeth
8 Boomerang Backpackers
9 Broadway Inn
10 Chamberlain Hotel
11 City Central Backpackers
12 City Resort Hostel
13 Forbes Terrace (G'day Backpackers)
14 The George
15 Harbour City Backpackers
16 Home Backpackers
17 Hyde Park Backpackers
18 Legend Has It... Westend
19 Maze Backpackers
20 Mountbatten Hotel
21 Railway Square YHA
22 Strattons Hotel
23 Sydney Backpackers
24 Sydney Central YHA
25 Sydney Star Accommodation
26 Tokyo Village
27 Wake Up!
28 Wood Duck Inn
29 Y on the Park

hostel's facilities include the usual TV lounge and kitchen but it is a dreary building that doesn't have much atmosphere

2 Buckland Street, Chippendale
(02) 9281 0165
Website *www.broadwayinn.com.au*
Dorm bed *$28-30*
Reception open *9am-10.30pm*

Maintenance & cleanliness	★★★★
Facilities	★½
Atmosphere & character	★★
Security	★★★½
Overall rating	★★★

Chamberlain Hotel

The Chamberlain Hotel is a pub close to Chinatown and Central Station that has hostel accommodation upstairs. It is a very clean and well maintained hostel with TVs and fridges in the double rooms and lockers for each bed in the dormitories. However there are no common areas other than a small room with a microwave (it really isn't equipped enough to be called a kitchen), but there is a good bar downstairs with good value meals.

421 Pitt Street, Sydney
Central Station, Museum *Capitol Square*
(02) 9288 0888
Website *www.chamberlainhotel.com.au*
Dorm bed *$35 per night, $210 per week;* **double room** *$100 per night, $610 per week*
Credit cards *Amex, Diners, MC, Visa*
Reception open *Mon-Thu 10am-2am, Thu-Sat 10am-4am, Sun noon-midnight*

Maintenance & cleanliness	★★★★★
Facilities	★
Atmosphere & character	★★
Security	★★★★
Overall rating	★★★

City Central Backpackers

This hostel is tiny and stuffy, and badly in need of renovations or at least some maintenance. Some may find it characterful, however, with the eccentric artwork lining the hallways and the offbeat crowd who stays here. The kitchen is dirty and old, and the common area/TV lounge needs new furniture, but the toilets are exceptionally clean. Reception staff are indifferent and security is not great for being located on a busy street. Dorms are sparse and ugly and they need a paint job. It is less expensive than most, though, and there is one computer with free internet.

752 George Street, Sydney
412, 413, 431, 432, 433, 436, 437, 438, 440, 461, 470, 480, 483, 501, L38, L88, L90 *Capitol Square*
Central, Town Hall
(02) 9212 4833
Website *www.ccbackpack.com.au*
Dorm bed *$20-27;* **double/twin room** *$75;* **triple room** *$90*
Credit cards *MC, Visa*
Reception open *7am-10pm*

New South Wales

Maintenance & cleanliness	★★½
Facilities	★★
Atmosphere & character	★★★
Security	★★½
Overall rating	★★½

The George

This small, austere hostel has nice carpet and new paint, but barely any character to speak of, and it feels old. There is not much of an atmosphere here, and every room except for one is girls only. The paint and carpet are new, but the rooms are bare. Bathrooms are clean and well maintained. Staff are on the cold side. There are pay internet stalls in the boring common area.

700a George Street, Sydney
412, 413, 431, 432, 433, 436, 437, 438, 440, 461, 470, 480, 483, 501, L38, L88, L90 *Capitol Square* *Central, Town Hall*
(02) 9211 1800
***Website** www.thegeorge.com.au*
***Dorm bed** $29-32; **single room** $61; **double room** $78*
***Credit cards** MC, Visa*
***Reception open** 7am-midnight*

Maintenance & cleanliness	★★★
Facilities	★½
Atmosphere & character	★★
Security	★★
Overall rating	★★½

Home Backpackers

This hostel is located in a rickety old building on a busy street. It is actually a combination of two old small hotels, with one side used as the hostel and the other side full of double and twin rooms. The kitchen is teeny and dirty, bathrooms are slightly mouldy, and dorms are in need of a facelift. But the rooftop sundeck is being improved and looks nice, and one half of the hostel is beautifully decorated with wall murals. Reception tends to be nonexistent or rude. Internet is $3 per hour in the downstairs lobby.

240A Elizabeth Street, Sydney
308, 309, 310, 311, 339, 343, 372, 378, 393, 395 *Central* *Central*
(02) 9211 9111
***Website** www.homebackpackers.com*
***Dorm bed** $20-25; **single room** $40; **double/twin room** $55-65*
***Credit cards** MC, Visa*
***Reception open** 8am-8pm*

Maintenance & cleanliness	★★
Facilities	★½
Atmosphere & character	★★★
Security	★★
Overall rating	★★

Hyde Park Backpackers

Hyde Park Backpackers is a small hostel upstairs from a good café. It is a quiet place that is currently undergoing renovations, which look promising. Rooms have high ceilings and tall, breezy windows. It is cheerful, if a bit rough around the edges. Bathrooms could be updated, but they are spotlessly clean. The kitchen and common room are very small and staff are easy going and kind.

88-90 Wentworth Avenue, Sydney
308, 309, 310, 311, 339, 343, 372, 378, 393, 395 *Central* *Central, Museum*
(02) 9282 9266
***Website** www.hydeparkbackpackers.com.au*
***Dorm bed** $25-35; **double room** $79-94; prices include breakfast*
***Credit cards** MC, Visa*
***Reception open** 8am-1.30pm & 6pm-8pm*

Maintenance & cleanliness	★★★
Facilities	★½
Atmosphere & character	★★★
Security	★★★
Overall rating	★★½

Kangaroo Bakpak

Kangaroo Bakpak is a tiny, funky old townhouse-turned-hostel with very little in the way of facilities. It is a bit difficult to locate, but that means it is also quiet. Many staff members live there and know each other well, giving it a homey atmosphere. It is also not a place to party. There is a small, messy kitchen and an outside common area. The bathrooms are clean and the dorms are very large and nice. The TV lounge is dark, but well stocked with movies and books. The staff are all friendly.

665 South Dowling Street, Surry Hills
393, 395, 341, 372 (from Central Station)
(02) 9319 5915
***Website** www.kangaroobakpak.com.au*
***Dorm bed** $26-28; **double/twin room** $70*
***Credit cards** MC, Visa*
***Reception open** Mon-Fri 8am-1pm & 6.30pm-7.30pm, Sat 8.30am-10.30am & 6pm-7pm, Sun 9.30am-10.30am & 6pm-7pm*

Maintenance & cleanliness	★★
Facilities	★★½
Atmosphere & character	★★★½
Security	★★★
Overall rating	★★

Legend Has It... Westend

This place has a reputation as a party hostel, and for good reason – the entire first floor is dedicated to fun and games. The TV lounge is plush and inviting, the kitchen is clean, and there is a nice red pool table and modern furnishings in the common area. The sound system is configured to be able to quickly organise a party. At the top of the nine story building is the Church, a 27-bed dorm with stained glass windows that is rumoured to have more to do with sin than salvation. The interior is cool and sleek, and the daily activities are well planned and fun. It's a great place to meet people.

412 Pitt Street, Sydney
339 Capitol Square Central, Museum
(02) 9211 4588 or 1800 013 186
***Website** www.legendhasitwestend.com.au*
***Dorm bed** $21-30; **double room** $80-85; prices include breakfast*
***Credit cards** MC, Visa*
***Reception open** 24 hours*

Maintenance & cleanliness	★★★
Facilities	★★★
Atmosphere & character	★★★★
Security	★★★
Overall rating	★★★½

Maze Backpackers

This place really lives up to its name. A funky but inviting reception area leads to staircases and snaking hallways on three floors. The building is quite old and run down, but it has character to spare and feels like home. A big, comfy movie room is usually packed with travellers. The kitchen is plain and the toilets are aging but kept clean. Dorm rooms are really tiny and bare. Reception staff are energetic and friendly, and always seem to have activities planned. Internet is a relatively cheap $2 per hour.

417 Pitt Street, Sydney
339 Capitol Square Central, Museum
(02) 9211 5115 or 1800 813 522
***Website** www.mazebackpackers.com*
***Dorm bed** $27-35 (Nomads $26-24); **single room** $55-57 (Nomads $54-56); **double room** $76-80 (Nomads $74-78)*
***Credit cards** MC, Visa*
***Reception open** 24 hours*

Maintenance & cleanliness	★★★
Facilities	★★
Atmosphere & character	★★★½
Security	★★★½
Overall rating	★★★

Mountbatten Hotel

This is a hostel attached to a hotel between Central Station and Chinatown. It has nice hardwood floors and huge airy dorm rooms with new beds. Breakfast is served in the small but clean kitchen and toilets are simple and spotless. There is not much in the way of facilities besides the kitchen and laundry but there is free Wi-Fi access. Management is very kind but the hostel does have sort of a hotel feel to it, so the atmosphere is not the best.

701 George Street, Sydney
Central Capitol Square
(02) 9211 4894
***Website** www.mountbattenhotel.com.au*
***Dorm bed** $26-34; **double room** $80; prices include breakfast*
***Credit cards** MC, Visa*
***Reception open** 8.30am-7pm*

Maintenance & cleanliness	★★★
Facilities	★★
Atmosphere & character	★★★
Security	★★★
Overall rating	★★★

Railway Square YHA

Railway Square YHA is literally next to Central Station, with some reconstructed rail carriages turned into dorm rooms right next to the railway platform. They are small, but impeccably clean and well insulated to keep the train noise out. The hostel has a large kitchen and dining area, and a café with snacks. It is large and open inside, and while the rooms are quite spartan, it still maintains an intimate feel and a laid-back atmosphere. Staff are pleasant and organise tours daily. Internet kiosks cost $3 per hour. Outside there is a huge spa pool and lounge area which is fun at night.

8a Lee Street, Sydney
311, 339, 372, 374, 376, 378, 391, 393, 395, 412, 413, 431, 432, 433, 436, 437, 438, 440, 461, 470, 480, 483, 501, L38, L88, L90 *Central*
Central
(02) 9281 9666
Website *www.yha.com.au*
Dorm bed *$33-40.50 ($29.50-36 HI/YHA);* ***double room*** *$98 ($88 HI/YHA)*
Credit cards *MC, Visa*
Reception open *24 hours*

Maintenance & cleanliness	★★★★½
Facilities	★★½
Atmosphere & character	★★★½
Security	★★★★★
Overall rating	★★★★

Strattons Hotel

Stratton's Hotel is a pub right in the heart of the city with cheap meals and good value hostel accommodation upstairs. There are around 70 beds and very limited amenities such as a small kitchen (only one microwave and one cooker). The accommodation is clean and quiet but there are no common areas, which mean not much atmosphere as there is nowhere to meet other travellers apart from your dormitory or the bar downstairs.

149 Castlereagh Street, Sydney
Museum
(02) 9267 5616 or 1800 337 661
Website *www.strattonshotel.com.au*
Dorm bed *$20-28*
Credit cards *MC, Visa*
Reception open *Mon 7am-1pm & 3pm-8pm, Tue-Thu 7am-8pm, Fri-Sun 7am-1pm & 3pm-8pm*

Maintenance & cleanliness	★★★½
Facilities	★
Atmosphere & character	★★
Security	★½
Overall rating	★★½

Sydney Backpackers

This hostel is halfway finished with renovations, which were badly needed. It is a hit or miss here, as some rooms are spacious and clean, while others are old and depressingly dark. Some also have a stale smell to them. All of the carpets are new, but only half the bathrooms are new, the others are a bit mouldy. There is not much in the way of facilities here. The kitchen is tiny, so they encourage guests to eat downstairs in the Asian restaurant. Reception staff are not very outgoing or friendly. It is not the most convivial place but has a rooftop sundeck with a barbecue and nice views.

7 Wilmot Street, Sydney
412, 413, 431, 432, 433, 436, 437, 438, 440, 461, 470, 480, 483, 501, L38, L88, L90 *World Square*
Town Hall
(02) 9267 7772
Website *www.sydneybackpackers.com*
Dorm bed *$26-39;* ***single room*** *$69;* ***twin room*** *$89*
Credit cards *MC, Visa*
Reception open *7.30am-11pm; 24 hour check in available*

Maintenance & cleanliness	★★★
Facilities	★½
Atmosphere & character	★★
Security	★★★★
Overall rating	★★½

Sydney Central YHA

This huge hostel is colourful and fun. It packs a lot of facilities into a huge ornate building next to Central Station. The excellent rooftop pool and sauna are a highlight, as is the cinema, barbecue area, and view from the balcony. The downstairs café sits on the corner of a busy street, offers good value food and drinks, and attracts large crowds. Two kitchens bookend a nice dining area and nice paintings adorn the otherwise plain walls. Dorms are extremely clean and well maintained, and staff are attentive. There is a full service travel agency beside the reception area, and there are loads of activities to choose from every day. They offer free laundry and internet/Wi-Fi access at $3 per hour. Security is great.

11 Rawson Place, Sydney, NSW 2000
311, 339, 372, 374, 376, 378, 391, 393, 395, 412, 413, 431, 432, 433, 436, 437, 438, 440, 461, 470, 480, 483, 501, L38, L88, L90 *Central*
Central
(02) 9281 9111
***Website** www.yha.com.au*
***Dorm bed** $33.50-41.50 ($32-37 HI/YHA); **double room** $112-123 ($100-110 HI/YHA); **twin room** $96-107 ($88-96 HI/YHA)*
***Credit cards** MC, Visa*
***Reception open** 24 hours*

Maintenance & cleanliness	★★★★★
Facilities	★★★★
Atmosphere & character	★★★½
Security	★★★★½
Overall rating	★★★★½

Tokyo Village

Tokyo Village is a sprawling house south of the city centre that is popular with Asian travellers. It has a TV room with table football; two small, but fully-equipped, kitchens; internet access; a laundry and an outdoor barbecue area. It is a bit cluttered but some travellers like the atmosphere.

243-247 Cleveland Street, Surry Hills
Central
(02) 9698 8839 or 1800 996 488
***Website** www.tokyovillage.com.au*
***Dorm bed** $22.50; **double/twin room** $55-65*
***Credit cards** MC, Visa*
***Reception open** 8am-noon & 4.30pm-8.30pm*

Maintenance & cleanliness	★★
Facilities	★½
Atmosphere & character	★★★
Security	★★½
Overall rating	★★

Wake Up!

Just across the street from Central Station, Wake Up! hostel is in a nice nine-story building packed with amenities. Besides kitchen, laundry, and an good TV lounge, they have a travel desk, a street side café, and a lively downstairs bar. Every weekday they offer free walking tours and excursions, which draw good crowds and could be a great way to sightsee while meeting some of the international travellers staying here (if you didn't do so last night in the SideBar). The funky interior is clean, air-conditioned and spacious, each floor themed for a different region of the world. Internet runs $2.50 per hour and Wi-Fi access is $3 per hour. Security is air-tight and reception staff are very helpful. It's a bit pricey, but for the location and facilities it just might be worth it.

509 Pitt Street, Sydney
311, 339, 372, 374, 376, 378, 391, 393, 395, 412, 413, 431, 432, 433, 436, 437, 438, 440, 461, 470, 480, 483, 501, L38, L88, L90 *Central*
Central
(02) 9288 7888 or 1800 800 945
***Website** www.wakeup.com.au*
***Dorm bed** $28-36 (HI/YHA, ISIC, Nomads, YHA $17-35); **single room** $98-108 (HI/YHA, ISIC, Nomads, YHA $97-107); **double/twin room** $98-108 (I/YHA, ISIC, Nomads, YHA $96-106)*
***Credit cards** MC, Visa*
***Reception open** 24 hours*

Maintenance & cleanliness	★★★★★
Facilities	★★½
Atmosphere & character	★★½
Security	★★★★★
Overall rating	★★★★

Y on the Park Hotel

This is part of the YWCA hotel, a large building with clean lines and modern furnishings. The dorms have single beds instead of bunks, and are clean if a bit spartan. They are small with plain grey walls and boring duvets- like an old motel room with new paint. There is barely enough room to turn around in the kitchen; it is more like a kitchenette. But there is a bright self-service café on

the ground floor where they serve free breakfast. This is probably not a good place to meet other travellers, and definitely not the place to find a party, but it is clean and safe.
5-11 Wentworth Avenue, Sydney
311, 333, 371, 373, 377, 380, 391, 392, 394, 396, 397, 399, 890, L94 *Museum*
(02) 9264 2451 or 1800 994 994
***Website** www.yhotel.com.au*
***Dorm bed** $35; **single room** $76-120; **double room** $92-134; prices include breakfast*
***Credit cards** Amex, Diners, JCB, MC, Visa*
***Reception open** 24 hours*

Maintenance & cleanliness	★★★½
Facilities	★½
Atmosphere & character	★★½
Security	★★★★★
Overall rating	★★★

COOGEE

This suburban beach is a popular alternative to Bondi and it has a good selection of budget accommodation geared towards long-term guests, but it is an inconvenient location if you're only in Sydney for a few days.

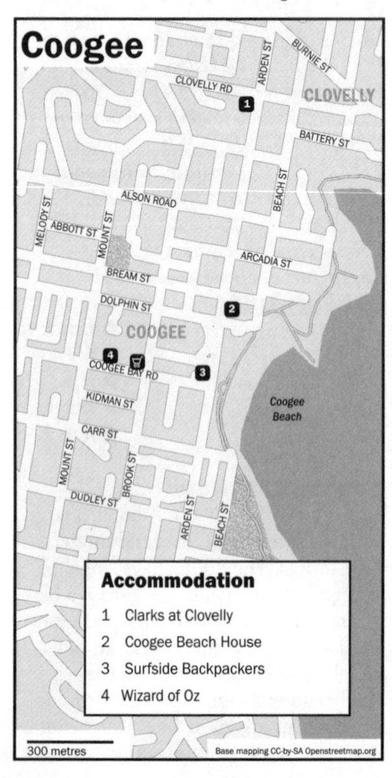

Clarks at Clovelly

Clarks is a big hostel geared to travellers on a working holiday, but there are also some Australians staying here as permanent guests. It has the usual kitchen and TV lounge and a couple of outdoor decks with seaviews.
272 Clovelly Road, Clovelly
339, X39, 360, 353
(02) 9665 1824 or 1800 551 415
***Website** www.clarksatclovelly.com.au*
***Dorm bed** $25-40*
***Credit cards** Amex, MC, Visa*

Maintenance & cleanliness	★★½
Facilities	★★
Atmosphere & character	★★½
Security	★½
Overall rating	★★½

Coogee Beach House

Coogee Beach House is a clean hostel that has the usual amenities such as a kitchen, internet access (including Wi-Fi), TV lounge and a barbecue. However some rooms have TVs, which detracts from the atmosphere. Guests have free use of surfboards.
171 Arden Street, Coogee Beach
313, 314, 353, 370, 372, 373, 374, X73, X74
(02) 9665 1162
***Website** www.coogeebeachhouse.com*
***Dorm bed** $25; price includes breakfast*
***Credit cards** MC, Visa*
***Reception open** 8am-1pm & 3pm-8pm*

Maintenance & cleanliness	★★★½
Facilities	★½
Atmosphere & character	★½
Security	★★½
Overall rating	★★½

Surfside Backpackers

Surfside has Coogee's best location, upstairs from McDonalds and right across the road from the beach. It is an old building but the penthouse common area is quite nice with a big screen telly, a kitchen and lovely sea views.

186 Arden Street, Coogee
🚌 *313, 314, 353, 370, 372, 373, 374, X73, X74*
☎ *(02) 9315 7888*
Website *www.surfsidebackpackers.com.au*
Dorm bed *$26-46 ($24-43 HI/YHA, $22-40 VIP);* ***double/twin room*** *$85-140 ($80-130 HI/YHA, $75-120 VIP)*
Credit cards *MC, Visa*
Reception open *8am-1pm & 5pm-8pm*
TV K L

Maintenance & cleanliness	★★★½
Facilities	★½
Atmosphere & character	★★★½
Security	★★★
Overall rating	★★★

Wizard of Oz

The Wizard of Oz is a clean hostel in a nicely renovated house. It has the usual kitchen and TV lounge and laundry plus a big backyard. It has a great atmosphere and it's close to shops and a short walk from the beach.
172 Coogee Beach Road, Coogee
🚌 *313, 314, 353, 370, 372, 373, 374, X73, X74*
☎ *(02) 9315 7876*
Website *www.wizardofoz.com.au*
Dorm bed *$25-45;* ***double/twin room*** *$60-120*
Credit cards *MC, Visa; 3% credit card surcharge*
Reception open *8am-1pm & 5pm-8pm*
TV K L

Maintenance & cleanliness	★★★★
Facilities	★½
Atmosphere & character	★★★★
Security	★★
Overall rating	★★★

DARLINGHURST & WOOLLOOMOOLOO

These two inner-city neighbourhoods are located east of the city centre. Woolloomooloo is the harbour side area in the valley between the city centre and Kings Cross and is home to a naval base. Darlinghurst is the area south of William Street with a diverse atmosphere that encompasses everything from prostitution to quaint Victorian architecture. The Kings Cross end of William Street can feel a little threatening at times, but it is a convenient area to base yourself and is within walking distance to both Kings Cross and the city centre.

Australian Backpackers

Although this hostel has sort of a party reputation, it is actually more on the quiet side, and would be better described as laid-back. It is small and plain, with some maintenance issues. Staff are very friendly and talkative, and the rooftop terrace is nice to hang out and chat. Free barbecues are quite popular here. Bathrooms are newly renovated but not the cleanest, and dorms are simple but comfortable. Staff are extremely helpful and pleasant, and Wi-Fi is free.
132 Bourke Street, Woolloomooloo
🚌 *200, 311, 324, 325, 326, 327*
🚆 *Kings Cross, Museum*
☎ *(02) 9331 0822*
Website *www.australianbackpackers.com.au*
Dorm bed *$25;* ***double/twin room*** *$65;* ***twin room*** *$60; prices include breakfast*
Credit cards *MC, Visa*
Reception open *8am-8pm*
TV K L

Maintenance & cleanliness	★★½
Facilities	★★
Atmosphere & character	★★½
Security	★★★
Overall rating	★★½

Boomerang Backpackers

This is a pretty run-down and bland little hostel near King's Cross. The kitchen is old but clean. Bathrooms are quite dirty and desperately need some maintenance. There is no internet, but at reception they offer vouchers for free internet in a café down the street. The rooftop has a barbecue and a nice view of the Harbour Bridge, but the old plastic furniture does not provide much in the way of atmosphere. The television lounge has a nice TV but the carpet and couches are old and torn.
141 William Street, Darlinghurst
🚌 *200, 311, 324, 325, 326, 327*
🚆 *Kings Cross, Museum*
☎ *(02) 8354 0488*
Website *www.boomerangbackpackers.com*

***Dorm bed** $25-28; **double/twin room** $70*
***Credit cards** MC, Visa*
***Reception open** 7am-1pm & 4.30pm-10pm; later check in with prior arrangement*

Maintenance & cleanliness	★★
Facilities	★★½
Atmosphere & character	★★
Security	★★★
Overall rating	★★

City Resort Hostel

This hostel is located just off a busy highway near King's Cross. The interior is cramped and old, with colourful but peeling walls. Maintenance is poor, and the dorms show their age. The kitchen is on the top floor next to the nice rooftop common area, but there is really no atmosphere to speak of here. Reception staff are cold, and there are not many opportunities for meeting other travellers. Facilities and activities are very limited.

103 Palmer Street, Woolloomooloo
200, 311, 324, 325, 326, 327
Kings Cross
(02) 9357 3333 or 1800 688 335
***Website** www.cityresort.com.au*
***Dorm bed** $23-26*
***Credit cards** Amex, Diners, MC, Visa*
***Reception open** 7am-10pm*

Maintenance & cleanliness	★½
Facilities	★½
Atmosphere & character	★★½
Security	★★★
Overall rating	★★

Forbes Terrace (G'Day Backpackers)

Forbes Terrace is a nice clean hostel just off William Street within walking distance to both Kings Cross and the city centre. All the rooms have a fridge and TV and come with made up beds. The hostel's facilities include the usual kitchen, plus a room with a pool table and a pleasant shady courtyard.

153 Forbes Street, Woolloomooloo
200, 311, 324, 325, 326, 327

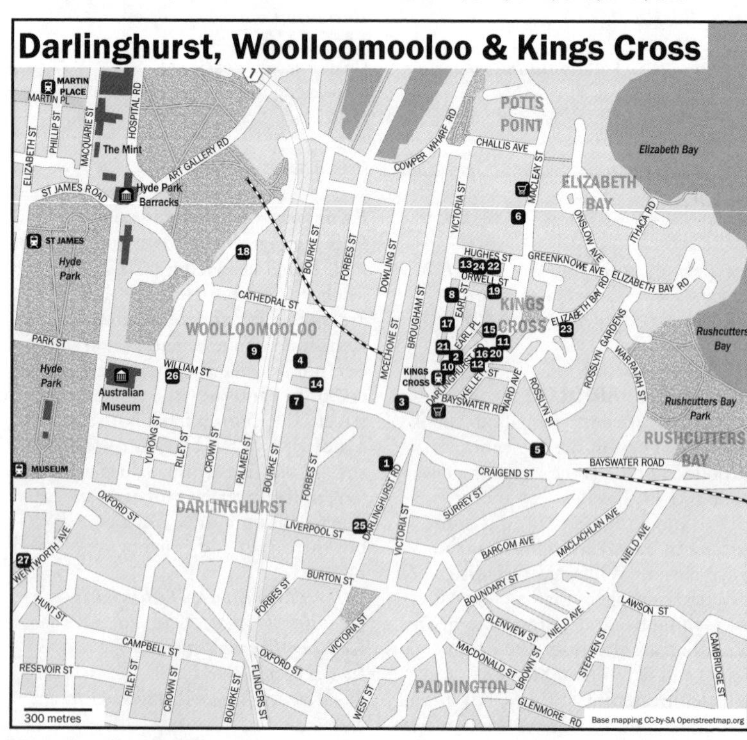

Kings Cross
(02) 9358 4327
Website *www.g-day.com.au*
Dorm bed *$20-24*
Credit cards *MC, Visa*
Reception open *8am-10pm*

Maintenance & cleanliness	★★★½
Facilities	★½
Atmosphere & character	★★
Security	★★★½
Overall rating	★★

Harbour City Backpackers

Harbour City Backpackers is a big hostel in a nice old Victorian building that has 220 beds on three floors. It is very roomy and has a nice wooden railing staircase. The kitchen is large but a bit dirty. The hostel has a good social atmosphere and there are plenty of activities going on everyday. The main TV lounge has a large screen TV but only a couple of old couches in an unventilated room. The rooftop sundeck has great views of the park and St Mary's Cathedral, and often gathers a good crowd at night. Reception staff are friendly and the price includes breakfast.

50 Sir John Young Crescent, Woolloomooloo
200, 311, 324, 325, 326, 327
St James
(02) 9380 2922
Website *www.harbourcityhotel.com*
Dorm bed *$24-27 ($23-26 VIP);* ***double/twin room*** *$75 ($73 VIP); prices include breakfast*
Credit cards *MC, Visa*
Reception open *7.30am-9pm*

Maintenance & cleanliness	★★★
Facilities	★½
Atmosphere & character	★★★★
Security	★★★★
Overall rating	★★★

Accommodation

1 Hotel Altamont
2 Ambassador Backpackers
3 Asylum Sydney
4 Australian Backpackers
5 Backpackers Headquarters
6 Blue Parrot Backpackers
7 Boomerang Backpackers
8 Chili Blue Backpackers
9 City Resort Hostel
10 Cooee Backpackers
11 D*lux Backpackers
12 Dury House Hostel
13 Eva's Backpackers
14 Forbes Terrace
15 Funk House
16 The Globe
17 Great Aussie Backpackers
18 Harbour City Backpackers
19 Jolly Swagman Backpackers
20 Mate's Place
21 The Original Backpackers' Hostel
22 The Palms
23 The Pink House
24 Sydney Central Backpackers
25 Sydney Star Accommodation
26 Wood Duck Inn
27 Y on the Park

Hotel Altamont

This is a 13-room hotel that includes one dormitory for backpackers so it is basically a small eight-bed hostel inside a boutique hotel. It is a trendy place with a unique industrial/medieval décor. There is a bar with a pool table in the foyer and other amenities include an en suite bathroom, a TV in the dorm, laundry and a small kitchen plus a nice rooftop terrace. It represents good value, but with only eight beds it fills up quickly.

207 Darlinghurst Road, Darlinghurst
200, 311, 324, 325, 326, 327
Kings Cross
(02) 9360 6000
Website *www.altamont.com.au*
Dorm bed *$25*
Credit cards *Amex, MC, Visa*
Reception open *8am-8pm daily; late check in by prior arrangement*

Maintenance & cleanliness	★★★★
Facilities	★★
Atmosphere & character	★★★★
Security	★★
Overall rating	★★★½

Sydney Star Accommodation

Sydney Star Accommodation is a small hostel in Darlinghurst, which is just a short walk from Kings Cross. The hostel's amenities include a courtyard with a barbecue, laundry, a small fully-equipped kitchen plus a TV lounge. All the rooms are self-contained with a fridge, microwave and TV, which tends to keep travellers in their rooms rather than hanging out in the common areas.

273 Darlinghurst Road, Darlinghurst
311 Kings Cross
(02) 9232 4455 or 1800 13 44 55
***Website** www.sydneystar.com.au*
***Dorm bed** $25-30; **double room** $60-80*
***Credit cards** MC, Visa*
***Reception open** 9am-11am & 5pm-7pm*

Maintenance & cleanliness	★★½
Facilities	★★
Atmosphere & character	★★
Security	★★½
Overall rating	★★½

The Wood Duck Inn

The Wood Duck Inn is a small, colourful hostel that has narrow halls and high ceilings, and you must walk up three flights to get to the rooftop reception and common area. It has a tiny kitchen and TV room, and dorms have good beds although some are crowded. There are only 50 beds and the bathrooms are dark and shabby. It is a friendly hostel, and reception staff are helpful. There are nice city views from the roof-top deck where everyone hangs out there at night so it can have a rather good atmosphere. It is located near the Australian Museum and is just a short walk from the city centre. Internet kiosks cost $4 per hour.

49 William Street, East Sydney
200, 311, 324, 325, 326, 327, 389
Museum
(02) 9358 5856 or 1800 110 025
***Website** www.woodduckinn.com.au*
***Dorm bed** $24; **twin room** $60*
***Credit cards** MC, Visa*
***Reception open** 8am-12.30pm & 4.30pm-8pm*

Maintenance & cleanliness	★★½
Facilities	★½
Atmosphere & character	★★★½
Security	★★★★½
Overall rating	★★½

GLEBE

Glebe is a quiet neighbourhood with a sizable student population a short distance west of the city centre. Although it isn't served by Sydney's rail system, there are plenty of buses and the Metro Light Rail tram stops here.

Alishan International Guest House

This hostel is located in a beautiful building that has been tastefully decorated. There is a very nice common room with Internet access and a clean kitchen. The bathrooms are spotless. There is also a backyard with a barbecue and picnic tables and a balcony overlooking the street. It is a quiet hostel with a pleasant relaxed atmosphere. It has the best location of Glebe's hostels right in Glebe's main shopping area and close to shops, restaurants and cafés.

100 Glebe Point Road, Glebe
431, 432, 433, 434 Glebe
(02) 9566 4048
***Website** www.alishan.com.au*

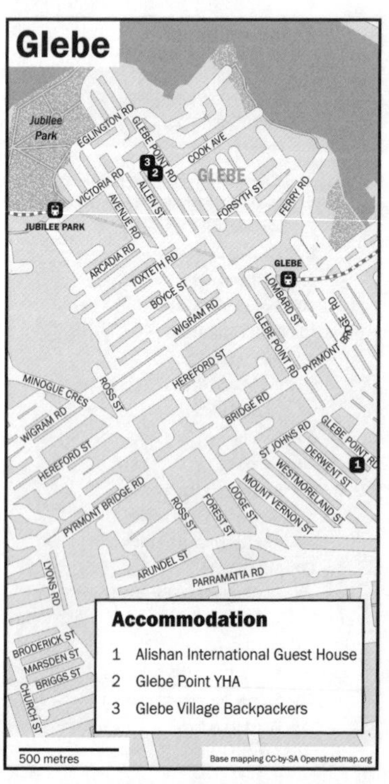

***Dorm bed** $25; **single room** $60-88; **double room** $80-105; **family room** $154*
***Credit cards** Amex, MC, Visa*
***Reception open** 8am-10.30pm*
TV K L

Maintenance & cleanliness	★★★★
Facilities	★★
Atmosphere & character	★★★½
Security	★★½
Overall rating	★★★

Glebe Point YHA

Glebe Point YHA is a clean hostel at the quiet end of Glebe Point Road. Common areas include a games room with a pool table, a kitchen, a big dining room and a TV lounge plus internet access including a Wi-Fi hotspot ($4 per hour, YHA Connect). There's also a great rooftop barbecue area. All the bunk beds have their own locker and reading light and there's a sink in each room.

262 Glebe Point Road, Glebe
431, 432, 433, 434 Glebe, Jubilee Park
(02) 9692 8418
***Website** www.yha.com.au*
***Dorm bed** $28-32.50 ($25-29 HI/YHA); **single room** $67 ($60 HI/YHA); **double/twin room** $78 ($70 HI/YHA)*
***Credit cards** MC, Visa*
***Reception open** 7am-10.45pm*
TV K L

Maintenance & cleanliness	★★★½
Facilities	★★
Atmosphere & character	★★★
Security	★★★½
Overall rating	★★★

Glebe Village Backpackers

Glebe Village Backpackers has the best atmosphere of Glebe's hostels and this is noticeable as soon as you walk through the front door. It consists of four old buildings (including a female-only building) that all have loads of character with hardwood floors, stained glass and exposed brickwork. Accommodation is in spacious rooms and there are several small lounge rooms scattered throughout the hostel plus a TV lounge and internet access but the best feature is the laid-back front yard with picnic tables.

256 Glebe Point Road, Glebe
431, 432, 433, 434 Glebe
(02) 9660 8133 or 1800 801 983
***Website** www.bakpak.com/glebevillage/*
***Dorm bed** $26-28; **single room** $65; **double room** $80; prices include breakfast*
***Credit cards** MC, Visa*
***Reception open** 8am-1am*
TV K L

Maintenance & cleanliness	★★½
Facilities	★★
Atmosphere & character	★★★★½
Security	★★½
Overall rating	★★★

KINGS CROSS

Kings Cross is backpacker central with loads of hostels, particularly along quiet tree-lined Victoria Street. Many of the hostels in Kings Cross have rooftop sundecks with amazing city views. The neighbourhood has plenty of cheap eats; great transport connections and is only a 15-minute walk from the heart of the city. However the Cross is also Sydney's red light district and some people may not feel comfortable walking alone at night among the brothels and sex shops.

Ambassador Backpackers

Ambassador Backpackers is a dull hostel in a charmless building in a back alley in the centre of Kings Cross. The hostel doesn't have many common areas – just a kitchen and a rooftop deck with nice views. There's no TV lounge but all the rooms have TVs, which keep travellers in their room and kills any chance of a social atmosphere. Apart from that there are en suite bathrooms in most rooms.

15 Earl Place, Kings Cross
311, 324, 325, 326, 327 Kings Cross
(02) 9331 6664 or 1800 005 331
***Dorm bed** $20-23; **double/twin room** $60-80*
***Credit cards** MC, Visa*
***Reception open** 8am-noon & 4pm-8pm*
TV K L

Maintenance & cleanliness	★★½
Facilities	★½
Atmosphere & character	★
Security	★★★
Overall rating	★★

Asylum Sydney

This mid-size hostel is in a terrace house one block from where Darlinghurst Road and Victoria Street intersect. It is relatively clean and well maintained when compared with other hostels in Kings Cross. Facilities include a small TV lounge with free internet access and a small kitchen (no oven) and there are TVs in some dormitories. It is quite good value when you consider that the price includes breakfast and an evening meal.

201-203 Brougham Street, Kings Cross
200, 311, 323 Kings Cross
(02) 9368 1822
Website *www.asylumsydney.com*
Dorm bed *$25-30;* ***double room*** *$70-100*
Credit cards *MC, Visa*
Reception open *7am-10pm*
L

Maintenance & cleanliness	★★★
Facilities	★★
Atmosphere & character	★★★
Security	★★½
Overall rating	★★½

Backpackers Headquarters

Backpackers Headquarters is quite a good hostel when compared to others in Kings Cross. It is clean although it is starting to show its age. There is a small kitchen and a lounge with a big TV on the ground floor near the reception plus a laundry and rooftop sundeck. This hostel also offers a free pick up service from the airport. It is at the quiet Rushcutters Bay end of Kings Cross.

79 Bayswater Road, Kings Cross
311, 324, 325, 326, 327 Kings Cross
(02) 9331 6180
Website *www.headquartershostel.com.au*
Dorm bed *$25 per night, $160 per week*
Credit cards *MC, Visa*
Reception open *7am-9pm*
TV K L

Maintenance & cleanliness	★★½
Facilities	★★
Atmosphere & character	★★★
Security	★★★
Overall rating	★★½

Blue Parrot Backpackers

This family-run hostel is clean and charming. It has a comfy TV room and a brand new clean kitchen. The open courtyard in the back is great for barbecues and meeting fellow backpackers. The large dorms are spotless and breezy, with skylights and fans and some with nice views. Dorm rooms are spotless and freshly painted in muted colours with comfortable beds. Toilets are not quite as new but well maintained. Lots of travellers relax and watch movies in the common room. It is not a party hostel, but it can still be fun. Staff are extremely friendly and warm. Although it is pricey, it is central and safe – perfect for women travelling alone, since technically it is located in Potts Point, but just a few steps from the dodgier area of Kings Cross. Internet access (including Wi-Fi) is free.

87 Macleay Street, Potts Point
311, 324, 325, 326, 327 Kings Cross
(02) 9356 4888 or 1800 252 299
Website *www.blueparrot.com.au*
Dorm bed *$25-35;* ***double/twin room*** *$85*
Credit cards *MC, Visa*
Reception open *9am-8.30pm*
TV K L

Maintenance & cleanliness	★★★★
Facilities	★★★
Atmosphere & character	★★★★
Security	★★★★
Overall rating	★★★★

Chili Blue Backpackers

Chili Blue is a small hostel with tiny, messy rooms and old beds. The courtyard with barbecue and cosy TV lounge can be a good place to mingle and the kitchen is brand new, but bathrooms need serious work and some of the dorms are dark and unventilated. Reception can be a bit cold. Free internet and free brekfast are perks. Security could be improved as well, as the reception area opens widely onto the walkway and anyone can walk in.

144 Victoria Street, Kings Cross
311, 324, 325, 326, 327 Kings Cross
(02) 9357 4733 or 1800 667 225
Website *www.chiliblue.com.au*

Dorm bed *$23-26;* ***double room*** *$65; prices include breakfast*
Credit cards *MC, Visa*
Reception open *7.30am-10.30pm*

Maintenance & cleanliness	★★½
Facilities	★★
Atmosphere & character	★★★
Security	★★★
Overall rating	★★½

Cooee Backpackers

This hostel in King's Cross is really old and run-down but is cleaned well. Reception staff are very open and helpful, and they try to provide a standard of accommodation which the structure does not really allow for. It has a slightly institutional feel, and dorm rooms are very old and dirty. The common area fills up at night with travellers, but it does not have a great atmosphere. Internet kiosks are free. The location is a bit dodgy and security is not very good.
107-109 Darlinghurst Road, Kings Cross
311, 324, 325, 326, 327 Kings Cross
(02) 9332 3244 or 1800 110 690
Website *http://cooeekingscross.com*
Dorm bed *$21-24;* ***double/twin room*** *$58-62*
Credit cards *MC, Visa*
Reception open *7am-2am*

Maintenance & cleanliness	★★
Facilities	★½
Atmosphere & character	★★★
Security	★★½
Overall rating	★★

D.lux Budget Hotel

In an old apartment building in King's Cross, this hostel has good presentation and good security. The lobby and common areas are gorgeous and the rooftop sundeck is a great place to hang out and have a barbecue with a view of the Harbour Bridge and the Opera House. They offer loads of activities and even have their own yacht to use for Harbour tours. The TV lounge has plenty of seating and big bean bag chairs to watch movies. The dorms, however, are nothing special. Some of them smell a bit musty, but the bathrooms are very clean and well maintained. Staff are very friendly.
30 Darlinghurst Road, Kings Cross
311, 324, 325, 326, 327 Kings Cross
1800 236 213
Website *www.dluxbudgethotel.com.au*
Dorm bed *$17-26;* ***double room*** *$70-90;* ***family room*** *$85-125*
Credit cards *JCB, MC, Visa*
Reception open *24 hours*

Maintenance & cleanliness	★★★
Facilities	★★½
Atmosphere & character	★★★
Security	★★★★★
Overall rating	★★★

Dury House

This is one of the worst hostels in King's Cross. Dorm rooms are small and cluttered, with old beds and no character. Bathrooms are really dirty with mouldy shower curtains and peeling paint. The kitchen is teeny and crowded, with a one-table dining area which doubles as a common room. It seems to cater mostly to Asian travellers and guests don't appear to socialise much, so there's not much of a backpacker atmosphere. The one good point is free internet (though there is only one computer) and wireless access.
48A Darlinghurst Road, Kings Cross
311, 324, 325, 326, 327 Kings Cross
(02) 9357 2255 or 1800 778 282
Website *www.duryhouse.com*
Dorm bed *$22-23*
Credit cards *Amex, MC, Visa*
Reception open *7.30am-10pm*

Maintenance & cleanliness	★
Facilities	★★
Atmosphere & character	★½
Security	★★★
Overall rating	★½

Eva's Backpackers

A cheerful, unassuming hostel on a quiet street, Eva's is family run and charming. It has a new, clean kitchen and a bright, sunny dining area. The lounge is really small, but the well-kept rooftop terrace has a barbecue and stunning city views. Dorms are spacious with huge lockers, and the bathrooms are brand new and meticulously clean. Prices are relatively steep, but if you are looking for a comfortable and quiet spot, it can't be beat. Staff are extremely friendly. It is the perfect place for women travelling alone.

6-8 Orwell Street, Kings Cross
311, 324, 325, 326, 327 Kings Cross
(02) 9358 2185 or 1800 802 517
***Website** www.evasbackpackers.com.au*
***Dorm bed** $28-40; **double/twin room** $75-90; prices include breakfast*
***Credit cards** Amex, MC, Visa*
***Reception open** Mon-Sat 7am-7pm, Sun 7am-2pm*

Maintenance & cleanliness	★★★★
Facilities	★★½
Atmosphere & character	★★★★
Security	★★★½
Overall rating	★★★½

Funk House Backpackers

Funk House is a very convivial little place with psychedelic paintings in the halls and on doors. Dorms are cramped but clean, with new bright paint and good beds. There is a Peter Pan travel agency in reception, and they organize nightly events such as pub crawls. It is a good place to meet party-minded travellers, and reception staff are warm and welcoming. Across the street you can get 15 minutes of free internet with your hostel key card. It has a good location and a nice rooftop barbecue area.

23 Darlinghurst Road, Kings Cross
311, 324, 325, 326, 327 Kings Cross
(02) 9358 6455 or 1800 247 600
***Website** www.funkhouse.com.au*
***Dorm bed** $21-27; **double/twin room** $60-80*
***Credit cards** MC, Visa*
***Reception open** Mon-Sat 7am-10pm, Sun 8am-8pm; 24 hours on summer weekends*

Maintenance & cleanliness	★★★
Facilities	★★
Atmosphere & character	★★★★½
Security	★★★
Overall rating	★★★

The Globe Backpackers

This backpackers' hostel is a pretty social place. It is a bit dingy in spots, but overall it's not bad. The kitchen doesn't offer much in the way of facilities. Rooms are on the grubby side, but they get better toward the top floors and some are ensuite. There is a cool little courtyard where they have barbecues often. There are no lockers, just a storage room. But reception staff are nice enough, and the TV lounge is convivial.

40 Darlinghurst Road, Kings Cross
311, 324, 325, 326, 327 Kings Cross
(02) 9326 9675
***Website** www.globebackpackers.com*
***Dorm bed** $21-27 ($20-26 HI/YHA, ISIC, VIP); **twin room** $75 ($73 HI/YHA, ISIC, VIP); prices include breakfast*
***Credit cards** MC, Visa*
***Reception open** Mon-Fri 8am-8pm, Sat-Sun 9am-8pm*

Maintenance & cleanliness	★½
Facilities	★★
Atmosphere & character	★★★½
Security	★★½
Overall rating	★★

Great Aussie Backpackers

This hostel is probably a good choice if you are looking to party. It is large and offers loads of daily organised tours and events. Young travellers gather in the covered courtyard where there is a good free barbecue every Friday night. At check-in you are given 15 free drinks at various bars around town, and the pub crawl has a good reputation among guests. But if you want a clean or quiet room, it may not be all that great. The paint is peeling, the bathrooms are unclean, and it is noisy at night. Security is below par as well. The building needs a bit of work, but the party atmosphere and friendly staff help to make up for it.

174 Victoria Street, Kings Cross
311, 324, 325, 326, 327 Kings Cross
(02) 9356 4551 or 1800 006 613
***Website** www.greataussiebackpackers.com.au*

Dorm bed *$26b;* ***double/twin room*** *$70-80; prices include breakfast*
Credit cards *MC, Visa*
Reception open *Mon-Fri 7am-9pm, Sat-Sun 8am-8pm*

Maintenance & cleanliness	★½
Facilities	★½
Atmosphere & character	★★★½
Security	★★★
Overall rating	★★

Jolly Swagman

This large, bright hostel attracts a party-minded crowd who hang out in the downstairs common area which opens onto the footpath. Reception doubles as a travel booking agency and tour organiser, and staff have tons of advice on things to do and see in Sydney. Big yellow dorms have plenty of locker space and sinks. The kitchen is roomy but lacking in facilities and maintenance. It is not the cleanest place in town, but it has good security and location.
27 Orwell Street, Kings Cross
311, 324, 325, 326, 327 *Kings Cross*
(02) 9358 6400
Website *www.jollyswagman.com.au*
Dorm bed *$25-29 ($24-28 VIP);* ***double room*** *$70-78 ($68-76 VIP); prices include breakfast*
Credit cards *MC, Visa*
Reception open *24 hours*

Maintenance & cleanliness	★★★
Facilities	★★
Atmosphere & character	★★★★
Security	★★★★
Overall rating	★★★

Kanga House

This funky hostel has three courtyard areas and a good barbeque night. The dorm rooms are small and simple and the bathrooms could do with a good scrubbing, but it has a large, clean kitchen with plenty of cooking equipment. Some of the upper floor rooms have great city views. The TV lounge is quietly convivial, with lots of books and movies available.
141 Victoria Street, Kings Cross
311, 324, 325, 326, 327 *Kings Cross*
(02) 9357 7897 or 1800 4 KANGA
Website *www.kangahouse.com.au*
Dorm bed *$22-25*
Credit cards *MC, Visa*
Reception open *7.30am-7pm; check in till 11pm*

Maintenance & cleanliness	★★½
Facilities	★★
Atmosphere & character	★★★
Security	★★½
Overall rating	★★½

Mate's Place

Mate's Place is a grungy hostel in the centre of Kings Cross. The hostel's facilities include a fully equipped kitchen, a TV lounge and free internet access (including Wi-Fi). All the rooms have fridges and air-conditioning and there's a locker for each bed. The hostel is messy but there is a good atmosphere and the guests seem happy enough.
7/1 Roslyn Street, Kings Cross
311, 324, 325, 326, 327 *Kings Cross*
Dorm bed *$18-25*
Credit cards *Amex, MC, Visa*
Reception open *8am-4pm & 5pm-1am*

Maintenance & cleanliness	★½
Facilities	★★
Atmosphere & character	★★★
Security	★★★
Overall rating	★★

Sydney Central Backpackers

Sydney Central Backpackers has polished floorboards in the reception and nice clean bathrooms. It also has a good kitchen area, a TV lounge and a brilliant rooftop sundeck with a pool table, barbecue and brilliant city views.
16 Orwell Street, Kings Cross
311, 324, 325, 326, 327 *Kings Cross*
(02) 9358 6600 or 1800 440 202
Website *www.sydneybackpackers.com.au*
Dorm bed *$27;* ***single/double/twin room*** *$70; prices include breakfast*
Credit cards *MC, Visa*
Reception open *7am-2pm & 4pm-9pm*

Maintenance & cleanliness	★★★
Facilities	★★½
Atmosphere & character	★★★½
Security	★★½
Overall rating	★★★

The Original Backpackers Lodge

Set in a lovely old building with moulded ceilings and nice furnishings, this hostel offers quite a bit of charm. Dorm rooms are spacious with high ceilings and wood floors; some of them have their own balconies. All of them have their own television. Toilets are pretty standard and the kitchen is well stocked. The courtyard has a great atmosphere especially at night and when they have barbecues. It is a good place to chill out and meet people.

160-162 Victoria Street, Kings Cross
311, 324, 325, 326, 327 *Kings Cross*
(02) 9356 3232
Website *www.originalbackpackers.com.au*
Dorm bed *$25-32 ($24-31 VIP);* ***single room*** *$65 ($64 VIP);* ***double/twin room*** *$75-95 ($73-93 VIP)*
Credit cards *MC, Visa; $2 credit card surcharge*
Reception open *24 hours*

Maintenance & cleanliness	★★★½
Facilities	★★
Atmosphere & character	★★★★
Security	★★★★
Overall rating	★★★½

The Palms

The Palms is a small friendly hostel on a quieter street in King's Cross. It is quite small and simple with a laid-back, friendly atmosphere. Free internet (including Wi-Fi) and a cosy lounge area with a large TV are highlights. Dorms tend to be cluttered and in poor shape, but the beds are good. Each has a clean en suite bathroom. The balcony in front is a nice place to hang out at night. The kitchen is well equipped, and there is free breakfast and free tea and coffee. Staff are fun and outgoing.

23 Hughes Street, Kings Cross
311, 324, 325, 326, 327 *Kings Cross*
(02) 9357 1199
Website *www.thepalmsbackpackers.com*
Dorm bed *$20-25;* ***double/twin room*** *$60; prices include breakfast*
Credit cards *MC, UnionPay, Visa*
Reception open *Mon-Fri 8am-noon & 5pm-8pm, Sat 8.30am-noon & 5pm-8pm, Sun 10am-noon & 5pm-8pm*

Maintenance & cleanliness	★★★
Facilities	★★½
Atmosphere & character	★★★
Security	★★★
Overall rating	★★★

The Pink House

The Pink House is a big old house on a leafy residential street but close to the heart of Kings Cross. The building has loads of character with high ceilings but it shows its age. It has the usual facilities including a kitchen and TV lounge plus free Internet access (Wi-Fi isn't free but you get unlimited Wi-Fi access for only $2) and several quiet shady courtyard areas including one with a barbecue. There are TVs in all the rooms. It is a fun place to stay.

6-8 Barncleuth Square, Kings Cross
311, 324, 325, 326, 327 *Kings Cross*
(02) 9358 1689 or 1800 806 385
Website *www.pinkhouse.com.au*
Dorm bed *$24-28 ($23-27 HI/YHA, ISIC, VIP);* ***double room*** *$75-85 ($73-83 HI/YHA, ISIC, VIP);* ***twin room*** *$75 ($73 HI/YHA, ISIC, VIP)*
Credit cards *MC, Visa*
Reception open *8.30am-12.30pm & 2pm-9pm*

Maintenance & cleanliness	★★½
Facilities	★★
Atmosphere & character	★★★★½
Security	★★
Overall rating	★★★

Travellers Rest

This place is a bit out-dated but comfortable. The carpets are old and some of the fixtures are broken, and there is no real common area to hang out in. The kitchen is very minimal, and ends up doubling as a common room. There is a small courtyard in the back as well. Many of the guests are in Sydney for

work, so it is not a very lively place. You must be buzzed into the front door, but there are no lockers. The hostel staff are sociable with the guests.
156 Victoria Street, Kings Cross
311, 324, 325, 326, 327 Kings Cross
(02) 9380 2044
Website *www.travellersrest.com.au*
Dorm bed *$24;* ***double room*** *$65*
Credit cards *MC, Visa; 3% credit card surcharge*
Reception open *8am-noon & 2pm-6pm*

Maintenance & cleanliness	★★
Facilities	★½
Atmosphere & character	★★★½
Security	★★
Overall rating	★★

KIRRIBILLI
Kirribilli is one of Sydney's oldest suburbs. It is a quiet residential neighbourhood at the northern end of the Sydney Harbour Bridge. It is an upmarket area that is home to the official Sydney residences of both the Governor-General and the Prime Minister.

Carnarvon Lodge
This hostel is down a small side street in Kirribilli. It is quiet and small; there is definitely no party atmosphere here at all. It seems to have been converted into a hostel from someone's house. The main common area is simply a few couches, a big television and some books. The kitchen is small and well stocked, if a bit messy. Toilets are bland but clean enough.
10 Parkes Street, Kirribilli
269 Kirribilli
(02) 9925 0517
Website *www.carnarvonlodge.com*
Dorm bed *$35;* ***single room*** *$70;* ***double/twin room*** *$95-110*
Credit cards *MC, Visa*
Reception open *11am-6pm*

Maintenance & cleanliness	★★★
Facilities	★
Atmosphere & character	★★½
Security	★½
Overall rating	★★

Glenferrie Lodge
This is a three-star hotel that has two four-bed dorms rather than a proper backpackers' hostel. It is the best place to stay in Kirribilli, if you can get in. Glenferrie Lodge is set in an old manor house that is beautifully maintained; they offer free hot breakfast and nightly dinners are available in the dining area. There is a lovely garden in the back and it has a good amount of character with stained glass windows and chandeliers. The dorms are cosy and plain white, the beds are of high quality, and each has a small fridge and a telly. There is wireless access at $6 per hour or $15 per day. It is in a very quiet neighbourhood and the staff are pleasant.
12a Carabella Street, Kirribilli
269 Kirribilli
(02) 9955 1685 or 1800 121 011
Website *www.glenferrielodge.com*
Dorm bed *$40-45; single room $69-99;* ***double/twin room*** *$109-129; prices include breakfast*
Credit cards *Amex, MC, Visa*
Reception open *6am-11pm*

Maintenance & cleanliness	★★★½
Facilities	★★
Atmosphere & character	★★★
Security	★★★
Overall rating	★★★

Tremayne Backpackers
Set in a nice large building on a leafy street, this place feels more like an old hotel. It doesn't have much in the way of facilities, and seems to cater to an older crowd of travellers rather than backpackers. The common area is a bit drab - just a small television, some old couches and metal tables. The dorms and toilets are nice and clean, but the kitchen is nothing special. There is no internet and there are no lockers. For the price, it doesn't quite measure up.
89 Carabella Street, Kirribilli
269 Kirribilli
(02) 9955 4155
Dorm bed *$30*
Reception open *Mon-Fri 9.30am-6pm, Sat 9.30am-noon*

New South Wales

Maintenance & cleanliness	★★★½
Facilities	★
Atmosphere & character	★★★½
Security	★★★½
Overall rating	★★

MANLY

Although a half-hour ferry ride from the centre of Sydney, this beachside suburb is a nice spot with a lively atmosphere, good pubs and a great beach. There are frequent ferries from Circular Quay.

Boardrider Backpacker

This place is popular despite the relatively low standard of accommodation. Posters and ads selling surfboards fill the walls (covering the peeling paint), and some of the dorms are cluttered and badly maintained. The kitchen is messy, and the toilets could be cleaner, too. But the location is great, and tanned surfers hang out watching movies in the common room, giving the place a fair amount of atmosphere. They offer free use of body boards and have good security. Internet, including wireless, is $3 per hour.

63 The Corso, Manly
151, 169, E69, E71 *Manly*
(02) 9977 6077
Website *www.boardrider.com.au*
Dorm bed *$33;* ***double/twin room*** *$100-120*
Credit cards *MC, Visa*
Reception open *8am-8pm*

Maintenance & cleanliness	★★★½
Facilities	★★★½
Atmosphere & character	★★★★
Security	★★★★★
Overall rating	★★★

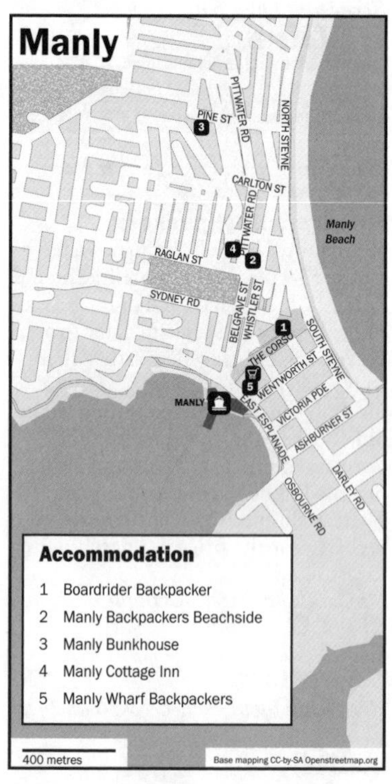

Manly Backpackers Beachside

This hostel is in a cool building in a good location, but the charm is all in the façade. Inside there is a cold, institutional feel and the main common area is just a big empty room with a television and a few couches. The kitchen is a bit messy, as are most dorms. Toilets are a bit grimy. They have bikes and body boards available for use. It attracts a good crowd, but security is lacking and there is not enough locker space.

28 Raglan Street, Manly
151, 169, E69, E71 *Manly*
(02) 9977 3411 or 1800 656 299
Website *www.manlybackpackers.com.au*
Dorm bed *$35 ($34 VIP);* ***twin room*** *$65-100 ($653-98 VIP)*
Credit cards *MC, Visa*
Reception open *9am-7pm*

Maintenance & cleanliness	★★★½
Facilities	★★★½
Atmosphere & character	★★★
Security	★★★½
Overall rating	★★★½

Manly Bunkhouse

A bit farther from the centre than the other Manly hostels, the Manly Bunkhouse is in a residential neighbourhood in a small run-down building. The kitchen is tiny and badly maintained. A dark and stuffy television room is the only real common area although there is also a sunny backyard with a barbecue.

35 Pine Street, Manly

151, 169, E69, E71 *Manly*
(02) 9976 0472 or 1800 657 122
Website *www.bunkhouse.com.au*
Dorm bed *$26-30 ($25-29 VIP);* ***double/twin room*** *$66-80 ($65-79 VIP)*
Credit cards *MC, Visa*
Reception open *Mon-Fri 8.30am-1pm & 2pm-6pm; Sat-Sun 9am-noon & 5pm-6pm*

Maintenance & cleanliness	★★½
Facilities	★½
Atmosphere & character	★★
Security	★★
Overall rating	★★

Manly Cottage Inn

This is a small hostel with 30 beds and a nice family atmosphere. Dorms are spacious and clean with large windows and bright yellow walls. Toilets are impeccable. A small and shabby kitchen and common area fills with travellers and people doing temporary work in Manly. Security is good as there are lockers and you must ring the bell to get in. There is no internet. Reserve ahead in summer.
25 Pittwater Road, Manly
151, 169, E69, E71 *Manly*
(02) 9976 0297
Website *www.users.bigpond.com/manlycottage/*
Dorm bed *$30*
Credit cards *MC, Visa*
Reception open *9am-8pm*

Maintenance & cleanliness	★★★
Facilities	★
Atmosphere & character	★★★★
Security	★★★½
Overall rating	★★½

Manly Wharf Backpackers

This small hostel is dark and run-down. The TV lounge is musty and cluttered with books, old ripped couches and a simple television. This is where everyone (read: a group of surfer guys) gather when they're not out partying. Security could be better; you must ring the bell to get in, but anyone can come to let you in if reception is not around. Dorms and toilets are average. You pay for the location.
48 East Esplanade, Manly
151, 169, E69, E71 *Manly*
(02) 9977 2800
Dorm bed *$25-30*
Reception open *Mon-Fri 8am-8pm, Sat 8.30am-8pm, Sun 8.30am-7pm*

Maintenance & cleanliness	★★
Facilities	★
Atmosphere & character	★★★
Security	★★★½
Overall rating	★★

NEWTOWN

Newtown is a vibrant neighbourhood with lots of pubs, restaurants and cafés. It is about 10 minutes from the city centre by bus or train. Parking is very difficult to find here so you may want to avoid staying here if you have a car.

Abbey on King

Abbey on King is a very clean and secure hostel above a café near Newtown station. It is well maintained with top quality fittings but facilities are limited to a TV lounge, Internet access and a small, but fully equipped, kitchen. Although on first glance it seems a bit sterile, the atmosphere is actually pretty good making it a good value accommodation option.
379 King Street, Newtown
422, 423, 426, 428 *Newtown*
(02) 9519 2099 or 1800 219 999
Website *www.theabbeyonking.com.au*
Dorm bed *$15-24; single room $30;* ***double room*** *$50*
Credit cards *Amex, Diners, MC, Visa*
Reception open *8am-1pm & 5pm-8pm*

Maintenance & cleanliness	★★★★½
Facilities	★½
Atmosphere & character	★★★½
Security	★★★★½
Overall rating	★★★½

Billabong Gardens

Billabong Gardens is a nice purpose-built hostel behind a terrace house, which is centred on a courtyard with a swimming pool. It has a fully-equipped kitchen plus a barbecue and TV lounge with free internet access

including Wi-Fi. Most rooms have en suite bathrooms and all beds come with linen. Private rooms have fridges and TVs. The hostel has good security with lockers in the dorms. There is also secure off-street parking ($5 per night).
5-11 Egan Street, Newtown
422, 423, 426, 428 *Newtown*
(02) 9550 3236
Website *www.billabonggardens.com.au*
Dorm bed *$25-27*
Credit cards *MC, Visa*
Reception open *8.15am-noon & 6pm-10pm*

Maintenance & cleanliness	★★★
Facilities	★★★
Atmosphere & character	★★★
Security	★★★½
Overall rating	★★★

NORTHERN BEACHES

Sydney's northern beaches are a long way from the city centre, but the beaches are great and the hostels are generally worth the trip.

Avalon Beach Hostel

The Avalon Beach Hostel is a good accommodation choice for travellers wanting a fun place to stay in Sydney's Northern Beaches. It has a kitchen and a big common area with a fireplace and a balcony where rainbow lorikeets often come to perch. Downstairs there is a laundry and a TV lounge with table tennis. It has a really great atmosphere, making it one of the most fun places to stay in the Sydney area.
59 Avalon Parade, Avalon
L90
(02) 9918 9709
Dorm bed *$25*
Credit cards *MC, Visa*
Reception open *8am-noon & 4.30pm-9pm*

Maintenance & cleanliness	★★
Facilities	★★
Atmosphere & character	★★★★★
Security	★
Overall rating	★★½

Sydney Beachouse YHA

This is an excellent purpose-built hostel with very good facilities. The hostel features two TV lounges; a kitchen; a lounge/dining area with a TV, pool table and a fireplace; a games room with table tennis and an outdoor area with a swimming pool and barbecue. This hostel has excellent security with key card access, lockers in all dorms, video surveillance and secure parking. Guests have free use of bicycles, surfboards, bodyboards and snorkelling gear. It is close to shops and Collaroy Beach, but it's around a one hour bus ride to the city centre.
4 Collaroy Street, Collaroy
151, 155, 156, L88, L90
(02) 9981 1177
Website *www.sydneybeachouse.com.au*
Dorm bed *$29.50-31.50 ($26-28 HI/YHA);* ***double/twin room*** *$71-75 ($64-68 HI/YHA)*
Credit cards *MC, Visa*
Reception open *Jan-Feb 8am-8pm; Mar-Nov 8.30am-7pm; Dec 8am-8pm*

Maintenance & cleanliness	★★★★
Facilities	★★★★½
Atmosphere & character	★★★½
Security	★★★★½
Overall rating	★★★★

OTHER AREAS

Many of the hostels located in other parts of Sydney cater primarily to travellers on a working holiday and offer basic facilities at a lower cost. There are some nice areas away from the main backpackers' neighbourhoods that offer great beaches and are a pleasant spot to base yourself while in Sydney.

The hostels listed below vary from a 10-minute bus ride to a one-hour train trip from the city centre.

Balmain Backpackers

Balmain Backpackers caters mainly to long term guests who are working in Sydney and there is a minimum three-night stay. It's a relatively clean and well maintained place and it has a good atmosphere. Facilities include the usual internet access, a TV lounge, kitchen and a veranda with a barbecue. It is on a busy intersection about a 10-minute bus ride from the city centre.
675 Darling Street, Balmain

432, 433, 434, 440, 500, 501, 504, 506, 520
(02) 9555 6436
Website *www.backpackersydney.com*
Dorm bed *$18-20 per night, $140 per week; price includes breakfast*
Credit cards *MC, Visa*
Reception open *10am-6pm*

Maintenance & cleanliness	★★★½
Facilities	★★½
Atmosphere & character	★★★½
Security	★★★
Overall rating	★★★

Cronulla Beach YHA

Cronulla Beach YHA is a clean and well-maintained hostel that has a very good atmosphere for a YHA. Common areas include a TV lounge with comfy bean bags plus big kitchen/dining room with a pool table; internet access including Wi-Fi ($5 per hour, YHA Connect), a laundry and a small courtyard. It's located in the heart of Cronulla – a distant beachside suburb with a resort feel to it – 45 minutes by train from the city centre.
40-42 Kingsway, Cronulla
Cronulla
(02) 9527 7772
Website *www.cronullabeachyha.com*
Dorm bed *$28-29 ($25-26 HI/YHA);* ***double/twin room*** *$85 ($76.50 HI/YHA)*
Credit cards *MC, Visa*
Reception open *8.30am-10pm*

Maintenance & cleanliness	★★★½
Facilities	★★
Atmosphere & character	★★★★
Security	★★★
Overall rating	★★★

Eating & Drinking

Sydney is a good city for eating. It's not quite up there with Melbourne, but it is good value with a lot of cheap meal deals.

There are plenty of fast food joints and food courts and some of the hostels organise regular cheap meals. There is also a good range of 24-hour places to satisfy those midnight cravings.

A lot of pubs advertise $7 steak and $10 steak and beer deals. It's usually a cheap cut, like rump, but it fills you up and usually comes with chips and salad. A lot of pubs advertise these cheap deals to pull in the punters so they can sell them more beer. It's not a bad deal when you consider that it's not much more expensive than a McDonald's meal. Just look for the "$7 Steak" signs in pub windows.

Sydney's favourite fish and chips is Doyles at Watsons Bay – avoid the fancy upmarket restaurant of the same name and head to the cheaper fish and chip place across the road. It involves a ferry ride from Circular Quay so it is only a cheap meal if you have a TravelPass.

If you're hankering for a meat pie, then **Harry's Cafe de Wheels** is a Sydney institution worth visiting for a late night snack. The original pie cart is on Cowper Wharf Road in Woolloomooloo, but there is a more central one on Capitol Square in the city centre. Harry's clientele has included Frank Sinatra, Marlene Dietrich and Colonel Sanders and it has also featured in the second season of *the Amazing Race* TV show.

If you're preparing your own food there are several supermarkets in the city centre including a **Coles** in World Square *(650 George Street, Sydney; Town Hall)* and at Wynyard Station *(289-307 George Street, Sydney; Wynyard)* and a **Woolworths** next to Town Hall Station *(corner Park & George Streets, Sydney)*. In Kings Cross you'll find a **Coles** in the Hyatt Kingsgate Shopping Centre *(88-94 Darlinghurst Road, Kings Cross; Kings Cross)* underneath the big Coca Cola sign, and a **Woolworths** in the Icon Building in Potts Point *(81 Macleay Street, Potts Point; Kings Cross)*. If you're staying in Glebe your best bet are the Bi-Lo and Coles supermarkets in the Broadway Shopping Centre on Bay Street near the southern end of Glebe Point Road.

Sydney has a growing café scene with plenty of good cafés in all the neighbourhoods frequented by backpackers but pubs are more popular with most travellers. The best pubs are generally those in the more established areas such as The Rocks, Surry Hills, Woolloomooloo and the city centre.

A couple of the more centrally located Irish pubs are **Paddy Maguire's** on Capitol Square *(corner George & Hay Streets, Sydney; Capitol Square)* and **Scruffy Murphy's** *(43-49 Goulburn Street, Sydney; Town Hall)*. Paddy's is probably the better of the two and its convenient location means that a lot of visitors to Sydney end up here on some point of their travels, but a lot of travellers prefer the more rowdy atmosphere at Scruffy Murphy's. The **Three Wise Monkeys** *(555 George Street, Sydney; Town Hall)* is a good city pub in a former bank that is a popular backpackers' haunt with three floors of bars, a good atmosphere and live music. **Scubar**, in the basement of the Sydney Central YHA *(2-24 Rawson Place, Sydney; Central)*, is probably the best known backpackers' bar in Sydney. It features theme nights including its famous crab races on Monday nights. The **Side Bar** in the basement of Wake Up! *(509 Pitt Street, Sydney; Central)* is another major backpackers' bar with pool tables, drinking games and food specials.

Backpackers staying in Kings Cross, Darlinghurst and Woolloomooloo hang out at the **Empire Hotel** *(2A Roslyn Street, Potts Point; Kings Cross)*, which is open 24 hours and attracts a mixed crowd. The **World Bar** *(24 Bayswater Road, Kings Cross; Kings Cross)* is another popular Kings Cross backpackers' bar that has more of a nightclub feel with thumping dance music.

Pubs in beachside suburbs are known for their outdoor areas and beer gardens and many beach pubs boast sea views. The **Coogee Beach Palace Hotel** *(169 Dolphin Street, Coogee; 313, 314, 370, 372, 373, 374, X73, X74)* is the most popular pub among backpackers staying in Coogee and the **Bondi Hotel** *(178 Campbell Parade, Bondi Beach; 333, 380, 381, 382, X84)* is the main drinking spot in Bondi.

Many of Sydney's hostels have excellent rooftop decks that make a good venue for drinking back at the hostel. Buy a six-pack from the local bottle shop, head back to your hostel and enjoy Sydney's cheapest drinking option.

Sights

CITY CENTRE

The Central Business District (known as either the CBD or simply the City) stretches from Circular Quay at the harbour south to Central Station and encompasses the cluster of high-rise office buildings in between. Most of Sydney's sights are here and other neighbourhoods such as Darling Harbour and The Rocks are within easy walking distance.

Sydney Tower

Sydney's tallest building offers great views over the city centre and Sydney Harbour. Entry to the observation deck also includes OzTrek, a 35-minute virtual reality tour featuring 3D holograms and 180 degree cinema screens.

100 Market Street, Sydney
City Centre St James, Town Hall
(02) 9333 9222
Website *www.sydneytower.com.au*
Admission *$25 ($19.50 students)*
Open *Mon-Fri 9am-10.30pm, Sat 9am-11.30pm, Sun 9am-10.30pm*

Sydney Tower Skywalk

The Centrepoint Tower is also the venue for the Sydney Tower Skywalk. This adventure activity involves getting into a harness and venturing out onto the roof of the tower and walking along external walkways to a platform suspended over the edge of the tower that offers even better city views than the observation deck.

Admission *$40 (in addition to Sydney Tower entry fee)*
Open *9.30am-8.45pm daily*

Art Gallery of NSW

A good collection of permanent exhibits ranging from Australian artists and even including a few European masters. The Art Gallery of New South Wales also hosts a number of excellent temporary exhibits.

Art Gallery Road, The Domain, Sydney
441 Martin Place, St James
(02) 9225 1744
Website *www.artgallery.nsw.gov.au*
Admission *free, charge for temporary exhibits*

Open *10am-5pm daily*

Australian Museum

Australia's first museum is home to impressive displays of Australian culture as well as stuffed animals and interactive science exhibits.
6 College Street, Sydney
200, 311, 312, 323, 324, 325, 326, 327, 389 *Museum*
(02) 9320 6000
Website *www.amonline.net.au*
Admission *$10*
Open *9.30am-5pm daily*

Government House

Although no longer the governor's residence, Government House is still used for official functions. At other times visitors can enjoy one of Australia's best examples of Gothic Revival architecture.
Macquarie Street, Royal Botanic Gardens, Sydney
L82, L94, X94, X98, 301, 302, 303, 304, 308, 309, 310, 311, 323, 324, 325, 327, 373, 374, 376, 377, 380, 382, 389, 390, 391, 392, 394, 396, 397, 398, 399, 438, 888 *Circular Quay* *Circular Quay*
(02) 9931 5222
Website *www.hht.nsw.gov.au*
Admission *free*
Open *house Fri-Sun 10am-3pm; grounds 10am-4pm daily*

Hyde Park Barracks

Designed by convict architect, Francis Greenway, Hyde Park Barracks have endured a colourful history as a home for convicts, an immigration depot and an asylum. It has now been converted into a museum with exhibits on convict life.
Queens Square, Macquarie Street, Sydney
X90, X96 *Martin Place, St James*
(02) 9223 8922
Website *www.hht.nsw.gov.au*
Admission *$10*
Open *9.30am-5pm daily*

Justice & Police Museum

Formerly a police station and courtroom, the Justice & Police Museum has an interesting series of exhibits on crime, law and policing in New South Wales. Visitors have the opportunity to see mug shots of early criminals, weapons and forensic evidence as well as seeing the inside of a police charge room and a remand cell.
Corner Albert & Phillip Streets, Sydney
L82, L94, X94, X98, 301, 302, 303, 304, 308, 309, 310, 311, 323, 324, 325, 327, 373, 374, 376, 377, 380, 382, 389, 390, 391, 392, 394, 396, 397, 398, 399, 438, 888 *Circular Quay* *Circular Quay*
(02) 9252 1144
Website *www.hht.nsw.gov.au*
Admission *$8*
Open *Jan 10am-5pm daily; Feb-Dec Sat-Sun 10am-5pm*

Museum of Sydney

Situated on the site of the original Government House, the Museum of Sydney delves into the history of Sydney from early Aboriginal culture through colonial times to the modern city that you see today.
Corner Bridge & Phillip Streets, Sydney
L82, L94, X94, X98, 301, 302, 303, 304, 308, 309, 310, 311, 323, 324, 325, 327, 373, 374, 376, 377, 380, 382, 389, 390, 391, 392, 394, 396, 397, 398, 399, 438, 888 *Circular Quay* *Circular Quay*
(02) 9251 5988
Website *www.hht.nsw.gov.au*
Admission *$10*
Open *9.30am-5pm daily*

Queen Victoria Building

The Queen Victoria Building, or QVB, is an opulent Romanesque Revival shopping centre that fills the city block bordered by Druitt, George, Market and York Streets. It was built in 1898 and although threatened with demolition in the late 1950s, it reopened as an upmarket shopping centre in 1986. Although it is hardly a place where most backpackers come to shop, it's a nice building to saunter through.
455 George Street, Sydney
151, 169, 175, 178, 180, 183, 184, 190, 200, 247, 254, 261, 264, 286, 288, 289, 290, 291, 292, 293, 294, 441, 442, 461 *Park Plaza* *Town Hall*
(02) 9264 1955
Website *www.qvb.com.au*
Admission *free*

Open Mon-Sat 9am-6pm, Sun 11am-5pm

Royal Botanic Gardens
The Royal Botanic Gardens occupies the large area of parkland at the north eastern edge of the city centre. It is home to Government House, ponds, gardens and lots of fruit bats.
Mrs Macquaries Road, Sydney
L82, L94, X94, X98, 301, 302, 303, 304, 308, 309, 310, 311, 323, 324, 325, 327, 373, 374, 376, 377, 380, 382, 389, 390, 391, 392, 394, 396, 397, 398, 399, 438, 888 Circular Quay Circular Quay
(02) 9231 8125
***Website** www.rbgsyd.nsw.gov.au*
***Admission** free*
***Open** 6.30am-sunset*

State Library of NSW
This impressive library contains more than two million books including historical treasures such as the logbooks of Captain Bligh and Captain Cook's original journals.
Macquarie Street, Sydney
200 Martin Place
(02) 9273 1414
***Website** www.slnsw.gov.au*
***Admission** free*
***Open** Mon-Fri 9am-9pm, Sat-Sun 11am-5pm*

Sydney Opera House
The Sydney Opera House was designed by Danish architect Jørn Utzon and built over a 14-year period. It was finally completed, way over budget, in 1973. The Opera House is one of Australia's two internationally recognised urban landmarks (the Harbour Bridge is the other) and is widely recognised for its unique design and imposing position overlooking the harbour at the tip of Bennelong Point. The Opera House has four auditoria and features ballet, classical music, theatre and opera performances. Front of house tours run frequently but backstage tours run less often and need to be booked in advance.
Bennelong Point, Sydney
all Circular Quay buses Circular Quay Circular Quay
(02) 9250 7777
***Website** www.sydneyoperahouse.com*
***Tours cost** $35 ($27.50 online); backstage tour $150*
***Tours depart** every 30mins 9am-5pm daily*

Town Hall
Sydney's Town Hall is a fine example of Victorian architecture featuring a clock tower, while the interior contains a concert hall with an impressive 8,500-pipe organ.
483 George Street, Sydney
151, 169, 175, 178, 180, 183, 184, 190, 200, 247, 254, 261, 264, 286, 288, 289, 290, 291, 292, 293, 294, 441, 442, 461 Park Plaza Town Hall
(02) 9265 9007
***Admission** free*
***Open** Mon-Fri 8am-6pm*

DARLING HARBOUR
Just a short walk from the heart of the city centre, this harbour side precinct has been developed as new tourist area with hotels, museums, parks, shopping centres and plenty of fast food shops. Everything of interest in Darling Harbour was built in the last 20 years and parts of it seem quite sterile, however the area is home to several attractions including the Sydney Aquarium, Sydney Wildlife World, the National Maritime Museum and the Powerhouse Museum.

Australian National Maritime Museum
An excellent maritime museum with exhibits which include the submarine *HMAS Onslow*.
2 Murray Street, Pyrmont
888 Darling Harbour Harbourside Pyrmont Bay
(02) 9298 3777
***Website** www.anmm.gov.au*
***Admission** museum free; boats & submarine $30*
***Open** Jan 9.30am-6pm daily; Feb-Dec 9.30am-5pm daily*

Powerhouse Museum
One of Australia's largest museums has some excellent interactive displays and is host to a number of very good tem-

porary exhibits. It is definitely one of Australia's more enjoyable museums.
500 Harris Street, Ultimo
501 Darling Harbour Haymarket Haymarket
(02) 9217 0100 or 9217 0444
***Website** www.phm.gov.au*
***Admission** $10 ($6 students)*
***Open** 10am-5pm daily*

Sydney Aquarium

This aquarium is excellent and shows underwater life in different ecosystems from mangrove swamps to rivers and the Great Barrier Reef and features glass tunnels where you are surrounded by water.
Wheat Street, Sydney
Darling Harbour Darling Park
Town Hall
(02) 9262 2300
***Website** www.sydneyaquarium.com.au*
***Admission** $29.50 ($20.50 students)*
***Open** 9am-10pm daily (last entry 9pm)*

Sydney Wildlife World

This small wildlife park has 65 exhibits with 100 different Australian species over three levels. It fits quite a lot into a small space and gets good reports from travellers, but it is really small and much larger wildlife parks outside Sydney are a lot cheaper.
Lime Street, Darling Harbour, Sydney
Darling Park Town Hall
Convention, Pyrmont Bay
(02) 9333 9288
***Website** www.sydneywildlifeworld.com.au*
***Admission** $29.50 ($26.55 online)*
***Open** 9am-10pm daily (last entry 9pm)*

THE ROCKS

This area at the southern end of the Harbour Bridge is Sydney's oldest neighbourhood and is a welcome departure from the towers of glass and steel just a few minutes walk away. Much of the area has been renovated with plenty of expensive restaurants and boutiques. The Rocks is also home to some of the city's best pubs and can get quite busy on a Friday or Saturday night.

Museum of Contemporary Art

With an enviable location overlooking Sydney Cove from Circular Quay West, the Museum of Contemporary Art has a good collection of artworks including a number of excellent temporary exhibits.
140 George Street, The Rocks
435, 436, 437, 438, 440, 443, 470, 500, 501, 504, 506, 508, 510, 520, 888
Circular Quay Circular Quay
(02) 9252 4033
***Website** www.mca.com.au*
***Admission** free*
***Open** 10am-5pm daily*

Sydney Harbour Bridge

The world's widest long-span bridge and tallest (134m), but not the longest, steel arch bridge opened in 1932 becoming Sydney's first internationally recognised landmark. The bridge is such an enduring symbol of the city that it deserves more than just a quick look. Walking across is the cheapest and one of the best ways to experience the bridge, although you can also take a bus or train across. If you've got the money the best experience by far is the BridgeClimb. One of the bridge's southern pylons houses the Harbour Bridge Museum that has great views from the top.
Access to the pedestrian lane is via the Bridge Stairs on Cumberland Street between Argyle and Gloucester Streets, The Rocks.
X39, 339, X43, 343, 431, 432, 433, 434 Wynyard, Milsons Point

BridgeClimb

The BridgeClimb offers a once in a lifetime opportunity to climb the outer arch of the Sydney Harbour Bridge. Although expensive and out of many backpackers' budgets the BridgeClimb is established as Sydney's top attraction. The BridgeClimb bills itself as an adventure activity although it's not in the same league as skydiving or bungee jumping. The experience lasts for 3½ hours and gives you a fantastic view of the city and an appreciation of the Sydney Harbour Bridge.

All climbers are fitted with a bridge suit and safety harness and given a safety briefing before heading out on to the bridge. Then small groups of around ten climb a series of ladders to the lower

area of the top arch, from where they climb to the top of the bridge. There's a photo session at the top, then you walk across a walkway to the other side where you descend back to street level. Bookings are essential and don't go out on the town the night before as everyone is breathalysed before the climb.
5 Cumberland Street, The Rocks
all Wynyard & Circular Quay buses
Circular Quay *Circular Quay*
(02) 8274 7777
Website *www.bridgeclimb.com.au*
Admission *$179-295*
Open *8am-5pm daily*

Harbour Bridge Pylon Lookout

The climb up the stairs inside one of the bridge's southern pylons is a cheaper alternative to the BridgeClimb although the experience isn't quite the same. There are great views from the top and the museum inside the pylon has exhibits about the bridge's construction.
Hickson Road, Dawes Point. South East Pylon (access is via the pedestrian pathway on the Eastern side of the bridge).
X39, 339, X43, 343, 431, 432, 433, 434, 435, 436, 437, 438, 440, 443, 470, 500, 504, 506, 888 *Circular Quay* *Circular Quay*
(02) 9240 1100
Website *www.pylonlookout.com.au*
Admission *$9.50*
Open *10am-5pm daily*

Sydney Observatory

Australia's oldest observatory features an exhibition on astronomy and its context in Australian history.
Watson Road, Observatory Hill, The Rocks
X39, 339, X43, 343, 431, 432, 433, 434 *Circular Quay* *Circular Quay*
(02) 9217 0485
Website *www.sydneyobservatory.com.au*
Admission *daytime $7; night time $15*
Open *10am-5pm daily; night time hours vary*

OTHER AREAS

Sydney's suburbs go on and on and on so allow plenty of travelling time to get to the city's more far-flung sights.

Taronga Zoo

Taronga Zoo is one of Sydney's most popular attractions. It is known as the zoo with a view and is one of the world's more enjoyable zoos, partly because of its lovely harbour side setting. The zoo has the usual collection of animals from around the globe and a couple of good picnic and barbecue areas.
Bradleys Head Road, Mosman
Taronga Zoo
(02) 9969 2777
Website *www.zoo.nsw.gov.au*
Admission *$37 ($23 students); combined ferry & admission tickets available*
Open *9am-5pm daily*

Around Sydney

There are plenty of interesting excursions that can be made from Sydney and most can be made as either a day trip or a weekend getaway.

Attractions around Sydney range from industrial cities like Newcastle and Wollongong to the vineyards of the Hunter Valley and hiking in the Blue Mountains and Ku-Ring-Gai Chase National Park.

Newcastle

At first glance, Newcastle seems like an underwhelming place, but if you dig a little deeper you will uncover some of the great activities it has to offer. An industrial town with an uneasy past and a stagnant reputation, Newcastle today is growing in popularity among backpackers. Its proximity to the Hunter Valley wine region and adventure tours makes it the perfect home base for day trips.

The city has undergone a serious facelift in the past decade and now has a few good hostels and a healthy café scene. Surfers hone in on Newcastle for the great waves, while beach-goers are equally delighted to wade in the mild ocean baths along the shoreline. Nightlife is surging these days with a large concentration of live music and all-night pubs. Darby and Beaumont streets are the main arteries of the city, with loads of cafes, restaurants, and bars.

Beaumont Street boasts free wireless internet access from any point along the road and in restaurants. There are a few more galleries and exhibitions springing up these days as well; it's worth a bit of investigation. Fort Scratchley is an interesting sight, as is the Newcastle Regional Art Gallery.

Practical Information

Newcastle Visitor Information Centre

363 Hunter Street, Newcastle
☎ *(02) 4974 2999*
Website *www.visitnewcastle.com.au*
Open *Mon-Fri 9am-5pm, Sat-Sun 10am-3.30pm*

INTERNET ACCESS

There is a free Wi-Fi hot zone on Beaumont Street between Tudor Street and Maitland Road in the suburb of Hamilton. There is also free wireless internet access at Newcastle Airport provided by Internode *(**website** www.internode.on.net)*.

The Battleground

Shop 2, 169/173 King Street, Newcastle
☎ *(02) 4926 3898*
Website *www.thebattleground.com.au*
Open *Tue-Thu 9am-7.30pm, Fri 9am-9pm, Sat 10am-9pm, Sun 10am-5pm*

Coming & Going

Newcastle has good transport connections including an airport plus bus and train services. Generally the train is the cheaper way to get to Sydney whereas buses are cheaper for places north of Newcastle.

AIR

Newcastle Airport *(**website** www.newcastleairport.com.au)* is at Williamtown at the western end of Port Stephens. It is a fast-growing airport with flights to Adelaide, Canberra, Brisbane and Melbourne. It is served by Jetstar, Qantas, Tiger Airways and Virgin Blue.

The bus between Newcastle Airport and the train station in the city centre costs $4.80.

BUS

The bus terminal is behind the Train station. There are buses to destinations all the way up the east coast as far as Cairns as well as buses to Sydney and Port Stephens.

TRAIN

Newcastle is part of the CityRail network with frequent trains to Sydney. The train journey between Newcastle and Sydney Central should take around three hours. Trains heading further north stop at Broadmeadow station, which is about five stations out of town on the CityRail system. The train from Sydney Central to Newcastle costs $18 one-way and $25 for an off-peak return.

Local Transport

Newcastle has a good public transport network that is made up of buses, trains and ferries.

BUS

Buses *(**website** www.newcastlebuses.info)* are the most common form of transport for most travellers.

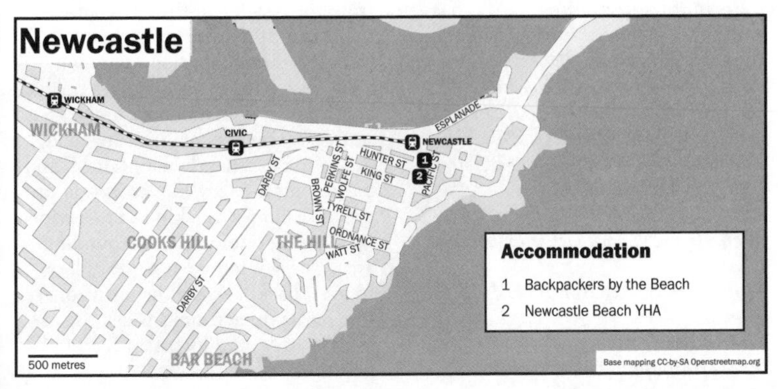

All bus tickets are good for unlimited rides within a one-hour, four-hour or all day period.

A one-hour ticket is $3, four-hour tickets cost $5.90 and an all day ticket costs $9. A ten-trip ticket is also available and costs $24.70. Weekly passes cost $39 for bus and ferry travel and $47-50 for bus, ferry and train travel.

FERRY

Ferries run at half-hour intervals between Queens Wharf near the main train station and Stockton on the north shore of the Hunter River. The ferry costs $2.10 one-way.

TRAIN

The CityRail *(website www.cityrail.info)* network serves the western and southern suburbs.

Train fares in the Newcastle area generally cost between $2.60 and $4.60 for a one-way ticket. Return tickets cost twice the one-way fare with the exception of off-peak return tickets that cost between $3.60 and $6.40. Off-peak return tickets are equivalent to a cheap day return and must be purchased after 9am.

Accommodation

Backpackers by the Beach

Backpackers by the Beach is a simple hostel in an older building just across from the beach. The reception area is also the kitchen and common room, and there is a games room with internet access ($4 per hour) downstairs. Rooms are very plain and clean, and toilets are shiny. There are not many facilities here but they do organise tours in the surrounding area. It has a bit more of a party atmosphere than the other hostels in Newcastle.

34-36 Hunter Street, Newcastle
100, 101, 103, 104, 107, 108, 111, 201, 222, 224, 225, 226, 230, 231, 235, 310, 317, 322, 334, 349, 350, 351, 363 *Newcastle*
(02) 4926 3472
***Website** www.backpackersbythebeach.com.au*
***Dorm bed** $28 ($26 HI/YHA, ISIC, Nomads, VIP)*
***Credit cards** MC, Visa*
***Reception open** 7am-11pm*

TV K

Maintenance & cleanliness	★★★
Facilities	★★½
Atmosphere & character	★★★
Security	★★★
Overall rating	★★★½

Backpackers Newcastle

This hostel is located in a residential neighbourhood convenient to central attractions. It has a summer cottage feel to it, with a nice swimming pool in the back. The walls are freshly painted, and more (much needed) renovations are in order. Facilities include table tennis, DVDs and a laundry. The kitchen facilities could be better and the bathrooms are run-down, but the hostel has potential. It is under new management, and the owner is talkative and helpful.

42-44 Denison Street, Hamilton
201, 222, 226, 230, 231, 317, 322, 334, 349, 350, 363 *Hamilton*
(02) 4969 3436 or 1800 333 436
***Website** www.newcastlebackpackers.com*
***Dorm bed** $28 ($27 HI/YHA, ISIC, VIP); **double/twin room** $60-85*
***Credit cards** MC, Visa*
***Reception open** 8am-10am & 4pm-8pm*

TV K L

Maintenance & cleanliness	★★
Facilities	★★★
Atmosphere & character	★★★
Security	★½
Overall rating	★★½

Newcastle Beach YHA

Set in a unique old building not far from the beach and the city centre, this YHA hostel has great presentation. It has large spacious common areas with rows of aged leather couches and fireplaces, chandeliers, and a grand staircase. Kitchen facilities are good, dorms are excellently maintained, and bathrooms are flawless. Reception can organise almost any kind of excursion you can think of in the surrounding area. The TV lounge is a great place to meet backpackers. The hostel offers free meals three times a week, use of body boards, and internet access ($4 per hour).

30 Pacific Street, Newcastle
100, 101, 103, 104, 107, 108, 111, 201, 222, 224, 225, 226, 230, 231, 235, 310, 317, 322, 334, 349, 350, 351, 363 *Newcastle*
(02) 4925 3544
***Website** www.yha.com.au*
***Dorm bed** $30 ($27 HI/YHA); **single room** $50 ($45 HI/YHA); **double room** $72.50 ($65 HI/YHA)*
***Credit cards** MC, Visa*
***Reception open** 7am-10.30pm*

Maintenance & cleanliness	★★★★½
Facilities	★★½
Atmosphere & character	★★★
Security	★★½
Overall rating	★★★½

Eating & Drinking

For a mostly industrial city, Newcastle has a surprisingly good restaurant, café and pub scene. Newcastle has the usual selection of fast food places in the city centre, but there are more diverse eating and drinking options just outside the centre in Cooks Hill and Hamilton.

Beaumont Street in Hamilton (*201, 222, 226, 230, 231, 235, 317, 322, 334, 349, 350, 363* *Hamilton*), a couple of kilometres west of the city centre, is a good spot for Mediterranean influenced food with a selection of Greek and Italian restaurants as well as a thriving café and pub scene. This neighbourhood is a handy place to eat and drink for travellers staying at Backpackers Newcastle.

Darby Street in Cooks Hill (*310, 311*), just south of the city centre, is a diverse neighbourhood with a vibrant café scene and some nice restaurants.

Sights

Fort Scratchley

Built in the 1880s, this former defence post now contains a military and maritime museum. The fort offers good views of both the harbour and city centre. There is an extensive system of tunnels linking the complex.
Corner Nobbys & Wharf Roads, Newcastle East
100, 101, 103, 104, 107, 108, 111, 201, 222, 224, 225, 226, 230, 231, 235, 310, 317, 322, 334, 349, 350, 351, 363 *Newcastle*
(02) 4929 2588
***Website** www.fortscratchley.org*
***Admission** Maritime Museum free, Military Museum free, tours of the tunnel system $1.50*
***Open** Maritime Museum Tue-Fri 10am-4pm, Sat-Sun noon-4pm, Military Museum Sat-Sun noon-4pm*

Hunter Wetlands Centre

More than 170 bird species have been recorded in this 45-hectare wildlife sanctuary in the suburbs. There are hiking trails and canoes can be rented.
Sandgate Road, Shortlands
103, 108 *Sandgate*
(02) 4951 6466
***Website** www.wetlands.org.au*
***Admission** $4.50*
***Open** Mon-Fri 9am-3pm, Sat-Sun 9am-5pm*

Newcastle Region Art Gallery

For a regional art gallery, there is a decent collection of Australian and international exhibits.
Laman Street, Newcastle
100, 101, 103, 104, 107, 111, 201, 222, 225, 226, 230, 231, 235, 317, 322, 334, 349, 350, 351, 363 *Civic*
(02) 4974 5100
***Website** www.ncc.nsw.gov.au/discover_newcastle/region_art_gallery*
***Admission** free*
***Open** Tue-Sun 10am-5pm*

Hunter Valley

A pleasant two-hour drive north of Sydney, the Hunter Valley is one of Australia's oldest and most visited wine producing regions. It is split into the Upper and Lower Hunter regions, with wineries and accommodation concentrated in the Lower Hunter around Cessnock and Pokolbin. There are some truly world-class wines made here, and the range of cellars within a small area offers you a chance to taste some of the famous names. Tastings are usually free, although some cellar doors have recently added fees, and many wineries also offer very informative tours of their vineyards. Some tours include lunch and discounted bottles, and there is even an opportunity to take part in grape crushing, the old-fashioned way – with your bare feet.

Hotels and hostels often have maps of the region with all of the cellar doors marked. There are many weekenders coming from Sydney these days, so the tourist infrastructure has blossomed with hotels, resorts and attractions catering to a relatively affluent crowd. There is only one hostel and it is a good one, so it is best to book ahead or come as a day trip from somewhere else. The best way to get around (since drinking alcohol means you cannot drive and there is no public transport) is by bike, and there are loads of bike rentals available. Other options include several tour companies, but if you have a designated driver, going by car would be ideal.

The region is lovely to tour through, but the roads are narrow and winding, so drive with caution. Besides the scenery there are a couple of attractions the non-wine-drinker can enjoy. The Hunter Valley Gardens are a gorgeous place to visit or to have a picnic, and the Bluetongue Brewery is reputed to have some of the best and most innovative beers in the state. Fittingly, there are also some fine cheese and chocolate companies to visit.

The main towns in the region are Cesnock, Pokolbin and Branxton.

Practical Information

Wine and Visitors Centre

111 Main Road, Polkolbin
☎ *(02) 4990 4477*
Website *www.winecountry.com.au*
Open *Mon-Thu 9am-5pm, Fri 9am-6pm, Sat 9.30am-5pm, Sun 9.30am-3.30pm*

Coming & Going

Cessnock is most easily accessible from Newcastle. If you're visiting Newcastle you can make the Hunter Valley a day trip, catching a bus from there or alternatively taking a train to Maitland and the getting a connecting bus.

Coming from Sydney you have the option of going via Newcastle or Maitland or catching a less frequent direct bus. Keans Travel Express (☎ *(02) 9281 9366)* runs a daily service to Scone, which passes through the Hunter Valley.

Local Transport

There's no public transport between the wineries in the Hunter Valley, so your best bet is to tag along with someone who's driving or rent a bike. Bicycle rental is available from Hunter Valley Cycling (☎ *0418 281 480;* ***website*** *www.huntervalleycycling.com.au).*

Accommodation

Hunter Valley YHA

This hostel sits among 26 acres of vineyards and verdant fields in the heart of the Hunter Valley wine country. During the grape harvest (January to March) it is often full of international travellers staying here to pick grapes. The hostel is a large purpose-built cabin with nice dorms and good quality fittings. Guests mingle on the veranda and enjoy the lovely swimming pool, sauna and barbecue area. They have pizza nights and offer bike hire and winery tours. There is also a volleyball court and a funky common area/bar. Management and staff are friendly and knowledgeable.

100 Wine Country Drive, Nulkaba
☎ *(02) 4991 3278*
Website *www.yha.com.au*
Dorm bed *$29-32 ($26.10-28.80 HI/YHA);* ***double room*** *$65-92 ($58.50-82.80 HI/YHA);* ***twin room*** *$65-77 ($58.50-69.30 HI/YHA)*
Credit cards *MC, Visa*
Reception open *8am-noon & 5pm-8pm*

Maintenance & cleanliness	★★★★
Facilities	★★★½
Atmosphere & character	★★★★½
Security	★★★
Overall rating	★★★★

Ku-Ring-Gai Chase National Park

Ku-Ring-Gai Chase National Park is just 24km north of central Sydney. It is Australia's second-oldest national park and features numerous coves and inlets along Broken Bay. The park is easily accessible by public transport making it a great day-trip or weekend destination. The park has some good bush walks, including a couple of easy 20-minute walks.

The Pittwater YHA hostel is located here, making the national park a popular destination with backpackers.

Practical Information

Bobbin Head Visitor Centre

Bobbin Head, Ku-Ring-Gai Chase National Park
☎ *(02) 9472 8949*
Open *Mon-Fri 1pm-4pm, Sat-Sun 10am-5pm*

Kalkari Visitor Centre

Ku-Ring-Gai Chase Road, Ku-Ring-Gai Chase National Park
☎ *(02) 9472 9300*
Open *9am-5pm daily*

Coming & Going

This national park is unique in its easy accessibility by public transport.

To get to the Bobbin Head entrance at the southern end of the park take a train to Turramurra (on the North Shore line) and then transfer to bus 577.

If you want to get to the Pittwater YHA hostel at the eastern end of the national park, take bus E86 from Wynyard Station, or bus 156 from Manly, to Church Point and then take the ferry (☎ *9999 3492; **website** www.churchpointferryservice.com)* to the hostel. The ferry costs $5.40 each way or $8.50 return and runs approximately every 45 minutes.

Accommodation

Pittwater YHA Hostel

This is one of Australia's most beautifully located hostels. It is on a secluded hilltop overlooking Pittwater and the surrounding area is home to wildlife including wallabies and cockatoos. The hostel is a big old house with loads of charm. The hostel's facilities include a big common room with a fireplace and lots of books plus a fully equipped kitchen and an outdoor area with a barbecue. Accommodation is in small dorms with verandas where you can sit and enjoy the stunning views. It is a low-tech hostel with no TV so you can enjoy the ancient art of conversation.

Halls Wharf via Church Point, Morning Bay, Pittwater
156, E86 to Church Point then ferry to Halls Wharf
☎ *(02) 9999 5748*
Website *www.yha.com.au*
Dorm bed *$27.50 ($24 HI/YHA);* ***double/twin room*** *$69 ($62 HI/YHA)*
Credit cards *MC, Visa*
Reception open *8am-11am & 5pm-8pm*
K L

Maintenance & cleanliness	★★★
Facilities	★★½
Atmosphere & character	★★★★★
Security	★
Overall rating	★★★

Blue Mountains

Named for their distinctive blue haze, a result of eucalyptus oil evaporating from gum trees, the Blue Mountains have long been a popular destination. They are famous for their scenery that features spectacular rock formations, vast gorges and sandstone cliffs hundreds of metres high. Situated on the Great Dividing Range at an average altitude of 1,000m above sea level, the Blue Mountains is a vast and rugged natural wilderness area containing three National Parks totalling almost 250,000 ha. The Blue Mountains is classified as a World Heritage site.

The Blue Mountains were initially perceived as an impenetrable barrier for early explorers and a route through them was not found until 1813. Today the Great Western Highway closely follows the route blazed by the early explorers, winding its way along a string of 26 mountain townships and it is now easily accessible by train from Sydney.

The Three Sisters rock formation is the most famous Blue Mountains attraction and there are plenty of hiking trails in the surrounding area.

Other attractions include the world's steepest railway, the Katoomba Scenic Railway, which travels from the cliff top at Katoomba down into the Jamison Valley. Above, the Skyway carries passengers along a ropeway 206m above the valley floor.

Katoomba is the major town in the region and caters to day-trippers from Sydney with plenty of pricey boutiques, craft shops and cafés. Katoomba is the best place to base yourself in the Blue Mountains; it has easy access to the Scenic Railway, scenic lookouts and hiking trails and good rail access from Sydney.

Practical Information

Blue Mountains Visitor Centre

Echo Point Road, Katoomba
☎ *1300 653 408*
Website *www.visitbluemountains.com.au*
Open *9am-5pm daily*

Coming & Going

CityRail *(☎ 131500; **website** www.cityrail.info)* operate an hourly train service between Sydney Central station and the Blue Mountains with stops at Katoomba, Leura and Wentworth Falls. The train from Sydney Central costs $12.20 one-way and $16.80 for an off-peak return.

Local Transport

The Blue Mountains Bus Company *(☎ (02) 4782 4213; **website** www.bmbc.com.au)* operate local public transport with regular bus services through most of the day, although services become much less frequent after 6pm.

There is also the Blue Mountains Explorer *(☎ 1300 300 915; **website** www.explorerbus.com.au)* tourist bus service that runs a loop of the main sights in Leura and Katoomba. However this is overpriced at $32 ($26 HI/YHA, ISIC, Nomads, VIP) and Katoomba is compact enough to walk around.

If you arrive at Katoomba station, walk down Katoomba Street, which will take you to the cliff-face overlooking Jamison Valley. This is where most of the hiking trails depart from and it's also where you'll find the Scenic Skyway, Scenic Railway, the Three Sisters lookout and the information centre at Echo Point.

Accommodation

Blue Mountains YHA

The Blue Mountains YHA is a big youth hostel housed in a National Trust listed historic building that was home to a cabaret club in the 1930s and has been renovated retaining its art deco character. This hostel has top quality fittings and facilities include a fully equipped kitchen; a big dining area/common room with pool table and table football; a room with internet and also Wi-Fi access ($4 per hour, YHA Connect); and there is a TV lounge downstairs. There is excellent security with key card access and a locker for each bed.

207 Katoomba Street, Katoomba
☎ *(02) 4782 1416*
Website *www.yha.com.au*
Dorm bed *$27-29 ($24-26 HI/YHA);* ***double/twin room*** *$82-92 ($73-82 HI/YHA);* ***family room*** *$116-129 ($104-116 HI/YHA)*
Credit cards *MC, Visa*
Reception open *7am-10pm*

[parking] [wheelchair] [lockers] TV K L

Maintenance & cleanliness	★★★★★
Facilities	★★★
Atmosphere & character	★★★½
Security	★★★★½
Overall rating	★★★★

Central Blue Mountains Backpackers

Central Blue Mountains Backpackers is a large hostel with around 130 beds in a former nursing home. It is bright and clean but it is also feels a bit sterile. The hostel's facilities include a bright spacious common room with TV and internet access plus a pool table and table football. It is the closest hostel to the train station.

144 Bathurst Road, Katoomba
☎ *(02) 4782 9630 or 1800 287 370*
Website *www.centralblue.com.au*
Dorm bed *$24-25;* ***double room*** *$90*
Credit cards *MC, Visa*
Reception open *Mon-Thu 8.30am-8.30pm, Fri-Sat 8.30am-10pm, Sun 8.30am-8.30pm*

TV K L

Maintenance & cleanliness	★★★★★
Facilities	★★
Atmosphere & character	★½
Security	★★½
Overall rating	★★★

The Flying Fox

The Flying Fox is a small clean hostel in an old house just a short walk

from the centre of Katoomba. It has a friendly home-style feel with eclectic retro furnishings and loads of character. Amenities include a cosy lounge with a fireplace, guitars and lots of books plus a kitchen and a small TV lounge. There is also an outdoor barbecue area outside.
190 Bathurst Road, Katoomba
☎ *(02) 4782 4226 or 1800 624 226*
Website *www.theflyingfox.com.au*
Dorm bed *$27;* ***double room*** *$68;* ***camping*** *$17-23 per person; prices include breakfast*
Credit cards *MC, Visa*
🚗 TV K L

Maintenance & cleanliness	★★★
Facilities	★★
Atmosphere & character	★★★★★
Security	★★★
Overall rating	★★★

Katoomba Mountain Lodge
Katoomba Mountain Lodge is a big old building tucked behind the main street. It has a pretty good atmosphere but it feels dated with old furniture and old fashioned décor. Amenities include a couple of kitchens; and a games room with table tennis and two TV lounges, both lounges have fireplaces and one has a piano. There is also big veranda at the front of the building with lovely views of the mountains.
31 Lurline Street, Katoomba
☎ *(02) 4782 3933*
Website *www.katoombabackpackers.com.au*
Dorm bed *$18-20;* ***single room*** *$42-48;* ***double/twin room*** *$58-68*
Credit cards *MC, Visa*
Reception open *8am-10pm*
🚗 TV K L

Maintenance & cleanliness	★★½
Facilities	★★½
Atmosphere & character	★★★½
Security	★★
Overall rating	★★½

Number 14
Number 14 is a small hostel in a tastefully decorated cute old wooden house with nice polished floorboards and a cosy atmosphere. Accommodation is in mostly double and twin rooms but there are also a few small dormitories. Facilities include a cosy lounge plus a kitchen and there is also a nice shady veranda. It is about a 10-minute walk to the town centre.
14 Lovel Street, Katoomba
☎ *(02) 4782 7104*
Website *www.bluemts.com.au/no14/*
Dorm bed *$22-25;* ***double/twin bed*** *$59-69*
Credit cards *MC, Visa*
Reception open *8am-11am & 5pm-8pm*
K

Maintenance & cleanliness	★★★★
Facilities	★
Atmosphere & character	★★★★½
Security	★½
Overall rating	★★★

Hiking
There are some excellent hiking trails around the Blue Mountains with most of the walks originating around Katoomba.

The most popular include the Giant Stairway Walk that descends the Jamison Valley from Echo Point and the Federal Pass Trail that passes along the floor of the valley and includes the Katoomba Falls and Orphan Rock.

Activities
Scenic Railway
With an incline of 52°, the Scenic Railway is the world's steepest inclined railway. It is very popular and feels a bit like a slow roller coaster ride.
Corner Violet Street & Cliff Drive, Katoomba
☎ *(02) 4752 2699*
Website *www.scenicworld.com.au*
Tickets *$10 one-way, $19 return*
Open *9am-5pm daily*

Scenic Skyway
The Scenic Skyway cable gondola travels over the Jamison Valley and provides an impressive view of Katoomba and the Blue Mountains.
Corner Violet Street & Cliff Drive, Katoomba
☎ *(02) 4752 2699*
Website *www.scenicworld.com.au*
Tickets *$16*
Open *9am-5pm daily*

Wollongong

Wollongong is New South Wales' third largest city. It is located less than two hours south of Sydney and has a busy port, coal and steel industries. The city also has a few attractions worth visiting that include centrally located surf beaches and the Nan Tien Buddhist Temple, which is the largest in the Southern hemisphere. The city makes a good base for exploring the surrounding Illawarra region.

Practical Information

Tourism Wollongong

93 Crown Street, Wollongong
☎ *(02) 4227 5545*
Website *www.tourismwollongong.com*
Open *Mon-Fri 9am-5pm, Sat 9am-4pm, Sun 10am-4pm*

INTERNET ACCESS

Network Café

Crown Street Mall, Wollongong
☎ *(02) 4228 8686*
Website *www.networkcafe.com.au*
Open *Mon-Wed 9.45am-6pm, Thu 9.45am-8.30pm, Fri 9.45am-6pm, Sat 9.45am-4pm*

If you're travelling with your own computer, consider staying at Wollongong Backpackers Keiraleagh, which has free wireless internet.

Coming & Going

The easiest way to get in and out of Wollongong is by train. The CityRail network covers the city and its surrounding area and there are frequent trains between Wollongong and Sydney as well as trains further south to Kiama and Nowra. The train from Sydney Central to Wollongong costs $9.60 one-way or $13.20 for an off-peak return.

Buses go to destinations south of Nowra as well as to Canberra and Melbourne. Buses terminate at the bus station on the corner of Campbell and Keira Streets.

Local Transport

The CityRail network serves the metropolitan area including Port Kembla. Buses supplement the suburban rail system although the central area is compact enough to get around on foot.

Accommodation

Wollongong Backpackers Keiraleagh

Wollongong Backpackers Keiraleagh is a big old house near the centre of Wollongong. The old building has loads of character and facilities include a cosy TV lounge with free Wi-Fi access, a small kitchen and a backyard with barbecue. Some parts of the hostel feel a bit cluttered, but it adds to the hostel's character.

60 Kembla Street, Wollongong
☎ *(02) 4228 6765*
Dorm bed *$20;* ***single room*** *$30;* ***double/twin room*** *$50-60;* ***three to four-bed private room*** *$80-100*
TV K L

Maintenance & cleanliness	★★½
Facilities	★★
Atmosphere & character	★★★★★
Security	★★½
Overall rating	★★★

Wollongong YHA (Keiraview Accommodation)

Wollongong's YHA hostel is a relatively large complex with three types of accommodation: a three-star hotel, student accommodation and the YHA hostel. It is a big modern hostel that is clean and well maintained. Facilities include several kitchens, a big TV lounge with internet access including Wi-Fi access ($2.50 per hour; Everywhere Internet) and a courtyard barbecue area. It is run by the University of Wollongong but don't expect a frat house atmosphere as the no alcohol rule ensures that any attempt at a party is out of the question.

75-79 Keira Street, Wollongong
☎ *(02) 4229 1132*
Website *www.keiraviewaccommodation.com.au*
Dorm bed *$26 ($24-25 HI/YHA);* ***twin room*** *$81.53 ($72 HI/YHA);* ***family room*** *$87 ($78 HI/YHA)*
Credit cards *Amex, MC, Visa*
Reception open *8am-8.30pm*

Maintenance & cleanliness	★★★★★
Facilities	★★
Atmosphere & character	½★
Security	★★★
Overall rating	★★★

Sights

Australia's Industry World

Port Kembla, near Wollongong, is home to one of Australia's highest concentrations of heavy industry. Australia's Industry World consists of a visitors' centre where tours depart for the nearby steel making and port facilities.

Springhill Road, Coniston (Visitor Centre at the Northgate Entrance)
Coniston
(02) 4275 7023
Website *www.aiw.org.au*
Admission *$18*
Tours depart *Wed, Fri 9.30am*

Illawarra Museum

This small museum has a focus on local history.

11 Market Street, Wollongong
Wollongong
(02) 4228 7770
Website *www.illawarramuseum.com*
Admission *$4 ($2 students)*
Open *Wed-Thu noon-3pm, Sat-Sun 1pm-4pm*

Nan Tien Buddhist Temple

The Nan Tien Buddhist Temple is the largest in the Southern Hemisphere. The temple has become an integral part of Wollongong's multicultural community with an increasing number of locals adopting Buddhism.

Berkeley Road, Berkeley
34, 43, 67, 69 Unanderra
(02) 4272 0600
Website *www.nantien.org.au*
Admission *museum $1.10; guided tour $4*
Open *Tue-Sun 9am-5pm; tours Sat-Sun 1pm*

Wollongong City Gallery

This art museum features a small collection of Aboriginal and contemporary art.

Corner Kembla & Burelli Streets, Wollongong
Wollongong
(02) 4228 7500
Website *www.wollongongcitygallery.com*
Admission *free*
Open *Tue-Fri 10am-5pm, Sat-Sun noon-4pm*

Wollongong Science Centre & Planetarium

This science museum north of the city centre has over 120 hands-on exhibits plus a fully featured planetarium.

Squires Way, Brandon Park, Fairy Meadow
Fairy Meadow
(02) 4286 5000
Website *http://sciencecentre.uow.edu.au/*
Admission *museum $10; planetarium $6; combined entry to museum & planetarium $13*
Open *10am-4pm daily; planetarium shows Sat-Sun noon & 3pm*

North Coast

The North Coast of New South Wales starts just north of Newcastle and stretches to Tweed Heads on the Queensland border. The most notable stops along the way are Coffs Harbour and Byron Bay, but these are well on the beaten path, and it is worth it to take a few detours inland if you can.

On a scenic drive up the Pacific Highway, the North Coast is the calm before the Queensland storm, with some eccentric towns and awesome national parks where you can get a taste of the real Australia. The lovely towns of the far north hinterland are packed with laid-back country folk and new-age hippies, giving the area an interesting vibe. The highway passes through quite a few lush river deltas and serene estuaries, and scenic views of mountain ranges and coastline abound.

This is the perfect area for the outdoorsy type. Activities range from horseback riding, jet boating, surfing, kayaking, white water rafting and much more. Any hostel you stay in will have flyers and information ready for whatever adventure takes your fancy. Since there are so many companies running tours, most of them are surprisingly inexpensive considering what you get. Look into it; it is a great way to spend a day and make some friends.

Port Stephens

Port Stephens is a sleepy peninsula with small towns and fertile bush land about a one-hour drive north from Newcastle. Travellers come here for the natural beauty, adventure activities and wildlife tours. Nelson Bay, the main town, is famous for its dolphin and whale watching excursions (best Jun-Oct for whale sightings) and great fishing. The little seaside village of Anna Bay has nothing of much interest, but is a good place to stop for lunch. One Mile Beach is a tranquil crescent of soft sand and gentle waves, while Samurai Beach is clothing optional and has great surf. The Stockton Sand Dunes are the largest moving dunes in the southern hemisphere and are an exhilarating place for a 4WD trip.

The two hostels in the area are beautiful and located in lovely bushland settings. They offer peaceful retreat-like getaways with great wildlife, and are worth a night or two. Port Stephens is a sleepy place that doesn't get a lot of press but is well worth a short side trip - more so than its industrial neighbours, anyway.

Practical Information

Tourist Information Centre

Victoria Parade, Nelson Bay
☎ *(02) 4981 1579*
Website *www.portstephens.org.au*
Open *Mon-Fri 9am-5pm, Sat-Sun 9am-4pm*

Coming & Going

AIR

Newcastle Airport *(**website** www.newcastleairport.com.au)* is at Williamtown at the western end of Port Stephens. It is a fast-growing airport with flights to Adelaide, Canberra, Brisbane and Melbourne. It is served by Jetstar, Qantas, Tiger Airways and Virgin Blue.

BUS

Port Stephens Coaches *(☎ (02) 4982 2940; **website** www.pscoaches.com.au)* runs buses connecting Port Stephens with Newcastle that stop at Newcastle Airport, Anna Bay and Nelson Bay. A one-way fare between Newcastle and Port Stephens costs $5.80. They also operate express buses to Sydney ($33 one-way/$50 return).

The Port Stephens Explorer *(☎ (02) 4980 6900)* is another direct coach to Sydney. Tickets cost $40 one-way or $70 return. The return ticket includes a free Port Stephens Explorer Pass good for seven days travel on the Tomaree Peninsula.

Local Transport

Port Stephens Coaches *(☎ (02) 4982 2940; **website** www.pscoaches.com.au)* operate local bus services in the Port Stephens area. A one-day Bay Explorer ticket costs $10.

Accommodation

Melaleuca Backpackers

On six acres of peaceful bush land, Melaleuca offers dorm accommodation with a retreat ambience. The rustic cabins are scattered on the grounds around an attractive main building with a big kitchen and comfortable common room. Bathrooms, which are remarkably clean, are connected to this by way of a boardwalk. The owners are affiliated with wildlife protection, and are keen on introducing you to some of the animals which inhabit the area such as koalas, possums, sugar-gliders, and even a temporary resident kangaroo. It is a five minute walk to the lovely One Mile Beach and a short drive from the Stockton sand dunes.

2 Koala Place, One Mile Beach, Port Stephens, NSW 2316
☎ *(02) 4981 9422*
Website *www.melaleucabackpackers.com.au*
Dorm bed *$28-32 ($27-31 VIP);* ***double room*** *$80 ($78 VIP);* ***camping*** *$15 ($14 VIP) per person*
Credit cards *MC, Visa; 5% credit card surcharge*

Maintenance & cleanliness	★★★★
Facilities	★
Atmosphere & character	★★★★★
Security	-
Overall rating	★★★

Samurai Beach Bungalows YHA

The Samurai Bungalows are dotted among three acres of tranquil bush land and offer good quality accommodation with well-maintained rooms and sparkling bathrooms. The shed, a common room decorated with a telly, a pool table, and quirky bits and pieces, is a great place to hang out and has undoubtedly seen some late nights. Other amenities include internet access ($3 per hour) including Wi-Fi ($8 per day), an outdoor kitchen that is a great place for a barbecue plus a beautiful saltwater swimming pool that is a favoured daytime hangout for travellers. The family who own the place are gracious and helpful, and give good travel advice. They share the property with koalas and other wildlife.

Corner Frost Road & Robert Connell Close, Anna Bay, Port Stephens
☎ *(02) 4982 1921*
Website *www.samuraiportstephens.com*
Dorm bed *$25-29;* ***double room*** *$85-104*
Credit cards *MC, Visa; $50 minimum for credit card transactions*
Reception open *8.30am-9.30pm*

Maintenance & cleanliness	★★★½
Facilities	★★★
Atmosphere & character	★★★★½
Security	★
Overall rating	★★★½

Sights & Activities

Stockton Beach Sand Dunes

Stockton Beach extends from Port Stephens to Newcastle and is best known for its impressive sand dunes. If you have your own 4WD vehicle you can buy a permit for $10 that allows you to drive on the beach (permit valid for three days), otherwise you will have to take a tour. Dawsons Scenic Tours *(☎ 0425 213 096;* ***website*** *www.portstephensadventure.com.au)* operate 4WD tours on the dunes that cost between $20 and $45.

Surfing

Anna Bay Surf School *(☎ (02) 4981 9919;* ***website*** *www.annabaysurfschool.com.au)* runs surfing lessons for $55 ($50 HI/YHA, Nomads, VIP) and also rents surf gear.

Port Macquarie

Port Macquarie is a popular holiday destination for Sydneysiders and is also popular with backpackers who stop over to take advantage of the cheaper prices on adventure activities compared to destinations further north. Although much of Port Macquarie feels like a featureless Australian suburb, there are some good beaches and it is well situated for exploring nearby lakes and rainforest.

Practical Information

Port Macquarie Visitor Information Centre

Corner Gordon & Gore Streets, Port Macquarie
☎ *1300 303 155 or (02) 6581 8000*
Website *www.portmacquarieinfo.com.au*
Open *Mon-Fri 8.30am-5pm, Sat-Sun 9am-4pm*

INTERNET ACCESS

Port Surf Hub

57 Clarence Street, Port Macquarie
☎ *(02) 6584 4744*
Open *Sun-Wed 9am-6/7pm, Thu-Sat 9am-7/9pm*

Coming & Going

AIR

Port Macquarie's small airport has flights to Canberra and Sydney. The airport is served by Brindabella Airlines *(☎ 1300 66 88 24;* ***website*** *www.brindabella-airlines.com.au)*; Qantaslink *(☎ 13 13 13;* ***website*** *www.qantas.com.au)* and Virgin Blue *(☎ 13 67 89;* ***website*** *www.virginblue.com.au)*.

BUS

Greyhound Australia *(☎ 1300 473 946;* ***website*** *www.greyhound.com.au)* and Premier Motor Service *(****website*** *www.premierms.com.au)* buses run up and down the coast stopping at the transit centre at 28 Hayward Street.

TRAIN

The closest train station to Port Macquarie is in Wauchope. A connecting bus service meets CountryLink (☎ *13 22 32;* ***website*** *www.countrylink.com.au)* trains from Sydney.

Accommodation

Limeburners Lodge

Unless everything is full and you're heading this way, Limeburners Lodge is too far away from anything to be worth the effort; as you have to take a car ferry to the north shore of Port Macquarie to get here. That said, it is a peaceful retreat set in an old manor house next to a tranquil lagoon. The hostel is under new management and undergoing numerous renovations and improvements. It has a swimming pool, a spa, and a nice outdoor kitchen/barbecue area. Dorms are large and newly redone, with brick walls and clean bathrooms. Unfortunately it attracts a lot of groups, so the social atmosphere is compromised, and there is currently no internet access.

353 Shoreline Drive, Port Macquarie
☎ *(02) 6583 3381*
Website *www.limeburnerslodge.com.au*
Dorm bed *$30*
Credit cards *MC, Visa*
Reception open *7am-10pm; late check in with prior arrangement*

Maintenance & cleanliness	★★★★
Facilities	★★★★½
Atmosphere & character	★★★
Security	★★½
Overall rating	★★★★

Ozzie Pozzie Backpackers

This small hostel has dorms laid out around a cosy centre courtyard. It has clean toilets and showers, a big kitchen, and a barbecue. Guests hang out in hammocks around the courtyard and have barbecues at night. It is a very convivial setting. They offer free body boards and bicycles, and staff offer loads of advice about activities. Everything is cheerful and bright, with friendly reception staff and a laid-back atmosphere. It is off the main road, so phone ahead and they will give you directions.

36 Waugh Street, Port Macquarie

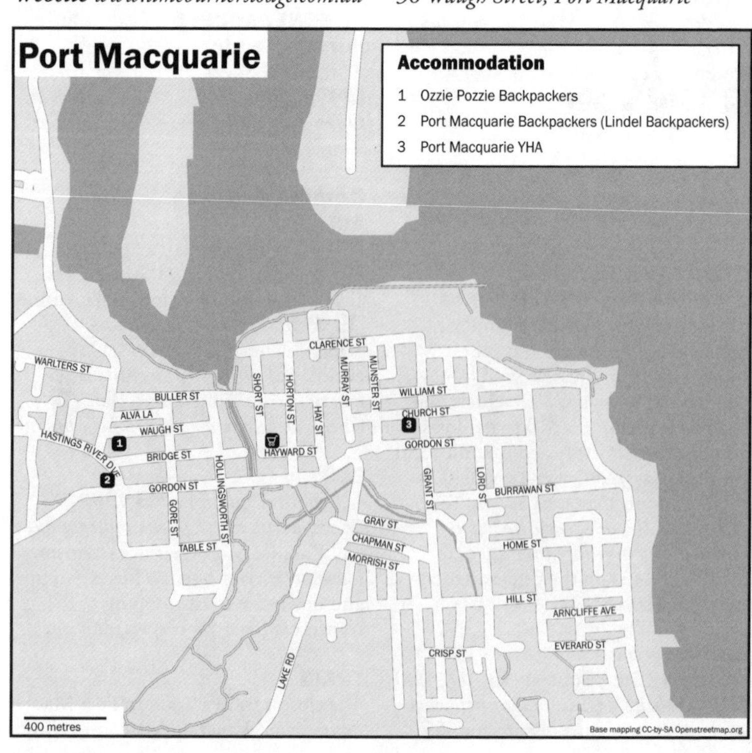

☎ *(02) 6583 8133 or 1800 620 020*
Website *www.ozziepozzie.com*
Dorm bed *$22-28; price includes breakfast*
Credit cards *MC, Visa*
Reception open *8am-11am & 3pm-9pm*

Maintenance & cleanliness	★★★½
Facilities	★★½
Atmosphere & character	★★★★½
Security	★★
Overall rating	★★★½

Port Macquarie Backpackers (Lindel Backpackers)

Just off the main highway leading to town, Lindel is in a big house and has a family atmosphere. The kitchen is spacious, and the dorms are clean and have good beds. Common areas, including a veranda, fill up with cheerful travellers. Bathrooms are modern and well maintained. They offer free breakfast, a swimming pool, and free use of body boards. Security could be better, but for the price, this hostel is a good bet.
2 Hastings River Drive, Port Macquarie
☎ *(02) 6583 1791*
Website *www.portmacquariebackpackers.com.au*
Dorm bed *$24-27 ($23-26 VIP);* ***double/twin room*** *$65-75; prices include breakfast*
Credit cards *MC, Visa*
Reception open *8am-10pm*

Maintenance & cleanliness	★★★½
Facilities	★★★
Atmosphere & character	★★★★
Security	★½
Overall rating	★★★½

Port Macquarie YHA

This is a small and colourful hostel farther from town centre than the others, and a little more run-down. The atmosphere is a bit quieter here and the bathrooms need some maintenance, but dorms are fresh and breezy, and the kitchen is not bad. They have nightly events like dinners and movies, and this place has relatively high security. They offer free use of body boards.
40 Church Street, Port Macquarie
☎ *(02) 6583 5512*
Website *www.yha.com.au*
Dorm bed *$28-33.50 ($25-30 HI/YHA);* ***twin room*** *$70-78 ($67-78 HI/YHA)*
Credit cards *MC, Visa*
Reception open *8am-10pm*

Maintenance & cleanliness	★★★½
Facilities	★★
Atmosphere & character	★★
Security	★★★½
Overall rating	★★★

Eating & Drinking

If you're preparing your own food there is a **Coles** supermarket in the Palms Centre (corner Short & Haywood Streets, Port Macquarie) and a Woolworths at the corner of Bay and Park Streets.

Sights

Port Macquarie Historical Museum

This small museum features exhibits on Port Macquarie's convict heritage, including the obligatory display of store dummies in period costume.
22 Clarence Street, Port Macquarie
☎ *(02) 6583 1108*
Website *www.port-macquarie-historical-museum.org.au*
Admission *$4.50*
Open *Mon-Sat 9.30am-4.30pm*

Timbertown

This open-air museum west of Port Macquarie offers a glimpse of life in the 1900s. It features paddle steamer, stage coach and steam train rides.
Oxley Highway, Wauchope
☎ *(02) 6585 2322*
Website *www.timbertown.com.au*
Admission *$5*
Open *9.30am-3.30pm daily*

Port Macquarie Maritime Museum

The Port Macquarie Maritime Museum is much like other maritime museums around Australia and it includes the usual collection of model ships and all things nautical. Visitors can take a cruise on some of the museum's historic boats.
6 William Street, Port Macquarie

(02) 6583 1866
Website *www.hastings.nsw.gov.au/www/html/974-maritime-museum.asp*
Admission *$6*
Open *Mon-Sat 11am-3pm*

Sea Acres Rainforest Centre
This rainforest centre south of the town centre is set among 72 hectares of coastal rainforest and it features a 1.3km boardwalk through the rainforest canopy.
Pacific Drive, Shelly Beach
(02) 6582 3355
Admission *$8*
Open *9am-4.30pm daily*

Bellingen

A 13km drive inland from the Pacific Highway, about halfway between Nambucca Heads and Coffs Harbour, is the sleepy little mountain town of Bellingen. Its quaint streets are lined with heritage architecture, with charming cafés and craft shops showcasing the residents unique artistic flair. The town's alternative edge is offset by a cosmopolitan feel, as many of the current residents have moved here from the bigger cities in search of rural calm.

The Bellinger River, Dorrigo Plateau, and the surrounding valley offer stunning vistas and outdoor recreational activities. A visit to the Dorrigo National Park makes for a good day trip. There are also many places to go swimming and canoeing, and fishing in the valley is great. Bellingen is host to a few good music festivals and the pubs in town often have live entertainment. The monthly Bellingen markets draw huge crowds to sample many of the regional products. The hostel in town is great, so plan a night here and be prepared to extend your visit, or at least be tempted to.

Coming & Going

Because of its location off the highway, many buses running up and down the east coast don't stop at Bellingen. However there are some buses stopping in Bellingen that depart from Coffs Harbour, Port Macquarie and Armidale although they don't always run every day.

Accommodation

Bellingen Backpackers YHA
Located just off the main street in Bellingen, this YHA hostel is in an old building, but well maintained. Dorms are spacious, colourful, and have nice wooden bunks. There are outside beds on the veranda with mosquito nets and wonderful views of mountains and valleys. The kitchen is fully-equipped, there is internet access ($4 per hour and $8 per day for Wi-Fi) and the common area on the veranda has hammocks and a pool table. Reception organises canoeing tours, Dorrigo rainforest tours, and even a weekly trip to the nudist beach Bundagen. They also do free river tubing trips.
2 Short Street, Bellingen
(02) 6655 1116
Website *www.bellingenyha.com.au*
Dorm bed *$28-30 ($25-27 HI/YHA);* ***double room*** *$72-78 ($64-70 HI/YHA)*
Credit cards *MC, Visa*
Reception open *Mon-Fri 8am-8pm, Sat-Sun 8am-11am & 4pm-8pm*
TV K L

Maintenance & cleanliness	★★★½
Facilities	★★½
Atmosphere & character	★★★★
Security	★★
Overall rating	★★★

Activities

Canoeing

Bellingen Canoe Adventures (*(02) 6655 9955;* ***website*** *www.canoeadventures.com.au)* operates canoeing trips on the Bellinger River. These start at $20 for a one-hour sunset tour and increase to $88 for a full day guided tour with a gourmet lunch.

Coffs Harbour

Coffs Harbour lies on the Pacific Highway just over halfway between Sydney and Brisbane. It has some great beaches and endless choices of water sports to take part in. It is a popular spot for backpackers with its adrenaline-pumping activities like skydiving and white water rafting and it's one of the cheapest places on the east coast for diving lessons. Coffs also has a large surfing community and regularly holds regional competitions.

Jetty Beach is a protected cove good for swimming, but Park Beach is more popular and patrolled. Diggers Beach is the favorite spot for surfers, especially at Macauleys Headland, but the surf stays good at many beaches continuing north. The town itself is larger than the others of the region, but it has a very suburban feel and can sometimes seem boring. Still, there are some nice shops and cafes in the centre of town and it may be the best place to stay while enjoying the surrounding towns and attractions since there is a good choice of hostels here.

Practical Information

Coffs Coast Visitor Information Centre

Corner Pacific Highway & McLean Street, Coffs Harbour
☎ *(02) 6652 1522*
Website *www.coffscoast.com.au*
Open *9am-5pm daily*

Coming & Going

AIR

Coffs Harbour Airport *(**website** www.coffsharbour.nsw.gov.au/www/html/425-airport-.asp)* has flights to Brisbane, Canberra, Lord Howe Island, Melbourne, Newcastle, Port Macquarie and Sydney. Brindabella, Qantas and Virgin Blue are the main airlines serving Coffs Harbour.

BUS

Both Greyhound Australia *(☎ 1300 473 946; **website** www.greyhound.com.au)* and Premier Motor Service *(**website** www.premierms.com.au)* buses stop in Coffs Harbour with services to Brisbane and Sydney. Buses stop at the coach station near the information centre on the Pacific Highway.

TRAIN

CountryLink stop in Coffs Harbour en route between Brisbane and Sydney. The train station is on Angus McLeod Street across from Jetty Beach.

Local Transport

Busways *(☎ (02) 6652 2744; **website** www.busways.com.au)* and Ryans Bus Service *(☎ (02) 6652 3201; **website** www.ryansbusservice.com.au)* provide local bus services in Coffs Harbour. Fares within the city vary from $1.90 to 3.50.

Accommodation

Aussitel Backpackers

Aussitel is a small hostel without much to write home about. The bathrooms are in need of an update, and the dorm rooms are ugly and ill-ventilated. The kitchen is average, but could use some maintenance as well. There is laundry, internet ($4 per hour), and a nice TV lounge with a fish tank and comfortable couches. The common area, though outside, is covered and gets smoky quickly. They have barbecues a few times a week and organise a lot of activities, specialising in dive trips, since there is a dive shop next door.

312 Harbour Drive, Coffs Harbour
☎ *(02) 6651 1871*
Website *www.aussitel.com.au*
Dorm bed *$20-26;* ***double/twin room*** *$50-65*
Credit cards *MC, Visa*
Reception open *8am-10.30am & 1.30pm-8pm*

Maintenance & cleanliness	★★½
Facilities	★★½
Atmosphere & character	★★★½
Security	★½
Overall rating	★★½

Barracuda Backpackers

Barracuda Backpackers is cosy but it shows its age. The kitchen is homely and well equipped and there is a pool table, barbecue and swimming pool area with a fire pit that guests make good use of. They also offer free use of surfboards, a free city tour, and free pickup from the bus station. The atmosphere is potentially very fun, but they need to do a bit of renovating to keep the standards up. This hostel is located close to Park Beach Plaza shopping centre.

19 Arthur Street, Coffs Harbour
365 (Busways)

(02) 6651 3514
Website *www.backpackers.coffs.tv*
Dorm bed *$22;* ***double/twin room*** *$55*
Credit cards *MC, Visa*
Reception open *6am-10.30pm*

Maintenance & cleanliness	★★
Facilities	★★½
Atmosphere & character	★★½
Security	★★
Overall rating	★★½

Coffs Harbour YHA

This YHA is a new purpose-built hostel near the jetty, beach, and shops, with a swimming pool and a barbecue area. The dorms are extremely clean to the point of seeming sterile. The kitchen is well equipped and even has a walk-in refrigerator. There are endless activities available through reception, and the common room is cosy. It has great security as well but it may not have quite the lively atmosphere that the other hostels do.
51 Collingwood Street, Coffs Harbour
365 (Busways)
(02) 6652 6462
Website *www.yha.com.au*
Dorm bed *$23-33*
Credit cards *MC, Visa*
Reception open *8am-10pm*

Maintenance & cleanliness	★★★★½
Facilities	★★★
Atmosphere & character	★★★
Security	★★★★½
Overall rating	★★★★

Hoey Moey Backpackers

Hoey Moey is in a dated and run down motel, but it is popular with the party-minded because it shares the property with a lively pub & restaurant. There is live music and entertainment on the weekends. It has private access, via boardwalk, to the beach, and they offer free use of body boards and surfboards. There is also free pizza night on Monday and a bottle shop next door. It is relatively cheap and it may be the best place to party, but it is pretty grimy and security is limited. It

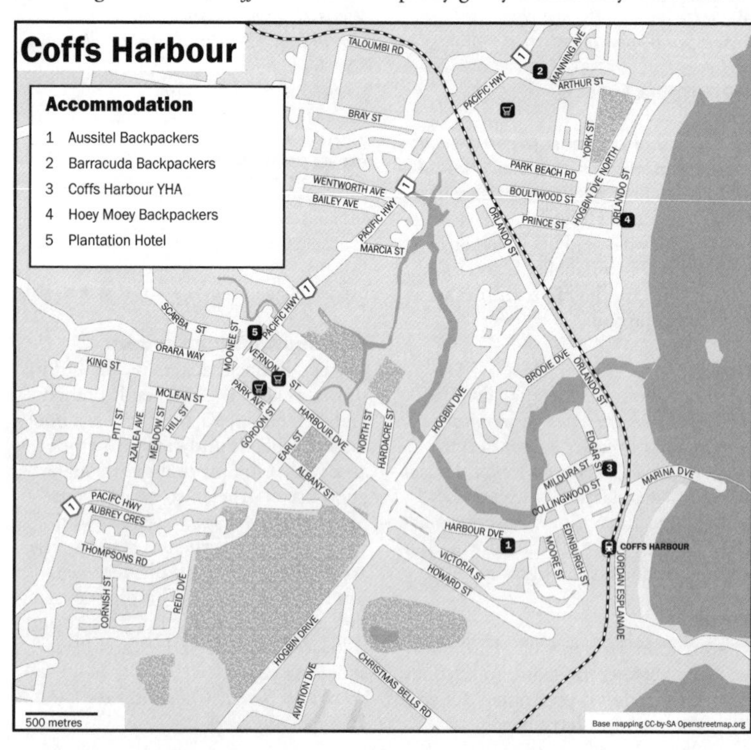

would be better to stay somewhere else and come to the bar to party.
Ocean Parade, Coffs Harbour
365 (Busways)
(02) 6651 7966
***Website** www.hoeymoey.com.au*
***Dorm bed** $22-26 ($20-24 HI/YHA, VIP); **double room** $54-58 ($52-55 HI/YHA, VIP)*
***Credit cards** MC, Visa*
***Reception open** 8am-6pm, check in at the bar till midnight*

Maintenance & cleanliness	★★
Facilities	★★½
Atmosphere & character	★★★
Security	★
Overall rating	★★½

Plantation Hotel
The huge, modern restaurant and bar on the ground level of this building is quite inviting. Unfortunately the hostel upstairs is disappointing in comparison. The kitchen is a mess and the common area is small. Bathrooms and dorms are dark and plain, and need a bit of attention. There isn't much else to it, except for the pool table downstairs and the fact that the basement nightclub is the best in town.
88 Grafton Street, Coffs Harbour
(02) 6652 3855
***Website** www.plantationhotel.com.au*
***Dorm bed** $20-22; **double room** $55*
***Credit cards** MC, Visa*
***Reception open** 9am-noon & 4pm-7pm; 24 hour check-in available with prior arrangement*

Maintenance & cleanliness	★★
Facilities	★★
Atmosphere & character	★★★½
Security	★★
Overall rating	★★½

Eating & Drinking
Nobody goes to Coffs Harbour for the food, but you won't starve as there is a good selection of fast food places that are clustered around the town centre and also in the Park Plaza shopping centre.

If you're preparing your own food, there is a **Coles** supermarket in the Palms Centre (31-65 Harbour Drive, Coffs Harbour) and **Woolworths** in the Park Beach Plaza shopping centre and at 7 Park Avenue in the city centre.

Sights
Big Banana
One of the more famous of Australia's big things, this huge concrete banana is the focal point of a tourist complex that features monorail tours of a banana plantation.
Pacific Highway, Coffs Harbour
(02) 6652 4355
***Website** www.bigbanana.com*
***Admission** free; charge for tours*
***Open** 9am-4.30pm daily*

Coffs Harbour Historical Museum
This small museum focuses on the region's history.
191A High Street, Coffs Harbour
365 (Busways)
(02) 6652 5794
***Admission** $3*
***Open** Tue-Sat 10am-4pm*

Muttonbird Island Nature Reserve
Overlooking the harbour and marina, Muttonbird Island is a great retreat and ideal spot for whale watching. It is accessible by foot via the causeway from Marina Drive.

Oceanarium (Pet Porpoise Pool)
This marine-themed animal park has performing dolphins and seals as well as native fauna such as cockatoos and kangaroos.
Orlando Street, Coffs Harbour
365 (Busways)
(02) 6652 2164
***Website** www.petporpoisepool.com*
***Admission** $27($21 HI/YHA, Nomads, VIP; $19 students)*
***Open** 9am-4pm daily*

Activities
Diving
Coffs Harbour is a popular place to learn to dive. Diving here is considerably cheaper than in Queensland and the nearby Solitary Islands Marine Park is a top diving spot.

Expect to pay around $395 for a four-day PADI dive course although shorter courses are also available. Dive courses are run by **Jetty Dive Centre** *(☎ (02) 6651 1611; **website** www.jettydive.com.au).*

Sea Kayaking

Liquid Assets *(☎ (02) 6658 0850; **website** www.surfrafting.com)* run good value sea kayaking trips to the Solitary Islands Marine Park that give you the opportunity to see dolphins, turtles and whales. Half-day trips cost $50.

Skydiving

Coffs is a popular skydiving destination. **Coffs City Skydivers** *(☎ (02) 6651 1167; **website** www.coffscentral.dnet.tv/CoffsCitySkyDivers/)* offers tandem skydiving.

Surfing

There is good surfing available around Coffs Harbour. **East Coast Surf School** *(☎ (02) 6651 5515; **website** www.east coastsurfschool.com.au)* offers how-to-surf lessons for $50 for one lesson or $200 for a five-day course.

Whale Watching

Up to 4,000 hump back whales migrate through the Coffs Coast. **Cougar Cat 12** *(☎ (02) 6651 6715; **website** www.cougarcat12.com.au)* run whale watching cruises between June and November that cost $44 for a 2½ hour cruise.

White Water Rafting

There are several companies operating white water rafting trips on rivers between Coffs Harbour and Byron Bay with pickups from Coffs Harbour hostels. The Nymboida River is the closest to Coffs Harbour and is a popular river for rafting. A one-day rafting trip on the Nymboida River costs around $160. White water rafting companies include: **Liquid Assets Adventure Tours** *(☎ (02) 6658 0850; **website** www.surfrafting.com)*, **Rapid Rafting** *(☎ (02) 6652 1741; **website** www.coffscentral.com/RapidRafting/)* and **Wild Scenic Rivers** *(☎ (02) 6651 4575; **website** www.coffscentral.com/WildScenicRivers/).*

Ballina

Around 30 minutes south of Byron Bay, Ballina has some good beaches and is an alternative when Byron Bay is booked out, although it is more of a spot to come to make transport connections rather than a destination in its own right. Ballina's attractions include a maritime museum and the Big Prawn.

Practical Information

Ballina Tourist Information Centre

Las Balsas Plaza, River Street, Ballina
☎ (02) 6686 3484
***Open** Mon-Fri 9am-5pm, Sat-Sun 9am-4pm*

Coming & Going

AIR

Ballina Airport *(☎ (02) 6686 8385; **website** www.ncas.com.au/html/ballina airport.html)* has several daily flights to Sydney and you can fly here with a Rex backpacker pass.

BUS

Ballina is on the Brisbane to Sydney bus route and also has local buses to nearby towns including Lennox Head, Byron Bay and Mullumbimby. Buses stop at the Big Prawn on the Pacific Highway south of the town centre.

Accommodation

Ballina Travellers Lodge YHA

This hostel doubles as a motel in a leafy residential side street in central Ballina. It has a very nice swimming pool and attractive brick walls. Bathrooms are recently redone and kept very clean, and the kitchen is simple and neat. Dorms, however, need an update and a paint job. Old furniture and stained carpet ruin the ambience. It is a very quiet place.

36-38 Tamar Street, Ballina
☎ (02) 6686 6737
***Website** www.yha.com.au*
***Dorm bed** $23-30.50 ($20.70-27.45 HI/YHA); **double room** $56-78 ($50.40-70.20 HI/YHA)*
***Credit cards** Amex, MC, Visa*
***Reception open** 7am-10pm*

TV K L

Maintenance & cleanliness	★★★½
Facilities	★★½
Atmosphere & character	★★★½
Security	★½
Overall rating	★★★

Lennox Head

Lennox Head is a small town of 6,000 people just 15 minutes south of Byron Bay. It is popular with surfers who come to ride the internationally famous right-hand point break at the southern end of town. The town holds the biannual Lennox Masters Surf Classic and the annual Gromfest Junior Surf Contest. The beach is long and sandy, and good for sunbathing or body boarding. Pat Morton Lookout is the perfect take-off spot for hang-gliding, and Lake Ainsworth is celebrated for its therapeutic waters tinged with tea tree oils. Families often head for the lake to have picnics and practice water sports such as kayaking and sailing, and it is home to the wonderful Lenox Head Markets, where locally grown fruit and vegetables are sold alongside local art and handicrafts. The market is worth a look and is cheaper than the Byron Market but just as bustling.

The town is more of a village, with a short main street lined with cafés, restaurants and surf shops which you can walk through in a few minutes. It is quite a charming place to spend a day, and many Byron residents head here to escape the crowds during peak summer months.

Coming & Going

Bus 640 runs between Ballina and Byron Bay stopping en route at Lennox Head. This bus stops in the town centre and also outside Lennox Head Backpackers.

Premier Motor Service coaches also stop at Lennox Head, but Greyhound doesn't come here.

Accommodation

Lennox Head Backpackers

Right down the street from the centre of town, this little place is charming and laid-back. It is usually full of surfers who come for the great point break at the beach across the street, and backpackers who stop in before heading to Byron. The kitchen and the toilets are in bad repair, and the TV room is dark and stuffy but the dorms are extremely clean and well maintained. They offer free use of surfboards and body boards.

2-3 Ross Street, Lennox Head
☎ *(02) 6687 7636*
Website *www.yha.com.au*
Dorm bed *$26-34;* ***double room*** *$62-76*
Credit cards *MC, Visa*
Reception open *8am-10pm*

Maintenance & cleanliness	★★★
Facilities	★★
Atmosphere & character	★★★½
Security	★★½
Overall rating	★★★

Byron Bay

Byron Bay is a small town with a big personality. It lies at Australia's easternmost point and the subtropical weather and laid-back ambiance is famous with surfers, hippies, writers and celebrities, as well as travellers in search of the quintessential Australian beach town. They are never disappointed.

The beaches are the main attraction here. Off Cape Byron are the Pass and Watego's Beach, which are famous among surfers. Continuing north is Clarks Beach, which has smaller surf. After that is Main Beach, the swimming and sunbathing spot with much calmer waters. Belongil Beach, also good for surfing, is clothing optional. South of the cape is Tallow Beach, a long sandy strip in front of the Arakwal National Park that often has rough seas but is good for a walk. On top of Cape Byron is the Lighthouse, a beautiful beacon of Byron's maritime heritage. Park a third of the way up and walk; otherwise, parking costs $7.

Just walking through the fascinating streets of Byron is pleasing enough. Its residents, though bombarded by tourists daily, are welcoming and friendly. And walking is the preferred mode of transport as the town is so small. If you want to visit another town in the area, there are regional buses with regular service. You can also rent bikes from almost any hostel.

There are many activities in the area to choose from, the most popular of course being surfing lessons.

The International Blues & Roots Music Festival takes over town each Easter. The Byron Bay Writers Festival in July also attracts a crowd.

The café scene here is brilliant, and the bars off Jonson Street are packed with models and pro surfers nightly. All these things combine to give Byron an infectious vibe; one which causes many backpackers to find jobs and stay much longer than they had planned.

Practical Information

INFORMATION & BOOKING CENTRES

Byron Bus & Backpacker Centre

84 Jonson Street, Bryon Bay
☎ *(02) 6685 5517*
Open *Mon-Fri 7.30am-7pm, Sat-Sun 8am-7pm*

Visitor Information Centre

Stationmaster's Cottage, 80 Jonson Street, Byron Bay
☎ *(02) 6680 8558*
Website *www.visitbyronbay.com*
Open *9am-5pm daily*

Peter Pan Adventures

87 Jonson Street, Byron Bay
☎ *1800 252 459*
Website *www.peterpans.com*
Open *9am-8pm daily*

INTERNET ACCESS

Byron Bay's internet cafés include:

Backpackers World

Shop 6, Byron Street, Byron Bay
☎ *(02) 6685 8858*
Website *www.byron-bay.com/backpackersworld/*
Open *Mon-Fri 9am-8pm, Sat 9.45am-6pm, Sun 11am-5pm*

Global Gossip

84 Jonson Street, Byron Bay
☎ *(02) 6680 9140*

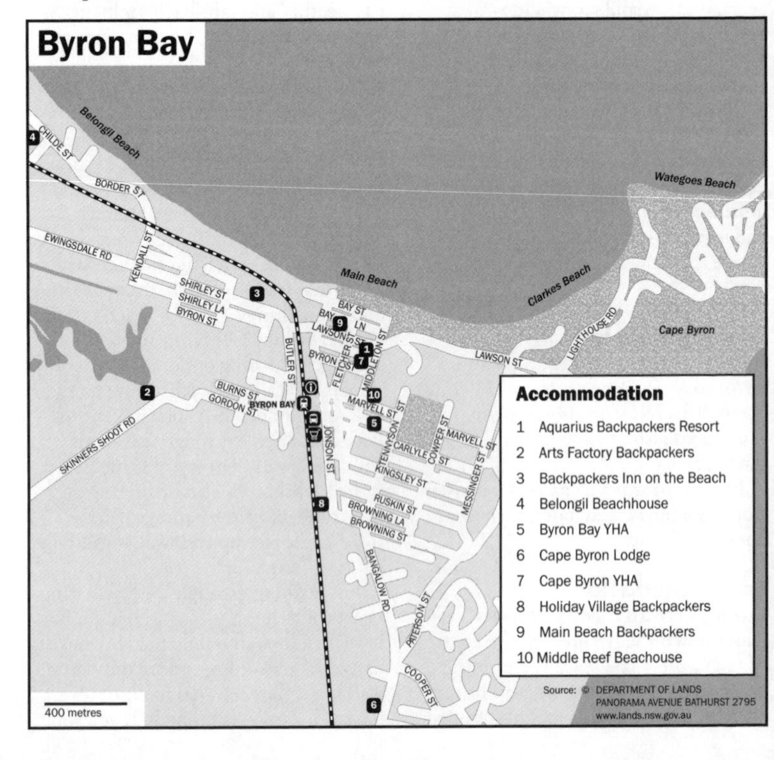

Website *www.globalgossip.com*
Open *Mon-Fri 9am-11pm, Sat-Sun 10am-11pm*

Coming & Going

AIR

Byron Bay is located between Ballina and Coolangatta Airports. Ballina Airport has flights to Sydney and regional destinations in NSW while the busier Coolangatta Airport has flights to most parts of Australia as well as some international flights. There are airport buses that connect Byron Bay with both airports. These include Airlink (☎ *(02) 6684 3232;* ***website*** *www.airlinkbyron bay.com.au)*; Airport Transfers Byron Bay *(☎ (02) 6620 9200;* ***website*** *www.airporttransfersbyronbay.com)*; Byron easyBus *(☎ (02) 6685 7447;* ***website*** *www.byroneasybus.com.au)* and Steve's Tours Airport Express *(☎ 0414 660 031;* ***website*** *www.stevestours.com.au).*

TRAIN

Byron Bay is on the Sydney-Brisbane train line with two daily trains in each direction. The train station is on Jonson Street in the centre of town.

BUS

Because Byron Bay is off the main highway some buses don't stop here, but most buses on the Brisbane-Sydney route do. They stop near the information centre on Jonson Street outside the train station.

Brisbane 2 Byron *(☎ 1800 626 222;* ***website*** *www.brisbane2byron.com)* operates a minibus service between Brisbane and Byron Bay. The trip takes two hours and costs $30.

There are several companies offering day trips to Nimbin, these trips range from a simple shuttle bus to tours that stop by at a number of local attractions. Because of competition, there are some good deals available. See the Nimbin section for more information.

Accommodation

The selection of hostels in and around Byron Bay is excellent, but accommodation can be booked weeks in advance during summer. Take that as a warning, or you may have to sleep in the back of a Kombi van (not such a bad prospect for the hippy population in Byron).

Aquarius Backpackers Resort

Aquarius Backpackers is located in the town centre just a two-minute walk from the beach. It has a great layout with an outside bar, three televisions, a pool table and a clay fireplace. They have an internet room ($4 per hour), a large kitchen, laundry and a travel booking agency. The on-site café has a cool veranda and good breakfast. Dorms are all en suite and have rustic lofts, some with comfortable single beds instead of bunks. Nights here can get pretty wild, so don't come here if you want a good night's sleep.

16 Lawson Street, Byron Bay
☎ *(02) 6685 7663 or 1800 028 909*
Website *www.aquarius-backpack.com.au*
Dorm bed *$33;* ***double room*** *$90-130*
Credit cards *MC, Visa*
Reception open *7am-midnight*

Maintenance & cleanliness	★★★★
Facilities	★★★★½
Atmosphere & character	★★★★½
Security	★★½
Overall rating	★★★★

Arts Factory Backpackers

This place is more of a compound than a hostel. Spread over five acres of subtropical bush land and gardens, the Arts Factory boasts such facilities as a cinema, the Buddha Bar restaurant, a beautiful heated pool and sauna, a day spa, beach volleyball, and a café with food, drinks and souvenirs, as well as the usual kitchen, internet kiosks, and plenty of chilled-out common areas. Guests lounge by the lake in hammocks, or take part in didgeridoo lessons, yoga classes, and guided bush walks. In addition to the well-kept dorms, there is an eclectic range of accommodation options including canvas & wood huts, a tepee, an old double-decker bus, and the nunnery, a girls-only air-conditioned dorm. It is not far from town and the beach, and they have regular shuttle services.

Skinners Shoot Road, Byron Bay

(02) 6685 7709
Website *www.artsfactory.com.au*
Dorm bed *$28-36;* **double/twin room** *$75-95*
Credit cards *MC, Visa*
Reception open *7am-9pm*

Maintenance & cleanliness	★★★
Facilities	★★★★½
Atmosphere & character	★★★★★
Security	★★
Overall rating	★★★★

Backpackers Inn on the Beach

This hostel is the perfect place for surfers, since it has private access via a sandy path to Main Beach. It is an open, airy complex of palm trees, hammocks and outdoor common areas. The colourful dorms are well-kept and clean, and the kitchen is bright and well stocked, though the bathrooms are lacking maintenance. There is a swimming pool and a beach volleyball court, and they offer free use of body boards and bikes. It has a mellow vibe to it, with very friendly staff.
29 Shirley Street, Byron Bay
(02) 6685 8231
Website *www.backpackersinnbyronbay.com.au*
Dorm bed *$29-32 ($26-30 HI/YHA, ISIC, VIP);* **double/twin room** *$75-92*
Credit cards *MC, Visa*
Reception open *8am-8pm*

Maintenance & cleanliness	★★★½
Facilities	★★★★
Atmosphere & character	★★★★½
Security	★★½
Overall rating	★★★★

Belongil Beachhouse

This hostel has a retreat feel to it, with large open-beamed cabins surrounding lush gardens and wooden pathways. It has a big upstairs kitchen and an outdoor barbecue area. There is also a café on site, as well as the Relax Haven massage therapy rooms. It is just across from the quiet Belongil Beach, and not too far from town. Some of the areas are a bit run-down and could use an update, but it is kept clean and has character. It is the perfect place to stay for a night of relaxation.
Childe Street, Byron Bay
(02) 6685 7868
Website *www.belongilbeachouse.com*
Dorm bed *$28 ($27 HI/YHA, VIP)*
Credit cards *MC, Visa*
Reception open *8am-7pm*

Maintenance & cleanliness	★★★
Facilities	★★½
Atmosphere & character	★★★★
Security	★½
Overall rating	★★★

Byron Bay YHA

Byron Bay YHA is a beautifully maintained hostel with a heated swimming pool and an outside kitchen/barbecue area. The TV lounge has cheap internet access ($3 per hour), and the upstairs deck has hammocks overlooking the pool. Dorm rooms and bathrooms are new and sparkling and the kitchen is large and well equipped for cooking. It attracts a mellow crowd of travellers who lounge on the deck and beside the pool. It's not too far from town and the beach and they have bikes and good surfboards available for rent.
7 Carlyle Street, Byron Bay
(02) 6685 8853 or 1800 678 195
Website *www.yha.com.au*
Dorm bed *$25-39;* **double room** *$82-112*
Credit cards *MC, Visa*
Reception open *8am-9pm*

Maintenance & cleanliness	★★★★
Facilities	★★★
Atmosphere & character	★★★★½
Security	★★
Overall rating	★★★½

Cape Byron Lodge

This hostel is a bit farther from town and the beach, and consequently quieter. It's a small place with bare dorms and average bathrooms, all curving around little courtyards and gardens. The kitchen is small but well equipped, and the common area/TV lounge is comfortable and packed. If you are looking for a relaxing place to stay, this is a good deal as there is still a convivial atmosphere and it's a lot cheaper.
78 Bangalow Road, Byron Bay

☎ *(02) 6685 6445*
Website *www.capebyronlodge.com*
Dorm bed *$20-29;* ***double room*** *$55-80*
Credit cards *MC, Visa*
Reception open *9am-1pm & 5pm-9pm; late check-in with prior arrangement*

Maintenance & cleanliness	★★★
Facilities	★★★½
Atmosphere & character	★★★
Security	★★
Overall rating	★★★

Cape Byron YHA

This clean, purpose-built hostel is located in the town centre and has loads of shops surrounding it. The simple, comfortable dorms circle a huge heated swimming pool with palm trees and a barbecue and the bathrooms are all shiny new white tile. There is a TV lounge with a large screen and rows of nice leather couches, which doubles as a reading room during the day. Reception staff are nice, and internet costs $3 per hour. There is a café and a dive centre on site. The atmosphere is just right – not too quiet, but not too rowdy, either.

Corner Byron & Middleton Streets, Byron Bay
☎ *(02) 6685 8788 or 1800 652 627*
Website *www.yha.com.au*
Dorm bed *$25-38;* ***double/twin room*** *$80-125*
Credit cards *MC, Visa*
Reception open *9am-1pm & 5pm-9pm*

Maintenance & cleanliness	★★★★
Facilities	★★★
Atmosphere & character	★★½
Security	★★
Overall rating	★★★½

Holiday Village Backpackers

Holiday Village is a complex of brick and wood buildings tucked away off the main street coming into Byron Bay. It is a lively place, with bi-weekly barbecues, a volleyball court and a good swimming pool. They also offer free use of bikes, body boards and surfboards. But the TV lounge is just a box with some torn couches thrown in, and the kitchen is spacious but rather empty. Dorms could use some work, and some of the linen is stained and needs replacing. Also, security is seriously lacking. But the potential for partying is high here since it is right across the street from the best nightclub in town and young backpackers revel in the streets well into the morning.

116 Jonson Street, Byron Bay
☎ *(02) 6685 8888*
Website *www.byronbaybackpackers.com.au*
Dorm bed *$25-33; double room $75-100*
Credit cards *MC, Visa*
Reception open *7am-9pm; 24 hour check-in with prior arrangement*

Maintenance & cleanliness	★★★★
Facilities	★★★½
Atmosphere & character	★★★½
Security	★
Overall rating	★★★½

Main Beach Backpackers

This hostel is in a great location just off the main street in Byron. It is spacious and modern, but a bit rough around the edges. There is a large rooftop sundeck looking onto the street and the kitchen is fresh and clean, but the dorms are sparse and the bathrooms are in disrepair. They have a small swimming pool, but it can get murky. They are one of the only hostels that offers an hour of free internet. Reception staff are enormously friendly and helpful.

Corner Fletcher & Lawson Streets, Byron Bay
☎ *(02) 6685 8695 or 1 800 150 233*
Website *www.mainbeachbackpackers.com*
Dorm bed *$23-33;* ***double room*** *$60-110*
Credit cards *MC, Visa*
Reception open *8am-9pm*

Maintenance & cleanliness	★★★
Facilities	★★★
Atmosphere & character	★★★½
Security	★★★½
Overall rating	★★★

Middle Reef Beachouse

Middle Reef Beachouse takes up three large houses next to each other in a good location near the beach, and with a relaxed atmosphere. They offer free wireless internet and free use of body boards and surfboards. Dorm rooms are clean and painted with different shades of blue with nice wooden flooring. Most of them have en suite bathrooms with new clean showers. The atmosphere here is slightly more subdued than the other places. Management are knowledgeable and friendly.

13 Marvel Street, Byron Bay
☎ *(02) 6685 5118*
Website *www.byron-bay.com/middlereef/*
Dorm bed *$20-35*
Credit cards *MC, Visa*
Reception open *9am-9pm*

Maintenance & cleanliness	★★★½
Facilities	★★★
Atmosphere & character	★★★½
Security	★★
Overall rating	★★★½

Eating & Drinking

Byron's abundance of surfers and hippies mean that there are tons of healthy eating options in town, as well as fresh fruit stands and juice bars.

Once a month the **Byron Farmers Market** takes over the town and sells heaps of organic produce and locally grown fruit. There are some great new places for cheap and healthy sandwiches and wraps. Try **Krave** across from the bus station. Indian restaurants and Middle Eastern joints are widespread, with some seriously good falafel (**Orgasmic Café** makes great balls – with love) and kebabs. There is even a great raw food restaurant in town, but the prices are lofty. Another good place for the health-conscious is **Mokha** café on Lawson Street, the only restaurant with free wireless access and awesome salads.

The **Woolworths** on Jonson Street sometimes seems like the town meeting point. Cooking your own food will always be cheaper in Byron Bay due to the high tourist prices. Fiercely protective citizens are a force to be reckoned with here, evidenced by the absence of fast food, including McDonald's. But there are still some cheap options. Locals head to **Mac's Milk Bar** on Bangalow Road for great fish and chips.

Cafés are dotted along the main roads in town, and local coffee farmers take pride in their harvest for good reason.

There are only a few nightclubs in town and the **Cheeky Monkey** is usually the first stop for partiers. Live music is big here, especially reggae and blues.

Alcohol here is seriously expensive in Byron Bay. Going out to a nightclub can easily rack up a $100 tab on beer alone. Hostels often have happy hours or drink specials, and a visit to the bottle shop on the way to the beach could make for a better night than one in any club; but that's the Byron talking.

Activities

Hang Gliding

Seabreeze Hang Gliding (☎ *0428 560248; **website** www.seabreezehanggliding.com)* runs tandem hang gliding flights from Cape Byron or Lennox Head. A tandem flight costs $145.

Sea Kayaking

Sea kayaking puts you in a unique position to discover Byron Bay's marine life, which includes dolphins. Sea kayaking trips cost around $60 per person.

Byron Bay Sea Kayaks (☎ *0416 222 344; **website** www.byronbay-seakayak.com.au)*; **Cape Byron Kayaks** (☎ *(02) 6680 9555; **website** www.capebyron kayaks.com)* and **Dolphin Kayaking** (☎ *(02) 6685 8044; **website** www.dolphinkayaking.com.au)* operate sea-kayaking trips.

Surfing

Byron Bay has excellent beginners waves and it's a popular spot to learn to surf. One-day lessons cost between $49 and $65 and two-day courses cost from $85 to $105. Three and five-day courses are also available.

There are loads of surfing schools in Byron Bay including **Black Dog Surfing** (☎ *(02) 6685 8858; **website** www.blackdogsurfing.com)*, **Byron Bay Surf School** (☎ *1800 707 274; **website** www.byronbaysurfschool.com)*, **Style Surfing** (☎ *(02) 6685 5634; **website** www.stylesurfingbyronbay.com)*, **Surfing Byron Bay** (☎ *(02) 6685 7099; **website** www.gosurfingbyronbay.com)* and the cheapest, **Kool Katz** (☎ *(02) 6685 5169; **website** www.koolkatzsurf.com)*.

Lismore

With around 50,000 people, Lismore is the main town in the far north of the state and it's where people from neighbouring towns come to get things done. Lismore has a university and a much more sophisticated air to it than most other regional towns of a similar size – probably due to the alternative/new-age influence of nearby places like Byron Bay and Nimbin.

Practical Information

Lismore Tourist Information Centre

Corner Ballina & Molesworth Sts, Lismore
☎ *(02) 6622 0122*
***Website** www.liscity.nsw.gov.au*
***Open** 9.30am-4pm daily*

INTERNET ACCESS

The Bush Telegraph

50 Magellan Street, Lismore
☎ *(02) 6621 5324*

SHOWERS

There are public showers in the transit centre that cost $2.

Coming & Going

Lismore is accessible by both train and bus. The Train station is on Union Street with trains to Brisbane, Sydney and Murwillumbah.

Some Brisbane-Sydney buses bypass Lismore so check first if you want to get off here. Most buses, including Kirklands and Greyhound Australia, stop at the Transit Centre at the corner of Magellen and Molesworth Streets.

Murwillumbah

Murwillumbah is a charming town on the banks of the Tweed River about 30km from Byron Bay. Its location is perfect for exploring nearby Mount Warning and the subtropical rainforests of Nightcap National Park. There are many historic buildings along Main Street and elsewhere in the commercial centre. Cafés and hotels are concentrated here as well. Shady parks and gardens are dotted throughout the town, many offering superb views of the surrounding hills and Mt Warning. The Tweed River National Gallery is renowned for its collection and exhibitions, and the region's famous markets also make a stop here on the forth Sunday of each month.

Murwillumbah is the commercial hub for the region and its many small villages. Many dairy and beef farms and fruit orchards in its environs depend on the town for business purposes. Besides the scenery, there are not many other attractions in Murwillumbah, but it is a nice place to stop for a coffee on one of the small cafes on Main or Brisbane Streets. If you are heading into the rainforests or hinterland for outdoor activities, the hostel in town is the perfect place to stay.

Practical Information

World Heritage Rainforest & Information Centre

Corner Alma Street & Pacific Highway, Murwillumbah
☎ *(02) 6672 1340*
***Website** www.nationalparks.nsw.gov.au*
***Open** 9am-4.30pm daily*

Coming & Going

Murwillumbah is at the end of the Sydney-Murwillumbah train line with daily trains to Sydney. There are also frequent buses to Brisbane, Sydney as well as Byron Bay and the Gold Coast that depart from the bus terminal on Murwillumbah Street.

Accommodation

Murwillumbah Hotel

This is just a few dorm rooms above the local bar. The bathrooms are rather shoddy and the kitchen is very minimal, but otherwise it is clean and well maintained. There is a large bar downstairs where town regulars share morning beers. It is a bit of a time warp in here, but cheap and adequate. Surprisingly, they are one of the few places to offer free Wi-Fi access. Reception is in the bar and the staff here are a good-humoured lot. Few backpackers make it here, so don't expect to meet

many other travellers, though you may meet some of the permanent residents upstairs.
13 Wharf Street, Murwillumbah
☎ *(02) 8872 1129*
Website *www.murwillumbahhotel.com.au*
Dorm bed *$20*
Credit cards *MC, Visa*
Reception open *Mon-Fri 10am-10pm, Sat-Sun 10am-1am*

Maintenance & cleanliness	★★★
Facilities	★★
Atmosphere & character	★★½
Security	★★★
Overall rating	★★½

Riverside YHA Backpackers

With a large riverside balcony and views of Mt Warning, the location of this hostel is perfect. It is a cheerful little place with only 24 beds and colourful murals painted on the walls, accented with nice wooden tables and benches. The management is easygoing and amiable and offer free ice cream to guests every night. If you stay for three nights, you get a free trip to Mt Warning with bikes and canoes. The TV room is in a small shed set away from the house to keep the noise down at night. The atmosphere here is quiet and pleasant.
1 Tumbulgum Road, Murwillumbah
☎ *(02) 6672 3763*
Website *www.yha.com.au*
Dorm bed *$29 ($26 HI/YHA);* ***double/twin room*** *$62.50 ($56 HI/YHA)*
Credit cards *MC, Visa*
Reception open *8am-11pm*

Maintenance & cleanliness	★★★
Facilities	★★½
Atmosphere & character	★★★½
Security	★★
Overall rating	★★★

Activities

Mount Warning

Mount Warning is the main reason most travellers visit Murwillumbah. The staff at the YHA hostel know all about climbing the mountain and they may even arrange your transport in time for a pre-sunrise climb.

Nimbin

This tiny village high in the hills of the far north coast hinterland is Australia's hippy haven. Since the first Aquarius Festival in 1973, it has grown steadily to become one of the most popular day trips from Byron Bay. It is still a very small village, with all the shops and cafes crammed onto the short stretch of Cullen Street. Amid the scents of patchouli and spices, vendors sell their crafts and food on makeshift street side stalls.

Surrounding Nimbin are lush forests and some of the most spectacular scenery in New South Wales. It is home to numerous organic farms as well as a prominent Aboriginal population. The large Nimbin Market twice a month brings live music and a range of fresh organic produce which is popular with residents of the region and visitors alike. The Nimbin Museum is a record of Nimbin's hippy history and culture, and the Hemp Embassy is where travellers go to stock up on souvenirs and paraphernalia. The Nimbin Rocks are a spectacular sight to see if you are driving south from town.

Practical Information

LAUNDRY

Village Wash House

Shop 5, 45 Cullen Street, Nimbin
☎ *(02) 6689 1799*
Open *8am-6.30pm daily*

Coming & Going

There are several companies offering day trips to Nimbin from Byron Bay. These trips range from simple shuttle buses to tours that call in at a number of local attractions. Because of intense competition, there are some good deals available – check the brochures at your hostel for the best prices.

A couple of the tours and bus services between Byron Bay and Nimbin include:

Jim's Alternative Tours

Jim's is a popular tour that goes to Nimbin via the Minyon Falls, a country pub and World Heritage rainforest.
☎ *(02) 6685 7720*
Website *www.jimsalternativetours.com*

***Day trip** $35*
Departs Byron Bay 10am, returns 6pm

Nimbin Shuttle Bus
The Nimbin Shuttle Bus makes a daily return trip between Byron and Nimbin.
☎ *(02) 6680 9189*
***Website** www.nimbinaustralia.com/nimbinshuttle/*
***Return trip** $25-26; **one-way** $14*
Departs Byron Bay Mon-Sat 10am, returns 4pm

Accommodation

Nimbin Hotel & Backpackers
This hostel is located above Nimbin's pub and offers basic but clean accommodation and is undergoing renovation, which should see an improvement in standards.
55 Cullen Street, Nimbin
☎ *(02) 6689 1246*
***Dorm bed** $25*
***Credit cards** MC, Visa*
***Reception open** Mon-Fri 10.30am-10.30pm, Sat-Sun 10.30am-midnight*

Maintenance & cleanliness	★★½
Facilities	★
Atmosphere & character	★★
Security	★½
Overall rating	★★

Nimbin Rox YHA
This is by far the best place to stay in Nimbin. A colourful and extremely well maintained complex of dorms and common areas are tucked away beneath palm trees and gardens, and look out to a beautiful view of the hills and Mt Warning. The accommodation options include a huge tepee with mattresses on the floor, and a nice yurt with a double bed. The pool is beautiful and the kitchen is newly renovated and clean. There is a quiet, relaxing feel to the place, and it attracts a lot of backpackers from all over the world.
74 Thorburn Street, Nimbin
☎ *(02) 6689 0022*
***Website** www.yha.com.au*
***Dorm bed** $27-30 ($24-27 HI/YHA); **double room** $55-60; yurt $70*
***Credit cards** MC, Visa*
***Reception open** 9am-9pm*

Maintenance & cleanliness	★★★★
Facilities	★★½
Atmosphere & character	★★★★½
Security	★
Overall rating	★★★½

Rainbow Retreat
This place is definitely more of a retreat than a backpackers. Do not come here expecting cleanliness or a party atmosphere. For that matter, don't even expect to have four walls. Dorms are set up in an eccentric range of accommodation including an old wagon and an open theatre stage. There is also a mountain hut, a love shack, and an Indonesian-themed room. When it rains, expect mud. That said, the owner of this place is caring and compassionate, and looks after things in his own way. It is not for everyone, but if you don't mind roughing it, this place might be the authentic and rustic experience you are looking for.
75 Thornburn Street, Nimbin
☎ *(02) 6689 1262*
***Website** www.rainbowretreat.net*
***Dorm bed** $20; **double room** $40-50; **camping** $13 per person*
***Reception open** 8am-10.30am & 3.30pm-8pm*

Maintenance & cleanliness	★
Facilities	★½
Atmosphere & character	★★★½
Security	½
Overall rating	★½

Sights

Nimbin Museum
This unique museum shows things from the hippy perspective. Exhibits include psychedelic art and marijuana paraphernalia.
62 Cullen Street, Nimbin
☎ *(02) 6689 1123*
***Website** www.nimbinmuseum.com*
***Admission** free*
***Open** 8am-5.30pm daily*

New England
New England is the inland region behind the New South Wales north

coast. This is traditionally farming country and is usually bypassed by travellers making their way up the coast, although the more direct route between Queensland and Melbourne or Sydney passes through this area.

Armidale

This small university town is one of the nicer regional towns in New South Wales with some attractive old buildings and more culture than other country towns of a similar size. Armidale is a convenient base if you're exploring nearby national parks.

Practical Information

Armidale Tourist Information Centre

82 Marsh Street, Armidale
480, 481, 482, 485
1800 627 736
***Website** www.armidaletourism.com.au*
***Open** Mon-Fri 9am-5pm, Sat 9am-4pm, Sun 10am-4pm*

Coming & Going

BUS

Armidale is connected by buses to Brisbane, Sydney and other towns in New England and along the north coast. The bus station is located at the information centre on Marsh Street.

TRAIN

CountryLink's *(**website** www.countrylink. info)* Xplorer train service runs to Armidale from Sydney and Newcastle.

Local Transport

Armidale has six local bus routes operated by Edwards Coaches *((02) 6772 3116; **website** www.edwardscoaches.com. au)*. Bus fares vary between $1.80 and $4.50 depending on the distance travelled.

Accommodation

Pembroke Tourist & Leisure Park

This hostel shares premises with a caravan park on the edge of town about 3km from the train station. It is a clean and well-maintained building with a kitchen, TV lounge and a games room with table tennis and pool table. Accommodation is in four 10-bed dormitories. Guests can use caravan park facilities that include tennis courts and a swimming pool.
39 Waterfall Way (entrance in Cookes Road), Armidale
(02) 6772 6470
***Website** www.yha.com.au*
***Dorm bed** $28.50 ($25 HI/YHA)*
***Credit cards** MC, Visa*
***Reception open** 7.30am-7.30pm*

Maintenance & cleanliness	★★★½
Facilities	★★★★
Atmosphere & character	★½
Security	★½
Overall rating	★★★

Glen Innes

With a rich Celtic heritage, Glen Innes is a pleasant stop if you're driving through New England but it isn't a destination in its own right. The main attraction is the Standing Stones at Martins Lookout.

Practical Information

Glen Innes Visitor & Coach Centre

152 Church Street, Glen Innes
(02) 6732 2397
***Website** www.gleninnestourism.com*
***Open** Mon-Fri 9am-5pm, Sat-Sun 9am-3pm*

Coming & Going

CountryLink *(**website** www.countrylink. com.au)* buses go to Brisbane, Grafton, Inverell, Moree and Sydney. Greyhound *(1300 473 946; **website** www.grey hound.com.au)* buses go to Brisbane, Melbourne and Sydney. Greyhound buses stop at the Caltex service station.

Sights

Land of the Beardies History House Museum

The region was first settled by a couple of bearded men from whom this museum takes its name. The museum delves into the town's history with an interesting array of exhibits.
Corner Fergusson Street & West Avenue, Glen Innes

☎ *(02) 6732 1035*
Website *www.beardieshistoryhouse.info*
Admission *$4*
Open *Mon-Fri 10am-noon & 1pm-4pm, Sat-Sun 1pm-4pm*

Standing Stones
Based upon the Ring of Brodgar in Scotland, Glen Innes's Standing Stones are a reflection of the town's Celtic heritage.
Martins Lookout, Watsons Dve, Glen Innes
Website *www.australianstandingstones.com*
Admission *free*
Always open

Scone
Located west of Newcastle, this small town is closer to the Hunter Valley than the other New England towns further to the north and the frequent Trains from Newcastle make it accessible enough for a day-trip. Scone is one of the most important towns in New South Wales' horse breeding and racing industry and calls itself 'the horse capital of Australia'.

Practical Information
Scone Tourist Information Centre
Corner Kelly & Susan Streets, Scone
☎ *(02) 6545 2907*
Website *www.upperhuntertourism.com.au*
Open *9am-5pm daily*

Coming & Going
Although it is accessible by bus from Sydney, Newcastle and the Hunter Valley, the train is the best way to visit Scone. Scone lies at the western terminus on the Hunter line on the CityRail network and the frequent trains put it almost within commuting distance of Newcastle.

Tamworth
Tamworth is the country music capital of Australia and the home of the annual Tamworth Country Music Festival as well as the big guitar. Country music is especially evident during the festival in late January, although at other times Tamworth is just another small regional city.

Practical Information
Tourist Information Centre
561 Peel Street, Tamworth
☎ *(02) 6755 4300*
Website *www.visittamworth.com*
Open *Mon-Fri 8.30am-4.30pm, Sat-Sun 9am-3pm*

Coming & Going
Tamworth has pretty good transport connections including buses to Sydney, Brisbane, Melbourne and towns in New England and the New South Wales north coast. Buses stop at the bus terminal near the corner of Murray and Peel streets.

Tamworth is also accessible by train with a station at the corner of Brisbane and Marius Streets. Countrylink runs one train a day to and from Sydney.

Accommodation
Tamworth YHA
Tamworth YHA is a fairly standard youth hostel with the usual kitchen, TV lounge and barbecue facilities. Accommodation is in six and eight-bed dormitories with made up beds. The sign at reception asking guests to "speak English in the kitchen and eating area" implies a feeling of xenophobia that may make some guests feel unwelcome. It is in the centre of Tamworth, across the road from the train station.
169 Marius Street, Tamworth
☎ *(02) 6761 2600*
Website *www.yha.com.au*
Dorm bed *$26-28 ($23-25 HI/YHA);* ***double room*** *$56 ($50 HI/YHA)*
Credit cards *MC, Visa*
Reception open *7am-12.30pm & 4pm-9.30pm*
TV K L

Maintenance & cleanliness	★★★
Facilities	★★★½
Atmosphere & character	★★½
Security	★★½
Overall rating	★★★½

Sights
Tamworth Country Centre
This is a tacky collection of country music memorabilia that includes a

small wax museum and the big guitar.
2 Ringers Road, South Tamworth
☎ *(02) 6765 2688*
Website *www.biggoldenguitar.com.au*
Admission *$8*
Open *9am-5pm daily*

Central West New South Wales

Central Western New South Wales consists mainly of fairly non-descript rural towns and farming land. You're most likely to pass through this area if you're travelling between Brisbane and Melbourne bypassing Sydney and the coast. If you're taking the bus, it's a 24-hour stretch and you may want to break the journey.

Bathurst

An attractive town west of the Blue Mountains, Bathurst is known throughout Australia as the home of the Mount Panorama racetrack and the annual Bathurst 1000 motor race. When the race isn't being run, the six-kilometre track up Mount Panorama is a public road and virtually everyone with a car who visits Bathurst does a lap of the famous circuit – but it isn't quite the same when you stick to the 60km/h speed limit.

Other attractions in Bathurst are the National Motor Racing Museum and the Sir Joseph Banks Nature Park.

Practical Information

Bathurst Visitor Information Centre

28 William Street, Bathurst
☎ *(02) 6332 1444*
Website *www.bathurstregion.com.au/visitors/*
Open *9am-5pm daily*

Coming & Going

Most people visit Bathurst en route to someplace else, although you may want to make the trip out from Sydney for the big race. Bathurst is at the end of the CityRail network and is also served by CountryLink trains with regular services from Sydney. Buses stop at the train station.

Local Transport

Bathurst has a local bus service comprised of seven routes; all run along Wilson Street and terminate at the Howick Street terminus. Routes 526 and 527 are useful for getting to the National Motor Museum.

Sights

Bathurst & District Historical Museum

This small museum features exhibits on regional history. It is housed in the old courthouse, which is the most impressive of Bathurst's architectural gems.
Russell Street, Bathurst
🚌 *520, 522, 523, 524, 525, 526, 527*
☎ *(02) 6332 4755*
Admission *$3*
Open *Tue-Wed & Sat-Sun 10am-4pm*

National Motor Racing Museum

This is worth seeing if you're a motor racing fan and interested in learning more about the sport from an Australian perspective.
Murrays Corner, Mount Panorama
🚌 *526, 527*
☎ *(02) 6332 1872*
Website *www.nmrm.com.au*
Admission *$8*
Open *9am-4.30pm daily*

Cowra

This small country town on the banks of the Lachlan River was the scene of the Cowra Breakout – an escape attempt by Japanese prisoners of war that took place in 1944. Although more than 200 prisoners died during the breakout, the incident has gone a long way in building Australian-Japanese relations and Cowra is now home to Japanese war cemeteries, gardens and a cultural centre.

Practical Information

Cowra Tourism Centre

Corner Boorowa Road and Mid Western Highway, Cowra

☎ *(02) 6342 4333*
***Website** www.cowratourism.com.au*
***Open** 9am-5pm daily*

Coming & Going

CountryLink *(**website** www.countrylink.info)* buses go to Cowra from Bathurst, Cootamundra, Grenfell and Orange. Buses depart from the Bus Zone on Macquarie Street.

Sights

Japanese Gardens & Cultural Centre

Cowra's biggest attraction is the Japanese Gardens and the adjoining cultural centre. It is the setting for many Japanese festivals and public holidays that are celebrated in Cowra.
Scenic Drive, Cowra
☎ *(02) 6341 2233*
***Website** www.cowrajapanesegarden.com.au*
***Admission** $7.70*
***Open** 8.30am-5pm daily*

Cowra Breakout Memorial & Japanese War Cemetery

The memorial is situated at the scene of the Cowra Breakout while the Australian and Japanese War Cemetery lies several kilometres north.
***Memorial** Corner of Farm Street & Sakura Avenue, Cowra*
***Cemetery** Doncaster Drive, Cowra*
***Admission** free*

Mudgee

Although not in the same league as Coonawarra, or the Barossa, Hunter or Yarra Valleys, Mudgee is an important wine producing area that is a pleasant place to pass through.

Some travellers find work here during the harvest.

Practical Information

Mudgee Visitors Information Centre

84 Market Street, Mudgee
☎ *(02) 6372 5875*
***Website** www.visitmudgeeregion.com.au*
***Open** Mon-Fri 9am-5pm, Sat 9am-3.30pm, Sun 9.30am-2pm*

Coming & Going

CountryLink *(**website** www.countrylink.info)* buses run between Mudgee and Lithgow with connecting train services to Sydney.

Orange

This orchard town between Bathurst and Dubbo has a thriving apple and cherry growing industry.

Fruit picking work attracts most travellers to Orange, who come to pick apples during February and March and cherries later in the year around November to December.

Practical Information

Orange Visitors Centre

Corner Byng & Peisley Streets, Orange
☎ *(02) 6361 5226 or 1800 069 466*
***Website** www.orange.nsw.gov.au*
***Open** 9am-5pm daily*

Coming & Going

CountryLink *(**website** www.countrylink.info)* trains connect Orange with Broken Hill, Dubbo and Sydney.

Dubbo

A busy town and the main centre of the state's central west, Dubbo is a good place to break your journey. The town has a good range of attractions but the highlight is the excellent Western Plains Zoo.

Practical Information

Dubbo Visitors Centre

Corner Brisbane & Erskine Streets, Dubbo
☎ *(02) 6884 1422*
***Website** www.dubbotourism.com.au*
***Open** 9am-5pm daily*

Coming & Going

CountryLink *(**website** www.countrylink.info)* trains connect Dubbo with Sydney and Greyhound Australia *(☎ 1300 473 946; **website** www.greyhound.com.au)* buses stop in Dubbo en route between Melbourne and Brisbane.

Local Transport

Dubbo Buslines *(**website** www.dubbobuslines.com.au/dubbo/)* run Dubbo's

New South Wales

local bus services. Bus fares range from $1.90 to $6 depending on the distance travelled.

Accommodation

Dubbo YHA Hostel

Dubbo's YHA is a small youth hostel on a quiet residential street close to the town centre. The hostel features a TV lounge with a log fire and a small kitchen. It's off the main backpackers' trail and subsequently the hostel has a different clientele to the average coastal hostel, which means that the atmosphere can feel a bit dead.

87 Brisbane Street, Dubbo
☎ *(02) 6882 0922*
Website *www.yha.com.au*
Dorm bed *$27.50 ($24.50 HI/YHA); **single room** $33.50 ($30 HI/YHA); **double/twin room** $55 ($49 HI/YHA)*
Credit cards *MC, Visa*
Reception open *8am-10am & 3pm-10pm*

Maintenance & cleanliness	★★★½
Facilities	★★½
Atmosphere & character	★★★½
Security	★★½
Overall rating	★★

Sights

Dubbo Regional Gallery

The Dubbo Regional Gallery features four galleries with space for temporary exhibits. The Armati Bequest is a new branch of the Dubbo Regional Gallery at the Western Plains Cultural Centre *(76 Wingewarra Street, Dubbo)*, which specialises in the Animal in Art theme with works featuring animals in a variety of media.

165 Darling Street, Dubbo
☎ *(02) 6881 4342*
Website *www.wpccdubbo.org.au/regional-gallery.html*
Admission *free*
Open *Mon & Wed-Sun 10am-4pm*

Dubbo Regional Museum

This regional museum at the Western Plains Cultural Centre has a permanent exhibit on the people of Dubbo, which chronicles the changing face of the city. There is also a space for temporary exhibits.

76 Wingewarra Street, Dubbo
☎ *(02) 6801 4444*
Website *www.wpccdubbo.org.au/regional-museum.html*
Admission *free*
Open *Mon & Wed-Sun 10am-4pm*

Old Dubbo Gaol

This old prision is now a museum that features animatronic mannequins.

90 Macquarie Street, Dubbo
☎ *(02) 6882 8122*
Website *www.olddubbogaol.com.au*
Admission *$15*
Open *9am-5pm daily (last entry 4.30pm)*

Taronga Western Plains Zoo

The Western Plains Zoo is Australia's first open range zoo and one of the countries best zoos. The zoo was established to provide open spaces for – mostly African – animals that need more extensive grounds than could be provided in city zoos. It is home to 82 different species. Although the zoo has a focus on African wildlife, there are animals from around the world including many native Australian animals. There are extensive cycling and walking paths around the zoo. The zoo covers around 300 hectares so renting a bike is probably the best way to see it.

Obley Road, Dubbo
☎ *(02) 6882 5888*
Website *www.zoo.nsw.gov.au*
Admission *$37 ($23 students)*
Open *9am-5pm daily (last entry 4pm)*

South Coast

Heading south from Wollongong, the New South Wales south coast is made up of pleasant beach resorts and fishing towns. Travelling this route between Melbourne and Sydney is a great alternative to the busy Hume Highway.

Kiama

Kiama is 45 minutes south of Wollongong and two hours from Sydney and has more character than most other towns on the south coast. There are good surf beaches here as well as hiking trails in nearby nature reserves.

Kiama's main attraction is the blowhole, which is a natural formation that, in big seas, spurts water hundreds of metres into the air through two rock caverns.

Practical Information

Kiama Tourist Information Centre

Blowhole Point Road, Kiama
☎ *(02) 4232 3322 or 1300 654 262*
Website *www.kiama.com.au*
Open *9am-5pm daily*

Coming & Going

Kiama is on the CityRail network and the train is by far the best way to get here if you're travelling from Wollongong or Sydney, although the bus is better if you're coming from destinations inland and further down the coast.

The train station on Bong Bong Street has frequent trains to Sydney (2 hours) and Wollongong (45 minutes).

Premier Motor Service *(**website** www.premierms.com.au)* buses stop at the Bombo Station just north of Kiama en route between Melbourne and Sydney.

Accommodation

Kiama Backpackers Hostel

Kiama Backpackers is a small hostel in a dreary looking brick building that has basic facilities that include a small kitchen, TV lounge and internet access. It has a dull atmosphere and a dated feel with old furnishings but it does have a handy location next to the train station.

31 Bong Bong Street, Kiama
☎ *(02) 4233 1881*
Dorm bed *$20*
Reception open *10am-10pm*
TV K

Maintenance & cleanliness	★★★
Facilities	★★½
Atmosphere & character	★★½
Security	★
Overall rating	★★

Sights

Kiama Blowhole

Kiama's major attraction is a blowhole that, under certain conditions, can spray water up to 25m in the air. A smaller one, called the Little Blowhole is located just a short distance south of the Kiama Blowhole.

Nowra

Nowra is the biggest city on the NSW coast south of Wollongong. It is an ugly place with the town centre cut in half by a multi-lane highway, but it does have the best shopping on the south coast and some travellers stop in Nowra to stock up on supplies before exploring the surrounding region, which includes the glistening white sand beaches at nearby Jervis Bay as well as the pretty towns of Berry and Kangaroo Valley.

Practical Information

Shoalhaven Visitors Centre

Corner Pleasant Way & Princes Highway, Nowra
☎ *(02) 4421 0778 or 1800 024 261*
Website *www.shoalhavenholidays.com.au*
Open *9am-4.30pm daily*

INTERNET ACCESS

Flat Earth Internet Café

Level 1, Nowra Mall, Junction Court, Nowra
☎ *(02) 4423 7771*
Website *www.flatearth.net.au/cafe.php*
Open *Mon-Fri 8.30am-5pm daily*

Coming & Going

Bomaderry is just north of Nowra's centre and is the southern terminus for the CityRail *(**website** www.cityrail.info)* network with frequent trains to Kiama, Wollongong and Sydney. The station is on Railway Street in Bomaderry.

Premier Motor Service *(**website** www.premierms.com.au)* buses stop at Stewart Place in the centre of Nowra.

Sights & Activities

Nowra Wildlife Park

The south coast's largest wildlife park, on the banks of the Shoalhaven River north of Nowra, features a variety of Australian wildlife including koalas, kangaroos, wallabies and wombats.

New South Wales

Rockhill Road, North Nowra
(02) 4421 3949
***Website** www.nowrawildlifepark.com.au*
***Admission** $16*
***Open** 9am-5pm daily*

Rock climbing

The sandstone cliffs around Nowra offer very good rock climbing with some challenging climbs for more advanced climbers, however there isn't so much here for beginners.

Jervis Bay Region (NSW)

Only 20 minutes from Nowra, Jervis Bay is noted for having Australia's whitest sand beaches.

The waters around Jervis Bay are protected as Jervis Bay Marine Park and they are home to dolphins, whales, seals and penguins. The marine park is a popular spot for scuba diving.

Much of the area is national park, with the NSW Jervis Bay National Park in NSW and Booderee National Park in Jervis Bay Territory.

Huskisson and Vincentia are the two main towns in the region although many travellers base themselves in Nowra, which is less than 30 minutes away.

Coming & Going

Nowra Coaches (*(02) 4423 5244; **website** www.nowracoaches.com.au*) run buses linking Nowra and Bomaderry with towns in the Jervis Bay region, including Huskisson and Vincentia. The bus runs four to five times each weekday and two to three times a day on weekends.

Accommodation

Jervis Bay Backpackers

Jervis Bay Backpackers consists of three separate houses in Huskisson and Vincentia on Jervis Bay. The main house on Elizabeth Drive about midway between Huskisson and Vincentia is a six-bed backpackers hostel consisting of one four-bed dorm and a double room in a house near the beach. It has a fully equipped kitchen and a small TV lounge. You will need to phone before arriving to get the address of the property with available accommodation.

Elizabeth Drive, Vincentia
(02) 4441 6880 or 0402 299 309
***Website** www.jervisbaybackpackers.com.au*
***Dorm bed** $25; **double/twin room** $60-100; prices include breakfast*

Maintenance & cleanliness	★★★★
Facilities	★½
Atmosphere & character	★★★★
Security	★
Overall rating	★★★

Sights & Activities

Dolphin & Whale Cruises

Dolphin and whale watching is Jervis Bay's big attraction and cruises depart from Huskisson.

50 Owen Street, Huskisson
(02) 4441 6311 or 1800 246 010
***Website** www.dolphinwatch.com.au*
***Dolphin watching cruise** $24 ($20 students), departs 10am daily; **dolphin & bay cruise** $30 ($24 students), departs 1pm daily; **whale watching cruise** $60 ($47 students), Jun-Jul & mid-Sep to mid-Nov*

Lady Denman Maritime Museum

This museum features the *Lady Denman* Ferry and several other historic vessels as well as exhibits on the heritage of Jervis Bay.

Corner Dent Street and Woollamia Road, Huskisson
(02) 4441 5675
***Website** www.ladydenman.asn.au*
***Admission** $8*
***Open** 10am-4pm daily*

Scuba Diving

Jervis Bay is the best dive destination on the New South Wales coast and it is well known for its marine life and crystal-clear waters. Dive trips can be organised through companies in Huskisson and it is also possible to do a PADI dive course here. **Deep Six Diving Jervis Bay** (*64 Owen Street, Huskisson; (02) 4441 5255; **website** www.deep6divingjervis bay.com.au*) operate scuba diving trips and also run PADI dive courses.

Jervis Bay Territory

Jervis Bay was originally earmarked as Canberra's port with the bay's southern peninsula administered from Canberra as a separate territory to New South Wales. It is now mostly made up of a military base, an Aboriginal community and a national park and it is relatively untouched considering its close proximity to Canberra and Sydney, which are both only three hours away. It is the smallest of Australia's mainland states and territories and has a population of less than 800 permanent residents.

The main attraction here is Booderee National Park (***website*** *www.environment.gov.au/parks/booderee/*), which is known for its wildlife and pristine beaches. Admission to the national park is $10 per car or $3 if you arrive by bus.

Green Patch is one of the more popular spots in the national park. Kangaroos and colourful rainbow lorikeets frequent this lovely beach. Further east is Murrays Beach, another beautiful beach that is a popular swimming spot.

Practical Information

Jervis Bay Visitor Information Centre

Jervis Bay Road, Jervis Bay Territory
☎ *(02) 4443 0977*
Website *www.environment.gov.au/parks/booderee/*
Open *9am-4pm daily*

Accommodation

Although many people stay in Huskisson and Vincentia in the NSW part of Jervis Bay, some people choose to camp in the Booderee National Park. The park has camping areas at Cave Beach and Green Patch; with another area at Bristol Point that is reserved for large groups.

The camping fee is $10-20 for the site plus $5-10 per person.

Ulladulla

Situated between Nowra and Bateman's Bay, this small seaside town is a popular weekend getaway for people from Canberra, Sydney and Wollongong. Most backpackers use Ulladulla as a stop over on the Melbourne-Sydney coastal drive and some people base themselves here to visit Pebbly Beach and Murramarang National Park.

Practical Information

Ulladulla Tourist Information Centre

Princes Highway, Ulladulla
☎ *(02) 4455 1269*
Website *www.ulladulla.info*
Open *Mon-Fri 10am-5pm, Sat-Sun 9am-5pm*

Coming & Going

Premier Motor Services (☎ *13 34 10;* ***website*** *www.premierms.com.au*) stop at Ulladulla on their Sydney-Melbourne run. Buses stop outside the Marlin Hotel (southbound) and outside the Traveland travel agency (northbound).

Accommodation

South Coast Travellers Rest

This is a small hostel in a nice house with polished hardwood floors, a fully equipped kitchen, a TV lounge with a fireplace and a nice outdoor area with hammocks and a barbecue. It has a cosy atmosphere. Guests have free use of bicycles, boogie boards, surfboards and fishing gear. It is located on the highway north of the town centre.

63 Princes Highway, Ulladulla
☎ *(02) 4454 0500*
Website *www.southcoastbackpackers.com.au*
Dorm bed *$25;* ***double/twin room*** *$55*
Reception open *8am-8.30pm*

Maintenance & cleanliness	★★★½
Facilities	★★
Atmosphere & character	★★★
Security	★½
Overall rating	★★★

Murramarang National Park National Park & Pebbly Beach

For many travellers, Pebbly Beach (in Murramarang National Park) is the highlight of the New South Wales South Coast.

Located less than 30 minutes north of Batemans Bay, Pebbly Beach consists of a sheltered cove with a beautiful sandy beach that is frequented by abundant wildlife including scores of kangaroos. This is better than any wildlife park as you get to see animals in their natural habitat rather than in an enclosure.

There are some good hiking trails that depart from Pebbly Beach, including one to Durras Mountain (4 hours return), Depot Beach (30 minutes) and the Discovery Trail (45 minutes). Entry to the park is $7 per car.

Coming & Going

There is no public transport to Pebbly Beach although the YHA in Batemans Bay runs daytrips that allow for five hours in the park. The return trip costs $15.

Accommodation

Most backpackers visit on a day trip from Batemans Bay or Ulladulla, but you can camp at Pebbly Beach. Camping costs $10 per person, in addition to the vehicle entry fee. It is a good idea to book ahead on (02) 4478 6023 if you plan on staying here during peak periods.

Batemans Bay

Batemans Bay is around 150km east of Canberra and is a popular weekend destination for families from the capital. Although there aren't a lot of things to see or do in Batemans Bay, the town is one of the nicer holiday destinations on the coast. Many travellers stay in Bateman's Bay and make a day trip to Pebbly Beach in Murramarang National Park, which is only about 30 minutes north of here.

Practical Information

Batemans Bay Tourist Information Centre

Corner Beach Road & Princes Highway (near McDonalds), Batemans Bay
☎ *(02) 4472 6900*
Website *www.naturecoast-tourism.com.au*
Open *9am-5pm daily*

Coming & Going

Premier Motor Services *(**website** www.premierms.com.au)* run buses to destinations up and down the coast including services to Sydney and Melbourne. There are also daily buses to Canberra run by Transborder Express *(**website** www.transborder.com.au)*. All buses stop at the Orient Street bus bay and Transborder buses also stop at the Shady Willows YHA.

Although there is no regular public transport from Batemans Bay to Pebbly Beach, the Shady Willows YHA runs daytrips that allow for five hours in Murramarang National Park. The return trip costs $15.

Accommodation

Kooringa Coastal Retreat

Kooringa has accommodation in several concrete block buildings across the road from Caseys Beach, about 4km from the centre of Batemans Bay. Shared facilities include a TV lounge plus a riverfront outdoor area with a pool table and table tennis and the dorms have good quality bunk beds. This hostel is often booked by church groups on weekends so it is best to stay on a weekday.

410 Beach Road, Sunshine Bay
☎ *(02) 4472 4942*
Website *www.kooringa.org.au*
Dorm bed *$20*
[car] [TV] [K]

Maintenance & cleanliness	★★½
Facilities	★★
Atmosphere & character	★★
Security	★
Overall rating	★★

Shady Willows YHA

Batemans Bay YHA is a small hostel with a basic kitchen and TV lounge. The accommodation is clean but basic with old lino floors and cheap furniture. It is part of a larger caravan park and guests have use of the swimming pool and barbecue areas. It is in a residential street a short walk from the town centre.

Corner Old Princes Highway & South Street, Batemans Bay
☎ *(02) 4472 4972*
Website *www.shadywillows.com.au*

***Dorm bed** $25-27 ($22-24 HI/YHA);*
***double/twin room** $55 ($48 HI/YHA);*
***camping** $12 per person*
***Credit cards** MC, Visa*
***Reception open** 8am-9pm*

Maintenance & cleanliness	★★½
Facilities	★★½
Atmosphere & character	★★½
Security	★★½
Overall rating	★★½

Eating & Drinking
There are several cheap places to eat on Clyde Street and Orient Street along the waterfront. If you're preparing your own food, you can find Aldi, Coles and Woolworths supermarkets in the Stockland Shopping Centre on the corner of Princes Highway and Beach Road.

Bega
This small town north of Merimbula is best known for its cheese. There is a small hostel here where some travellers make an overnight stop on the Melbourne-Sydney coastal drive.

Practical Information
Bega Visitor Information Centre
Lagoon street, Bega
(02) 6491 7645
***Open** 9am-5pm daily*

Coming & Going
CountryLink *(**website** www.countrylink.info)* buses go to Canberra and Premier Motor Services *(**website** www.premierms.com.au)* stop here en route between Melbourne and Sydney.

Local Transport
Deanes Buslines *(**website** www.deanes-buslines.com.au/southcoast/)* run local bus services in Bega with buses going as far south as Merimbula, Pambula and Eden. Most bus fares within Bega cost between $1.80 and $3.40.

Accommodation
Bega Valley Backpackers
Bega's backpackers' hostel is a purpose-built mud brick building on the northern edge of town and it has a cosy atmosphere. The hostel features a lounge with a pool table, TV and organ and there is a balcony that overlooks a park. The building is well maintained but it is cluttered and furnishings are old and need to be replaced.
Princes Highway, Bega
(02) 6492 3103
***Dorm bed** $20*

Maintenance & cleanliness	★★★
Facilities	★
Atmosphere & character	★★★★
Security	★
Overall rating	★★½

Merimbula
Merimbula is the nicest town on the south coast and it is a popular spot for holidaymakers from Victoria and Canberra. It has nice beaches that are good for fishing, surfing and swimming. Whales can be seen off the coast (Oct-Nov).

Practical Information
Merimbula Visitor Information Centre
Beach Street, Merimbula
(02) 6495 1129
***Website** www.sapphirecoast.com.au*
***Open** 9am-4.30pm daily*

Coming & Going
Rex *(**website** www.rex.com.au)* has daily flights from Merimbula Airport to Melbourne and Sydney. Buses 790, 791 and 792 run into town from the airport but services are infrequent and it is usually easier to just walk the 25 minutes to the YHA hostel. The bus from the airport into the town centre costs $2.70.

Buses run to Melbourne, Sydney and Canberra and stop at the Caltex service station on the Princes Highway.

Local Transport
Deanes Buslines *(**website** www.deanes buslines.com.au/southcoast/)* run local bus services in Merimbula with buses to neighbouring towns including Bega, Eden and Pambula. Most bus fares within Merimbula cost between $1.80 and $3.40.

Accommodation

Wandarrah Lodge YHA

Merimbula's YHA hostel is a good quality purpose-built hostel with facilities that include a kitchen, a lounge/dining room with a pool table, plus a TV room and another TV lounge upstairs with table tennis. It is located on a quiet street across the lake from the town centre (a 15-minute walk away) and just a two-minute walk from the beach.

8 Marine Parade, Merimbula
(02) 6495 3503
***Website** www.yha.com.au*
***Dorm bed** $25.50-30.50 ($22-27 HI/YHA); **double/twin room** $55-65 ($48-58 HI/YHA)*
***Credit cards** MC, Visa*
***Reception open** 8am-11am & 4pm-7pm*

Maintenance & cleanliness	★★★★
Facilities	★★
Atmosphere & character	★★★½
Security	★★
Overall rating	★★★

Eden

If you're taking the coastal route between Melbourne and Sydney, Eden is the first town on the New South Wales coast after crossing the Victorian border. It is a quiet holiday resort with several attractions including the Killer Whale Museum, although it is less touristy than places further up the coast.

Practical Information

Eden Gateway Visitor Information Centre

Princes Highway, Eden
(02) 6496 1953
***Website** www.sapphirecoast.com.au*
***Open** 9am-5pm daily*

Coming & Going

CountryLink *(**website** www.countrylink.info)* buses go to Canberra and Premier Motor Services *(**website** www.premierms. com.au)* buses go to Melbourne and Sydney. Buses stop at the Caltex service station on the Princes Highway.

Deanes Buslines *(**website** www.deanesbuslines.com.au/southcoast/)* run buses to nearby Pambula, Merimbula and Bega.

Local Transport

Deanes Buslines *(**website** www.deanesbuslines.com.au/southcoast/)* run local bus services in Eden with buses going as far north as Pambula, Merimbula and Bega. Most bus fares within Eden cost between $1.80 and $3.40.

Sights

Killer Whale Museum

Eden's top attraction, the Killer Whale Museum has interesting exhibits on Killer Whales and the history of the region's whaling industry.

94 Imlay Street, Eden
(02) 6496 2094
***Website** www.killerwhalemuseum.com.au*
***Admission** $750*
***Open** Mon-Sat 9.15am-3.45pm, Sun 11.15am-3.45pm*

Snowy Mountains

Just six hours drive south of Sydney, the Snowy Mountains includes Australia's highest peak, Mount Kosciuszko.

Settled in the mid-1800s, the area was originally used by cattlemen to feed cattle during long, hot summers. In 1964 the area was declared a National Park and grazing ceased.

The seven ski resorts in the region have more than 50 ski lifts and the official ski season runs from June to October.

Serious adventurers will thrive on challenging treks, rock and mountain climbing, cross country skiing and heart-stopping downhill ski runs. Ski resorts such as Kosciuszko-Thredbo, Perisher Blue, Charlotte's Pass and Mount Selwyn each have their own character and village atmosphere.

If you're coming here for the skiing, the easiest option is to organise a ski package from Canberra or Sydney.

Cooma

Situated midway between Canberra and the Victorian border, Cooma is far enough from the main ski resorts to be an affordable place to base yourself but close enough to the action to enjoy the region.

Practical Information

Cooma Tourist Information Centre

119 Sharp Street, Cooma
☎ *(02) 6450 1742 or 1800 636 525*
***Website** www.visitcooma.com.au*
***Open** 9am-5pm daily*

Coming & Going

CountryLink *(**website** www.countrylink.info)* and Transborder Express *(**website** www.transborderexpress.com.au)* buses go to Canberra, Merimbula and Eden. CountryLink buses stop at the Snowstop Village on Sharp Street (Monaro Highway) and Transborder Express buses stop at Centennial Park on Bombala Street.

Accommodation

Cooma Bunkhouse Backpackers

This motel has small self-contained units for backpackers with dorm beds, TV and a small kitchen. There is a nice courtyard but other facilities are limited and the place feels a bit shabby.
28 Soho Street, Cooma
☎ *(02) 6452 2983*
***Website** www.bunkhousemotel.com.au*
***Dorm bed** $30; single room $40; **double room** $55*
***Credit cards** MC, Visa*
***Reception open** 6.45am-10.30pm*

Maintenance & cleanliness	★★
Facilities	★
Atmosphere & character	★
Security	★½
Overall rating	★½

Sights

Snowy Mountains Hydro-Electric Scheme

One of Australia's biggest engineering feats involves 16 large dams on the Snowy River that produce huge amounts of electricity and irrigate large areas of farmland. The scheme's headquarters is located about 3km from the centre of Cooma and includes a visitor centre with information on touring the facilities.
Yulin Avenue, Cooma
☎ *1800 623 776*
***Website** www.snowyhydro.com.au*
***Open** Mon-Fri 8am-5pm, Sat-Sun 8am-1pm*

Jindabyne

During the ski season this resort town on the shore of Lake Jindabyne is a cheaper place to stay than Thredbo and there are frequent buses and trains that bring it within commuting distance of the ski slopes.

Jindabyne is a nice town and outside the ski season, it is a popular base for bush walking in Kosciuszko National Park.

Practical Information

Snowy Region Visitor Information Centre

Kosciuszko Road, Jindabyne
☎ *(02) 6450 5600*
***Open** winter 8am-5.30pm daily; summer 8.30am-5pm daily*

INTERNET ACCESS

There's an internet café on the ground floor of **Snowy Mountain Backpackers** *(7-8 Gippsland Street, Jindabyne)* and Wi-Fi internet access throughout Jindabyne is provided by **Airlan** *(**website** www.airlan.com.au)*.

Coming & Going

In the ski season (May-Oct) Transborder Express *(**website** www.transborderexpress.com.au)* buses connect Jindabyne with Canberra and Thredbo.

Mojo Snow *(☎ (02) 8558 8888 or 1300 850 380; **website** www.mojosnow.com)* run snow tours with transport from Sydney and accommodation in Jindabyne.

Accommodation

Snowy Mountain Backpackers

Snowy Mountain Backpackers is a very nice hostel right in the town centre. It doesn't have a lot of facilities but there is the usual internet access, laundry, kitchen and TV lounge and the hostel is very clean and well maintained.
7-8 Gippsland Street, Jindabyne
☎ *(02) 6456 1500 or 1800 333 468*
***Website** www.snowybackpackers.com.au*

***Dorm bed** $30-45; **double room** $90-130*
***Credit cards** MC, Visa*
***Reception open** Mon-Sat 9am-1pm*

Maintenance & cleanliness	★★★★★
Facilities	★★½
Atmosphere & character	★★★
Security	★★½
Overall rating	★★★½

Thredbo

Arguably Australia's top ski resort, Thredbo is a party town with 11 ski lifts and plenty of challenging runs. The village is lovely and has a European feel to it. Like any ski resort, it can be expensive, but at least you have the option of commuting in from Jindabyne or even Cooma if you can't afford to stay here. Outside the ski season, Thredbo is a useful base for hiking in Mount Kosciuszko.

Practical Information

Thredbo Tourist Information Centre
6 Friday Drive, Thredbo
(02) 6459 4198
***Website** www.thredbo.com.au*
***Open** summer 9am-5pm daily; winter 8am-6pm daily*

INTERNET ACCESS

There are internet terminals at the **YHA** hostel *(8 Jack Adams Path, Thredbo)* and Wi-Fi internet access throughout Thredbo Village is provided by **Airlan** *(**website** www.airlan.com.au)*.

Coming & Going

In the ski season (May-Oct) Transborder Express *(**website** www.transborderexpress.com.au)* buses connect Thredbo with Jindabyne and Canberra.

Accommodation

Thredbo YHA Hostel

This purpose-built hostel in Thredbo Village is a top quality hostel surrounded by expensive ski lodges and is just a short walk to the centre of the village, but the closest parking is a decent walk away. Facilities include a kitchen, a cosy lounge with a fireplace and a balcony with a barbecue and views of the ski fields. There's also a TV lounge, but it's only open during summer. During the ski season accommodation here is restricted to HI/YHA members and during this period the prices skyrocket.

8 Jack Adams Path, Thredbo
(02) 6457 6376
***Website** www.yha.com.au*
***Dorm bed** $29-44 ($26-40 HI/YHA); **double/twin room** $67-78 ($60-70 HI/YHA); prices are higher during the ski season*
***Credit cards** MC, Visa*
***Reception open** summer 8.30am-10am & 3pm-8pm daily; winter 7am-10am & 4pm-9pm daily*

Maintenance & cleanliness	★★★★
Facilities	★★
Atmosphere & character	★★★★
Security	★★½
Overall rating	★★★½

Hume Highway

The Hume Highway is the quickest route between Melbourne and Sydney. Although it is generally a quick boring route, there are a few places of interest along the way such as Gundagai and Albury.

Goulburn

Goulburn was proclaimed a City by Queen Victoria in 1863 and was the first inland city in Australia. It was also the location of the State's last public hanging. Inspired by the region's sheep farming industry, Goulburn's main landmark is an enormous sheep where many of the Melbourne-Sydney buses stop for a meal break.

Practical Information

Goulburn Tourist Information Centre
201 Sloane Street, Goulburn
(02) 4823 0492
***Website** www.igoulburn.com*
***Open** 9am-5pm daily*

Coming & Going
Goulburn is easily accessible by both rail and bus. Melbourne-Sydney buses stop in the edge of town at the Big Merino, while trains stop in the more centrally situated station on Sloane Street. Goulburn has Countrylink Trains to Melbourne and Sydney and is also the southern terminus for CityRail Trains that provide a cheaper and more frequent, although slower, rail transport option to Sydney and Newcastle.

Gundagai
Gundagai was a popular stopover for early settlers and the town is frequently mentioned in early Australian literature. Australian poet Jack Moses wrote the famous line "and the dog sat on the tuckerbox nine miles from Gundagai" although this was adapted from an earlier poem where "the dog shat on the tuckerbox five miles from Gundagai". The early folk song *Along the Road to Gundagai* is almost as well known among Australians.

The town is best known for the Dog on the Tucker Box monument at Five Mile Creek, 8km north of town, and many people stop here for a bite to eat before continuing on. Gundagai is a nice place with some old historic buildings and there is definitely more to the town than the tacky monument and adjoining souvenir shop.

Practical Information
Gundagai Visitor Information Centre
249 Sheridan Street, Gundagai
☎ *(02) 6944 0250*
Website *www.gundagaishire.nsw.gov.au*
Open *Mon-Fri 8am-5pm, Sat-Sun 9am-5pm*

Coming & Going
Firefly Express *(**website** www.fireflyexpress.com.au)* and Greyhound *(☎ 1300 473 946; **website** www.greyhound.com.au)* buses stop in Gundagai en route between Melbourne and Sydney. Buses stop at the tourist information centre on Sheridan Street.

Accommodation
Blue Heeler Guesthouse
The Blue Heeler is a big old building in the town centre with a big kitchen, TV lounge, games room with table tennis and a big balcony that looks over the main street. It is pretty clean but parts of the hostel need a bit of work.
Sheridan Street, Gundagai
☎ *(02) 6944 2286*
***Dorm bed** $20; **double room** $30-40; **twin room** $30*
TV K

Maintenance & cleanliness	★★★
Facilities	★
Atmosphere & character	★★★½
Security	★½
Overall rating	★★½

Sights
Gundagai Historical Museum
Gundagai's small museum has an interesting collection of exhibits about pioneer life. These exhibits include an old drover's cart, Phar Lap's saddlecloth and the shirt and jacket worn by Kiley of *Kiley's Run* (the poem by Banjo Patterson).
Homer Street, Gundagai
☎ *(02) 6944 1995*
***Admission** $3*
***Open** 9am-3pm daily*

Albury
Sitting on the Murray River just north of Wodonga in Victoria, Albury is a major regional centre that is a good base for exploring the surrounding countryside. At Albury the Murray River has been dammed to form Lake Hume, a popular spot for boating, water-skiing, sail boarding and fishing.

Practical Information
Albury Visitor Information Centre
Gateway Village, Hume Highway, Albury
☎ *(02) 6041 3875 or 1800 800 743*
Website *www.alburywodongaaustralia.com.au*
Open *9am-5pm daily*

Coming & Going
Most Melbourne-Sydney buses and trains pass through Albury. The bus

and train station is on Young Street (Hume Highway) near the town centre.

Accommodation

Albury Motor Village YHA

Albury's YHA hostel is a good quality accommodation option although the complex also includes motel cabins and caravan sites so it doesn't have a proper backpackers' atmosphere. It is a clean and well-maintained place to stay with facilities that include a guest lounge with a TV and basic kitchen facilities plus a swimming pool and barbecue area. The hostel is located in Lavington in Albury's northern suburbs.

372 Wagga Road, Lavington
(02) 6040 2999
Website *www.alburymotorvillage.com.au*
Dorm bed *$28 ($25.20 HI/YHA)*
Credit cards *Amex, Diners, MC, Visa*

Maintenance & cleanliness	★★★★
Facilities	★★
Atmosphere & character	★★★
Security	★★½
Overall rating	★★★

Sodens Australia Hotel

This place is just a few blocks north of the city centre but it is basically just rooms above a pub. It feels very dated with old furnishings and a depressing lifeless atmosphere and there are no common areas for backpackers to hang out in. Although this is Albury's most central backpackers' accommodation option, you're still better off staying at the YHA in Lavington.

Corner David & Wilson Streets, Albury
(02) 6021 2400
Dorm bed *$20;* ***single room*** *$50;* ***double room*** *$60*
Credit cards *Amex, MC, Visa*

Maintenance & cleanliness	★½
Facilities	★
Atmosphere & character	½
Security	★
Overall rating	★

Sights

Albury Botanic Gardens

The 4 ha Albury Botanic Gardens at the western end of Albury's city centre have an impressive collection of plants and features a rainforest walk.

Wodonga Place, Albury
(02) 6023 8769
Website *www.alburycity.nsw.gov.au/gardens/*
Admission *free*

Albury LibraryMuseum

Albury's LibraryMuseum features a gallery with exhibits relating to Albury's history and culture.

Corner Kiewa & Swift Streets, Albury
(02) 6023 8333
Website *www.alburycity.nsw.gov.au/librarymuseum/*
Admission *free*
Open *Mon 10am-7pm, Tue 10am-5pm, Wed-Thu 10am-7pm, Fri 10am-5pm, Sat 10am-4pm, Sun noon-4pm*

Riverina

Watered primarily by the Murrumbidgee River, this area produces citrus and stone fruits, vegetables, wines, rice, canola, wheat, sheep, cattle, pistachio nuts, olives and much more. The fertile farmlands have attracted migrants from many nations, creating a surprising and eclectic mix of cuisines and cultures.

Fruit picking work draws most backpackers here. There is work at most times throughout the year, but December to April is the busiest period when work is easiest to find.

Griffith

Walter Burley Griffin – the American architect and town planner who also designed Canberra – designed Griffith. Although Griffith shares some similarities with Australia's capital, it lacks Canberra's monuments and museums. In other words, it's like Canberra with even less things to see and do.

The surrounding region is home to many orchards, vineyards and even rice paddies and many backpackers come here for fruit picking rather than to see the sights.

Practical Information

Griffith Tourist Information Centre

Corner Banna & Jondaryan Avenues, Griffith
☎ *(02) 6962 4145*
Website *www.riverinatourism.com.au*
Open *9am-5pm daily*

Coming & Going

CountryLink *(**website** www.countrylink.info)* has buses to Mildura in Victoria and trains to Sydney. Greyhound *(☎ 1300 473 946; **website** www.greyhound.com.au)* buses stop in Griffith en route between Adelaide and Sydney.

Accommodation

Griffith International Hostel

The Griffith International is a big concrete block and brick building that provides work and accommodation for working travellers. It features a large kitchen and TV lounge and it has an outdoor barbecue area.
112 Binya Street, Griffith
☎ *(02) 6964 4236*
Website *www.griffithinternational.com.au*
Dorm bed *$20 ($18 VIP) per night, $110 ($105 VIP) per week*
Credit cards *MC, Visa*
Reception open *Mon-Fri 10am-11am & 5pm-6pm, Sat-Sun 5pm-6pm*
TV K L

Maintenance & cleanliness	★★
Facilities	★★
Atmosphere & character	★★
Security	★★★½
Overall rating	★★

Shearer's Quarters at Pioneer Park Museum

The Shearer's Quarters at Pioneer Park Museum consists of accommodation in old corrugated iron buildings arranged around a courtyard. It has a kitchen/TV lounge and the clean bathrooms are in a separate building.
Remembrance Drive, Griffith
☎ *(02) 6962 4196*
Dorm bed *$15 per night, $85 per week*
Credit cards *MC, Visa*
Reception open *9am-4.30pm*
TV K

Maintenance & cleanliness	★★★½
Facilities	★½
Atmosphere & character	★★★½
Security	★
Overall rating	★★

Eating & Drinking

Griffith has a large Italian population that ensures plenty of good pizza and pasta joints.

If you're preparing your own food you can find a **Coles** supermarket in the Griffith Plaza *(corner Crossing & Yambil Streets, Griffith)* and **Woolworths** at the corner of Banna Avenue and Crossing Street.

Sights

Pioneer Park Museum

This open-air museum features restored buildings and working machinery to portray the history of the Murrumbidgee Irrigation Area.
Corner Remembrance & Scenic Drives, Griffith
☎ *(02) 6962 4196*
Admission *$7 ($5 students)*
Open *9am-4.30pm daily*

Hay

This town is home to some interesting museums that showcase the culture of rural Australia and it is one of the more interesting towns in the Riverina region.

Practical Information

Hay Visitor's Centre

Hay's information centre has free showers, which makes it an essential stop if you're travelling by campervan.
407 Moppett Street, Hay
☎ *(02) 6993 4045*
Website *www.visithay.com.au*

Coming & Going

CountryLink *(**website** www.countrylink.info)* buses stop in Hay en route between Mildura and Griffith. Buses stop at the Caltex service station in South Hay.

Sights

Hay Gaol Museum

This old prison has a variety of local history exhibits.

Church Street, Hay
☎ *(02) 6993 4045*
Website *www.visithay.com.au/haygaol.html*
Admission *$2*
Open *9am-5pm daily*

Hay Prisoner of War & Internment Camp Interpretive Centre
Two old Train carriages at Hay's Train station contain exhibits about prisoners of war who were held at Hay during World War II.
Hay Train Station, Murray Street, Hay
☎ *(02) 6993 2112*
Website *www.visithay.com.au/pow.html*
Admission *$2*
Open *9am-6pm daily*

Shear Outback
Hay's top attraction is this flash new museum dedicated to sheep, sheep shearers and sheep dogs.
Corner Cobb & Sturt Highways, Hay
☎ *(02) 6993 4000*
Website *www.shearoutback.com.au*
Admission *$15*
Open *9am-5pm daily; shearing demonstrations 10.30am, 1pm, 3.30pm*

Wagga Wagga

New South Wales' largest inland city lies on the Sturt Highway and many travellers pass through here on the way to somewhere else. There's not a lot to draw you to town but it's a good place to take a break if you're driving.

Practical Information

Wagga Wagga Tourist Information Centre
Tarcutta Street, Wagga Wagga
☎ *(02) 6926 9621*
Website *www.tourismwaggawagga.com.au*
Open *9am-5pm daily*

Coming & Going

Both Wagga's bus and train station are located on Baylis Street although buses better serve the city. Buses run from Wagga Wagga to Adelaide, Canberra, Melbourne, Sydney as well as many regional destinations throughout New South Wales.

Sights

National Art Glass Gallery
Wagga's unique National Art Glass Gallery has two storeys of glass artwork exhibits.
Baylis Street, Wagga Wagga
☎ *(02) 6926 9660*
Website *www.waggaartgallery.org*
Admission *free*
Open *Tue-Sat 10am-5pm, Sun noon-4pm*

Wagga Wagga Art Gallery
Wagga's main art museum has an expansive exhibition space that is host to a programme of temporary exhibits.
Baylis Street, Wagga Wagga
☎ *(02) 6926 9660*
Website *www.waggaartgallery.org*
Admission *free*
Open *Tue-Sat 10am-5pm, Sun noon-4pm*

Outback NSW

Although not as wild as the outback regions in other states, the New South Wales outback is more accessible, particularly if you don't have the time to visit South Australia or the Northern Territory.

Bourke

The Australian expression "back of Bourke" means a long way from anywhere and it is generally assumed that this is where the outback starts. Although Bourke is a remote town by anyone's standards, it is the closest bit of outback to Sydney.

The area around Bourke is surprisingly fertile and there is quite a bit of fruit picking work (Nov-Feb) although there are nicer spots elsewhere in Australia for this sort of work.

Practical Information

Bourke Visitor Information Centre
Anson Street, Bourke
☎ *(02) 6872 2280*
Website *www.visitbourke.com*
Open *9am-5pm daily*

Coming & Going

Most travellers arrive in Bourke either by car or bus. Buses depart from the tourist information centre on Anson Street and run to Dubbo and Sydney.

Accommodation

Gidgee Guesthouse

Burke's centrally located youth hostel is in an historic building that was built as a bank in 1888. Accommodation is arranged around a shady courtyard garden with a barbecue and a fountain.
17 Oxley Street, Bourke
☎ *(02) 6870 1017*
Website *www.gidgeeguesthouse.com.au*
Dorm bed *$25;* ***single room*** *$40;* ***double/twin room*** *$60*
Credit cards MC, Visa
TV K L

Maintenance & cleanliness	★★★
Facilities	★★½
Atmosphere & character	★★★½
Security	★
Overall rating	★★★

Sights

Back O'Bourke Exhibition Centre

The Back O'Bourke Exhibition Centre has displays about outback New South Wales including early explorers, bush poets, outlaws and the development of the grazing industry. It's an excellent museum for such a small town.
☎ *(02) 6872 1321*
Website *www.backobourke.com.au*
Admission *$17.50*

Broken Hill

Broken Hill is the major city in the New South Wales outback. It is a busy mining town and the original home of Broken Hill Proprietary (BHP), now called BHP Billiton, which started out mining silver here and grew to become Australia's largest company.

Broken Hill is a great opportunity to see what life is like in an outback mining town and you can also experience some real outback institutions including the Royal Flying Doctor Service and the School of the Air.

Unusually for an outback mining town, Broken Hill has a thriving arts scene and is home to many artists, the most well-known being Jack Absalom and Pro Hart. Many people come to Broken Hill to visit the city's many art galleries.

Broken Hill runs on South Australian time and also uses South Australia's 08 telephone area code.

Practical Information

Broken Hill Visitor Information Centre

Corner Blende & Bromide Streets, Broken Hill
☎ *(08) 8080 3560*
Website *www.visitbrokenhill.com.au*
Open *8.30am-5pm daily*

Coming & Going

Despite its remote location, Broken Hill is easy to get to. If you're driving in the region around the Murray River then Broken Hill is just a three-hour drive north of Mildura. It is also on the train and bus route that connects Adelaide with Sydney.

Broken Hill's airport handles flights from Adelaide, Melbourne and Sydney but there is no public transport from the airport so you'll have to take a taxi in town.

The train is the best way to get here; the *Indian Pacific* stops here between Adelaide and Sydney. This train is considered one of Australia's classic train journeys, particularly if you travel all the way to Perth. The train station is on Crystal Street in the city centre near the corner of Chloride Street.

Buses stop at the tourist information centre at the corner of Blende and Bromide Streets. Buses go to Adelaide, Dubbo and Mildura. Take a bus to Dubbo to connect with buses to other destinations in New South Wales or Mildura for connections in Victoria.

Accommodation

Tourist Lodge YHA

Broken Hill's centrally located YHA hostel is comprised of two main buildings: a brick building at the front and an old corrugated iron building out back. The hostel is built around a courtyard with a barbecue and swimming pool. Inside there is a plain lounge with a TV and basic cooking facilities – just a toaster, microwave and kettle. The hostel is overdue for renovation and the interior feels very dated.

100 Argent Street, Broken Hill
☎ *(08) 8088 2086*
Website *www.yha.com.au*
Dorm bed *$24.50 ($20 HI/YHA);* ***double room*** *$54 ($50 HI/YHA);* ***twin room*** *$49 ($44 HI/YHA);* ***family room*** *$70 ($60 HI/YHA)*
Credit cards *MC, Visa*
Reception open *7am-11pm*

Maintenance & cleanliness	★★
Facilities	★★★½
Atmosphere & character	★★½
Security	★★
Overall rating	★★

New South Wales

Sights

Broken Hill Regional Art Gallery

Located in the historic Sully's Emporium on Argent Street, the Broken Hill Regional Art Gallery has an important collection of over 1700 Australian artworks including works by many leading Aboriginal artists. It is also noted for its collection of work by local artists including Pro Hart.
404-408 Argent Street, Broken Hill
☎ *(08) 8080 3440*
Website *www.brokenhill.net.au/bhart/main.html*
Admission *$2*
Open *10am-5pm daily*

Broken Hill Heritage Trail

Broken Hill is much more prosperous than most other outback towns and over the years many grand old buildings have been erected. The Broken Hill Heritage Trail is a walking tour that takes you around the city's most historic buildings. You can either take a guided tour or follow the trail yourself.
Tours depart *from the information centre (Corner Blende & Bromide Streets, Broken Hill)*
Tours *Mon, Wed, Fri & Sat 10am*

Line of Lode

Line of Lode is a striking structure that is a memorial to over 800 miners who died working along the Line of Lode. The memorial features audio-visual exhibits and offers spectacular views over Broken Hill.
Federation Road, Broken Hill
☎ *(08)8088 9700*
Admission *free*
Open *10am-10pm daily*

Royal Flying Doctor Service

This outback institution provides medical support in isolated communities. The RFDS maintains visitors centres in several outback towns and this one is a working base with a museum on site. A visit includes a one-hour tour of the base.
Broken Hill Airport
☎ *(08) 8080 3714*
Website *www.flyingdoctor.net/Broken-Hill.html*
Admission *$5.50*
Open *Mon-Fri 9am-5pm, Sat-Sun 11am-4pm*

School of the Air

While the Flying Doctor looks after medical problems in the outback, the School of the Air educates the outback. This unique correspondence school allows visitors to experience what life is like for children in the more remote parts of the outback. It is essential to book ahead through the tourist office.
Lane Street, Broken Hill
Book ahead through the tourist information centre at ☎ *(08) 8080 3560*
Admission *$3.30*
Tours *Mon-Fri 8.20am school days (you must arrive between 8.15am & 8.20am)*

Silverton

Silverton is an easy day-trip from Broken Hill making it an easily accessible yet quintessential outback town. The local pub – the Silverton Hotel – is the main attraction and the classical image of a pub sitting smack-bang in the middle of the desert has made it a popular film set.

Although many travellers spend most of their time in the pub, there is a walking tour around town that passes the more historic buildings and there are also couple of art galleries that are worth visiting.

Practical Information

Silverton Visitor Information Centre

2 Layard Street, Silverton
☎ *(08) 8088 7566*

Website *www.silverton.org.au*
Open *9am-5pm daily*

Coming & Going

Silverton is only a short drive (25km) from Broken Hill and it is best visited by car. Although there is no proper bus service between Broken Hill and Silverton, several companies operate overpriced day tours.

Sights & Activities

Camel Riding

Riding a camel is a great way to experience the outback landscape around Silverton. Silverton Camels (☎ *(08) 8088 5316;* ***website*** *www.silvertoncamels.com)* on Silverton Road, 2km before Silverton, run camel rides that cost $15 for a 15-minute ride and $30 for a one-hour ride.

Silverton Gaol Museum

This museum in Silverton's former four-cell prison features exhibits on Silverton and Broken Hill.
8 Burke Street, Silverton
☎ *(08) 8088 5317*
Website *www.silverton.org.au/museum.htm*
Admission *$2.50*
Open *9.30am-4.30pm daily*

Northern Territory

The Northern Territory covers one-sixth of Australia and is split into two regions: the Top End, which includes the capital Darwin, and Central Australia, home to Uluru and Alice Springs.

The Northern Territory remains Australia's most sparsely populated region and is an area rich in Aboriginal culture and natural attractions.

Darwin

Darwin, with its lush vegetation and diverse population, is a surprisingly vibrant city considering its small size. The city's diversity is reflected in the its array of Asian and Western eating places, ranging from upmarket restaurants to budget-priced food stalls at the Mindil Beach Sunset Markets.

Practical Information

INFORMATION CENTRES & USEFUL ADDRESSES

Darwin Visitor Information Centre
Corner Mitchell & Knuckey Streets, Darwin
4, 5, 6, 8, 10
(08) 8936 2499
Website *www.tourismtopend.com.au*
Open *Mon-Fri 9am-5pm, Sat 9am-3pm, Sun 10am-3pm*

INTERNET ACCESS

Internode *(website https://hotspot.inter node.on.net/)* provides free Wi-Fi access at Darwin Airport. In the city centre there are several Wi-Fi hotspots along Mitchell Street between Knuckey Street and Shenannigans pub, although there are strings attached – you either have to be a customer at one of the cafés and restaurants or pay (around $6 an hour) to access one of the hostel hotspots, most of which are run by **Global Gossip Connect** *(website www.globalgossip.com)*.

Global Gossip
44 Mitchell Street, Darwin
4, 5, 6, 8, 10
(08) 8942 3044
Website *www.globalgossip.com*
Open *Mon-Fri 8am-midnight, Sat-Sun 9am-midnight*

Must do in the Northern Territory

- Feed the fish at Aquascene in Darwin
- Visit the Mindil Beach Markets in Darwin
- Visit Litchfield National Park
- Visit Kakadu National Park
- Canoe or cruise Katherine Gorge in Nitmiluk National Park
- Swim in the thermal pool at Elsey National Park near Mataranka
- Visit Uluru-Kata Tjuta National Park

Coming & Going

AIR

Darwin is the closest Australian city to Asia. Its airport handles many of the cheapest international flights into and out of Australia, making Darwin a popular gateway.

Darwin International Airport (*(08) 8920 1811;* ***website*** *www.darwinairport.com.au)* is 10km northeast of the city centre and is served by the airport shuttle bus *((08) 8981 5066)* that meets most (but not all) flights and drops off at hostels. The one-way fare is $10.

BUS

Greyhound (*1300 473 946;* ***website*** *www.greyhound.com.au)* coaches terminate at the Transit Centre *(69 Mitchell Street, Darwin)*, which is between Chilli's and the Youth Shack.

TRAIN

Great Southern Railway's Ghan train service runs from Darwin to Adelaide three times a week. The station is located at Berrimah in Darwin's outer suburbs. There are no scheduled bus services between the station and the city centre but shuttle buses meet the train; the fare into the city centre is around $8.

HITCHHIKING

The Stuart Highway is the only major road out of Darwin, which makes it fairly easy to hitchhike from. Take bus 5 or 8 to get out on the Stuart Highway from the city centre.

The Stuart Highway continues south to Alice Springs and Adelaide, while the Victoria Highway to Western Australia branches off near Katherine. The Barkly Highway to Cairns and Townsville joins the Stuart Highway at Three Ways, just north of Tennant Creek. If you are heading to Queensland or Western Australia, it would be a good idea to use a destination sign.

Because Darwin is so isolated, you can get some long rides. But you can also get dropped off in some pretty remote places, which means that it's a good idea to take plenty of drinking water.

Local Transport

Darwin has a relatively good bus network for a small city. Darwin's buses are supplemented by minibuses, which

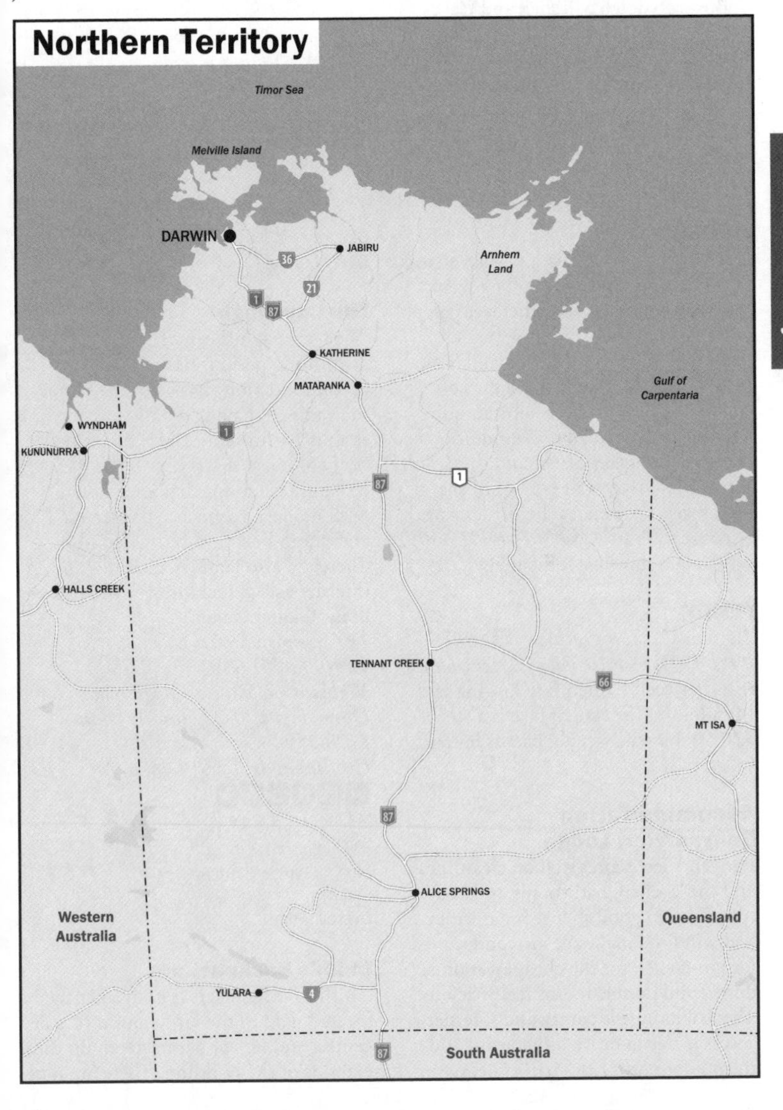

are a good way to get around.

The city centre is small enough to easily walk to most destinations.

BUS

Darwinbus (*(08) 8924 7666; **website** www.nt.gov.au/transport/public/*) operates 14 bus routes, which are a handy way to get around suburban areas. The most useful routes are routes 4 and 10, which run between the city centre and Casuarina Shopping Centre via the Mindil Beach and Parap markets.

Buses go down Mitchell and Cavenagh Streets with the main terminus on Harry Chan Avenue. On weekdays most buses run at half-hourly intervals.

Single fares cost $2 for three hours unlimited bus travel and a pack of 10 tickets costs $18. A Show&Go daily ticket costs $5 and a weekly pass is $15.

MINIBUS

Darwin's minibuses are a bit like a cross between a bus and a taxi. For a flat $3 fare, they will take you wherever you want to go in the city centre, which includes Cullen Bay Marina and Stokes Hill Wharf. Once you leave the central area, prices increase substantially. Minibuses depart from a stand near the corner of Knuckey Street and the Smith Street Mall; they wait here until they have several passengers before leaving.

Arafura Shuttle (*(08) 8981 3300*) is the main minibus company.

FERRY

The Sea-Cat ferry service (*(08) 8941 1991; **website** www.seacat.com.au*) runs between Cullen Bay marina and Mandorah. The return fare is a steep $20.50, but the weekly pass is better value at $62.

Accommodation

Banyan View Lodge

Banyan View scores well on cleanliness and the kitchen, bathrooms and bedrooms are in good shape. Big mirrors and windows make the air-conditioned (or fan-cooled for the cheapest rooms) dorms and double rooms feel spacious. The TV lounge is comfy and internet access is free (a rarity in Darwin) and the outdoor area has a barbecue, swimming pool and a nice spa pool. Banyan View is a part of the YWCA and there is an institutional feel that comes with being run by a large organisation. Party animals might look elsewhere though, as it seems like alcohol is more accepted than encouraged. The hostel has a room full of toys for the little ones so the doors are obviously open for families.

119 Mitchell Street, Darwin
4, 5, 6, 8, 10
(08) 8981 8644
***Website** www.banyanviewlodge.com.au*
***Dorm bed** $21-25 (dry season); $19-23 (wet season); **single room** $60 (dry season); $50 (wet season)*
***Credit cards** MC, Visa*
***Reception open** 8am-noon & 4pm-8pm*

Maintenance & cleanliness	★★★
Facilities	★★★
Atmosphere & character	★★★½
Security	★½
Overall rating	★★★

The Cavenagh

The Cavenagh is centred on a big swimming pool. It has two levels of accommodation that could be better maintained, having a basic kitchen and shabby bathrooms. The accommodation contrasts sharply with the flash bar and restaurant that is complete with modern furniture, flat screen TVs and cheap beer-and-burger combos. There are also laundry facilities and internet access including Wi-Fi ($6 per hour, Global Gossip).

12 Cavenagh Street, Darwin
(08) 8941 6383
***Website** www.thecavenagh.com*
***Dorm bed** $20-27, **double room** $100-150*
***Credit cards** Amex, Diners, MC, Visa*

Maintenance & cleanliness	★★
Facilities	★★★
Atmosphere & character	★★★★½
Security	★½
Overall rating	★★½

Chilli's Backpackers

Chilli's Backpackers is conveniently located next to the Greyhound transit centre, and lots of plants green up the exterior of the building. There are nice open-air common areas on the balcony and the dorms are clean and in fairly good shape with proper inner-spring mattresses, but the overall maintenance could be better (especially the bathrooms). Like most hostels in Darwin, there is internet access plus a kitchen and laundry facilities. There are two spa pools on the rear deck and guests can cool down in the swimming pool at Youth Shack, just up the road.

69a Mitchell Street, Darwin

4, 5, 6, 8, 10

(08) 8980 5800 or 1800 351 313

Website *www.chillis.com.au*

Dorm bed *$19-26 ($17-24 HI/YHA, ISIC, VIP);* ***double/twin room*** *$50-56 ($48-54 HI/YHA, ISIC, VIP); prices include breakfast*

Credit cards *MC, Visa*

TV K L

Maintenance & cleanliness	★★★
Facilities	★★★½
Atmosphere & character	★★★
Security	★★★
Overall rating	★★★

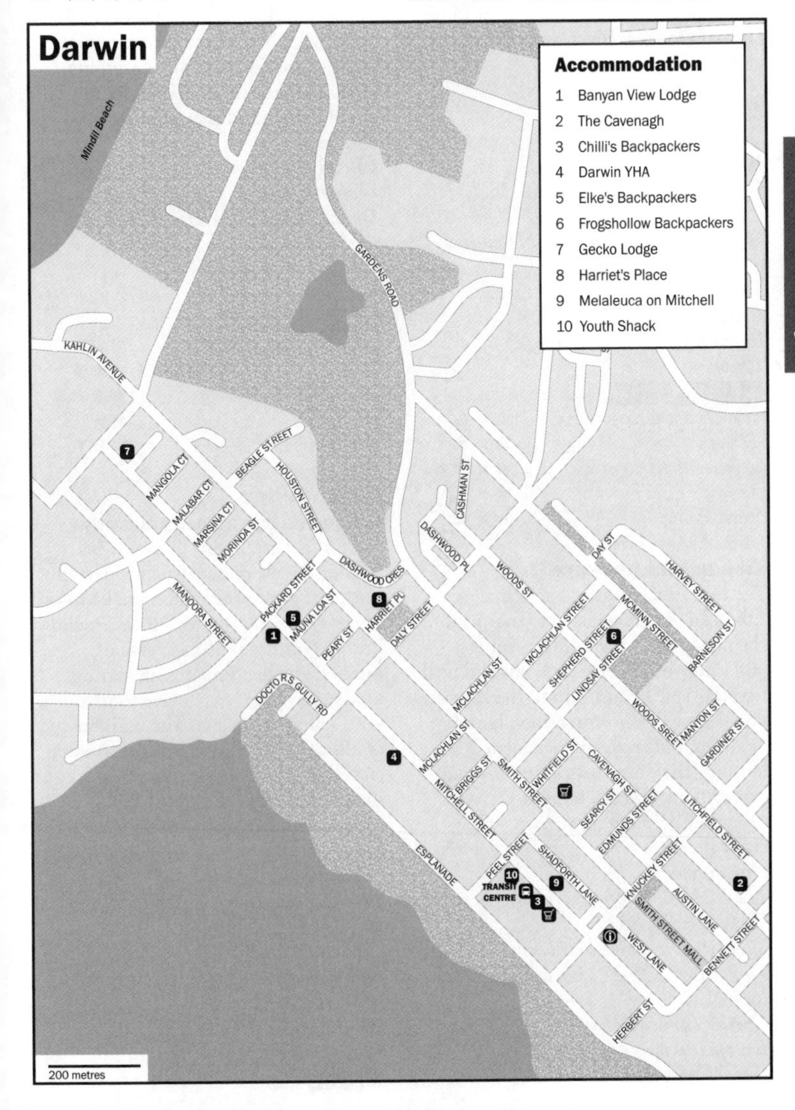

Darwin YHA

Darwin YHA is really an old motel-turned-hostel, with drive-in parking right outside the dorms. There are fridges in the rooms (another leftover from the motel-era), a swimming pool, and a good TV lounge. The excellent bar is the social centre of the hostel but the hostel isn't so lively when the bar is closed. Cleanliness is acceptable, but maintenance is below average, although the building is slowly undergoing a renovation. There are no lockers, which could be an issue for travellers with expensive gadgets.

97 Mitchell Street, Darwin
4, 5, 6, 8, 10
(08) 8981 5385
***Website** www.yha.com.au*
***Dorm bed** $33.50-37 ($30-33.50 HI/YHA) dry season; $21-24 ($18.50-21.50 HI/YHA) wet season; **double/twin room** $87 ($83.50 HI/YHA) dry season; $62.50 ($56 HI/YHA) wet season*
***Credit cards** MC, Visa*
***Reception open** 6am-9am & 6pm-10pm*

Maintenance & cleanliness	★★★½
Facilities	★★★
Atmosphere & character	★★★★½
Security	★★
Overall rating	★★★

Elke's Backpackers

The lush green outdoor area makes Elke's an attractive hostel. Thanks to the newly-renovated dorms, toilets and kitchen, Elke's feels clean and well maintained. In addition to the kitchen, you'll find a swimming pool, laundry facilities, barbecue and a decent TV lounge. The dormitories are air-conditioned, which is essential in Darwin. Overall Elke's is a nice place – especially if you're looking for a peaceful atmosphere.

112 Mitchell Street, Darwin
(08) 8981 8399
***Website** www.elkesbackpackers.com.au*
***Dorm bed** $25-27 ($24-26 HI/YHA, ISIC, VIP)*
***Credit cards** Amex, JCB, MC, Visa*
***Reception open** 6am-9pm*

Maintenance & cleanliness	★★★★½
Facilities	★★★½
Atmosphere & character	★★★
Security	★
Overall rating	★★★½

Frogshollow Backpackers

The hostel is painted half-and-half in pink and green, and the building looks good with its wooden balcony, which is a nice place to eat your home-made meals – a well-equipped kitchen is available for use. We found a pretty unclean and badly maintained bathroom when we visited, but the kitchen and the dorms are at an acceptable level. Lockers are available, so are board games and a swimming pool.

27 Lindsay Street, Darwin
(08) 8941 2600
***Website** www.frogs-hollow.com.au*
***Dorm bed** $23 per night, $140 per week*
***Credit cards** MC, Visa*
***Reception open** 6am-noon & 4pm-9pm*

Maintenance & cleanliness	★★★½
Facilities	★★★½
Atmosphere & character	★★★
Security	★★
Overall rating	★★★½

Gecko Lodge

Gecko Lodge is a small and fairly worn-out hostel with 30 dorm-beds. It's not the cleanest hostel in Darwin; but there's certainly a laid-back atmosphere with a family-feel in this mellow hostel. Comfy old sofas, a small kitchen and accompanying seating area makes it an easy place to socialise with fellow travellers. The maintenance could certainly be better, but to some travellers, the pancake breakfast might make up for it. Outdoors there is a nice swimming pool and barbecue area. You can rent bicycles here for just $12 a day.

146 Mitchell Street, Darwin
(08) 8981 5569
***Website** www.geckolodge.com.au*
***Dorm bed** $18-20; **double room** $55; prices include breakfast*
***Credit cards** MC, Visa*
***Reception open** 8am-7pm*

Maintenance & cleanliness	★★½
Facilities	★★
Atmosphere & character	★★★½
Security	★
Overall rating	★★

Harriet's Place

Harriet's Place is a small hostel that caters primarily to backpackers working in Darwin and it is one of Darwin's few places with weekly rates. It is relatively clean but has basic facilities that include a small kitchen and a nice outdoor TV lounge.

4 Harriet Place, Darwin
☎ *(08) 8981 5694*
Dorm bed *$23-30 per night, $140-200 per week*
Reception open *8.30am-6pm*

Maintenance & cleanliness	★★★
Facilities	★★½
Atmosphere & character	★★★½
Security	★
Overall rating	★★½

Melaleuca on Mitchell

Melaleuca on Mitchell is a new purpose-built hostel right in the hubbub of Mitchell Street's nightlife. It feels surprisingly worn around the edges for a building that's only a few years old, but it is still a top choice. Accommodation is in clean air-conditioned rooms with a locker for each bed but some travellers find the plastic mattresses a bit uncomfortable. The main focus of the hostel is the open-air common area upstairs that features a bar, TV area, swimming pool and spa pool. There are also kitchen and laundry facilities. All things considered it is Darwin's best budget accommodation option.

52 Mitchell Street, Darwin
4, 5, 6, 8, 10
☎ *(08) 8941 7800 or 1300 723 437*
Website *www.momdarwin.com*
Dorm bed *$20-33;* ***double room*** *$55-150*
Credit cards *Amex, Diners, JCB, MC, Visa*
Reception open *24 hours*

Maintenance & cleanliness	★★★½
Facilities	★★★½
Atmosphere & character	★★½
Security	★★★★
Overall rating	★★★½

Youth Shack

Youth Shack is a relatively good hostel that has a big kitchen, TV lounge, pool table and a large air-conditioned lobby with internet access including Wi-Fi ($6 per hour, Global Gossip Connect). There is also a nice swimming pool that attracts guests from the affiliated Chilli's Backpackers just up the road. Although the swimming pool area has the potential to be a sociable spot, the no-alcohol rule keeps a lid on the hostel's atmosphere.

69 Mitchell Street, Darwin
4, 5, 6, 8, 10
☎ *(08) 8923 9790*
Website *www.youthshack.com.au*
Dorm bed *$19 ($18 HI/YHA, ISIC, VIP);* ***double/twin room*** *$50 ($48 HI/YHA, ISIC, VIP)*
Credit cards *MC, Visa*
Reception open *6am-10pm*

Maintenance & cleanliness	★★★
Facilities	★★★
Atmosphere & character	★★★
Security	★★★
Overall rating	★★★

Eating & Drinking

Darwin has a good choice of eating and drinking options.

Smith Street Mall in the city centre has plenty of good value food courts and there are a few fast food places around Knuckey Street.

Mitchell Street is Darwin's main bar and pub strip with **Monsoon's** *(46 Mitchell Street, Darwin)*, **Shennanigans** Irish pub *(69 Mitchell Street, Darwin)* next to the YHA, **Duck's Nuts** *(75 Mitchell Street, Darwin)* and the Lizard Bar in the **Top End Hotel** *(corner Daly & MItchell Streets, Darwin)*, which has Darwin's best beer garden. There are also a couple of other bars and restaurants popular with backpackers, including the **Vic** *(27 Smith Street, Darwin)* in the Smith Street Mall.

If you're preparing your own food, there's a **Woolworths** supermarket on the corner of Cavenagh and Whitfield

Streets and a **Coles** supermarket in the Mitchell Centre next door to Chilli's Backpackers on Mitchell Street.

Sights

Aquascene

Darwin's most unique and fun attraction involves feeding the fish that arrive at each high tide at a small bay in Doctors Gully at the northern end of the city centre. Thousands of milkfish, mullet, catfish and barramundi as well as stingrays come to be handfed.

28 Doctors Gully Road, Darwin
4, 5, 6, 8, 10
(08) 8981 7837
***Website** www.aquascene.com.au*
***Admission** $8*
***Open** at high tide, call (08) 8981 7937 for current opening hours*

Crocodylus Park

This popular wildlife park is home to a variety of Australian wildlife with an emphasis on crocodiles.

815 McMillans Road, Knuckey Lagoon, Berrimah
5, 9
(08) 8922 4500
***Website** www.crocodyluspark.com*
***Admission** $25*
***Open** 9am-5pm daily; tours and feeding: 10am, noon, 2pm*

Fannie Bay Gaol

Fannie Bay Gaol is a former prison that has been turned into a museum. It provides an insight into the early Northern Territory penal system.

Dick Ward Drive, Fannie Bay
4, 6
(08) 8999 8290
***Admission** free*
***Open** 10am-4pm daily*

Mindil Beach Sunset Market

This is one of Australia's top markets with an excellent selection of food stalls plus the usual art and craft items.

Mindil Beach
4, 6
(08) 8981 3454
***Website** www.mindil.com.au*
***Admission** free*
***Open** last Thu Apr-last Thu Oct, Thu 5pm-10pm, Sun 4pm-9pm*

Museum & Art Gallery of the Northern Territory

This is an excellent museum with exhibits focusing on the cultural, social and natural history of the Northern Territory. Some of the better displays include the Aboriginal Art Gallery, exhibits on Cyclone Tracy and a five-metre crocodile named 'Sweetheart'.

Conacher Street, Fannie Bay
4, 6
(08) 8999 8264
***Website** www.nt.gov.au/nreta/museums/*
***Admission** free*
***Open** Mon-Fri 9am-5pm, Sat-Sun 10am-5pm*

Northern Territory Parliament House

Australia's newest parliament house is an imposing modern building at the southern end of Mitchell Street. Guided tours are conducted on Saturdays.

Mitchell Street, Darwin
(08) 8946 1414
***Website** www.nt.gov.au/lant/parlhouse/features.shtml*
***Admission** free*
***Open** 8am-6pm daily; tours 9am, 11am*

Territory Wildlife Park

Run by the NT Parks & Wildlife Commission, this accessible wildlife park features 6km of walking trails as well as an excellent collection of native animals.

Cox Peninsula Road, Berry Springs (45 minutes from Darwin)
(08) 8988 7200
***Website** www.territorywildlifepark.com.au*
***Admission** $20 ($14 students)*
***Open** 8.30am-6pm daily (last entry 4pm)*

The Top End

Australia's Top End juts northward into the Arafura and Timor Seas. Its magnificent scenery includes escarpments, gorges and broad wetlands that experience a spectacular tropical summer season (October to May), when monsoon rains bring on a renewal of lush vegetation; and the cooler dry season (May to September), when it's the best time to pursue outdoor activities.

The Top End's two big attractions are Kakadu and Litchfield National Parks.

Litchfield National Park

Although not as well known as Kakadu, this compact national park also features spectacular scenery including gorges and waterfalls. Litchfield National Park *(**website** www.nt.gov.au/nreta/parks/find/litchfield.html)* is only 45 minutes from Darwin and many travellers visit as a day trip. Because Litchfield is smaller and closer to Darwin than Kakadu, it can become more crowded, but it is still a worthwhile trip.

Because the park is accessible by sealed roads, it is easy to visit year-round but most 4WD tracks within the park are closed during the wet season and some swimming spots are closed after heavy rain.

There are several short hiking trails in the park, mostly 1-3km long; the more spectacular trails go past waterfalls, for which Litchfield is famous.

Litchfield's waterfalls include the Florence, Tjaynera, Tolmer and Wangi Falls. These pretty waterfalls are fantastic swimming spots. Many people also take a dip in the popular Buley Rockhole, but swimming is not permitted in the Reynolds River.

Coming & Going & Local Transport

Hostels in Darwin can book tours to Litchfield. One-day tours generally cost around $100 and visit all the main sights. Two-day tours are only a little more expensive (around $135) and offer a better opportunity to experience the park.

Tour companies running tours of Litchfield National Park from Darwin include **AAT Kings** *(☎ 1300 556 100; **website** www.aatkings.com)*, **Goanna Eco Tours** *(☎ 1800 003 880; **website** www.goannaecotours.com.au)*, **Kakadu Dreams** *(☎ 1800 813 266; **website** www.kakadudreams.com.au)*, **Top End Escapes** *(☎ 1300 736 892; **website** www.topendescapes.com.au)* and **Walaroo Eco Tours** *(☎ (08) 8983 2699; **website** www.litchfielddaytours.com)*.

Accommodation

Most people stay in hostels in Darwin and visit Litchfield as a day trip, although camping is possible within the park. The main camping sites are located at Buley Rockhole, Walker Creek, Florence Falls and Wangi Falls. The Wangi Falls campground is the most crowded, but has better facilities than the others. Camping in the park costs $6.60 per person.

Lower Adelaide River District

The area where the Adelaide River crosses the Arnhem Highway is popular with travellers stopping en route to Kakadu and it is also a popular daytrip from Darwin, only 70km away.

The popular river cruises allow you to see crocodiles in their natural habitat.

Practical Information

Window on the Wetlands Visitor Centre

This excellent information centre has exhibits about the flora and fauna of the wetlands in the Top End.

Arnhem Highway
☎ (08) 8988 8188
***Website** www.nt.gov.au/nreta/parks/find/windowwetlands.html*
***Open** 8am-7pm daily*

Crocodile Cruises

There are several companies that operate cruises departing from the Windows on the Wetlands Visitor Centre and from the Adelaide River Bridge.

These include the **Adelaide River Queen** *(☎ (08) 8988 8144; **website** www.jumpingcrocodilecruises.com.au)* and **Jumping Crocodile** *(☎ (08) 8988 4547; **website** www.jumpingcrocodile.com.au)*. A 90- minute cruise costs from $25 to $30.

Mary River National Park (proposed)

Located between Darwin and Kakadu National Park, the proposed Mary

River National Park *(**website** www.nt.gov.au/nreta/parks/find/maryriver.html)* is an excellent spot for crocodile spotting and bird watching.

The highlight of the park is Bird Billabong, which is a fantastic spot for bird watching.

If you're staying at the Mary River Park, they have their own 500-acre park with an excellent Bamboo Walk (4.5km, 2 hours) that takes you past shady native bamboo to a billabong, returning along the river.

There are a number of excursions that you can organise from **Mary River Park** tourist complex *(Mary River Crossing, Arnhem Highway; ☎ (08) 8978 8877 or 1800 788 844; **website** www.maryriver park.com.au)* that include their popular wildlife river cruise that is ideal for spotting crocodiles and birds and costs $46. It is common to see between 20 and 50 crocodiles if you go on a cruise between April and August (which is the best time of year to visit). Mary River Park also runs sunset star-gazing and dinner cruises ($79.50).

Coming & Going

Greyhound Australia *(☎ 1300 473 946 (1300 GREYHOUND); **website** www.grey hound.com.au)* buses stop at Mary River Park tourist complex on their Darwin to Kakadu service. Adventure Tours *(☎ 1300 654 604; **website** www.adven turetours.com.au)* have an overnight stop at Point Stuart Wilderness Lodge.

Accommodation

Point Stuart Wilderness Lodge

This hostel/campground has nice air-conditioned dormitories with en suite bathroom facilities plus a good swimming pool and a bar/restaurant, but there are no other common areas apart from the pool and bar. It is a bit off the beaten track but abundant wildlife means that you have a good chance of seeing wallabies hopping around the grounds. Adventure Tours maintain a permanent camp here so you'll stay here if you take one of their tours.

Point Stuart Road off Arnhem Highway, Mary River Wetlands
☎ (08) 8936 1311 or 1800 654 604
***Website** www.pointstuart.com.au*
***Dorm bed** $32; **double room** $145-205; **twin room** $85; **camping** $12-15 per person*
***Credit cards** MC, Visa; 2% credit card surcharge*
***Reception open** 7.30am-5pm*

Maintenance & cleanliness	★★★★
Facilities	★★
Atmosphere & character	★★
Security	★
Overall rating	★★★

Kakadu National Park

The World Heritage listed Kakadu National Park *(**website** www.environ ment.gov.au/parks/kakadu/)* is regarded by many to be Australia's best national park.

At almost 20,000km², Kakadu covers a large area but only a relatively small part of the park can easily be explored in a car.

Many travellers organise tours from Darwin that take in the main attractions, but independent travel is also possible with accommodation and other services available from areas within Kakadu.

Jabiru is the main town serving the park and it has accommodation, shops, a visitor centre and an airport. The East and South Alligator areas are two other accessible parts of Kakadu, each with accommodation and other services.

Kakadu is a very different park in the wet (Nov-Mar) and dry (Apr-Oct) seasons. Most backpackers visit in the dry when it is easier to travel and more comfortable. However Kakadu is much greener in the wet when it teems with wildflowers and the waterfalls are at their most powerful, but it is harder to get around as some roads are closed – even to 4WD vehicles. A wider variety of boat cruises operate during the wet and are an enjoyable way to see Kakadu at this time of year.

Tours from Darwin operate throughout the year and they tailor their itinerary to capture the best sights in each season.

Highlights of the park, which are accessible in both the wet and dry seasons, include the Mamukala Wetlands, Nourlangie rock art site and Yellow Water.

Entry to the park is free.

Practical Information

Bowali Visitor Centre

The Bowali Visitor Centre has a café, shop, theatrette and a small museum with exhibits on the park and Aboriginal culture.

Kakadu Highway, Jabiru
☎ *(08) 8938 1120*
Website *www.environment.gov.au/parks/kakadu/*
Admission *free*
Open *9am-5pm daily*

Coming & Going & Local Transport

Greyhound (☎ *1300 473 946 (1300 GREYHOUND);* ***website*** *www.greyhound.com.au)* buses operate between Darwin and Kakadu National Park with stops at Jabiru and other areas of interest. The bus service is a little like a mini-tour and is included in some of Greyhound's bus passes.

Other options include a wide range of tours that can be booked from Darwin including a good selection catering to backpackers. Tour prices range from $460 for a three-day tour to more than $1000 for a five-day 4WD safari. A day trip from Darwin starts at around $100, although one day isn't long enough to properly experience Kakadu.

Kakadu Dreams (☎ *1800 813 266;* ***website*** *www.kakadudreams.com.au)* is one of the most popular tour companies with backpackers. They have three-day tours for $460 and five-day tours for $700. Other tour companies running tours from Darwin include AAT Kings (☎ *1300 556 100;* ***website*** *www.aatkings.com)*, Aussie Adventures (☎ *1300 721 365;* ***website*** *www.aussieadventure.com.au)*, and Top End Escapes (☎ *1300 736 892;* ***website*** *www.topendescapes.com.au)*.

Accommodation

Gagudju Lodge – Cooinda YHA

Gagudju is a large accommodation complex that attracts lots of tourists but the backpackers' accommodation here isn't as well maintained as the rest of the resort. The clean air-conditioned dorms are located in a set of prefabricated units that feel a bit barren and there is a small, shabby camp-kitchen with a barbecue but few other facilities. However there are many other amenities throughout the resort that include an ATM, internet access, a nice swimming pool and a good bar/restaurant (but with prices generally not suited to budget travellers).

Cooinda, off Kakadu Highway, Kakadu National Park
☎ *(08) 8979 0145 or 1800 500 401*
Website *www.gagudjulodgecooinda.com.au*
Dorm bed *$35 ($31.50 HI/YHA);* ***double room*** *$80 ($70 HI/YHA)*
Credit cards *Amex, Diners, JCB, MC, Visa*
Reception open *6.30am-7pm (wet season); 6am-10pm (dry season)*

Crocodile Warning

Kakadu is a great place to spot crocodiles – unfortunately this also makes swimming in the park's waters dangerous.

Some visitors risk swimming at some beautiful spots such as Gubara, Maguk Gorge, Jim Jim Falls and Twin Falls. However freshwater crocodiles live here and the more dangerous estaurine (or saltwater) crocs sometimes move into these areas.

These areas are surveyed at the opening of each dry season and information is posted next to crocodile warning signs at each gorge and plunge pool area.

Park rangers recommend that the only safe places to swim are the pools at the hostels and the swimming pool at Jabiru.

PHOTO: TIM UDEN

Northern Territory

Maintenance & cleanliness	★★★
Facilities	★★★
Atmosphere & character	★★½
Security	★
Overall rating	★★½

Kakadu Lodge

Kakadu Lodge is a large caravan park complex that also includes backpackers' accommodation in several concrete-block lodges with clean air-conditioned dorms. There is also a small camp kitchen (no oven) with a TV and laundry facilities but the nicest part of the park is the swimming pool and the poolside bar and bistro. There is very little character around the backpackers' accommodation block but the area around the poolside bar has a much better atmosphere than most other caravan park bars.

Jabiru Drive, Jabiru
(08) 8979 2422
Website *www.auroraresorts.com.au*
Dorm bed *$35*
Credit cards *Amex, Diners, MC, Visa*
Reception open *8am-6pm, check in at bar till 10pm*

Maintenance & cleanliness	★★★½
Facilities	★★★½
Atmosphere & character	★★
Security	★
Overall rating	★★½

Lakeview Park YHA

Lakeview Park is a large accommodation complex in Jabiru that offers a range of accommodation options including the Bush Bungalows for backpackers. The Bush Bungalows are unique structures that have good ventilation and a tent-like roof that is high enough to accommodate a ceiling fan. Each of these structures accommodates four people in two bunk beds and includes a fridge and tea and coffee making facilities. It is a nice place to stay but like many caravan park/hostels the focus isn't solely on the backpacker so it doesn't really have a hostel feel to it.

Lakeside Drive, Jabiru
(08) 8979 3144
Website *www.lakeviewkakadu.com.au*
Dorm bed *$27-30;* ***double room*** *$67.50-110*
Credit cards *MC, Visa*
Reception open *Jan-Mar 8am-6pm; Apr-Nov 7am-7pm; Dec 8am-6pm*

Maintenance & cleanliness	★★★
Facilities	★½
Atmosphere & character	★★½
Security	★
Overall rating	★★½

Mary River Roadhouse

Mary River Roadhouse is the best value of the Kakadu hostels and it is just a couple of kilometres from the park's southern entrance. However it is very basic with accommodation in air-conditioned pre-fabricated units like you find on a construction site. Atmosphere is almost non-existent and there isn't much in the way of facilities but there is a swimming pool and small shop where you can buy food and drinks.

Kakadu Highway via Pine Creek
(08) 8975 4564
Dorm bed *$17;* ***single room*** *$30;* ***double/twin room*** *$40*
Credit Cards *MC,Visa*
Reception open *7am-11pm*

Maintenance & cleanliness	★★
Facilities	★½
Atmosphere & character	★
Security	★
Overall rating	★½

Sights

Jim Jim Falls

The spectacular Jim Jim Falls stop flowing in the dry season, which unfortunately is the only time when the falls are accessible by road (4WD only). Kakadu Air (*1800 089 113;* ***website*** *www.kakadutours.com.au)* operate scenic flights in the wet season, which cost $195 and is the only way to see the falls in their full glory. Flights depart from the Cooinda and Jabiru East airstrips.

103km south of the Bowali Visitor Centre, Jim Jim, Kakadu National Park

Mamukala wetlands

The Mamukala wetlands is a great place to see bird life including thousands of magpie geese that flock here towards the end of the dry season

(Sep-Oct). There is an observation platform and a couple of short walks (1km; 20 mins and 3km; 2 hours) that allow you to see more of the wetlands.
Arnhem Highway, 7km east of South Alligator River

Nourlangie rock art site

A short (1.5km) walk takes you past the exceptional Nourlangie rock art site and there is also a short climb to the Gunwarddehwardde lookout with views of the surrounding area. Rangers give talks about Aboriginal art and culture here three times a day during the dry season.
20km south of the Bowali Visitor Centre, Nourlangie area, Kakadu National Park

Ubirr

At Ubirr a short walk (1¼km; 1 hour) takes you past Aboriginal rock art sites and climbs to a lookout offering fantastic views that are particularly magnificent at sunset.
East Alligator area, Kakadu National Park
***Open** Apr-Nov 8.30am-sunset; Dec-Mar 2pm-sunset*

Warradjan Aboriginal Cultural Centre

The Warradjan Aboriginal Cultural centre features displays on Aboriginal culture and it also includes a small video theatre.
Cooinda, off Kakadu Highway 50km south of Bowali Visitor Centre, Kakadu National Park
☎ *(08) 8979 0051*
***Admission** free*
***Open** 9am-5pm daily*

Yellow Water

The Yellow Water wetlands are a popular spot to see crocodiles as well as bird life including Jabiru storks. The seasons dictate how you will visit this area. A boardwalk provides a good vantage point for observing wildlife during the early dry season; later in the dry (when the water has dried up) there is a walk (1km) across the floodplains to a viewing platform. In the wet you'll need to take a cruise on the river, although these cruises operate year round.
Cooinda, off Kakadu Highway 50km south of Bowali Visitor Centre, Kakadu National Park
☎ *(08) 8979 0145*
***Website** www.yellowwatercruises.com*
***Cruises cost** $50-70*

Katherine

Katherine is the most popular stop on the highway between Darwin and Alice Springs. The town is nothing special, but it's a good place to base yourself if you want to explore the nearby Katherine Gorge.

Practical Information

Visitor Information Centre

Corner Katherine Terrace & Lindsay Street, Katherine
☎ *(08) 8972 2650*
***Website** www.visitkatherine.com.au*
***Open** Mon-Fri 8.30am-5pm*

Coming & Going

BUS

Greyhound (☎ *1300 473 946 (1300 GREYHOUND); **website** www.greyhound.com.au*) buses travelling between

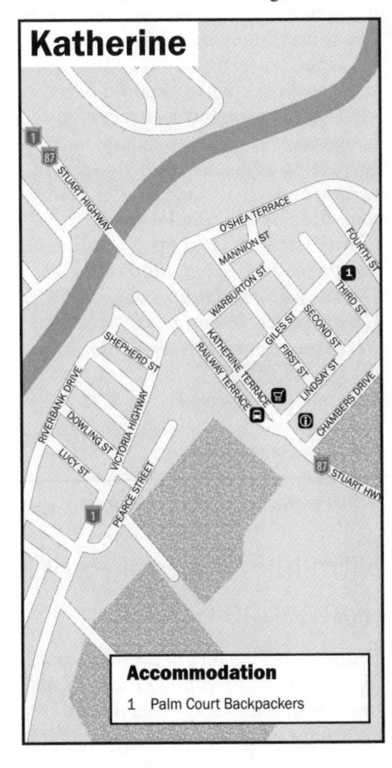

Alice and Darwin stop at the BP service station on Katherine Terrace (Stuart Highway) opposite the tourist information centre. Buses go to Alice Springs, Broome and Darwin.

TRAIN

The *Ghan (**website** www.gsr.com.au)* stops in Katherine en route from Adelaide to Darwin. The station is 8km outside town on the Victoria Highway. Travel North *(☎ (08) 8971 9999 or 1800 089 103; **website** www.travelnorth.com.au)* run a shuttle bus between the train station and the town centre, which costs $12. The bus departs from the BP service station.

Northern Territory

Accommodation

Palm Court Backpackers Hostel

Backpackers travelling through Katherine might end up spending the night at Palm Court, simply because the town doesn't have any alternatives – at the time of writing all other hostels were closed. Palm Court feels a bit shabby, the maintenance could definitely have been better, and the overall cleanliness is not exactly top-notch. However, you'll find most of the facilities a backpacker-place should have: kitchen, laundry, internet access and book-swap. There's also a quite nice swimming pool area, with wooden seating and a barbecue. All the dorms have fridges, TVs and lockers.

Corner Gilles & Third Streets, Katherine
☎ (08) 8972 2722 or 1800 626 722
***Dorm bed** $24; **double room** $58-82*
***Credit cards** Amex, Diners, MC, Visa*
***Reception open** 7am-1pm & 3pm-7pm*

Maintenance & cleanliness	★★
Facilities	★★★½
Atmosphere & character	★½
Security	★½
Overall rating	★★

Nitmiluk National Park (Katherine Gorge)

Nitmiluk National Park *(**website** www.nt.gov.au/nreta/parks/find/nitmiluk.html)* in the Katherine Gorge area is well known for its system of 13 giant gorges.

The park offers a wide range of hiking trails ranging from walks lasting a couple of hours to challenging 65km overnight hikes. An easier – and more popular – option is a cruise on the Katherine River.

Many of the shorter walks depart from the visitors centre. These include the Butterfly Gorge, Lookout Loop and Windolf walks. The demanding **Butterfly Gorge walk** *(12km; 4½ hours)* takes you through a varied landscape and ends at a good swimming spot. The **Lookout Loop** *(3.6km; 2 hours)* takes you up the side of the gorge and offers great views of the river. The **Windolf walk** *(8.4km; 3½ hours)* features Aboriginal art and also has lovely views.

The most taxing of the overnight hikes is the **Jatbula Trail** *(65km; 5 days)*. This one-way hike starts at the visitor centre and takes you past rainforests, gorges and waterfalls before finishing at Edith Falls. It is essential to register with the visitors centre if you're walking the Jatbula Trail or any of the other overnight hikes in Nitmiluk.

The park is also a popular spot for canoeing; but it can be tough going at times, as you'll have to carry your canoe over the rocks that separate each gorge. There are several camping areas set aside for canoeists, although registration is required at the visitor centre.

Boat cruises on the Katherine River are popular with many tourists and are the easiest way to see the gorge, but they are touristy and it can feel like you're being rushed. The two-gorge cruise (1½-2 hours) costs $53; the three-gorge cruise (3½-4½ hours) costs $69 and the five-gorge cruise (8 hours) costs $110. Cruises are operated by **Nitmiluk Tours** *(☎ (08) 8972 1253 or 1300 146 743; **website** www.nitmiluktours.com.au)*, who also organise canoe rental ($29.50-39.50 for four hours).

May to Sep is the best time to visit. In the wet season, parts of the park are subject to flooding and some trails, including the Jatbula Trail, are closed.

Practical Information

Nitmiluk Visitor Centre

Gorge Road, Nitmiluk National Park
☎ (08) 8972 3150

***Website** www.nitmiluktours.com.au*
***Open** 7am-6pm daily*

Coming & Going

Travel North (☎ *1800 089 103; **website** www.travelnorth.com.au)* operates a bus service connecting the national park and Katherine. The return fare is $24.

Mataranka & Elsey National Park

This small village is a handy base for exploring the nearby Elsey National Park where the main attractions are the Mataranka Homestead and swimming at the thermal pool.

Elsey National Park is 9km from Mataranka. It features a palm forest that is home to wildlife including hundreds of bats and it feels like a bit of an oasis, particularly if you've just arrived from Alice Springs. There is great swimming at the thermal pool, Bitter Springs and also in the Roper River.

Coming & Going

Greyhound (☎ *1300 473 946 (1300 GREYHOUND); **website** www.greyhound.com.au)* buses stop at both the town centre and the homestead on their Alice Springs-Darwin run. It sometimes stops for enough time to see the thermal pool, but usually not for long enough to get wet.

Accommodation

Mataranka Homestead

This hostel offers very basic accommodation in the original homestead that was established in 1916. Accommodation is in mostly small two-bed dorms although there are a couple of larger ones. Facilities include a laundry, limited kitchen facilities and a bar, restaurant and a shop. Camping is also possible at the homestead complex. It is 9km from Mataranka town and right next to Elsey National Park and only 100 metres from the thermal springs.

Homestead Road, Mataranka
☎ *(08) 8975 4544 or 1800 754 544*
***Dorm bed** $19; **twin room** $42; **camping** $20-24 (for 1-2 people)*
***Credit cards** MC, Visa*
***Reception open** peak season 7am-8pm daily; off-peak season 9am-5pm daily; check in at bar when the reception is closed*

Maintenance & cleanliness	★
Facilities	★
Atmosphere & character	★★
Security	★
Overall rating	★★½

Central Northern Territory

There's not a lot to see between Alice Springs and Katherine and many travellers travel straight through without stopping, but it's a long way so you may want to make a few stops en route.

Tennant Creek

In 1872 a station was established 11km north of town to service the overland telegraph and in the 1930s gold was discovered in the area and the town developed around this time.

Although there are only 3500 people in Tennant Creek, it is the Northern Territory's fifth-largest town. It is 500km north of Alice Springs and 1000km south of Darwin.

If you're travelling on the Stuart Highway between Alice Springs and Darwin you may want to break your journey at this small mining town, even though there isn't really a lot to see here. It's the only town of any size for at least 500km in any direction and it has ATMs, grocery stores and a hospital.

Practical Information

Tennant Creek Tourist Information Centre

58 Peko Road, Tennant Creek
☎ *(08) 8962 3388*
***Website** www.tennantcreek.nt.gov.au/visit-us/*
***Open** Jan-Oct Mon-Fri 9am-5pm, Sat 9am-noon; May-Sep 9am-5pm daily; Oct-Dec Mon-Fri 9am-5pm, Sat 9am-noon*

Coming & Going

Greyhound *(☎ 1300 473 946 (1300 GREYHOUND); **website** www.greyhound.com.au)* buses to Alice Springs, Darwin and Townsville stop at the BP service station at 216 Patterson Street.

Accommodation

Tennant Creek has two basic hostels that are acceptable if you just need somewhere to stop for the night. However travellers with a campervan (or a car and a tent) are better off avoiding Tennant Creek altogether and camping 100km north of town at Banka Banka.

Garyochan's Backpackers

Garyochan's Backpackers is comprised of three buildings – two with en suite twin rooms and the other with common areas that include a TV lounge and kitchen. There's also a barbecue area near the car park. It is nothing special but it will do if you just need to stop for the night.

67 Schmidt Street, Tennant Creek
☎ (08) 8962 2024
***Dorm bed** $20; **single room** $38; **double/twin room** $40*

Maintenance & cleanliness	★½
Facilities	★★½
Atmosphere & character	★★★½
Security	★
Overall rating	★★

Tourist's Rest Youth Hostel

Tourist's Rest Youth Hostel is a shabby hostel that offers very basic accommodation. It has a barren common room with a kitchen, internet access and a TV plus an old above-ground swimming pool.

Corner Windy & Leichhardt Streets, Tennant Creek
☎ (08) 8962 2719
***Website** www.touristrest.com.au*
***Dorm bed** $20 ($18 HI/YHA, VIP; $19 ISIC); **double/twin room** $42 ($40 HI/YHA, VIP; $38 ISIC)*
***Credit cards** MC,Visa; $2 credit card surcharge*
***Reception open** 9am-1pm & 4pm-11pm*

Maintenance & cleanliness	★½
Facilities	★★½
Atmosphere & character	★★
Security	★
Overall rating	★★

Sights

Battery Hill Mining Centre

Battery Hill was named after the stamp battery that was built in 1939 to provide processing facilities for Tennant Creek's many small gold mines. The plant operated until the 1980s, although it closed during World War II and also for a few years in the late 1950s. The centre has a museum and you can take underground mine tours.

Peko Road, Tennant Creek
☎ (08) 8962 1281 or 1800 500 879
***Admission** free; underground tour $20*
***Open** 9am-5pm daily*

Devils Marbles

This rock formation is located about 100km south of Tennant Creek. There is a short walking track (30 minutes) with signs explaining how the 'marbles' were formed. There isn't enough to keep you busy for very long, but it is definitely worth a stop to break the journey.

Alice Springs

With a population of about 28,000, Alice Springs is much like any other small country town, but it is the only major town in central Australia and is almost 1000km to the nearest town of a similar size.

Alice is a good spot to explore the surrounding area. It lies at the foot of the world's oldest mountain range, the MacDonnell Ranges, and is a popular stopping-off point for travellers on their way to Uluru-Kata Tjuta National Park. Attractions and diversions include the Alice Springs Desert Park and several outback institutions such as the School of the Air and the Royal Flying Doctor Service.

Practical Information

Visitor Information Centre

Gregory Terrace, Alice Springs
☎ (08) 8952 5800

***Website** www.centralaustraliantourism.com*
***Open** Mon-Fri 8.30am-5.30pm, Sat-Sun 9am-4pm*

INTERNET ACCESS

Global Gossip have internet access at Backpackers World Travel *(70 Todd Street, Alice Springs; ☎ (08) 8953 0666; **website** www.backpackersworld.com.au)* and also Annie's Place hostel on Traeger Street.

If you're travelling with your own computer there free Wi-Fi access at Alice Lodge and Alice's Secret hostels. Wi-Fi is also available at Annie's Place, Haven Resort and the YHA although you'll need to pay to use it at these hostels.

Coming & Going

Alice Springs enjoys good transport connections with an airport plus buses and trains to Adelaide and Darwin.

AIR

Alice Springs Airport *(☎ (08) 8951 1211; **website** www.alicespringsairport.com.au)*, 15km south of town, has direct flights to most major cities in Australia.

Some hostels arrange pick-ups from the airport, particularly if several people book in advance, otherwise the best way into town from the airport is by the airport shuttle bus *(☎ (08) 8953 0310)* that meets most flights. It will drop you off at your hostel and costs $15. A taxi will cost about twice this, but may work out better value between a few people.

BUS

Greyhound *(☎ 1300 473 946 (1300 GREYHOUND); **website** www.greyhound.com.au)* buses stop at 113 Todd Street and go to Adelaide and Darwin.

TRAIN

The Ghan is one of Australia's great train journeys and it stops in Alice en route from Adelaide to Darwin. The train station is on George Terrace, about a 20-minute walk from the town centre.

Local Transport

Alice Springs has a local bus service *(**website** www.alicesprings.nt.gov.au/astc_site/services/public_transport)*, but it runs infrequently making it a difficult way to get around. There are four routes, the east route is handy for Alice Lodge and Alice's Secret and the south route goes to Toddy's hostel and Heavitree Gap Outback Lodge. Buses terminate on Railway Terrace near the Coles Complex.

The standard $2 fare gives you unlimited bus travel for three hours; a daily ticket costs $5; a weekly ticket costs $15 and a pack of 10 three-hour tickets costs $18.

Many travellers rent a bike or walk around town, although a lot of places are a long walk so it's a good idea to take along a bottle of water.

Accommodation

Alice Lodge Backpackers

Alice Lodge is a small hostel on a quiet residential street. It is basically a big house with facilities that include a small fully-equipped kitchen, laundry, a TV lounge and free internet access (including wireless) and there is also a backyard with a swimming pool. The place may not seem that flash, but it is relatively clean and the staff and other guests are friendly and welcoming.

4 Mueller Street, Alice Springs
East
☎ *(08) 8953 1975 or 1800 351 925*
***Website** www.alicelodge.com.au*
***Dorm bed** $20-24; **double room** $55; prices include breakfast*
***Credit cards** Amex, MC, Visa*
***Reception open** 8.30am-1.45pm & 4.30pm-7pm*

TV K L

Maintenance & cleanliness	★★½
Facilities	★★★
Atmosphere & character	★★★★
Security	★★
Overall rating	★★★

Alice Springs YHA

Alice Springs YHA is a nice hostel with a great location – it's the most centrally located hostel in town. The hostel is built in an old outdoor cinema with common areas like the kitchen, dining room, internet access (including Wi-Fi $4 per hour/$15 24 hours; Global Gossip Connect) and TV lounge in the original building and newer purpose-built accommodation. It has a nice outdoor setting centred on a swimming pool. It is clean and well-maintained but the atmosphere can feel a bit dull.

Corner Leichhardt & Parsons Streets, Alice Springs
☎ *(08) 8952 8855*
Website *www.yha.com.au*
Dorm bed *$21.50-28 ($19-25 HI/YHA);* ***double/twin room*** *$67 ($60 HI/YHA)*
Credit cards *MC, Visa*
Reception open *7.30am-8.30pm*

Maintenance & cleanliness	★★★½
Facilities	★★★
Atmosphere & character	★★½
Security	★★½
Overall rating	★★★

Alice's Secret Travellers Inn

This is a small hostel in a house in a quiet part of Alice Springs that has a good atmosphere. The hostel's

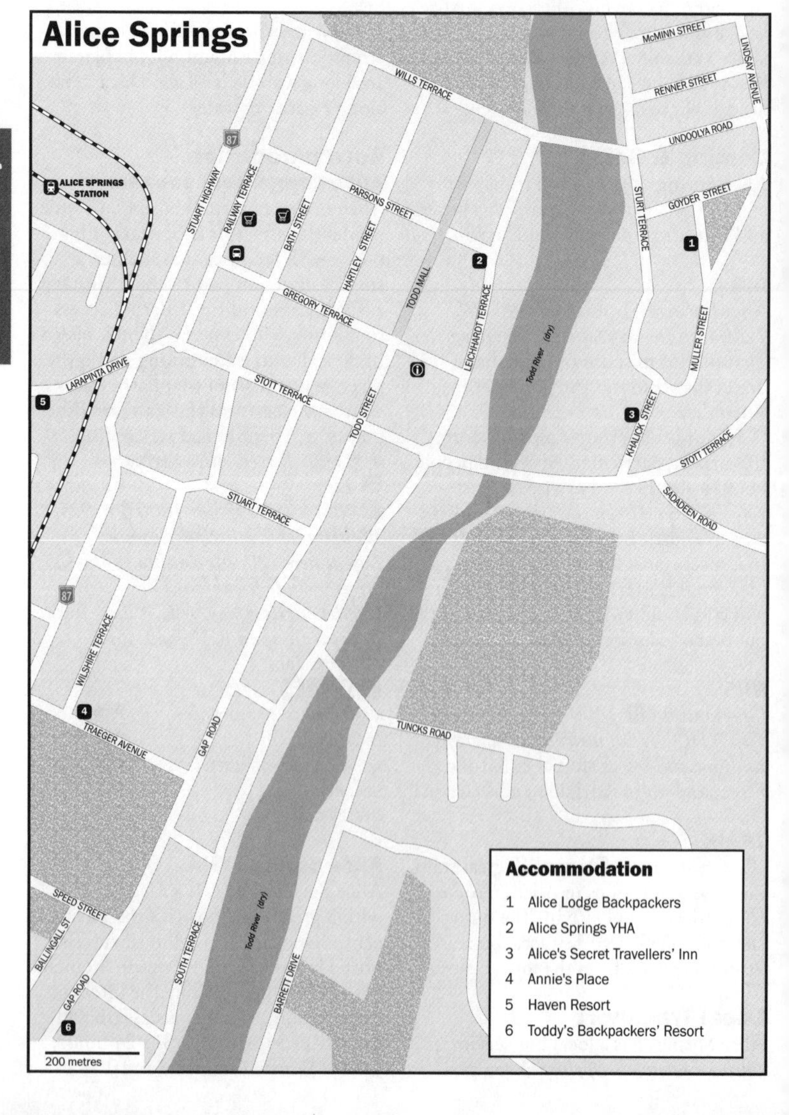

Northern Territory

amenities include a small TV lounge, a fully-equipped kitchen, internet access (including free Wi-Fi) and a backyard with a swimming pool, barbecue and trampoline.
6 Khalick Street, Alice Springs
East
(08) 8952 8686 or 1800 783 633
Website *www.asecret.com.au*
Dorm bed *$19-23 ($18-22 HI/YHA, ISIC, VIP);* ***single room*** *$40 ($38 HI/YHA, ISIC, VIP);* ***double room*** *$52-60 ($50-58 HI/YHA, ISIC, VIP); prices include breakfast*
Credit cards *MC, Visa*
Reception open *5.30am-6.30am & 8am-1pm & 4pm-7pm*

Maintenance & cleanliness	★★½
Facilities	★★★
Atmosphere & character	★★★
Security	★
Overall rating	★★½

Annie's Place

Annie's Place offers very good value accommodation on a quiet street near the hospital. The hostel feels a bit worn but is clean enough for most travellers. Facilities include a basic kitchen (no oven), a TV lounge, laundry and a swimming pool; however the hostel's best feature is the excellent bar that serves great value $5 meals. All the rooms are air-conditioned with TVs and most have en suite bathrooms.
4 Traeger Avenue, Alice Springs
(08) 8952 1545
Website *www.anniesplace.com.au*
Dorm bed *$18 ($17 VIP);* ***double room*** *$50-60*
Credit cards *MC, Visa*
Reception open *5.30am-8pm*

Maintenance & cleanliness	★★
Facilities	★★★
Atmosphere & character	★★★★
Security	★½
Overall rating	★★½

Haven Resort

The Haven is Alice Springs' best hostel. It is a big place on Larapinta Drive, east of the town centre that offers a high standard of accommodation in clean and well maintained rooms. Facilities include a kitchen, laundry, a nice TV lounge plus another TV in the dining room. There is internet access near the reception and a Wi-Fi connection ($5 per day). Outside there is a barbecue area plus a nice swimming pool. It is the closest hostel to the train station and a five to 10-minute walk to the centre of town.
3 Larapinta Drive, Alice Springs
(08) 8952 4663 (8952 HOME) or 1800 794 663 (1800 79 HOME)
Website *www.alicehaven.com.au*
Dorm bed *$24;* ***double room*** *$105; price includes breakfast*
Credit cards *Amex, Diners, MC, Visa*
Reception open *5am-8pm*

Maintenance & cleanliness	★★★★½
Facilities	★★★½
Atmosphere & character	★★★
Security	★★★½
Overall rating	★★★★

Heavitree Gap Outback Lodge

This is a large accommodation complex, just outside Heavitree Gap on the southern edge of town. It has a variety of accommodation options including air-conditioned motel-style dormitories that each have four single beds (not bunks) plus a fridge and en suite bathroom. The complex has laundry facilities, a barbecue area, a bar/restaurant and swimming pool. A unique feature of this place is the wallaby feeding each evening at sunset (you can buy a bag of wallaby food at reception for $1).
Palm Circuit, Alice Springs
South
(08) 8950 4444
Website *www.auroraresorts.com.au*
Dorm bed *$26-27;* ***double/twin room*** *$107*
Credit cards *Amex, MC, Visa*
Reception open *7am-9pm*

Maintenance & cleanliness	★★★½
Facilities	★★★
Atmosphere & character	★★½
Security	★
Overall rating	★★★

Toddy's Backpackers Resort

Toddy's is a large hostel complex at the southern end of Alice Springs that

is comprised of a couple of former motels. It offers poor quality accommodation with a barren and run-down kitchen, neglected bathrooms and old and worn furnishings in the common areas. However it has a relatively good bar and two swimming pools.
39 Gap Road, Alice Springs
South
(08) 8952 1322
***Website** www.toddys.com.au*
***Dorm bed** $20-22; **single/double/twin room** $58-90*
***Credit cards** MC, Visa*
***Reception open** 5.30am-8pm*

Maintenance & cleanliness	★½
Facilities	★★★½
Atmosphere & character	★★
Security	★
Overall rating	★★

Eating & Drinking

There are plenty of fast food restaurants in the centre of Alice Springs but in the evenings the cheapest place to eat is at the bar at Annie's Place on Traeger Avenue, which has meals for just $5.

If you're preparing your own food there are a few big supermarkets in the town centre where you can buy groceries and stock up on supplies for the long drive (or bus ride) that lays ahead. The two best supermarkets are **Coles** *(corner Gregory Terrace & Bath Street, Alice Springs)* and a **Woolworths** *(40 Hartley Street, Alice Springs)*, both in the town centre.

There are some good bars around Todd Street Mall but the best and most popular bar for backpackers is at **Annie's Place** *(4 Traeger Avenue, Alice Springs)*, which has a great atmosphere, cold beer and cheap food.

Sights

Alice Springs Cultural Precinct

The Alice Springs Cultural Precinct has a number of attractions including the Aviation Museum and the Museum of Central Australia.
Corner Memorial Avenue & Larapinta Drive, Alice Springs
(08) 8951 1122
***Website** www.nt.gov.au/nreta/arts/ascp/index.html*
***Admission** $10 for all attractions in the Cultural Precinct*
***Open** Mon-Fri 10am-4pm, Sat-Sun 11am-4pm*

Alice Springs Desert Park

Run by the NT Parks & Wildlife Commission, the Alice Springs Desert Park portrays the wildlife and plants that thrive in the harsh Central Australian landscape. The park features three different desert habitats with over 400 different types of plants and more than 120 different species of animals. There is also an exhibition centre and an area with rare and endangered nocturnal animals.
Larapinta Drive, 6km from central Alice Springs
(08) 8951 8788
***Website** www.alicespringsdesertpark.com.au*
***Admission** $20 ($14 students)*
***Open** 7.30am-6pm daily*

Anzac Hill

This is the best spot to watch the sun set over Alice Springs. You can get here by walking the Lions Walk trail, which is accessible via Wills Terrace.

Central Australian Aviation Museum

Plane spotters will love this museum, which is situated in the original hanger of Connellan Airways at what was the site of Alice Springs' first airport. The museum is home to several historic aircraft including early flying doctor planes and the remains of the *Kookaburra*, which crashed in the Tanami Desert in 1929.
Corner Memorial Avenue & Larapinta Drive, Alice Springs.
(08) 8951 1122
***Admission** $10, entry fee includes admission to other attractions in the Alice Springs Cultural Precinct*
***Open** Mon-Fri 10am-4pm, Sat-Sun 11am-4pm*

Frontier Camel Farm

This camel farm operates popular camel rides and also maintains a small museum containing exhibits of all things related to camels.
Ross Highway, Alice Springs

☎ *(08) 8953 0444*
Website *www.cameltours.com.au*
Museum admission *$6;* ***one-hour ride*** *$45 ($85-110 including breakfast or dinner)*
Open *9am-5pm*

Museum of Central Australia

This museum is a good introduction to Alice Springs and the surrounding region and it has an emphasis on Central Australia's natural history.
Corner Memorial Avenue & Larapinta Drive, Alice Springs
☎ *(08) 8951 1122*
Admission *$10, entry fee includes admission to other attractions in the Alice Springs Cultural Precinct*
Open *Mon-Fri 10am-4pm, Sat-Sun 11am-4pm*

National Pioneer Women's Hall of Fame

The National Pioneer Women's Hall of Fame is located in the old courthouse and has exhibits on the lives and achievements of pioneer women in central Australia.
27 Hartley Street, Alice Springs
☎ *(08) 8952 9006*
Website *www.pioneerwomen.com.au*
Admission *$6.50*
Open *Feb-mid Dec; 10am-5pm daily*

Old Ghan Train Museum & Heritage Railway

This museum about the old *Ghan* railway is a must for railway enthusiasts. It is situated about 10km out of town.
MacDonnell Siding, 1 Norris Bell Avenue, Alice Springs.
☎ *(08) 8955 5047*
Admission *$6*
Open *9am-5pm daily*

Royal Flying Doctor Service

The Alice Springs branch of the RFDS is open to visitors and includes a small museum with informative displays about this outback institution.
8-10 Stuart Terrace, Alice Springs
☎ *(08) 8952 1129*
Website *www.flyingdoctor.net/Alice-Springs.html*
Admission *$7*
Open *Mon-Sat 9am-4pm, Sun 1pm-4pm*

School of the Air

The Alice Springs branch of the School of the Air has a visitors' centre where you can learn about this unique education programme for students in remote areas.
80 Head Street, Alice Springs
🚌 *North*
☎ *(08) 8951 6834*
Website *www.assoa.nt.edu.au*
Admission *$6.50*
Open *Mon-Sat 8.30am-4.30pm, Sun 1.30pm-4.30pm*

Telegraph Station Historical Reserve

Alice Springs was originally established as a telegraph station in 1871. This 2,000-hectare reserve, 2km north of the centre of Alice Springs, is situated on the site of the original settlement. It features some of the original structures including the old telegraph station, which is open to the public.
Stuart Highway, Alice Springs
☎ *(08) 8952 3993*
Website *www.nt.gov.au/nreta/parks/find/astelegraphstation.html*
Admission *reserve free, buildings $6.50*
Open *reserve 8am-9pm daily, historic buildings 8am-5pm*

MacDonnell Ranges

The MacDonnell Ranges is the closest natural feature to Alice Springs and is a worthwhile detour en route to Uluru. The national parks in this region are home to surprising scenery of canyons and rugged gorges.

West MacDonnell National Park

The West MacDonnell National Park is the largest in the MacDonnell Ranges and features some of the best natural attractions in central Australia.

Simpsons Gap is close to Alice Springs and worth visiting as a daytrip from Alice even if you don't plan on visiting Uluru. This part of the park is a good place to see the black-footed rock wallaby, particularly at dawn or dusk.

Heading west, the next major attraction is Standley Chasm, a breathtakingly narrow canyon that is a big hit with bus tours. Standley Chasm is open 8am-6pm daily and admission is $6.50.

Ormiston Gorge and Pound is located further towards the western end of the park. There is a waterhole at the southern end of the gorge that is said to be up to 14 metres deep. Hiking the **Ormiston Pound Walk** *(7km, 3 hours)* is the best way to see the area; this walk starts at the visitors' centre and takes you through the Pound, returning along Ormiston Gorge via the waterhole. Shorter walks around Ormiston Gorge and Pound include trails to the **Waterhole** *(40 minutess return)* and **Ghost Gum Lookout** *(30 minutes return)*.

Glen Helen Gorge is nearby and is well worth visiting. The mostly dry Finke River passes through here, but the main feature of the gorge is the waterhole; a beautiful spot for a swim.

The most challenging hike in the park is the Larapinta Trail. The entire trail is not yet fully open, but will eventually be a 250km trek from Alice Springs to Mount Sonder. It is expected that most people will hike the trail in smaller sections. Eight of the 13 sections of the trail are open including Alice Springs to Simpsons Gap and Ormiston Gorge to Glen Helen.

Accommodation

West MacDonnell National Park offers a variety of camping sites that range in price from $3.30-6.60 per person. Alternatively the Glen Helen Resort has dorm accommodation for backpackers.

Glen Helen Resort

Glen Helen Resort is a remote roadhouse with a nice location at Glen Helen Gorge. It has a small outback pub, camping and very basic backpackers' accommodation. Backpackers stay in old and slightly run-down rooms, but it is kept clean enough. Although the hostel-style accommodation isn't too great, it is still a relatively good option if you want to camp or park your campervan.

Namitjira Drive, Glen Helen Gorge, West MacDonnell Ranges
☎ *(08) 8956 7489*
Website *www.glenhelen.com.au*
Dorm bed *$20;* ***double room*** *$130-160;* ***camping*** *$10 (1 person), $25 (2 people)*
Credit cards *MC, Visa*
Reception open *7am-11pm*

Maintenance & cleanliness	★★
Facilities	★
Atmosphere & character	★★
Security	★
Overall rating	★★½

Finke Gorge National Park

This national park, 138km west of Alice Springs, includes the impressive Palm Valley that is home to an abundance of rare flora including the Red Cabbage Palm.

There are several trails in the park. These include the **Kalaranga Lookout walk** *(1.5km, 45 minutes)*, which is an easy 20-minute climb with spectacular views of the rock amphitheatre encircled by rugged cliffs. Another popular walk is the **Mpaara Walk** *(5km, 2 hours)*, which introduces the mythology of the Western Arrernte Aboriginal culture.

Kings Canyon

This impressive natural feature in the Watarrka National Park is located between the West MacDonnell and Uluru-Kata Tjuta National Parks. Kings Canyon is a spectacular spot, but it is one of the more expensive destinations to stay in central Australia.

There are two hiking trails in the park. The **Canyon Walk** *(6km; 3-4 hours)* is the most rewarding walk and begins with a steep climb to the top of the Canyon, and then follows the Canyon rim around before descending again. The highlight of this walk is the 'Garden of Eden', an enchanting area of lush vegetation and cool waterholes. The **Kings Creek Walk** *(2.6km; one hour)* winds along Kings Creek ending at a lookout point.

Accommodation

Kings Canyon Resort

The backpackers' accommodation at the Kings Canyon Resort is part of a much larger accommodation complex. Backpackers can stay in four-bed dorms that each have their own TV, fridge and tea/coffee making facilities. There are also several very basic kitchens for travellers to use plus laundry, a swimming pool, tennis courts and several bar/restaurants. Overall, it is neat and tidy but also overpriced and charmless.

Luritija Road, Kings Canyon, Watarrka National Park
(08) 8956 7442 or 1800 817 622
***Website** www.voyages.com.au/experiences/backpacking/*
***Dorm bed** $39; **double/twin room** $100*
***Credit cards** Amex, Diners, MC, Visa; 1% credit card surcharge*
***Reception open** 6am-9.30pm*

Maintenance & cleanliness	★★★½
Facilities	★★★½
Atmosphere & character	★
Security	★
Overall rating	★★★

Uluru-Kata Tjuta National Park

Within the vast Uluru-Kata Tjuta National Park (***website** www.environment.gov.au/parks/uluru/*), 460km southwest of Alice Springs, lay many Aboriginal sacred sites, including Kata Tjuta (the Olgas) and Uluru (Ayers Rock), one of the world's largest monoliths.

This area is of vital significance to the Anangu people (the traditional Aboriginal owners), whose ancestors are thought to have lived in the area for at least 10,000 years and possibly far longer.

Entry to the national park costs $25, which allows the visitor to spend three days exploring the park. The park is only open during the following hours: Jan-Feb 5am-9pm, Mar 5.30am-8.30pm, Apr 6am-8pm, May 6am-7.30pm, Jun-Jul 6.30am-7.30pm, Aug 6am-7.30pm, Sep 5.30am-7.30pm, Oct 5am-8pm, Nov 5am-8.30pm, Dec 5am-9pm.

Practical Information

Uluru-Kata Tjuta Cultural Centre

Lasseter Highway, Uluru
(08) 8956 3138
***Website** www.environment.gov.au/parks/uluru/visitor-activities/cultural-centre.html*
***Admission** free*
***Open** 7am-6pm daily*

Uluru-Kata Tjuta Visitors Centre

Yulara Drive, Yulara
(08) 8956 7377
***Open** 8am-noon & 1pm-5pm daily*

Coming & Going

Driving is the best travel option, this way you can see the main sights in the MacDonnell Ranges on the way here and you can visit Uluru and Kata Tjuta at your own pace rather than when bus or tour schedules allow. There are plenty of car rental companies in Alice Springs and most hostels can organise rental cars for you, however most rental cars cannot be driven on unsealed roads.

If you don't have a car there are several tours catering to backpackers, that you can take from Alice Springs. Tours generally take in Uluru and Kata Tjuta, visiting the West MacDonnell National Park and either Finke Gorge or Kings Canyon en route. They can be booked through most hostels and start at around $200 for a daytrip, but can cost over $900 for a five-day tour.

Mulga's (*(08) 8952 1545 or 1800 359 089; **website** www.mulgas.com.au*) is the cheapest tour, but you get what you pay for and camp in the bush, rather than stay at a proper campsite. That means no showers! Mulga's gets mixed reviews and a lot of people do like the tour despite its drawbacks. Mulga's three-day Uluru tour includes Kings Canyon and costs $275 ($250 plus $25 park entry fee).

The **Rock Tour** (*1800 246 345; **website** www.therocktour.com.au*) is highly recommended and probably the best value. It visits Kings Canyon and has accommodation at proper campsites including Ayers Rock Resort. It costs $320 ($295 plus $25 park entry fee).

Wayoutback *(☎ (08) 8952 4324 or 1300 551 510; **website** www.wayoutback.com.au)* is a more expensive tour, although it offers unique experiences and many travellers say it is worth the extra money. It features small groups with transport in 4WD vehicles so you can get off the highway and onto outback dirt roads. It also includes the rare opportunity to visit an Aboriginal community. Wayoutback's three-day tour costs $565 ($535 HI/YHA, VIP, students), which is $510 or $480 plus a $55 local payment to cover park entry and fuel levy.

Wayward Bus *(☎ (08) 8132 8230 or 1300 653 510; **website** www.waywardbus.com.au)* is another good tour option that includes Kings Canyon with accommodation in permanent tents. It costs $410 ($375 plus $25 park entry fee and $10 fuel levy).

The **Wildway** *(☎ 1300 720 777; **website** www.wildway.com.au)* tour is a good value three-day trip that also includes Kings Canyon. It costs $375 ($295 plus $80 to cover food and the park entry fee).

Emu Run *(☎ (08) 8953 7057; **website** www.emurun.com.au)* operates day trips from Alice Springs, for $199. It is a rushed tour that crams a lot into one day, leaving Alice Springs at 6am and returning at midnight, but it is a good option if your time is limited.

Local Transport

There is a free shuttle bus operated by the Yulara Resort that runs to the main areas in Yulara. There is also a free shuttle between the airport and Yulara that picks up from all accommodation establishments including the hostel and meets all flights.

The best value and most flexible transport option is to drive yourself. Several rental car companies including Avis *(☎ (08) 8956 2266)*, Hertz *(☎ (08) 8956 2244)* and Thrifty *(☎ (08) 8956 2030)* can be booked through the airport or the visitor centre in Yulara.

The next best option is the Uluru Express *(☎ (08) 8956 2152; **website** www.uluruexpress.com.au)* shuttle bus, which operates a shuttle bus between Yulara, Uluru and Kata Tjuta. The first service to Uluru departs Yulara an hour prior to sunrise at the rock and runs regularly throughout the day with the last service back leaving Uluru after sunset. Buses leave Yulara for Kata Tjuta four times per day. The Yulara-Uluru service costs $40-45 return; a two-day pass for Uluru and Kata Tjuta costs $145 and a three-day pass costs $160.

Uluru (Ayers Rock)

One of the world's largest monoliths is the main attraction in Uluru-Kata Tjuta National Park. There is a walking trail around the base of the rock and a two-hour climb to the summit, which is not as popular as it used to be, as more people respect the wishes of the local Aboriginal people and choose not to climb.

There is an informative cultural centre located about 1km to the southwest of the rock, which is a good spot to learn more about the Anangu people and to understand their reasons for not climbing Uluru.

If you do decide to climb, you'll be rewarded by spectacular views that encompass Kata Tjuta and Mount Connor. Although the climb is relatively easy, it can be a dangerous venture and more than 30 people have died attempting it over the past 30 years. Hold on to the chain, wear hiking boots and take along a bottle of drinking water. As a safety precaution, the climbing route is closed during extreme weather conditions.

There are several hiking trails around the base of the rock; these include the 9.4km circuit walk that can take up to four hours. Shorter and easier walks include the **Mala Walk** *(2km; one hour)*, accessible from the western car park and the **Mutitjulu Walk** *(1km; 45 minutes)*, accessible from the southern car park.

After travelling so far, some travellers splurge on a scenic flight. **Ayers Rock Helicopters** *(☎ (08) 8956 2077)* and **Professional Helicopter Services** *(☎ (08) 8956 2003;*

***website** www.phs.com.au)* operate scenic helicopter flights over Uluṟu ($110-115) or both Uluṟu and the Kata Tjuṯa ($220).

Kata Tjuṯa (The Olgas)

Kata Tjuṯa, meaning 'many heads', is comprised of 36 rocks and in many ways this rock formation is a more rewarding destination than the more popular Uluṟu.

There are several hiking trails among Kata Tjuṯa that include the relatively easy **Wuḻpa Gorge Walk** *(2.6km; one hour)* that takes you between Mount Olga and Mount Wuḻpa – two of the more imposing rocks. Another popular hike is the **Valley of the Winds Walk** *(7.5km; three hours)*, which is a circuit taking in the Karingana and Karu lookouts.

Yulara

The Yulara resort complex is 20km from Uluṟu. Apart from accommodation, Yulara offers restaurants, bars and clubs and a giant telescope for night-sky viewing. This is the commercial centre of the national park featuring an airport and shopping centre and it is where virtually everyone stays regardless of their budget.

Accommodation

If you're driving, the cheapest option is the free camping at Curtin Springs Roadhouse, about a 45-minute drive from Uluṟu. Otherwise you have to stay at the overpriced campground or the hostel in Yulara.

Outback Pioneer Lodge

The Outback Pioneer Lodge is part of the large Ayers Rock Resort. It offers a relatively high standard of accommodation. Although some rooms have 20 beds, there are dividing walls that lend a degree of intimacy and four-bed dorms are also available for an additional cost. Shared facilities include a kitchen; TV lounge; laundry; internet access including Wi-Fi ($10 per hour, PIE); a bar and two restaurants, the Pioneer BBQ and the cheaper Pioneer Kitchen plus a swimming pool. There is a free shuttle bus that connects the hostel to other parts of the resort complex.

Ayers Rock Resort, Yulara
(08) 8957 7888 or 1300 139 889
***Website** www.voyages.com.au/experiences/backpacking/*
***Dorm bed** $33 (20-bed dorm), $41 (4-bed dorm)*
***Credit cards** Amex, Diners, JCB, MC, Visa; 1% credit card surcharge*
***Reception open** 24 hours*

Maintenance & cleanliness	★★★★
Facilities	★★★½
Atmosphere & character	★★★
Security	★★
Overall rating	★★★½

Eating & Drinking

Yulara is a resort town with a good selection of places to eat and drink, although most places are expensive.

In addition to the two, relatively affordable, restaurants at the hostel; Yulara has several posh restaurants, bars and cafés in the resort shopping centre. There is also an IGA supermarket, an ANZ bank, a post office and a newsagent.

Queensland

Queensland is a popular destination with thousands of backpackers drawn to the Sunshine State by the beaches, islands and the Great Barrier Reef.

Queensland's attractions range from theme parks and surf beaches to Fraser Island, the Great Barrier Reef, and the Daintree Rainforest.

The state also provides more active outdoor holiday pursuits – from white water rafting and whale-watching trips to hiking, paragliding and bungy jumping.

Brisbane

From its roots as a quiet rural hideaway, Brisbane has grown up and come into the limelight as one of todays most desirable places to live in Australia. Queensland's largest city now has almost as much urban sophistication as Sydney or Melbourne with its gleaming high-rises, ambitious restaurant scene and lively nightlife, while retaining an easygoing lifestyle cherished by its residents. Though it is often dubbed Brisneyland or Brisvegas by some, it is a more friendly and intimate city than some of its Australian counterparts. Modern high rises are interspersed with some beautiful colonial architecture and Queenslander-style houses.

Its warm climate and proximity to some of Queensland's most beautiful beaches and rugged natural wonders draws a steadily increasing number of tourists year-round. Moreton Bay has around 365 islands, the most popular being Moreton Island, where you can go from bushwalking to off-roading to sunbathing in one day. Around the other islands (the most developed and touristed being North Stradbroke), you can board ferries, take tours or go diving and meet some of the whales, dolphins and other marine life inhabiting the area.

Brisbane itself hosts year-round festivals, theatre and art exhibitions. Its attractions include museums, brewery tours, a zoo and an excellent wildlife park. The City Botanic Gardens is a popular quiet spot for lunch on the banks of the river, and the Roma Street Parklands are a must-see. Mt Coot-ha is a popular half-day excursion with stunning panoramas of the city and islands, and if you have time, Kangaroo Point Lookout is also highly recommended for the view (or climbing and abseiling for the adventurous). Backpackers flock to the South Bank Parklands for swimming and relaxing by the artificial beach. The main shopping and sightseeing district is centred on the Queen Street Mall, and is both walkable and interesting. Chinatown is small, but is bordered by Brunswick Street and the alternative, trendy area of Fortitude Valley.

Must do in Queensland

- Go on a club crawl on the Gold Coast
- Drive a 4WD on Fraser Island
- Sail among the Whitsunday Islands
- Go white water rafting on the Tully River
- Dive or snorkel on the Great Barrier Reef

Practical Information

INFORMATION CENTRES & USEFUL ADDRESSES

Brisbane Visitor Information Centre

Queen Street Mall, Brisbane
Central
(07) 3229 5918
Website *www.visitbrisbane.com.au*
Open *Mon-Thu 9am-6pm, Fri 9am-8pm, Sat 9am-5pm, Sun 9am-4.30pm*

Public Transport Hotline

13 12 30
Website *www.translink.com.au*

LAUNDRY

New Farm Launderette

Corner Brunswick & Harcourt Streets, New Farm
Brunswick Street *190, 191, 193, 194*

INTERNET ACCESS

There is free wireless internet access at the **Gloria Jeans** café in the Brunswick Street Mall in Fortitude Valley, **Urban Grind Café** *(33 Latrobe Terrace, Paddington; **website** www.urbangrind.com.au)*; **Queensland State Library** *(Stanley Place, Southbank)* and **Brisbane City Library** *(Brisbane Square, Brisbane)*.

If you don't have your own computer you can access the internet on computers at most hostels in Brisbane or at these internet cafés:

Global Gossip Brisbane
290 Edward Street, Brisbane
☎ *(07) 3229 4033*
***Website** www.globalgossip.com*

312 Brunswick Street, Fortitude Valley
☎ *(07) 3666 0800*
***Website** www.globalgossip.com*

Coming & Going

AIR

Brisbane is well connected by air and it is increasingly affordable to fly here.

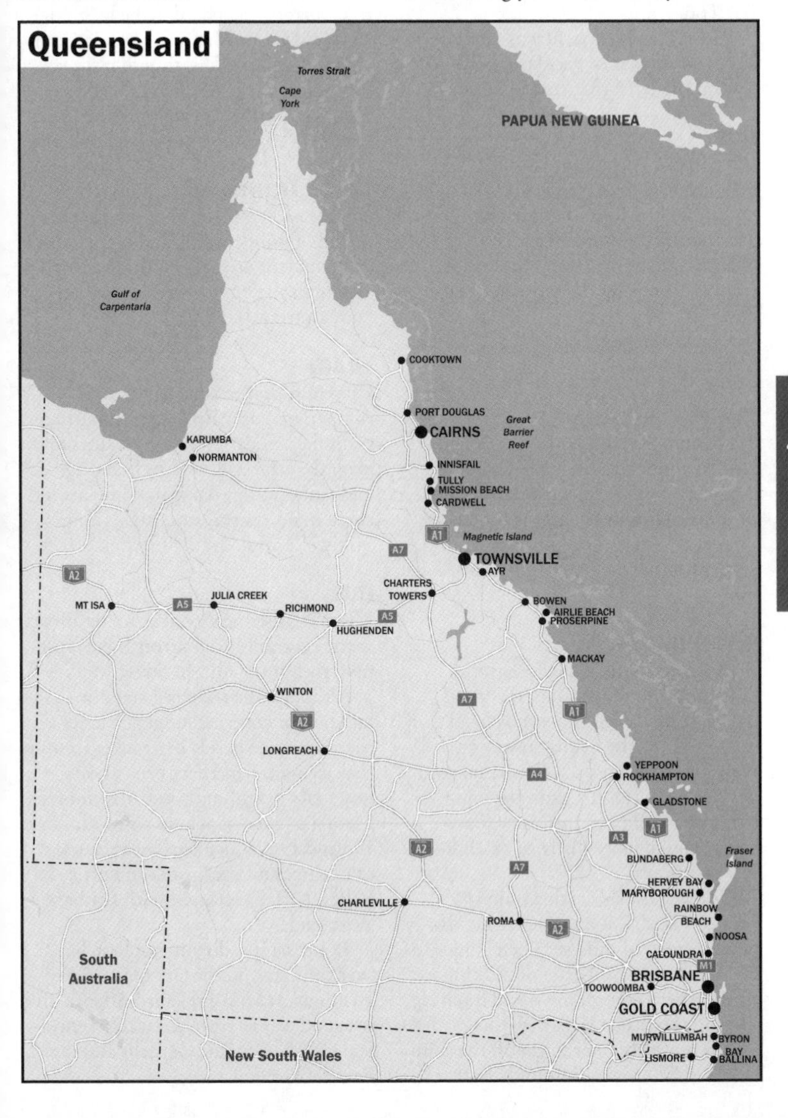

Brisbane Airport *(**website** www.brisbaneairport.com.au)* is about 16km northwest of the city centre and is comprised of two terminals – domestic and international – located 2km apart.

The easiest way to the airport is by the Air Train *(**website** www.airtrain.com.au)*. The Air Train runs to the city centre four times an hour and to the Gold Coast twice an hour. The trip between the airport and the city centre takes 22 minutes and costs $13. Many hostels sell discounted tickets for the Air Train.

Alternatively, Coachtrans *(**website** www.coachtrans.com.au)* run buses into central Brisbane that cost $12 each way.

BUS

Greyhound Australia *(☎ 1300 473 946; **website** www.greyhound.com.au)* and Premier Motor Service *(☎ 13 34 10; **website** www.premierms.com.au)* buses arrive at the Roma Street Transit Centre. There are daily buses to most destinations with more frequent services on the popular Sydney and Cairns routes.

TRAIN

The Roma Street Transit Centre is also Brisbane's main train station for long-distance travel with daily trains to most major destinations including interstate services to New South Wales and trains on the Brisbane-Cairns line.

HITCHHIKING

Because Brisbane is so close to the Sunshine and Gold Coasts, a lot of traffic heading out of town is local traffic bound for the nearby resort cities. If you're hitching from Brisbane, your best bet is to catch a train beyond either the Gold or Sunshine Coast where you're more likely to catch long-distance traffic.

Heading north, catch a train to Gympie. Both Citytrain and long-distance services should stop here. Once in Gympie, it's just a matter of walking to the northern edge of town and hitching a lift on the Bruce Highway.

Alternatively you can get off the train in either Cooroy or Eumundi, both a little closer to Brisbane (and cheaper to get to). However Cooroy and Eumundi are both located a couple of kilometres off the Bruce Highway, so you'll have a bit of a walk to get to the prime hitching spots.

Heading south from Brisbane, you'll need to get to Bilinga, near Coolangatta on the Gold Coast. You can take either a bus from Brisbane or a train to Robina and a connecting bus.

Once you're on the Gold Coast, you'll need to hop on a local bus heading south to Coolangatta and ask to be let off on the Gold Coast Highway outside Coolangatta Airport. This should place you just before the turn-off for the Tweed Heads Bypass where you can find a safe stretch of road to stick your thumb out.

Local Transport

Brisbane's transport network is comprised of buses, trains and ferries and is a convenient way to get around town, although the city centre is compact enough to walk around.

TRAIN

Citytrain *(**website** www.citytrain.com.au)* operates Brisbane's suburban train network that has seven lines and extends as far as Ipswich, Beenleigh and Caboolture. All trains stop at the three main central stations – Roma Street, Central and Brunswick Street.

BUS

Most of Brisbane's local buses terminate at the central Queen Street Bus Station underneath the Queen Street Mall.

Although the train is generally handier for covering longer distances, there are some handy bus routes around the city centre and between various inner-city neighbourhoods. The more useful bus routes include buses 190, 191, 193 and 194, which run between the city centre and the hostels in Fortitude Valley, New Farm and South Brisbane/West End.

There is a free downtown loop bus that runs around the city centre every 10 minutes (Mon-Fri 7am-5.50pm). This is a good way to travel between Central Station, the Botanic Gardens and the Eagle Street Pier.

FERRY
Brisbane has an efficient ferry network and it is a pleasant way to travel to destinations along the river. Ferries are divided between the City Cat that runs a route upriver stopping at a multitude of points along the way and the Cross-river ferries which operate a triangular route between Eagle and Edward Streets in the city centre and Thornton Street in Kangaroo Point. Ferries run about once every 20 minutes.

FARES
Fares are based on a zone system with 23 zones in south east Queensland and five zones in Brisbane, but most points of interest are located in zone one. A single trip within zone one is $2.30.

Single bus, ferry and train fares are listed below:

Zones	Fare
1 zone	$2.30
2 zones	$2.70
3 zones	$3.20
4 zones	$3.60
5 zones	$4.10

A single ticket allows you to transfer to other modes of transport within a two-hour period.

There are also a number of multi-trip tickets available for more frequent travellers. The various multiple trip tickets include:

Ten Trip Saver
The Ten Trip Saver ticket allows ten trips on buses, ferries and trains. They are a good idea if you're planning on spending a while in Brisbane. Bus travel with a Ten Trip Saver allows a two-hour transfer on every trip.

Zones	Fare
1 zone	$18.40
2 zones	$21.60
3 zones	$25.60
4 zones	$28.80
5 zones	$32.80

Daily & Weekly Tickets
Daily and weekly passes allow unlimited bus and ferry travel and are a good deal if you think you'll need to make at least two trips during the day. The daily off-peak ticket is valid for travel between 9am and 3.30pm and after 7pm Mon-Fri and all day on weekends.

Zones	Daily Peak	Daily Off-Peak	Weekly
1 zone	$4.60	$3.50	$18.40
2 zones	$5.40	$4.10	$21.60
3 zones	$6.40	$4.80	$25.60
4 zones	$7.20	$5.40	$28.80
5 zones	$8.20	$6.20	$32.80

Go Card
The go card is similar to London's Oyster card. It can be used to pay for bus, train and ferry services in Brisbane. Like the Oyster card you scan the card at the beginning and end of your journey and it will calculate your fare.

Accommodation
Aussie Way Hostel
Aussie Way is a small quiet hostel in a charming historic home. There's a small fully equipped kitchen, pool table, internet access, swimming pool and a nice balcony overlooking the street. The hostel is located on a quiet residential street close to bars and cafés on nearby Caxton Street and the Transit Centre is a short walk way.

34 Cricket Street, Petrie Terrace
350, 352, 355, 379, 380, 381, 384
Roma Street
(07) 3369 0711
***Website** http://users.bigpond.net.au/aussieway/*
***Dorm bed** $25 ($23.75 VIP); **single room** $45 ($42.75 VIP); **double room** $60 ($57 VIP)*
***Credit cards** MC, Visa*
***Reception open** 7.30am-2pm & 6pm-8pm*

TV K L

Maintenance & cleanliness	★★★½
Facilities	★★
Atmosphere & character	★★★
Security	★★½
Overall rating	★★★

Balmoral House
This is an old house down a side street in Fortitude Valley that has been turned into a hostel. It really has no atmosphere, as there are not many

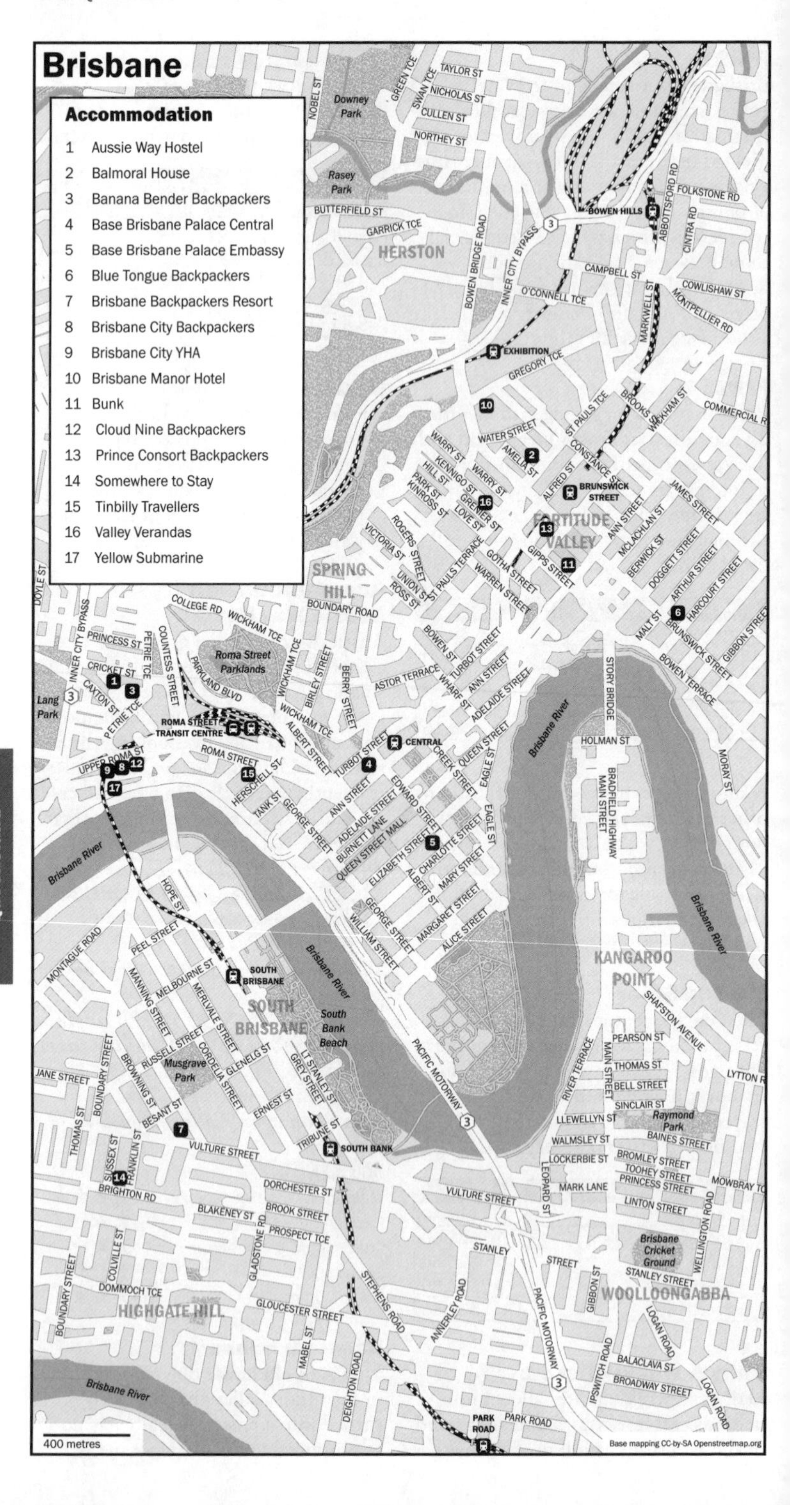
Brisbane
Accommodation
1 Aussie Way Hostel
2 Balmoral House
3 Banana Bender Backpackers
4 Base Brisbane Palace Central
5 Base Brisbane Palace Embassy
6 Blue Tongue Backpackers
7 Brisbane Backpackers Resort
8 Brisbane City Backpackers
9 Brisbane City YHA
10 Brisbane Manor Hotel
11 Bunk
12 Cloud Nine Backpackers
13 Prince Consort Backpackers
14 Somewhere to Stay
15 Tinbilly Travellers
16 Valley Verandas
17 Yellow Submarine
HERSTON
SPRING HILL
FORTITUDE VALLEY
SOUTH BRISBANE
KANGAROO POINT
WOOLLOONGABBA
HIGHGATE HILL
Brisbane River
Roma Street Parklands
ROMA STREET TRANSIT CENTRE
CENTRAL
BRUNSWICK STREET
EXHIBITION
BOWEN HILLS
SOUTH BRISBANE
SOUTH BANK
PARK ROAD
South Bank Beach
Musgrave Park
Raymond Park
Brisbane Cricket Ground
Downey Park
Rasey Park
Lang Park
STORY BRIDGE
400 metres
Base mapping CC-by-SA Openstreetmap.org

rooms and the owners keep things very quiet. The kitchen is tiny, and the dining area doubles as the common room with just a small television and some tables. The bathrooms are very old, and the dorms are shabby and cramped. The place has some character, though, and they offer internet and a shuttle service.

33 Amelia Street, Fortitude Valley

☎ *(07) 3257 0799*

Website *www.aussiecolonialinn.com.au*

Dorm bed *$25;* ***single room*** *$48;* ***double room*** *$58;* ***family room*** *$70;* ***apartment*** *$80; prices include breakfast*

Reception open *7am-11am & 3.30pm-8pm*

Maintenance & cleanliness	★★½
Facilities	★
Atmosphere & character	★★★
Security	★★
Overall rating	★★

Banana Bender Backpackers

Banana Bender is a nice hostel with a good TV lounge, internet access, bar, barbecue and a deck with nice views. Accommodation is mostly in four-bed dorms. It's located on the corner of Jessie Street and Petrie Terrace, close to the Transit Centre and the bars and cafés on nearby Caxton Street.

118 Petrie Terrace, Petrie Terrace

350, 352, 355, 379, 380, 381, 384

Roma Street

☎ *(07) 3367 1157 or 1800 241 157*

Website *www.bananabenders.com*

Dorm bed *$26-28 ($25-27 HI/YHA, VIP);* ***double/twin room*** *$66 ($64 HI/YHA, VIP)*

Reception open *7am-10pm*

Maintenance & cleanliness	★★★½
Facilities	★★
Atmosphere & character	★★★½
Security	★★
Overall rating	★★★

Base Brisbane Palace Central

Just across from Central Station in an old ornate building, this Base hostel has tons of character. The old rickety heritage-listed lift leads up to brightly coloured floors with spacious dorms. The Down Under Bar & Grill is a popular watering hole/nightclub, so expect a big party here most nights. They also offer cheap breakfast, happy hour, and pool tables. The hostel has a rooftop barbecue area with excellent views of the city, a large clean kitchen, an internet café, a job desk and a tour desk. Security is very good and the reception is open 24 hours. Since this (and the Embassy) is now a Base hostel, they are adding the Sanctuary – girls only dorms with special conveniences.

308 Edward Street (corner Ann Street), Brisbane

Central

☎ *(07) 3211 2433 or 1800 24 2273 (1800 24 BASE)*

Website *www.stayatbase.com/base-brisbane-palace-hostel/*

Dorm bed *$25-28 ($24-27 VIP);* ***single room*** *$45 ($44 VIP);* ***double room*** *$65 ($63 VIP)*

Credit cards *MC, Visa*

Reception open *24 hours*

Maintenance & cleanliness	★★★★
Facilities	★★★★
Atmosphere & character	★★★★½
Security	★★★★★
Overall rating	★★★★½

Base Brisbane Palace Embassy

This high-security hostel has a very low-key atmosphere compared to the Base Brisbane Palace Central, just two blocks away. Like the other Base hostel it has a great location, but has a more mature feel. The hostel is clean and modern, with nice furnishings and all the fittings. The kitchen is very well equipped, and the dorms are comfortable. The cinema room is beautiful, with plush pillows and a huge screen. They also have a good rooftop barbecue area with great city views. Reception staff are very nice and helpful.

214 Elizabeth Street, Brisbane (corner Edward Street), Brisbane

Central

☎ *(07) 3002 5777 or 1800 24 2273 (1800 24 BASE)*

Website *www.stayatbase.com/base-brisbane-embassy-hostel/*

Dorm bed *$27-30 ($26-29 VIP);* ***single room*** *$75-89 ($74-88 VIP);* ***double room*** *$75-89 ($74-88 VIP);*

***twin room** $75 ($73 VIP)*
***Credit cards** MC, Visa*
***Reception open** 7am-9pm daily*

Maintenance & cleanliness	★★★★
Facilities	★★★
Atmosphere & character	★★★★½
Security	★★★★★
Overall rating	★★★★

Blue Tongue Backpackers

This place caters to a lot of long-term guests on working holidays. The dorms are bare and boring, the kitchen is desperately in need of maintenance, and the common room is just like someone's messy living room. It doesn't offer much at all for facilities, either. But management is extremely friendly and can help you look for a job. It is a quiet homely spot if you want real no frills accommodation. Workers seem to love it as it is homely and quiet at night.

515 Brunswick Street, Fortitude Valley
190, 191, 193, 194 Brunswick Street
(07) 3254 1984 or 1800 808 941
***Website** www.bluetonguebackpackers.com*
***Dorm bed** $25; **double room** $60*
***Reception open** 9am-9pm daily*

Maintenance & cleanliness	★★
Facilities	★½
Atmosphere & character	★★★
Security	★½
Overall rating	★★

Brisbane Backpackers Resort

This is a bright hostel with heaps of facilities including a swimming pool/spa, tennis court, a bar, a café with cheap food, a movie room and a tour desk. Dorms all have en suite bathrooms and are clean and well maintained. There is an internet café and a nice outdoor common area with pool tables. The kitchen is not a strong point, as it is small and unclean. Reception staff are friendly and helpful with employment advice. They run free hourly shuttle bus into the city.

110 Vulture Street, West End
(07) 3844 9956 or 1800 626 452
***Website** www.brisbanebackpackers resort.com*
***Dorm bed** $24-28 summer, $22-26 winter; **double/twin room** $70-73*
***Credit cards** Amex, Diners, JCB, MC, Visa*
***Reception open** 24 hours*

Maintenance & cleanliness	★★★½
Facilities	★★★★
Atmosphere & character	★★★½
Security	★★½
Overall rating	★★★½

Brisbane City Backpackers

This hostel offers a good range of facilities including a lively bar and a rooftop swimming pool. The large but messy kitchen leads into a TV/internet room with unlimited free wireless access. There is a sundeck with great views of the city and Story Bridge, the dorms are quite old and the bathrooms could really use a renovation. They offer nightly events including pub crawls and barbecues. Reception staff can be rude and inattentive.

380 Upper Roma Street, Brisbane
470, 475 Roma Street
(07) 3211 3221 or 1800 062 572
***Website** www.citybackpackers.com*
***Dorm bed** $21-30; **single room** $79-99; **double room** $79-99*
***Credit cards** MC, Visa*
***Reception open** 24 hours*

Maintenance & cleanliness	★★½
Facilities	★★★½
Atmosphere & character	★★★½
Security	★★★½
Overall rating	★★★

Brisbane City YHA

This YHA is currently undergoing extensive remodelling and is poised to become one of the best hostels in Brisbane. By the time of publication it should have all brand new furnishings and fittings including a rooftop swimming pool and a bar/café. Half of it is done, and it is gorgeous. They have a travel desk specialising in northern Queensland and a games room with pool table. The modern dorms are all air conditioned spacious and clean, painted in pastels and muted browns. The atmosphere here is quiet, but plans to add a bar to the property and

upgrade the café are underway and should liven the place up quite a bit.
392 Upper Roma Street, Brisbane
470, 475 Roma Street
(07) 3236 1004
***Website** www.yha.com.au*
***Dorm bed** $28-29 (25-26 HI/YHA); **double/twin room** $71.50-87 ($64-78 HI/YHA)*
***Credit cards** MC, Visa*
***Reception open** 6.30am-11pm*

Maintenance & cleanliness	★★★★½
Facilities	★★★
Atmosphere & character	★★★★½
Security	★★
Overall rating	★★★★

Brisbane Manor Hotel

This hostel is in a rustic manor house full of antiques and old photos on the walls. It is brimming with character and the staff treat you like family. Unfortunately that means it has no social atmosphere and this may be as far away from a party you can get. The dorms are tidy and simple, they are all a bit different and some are nicer than others. The kitchen is limited. They offer a small TV lounge, laundry, internet and courtesy pick-ups.
555 Gregory Terrace, Fortitude Valley
Exhibition
(07) 3252 4171 or 1800 800 589
***Website** www.brisbanemanor.com*
***Dorm bed** $25; **single room** $55-70; **double/twin room** $65-80*
***Reception open** 8am-8pm daily*

Maintenance & cleanliness	★★★
Facilities	★½
Atmosphere & character	★★★½
Security	★★
Overall rating	★★½

Bunk

This flashy hostel offers an exceptional standard of accommodation. The exterior looks like a big cement block, but inside it is bright, comfortable and clean. Each of the five stories is themed with one of the natural elements. Dorms are a bit cramped, but have en suite and separate toilets and showers. The Birdie Num Num bar is a popular hotspot in town where people come to play pool, mingle, and hang out in some of the big round canvas huts. There is a lap pool and large spa with a retractable stage over it for live music nights, as well as a movie room with big plush pillows for seating. All of this combines to form a great atmosphere. Staff are friendly and the travel desk is helpful. It is a great place to stay near Chinatown and Brunswick Street.
Corner of Ann & Gipps Streets, Fortitude Valley
31,310,315,320 Brunswick Street
1800 682 865
***Website** www.bunkbrisbane.com.au*
***Dorm bed** $26-29; **single room** $70; **double room** $89-110*
***Credit cards** MC, Visa*
***Open** 24 hours*

Maintenance & cleanliness	★★★★½
Facilities	★★★★½
Atmosphere & character	★★★★★
Security	★★★★★
Overall rating	★★★★½

Cloud Nine Backpackers

Cloud Nine is a work in progress. Some areas of this small hostel – such as the common areas and dormitories – are gorgeous and while others – the bathrooms and kitchen – are lacking. To be fair, the kitchen was being renovated when we visited, but much of it appears to be dirty. They do have a bar, a movie room and a rooftop barbecue area with great views. It is quieter than its neighbour (Brisbane City Backpackers) but still has a cool atmosphere. For the price, it is a good choice.
350 Upper Roma Street, Brisbane
470, 475 Roma Street
(07) 3236 2300 or 1800 256 839
***Website** www.cloud9backpackers.com.au*
***Dorm bed** $17-27 ($16-26 HI/YHA, VIP); **single room** $79 ($78 HI/YHA, VIP); **double room** $85 ($83 HI/YHA, VIP)*
***Credit cards** MC Visa*
***Reception open** 24 hours*

Maintenance & cleanliness	★★★
Facilities	★★
Atmosphere & character	★★★½
Security	★★★
Overall rating	★★★

Homestead

This place is small and homely with some funky murals on the walls and hammocks to lounge in. The rooms are run down and a bit dirty and the bathrooms have surely seen better days. There are a lot of long term guests on working holiday here. Combined with an early curfew and a residential location, this place really has no atmosphere. They do have a regular shuttle bus and internet and guests have free use of bikes. At the time of writing, the swimming pool was empty. This place is under new management, so hopefully some improvements will be made in the near future.

57 Annie Street, New Farm
190, 191, 193, 194
(07) 3358 3538
***Dorm bed** $22-26 ($21-25 HI/YHA, VIP), **double room** $69 ($67 HI/YHA, VIP)*
***Credit cards** MC Visa*
***Reception open** 7am-7pm*

Maintenance & cleanliness	★★★
Facilities	★★★½
Atmosphere & character	★★★
Security	★
Overall rating	★★★

Moreton Bay Backpackers Lodge

This hostel has spacious and well maintained dorms creatively decorated with music themes. The sleek, modern bar is a highlight, with a wraparound balcony (with marina view), a cinema screen and pool table. It can get very lively at night. They offer $5 meals for guests, a free beer on arrival and a half hour of free internet (otherwise $5 per hour). There are also loads of activities available every day including powerboat cruises and free sailing on Wednesdays. The kitchen could use an update, but otherwise this place is great.

45 Cambridge Parade, Manly
Manly
(07) 3396 3824 or 1800 800 157
***Website** www.moretonbaylodge.com.au*
***Dorm bed** $20; **double room** $70*
***Credit cards** Amex, Diners, MC, Visa*
***Reception open** 8.30am-11am & noon-2pm & 5pm-midnight*

Maintenance & cleanliness	★★★
Facilities	★★★½
Atmosphere & character	★★★★½
Security	★★★½
Overall rating	★★★½

Prince Consort Backpackers

Located in a 100-year-old heritage building in the Valley, this hostel is understandably in a state of disrepair. There is currently scaffolding covering the façade of the building and they are planning massive renovations. For now, the dorms and common areas are bland and messy. The kitchen is small and poorly maintained. It is at the end of Brunswick Street near Chinatown, an interesting area just a short bus or train ride away from the city centre. Reception staff are very kind and helpful and keep the place rather quiet. Internet costs $4 per hour.

230 Wickham Street Fortitude Valley
190, 191, 193, 194 Brunswick Street
(07) 3257 2252
***Website** www.princeconsort.com.au*
***Dorm bed** $21-27 ($20-26 Nomads); **double room** $60 ($58 Nomads); **triple room** $79 ($76 Nomads)*
***Credit cards** Amex, MC, Visa*
***Reception open** 9am-6pm daily*

Maintenance & cleanliness	★★★
Facilities	★★
Atmosphere & character	★★★★
Security	★★★★
Overall rating	★★★

Somewhere to Stay

This old Queenslander house in southern Brisbane is nothing more than somewhere to stay. It is quite a mess, but OK for a night or two if there is nothing else available. The dorms are hot and stuffy and the bathrooms are wretched. The kitchen is standard but outdated. They do have a nice swimming pool area with hammocks and palm trees and a homely common room with a resident cat, but security is loose and there is not much of an atmosphere.

45 Brighton Road (corner Franklin Street), Highgate Hill

190, 191, 193, 194, 198
(07) 3846 2858 or 1800 812 398
Website *www.somewheretostay.com.au*
Dorm bed *$19-25;* ***single room*** *$39-45;* ***double room*** *$49-69;* ***triple room*** *$79*
Credit cards *Amex, JCB, MC, Visa*
Reception open *8am-8.30pm & 9pm-4am daily*

Maintenance & cleanliness	★★
Facilities	★★★★½
Atmosphere & character	★★★
Security	★★
Overall rating	★★★½

Tinbilly Travellers

This modern hostel is located next to its huge corner pub that gets really packed at night, but the hostel has little in the way of facilities otherwise. Dorms are modern with Ikea-like furniture, but are getting a little worn. The kitchen is large and well stocked and the TV room is relaxed and inviting. Security is first-rate. It has a great location and the reception staff are nice.

462 George Street, Brisbane
(07) 3238 5888 or 1800 446 646
Website *www.tinbilly.com*
Dorm bed *$ 28-29 ($26-27 Nomads);* ***double room*** *$99-109 ($95-105 Nomads)*
Credit cards *MC, Visa*
Reception open *24 hours*

Maintenance & cleanliness	★★★
Facilities	★★
Atmosphere & character	★★★½
Security	★★★★½
Overall rating	★★★

Valley Verandas

This hostel is in a nice old colonial home with wraparound verandas on two floors, but inside it is in quite a dismal state. The kitchen is small and messy, the dorms are stuffy and the bathrooms are filthy. There is a TV room with some couches and a backyard barbecue area, but again they are not well maintained. They offer very few facilities and the atmosphere is dull. For the price and the location, it is not really worth it unless it is a last resort.

11 Grenier Street, Spring Hill
(07) 3252 1820 or 1800 680 320
Website *www.valleyverandas.com.au*
Dorm bed *$22-26;* ***single room*** *$41-42;* ***double room*** *$64-66*
Credit cards *MC, Visa; 2.65% credit card surcharge*
Reception open *8am-10pm daily*

Maintenance & cleanliness	★½
Facilities	★★
Atmosphere & character	★★★
Security	★★½
Overall rating	★★

Yellow Submarine

Yes, it is definitely yellow and the writing on the walls is testament to some good times past and the happy, family-like atmosphere here. Reception staff are extremely nice and fun. There are a lot of travellers on Working Holiday visas living here long term, so it is relatively quiet. The kitchen is exceptionally clean but the dorms are a bit shabby. They have a swimming pool and do a free dinner on Sundays.

66 Quay Street Brisbane
Roma Street *470, 475*
(07) 3211 3424
Website *www.yellowsubmarinebackpackers.com*
Dorm bed *$25-27;* ***double room*** *$60;* ***twin room*** *$58*
Credit cards *MC, Visa*
Reception open *7am-10pm daily*

Maintenance & cleanliness	★★½
Facilities	★★½
Atmosphere & character	★★★★½
Security	★½
Overall rating	★★★

Eating & Drinking

Finding cheap eats in Brisbane is not difficult. There is a wide range of authentic and tasty international food, as well as the standard fast food restaurants and cheap pub meals. One of the best places to go for an inexpensive but quality meal is in Chinatown, where you can get great Asian food. **Pho B** *(28 Duncan Street, Fortitude Valley)* in the centre of Chinatown has great Vietnamese. For a real deal, check out **Fat Boys** *(323 Brunswick Street, For-*

titude Valley) for all day breakfast and other pub fare for bargain prices. Pizza is another cheap and ubiquitous staple in Brisbane, with many places staying open late in the city centre.

Open air food courts are a good place to grab a quick bite on the cheap. The Myer Centre in the city or the or the Riverside Centre in the northeast section of the city are both packed with options for a leisurely lunch. Eating out can get quite expensive in Brisbane, so the best bet is cooking at your hostel.

Supermarkets in the city centre include **Coles** in Queen's Plaza, *(corner Adelaide, Edward & Queen Streets, Brisbane)* and **Woolworths** *(256 Queen Street, Brisbane).*

Hostels often have special dinner deals or barbecues that can be a great deal and are worth it if the closest supermarket is too far away to walk to. It is always cheaper to buy your own alcohol in a bottle shop, but for the atmosphere there are plenty of bars and pubs in the city for a beer or two. **Irish Murphy's** *(175 George Street, Brisbane)* is a popular spot, as is the **Zi Bar** *(308 Edward Street, Brisbane)* and the **Belgian Beer Café** *(corner Edward & Mary Streets, Brisbane).*

Sights

Alma Park Zoo

As well as Australian animals like kangaroos, koalas, emus, wombats, dingoes, goannas and possums in their natural surroundings, Alma Park Zoo is home to a wide range of exotic animals including monkeys, baboon, red deer, fallow deer, leopards, camels, water buffalo and sun bears.

Alma Road, Kallangur (about 30 minutes north of Brisbane)
Dakabin, then courtesy bus (courtesy bus meets the 9.02am departure from Roma Street, 9.08am from Central, 9.10am from Brunswick Street)
(07) 3204 6566
***Website** www.almaparkzoo.com.au*
***Admission** $28 ($21 students)*
***Open** 9am-5pm daily*

Australian Woolshed

This animal park has the usual collection of native animals, but the focus is on sheep and sheep dogs.

148 Samford Road, Ferny Hills
Ferny Hills
(07) 3872 1100
***Website** www.auswoolshed.com.au*
***Admission** $17 ($12.50 students)*
***Open** 8.30am-4.30pm daily*

Carlton Brewery

The large Carlton Brewery, located in the southern suburbs on the way to the Gold Coast, brews Carlton, Fosters and Victoria Bitter and offers tours that include samples. Bookings essential, but it is difficult to get to without a car.

Corner Mulles Road & Pacific Highway, Yatala
(07) 3826 5858
***Website** www.visitfostersvenues.com/venues/carlton_brewhouse_yatala.asp*
***Admission** $20*
***Tours** Mon-Fri 10am & noon & 2pm, Sun noon & 2pm*

Castlemaine Brewery

There are regular tours of the brewery that produces XXXX beer. Each 75-minute tour gives you the chance to learn more about how beer is made, learn a few bits of useless trivia and most importantly taste the finished product. Bookings recommended.

Corner Black & Paten Streets, Milton
470, 475 Q Milton
(07) 3361 7597
***Website** www.xxxx.com.au*
***Admission** $20 ($18 students), includes four beers at the end of the tour*
Tours Mon-Fri 10am, 11am, noon, 1pm, 2pm, 3pm, 4pm, Sat 10.30am, 11am, noon

City Hall

City Hall is a major landmark in central Brisbane that features a clock tower with an observation deck with good views of the downtown area. The newly opened Museum of Brisbane (MoB) is on the ground floor.

King George Square, Brisbane
Central
(07) 3403 8888
***Website** www.brisbane.qld.gov.au/cityhall*
***Tours** $5; lift to clock tower free*
***Open** Mon-Fri 8am-5pm, Sat-Sun*

10am-5pm; tours Mon-Fri 9am-4pm; lift to clock tower 10am-3pm daily

Lone Pine Koala Sanctuary

Lone Pine is a large wildlife sanctuary with loads of native Australian animals including kangaroos and koalas as well as Tasmanian devils, wombats, dingoes and various reptiles. It is the world's largest koala sanctuary with over 130 koalas.
Jesmond Road, Fig Tree Pocket
430, 445
(07) 3878 1366
***Website** www.koala.net*
***Admission** $22, $18.70 (HI/YHA, Nomads, VIP)*
***Open** 8.30am-5pm daily*

Museum of Brisbane (MoB)

The Museum of Brisbane inside City Hall has exhibits about the city's history and culture.
King George Square, Brisbane
Central
(07) 3403 8888
***Website** www.museumofbrisbane.com.au*
***Admission** free*
***Open** 10am-5pm daily; free guided tours Tue, Thu, Sat 11am*

Parliament House

If you're interested in Queensland state politics, you may want to take advantage of the free tours of Parliament House, which run regularly.
Corner Alice & George Streets, Brisbane
Alice Street
(07) 3406 7111
***Admission** free*
***Tours** on sitting days, or when Parliament is in session, tours leave at 10.30am and 2.30pm. On non-sitting days tours leave at 9.30am, 10.30am, 11.15am, 2.30pm, 3.15pm and 4.15pm. The tours last 30 minutes. Sunday tours last for 20 minutes and operate between 10am and 2pm*

Queensland Art Gallery

Brisbane's major art gallery has a large collection of Australian artworks.
Queensland Cultural Centre, Melbourne Street, South Brisbane
South Brisbane F Convention Centre
(07) 3840 7303
***Website** www.qag.qld.gov.au*
***Admission** free, charge for special exhibits*
***Open** Mon-Fri 10am-5pm, Sat-Sun 9am-5pm*

Queensland Maritime Museum

The Queensland Maritime Museum is an excellent museum featuring a large range of nautical exhibits. The museum's collection includes several vessels including steam tug *SS Forceful* and frigate *HMAS Diamantina* as well as several smaller boats.
Sidon Street, South Brisbane
South Brisbane Convention Centre
(07) 3844 5361
***Website** www.maritimemuseum.com.au*
***Admission** $7; $11 with dry dock ticket*
***Open** 9.30am-4.30pm daily (last entry 3.30pm)*

Queensland Museum

This important museum features a diverse collection of artefacts ranging from dinosaur skeletons to exhibits on local history.
Queensland Cultural Centre, Corner Grey & Melbourne Streets, South Brisbane
South Brisbane Convention Centre
(07) 3840 7555
***Website** www.southbank.qm.qld.gov.au*
***Admission** free, charge for special exhibits*
***Open** 9.30am-5pm daily*

Riverside Craft Market

This is a great place if you love poking around markets.
123 Eagle Street, Brisbane
Eagle Street Pier Central
(07) 38702807
***Website** www.riversidemarkets.com.au*
***Admission** free*
***Open** Sun 8am-4pm*

Southbank Beach

Australia's only artificial inland city beach holds three mega litres of water or approximately three Olympic size swimming pools and is surrounded by 4000m^3 of sand from Rous Channel in Moreton Bay. It's a great place to chill out on a hot summer day.
South Bank, South Brisbane
South Brisbane Convention Centre
***Admission** free*

Story Bridge Adventure Climb

Brisbane's iconic Story Bridge was designed by John Bradfield – who also designed the Sydney Harbour Bridge – with a cantilever design based on Montréal's Jacques Cartier Bridge. The Story Bridge Adventure Climb is similar to Sydney's Bridge Climb; the 2½ hour experience involves a 1km climb route that takes you to a viewing platform 80 metres above the Brisbane River.

170 Main Street, Kangaroo Point
☎ *1300 254 627*
Website *www.storybridgeadventureclimb.com.au*
Admission *$110-130*

Moreton Bay

Despite its easy accessibility from Brisbane, Moreton Bay and its islands receive very few visitors. Moreton Bay is home to spectacular marine life and its islands are well worth visiting and are comparable to Fraser Island.

Moreton Island

This sand island, only 35km from Brisbane, is often compared to Fraser Island and offers pretty much the same attractions without the crowds. You can visit as a day trip from Brisbane, but a longer visit gives you a better experience of the island.

Coming & Going

Moreton Island is best reached by ferry from Lytton in Brisbane's southeastern suburbs or Scarborough on the Redcliffe Peninsula north of Brisbane.

Micat Moreton Island Ferries (☎ *(07) 3895 1000;* ***website*** *www.moretonventure.com.au)* charge $45 return or $190 return for a 4WD with up to two passengers. Their ferries depart from Howard Smith Drive in Lytton (with pick up service from Wynnum North train station) and sail to the Tangalooma Wreck.

The *Combie Trader II* (☎ *(07) 3203 6399;* ***website*** *www.moreton-island.com/how.html)* charges $40 return or $165-185 return for a car with two passengers. It sails between Scarborough and Bulwer.

Another option is the more expensive ferries that depart Brisbane at Holt Street Wharf, Pinkenba and go to the Tangalooma Resort. These ferries are popular with day-trippers and return fares are $70.

Local Transport

Because it is a sand island, you'll need a 4WD vehicle to explore Moreton Island, however there is a network of hiking tracks. There are plenty of places in Brisbane to rent a 4WD, and also a number of companies that organise affordable tours to the island. Moreton Island is a national park and you will have to pay $35.40 for a vehicle access permit, this permit is sometimes included if you're taking a tour. Companies operating tours of the island include:

Moreton Bay Escapes

This highly recommended company run tours to the island that includes sailing, snorkelling and hiking.
☎ *1300 559355*
Website *www.moretonbayescapes.com.au*
Day trip *$149 ($139 HI/YHA, VIP, students);* ***two-day overnight camping tour*** *$239 ($229 HI/YHA, VIP, students)*

Sunrover Expeditions

This tour operator runs day trips from Brisbane as well as longer two and three day camping safaris.
☎ *(07) 3203 4241*
Website *www.sunrover.com.au*
Day trip *$120;* ***two-day tour*** *$195;* ***three-day tour*** *$295*

Accommodation

There are five campgrounds on the island, which is really the only affordable accommodation option. You'll have to pay camping fees of $4 per person per night.

Sights & Activities

Tangalooma Wild Dolphin Resort

This is one of the few places in the world where visitors can hand feed wild

dolphins in their natural environment and every evening, several wild dolphins swim here. The resort's dolphin care programme staff supervises the nightly feedings to ensure the dolphins are not harmed in any way. Daily pelican feeding is another of Tangalooma's natural animal attractions.
Tangalooma Resort, Moreton Island
☎ *(07) 3268 6333*
Website *www.tangalooma.com*

Whale Watching

You can see humpback whales on their annual northern migration (Jun-Oct) from Antarctica. The whales put on a spectacular show and you can see them from Cape Moreton – the only part of the island that isn't sand – or you can take one of the whale watching trips that are offered by a number of operators; these trips depart from Manly and Scarborough.

St Helena Island

St Helena Island is Queensland's version of Alcatraz. This prison island is interesting although some of the trips are quite touristy with re-enactments of historical events in the same style you would expect from a tacky theatre restaurant.

Both day and night trips are available with ghost tours at night. Day trips cost $69, nighttime ghost tours $90. A B Sea Cruises *(☎ (07) 3396 3994; **website** www.sthelenaisland.com.au)* run the trips from Manly in Brisbane's southeast to St Helena Island. Manly is easily reached by train on the Cleveland line.

North Stradbroke Island

Also known as "Straddie", North Stradbroke Island is one of the world's largest sand islands and is home to the sprawling Blue Lake National Park plus some great beaches and tons of marine life. Point Lookout, at the northeast corner of the island, is the main hub of accommodation and dining and is surrounded by postcard-perfect beaches perfect for snorkelling. Most travellers come here to learn to dive or to dive the famous spots in front of Cylinder Beach, including a spectacular Manta Ray cleaning station. The surf is great and uncrowded at Main Beach just off Point Lookout. If you fancy a walk instead, the Gorge pathway around Point Lookout is a gorgeous half hour seaside stroll.

You can camp and four-wheel-drive along many of the beaches here, but you'll need to get a permit from the Stradbroke Visitors Centre before boarding the ferry in Cleveland. Access to the entire southern half of the island is prohibited due to mining.

Coming & Going

Frequent ferries run to North Stradbroke Island from Cleveland, 30km southeast of Brisbane city centre, which is reached by frequent trains on the Citytrain network.

Sea Stradbroke Ferries *(☎ (07) 3488 9777; **website** www.seastradbroke.com)* charge $10 return or $122 return for a car with passengers. Their ferries depart from Redland Bay.

Stradbroke Ferries *(☎ (07) 3286 2666; **website** www.stradbrokeholidays.com.au)* charge $17 return or $122 for a car with passengers. Stradbroke Ferries depart from Toondah Harbour, Middle Street, Cleveland. They have a courtesy bus that picks up from Cleveland train station and Cleveland Mall.

The Stradbroke Flyer *(☎ (07) 3286 1964; **website** www.flyer.com.au)* is a fast ferry that charges $17 return. Their ferries depart from Cleveland and they also have a courtesy bus that picks up from Cleveland train station.

Local Transport

North Stradbroke Island Bus Services *(☎ (07) 3415 2417; **website** www.stradbrokebuses.com)* is a reasonable local bus service on the island that meets all ferries. Buses run between Dunwich and Point Lookout with some services also going to Amity. The one-way fare from the ferry terminal to Point Lookout is $5 and a one-day pass costs $15.40.

Accommodation

Manta Lodge

This is the only hostel on North Stradbroke Island and is mainly focused on

the Manta Dive Centre, offering tours and PADI certification. It is usually a very quiet place, as most travellers come here on the weekends for diving. The dorms are very plain, but have comfortable beds and plenty of space. The shared bathrooms are a bit grimy. The common room has big plush couches perfect for lounging after a long day at the beach and the kitchen is clean and well equipped. The staff here are extremely friendly and helpful. The location just off the beautiful Cylinder Beach is nice.
1 East Coast Road, Point Lookout, North Stradbroke Island
☎ *(07) 3409 8888*
***Website** www.mantalodge.com.au*
***Dorm bed** $28 ($25 HI/YHA); **double/twin room** $70 ($63 HI/YHA)*
***Credit cards** MC, Visa*
***Reception open** 8am-5pm daily; late check in with prior arrangement*

Maintenance & cleanliness	★★★
Facilities	★★★
Atmosphere & character	★★★½
Security	★★
Overall rating	★★★

Eating & Drinking

There are a couple of shops in Point Lookout where you can buy supplies for cooking meals. Otherwise there are some nice cafés and restaurants but they can be pricey. The Point Lookout petrol station next to the Manta Lodge has a convenience store and café where you can get cheap sandwiches and snacks. A great dinner spot is the Bowls Club, just a bit further down the main road, where locals go for inexpensive quality meals. **Fishes** *(15 Mooloomba Road, Point Lookout)* is also a popular spot for lunch. For those on a strict budget, it is a good idea to stock up on food at a supermarket on the mainland before coming here.

Darling Downs

Backpackers seldom visit the part of southeast Queensland that lies inland from Brisbane although Stanthorpe attracts some travellers who come here to look for fruit picking work.

Toowoomba

Toowoomba is known for its gardens and it is a pleasant place but Australia's largest inland city doesn't hold the allure of the coast and not many backpackers visit here.

Practical Information

Toowoomba Tourist Information Centre

86 James Street, Rangeville
☎ *(07) 4639 3797*
***Website** www.toowoomba.com*
***Open** 9am-5pm daily*

Coming & Going

BUS

Greyhound *(☎ 1300 473 946; **website** www.greyhound.com.au)* is based in Toowoomba and has buses to Brisbane, Cunnamulla, Lightning Ridge and Rockhampton. The Greyhound terminal is at 28 Neil Street.

TRAIN

The *Westlander* train stops in Toowoomba en route between Brisbane and Charleville.

Sights

Cobb & Co Museum

This museum is home to Australia's largest collection of horse-drawn vehicles and it includes three stagecoaches from the Cobb & Co company that thrived during the 19th century.
27 Lindsay Street, Toowoomba
☎ *(07) 4639 1971*
***Website** www.cobbandco.qm.qld.gov.au*
***Admission** $9.50*
***Open** 10am-4pm daily*

Toowoomba Regional Art Gallery

Regional Queensland's oldest art gallery has a collection of over 400 Australian paintings as well as several important historical documents written by prominent historical figures including poet Henry Lawson, explorer Ludwig Leichardt and La Perouse.
Ruthven Street, Toowoomba

☎ *(07) 4688 6652*
***Admission** free*
***Open** Tue-Sat 10am-4pm, Sun 1pm-4pm*

Stanthorpe

This small town near the border with New South Wales is a popular spot with backpackers who come here for fruit picking work. Stanthorpe is around 1000m above sea level and it has a much cooler climate than elsewhere in Queensland, supporting 35 wineries in the surrounding countryside.

Practical Information

Stanthorpe Visitor Information Centre

28 Leslie Parade, Stanthorpe
☎ *(07) 4681 2057*
***Website** www.southerndownsholidays.com.au*
***Open** 8.30am-5pm daily*

Accommodation

Backpackers of Queensland

This purpose-built hostel is comprised of several buildings with a main building with common areas that include Internet access and dining areas with a TV. The kitchen facilities are limited to a toaster and five microwave ovens, but $5 cooked meals are served each evening. Accommodation is comprised of 10 five-bed air-conditioned dormitories with en suite facilities. Management organise work on nearby farms and also provide transport to and from work.
80 High Street, Stanthorpe
☎ *0429 810 998*
***Website** www.backpackersofqueensland.com.au*
***Dorm bed** $160 per week; price includes transport to work*
***Credit cards** MC, Visa*

Maintenance & cleanliness	★★★★½
Facilities	★★½
Atmosphere & character	★★★★
Security	★★
Overall rating	★★★½

Top of the Town

Top of the Town is a large accommodation complex encompassing a caravan park, cabins and a backpackers' hostel. Backpackers accommodation is split between two hostel buildings – the Lodge and the nicer Homestead – as well as bungalows and caravans. Each of the two hostel buildings have a TV lounge and kitchen (the Homestead has a brilliant fully equipped kitchen) and other facilities include a games room and swimming pool. Management organise work on nearby farms and provide transport to and from work.
10 High Street, Stanthorpe
☎ *(07) 4681 4888 or 1800 030 123*
***Website** www.topoftown.com.au*
***Dorm bed** $110 per week*
***Credit cards** MC, Visa*

Maintenance & cleanliness	★★★★
Facilities	★★★½
Atmosphere & character	★★½
Security	★½
Overall rating	★★★½

Sights

Stanthorpe Heritage Museum

This small museum, comprised of several historic buildings on High Street, has exhibits on local history.
12 High Street, Stanthorpe
☎ *(07) 4681 1711*
***Admission** $4.50*
***Open** Wed-Fri 10am-4pm, Sat 1pm-4pm, Sun 9am-1pm*

Gold Coast

The glamorous Gold Coast stretches 42km from Coolangatta to Surfers Paradise. It boasts beautiful beaches and beautiful people and takes pride in its extravagance. This is where the rich come to play and although afternoons on the beach are shadowed over by beachfront apartment towers, the energy before nightfall couldn't be higher. If there is anything residents are more dedicated to than their daily tanning sessions and shopping, it's the nightlife. Flashy, flaunting, and meticulously coiffed, Gold Coasters enjoy basking in the glory of their hedonistic lifestyle.

Most people stay in Surfers Paradise, which is the coast's accommodation, shopping and nightlife hub. Surfers' hostels are geared for busloads of party-seeking backpackers and organise loads of nightly activities so that, if you are so inclined, you can spend your entire holiday here in a blurry rotation of binge drinking, dancing and sleeping it off at the beach. Other things to do on the Gold Coast involve spending your time and money visiting the many theme parks plus skydiving, bungy jumping, horseback riding and visiting national parks and wildlife sanctuaries.

North of Surfers Paradise is Main Beach, which leads towards the Spit – a long sandbar stretching northwards with Sea World at its northernmost point.

Southport is a quieter residential and business area just north of Surfers Paradise past the Nerang River. It has a couple of good hostels with frequent buses to Surfers Paradise, so if you want to stay in a calmer area, the commute to the city is easy. The Australia Fair Shopping Centre on Scarborough Street in Southport is a huge but relaxed shopping centre good for shopping and cheap eats.

Coolangatta at the southern end of the Gold Coast is part of the same city but the atmosphere could be from a town a world away. Laid-back surfers lounge in hammocks in hostel gardens, mingle with the local fishermen and laze away sunsets talking about the best waves of the day. Things are cheaper, healthier and humbler here. Surf starts at the famous Kirra Point and Duranbah Beach, continuing to the famous Snapper Rocks and mellowing out at Greenmount and Rainbow Bay. The other great point break in the area is at Burleigh Heads 14km north of Coolangatta. The rip currents on these beaches can be dangerously strong, so always swim within the limits of the lifeguard flags.

Practical Information

Surfers Paradise Information & Booking Centre

2 Cavill Ave, Surfers Paradise
☎ *(07) 5538 4419*
Website *www.verygc.com*
Open *Mon-Fri 8.30am-5.30pm, Sat 8.30am-5pm, Sun 9am-4pm*

Coolangatta Information & Booking Centre

Shop 22 Showcase on the Beach, Griffith Street, Coolangatta
☎ *(07) 5569 3380*
Website *www.verygc.com*
Open *Mon-Fri 8.30am-5pm, Sat 9am-3pm, Sun 10am-3pm*

Harbour Town Information & Booking Centre

Kiosk 4 Harbour Town Shopping Centre, Biggera Waters
☎ *(07) 5563 7688*
Website *www.verygc.com*
Open *Mon-Wed 9am-5.30pm, Thu 9am-7pm, Fri-Sat 9am-5.30pm, Sun 10am-5pm*

INTERNET ACCESS

Free wireless hotspots are hard to find on the Gold Coast and **Gloria Jeans Coffee** *(3195 Gold Coast Highway, Surfers Paradise)* seems to be the only centrally located free Wi-Fi hotspot.

Otherwise you can access the net at most hostels or at Backpackers World Travel in Surfers Paradise.

Backpackers World Travel /Global Gossip

35 Orchid Avenue, Surfers Paradise
☎ *(07) 5561 0634*
Website *www.globalgossip.com*

Coming & Going

Many people travel to the Gold Coast via Brisbane, but the coast also has its own international airport at Coolangatta, plus bus links to destinations on the east coast.

AIR

Although the Gold Coast is close enough to make Brisbane's airport a convenient gateway, Coolangatta Airport *(**website** www.goldcoastairport.com.au)* at the southern end of the coast has frequent flights from most major destinations in Australia.

Surfside buses stop on the Gold Coast Highway outside Coolangatta Airport, and they also operate an airport shuttle service from both Brisbane and Coolangatta Airports with drop-offs to hostels and hotels along the Gold Coast. The shuttle costs around $18, so it's a much better idea to walk five minutes to the highway and catch the local bus (route 700 to Surfers Paradise) for just $4.10.

If you're travelling from Brisbane Airport, the Airtrain ***(website** www.airtrain.com.au)* operates twice an hour with a connecting bus to Surfers Paradise. It costs $25.80 from the airport to Robina station or $42 with a connecting shuttle bus to your hostel.

Alternatively, Coachtrans *(☎ (07) 3238 4700;* ***website** www.coachtrans.com.au)* run buses between Brisbane Airport and the Gold Coast that drop you off at the door of your hostel. The one-way fare is $39.

BUS

Greyhound buses stop at Coolangatta and Surfers Paradise. In Coolangatta, buses stop at the Coolangatta Transit Centre on the corner of Griffith and Warner Streets. The bus terminal in Surfers Paradise is at the corner of Beach and Cambridge Roads. In Coolangatta buses stop on Warner Street, between Chalk and Lanham Streets.

TRAIN

A train line runs through the Gold Coast Hinterland with stations at Nerang and Robina. Although it isn't on a main interstate rail line, there are frequent Citytrain services into Brisbane. Bus 745 goes to Surfers Paradise from Nerang Station and bus 750 runs from Robina Station.

Local Transport

There is a good local bus service along the coast that is supplemented by a rail line in the hinterland. Although services are frequent, it can take a while to travel the complete length of the coast.

TRAIN

Citytrain operate a rail line in the hinterland that connects to the Brisbane suburban rail network. The main stations on the Gold Coast are Coomera, Helensvale, Nerang and Robina. There are frequent buses that connect these stations with the coast, these include bus 750 from Robina station to Surfers Paradise and Sea World, bus 765 from Robina station to Coolangatta, bus 745 from Nerang station to Surfers Paradise, buses 1A, 1X, 3, 14 and 16 from Helensvale station to Southport and bus 709 from Helensvale station to Surfers Paradise and bus 715 from Helensvale to Sea World.

BUS

Surfside *(☎ (07) 5571 6555;* ***website** www.surfside.com.au)* operate a good bus network along the coast. Their routes that run along the Gold Coast Highway have stops around every 300 metres and operate 24 hours a day.

You're most likely to use the bus if you're staying at one of the hostels in Southport, Main Beach or Coolangatta. Buses 700, 702, 703, 704, 706, 707 and 709 run between Southport and Surfers Paradise; bus 750 runs between Main Beach and Surfers Paradise and bus 700 connects Coolangatta with Surfers Paradise.

The EZY Pass is a travel pass that offers unlimited bus travel. A three-day pass is $26 while the five-day pass costs $37 and a seven-day pass is $45.

Accommodation

SURFERS PARADISE

Backpackers in Paradise

This hostel is quite far from the beach, but still has a surfer vibe to it. The aqua green building is built around a sunny courtyard with hammocks. It has an onsite shop to buy groceries and toiletries, a café, a bamboo and tin bar, and a huge cinema room with funky couches and an underwater mural on the walls. Outside under a tin and palm leaf roof, there is another TV lounge popular with guests. They offer nightly activities including bar crawls. The dorms could do with a through renovation, though, and the bathrooms are quite dirty.

40 Peninsular Drive, Surfers Paradise
🚌 700, 702, 703, 704, 706, 707, 709, 745, 750, TX2
☎ (07) 5538 4344 or 1800 268 621
***Website** www.backpackersinparadise.com*
***Dorm bed** $23-26;* ***double room** $65-75*
***Credit cards** MC, Visa*

Queensland

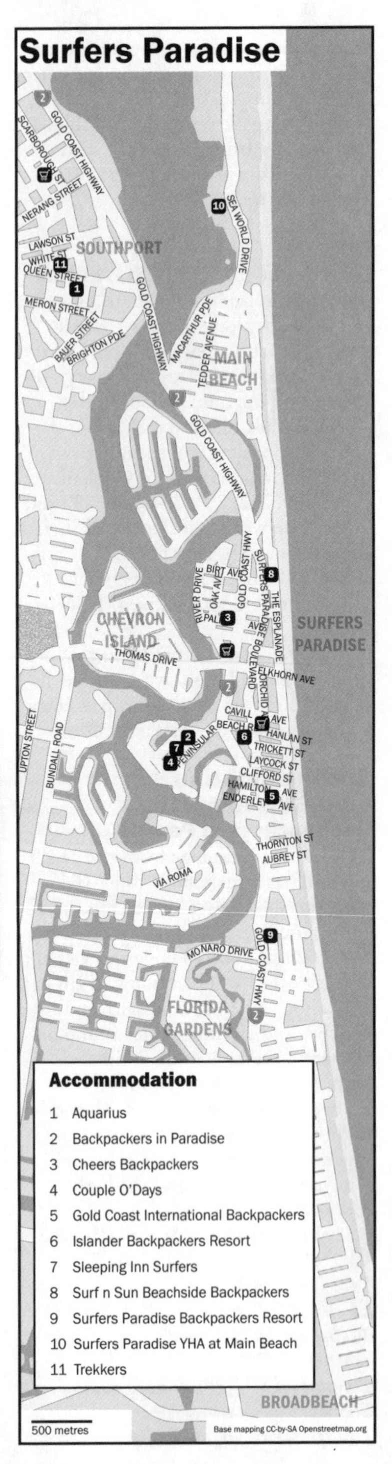

Reception open *8am-10.30pm daily*

Maintenance & cleanliness	★★
Facilities	★★★
Atmosphere & character	★★★★
Security	★★
Overall rating	★★★

Cheers Backpackers

This is a friendly place with a good bar and outside common area. They have a great barbecue every night and the swimming pool is nice. Bathrooms have just been redone, but the dorms are sparse and poorly-maintained. They offer free airport pickup. There are video games, a pool table and table football available in the bar. Staff are very friendly and interesting. It is not a big party hostel, so you will get a good night's sleep here.

8 Pine Avenue, Surfers Paradise
700, 702, 703, 704, 706, 707, 709, 745, 750, TX2
(07) 5531 6539 or 1800 636 539
Website *www.cheersbackpackers.com.au*
Dorm bed *$31;* ***double room*** *$78*
Credit cards *MC, Visa*
Recception open *7.30am-11pm*

Maintenance & cleanliness	★★½
Facilities	★★½
Atmosphere & character	★★★½
Security	★★★
Overall rating	★★★

Couple O' Days

This small hostel has serious maintenance issues and minimal facilities. The kitchen is bare and common areas are messy. Dorms all have en suite bathrooms, but they are old and falling apart. They do offer free internet and pub crawls and there is a nice swimming pool, but that's about it. They cater mostly to Asian backpackers. Reception staff are friendly.

18 Peninsular Drive, Surfers Paradise
700, 702, 703, 704, 706, 707, 709, 745, 750, TX2
(07) 5592 4200 or 1800 646 586
Website *www.coupleodays.com.au*
Dorm bed *$20-28;* ***double room*** *$52-72*
Reception open *7.30am-8pm*

Maintenance & cleanliness	★★½
Facilities	★★
Atmosphere & character	★★
Security	★★
Overall rating	★★

Gold Coast International Backpackers Resort

This hostel has a very institutional feel. The cramped dorms all have en suite bathrooms, but the showers are quite dirty. The kitchen is greasy and old, and the common room is dull and boring. Most rooms have balconies, some with views of the beach and the hostel has a great location, but the facilities here are very poor.

28 Hamilton Avenue, Surfers Paradise

700, 702, 703, 704, 706, 707, 709, 745, 750, TX2

(07) 5592 5888

Website *www.goldcoastbackpackers.com.au*

Dorm bed *$25-30;* ***double room*** *$70*

Credit cards *MC, Visa*

Reception open *7.30am-10pm*

Maintenance & cleanliness	★★
Facilities	★★½
Atmosphere & character	★★★½
Security	★★
Overall rating	★★

Islander Backpackers Resort

As part of a dated hotel in the city centre, guests at this place have access to a swimming pool, sauna, squash court and restaurant. There is a full arcade with great video games downstairs, as well as four pool tables and an internet café. Dorms are updated and clean, and bathrooms are just OK.

6 Beach Road, Surfers Paradise

700, 702, 703, 704, 706, 707, 709, 745, 750, TX2

(07) 5538 8000

Website *www.islander.com.au/backpackers.htm*

Dorm bed *$28; double room $85*

Credit cards *Amex, Diners, MC, Visa*

Reception open *24 hours*

Maintenance & cleanliness	★★★½
Facilities	★★★
Atmosphere & character	★★
Security	★
Overall rating	★★★½

Sleeping Inn Surfers

All of the dorms here have en suite kitchens and bathrooms, so there is not a great social atmosphere here. But they do have a gorgeous pool under a cinema screen, wooden deck chairs and palm trees set up for movie nights which is the highlight at this hostel. They also have an old bus that has been turned into a mini movie room. There is a common room with a pool table and they offer organised tours. Their most famous feature is the free airport pick up in a limousine.

26 Peninsular Drive, Surfers Paradise

700, 702, 703, 704, 706, 707, 709, 745, 750, TX2

(07) 5592 4455 or 1800 817 832

Website *www.sleepinginn.com.au*

Dorm bed *$26-31 (425-30 HI/YHA, VIP);* ***double/single/twin room*** *$68-88 ($66-86 HI/YHA, VIP)*

Credit cards *MC, Visa*

Reception open *7am-10pm*

Maintenance & cleanliness	★★★
Facilities	★★
Atmosphere & character	★★★
Security	★★★½
Overall rating	★★★

Surf n Sun Beachside Backpackers

A small hostel always packed with a cool crowd, the Surf n Sun has a great location just steps away from the beach. It has a nice pool with a lounge deck and a TV lounge where everyone hangs out watching movies. The dorms are quite messy and the staff are a bit careless with cleaning, but they all have en suite bathrooms, fans and TVs that show the movies being played in the common room. They offer barbeques and pool volleyball and free use of body boards. This is the place to meet people and party.

3323 Surfers Paradise Boulevard, Surfers Paradise

700, 702, 703, 704, 706, 707, 709, 745, 750, TX2

(07) 5592 2363 or 1800 678 194

Website *www.surfnsun-goldcoast.com*

Dorm bed *$26-31 ($25-30 VIP);* ***double room*** *$70-80 ($68-78 VIP)*

Credit cards *MC, Visa*

Reception open *7am-10pm*

Maintenance & cleanliness	★★½
Facilities	★★★
Atmosphere & character	★★★★
Security	★★½
Overall rating	★★★

Surfers Paradise Backpackers Resort

This hostel has average dorms and a good range of facilities including a swimming pool, tennis and basketball courts, a small gym and a bar. Guests also offer free use of bikes and body boards. The place has a pretty good atmosphere and the staff are very friendly. The only downside is the lack of security.

2837 Gold Coast Highway, Surfers Paradise

700, 702, 703, 704, 706, 707, 709, 745, 750, TX2

(07) 5592 4677 or 1800 282 800

Website *www.surfersparadisebackpackers.com.au*

Dorm bed *$31;* ***double/twin room*** *$39;* ***apartment*** *$35 per person*

Credit cards *MC Visa*

Reception open *8am-7pm*

Maintenance & cleanliness	★★★
Facilities	★★★★
Atmosphere & character	★★★★
Security	★½
Overall rating	★★★½

Surfers Paradise YHA at Main Beach

This is a quiet hostel north of Surfers Paradise near the marina and Main Beach. It has a modern TV lounge, clean bathrooms and a large kitchen with a barbecue on the balcony. It is surrounded by shops and restaurants and has barbecues every Tuesday. They also offer regular shuttle service to the airport and to town for pub crawls. Staff are welcoming and courteous.

Mariners Cove, 70 Seaworld Drive, Main Beach

715, 750

(07) 5571 1776

Website *www.yha.com.au*

Dorm bed *$33.50 ($26 HI/YHA);* ***double room*** *$76 ($66 HI/YHA)*

Credit cards *MC Visa*

Reception open *7am-10pm daily*

Maintenance & cleanliness	★★★
Facilities	★★
Atmosphere & character	★★★
Security	★★
Overall rating	★★½

SOUTHPORT

Aquarius

Aquarius is a very well maintained hostel with a pool and spa, an outside tropical themed bar, and comfortable TV lounge. The dorms are modern and clean with new bunks and nice carpet and the bathrooms are also very clean. They offer free barbeques and courtesy pick up and shuttle service. Southport is a bit further from the action, so it is quieter here, but they take part in the big hostel parties in town where guests get free drinks, food, and entry into nightclubs.

44 Queen Street, Southport

700, 702, 703, 704, 706, 707, 709, 715, TX2

(07) 5527 1300 or 1800 229 955

Website *www.aquariusbackpack.com.au*

Dorm bed *$26-32;* ***double room*** *$85*

Credit cards *MC, Visa*

Reception open *7am-midnight daily*

Maintenance & cleanliness	★★★
Facilities	★★★½
Atmosphere & character	★★★★
Security	★★½
Overall rating	★★★½

Trekkers

This homely place in Southport has a quiet location and laid-back atmosphere. The dorms are clean and very well maintained, but the beds are annoyingly squeaky and the showers need maintenance. They have a swimming pool and barbeque area and an upstairs sundeck. The common room has wooden furniture, a piano and a pool table. It is an intimate and comfortable setting that attracts a good crowd. They are now under new management and planning extensive remodelling in the next year.

22 White Street, Southport

700, 702, 703, 704, 706, 707, 709,

715, TX2
☎ *(07) 5591 5616*
Website *www.trekkersbackpackers.com.au*
Dorm bed *$28-31 ($27-30 HI/YHA, VIP);* ***double room*** *$76-80*
Credit cards *MC, Visa*
Reception open *7am-9.30pm*

Maintenance & cleanliness	★★★
Facilities	★★★
Atmosphere & character	★★★½
Security	★½
Overall rating	★★★

Eating & Drinking

Surfers Paradise often caters to a relatively affluent crowd and there are some fine five-star dining options. Although often it seems that in some of the cafés you are paying for the location and the view in lieu of quality fare, there are some hidden gems. The Surf Life Saving Clubs are one of the best deals in town for cheap meals and beer. Pubs also sometimes have incredible deals on dinner with a beer for the price you would pay for one beer alone later in the night at a club. Food courts abound as well with some good healthy options and juice bars. There are also loads of cheap, late-night kebab joints in town plus a plethora of fast food restaurants that stay open late to cater to the all-night party crowd.

If you are cooking your own food, there is a **Woolworths** supermarket in the basement of Paradise Centre and a **Coles** in the Chevron Renaissance Centre, both in the centre of Surfers Paradise.

Drinking in Surfers Paradise is a big business and there are several organised club crawls that are a good value way to party at Surfers' top clubs; these include **Plan B** *(**website** www.planbtours.com)* and the cheaper **Wicked Club Crawl** *(**website** www.wickedclubcrawl.com.au)*. Another is the **Big Night Out**, which is a club crawl run by seven hostels. Club crawls cost between $30 and $55 for the night and include drinks and nightclub entry in the ticket price. It is usually a great time and a great bargain, at least until the free drinks run out.

Sights & Activites

The Gold Coast's main attractions are the beaches and the nightlife, but there are plenty of other attractions including a host of amusement parks catering to Australian families. If you don't want to plough through a wad of cash it would be a good idea to stick to the beach or the natural attractions in the hinterland.

If you're planning on visiting several theme parks, you may want to consider a multi park Super Pass *(**website** www.myfun.com.au)* that allows 14 days unlimited entry to Movie World, Seaworld and Wet 'n' Wild for $177 or a single entry to each park for $142. A two-day World Pass *(**website** www.themeparksgoldcoast.com.au)* gives you entry to Dreamworld and WhiteWater World for $102.

Australian Outback Spectacular

This is essentially dinner and a show - on horseback. You get a three-course Aussie barbecue dinner while you watch an Australian-themed show with entertainment on horseback in the 1000-seat arena. It's expensive and geared mostly toward older international tourists who can't get to the outback. The show goes for 1½ hours or 2¼ hours including the pre-show entertainment.

Pacific Motorway, Oxenford
🚌 *TX1, TX2, TX5*
☎ *(07) 5573 3999 or 13 33 86*
Website *http://outbackspectacular.myfun.com.au*
Admission *$95*
Open *6.15pm*

Currumbin Wildlife Sanctuary

Currumbin Sanctuary is an excellent wildlife park at the southern end of the Gold Coast. The park is home to wombats, tree kangaroos, kangaroos, wallabies and Tasmanian devils; although birds are the main attraction.

Gold Coast Highway, Currumbin
🚌 *700, 760, 765, TX1*
☎ *(07) 5534 1266*
Website *www.currumbin-sanctuary.org.au*
Admission *$32*
Open *8am-5pm*

Dreamworld
Dreamworld is a big theme park that features the Tower of Terror – the world's tallest and fastest ride. Other features include an IMAX theatre and an animal park.
Dreamworld Parkway, Coomera
TX1, TX2, TX5
(07) 5588 1111 or 1800 073 300
Website *www.dreamworld.com.au*
Admission *$66, $102 including entry to Whitewater World*
Open *10am-5pm*

Lamington National Park
This national park in the Gold Coast hinterland has been classified by UNESCO as a World Heritage area and is home to unique flora and fauna. The park is close enough to the Gold Coast to make an easy day trip from either Coolangatta or Surfers and there is a good choice of both half-day and full-day walks.
Beechmont, via Nerang
(07) 5534 1266

Paradise Country
This is basically an oversized – and overpriced – petting zoo. You can cuddle a koala and feed kangaroos and watch sheep shearing demonstrations.
Entertainment Road, Oxenford
(07) 5573 8270
Website *http://paradisecountry.myfun.com.au/*
Admission *$57.50; price includes lunch*
Tours *9.30am, 11am, 11.45am, 1.45pm*

Sea World
Home to Australia's only polar bear enclosure, Polar Bear Shores, Sea World offers a range of shows and rides. The interactive marine programme offers visitors a chance to get up close to the park's popular residents, including going behind the scenes with Sea World's marine mammal trainers to meet the dolphins and sea lions, snorkelling and swimming with dolphins and, for the more adventurous, diving with sharks.
Seaworld Drive, The Spit
715, 750
(07) 5588 2222
Website *www.seaworld.com.au*
Admission *$66 or $142 for a 3 park pass*
Open *10am-5pm daily*

Q1 Observation Deck
The 322.5m-tall Q1 Tower is the world's 20th tallest building. It is the world's tallest residential building when measured to the top of its spire, but only the second tallest (to Melbourne's Eureka Tower) when measured to its top floor. It features the world's only beachside observation deck on the 77th and 78th floors, which offer breathtaking 360 degree views that allow you to see from Brisbane to Byron Bay.
Hamilton Avenue, Surfers Paradise
700, 702, 703, 704, 706, 707, 709, 745, 750, TX2
(07) 5630 4700
Website *www.qdeck.com.au*
Admission *$18.50*
Open *10am-late daily*

Warner Bros Movie World
The Warner Bros theme park has a good range of rides and areas themed on Warner Bros movies.
Pacific Highway, Helensvale
TX1, TX2, TX5
(07) 5573 8485
Website *www.movieworld.com.au*
Admission *$66 or $142 for a 3 park pass*
Open *9.30am-5.30pm daily*

Wet 'n' Wild Water World
Wet 'n' Wild features loads of water slides and many people find it is the most fun of the theme parks.
Pacific Highway, Oxenford
TX1, TX2, TX5
(07) 5573 2277
Website *www.wetnwild.com.au*
Admission *$45 or $142 for a 3 park pass*
Open *10am-5pm daily*

WhiteWater World
This new water themed park has loads of waterslides and aquatic-themed rides.
Dreamworld Parkway, Coomera
TX1, TX2, TX5
(07) 5588 1111 or 1800 073 300

Website *www.whitewaterworld.com.au*
Admission *$43, $102 including entry to Dreamworld*
Open *10.30am-4.30pm*

Sunshine Coast

The Sunshine Coast is an aptly named 100km stretch of beachside cities stretching from Caloundra to Noosa Heads. Besides the odd patch of high-rises and commercialised resort attractions, the Sunshine Coast puts the brakes on the late-night hedonism of the Gold Coast and Brisbane. There are great beaches with golden sand and uncrowded surf all along the coast. Outdoor activities abound, from hiking to windsurfing, and everything in between.

Caloundra is an unexceptional city surrounded by good swimming and surfing beaches. Kitesurfing is popular just south at Bulcock Beach and Moffat Beach has good waves. About 30km north are Mooloolaba, Alexandra Headland and Maroochydore, a strip of towns known for fishing and surfing, as well as shopping and luxury resorts. North of that is the quieter expanse from Coolum to Peregian Beach, with beautiful and secluded shoreline. Noosa is more of a five star resort town, and has high prices and sizeable crowds. But it still boasts some lovely natural wonders at the coast and inland, including the Teewah Coloured Sands accessible by four-wheel-drive on the beach.

Buses run frequently between all of the towns on the Sunshine Coast so it's easy to get around. In the hinterland are the Glass House Mountains and the Australia Zoo, Steve Irwin's famous wildlife park. Many travellers use the Sunshine Coast as a home base when trekking through the hinterland or travelling to Fraser Island.

Coming & Going

AIR

Sunshine Coast Airport (☎ *(07) 5453 1500)* has flights to most major destinations in Australia making it a viable alternative to Brisbane Airport. The airport is about 10km north of Maroochydore on the way to Noosa. Airport shuttle buses run from the airport to destinations up and down the Sunshine Coast. Sun-Air Bus Services *(**website** www.sunair.com.au)* goes to areas of the Sunshine Coast south of the airport including Maroochydore ($21) and Caloundra ($28). Henry's Airport Shuttle *(**website** www.henrys.com.au)* goes to Noosa ($22).
Sun-Air also run bus transfers between Brisbane Airport and the Sunshine Coast, which cost $32-33.

BUS

Some coaches run inland along the Bruce Highway, where it is possible to get off at either Nambour or Cooroy and get a connecting bus from there to the coast. However most coaches also call in at Maroochydore and Noosa. Both Greyhound (☎ *1300 473 946; **website** www.greyhound.com.au)* and Premier Motor Services (☎ *13 34 10; **website** www.premierms.com.au)* serve the Sunshine Coast.

TRAIN

Frequent trains run between Brisbane and the Sunshine Coast hinterland. Take the train to Cooroy, Eumundi or Nambour and take a connecting bus to Noosa or Maroochydore on the coast. You can get to Noosa by bus 630 from Eumundi station or bus 631 from Cooroy; buses 602 or 610 run between Nambour and Maroochydore.

Local Transport

The Sunshine Coast has a reasonably good local bus service *(**website** www.translink.com.au)* with buses running up and down the coast with connecting services to inland centres like Nambour, Cooroy and Eumundi.

Caloundra

Caloundra is an unsophisticated town, 96km north of Brisbane that sits on a tropical headland rich in fruit and vegetable farms. It is a well known holiday destination due to its excellent year-round climate and sandy beaches with good surf. It appeals to all ages, and is popular with families as well as independent travellers. Fishing is good here in the calm waters around Pumicestone Channel and off the jetty at Golden Beach, and there are several companies offering daily fishing trips. Snorkelling is also good in these calmer areas, especially off King's Beach.

Some other activities in the area are also worth visiting. Steve Irwin's Australia Zoo, although pricey, is a great place to see crocodiles and other wildlife. It is just off the highway before town, at the same turnoff for the spectacular Glass House Mountains. These are an ever-popular excursion with backpackers for the beautiful views and great opportunity for hiking. The Big Pineapple is the third big sight here, which is one of Australia's famed Big Things, as well as being a fully functional pineapple and macadamia nut plantation.

Caloundra itself doesn't have much to offer otherwise. People come here for the water sports and fishing; some also come for skydiving and flying lessons. The town is basically just a long strip of shops surrounded by suburban homes, with a few good cafés and cheap food. It is a business centre at heart, with a small-town feel and a barely blossoming tourist base.

Practical Information

Caloundra Tourism

7 Caloundra Road, Caloundra
600, 601, 602, 605, 607, 609
(07) 5491 9233 or 1800 644 969
***Website** www.caloundratourism.com.au*
***Open** 9am-5pm daily*

Coming & Going

Translink *(**website** www.translink.com.au)* bus route 605 connects Caloundra with Landsborough Station, route 602 goes to Nambour station via Maroochydore and routes 600 and 607 go up to coast to Maroochydore via Mooloolaba and Alexandra Headland.

Accommodation

Caloundra City Backpackers

This lovely hostel has only 20 rooms on two floors with large balconies on both sides. The whole place is painted in white and pastel yellow, giving it a very breezy feel. Everything here, especially the bathroom, is new and immaculately clean. There are two kitchens, which are small but also new and clean. They don't offer many on-site facilities but guests have free use of bikes and body boards. It is not a party hostel, but most travellers don't come to Caloundra to party anyway. Management couldn't be sweeter.

84 Omrah Avenue, Caloundra
600, 601, 602, 605, 607, 609
(07) 5499 7655
***Website** www.caloundracitybackpackers.com.au*
***Dorm bed** $25; **double room** $60-70*
***Credit cards** MC Visa*
***Reception open** 8.30am-9pm daily*

Maintenance & cleanliness	★★★★½
Facilities	★★★
Atmosphere & character	★★★★
Security	★★
Overall rating	★★★★

Sights & Activities

Kayaking

Blue Water Kayak Tours *(☎ (07) 5494 7789; **website** www.bluewaterkayaktours.com)* run kayaking trips to Pumicestone Passage and Moreton Bay Marine Park that allow you to paddle over to secluded beaches on Bribie Island. Half day tours cost $65 and full day tours are $130.

Queensland Air Museum

This aviation museum at Caloundra Aerodrome has around 40 historic aircraft.

Pathfinder Drive, Caloundra Aerodrome, Caloundra
(07) 5492 5930
***Website** www.qam.com.au*
***Admission** $9*
***Open** 10am-4pm daily*

Sky Diving

Caloundra is a great spot for skydiving and it is one of the very few places where you can have a beach landing. Most people jump from 12,000ft, which gives you 45 seconds of freefall, but you also have the option of a jump from 14,000ft with 60 seconds freefall or the budget option from 6,000ft with only 10 seconds freefall.

Pathfinder Drive, Caloundra Aerodrome, Caloundra

☎ *0500 522 533*
Website *www.scskydivers.com*
12000ft tandem skydive *$314;*
14000ft tandem skydive *$339*

Maroochydore & Mooloolaba

The Sunshine Coast's largest urban area encompasses the towns of Alexandra Headland, Maroochydore and Mooloolaba. This part of the coast has been overcome by high rise apartments and family-oriented resorts, but it still has great beaches and is a good place for fishing, surfing and swimming.

Maroochydore is the busiest spot on the Sunshine Coast with a commercial feel. Although it has some good water sports and nightlife, Maroochydore seems dull when compared to prettier Mooloolaba and the lusher beach towns on the Fraser Coast. Many backpackers use Maroochydore as a base for work during fruit picking season. The business centre here is a succession of shops along Aerodrome Road although the large Sunshine Plaza is the main shopping centre. Families come to Maroochydore to play on the protected beaches, while backpackers come for the skydiving and kayaking.

Mooloolaba is nice beach town with a lively atmosphere, despite several medium-rise oceanfront apartment towers. There are loads of eateries on the Esplanade where backpackers rub elbows with wealthy holiday-makers. The nightlife is good here as well and most backpackers choose to stay here for the combination of fun bars and sunny beaches. Mooloolaba's big attraction is UnderWater World, an oceanarium and marine park where you can walk through a huge glass tunnel surrounded by sharks, rays and tropical fish.

Practical Information

Mooloolaba Tourist Information Centre

Corner First Avenue & Brisbane Road, Mooloolaba
☎ *(07) 5444 5755*
Website *www.maroochytourism.com*
Open *Mon-Fri 8am-5.30pm, Sat-Sun 8am-5pm*

Maroochydore Tourist Information Centre

Corner Sixth Avenue & Melrose Place, Maroochydore
☎ *(07) 5479 1566*
Website *www.maroochytourism.com*
Open *Mon-Fri 9am-5pm, Sat-Sun 9am-4pm*

Sunshine Coast Airport Information Centre

Friendship Drive, Marcoola
☎ *(07) 5448 9088*
Website *www.maroochytourism.com*
Open *8.30am-3.45/4pm daily*

INTERNET ACCESS

Email Central Internet Lounge

19 The Esplanade, Cotton Tree, Maroochydore
☎ *(07) 5443 4440*
Open *9am-8pm daily*

Bluesurf Internet Cafe

Shop 11 Pacific Beach Resort, 95 Mooloolaba Esplanade, Mooloolaba
☎ *(07) 5477 7970*
Website *www.bluesurf.com.au*
Open *7am-7pm daily*

Coming & Going

Translink *(**website** www.translink.com.au)* bus routes 600, 601, 602, 619 and 622 run between Maroochydore and Mooloolaba. Buses 602 and 610 go to Nambour and bus 620 goes to Noosa.

Greyhound *(☎ 1300 473 946; **website** www.greyhound.com.au)* and Premier Motor Service *(**website** www.premierms.com.au)* buses stop in Maroochydore and Mooloolaba on their Brisbane to Cairns route. Greyhound stops at the tourist information centre on 6th Avenue in Maroochydore and Premier Motor Service stops at Scotlyn Fair on 1st Avenue in Maroochydore and the intercity stop at the Bowling Green in Mooloolaba.

Accommodation

MOOLOOLABA

Mooloolaba Beach Backpackers

This is a fun hostel in three colour-coded buildings – each with their own kitchen – in the heart of Mooloolaba. It has a great swimming pool with a volleyball net and a lively outside common area where they host events every night. There is a pool table, table tennis, a barbecue and guests have free use of bikes, surfboards, body boards and kayaks. It is located just two blocks from the beach, and they organise trips to the Glass House Mountains, the Eumundi market and the Australia Zoo, among others. Dorms have en suite bathroom facilities and are clean, if a bit old. It has a great party atmosphere but doesn't overdo it.

75 Brisbane Road, Mooloolaba
600, 619
(07) 5444 3399 or 1800 210 120
***Dorm bed** $26-29 ($25-28 VIP); **double room** $70 ($68 VIP); prices include breakfast*
***Credit cards** MC Visa*
***Reception open** Mon-Thu 8am-8pm; Fri-Sat 8am-10pm; Sun 8am-8pm*

Maintenance & cleanliness	★★★
Facilities	★★★★½
Atmosphere & character	★★★★½
Security	★★★½
Overall rating	★★★★

MAROOCHYDORE

Cotton Tree Backpackers

This homely hostel is full of bright yellows and blues and the walls are full of writing from previous happy guests, many of whom have stayed long-term to work in Maroochydore. It is a cheerful hostel, although quite run down and the bathrooms are tiny and dirty. Dorms are quirky and cluttered and some have a nice view over the Esplanade. Guests have free use of bikes, body boards, surfboards, kayaks and surf skis, and the hostel offers free pick up from the airport and bus stations. It has a great location and the management treat you like family.

15 The Esplanade, Cotton Tree
600, 610, 615, 622
(07) 5443 1755
***Website** www.cottontreebackpackers.com*
***Dorm bed** $23 per night, $63 for 3 nights, $138 per week; **double/twin room** $55-60*
***Credit cards** MC, Visa*
***Reception open** 8am-8pm daily*

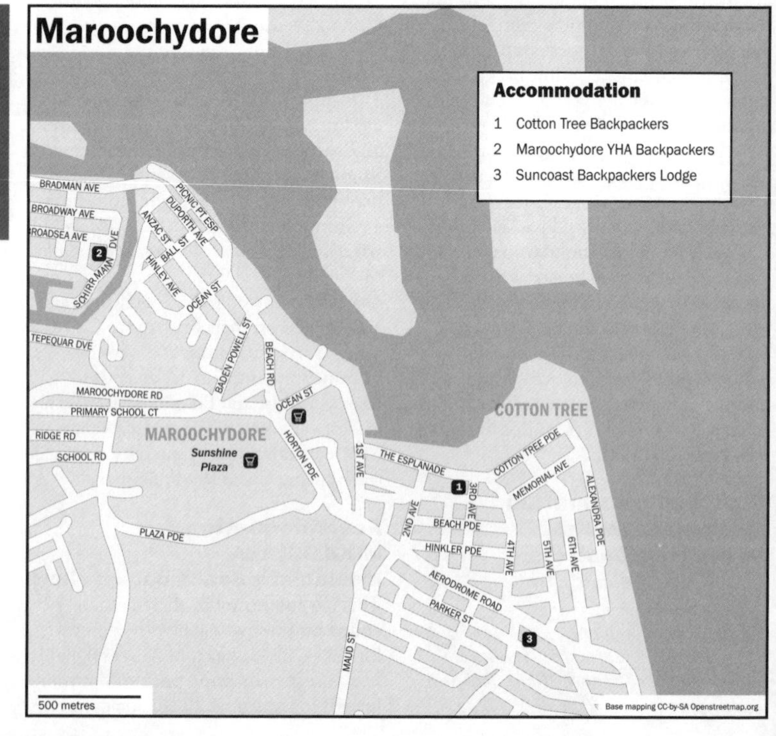

Maintenance & cleanliness	★★
Facilities	★★★
Atmosphere & character	★★★½
Security	★★
Overall rating	★★½

Maroochydore YHA Backpackers

This YHA has lots of colour but is looking rather weathered. The dorms are compact and quickly get cluttered. The bathrooms have old tiles and grimy showers. There is a good cinema room with soft couches and a chilled out atmosphere, and a hammock-lined backyard with a big swimming pool. They offer free breakfast, body boards and kayaks, yoga classes, and regular shuttle service, including a daily bus to the Australia Zoo and Underwater World. It is located in a quiet residential area.

24 Schirrmann Drive, Maroochydore

602, 620, 622

(07) 5443 3151 or 1800 302 855

***Website** www.yha.com.au*

***Dorm bed** $25 ($22.50 HI/YHA); **double/twin room** $64 ($57.60 HI/YHA); prices include breakfast*

***Credit cards** MC, Visa*

***Reception open** 8am-1pm & 2pm-7pm daily*

Maintenance & cleanliness	★★
Facilities	★★★★
Atmosphere & character	★★★
Security	★★½
Overall rating	★★★

Suncoast Backpackers Lodge

This hostel mainly caters to people on a working holiday. As such, the dorms are a complete wreck and the bathrooms are dirty. The common room is a funky old shed with knick knacks and flags scattered around the walls. The kitchen is surprisingly clean and well equipped, but still aging. The owners provide a real family atmosphere, and if you are here for temporary work, this is a great place to meet others doing the same.

50 Parker Street, Maroochydore

600, 610, 615, 622

(07) 5443 7544

***Dorm bed** $23 ($22 VIP); **double/twin room** $49 ($47 VIP)*

***Credit cards** MC, Visa*

***Reception open** Mon-Fri 8.30am-noon & 5pm-7pm, Sat-Sun 9am-noon & 5pm-6.30pm*

Maintenance & cleanliness	★★
Facilities	★★★
Atmosphere & character	★★★
Security	★★
Overall rating	★★½

Eating & Drinking

There are loads of fast food options both in Maroochydore and Mooloolaba, and some stay open late for the party crowd. Most of the big fast food chains can be found along Aerodrome Road in Maroochydore although the food court in the **Sunshine Plaza** is a better bet. There are also some cheap sandwich and wrap shops for travellers looking for a healthier option.

If you're preparing your own food there is a good choice of supermarkets along the coast. In Maroochydore there is are **Coles** and **Woolworths** supermarkets in the Sunshine Plaza and another **Woolworths** at the Big Top *(corner Ocean Street & Horton Parade)*. In Mooloolaba there is a **Coles** on the corner of Venning and Walan Streets.

Sights

UnderWater World

The largest aquarium in the southern hemisphere is worth a look. It is home to a wide variety of marine life ranging from crocodiles to colourful tropical fish, turtles and seals. You also have the opportunity to dive with sharks and stingrays.

The Wharf, Parkyn Parade, Mooloolaba

600, 601, 605

(07) 5444 2255

***Website** www.underwaterworld.com.au*

***Admission** $26.50*

***Open** 9am-5pm daily*

Coolum

Located around halfway between Maroochydore and Noosa, Coolum has great beaches backed by Mount Coolum National Park.

A hiking trail (800m, 2hrs return) climbs to the top of 208m Mount

Queensland

Coolum, rewarding the exhausted hiker with stunning 360-degree views.

Practical Information

Coolum Visitor Information Centre
Corner David Low Way & Williams Street, Coolum
☎ *(07) 5446 5910 or 1800 448 833*
Website *www.maroochytourism.com*
Open *9am-5pm daily*

Coming & Going

Translink *(**website** www.translink.com.au)* buses 620 and 622 go to Maroochydore. Bus 620 continues to Noosa and bus 622 goes via Mt Coolum.

Noosa

A two-hour drive north from Brisbane, Noosa is an upmarket resort town with prices to prove it. It boasts sunny beaches, lovely parklands, and a spattering of petite shopping centres and cafés. Although it is known as a glamorous holiday destination for the rich, the boutiques and fine dining restaurants share space with surf shops and fish and chip joints. There are upmarket condos side-by-side with hostels and motels, and sports cars glide by Kombi vans loaded with hippie surfers.

The main attractions here for backpackers are the beaches and water sports. It is surrounded by long stretches of protected sandy beach, and the Noosa River is a popular place for kayaking and canoeing. Surfing is great off the point at Sunshine Beach, while Main Beach has gentle waves good for beginners. The Noosa National Park has some wonderful walking tracks where you can look out over the surf breaks and spot koalas resting in the gum trees. On Saturdays, the Eumundi Market – 20km inland from Noosa – is a popular excursion, with most hostels running daytrips.

Practical Information

Noosa Visitor Information Centre
Corner Noosa Drive & Hastings Street, Noosa Heads
☎ *(07) 5447 4988*
Website *www.tourismnoosa.com.au*
Open *9am-5pm daily*

Great Sandy National Park Information Centre
Moorindil Street, Tewantin
☎ *(07) 5449 7792*
Website *www.epa.qld.gov.au*
Open *7am-4pm daily*

Coming & Going

Translink *(**website** www.translink.com.au)* bus 620 goes down the coast to Maroochydore; bus 627 goes to Sunshine Beach; 628 runs up Hastings Street to Noosa National Park and bus 630 goes to Eumundi.

Greyhound *(☎ 1300 473 946; **website** www.greyhound.com.au)* and Premier Motor Service *(**website** www.premierms.com.au)* buses stop at the bus stop opposite Lions Park in Noosa Heads.

Accommodation

NOOSA HEADS & NOOSAVILLE

Halse Lodge YHA

This youth hostel is in a beautifully restored manor house perched high on a hill just a short walk from Hastings Street. The furnishings are all well maintained with lots of wood and neutral colours. Dorms are clean and comfortable, the kitchen is small but well equipped, and there is a bar/café with cheap food and lots of character. The hostel is comprised of two buildings, both with large open-beam balconies where travellers read, hangout and mingle. The TV lounge is huge, with large screens, a piano, pool table, and old photographs on the walls. Reception staff are genuine and attentive.
Halse Lane, Noosa Heads
🚌 *628*
☎ *(07) 5447 3377 or 1800 242 567*
Website *www.yha.com.au*
Dorm bed *$32 ($29 HI/YHA, VIP);* **double room** *$82 ($74 HI/YHA, VIP);* **triple room** *$108 ($101 HI/YHA, VIP)*
Credit cards *MC, Visa; 1% credit card surcharge*
Reception open *7am-8.15pm daily; check in at bar until 11pm*

TV K L

Maintenance & cleanliness	★★★★
Facilities	★★½
Atmosphere & character	★★★½
Security	★★
Overall rating	★★★½

Koala Beach Resort

Koala is a party hostel. It has a great bar, a clear swimming pool, volleyball court, free use of bikes and surfboards, and a frequent shuttle service. There is also the usual laundry, internet access ($3 per hour) and barbecue. Unfortunately the rooms are bare and the bathrooms are hideous. The kitchen is basic and on the dirty side and the hostel is due for a facelift. It does have a good location, and surprisingly for a party hostel, reception staff are kind and attentive. They organise daily trips and nightly events and Koala Adventures travel agency has heaps of tours and excursions available.

44 Noosa Drive, Noosa Heads
620, 627, 628, 629, 630
(07) 5447 3355 or 1800 357 457
Website *www.koala-backpackers.com*
Dorm bed *$27 ($26 VIP);* ***double/twin room*** *$60*
Credit cards *MC, Visa*
Reception open *7.30am-8pm daily*

Maintenance & cleanliness	★★
Facilities	★★★★½
Atmosphere & character	★★★★½
Security	★★
Overall rating	★★★½

Noosa Backpackers Resort

This hostel is in the quiet residential area of Noosaville. It successfully combines a mild party atmosphere with a relaxed and clean daytime hangout. With its own bar and a palm-fringed restaurant that fills nightly, guests get a chance to mingle with the locals and socialise well into the night. The dorms all have en suite kitchen facilities, though everyone uses the large hostel kitchen. The bathrooms are sparkling clean. There is also a nice swimming pool plus a barbecue and table tennis. Internet, including Wi-Fi, is $4 per hour, and there is a good tour desk. Guests have free use of bicycles, body boards, surfboards, and kayaks. Reception staff are fun and helpful. If only they had better security.

9-13 William Street, Noosaville
626, 627, 630, 631
(07) 5449 8151 or 1800 626 673
Website *www.noosabackpackers.com*
Dorm bed *$24-28;* ***double room*** *$56-60;* ***family room*** *$72-96*
Credit cards *Amex, Diners, MC, Visa*
Reception open *8am-7.30pm daily*

Maintenance & cleanliness	★★★½
Facilities	★★★★½
Atmosphere & character	★★★★½
Security	★½
Overall rating	★★★★

SUNSHINE BEACH & SUNRISE BEACH

Dolphins Beach House

What this hostel lacks in maintenance, it makes up for in character with bright pink and aqua green walls surrounding island style furniture and Tibetan prayer flags. The leafy courtyard acts as a laid-back common area with a barbecue and stack of surfboards. There is also a small swimming pool, a pool table and table tennis table. The small dorms are in self-contained units with kitchens, bathrooms and televisions. There is also a "rainforest shower" in the back which is partly outdoors with mosaic tiles. With friendly staff, it is a good place to chill out.

14-16 Duke Street, Sunrise Beach
627
(07) 5447 2100
Website *www.dolphinsbeachhouse.com*
Dorm bed *$25*
Credit cards *MC, Visa*
Reception open *8am-8pm daily*

Maintenance & cleanliness	★★★
Facilities	★★★½
Atmosphere & character	★★★½
Security	★½
Overall rating	★★★

Melaluka on the Beach

This place feels more like an apartment building than a hostel. Each unit is entirely self-contained, each with its own small kitchen and lounge room so

there is no real atmosphere here unless you get along really well with the three or four other people in the same unit. The bathrooms are not particularly clean and the furnishings are dated. There are not many facilities besides laundry and free use of body boards. The doubles in the building next door are spotless and new. Management is friendly and knowledgeable.
7 Selene Street, Sunrise Beach
620
(07) 5447 3663 or 1800 003 663
***Website** www.melaluka.com.au*
***Dorm bed** $26; **double room** $60-70; **twin room** $52*
***Credit cards** MC, Visa*
***Reception open** Mon-Fri 9am-5.30pm, Sat 10am-5pm, Sun 10am-3pm*

Maintenance & cleanliness	★★
Facilities	★★
Atmosphere & character	★
Security	★½
Overall rating	★★

NOOSA RIVER & NORTH SHORE

Gagaju Bush Camp

Gagaju boasts a rustic bush setting on 2.4ha with accommodation in big tents. Facilities include a TV/video room, book exchange, a games room with table tennis, darts and a pool table, a gym, volleyball court and an outdoor kitchen with barbecues. Activities include didgeridoo making workshops and canoe trips and guests have free use of fishing rods. It is in a natural bush setting on the banks of the Noosa River, about 15km from Noosa. There's a good chance of seeing wildlife here.
118 Johns Road, Cooroibah
(07) 5474 3522
***Website** www.travoholic.com/gagaju/*
***Dorm bed** $15*
***Credit cards** MC, Visa*

Maintenance & cleanliness	★
Facilities	★½
Atmosphere & character	★★★★
Security	★
Overall rating	★★

Noosa North Shore Resort

Noosa North Shore Retreat is a wonderful place to stay for some rest and relaxation. It sits on 90 hectares of secluded bush land where kangaroos hop freely around the dorm buildings. Facilities are excellent and include a swimming pool, spa pool, barbecue area and an on-site equestrian centre. Guests have free use of bikes and kayaks. Accommodation is in self-contained units that are exceptionally clean and well maintained. The hostel is 1km from the beach and the onsite bar and restaurant offers discount backpacker meals.
Maximillian Road, Noosa North Shore
car ferry from Tewantin
(07) 5447 1225
***Website** www.noosanorthshorebackpackers.com.au*
***Dorm bed** $20; **double room** $50*
***Credit cards** Amex, Diners, MC, Visa*
***Reception open** 7am-8pm*

Maintenance & cleanliness	★★★★½
Facilities	★★★★½
Atmosphere & character	★★½
Security	★★
Overall rating	★★★★

Eating & Drinking

Noosa has a small-town vibe and a laid-back café scene with a nice atmosphere, but you'll pay for it. For the most part, Noosa cashes in on the influx of wealthy international visitors and domestic holiday-makers. There are a few good value eateries, but your best bet here is the supermarket.

Hastings Street in Noosa Heads is the trendy area with high priced Parisian-style cafés that are great for people-watching; while Sunshine Beach has sleepy, better value eateries and sandy feet with some nice spots for breakfast, lunch or a snack after you hit the beach. **Sunshine Foodstore** *(46 Duke Street, Sunshine Beach)* has a convivial setting and cheap healthy food.

There are plenty of fast food places near the shopping centres, but there are not many places that stay open late, so you'll need to stock up on snacks for the midnight munchies. Coffee in Noosa is usually great, and there are many juice bars with fresh juice and smoothies.

There are quite a few good nightclubs and bars in Noosa, but most of them have ridiculously overpriced drinks. Happy hour at the hostel bars is not such a bad idea and deals on jugs of beer are usually worth it.

Noosaville is the best part of Noosa to buy groceries. The cheapest supermarket is **Aldi** *(201 Weyba Road, Noosaville)*. There is also a **Coles** at the Noosa Fair Shopping Centre *(Lanyana Way, Castaways Beach)* and **Woolworths** at the corner of Gibson Road and Mary Street in Noosaville. Most of the hostels here have plenty of kitchen space and supplies.

Sights

Eumundi Markets

This large craft market takes place every Wednesday and Saturday and is one of the best markets in Australia. It is held in Eumundi, which is about 15km west of Noosa. Storeyline Tours (☎ *(07) 5474 1500)* run a shuttle bus from Caloundra, Mooloolaba, Maroochydore, Coolumn and Noosa that costs $12-16; but it is much cheaper to simply take bus 630 from Noosa.

Noosa National Park

This is a small, but excellent, national park easily accessible from the centre of Noosa Heads. The park has great beaches plus wildlife including koalas.

Sunshine Coast Hinterland

The area inland from the Sunshine Coast is home to natural attractions including the Glasshouse Mountains. Most of the sights in the hinterland are an easy daytrip from Maroochydore, Mooloolaba, Noosa or Brisbane.

Sights

Australia Zoo

Famed as the home of Steve Irwin, television's Crocodile Hunter, Australia Zoo was established in 1970 and is now home to more than 750 animals. The park features a large range of animals with a strong focus on Australian animals including giant pythons, some of the world's most venomous snakes, wild birds and native turtles and saltwater crocodiles.

Glasshouse Mountains Tourist Route, Beerwah
🚆 *Landsborough, then D 615 extension*
☎ *(07) 5494 1134*
Website *www.australiazoo.com.au*
Admission *$52 ($41 students)*
Open *9am-4.30pm daily*

Fraser Coast

The Fraser Coast is a relatively short stretch of coastal Queensland that offers some truly unique natural wonders. Although many of the towns are unremarkable, there are some pleasant places to spend a couple of days while you are off exploring.

First and foremost on everyone's agenda is the spectacular World Heritage-listed Fraser Island. At 120km from top to toe, it is the world's largest sand island. With endless beaches, headlands, rainforests and picture perfect freshwater lakes, it is a great place to escape. However with the increasing amounts of tour companies hawking "Fraser" like a cheap meal, during peak times it can get crowded with day-trippers.

Hervey Bay is the usual jumping off point to Fraser Island, but Rainbow Beach is gaining in popularity these days and Rainbow Beach's coloured sand cliffs are world famous.

Hervey Bay

Hervey Bay is a cluster of seaside suburbs that would otherwise never have made it onto the backpacker map. Its beachfront drive, the Esplanade, is not nearly as flashy as it sounds. There are some cheap restaurants, but otherwise it is a boring string of souvenir stores and overpriced surf shops. However Hervey is the most popular launching point for trips to Fraser Island, as it has an industrial and commercial infrastructure that makes it the ideal place to stock up on cheap supplies and organise your Fraser excursion. There is more than enough hostel accommodation here, from drab caravan park/hostels to party hostels, and not one of them misses a beat when it comes to the lucrative draw card of Fraser trips.

That said, it does have one other major attraction. Between August and October, humpback whales slowly cruise through Hervey Bay in the middle of their long migration. They stay in the area for a few months preparing the calves for the trip south to Antarctica. Several tours operate during this period; they can be expensive, but the sight of these creatures up close is definitely worth it. Many companies also offer guarantees, with a free trip if you don't spot any whales.

There are also good fishing spots, helicopter and skydiving trips, horseback riding and camel safaris. If you are in town for a few days, it is a good idea to rent a bike to get around, since the bus system in town is quite unreliable.

Practical Information

Hervey Bay Visitor Information Centre

Corner Maryborough-Hervey Bay & Urraween Roads, Urraween
🚌 *5*
☎ *(07) 4125 9855 or 1800 811 728*
Website *www.herveybay.qld.gov.au*
Open *9am-5pm daily*

Hervey Bay Visitor Information Centre

Hervey Bay Airport Terminal, Don Adams Drive, Urangan
☎ *1800 811 728*
Website *www.herveybay.qld.gov.au*

Coming & Going

AIR

Jetstar and Virgin Blue fly to Hervey Bay Airport *(**website** www.frasercoastairport.com.au)* from Sydney and Qantas has flights from Brisbane.

Airport Shuttle Hervey Bay *(☎ (07) 4194 6525; **website** http://airportshuttleherveybay.com.au/)* operates a door-to-door transport service picking up and dropping off at hostels in Hervey Bay. Fares start at $6.

BUS

Both Greyhound *(☎ 1300 473 946; **website** www.greyhound.com.au)* and Premier Motor Service *(**website** www.premierms.com.au)* serve Hervey Bay. Buses stop at the Bay Central Coach Terminal at the Bay Central Shopping Centre in Pialba.

TRAIN

The nearest train station to Hervey Bay is in nearby Maryborough. Wide Bay Transit's *(**website** www.widebaytransit.com.au)* bus route 5 runs between Maryborough and Hervey Bay.

Local Transport

Wide Bay Transit *(☎ (07) 4121 3719; **website** www.widebaytransit.com.au)* run local bus services in Hervey Bay. There are six bus routes in Hervey Bay and routes 5, 16 and 18 cover the part of town where most of the hostels are and route 5 goes as far as Marysborough. All bus routes terminate at the Centro Hervey Bay Shopping Centre.

One way fares cost $2.90 to $6.20 and you can buy a Day Rover ticket, which costs $7.30 and is good for one day's unlimited bus travel in Hervey Bay.

Accommodation

Aussie Woolshed Backpackers

Aussie Woolshed Backpackers has a few small dorms that are clean and well kept plus internet access ($4 per hour) and a kitchen/common area that is modelled after a traditional Australian woolshed. The kitchen is nothing special but it has all the necessary fittings. The beds are comfortable and the friendly and the family run hostel has a quiet homely atmosphere. Like most other hostels in Hervey Bay, they also organise tours to Fraser Island.

181 Torquay Road, Scarness
🚌 *5, 16, 18*
☎ *(07) 4124 0677*
Website *www.woolshedbackpackers.com*
Dorm bed *$18-22;* ***double/twin room*** *$46-64*
Credit cards *MC, Visa*
Reception open *7am-7pm daily*

Maintenance & cleanliness	★★★
Facilities	★★
Atmosphere & character	★★★½
Security	★★
Overall rating	★★★

Beaches Backpackers

Beaches has a good backpacker atmosphere. They organise tours daily and have a laid-back common room, internet access ($4 per hour) and clean kitchen. The dorms are nice, they are set in garden cabins although the carpets are old and stained. Bathrooms are also a bit rough around the edges. However there is a good swimming pool, a sleek bar with a large screen telly, and the friendliest staff in Hervey Bay.

195 Torquay Road, Scarness
5, 16, 18
(07) 4124 1322
Website *www.beaches.com.au*
Dorm bed *$22;* ***double/twin room*** *$60-65*
Credit cards *MC, Visa*
Reception open *7am-8pm daily*

Maintenance & cleanliness	★★½
Facilities	★★★½
Atmosphere & character	★★★★
Security	★½
Overall rating	★★★

Colonial Village YHA

This hostel has accommodation in cabins surrounded by gardens and ponds, with some nice water features. There are heaps of facilities including a swimming pool and spa, tennis court, basketball court and scooter hire. Dorms are a bit plain, but some have their own balconies. The large common room and kitchen are nice. Staff here can be very curt.

Corner Boat Harbour Drive & Pulgul Street, Urangan
5, 16
1800 818 280
Website *www.cvyha.com*
Dorm bed *$23-32 ($20-28 HI/YHA);* ***double room*** *$56-73 ($50-65 HI/YHA);* ***villa*** *$90-100;* ***camping*** *$18-24 per person*
Credit cards *MC, Visa*
Reception open *7am-8pm daily*

Maintenance & cleanliness	★★★
Facilities	★★★★½
Atmosphere & character	★★★½
Security	★★½
Overall rating	★★★½

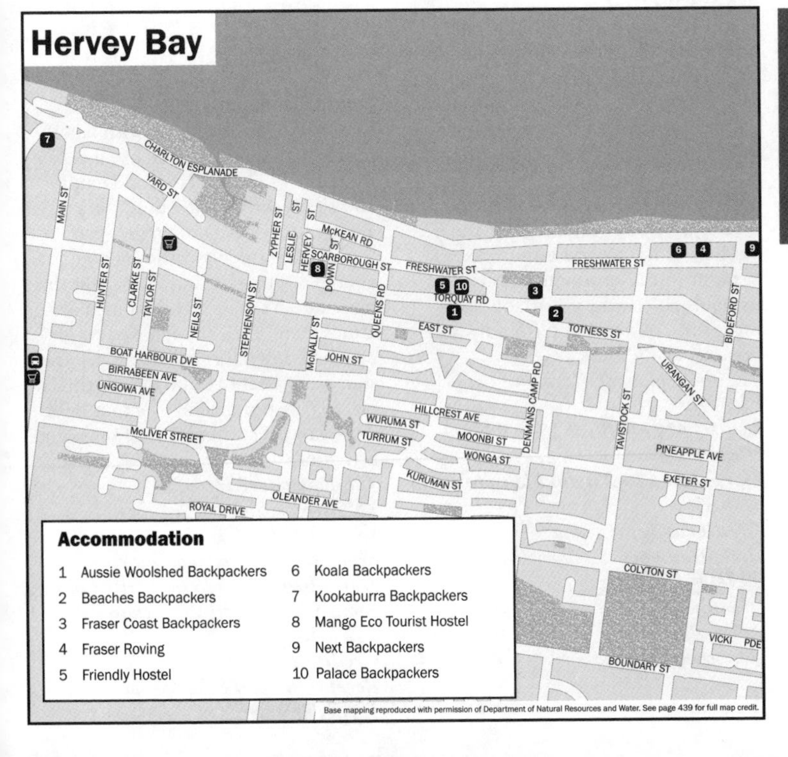

Fraser Coast Backpackers

Fraser Coast Backpackers is a mix of caravans, campsites and two unit self-contained dorms with kitchenettes and clean bathrooms. The large "Dingo Bar" has pool tables and theme nights. There is also laundry, internet access ($4 per hour), a barbecue area and tour desk. Reception staff are very friendly, but there is barely any backpackers' atmosphere. It is a good value for the price.

21 Denmans Camp Road, Scarness
(07) 4124 6237
Website *www.frasercoastbackpackers.com.au*
Dorm bed *$15-18;* ***double room*** *$40-60*
Credit cards *MC, Visa*
Reception open *7am-9pm daily*

Maintenance & cleanliness	★★½
Facilities	★★½
Atmosphere & character	★½
Security	★½
Overall rating	★★½

Fraser Roving

Fraser Roving is a large building with bright murals, simple dorms and clean bathrooms. The kitchen isn't much, but there is a bar/restaurant on site and it is located on the Esplanade near lots of shops and cheap cafés. They have a nice swimming pool, a mini golf course in front and a barbecue area in a small courtyard near the kitchen. It has a good atmosphere at night in the common area with its pool table and comfortable seating. Staff are warm and friendly and organise daily tours.

412 The Esplanade, Torquay
5, 16
(07) 4125 6386 or 1800 989811
Website *www.fraserroving.com*
Dorm bed *$20-23;* ***double/twin room*** *$60-65*
Credit cards *MC, Visa*
Reception open *5.30am-9pm daily*

Maintenance & cleanliness	★★★
Facilities	★★★½
Atmosphere & character	★★★★½
Security	★★★
Overall rating	★★★½

Friendly Hostel

This is a small place comprised of shared apartments, each with fully equipped kitchens, TV lounges and new, clean bathrooms. The beds are large and very comfortable and there is internet access ($5 per hour). Everything is well maintained, and although this place has a very quiet atmosphere, it is a good spot to relax. In the morning you can sit on the upstairs balcony with the lorikeets and watch the bats fly over in the evening. Definitely a friendly place.

182 Torquay Road, Scarness
5, 16, 18
1800 244 107
Website *www.thefriendly.com.au*
Dorm bed *$22-23;* ***single room*** *$47;* ***double/twin room*** *$50-70;* ***apartment*** *(2 or 3 bedrooms) $132-170*
Credit cards *MC, Visa; 1% credit card surcharge*
Reception open *7am-7pm daily*

Maintenance & cleanliness	★★★½
Facilities	★★★
Atmosphere & character	★★★
Security	★★½
Overall rating	★★★

Koala Backpackers

Koala's is a shabby hostel with bare rooms with flaking paint and mouldy tiles. The kitchen is large and empty and the bathrooms are dull. They have a bar, but it doesn't often get very lively. The garden swimming pool is a good place to hang out, but again this place doesn't seem to have much of an atmosphere, even though Koala's is usually known for its party style. The staff are inattentive and overall this place is unspectacular. The tour desk does, however, offer loads of tours and activities.

408 Esplanade, Torquay
5, 16
(07) 4125 360
Website *www.koalaadventures.com*
Dorm bed *$28 ($26.60 VIP);* ***double room*** *$72 ($68.40 VIP);* ***twin room*** *$62 ($58.90 VIP)*
Credit cards *MC, Visa*
Reception open *8.30am-9pm daily*

Maintenance & cleanliness	★★½
Facilities	★★★
Atmosphere & character	★★½
Security	★★½
Overall rating	★★½

Kondari Backpackers Resort

Kondari Backpackers Resort is another camping/caravan holiday resort that offers some backpackers' accommodation. Dorms have that "old motel room" feel, but they are kept clean and have en suite bathrooms. There is a large swimming pool, a bar and a drive-through bottle shop on site. It has a nice lakeside location, but is far from the beach and very quiet.

49/63 Elizabeth Street, Urangan
18
(07) 4128 9702 or 1800 072 131
***Website** www.kondari.com.au*
***Dorm bed** $20*
***Credit cards** Amex, MC, Visa*
***Reception open** Mon-Fri 6.30am-8pm, Sat 7am-7pm, Sun 8am-6.30pm*

Maintenance & cleanliness	★★½
Facilities	★★★★
Atmosphere & character	★★
Security	★½
Overall rating	★★★

Kookaburra Backpackers

This hostel does not have a very good location. It is in a nice old house, but it is not very well maintained. The outside kitchen is dirty and poorly equipped, but there is a nice swimming pool in the front plus a lacklustre TV room and internet access ($5 per hour). The atmosphere here is quiet and reception staff seem bored and can be unhelpful.

264 Charles Street, Pialba
16, 18
1800 111 442
***Dorm bed** $22; **double room** $45*
***Credit cards** MC, Visa*
***Reception open** 6.30am-10pm daily*

Maintenance & cleanliness	★★★
Facilities	★★½
Atmosphere & character	★★½
Security	★★½
Overall rating	★★★

Mango Eco Tourist Hostel

This tiny hostel is in a house with just a few small dorm rooms. It is nestled in overgrown gardens and offers comfortable, laid-back accommodation. There is just a small kitchen and outdoor balcony area to lounge in hammocks. The bathrooms are clean enough and the dorms are nicely decorated. The owner organises eco-tours and is very knowledgeable and helpful in planning excursions to Fraser Island. Guests love it here for the charm and good vibe.

110 Torquay Road, Scarness
5, 16, 18
(07) 4124 2832
***Website** www.mangohostel.com*
***Dorm bed** $22; **double/twin room** $48*
***Reception open** 7am-noon & 2pm-8pm*

Maintenance & cleanliness	★★★
Facilities	★★½
Atmosphere & character	★★★½
Security	★★
Overall rating	★★★

Next Backpackers

This brand new boutique hostel is modern and clean throughout and just steps from the beach. It has glossy hardwood floors, perfect showers and a common room with soft lighting and two nice televisions. The kitchen can get a bit messy but is spacious with all the mod-cons. Bathrooms are great besides some having those annoyingly tiny sinks. Girlzone is a girls-only dorm with hairdryers and other conveniences. There is also laundry and internet access. It is definitely a quiet hostel, but after a long day of outdoor activities, it is a welcome respite. Management are nice and eager to help.

10 Bideford Street, Torquay
5, 16, 18
(07) 4125 6600 or 1800 102 989
***Website** www.nextbackpackers.com.au*
***Dorm bed** $24-30; **double room** $69*
***Credit cards** MC, Visa*
***Reception open** 6.30am-9.30pm daily*

Maintenance & cleanliness	★★★★★
Facilities	★★★
Atmosphere & character	★★★
Security	★★★★
Overall rating	★★★★

Palace Backpackers
Palace Backpackers has accommodation in two-story self contained units with clean lounges and kitchens. The common room has a pool table and more kitchen facilities. There is a swimming pool and laundry, as well as internet access (including wireless) at $4 per hour. They organise tours, the most popular being Fraser Island and reception staff are extremely friendly.
184 Torquay Road, Scarness
5, 16, 18
1800 063 168
***Dorm bed** $20-25 ($19-23.75 VIP);*
***double room** $44 ($41.80 VIP)*
***Credit cards** MC, Visa*
***Reception open** 6am-8.30pm*

Maintenance & cleanliness	★★★
Facilities	★★★
Atmosphere & character	★★★★
Security	★★★
Overall rating	★★★½

Susan River Homestead Backpackers
This is an excellent place to stay with heaps of facilities, but it is rather quiet most of the time. Just outside of Hervey Bay on 650ha of bush land, they are most well known for their full-day package including horseback riding, a barbecue lunch, and waterskiing or wakeboarding. They also have a huge swimming pool and spa, two tennis courts, a trampoline, volleyball court, a bar and bistro, and a brand new movie room with cinema screen and rows of new plush couches. They have free internet access, campfire facilities, a new kitchen, laundry and a games room with an old jukebox. Dorms are clean with new comfortable beds. The family who run this place are extremely welcoming and kind. It is the perfect place for an authentic Aussie experience.
Bruce Highway (14km south of Hervey Bay)
5
(07) 4121 6846
***Website** www.susanriverresort.com*
***Dorm bed** $24-28*

Maintenance & cleanliness	★★★½
Facilities	★★★★½
Atmosphere & character	★★★½
Security	★
Overall rating	★★★½

Wanderer's Backpackers
Happy Wanderer Village is a camping and caravan park which happens to have a few dorm beds. They are in two old caravans with a kitchen and four beds. There is a big swimming pool and barbecue area, as well as a games room and TV room with internet ($8 per day). But there is absolutely no atmosphere as it caters mostly to older people and families camping.
Corner Ann & Truro Street, Torquay
16, 18
(07) 4128 9048 or 1800 444 040
***Website** www.wanderervillas.com.au*
***Dorm bed** $22*
***Credit cards** MC, Visa*
***Reception open** 7am-9pm daily*

Maintenance & cleanliness	★★½
Facilities	★★
Atmosphere & character	★½
Security	★★
Overall rating	★★

Maryborough

Maryborough is one of Queensland's oldest cities and during its heyday in the late 1800s it was the east coast's second most important port after Sydney. It once even rivalled Brisbane as the site for Queensland's state capital.

This small city is the closest place to Hervey Bay that has a train station and you'll have to stop here if you're travelling by rail and want to visit Hervey Bay or Fraser Island.

Although Maryborough is a bustling little city and in many ways a much nicer place than Hervey Bay, there's no backpackers' accommodation or enough attractions to keep you busy for very long and most travellers get off the train and get the first bus to Hervey Bay.

Practical Information

Maryborough-Fraser Island Visitor Information Centre
Bruce Highway, Maryborough

(07) 4121 4111
***Website** www.visitmaryborough.info*
***Open** Mon-Fri 8.30am-5pm, 10am-4pm daily*

Coming & Going

QR trains *(**website** www.traveltrain.com.au)*, Greyhound *(1300 473 946; **website** www.greyhound.com.au)* and Premier Motor Service *(**website** www.premierms.com.au)* coaches stop at the train station on Lennox Street. The train is met by Wide Bay Transit *((07) 4121 3719; **website** www.widebaytransit.com.au)* bus 5, which goes to Hervey Bay.

Rainbow Beach

Rainbow Beach is a tiny town at the foot of the Inskip Peninsula. It can be reached by highway from Gympie, or with 4WD from Noosa through the Great Sandy National Park. Driving along the Forty Mile Beach from Noosa requires some skill and careful attention to tides and weather conditions. This route gives you the best view of the sands and the wrecked *Cherry Venture*. The propeller from this vessel is placed on the headland at the edge of town.

There is some good surf here and it is one of the last places you can surf before the start of the Great Barrier Reef. Paragliding is also popular and is a great way to view the colours along the cliffs. Wolf Rock is known in diving circles to be one of Queensland's great dive sites.

The town gets its name from the vivid rainbow coloured sand cliffs at the edge of the town. It is closer to Fraser Island than Hervey Bay, its big sister to the north, and it is also cheaper and more laid-back. There is not much of anything to do here besides take trips to Fraser Island, but the town is steadily gaining in popularity due to that. There are some shops along the main street where you can gather cheap groceries and supplies for camping.

Practical Information

Queensland Parks & Wildlife Service

This small information centre has information about Fraser Island and also sells permits for the island.
Rainbow Beach Road, Rainbow Beach.
(07) 5486 3160
***Open** 7am-4pm daily.*

Shell Tourist Centre

Rainbow Beach Road, Rainbow Beach
(07) 5486 8888
***Website** www.rainbowbeach.info*

Coming & Going

Greyhound *(1300 473 946; **website** www.greyhound.com.au)* and Premier Motor Service *(**website** www.premierms.com.au)* stop on Spectrum Street in Rainbow Beach.

Accommodation

Dingo's Backpacker Adventure Resort

This hostel is the party spot in Rainbow Beach. It can be loud at night, but the dorms are air conditioned, very clean, and up-to-date. The swimming pool is good, and the airy TV room with a bar is always crowded with young backpackers coming from or going to Fraser Island. The kitchen is cramped and messy, but there are plans renovate it soon. There is a tropical pool and an outside gazebo where many backpackers also like to hang out. They offer free pancake breakfasts and $5 dinners, as well as internet ($5 per hour) and free use of body boards.
20 Spectrum Street, Rainbow Beach
(07) 5486 8222
***Website** www.dingosresort.com*
***Dorm bed** $22*
***Credit cards** MC, Visa*
***Reception open** 7am-7pm daily*

TV K L

Maintenance & cleanliness	★★★½
Facilities	★★★½
Atmosphere & character	★★★½
Security	★½
Overall rating	★★★½

Frasers on Rainbow Beach

This hostel gets it just right. Not too wild, but not boring either. It isn't the cleanest, though. Dorms are spacious and well maintained, but the bathrooms could do with a renovation. The common room is breezy and attractive, with open beam ceilings, a big TV, pool table and a good internet café.

There is also a swimming pool and hammocks strung between palm trees. Surfboards are free to use, and tours run daily. Reception staff are friendly.
18 Spectrum Street, Rainbow Beach
☎ *(07) 5486 4581*
Website *www.frasersonrainbow.com.au*
Dorm bed *$24 ($22 HI/YHA, VIP);* ***double room*** *$68 ($64 HI/YHA, VIP)*
Credit cards *MC, Visa*
Reception open *7am-7.30pm daily*

Maintenance & cleanliness	★★★
Facilities	★★★½
Atmosphere & character	★★★½
Security	★½
Overall rating	★★★

Pippie's

This is the quietest hostel in Rainbow Beach. The dorms are cared for and immaculate. They offer a wide range of facilities including a swimming pool, small kitchen, free body boards, free breakfast and free barbecues on Wednesdays. The hostel organises lots of tours and also has didgeridoo and boomerang making classes. It may not be the flashiest place on the block, but it still has a high standard of accommodation and keeps its guests comfortable.
22 Spectrum Street, Rainbow Beach
☎ *(07) 5486 8503 or 1800 425 356*
Website *www.pippiesbeachhouse.com.au*
Dorm bed *$22; price includes breakfast*
Credit cards *MC, Visa*
Reception open *7am-7pm daily*

Maintenance & cleanliness	★★★★½
Facilities	★★★½
Atmosphere & character	★★★
Security	★★½
Overall rating	★★★½

Fraser Island

Fraser Island is unique in that it is – at 120km by 15km – the world's largest sand bar. Despite being composed entirely of sand, the island boasts verdant rainforests and crystal clear lakes and is home to dingoes, wild horses and an abundance of bird life. Great Sandy National Park *(**website** www.epa.qld.gov.au/fraser)* comprises most of the island and there is a national park entry fee of $35.40 per vehicle.

Coming & Going

The central west coast of the island is connected to Hervey Bay by a ferry service. Ferries operate from River Heads (south of Hervey Bay) and Urangan Harbour in Hervey Bay and charge $140-150 return for a 4WD and three passengers.

Ferries from Inskip Point near Rainbow Beach work out cheaper, for example Rainbow Venture *(☎ (07) 5486 3154)* charge $80 return for a 4WD vehicle including three passengers.

You will need a vehicle permit if you are taking a vehicle across on the ferry. These cost $35.40 and let you take a 4WD onto the island for one month. The National Parks vehicle permit includes an information pack with a colour guide as well as details on camping and hiking on the island. National parks permits are available from the Marina Kiosk at Urangan boat harbour as well as from the Brisbane, Bundaberg, Maryborough, Rainbow Beach and River Heads offices of the Queensland Parks & Wildlife Service.

Local Transport & Tours

Because it is a sand island, a four-wheel-drive vehicle is essential for exploring Fraser Island; this explains why it is so expensive to get around the island. Renting your own 4WD (which usually comes complete with camping gear) is the way to go as it gives you much more independence than a tour, although you need to split the cost with a few others to make it affordable.

SELF-DRIVE SAFARIS

Most backpackers take advantage of the so-called self-drive tours of the island. These aren't really tours; they're more along the lines of car rental with a few extras thrown in. Generally a bunch of travellers each pay between $140 and $190 per person for a three-day trip and are given a 4WD and a lecture about what to see and the dos and don'ts of driving on Fraser Island. Ferry fares, camping gear and a vehicle permit are usually included in the price but a lot of the companies that organise these trips will charge you an extra $10 for fuel and $15 for insurance. These self-drive 'tours' give you the independence that comes with having your own set of wheels and no tour guide. Most hostels in Hervey Bay or Rainbow Beach can organise self-drive tours.

Hostels that organise self-drive safaris include: **Beaches** *($150-275; ☎ (07) 4124 1322; **website** www.beaches.com.au)*; **Colonial Village YHA** *($140; ☎ 1800 818 280; **website** www.cvyha.com)*; **Fraser Roving** *($160; ☎ (07) 4125 6386 or 1800 989811; **website** www.fraserroving.com)*; **Koala** *($140; ☎ (07) 4125 360; **website** www.koala adventures.com)*; **Next Backpackers** *($155; ☎ (07) 4125 6600 or 1800 102 989; **website** www.nextbackpackers.com.au)*. These prices are for a three day/two night self-drive safari.

If you would rather not organise a self-drive tour through a hostel you can organise everything yourself renting from **Aussie Trax** *(☎ (07) 4124 4433; **website** www.fraserisland4wd.com.au)*. If you already have a group organised, this can work out cheaper than the 4WD safaris organised by hostels in Hervey Bay.

GUIDED TOURS

There are also plenty of companies that offer more conventional guided tours, although these cost more and you miss out on the fun of driving off-road. Guided and self-drive tours of Fraser Island include:

Cool Dingo Tours

☎ (07) 4120 3333
***Website** www.cooldingotour.com*
***2 day/1 night guided tour** $289-339; **3 day/2 night guided tour** $359-409*

Fraser Explorer Tours

☎ (07) 4194 9222 or 1800 249 122
***Website** www.fraserexplorertours.com.au*
***1 day guided tour** $149; **2 day/1 night guided tour** $253-305*

Dingoes

Dogs are not permitted on Fraser Island and the lack of crossbreeding has resulted in Fraser Island's dingoes being the most pure breed in Australia. These native wild dogs are one of Fraser Island's attractions, however they can also be dangerous.

Because dingoes have many of the same characteristics as regular domestic dogs, many visitors feed them. This has made dingoes become less afraid of people, they have become dependent on handouts and their hunting skills have declined. Dingoes can also become aggressive towards people who do not feed them. In April 2001 a dingo on Fraser Island killed a nine-year-old boy.

The Queensland Parks & Wildlife Service has set a number of guidelines that are designed to protect you and ensure that dingoes retain their hunting skills and do not become too aggresive.

- Never feed dingoes.
- Lock food in strong lockable containers in your car. Dingoes can open iceboxes if they are left on the ground!
- Always stay close to children
- Walk in small groups
- Put rubbish in bins or keep it in your car.
- Keep your tent wide-open so dingoes can see that there is nothing to take.
- Bury fish waste at least 30cm deep in sand below high tide.

Don't leave expensive gear such as hiking boots or sleeping bags in your tent, as dingoes have been known to carry these off.

If you feel threatened by a dingo:

- stand up and face the dingo
- fold your arms and maintain eye contact
- calmly back away

PHOTO: © ISTOCKPHOTO/RAY HEMS

Driving a 4WD Vehicle

There's more to driving a 4WD vehicle than simply putting it in gear and heading off-road. You shouldn't run into too many problems if you follow these guidelines:

- The best time to travel is around low tide. Avoid two hours either side of high tide.
- When arriving on the island or before driving on to the beach, check that your wheel locks are in the right position to engage four-wheel drive.
- Tyre pressure should be adjusted before driving on the island. Generally, tyres should be 172kpa (25psi). Some areas on Fraser have signs suggesting specific reduced tire pressure to 103kpa (15psi) to enable driving through soft dry sand.
- The beach is a designated road and the normal "keep to the left" rules apply as well as using indicators for turning. Speed should be kept to below 80km/h on the beach and 35km/h on the inland roads. Police patrol the island and enforce speed limits and breathalyse drivers.
- There are stretches of the beach that are used as aircraft landing/take-off strips. Take note of the signs in designated areas and watch for aircraft.
- Drivers should note the numerous gutters that have been created by the creeks flowing into the sea from the island. Even gutters with small banks - if hit at speed - can overturn a vehicle.
- Drivers should beware the rising tide. Vehicles driven too close to the water can become trapped in wet sand. Drivers of hired vehicles lose their bond immediately if they drive in salt water.
- On "good beach days" the sand is hard-packed and makes for excellent driving conditions. On bad days, the tides may not have been high enough to wash way the ruts from the previous days' traffic - resulting in build-up of sand banks.
- When driving in deep banks of dry sand, keep the car in a low gear, do not change gears, keep the revs high and do not lose momentum.
- Where possible, follow someone else's tracks - choose a set of tracks and stay on them. Do not stop the vehicle in soft sand or in creek beds.

Fraser Island Company

☎ *(07) 4125 3933 or 1800 063 933*
Website *www.fraserislandco.com.au*
2 day/1 night guided tour *$269;* ***3 day/2 night guided tour*** *$435*

Accommodation

Camping is the main accommodation option on Fraser Island. Most campsites are operated by the national park and require camping permits that are available from shops, both in Hervey Bay, Rainbow Beach and on the island for $4.50 per person per night.

There are also a couple of resorts on the island that provide accommodation to some of the tour operators, so you may stay in a resort if you're taking a tour.

You should bring 50c coins for coin-operated showers and gas barbecues that are located at camping areas on the island.

Bundaberg Region

The region surrounding Bundaberg offers 140km of unspoilt coastline and glimpses of real Australian country life in small hinterland towns. Bundaberg is a good place to base yourself while exploring the area, as it is relatively cheap and there is plenty of accommodation. The city has nice Botanic Gardens and some attractive buildings, but it is mostly just used as a place to find fruit-picking work in the surrounding area or as a one night stopover before heading north.

Bargara, just 20 minutes east of Bundaberg, is a slow seaside getaway with a boardwalk and calm foreshore. Mon Repos is the most well-known beach for its hatchling turtles that you can see on summer evenings. Thirty minutes north is Moore Park Beach, where you can swim, surf and sailboard. This beach is also open to 4WD vehicles. Just a bit farther north is Miriam Vale Shire and the Discovery Coast, with excellent surf, national parks and estuaries.

Childers

Childers is a pleasant town between Hervey Bay and Bundaberg that dates mostly from 1903, when much of the town was re-built following a disastrous fire that destroyed the town a year earlier.

Many backpackers are more familiar with another tragic fire, which killed 15 backpackers when the Palace Backpackers Hostel burnt down in June 2000. The façade of the old hostel has been restored and it now houses the tourist information centre, an art gallery and a moving memorial to the backpackers who died in the fire.

Although it is an attractive town, most backpackers picking fruit in the region stay in nearby Bundaberg.

Practical Information

Childers Tourist Information Centre

Palace Memorial Building, Churchill Street (Bruce Highway), Childers
☎ *(07) 4126 3886*
Open *Mon-Fri 9am-4pm, Sat-Sun 9am-3pm*

Coming & Going

Greyhound *(☎ 1300 473 946; **website** www.greyhound.com.au)* and Premier Motor Service *(**website** www.premierms.com.au)* stops at the Shell service station on Churchill Street.

Sights

Flying High Bird Habitat

This 5000 square metre aviary at Apple Tree Creek, north of Childers, allows you to walk among a variety of Australian parrots and finches.
Corner Bruce Highway & Old Creek Road, Apple Tree Creek
☎ *(07) 4126 3777*
Admission *$18*

Palace Memorial Building

The re-constructed façade of the building that formerly served as the Palace Hotel, and later as the Palace Backpackers Hostel, houses an art gallery and memorial to the 15 backpackers who lost their lives to the tragic hostel fire of 23 June 2000.
Churchill Street (Bruce Highway), Childers
☎ *(07) 4126 3886*
Admission *free*
Open *Mon-Fri 9am-4pm, Sat-Sun 9am-3pm*

Snakes Down Under

This 1½ hour presentation lets you get up close to a variety of snakes. The show gives you a unique opportunity to handle snakes as well as learn more about these potentially dangerous animals.
51 Lucketts Road, Childers
☎ *(07) 4126 1853*
Website *www.snakesdownunder.com*
Admission *$18*
Open *Mon-Tue 9am-3pm, Thu-Sun 9am-3pm; show times 10am, 11.45am, 12.30pm*

Bundaberg

Most travellers who come to Bundaberg, come to work on the nearby fruit farms and there are quite a few hostels that cater almost exclusively to travellers staying here to pick fruit. Another big reason backpackers make a stop here is the cheap prices on diving courses, but there are also some nice things to see in the area.

Bundaberg is an industrial town full of farmers and families. There are several old heritage buildings of architectural interest along Bourbong Street, including the School of Arts and the Post Office clock tower. The Botanic Gardens, with its pretty lakes and shady trees, is also worth a visit. The Bundaberg Rum distillery is at the top of the list of must-do activities; you have a choice of tours and get a sample at the end.

If you're visiting between November and March you should make a trip to Mon Repos Beach to watch the loggerhead turtles come ashore to lay their eggs.

Practical Information

Bundaberg Visitor Information Centre

186 Bourbong Street, Bundaberg
☎ *(07) 4153 9289*
Website *www.bundabergregion.info*
Open *Mon-Fri 8.30am-4.45pm, Sat-Sun 10am-1pm*

INTERNET ACCESS

DataRite Enterprises

215 Bourbong Street Bundaberg
☎ *(07) 4154 3111*
Website *www.datarite.net/cafe/cafepage.htm*
Open *10am-8pm daily*

Coming & Going

Most travellers arrive by bus but the train is also a popular option. Greyhound *(☎ 1300 473 946; **website** www.greyhound.com.au)* and Premier Motor Service *(**website** www.premierms.com.au)* buses stop at the coach terminal at 66 Targo Street. The train station is on McLean Street in the town centre.

Local Transport

Duffy's City Buses *(☎ (07) 4151 4226; **website** www.duffysbuses.com.au)* run Bundaberg's local bus service. There are five bus routes with hourly services to most parts of the city.

Accommodation

Bundaberg Backpackers Travellers Hostel

This place is a large brick building with a wraparound veranda. It caters mostly to workers, so there is really no atmosphere here. There is internet access and a barbecue, both of which don't seem to get much use. The small kitchen gets very messy, as does the bathroom. The hostel is quite compact and stuffy inside with flaking paint and old, dirty beds. Management help to organise work, but tend to be very impatient. They also manage the Bus Stop backpackers.

2 Crofton Street, Bundaberg
☎ *(07) 4152 2080*
Dorm bed *$25 per night, $150 per week;* ***double room*** *$54 per night*
Credit cards *MC, Visa*
Reception open *8.30am-10.30am & 3pm-6pm daily*

Maintenance & cleanliness	★★½
Facilities	★½
Atmosphere & character	★★½
Security	★★½
Overall rating	★★½

Bus Stop Backpackers

Bus Stop is just across the street from the Bundaberg Backpackers Travellers and it has a more institutional feel, with bright blue walls and empty space. The communal areas have old futons, internet and a large TV. The kitchen is spacious but dirty. Bathrooms are filthy. Again, there are mostly workers staying here, so there is no backpacker atmosphere.

66 Targo Street
☎ *(07) 4151 8186*
Dorm bed *$25 per night, $150 per week*
Credit cards *MC, Visa*
Reception open *8.30am-10.30am & 3pm-6pm daily*

Maintenance & cleanliness	★★
Facilities	★½
Atmosphere & character	★★
Security	★★
Overall rating	★★

Queensland

Cellblock Backpackers

Cellblock Backpackers is in a nicely restored former prison. Most of the dorms are in old office rooms with high ceilings and large comfortable beds, but they are not particularly clean. The bathrooms are new, with spotless steel sinks and good showers. They have a good outside bar with pool tables and a heated swimming pool where they show movies at night on several large screens. The cells are an interesting place to stay, though there are only a few of them. It is worth it to book into an air-conditioned unit or risk stuffiness and heat. The staff have a tendency to be uncaring and unhelpful. Fittingly, the security here is great.

Corner Maryborough & Quay Streets, Bundaberg
☎ 1800 837 773
***Website** www.cellblock.com.au*
***Dorm bed** $26-30; **double room** $33*
***Credit cards** MC, Visa*
***Reception open** Mon-Fri 8.30am-6pm, Sat-Sun 9.30am-4pm*

Maintenance & cleanliness	★★★★½
Facilities	★★★★½
Atmosphere & character	★★★★
Security	★★★★★
Overall rating	★★★★

City Centre Backpackers

City Centre is in an old building with a nice wooden staircase and wraparound veranda. The dorms are basic and some of them need maintenance. There is a clean, spacious kitchen with a large walk-in fridge; a big TV lounge; a reading room and dormitories with good beds. It is family-run, with pleasant management who book tours and help guests to find jobs. This place is homely and comfortable compared to the other working hostels in town.

216 Bourbong Street, Bundaberg
☎ (07) 4151 3501
***Dorm bed** $25 per night, $140 per week*
***Credit cards** MC, Visa; 3% credit card surcharge*
***Reception open** 7.30am-10.30am & 3.30pm-8.30pm daily*

Maintenance & cleanliness	★★★½
Facilities	★★½
Atmosphere & character	★★★
Security	★★★
Overall rating	★★★½

Dingo Blue Backpackers

This workers' hostel has virtually no atmosphere and an alcohol ban (except on Saturday nights). The kitchen is absolutely filthy, as are the dorms and the small TV room. There are also no facilities besides a laundry. The reception staff are nice enough, but the entire place is in need of a renovation.

11 Burrum Street, Bundaberg
☎ 1300 782 385
***Dorm bed** $26 per night, $155 per week*
***Credit cards** MC, Visa*
***Reception open** 9am-10am & 5pm-6pm daily*

Maintenance & cleanliness	★
Facilities	★
Atmosphere & character	★
Security	★★
Overall rating	★

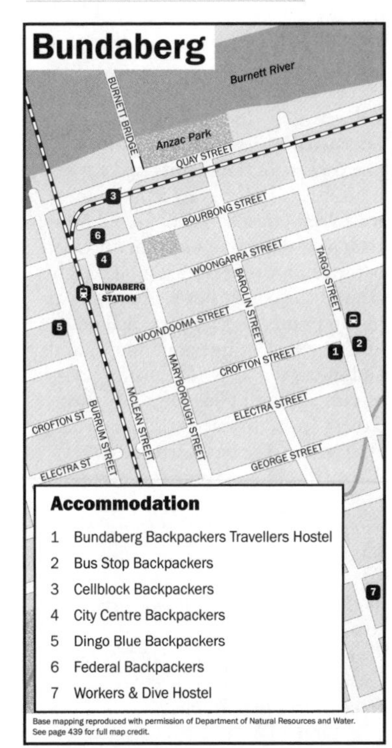

Federal Backpackers

The Federal is a large old building in dire need of a renovation. There are mostly workers living here, but it has more facilities than the other working hostels. The dorms are rickety with peeling paint, the bathrooms are aging and dirty and the dated TV lounge has graffiti covered walls. There is a large bar, with pool tables and a dancer's pole, which has live music every Friday. The hostel has a relatively good atmosphere here compared to the others in town, as the hostel's bar is a popular night-time hangout.

221 Bourbong Street, Bundaberg
(07) 4153 3711
Website *www.federalbackpackers.com.au*
Dorm bed *$23-25 per night, $133-140 per week*
Credit cards *MC, Visa; 2% credit card surcharge*
Reception open *Mon-Fri 9am-5.30pm, Sat-Sun 9.30am-noon &4pm-5.30pm*

Maintenance & cleanliness	★½
Facilities	★★½
Atmosphere & character	★★½
Security	★★★½
Overall rating	★★½

Footprints Feeding Grounds

The owners of Footprints make it what it is: a home away from home. It's a very small hostel in an old house with neat dorms and well maintained bathrooms. Footprints is a bit rough around the edges, but it's both charming and homely. Facilities include two kitchens and lounge areas plus laundry and internet access. They run a shuttle service and will take you to the Bundaberg Rum distillery and pick you up afterwards. They are also active with the turtle conservation and take guests to Mon Repos every night.

4 Hinkler Avenue, North Bundaberg
3
(07) 4152 3659
Website *www.footprintsadventures.com.au*
Dorm bed *$24 per night, $150 per week; price includes workers' transport*
Reception open *24 hours*

Maintenance & cleanliness	★★★
Facilities	★★
Atmosphere & character	★★★★½
Security	★½
Overall rating	★★★

Northside Backpackers

This bright blue hostel has a pretty quiet – you might say boring – atmosphere. The hostel is pretty clean throughout and the kitchen is well equipped, but the TV room is just a tiny box with a tiny box inside. Besides the nice swimming pool and barbecue area, there are not many facilities. Dorms are bland but reasonably clean. It is a good place for workers to stay as it is away from the noise of town. Reception staff are friendly.

12 Queen Street, North Bundaberg
(07) 4154 1166
Dorm bed *$20-21 per night, $120-125 per week;* ***double/twin room*** *$43 per night, $258 per week*
Reception open *Mon-Sat 8.30am-noon & 3.30pm-7.30pm, Sun 8.30am-noon & 4pm-7.30pm*

Maintenance & cleanliness	★★★
Facilities	★★★½
Atmosphere & character	★★
Security	★★
Overall rating	★★½

Workers & Dive Hostel

This hostel is also mainly used for workers. It is in a nice large building with verandas and a good swimming pool. The bathrooms are well maintained and clean, but the kitchens and dorms are a mess. Some of the dorms are in self-contained units which are just filthy. There is a pool table and TV room in the main building, but the place is boring, unorganised, and too far from the centre of town. It may be a better place to stay than some of the others if you are on a working holiday.

64 Barolin Street, Bundaberg
(07) 4151 6097
Dorm bed *$23-24 per night, $140-145 per week*
Credit cards *MC, Visa*
Reception open *Mon-Fri 8.30am-noon & 3.30pm-7.30pm, Sat-Sun 9am-noon & 4pm-7.30pm*

Maintenance & cleanliness	★★
Facilities	★★★
Atmosphere & character	★★
Security	★½
Overall rating	★★½

Sights

Bundaberg Distillery

Bundaberg Rum is Australia's biggest-selling spirit and Bundaberg's main attraction is the distillery where it is made. Distillery tours include a taste of Bundaberg's biggest export.
Avenue Street, East Bundaberg
4, 5
(07) 4131 2900
***Website** www.bundabergrum.com.au*
***Admission** $9.90, includes one drink*
***Open** Mon-Fri 10am-3pm, Sat-Sun 10am-2pm; tours leave every hour*

Hinkler House Museum

This museum focuses on the life of Bert Hinkler, a local lad who made the first solo flight to England.
Young Street, North Bundaberg
3
(07) 4152 0222
***Website** www.bundabergonthe.net/hinkler/*
***Admission** $5*
***Open** 10am-4pm daily*

Mon Repos

If you're visiting between November and March you should make a trip to Mon Repos Beach (15km from the town centre) to watch the loggerhead turtles come ashore to lay their eggs. It is a great experience to see the baby turtles digging through the sand and making their way to the sea. You must make a booking with the tourist office *((07) 4153 8888)* before you go as there are new regulations regarding the number of people allowed on the beach at a time, whether part of a tour or not. Your time of booking determines your time on the beach, so call early.

Agnes Water & Town of 1770

The tiny seaside towns of Agnes Water and Town of 1770 are steadily increasing in popularity with backpackers for their unspoilt beaches and lush green national parks. Captain Cook touched down here in 1770 (hence the name), for the first time in what is now called Queensland. This stakes the area's claim as the birthplace of Queensland.

Agnes Water is Queensland's most northerly surf beach and it has some spectacular breaks. Agnes Water also has the three backpackers' hostels, all of which are good accommodation options. There are a couple of small shopping centres and a good surf shop where you can rent longboards. The Town of 1770, just minutes away, is nothing more than a laid-back coastal settlement good for fishing, boating and cruising to the southern cays of Lady Musgrave and Lady Elliot Islands for diving. Overall, this area of the Discovery Coast is just a quiet rural hideaway with little in the way of tourist attractions but tons of charm.

Practical Information

The Discovery Centre (Visitor Information Centre)

Shop 12, Endeavour Plaza, Agnes Water
(07) 4974 7002
***Website** www.discover1770.info*
***Open** 9am-5pm daily*

Coming & Going

Greyhound *(1300 473 946; **website** www.greyhound.com.au)* and Premier Motor Service *(**website** www.premierms.com.au)* buses stop at the 1770 turnoff on Fingerboard Road about 30km outside town, however some Greyhound buses also go right into town with a stop opposite Cool Bananas.

Accommodation

1770 Backpackers

This is a tiny hostel with lots of character. The dorms are a little cramped, but the bathrooms are great and have huge showers with great water pressure. The kitchen doesn't have a microwave or stove but is well stocked with everything else. The outside common area is a good place to meet other travellers. 1770 Backpackers is laid-back and has a great atmosphere at night, but some-

times it gets a bit too noisy. One of the best things about this place is the staff, who are outgoing and friendly and make you feel instantly at home.
6 Captain Cook Drive, Agnes Water
☎ *1800 121 770*
***Website** www.the1770backpackers.com*
***Dorm bed** $25 ($24 HI/ YHA, VIP); **double room** $55 ($53 HI/ YHA, VIP)*
***Credit cards** MC, Visa*
***Reception open** 8am-8.30pm daily*

Maintenance & cleanliness	★★★
Facilities	★★½
Atmosphere & character	★★★★½
Security	★
Overall rating	★★½

Cool Bananas

This small and colourful hostel has a gorgeous common room with plush couches and television and a breezy outside lounge area with umbrellas and a fire pit. The kitchen is large and well equipped. Dorms are average but clean and the bathrooms are new. The reception staff are quite friendly and it is a good place to book tours and meet other travellers.
2 Springs Road, Agnes Water
☎ *(07) 4974 7660 or 1800 227 660*
***Website** www.coolbananas.net.au*
***Dorm bed** $25 ($24 HI/YHA, VIP)*
***Credit cards** MC, Visa*
***Reception open** 7am-midnight daily*

Maintenance & cleanliness	★★★½
Facilities	★★½
Atmosphere & character	★★★★
Security	★½
Overall rating	★★★

Southern Cross Tourist Retreat

This hostel consists of five cabins set around tropical gardens, each themed on a different country. The grounds include a beautiful swimming pool with palm trees and lush gardens. The cabins are spotless inside as are the en suite bathrooms. In the open-air common room there are new couches, a TV and pool table and an internet café. The kitchen is nothing special but it is kept clean. There is also a meditation area behind the common room.
2694 Round Hill Road, Agnes Water
☎ *(07) 4974 7225*
***Website** www.1770southerncross.com*
***Dorm bed** $24-25; **double room** $65; prices include breakfast*
***Credit cards** MC, Visa*
***Reception open** 8am-1pm & 4pm-8pm*

Maintenance & cleanliness	★★★★
Facilities	★★★★
Atmosphere & character	★★★★
Security	★
Overall rating	★★★★

Eating & Drinking

There literally are not many places to eat in Agnes Water and Town of 1770.

If you are staying in one of the hostels here, it's a good idea to make a trip to the **Foodworks** *(Round Hill Road, Agnes Water)* or **IGA supermarket** in Endeavour Plaza *(Captain Cook Drive, Agnes Water)* to buy supplies for a barbecue with some fellow travellers. There is not much going on in Agnes Water, so eating in will probably be an easy choice.

There is a nice café in the small shopping centre on Captain Cook Drive plus a low-key Thai restaurant. **Kahuna's** Italian restaurant *(40 Captain Cook Drive, Agnes Water)* has a Tuesday night $13 all-you-can-eat dinner special that draws a crowd. For an easy dinner in, go to the butcher in that same shopping centre and ask for the pre-made chicken stir fry.

There are also not many nightspots, but the **Agnes Water Tavern** *(1 Tavern Road, Agnes Water)* has cheap pub food, good beer and a relatively lively bar. Otherwise, there is a bottle shop in the main shopping centre.

Sights & Activities

Many travellers visit 1770 and Agnes Water for its easy access to Lady Musgrave Island (see following section), but there are also amphibious LARC trips and cruises to Pancake Creek and Fitzroy Reef Lagoon on the Great Barrier Reef.

AMPHIBIOUS LARC TRIPS

1770 Environmental Tours

(☎ *(07) 4974 9422; **website** www.1770larctours.com.au)* have a couple of pink amphibious vehicles that they use to run day tours to Eurimbula National Park, Bustard Head Lightstation and Middle Island. Day tours cost $121.50 ($115 plus $6.50 national park charges) and the shorter sunset cruises are $28.

REEF TRIPS

The **Reef Jet** *(☎ 1800 177 011; **website** www.1770holidays.com)* run trips to the relatively accessible Pancake Creek and Fitzroy Reef Lagoon. Both reefs offer excellent snorkelling. Trips to Fitzroy Reef Lagoon go every day except Wednesdays and Pancake Creek day trips run on Wednesdays and when weather conditions prevent travel to the outer reef.

Lady Musgrave Island

Lady Musgrave Island is one of the closest coral cays to Brisbane. It boasts a unique deep-water lagoon with brilliant snorkelling and diving opportunities. It is part of Capricornia Cays National Park.

Coming & Going

Lady Musgrave Island is accessible from both 1770 or Bundaberg with 1770 being the closest town to the island. Because 1770 is closer, daytrips from here allow you to spend longer on the reef.

From 1770 you can go to Lady Musgrave Island onboard MV Spirit of 1770 *(☎ (07) 4974 9077; **website** www.1770reefcruises.com)*, which takes 75 minutes and costs $165 for a daycruise. LM Cruises *(☎ (07) 4159 4519 or 1800 072 110; **website** www.lmcruises.com.au)* run trips from 1770 and Bundaberg, they charge $165 for day trips from 1770 and $185 from Bundaberg. The ferry costs considerably more if you plan on returning on a different day.

Accommodation

Camping is the only accommodation option on the island. There are no services on the island so you'll need to bring everything you need with you, including water.

Camping permits are available from the Queensland Parks & Wildlife Service *(**website** www.epa.qld.gov.au)* for $4.50 per night.

Ferry transfers are considerably more expensive if you plan on spending several nights on the island.

Capricorn Coast

The Capricorn Coast region, straddling the Tropic of Capricorn, is where tropical Queensland begins. Dramatic mountain ranges, gorges scoring deep into the earth, and dead flat plains stretching to the horizon are the hallmarks of this region.

The two major towns in the area include the port city of Gladstone and Rockhampton, the proud "beef capital of Australia". These are farming areas with a healthy dose of industrialism thrown in. Most visitors use the area as a jumping-off point for the secluded holiday resort of Great Keppel Island and the diver's paradise of Heron Island. There is a lot of good fishing along the coast here, from the quiet southerly beach town at Turkey Beach to Yeppoon and the Byfield National Park. Emu Park and Tannum Sands have nice protected beaches popular with families.

Gladstone

Gladstone is an industrial city with one of Australia's busiest ports, which handles most of Queensland's mineral and agricultural exports. The city is also home to the country's largest aluminium smelter and cement operation and Queensland's biggest power station. There is nothing of interest to backpackers in the city, but the marina is the main launching point for boats to the Great Barrier Reef's southern islands, as well as the diving in Fitzroy Bay near Heron Island.

The residents of Gladstone are active with marine activities and each Easter they celebrate the Gladstone Harbour Festival and the Brisbane to Gladstone Yacht Race. The Tondoon Botanic Gardens, Auckland Hill Lookout and Gecko Valley winery are some of the few attractions in the immediate area. There is only one hostel in town, but it is a great place to stay on your way through.

Practical Information

Visitor Information Centre

Marina Ferry Terminal, Gladstone
☎ *(07) 4972 9922*
Website *www.gladstoneregion.info*
Open *8.30am-5pm daily*

Queensland Parks & Wildlife Service

Floor 3, Centrepoint Building, 136 Goondoon Street, Gladstone
☎ *(07) 4971 6500*
Website *www.epa.qld.gov.au*

Coming & Going

Greyhound *(☎ 1300 473 946;* ***website*** *www.greyhound.com.au)* buses stop at the 24 hour Mobil service station on Dawson Road. Because it is located off the Bruce Highway, Gladstone may be bypassed by some buses.

Gladstone is on the main rail line between Brisbane and Rockhampton; the train station is in the city centre near the intersection of Tank and Toolooa Streets

Accommodation

Gladstone Backpackers

For an old house, Gladstone Backpackers has surprisingly modern furnished dorms and well maintained facilities. These include a swimming pool, barbecue and laundry. The kitchen is a bit old, but there are plans for a renovation. The hostel is within walking distance to shops and nightlife, and they organise trips to Heron and Curtis Islands. There is internet, including wireless, at $4 per hour. Though it has a very quiet atmosphere, staff are very friendly and they make you feel at home.

12 Rollo Street, Gladstone
☎ *(07) 4872 5744*
Dorm bed *$25 ($23.75 VIP);* ***double room*** *$55 ($52.25 VIP)*

Maintenance & cleanliness	★★★½
Facilities	★★★½
Atmosphere & character	★★★½
Security	★★½
Overall rating	★★★½

Sights & Activities

Gladstone Regional Art Gallery & Museum

This museum has displays on local history and a collection of artwork significant to the Central Queensland region.

Corner Bramston & Goondoon Streets, Gladstone
☎ *(07) 4970 1242*
Website *www.gladstone.qld.gov.au/gragm/*
Admission *free*
Open *Mon-Sat 10am-5pm*

Industry Tours

Informative tours of Gladstone's industrial plants take place on a regular basis. These tours can be very interesting if you've always wanted to know how aluminium, cement or petroleum is produced. Group sizes are generally small and you have a good opportunity to see behind the scenes. Bookings are essential and must be made through the information centre at the marina.

☎ *(07) 4972 9000*
Website *www.gladstoneholidays.info/places_to_visit/gladstone-city/industry-tours.cfm*
Admission *free*
Tours *Mon Queensland Alumina refinery; Tue Gladstone Ports Corporation; Thu NRG Gladstone Power Station; Fri Boyne Smelter & Rio Tinto Alcan Yarwun Refinery*

Rockhampton

Rockhampton is known as Australia's beef capital but it is known better by travellers as the gateway to Great Keppel Island and to outback Queensland (the highway to Mount Isa departs from here).

The town itself is a bit stuck in a time warp and there are plenty of historic buildings throughout the city from its days as a trading port and gold mining centre. The few hostels here are scattered and unspectacular. If you can make it through without stopping, you won't be missing much; besides, of course, the excellent steaks. On the way out of town is the Aboriginal cultural centre, which is interesting and worth a quick stop at least.

Practical Information

Rockhampton Tourist Information Centre

208 Quay Street, Rockhampton
(07) 4922 5339 or 1800 805 865
***Website** www.rockhamptoninfo.com*
***Open** Mon-Fri 8.30am-4.30pm, Sat-Sun 9am-4pm*

Coming & Going

Most buses going up the coast will stop at Rockhampton. Greyhound (*1300 473 946; **website** www.greyhound.com.au*) and Premier Motor Service (***website** www.premierms.com.au*) stop at the 24 hour Mobile roadhouse on George Street.

Rockhampton's train station is located at the end of Murray Street, southeast of the town centre.

Local Transport

Rockhampton's bus service (*(07) 4936 1002; **website** www.sunbus.com.au*) consists of nine routes connecting the city centre with outlying suburbs. It is handy for getting to hostels in North Rockhampton and Stockland shopping centre.

Accommodation

Ascot Backpackers

This hostel is in the old Ascot Hotel, a blue corner building with a huge elephant on the front – you can't miss it – and it says a bit about the character of the place. The hostel part is definitely aging, but well cared for by the owners, who are the most generous and kind hostel owners we've met. The dorms are spacious and the kitchen is well stocked. Downstairs is a bar, a bottle shop, slot machines and a restaurant serving the best steak in town (some say in Australia). It is north of the centre, but near lots of shops, and they will arrange buses wherever you need to go. They also help to find jobs in the area. It's an inexpensive and homely spot worth an overnight on your way north.

177 Musgrave Street, North Rockhampton
(07) 4922 4719
***Website** www.ascothotel.com.au*
***Dorm bed** $20; **double/twin room** $45*
***Credit cards** MC, Visa*
***Reception open** 6.30am-10pm*

Maintenance & cleanliness	★★★½
Facilities	★★★
Atmosphere & character	★★★★
Security	★★★½
Overall rating	★★★

Downtown Backpackers (Oxford Hotel)

Downtown Backpackers is located above the bar of the Oxford Hotel. The dorms are plain white with new carpets and mattresses. Bathrooms are showing their age, as the showers are mouldy and the paint is chipping. The kitchen is very small with one big wooden table in the middle and it leads into the common room with one couch, a big TV, and internet kiosks. It has a great location, but not much of a backpacker atmosphere.

Corner Denham & East Streets, Rockhampton
1, 2, 3, 4A, 5, 6, 10
(07) 4922 1837
***Dorm bed** $20*
***Credit cards** MC, Visa*
***Reception open** Mon-Tue 10am-8.30pm, Wed-Thu 10am-10pm, Fri-Sun 10am-midnight*

Maintenance & cleanliness	★★
Facilities	★★
Atmosphere & character	★★★½
Security	★½
Overall rating	★★

Rockhampton YHA

This hostel has very clean dorm rooms and cabins set in gardens north of the city centre. The kitchen and common room are well maintained and the hostel also has internet access, laundry and guests have free use of bikes. They are in the process of building a new swimming pool. Due to the location, it doesn't have a very good atmosphere although staff are helpful and friendly.

60 MacFarlane Street, Berserker
1, 3, 3A, 4A, 6, 10
(07) 4927 5288
***Website** www.yha.com.au*
***Dorm bed** $24.50 ($22 HI/YHA); **double room** $56-62.50 ($50-56 HI/*

Jellyfish Warning

Marine stingers, or box jellyfish, are among Australia's deadliest creatures. Swimmers who come into contact with the tentacles of these jellyfish have been known to die within five minutes and often become unconscious before they can get out of the water.

Box jellyfish are found in tropical waters between Gladstone in Queensland and Broome in Western Australia, but are not normally found on the Great Barrier Reef. The box jellyfish season is variable, although it is generally between November and March in southern areas and October to April in Far North Queensland and the Northern Territory. They are sometimes found a couple of weeks beyond the official close of the season.

Box jellyfish are also known as sea wasps and can weigh up to six kilograms and have a body 25-30cm in diameter with up to 60 tentacles, which can stretch for up to two metres.

It is best to ask locals first before swimming. Some beaches have jellyfish nets or stinger-resistant enclosures – if you're at a beach that has one of these, always swim inside the enclosure. These enclosures will keep out box jellyfish but not Irukandji, which can still get through. If no one else is swimming on the beach, there's probably a very good reason.

Some people wear a lycra suit, similar to a thin wetsuit, to protect themselves from stingers although there is no guaranteed way to avoid stingers other than sticking to swimming pools.

If you, or someone you're swimming with, are stung you should flood the stung area with vinegar (never use alcohol) for about half a minute and then seek immediate medical help. Mouth-to-mouth resuscitation may also be necessary. Many beaches in infected areas have vinegar on hand, but it's still a good idea to bring a big bottle of vinegar with you.

Although box jellyfish are found mostly in shallow water and not normally on the Great Barrier Reef, there are other jellyfish to watch out for including Irukandji. These small creatures have a body only around two centimetres in diameter and are usually found in deeper water making them a greater threat to divers. Every summer around 60 people are hospitalised from Irukandji stings. Although the sting is not as painful as other jellyfish, about 30 minutes after being stung the victim develops a series of symptoms including severe back and abdominal pain, nausea and vomiting, sweating and agitation.

Another potentially deadly jellyfish in Australian waters is the Portuguese man o war, or bluebottle. Vinegar is not recommended for bluebottle stings, although no deaths from these have been reported in Australia.

PHOTO: © ISTOCKPHOTO/JEANETTE ZEHENTMAYER

*YHA); **twin room** $50 ($40 HI/YHA)*
***Credit cards** MC, Visa*
***Reception open** 7am-7pm daily*

Maintenance & cleanliness	★★★
Facilities	★★★½
Atmosphere & character	★★★
Security	★★★
Overall rating	★★

Eating & Drinking

There is not a big variety of food in Rockhampton.

The big draw here of course is the excellent steak and you will see signs for cheap steak dinners on every street in the city centre. They are almost always a great deal as the steaks are exceptionally large. The unassuming restaurant below

Ascot Backpackers *(177 Musgrave Street, North Rockhampton)* is noted for its excellent stone grill steak and is a must if you're staying at their hostel.

There are also a few good Chinese restaurants that may not look like much, but they serve up generous meals at low prices. You will also find a lot of fast food like KFC, McDonalds and Pizza Hut along the main highway through town.

There are several supermarkets and more cheap places to eat in the **Stockland shopping centre** in North Rockhampton *(corner Musgrave Street & Bruce Highway, North Rockhampton).*

You can get a cheap hearty dinner at many of Rocky's pubs. The **Bush Inn Bar & Grill** *(corner Fitzroy & Quay Streets, Rockhampton)* is a favourite with locals and visitors alike; they also usually have long happy hours, but the nightlife from there fizzles out, so stop by a bottle shop for beer if you want to make it a long night. This is a hard working town, so many of the pubs are quiet at night. The pub beneath the **Downtown Backpackers** *(corner Denham & East Streets, Rockhampton)* can be an exception on the weekends, and they have cheap beer.

Sights & Activities

Dreamtime Cultural Centre

This interesting cultural centre focuses on the traditions of Aboriginal and Torres Strait Islanders. There are also displays on bush tucker and boomerang and didgeridoo demonstrations.

Corner Bruce Highway & Yeppoon Road, Parkhurst
🚌 *10*
☎ *(07) 4936 1655*
Website *www.dreamtimecentre.com.au*
Admission *$13.50 ($11 students)*
Open *Mon-Fri 10am-3.30pm; regular tours from 10.30am*

Rockhampton Art Gallery

Rocky's art gallery has exhibits of art by local artists with an emphasis on paintings from the 1940s to the 70s.

62 Victoria Parade, Rockhampton
☎ *(07) 4927 7129*
Admission *free*
Open *Tue-Fri 10am-4pm, Sat-Sun 11am-4pm*

Rockhampton Zoo & Botanic Gardens

Rockhampton has a surprisingly good zoo that is home to primates although the main focus is on native Australian fauna. Entry is free, which makes it a great alternative to the high priced wildlife parks in the bigger cities.

Spencer Street, South Rockhampton
🚌 *4A*
☎ *(07) 4922 1654*
Admission *free*
Open *8am-5pm daily*

Emu Park & Yeppoon

These two towns on the Capricorn Coast are an alternative to Rockhampton as gateways to Great Keppel Island. Both towns have a laidback and relaxed feel.

Practical Information

Capricorn Coast Visitor Information Centre

Fig Tree Creek Roundabout, Yeppoon
☎ *(07) 4939 4888*
Website *www.capricorncoast.com.au*
Open *9am-5pm daily*

Coming & Going

Young's Coaches *(☎ (07) 4922 3813; **website** www.youngsbusservice.com.au)* run regular buses from Rockhampton to Emu Park and Yeppoon. Route 20 goes from Rockhampton to Emu Park via Rosslyn Bay and Yeppoon and route 29 runs between Rocky and Emu Park.

Great Keppel Island

Great Keppel Island is one of the east coast's more accessible islands. From Rosslyn Bay Harbour (a 40-minute drive from Rockhampton), it is just 30 minutes by ferry to the island. This is a place to truly escape, to idle away days on the beach without any interruptions. Most of the island's 14km² are uninhabited and there are no paved roads on the island. The resort and Holiday Village Backpackers are both tucked into the bush in front of Fisherman's Beach, where the ferries come into shore.

The beaches here are superb. From Fisherman's Beach, there are hiking tracks that lead to the other four beaches on the other side of the island. Svendsen's Beach is heralded as the most beautiful and secluded, with just one small bed & breakfast near the beach. Though it is not on the Great Barrier Reef, the snorkelling here is great. The Watersports Hut hires out sailboards, catamarans, and fishing tackle and the hostel has snorkelling gear. There is a dive centre on the site of the old Keppel Haven that organises diving and supplies gear.

Coming & Going

Great Keppel Island is located 17km off the coast from Rosslyn Bay, which is near Yeppoon – about a 40-minute drive north of Rockhampton. You'll need to take the Young's bus *(☎ (07) 4922 3813; **website** www.youngsbusservice.com.au)* from Rockhampton to Rosslyn Bay, which costs $8.10 for the trip with buses departing from the corner of Bolsover & Denham Streets in Rockhampton.

Freedom Fast Cats *(☎ (07) 4933 6244; **website** www.keppelbaymarina.com.au)* run ferries to Great Keppel Island and the return ferry trip between Rosslyn Bay and Great Keppel Island costs $45.

It's worth checking the package deals offered by the hostels in Rockhampton before you book your transport to the island. There are often good deals that include both transport and accommodation on Great Keppel Island.

Accommodation

Great Keppel Island Holiday Village

This is where you go to really escape. The only activities here are bushwalks, some water sports and sunbathing. Otherwise, curl up with a book in one of the hammocks or get to know your neighbours in the tent cabin next door. There are a few standard dorms, some large canvas tents, a clean kitchen and plenty of time. It's a great place for the outdoorsy types, but not for night owls. The bathroom fittings are quite old, but otherwise it is well maintained. The management are good humoured and easygoing and guests have free use of snorkelling gear.

Great Keppel Island
☎ (07) 4939 8655
***Website** www.gkiholidayvillage.com.au*
***Dorm bed** $33 (after 3 nights, $30 each night for entire stay); **tent** $58 ($53 after 3 nights); **double room** $80 ($75 after 3 nights)*
***Credit cards** MC, Visa*
***Reception open** at boat arrival and departure times*

Maintenance & cleanliness	★★
Facilities	★★½
Atmosphere & character	★★★½
Security	★
Overall rating	★★

Eating & Drinking

Everyone will tell you the same thing when you are planning a trip to Keppel Island: bring your own food. Not only is there a severely limited selection of dining options on the island, but it is very expensive. Island Pizza is just around the corner from the hostel and they have good food but it is pricey. The resort also has snacks, a restaurant, and a bar (with a surprisingly good happy hour). The hostel has a few canned goods and snacks, as well as a large selection of frozen meats which you can buy.

The best option is to stop at the Coles or Woolworths supermarket in Rockhampton or Yeppoon and buy everything you need.

Whitsunday Coast

In the heart of the central Queensland coast, the 74 tropical Whitsunday Islands are the main reason to visit the Whitsunday Coast, which stretches from Mackay to Bowen. The islands form the border of the southern Great Barrier Reef, and are extremely popular not only with private yacht charters but also backpackers on a budget. With long white beaches and incredibly clear water bordered by palm trees and pristine wilderness, the islands are an irresistible outdoor playground for many visitors. There are opportunities for sailing, cruising, rainforest trekking, camping, snorkelling, and of course, spectacular diving.

Mackay, the region's sugar processing city, is often overlooked by travellers or used as a base to explore Eungella National Park, with its famous platypuses and other abundant wildlife. Finch Hatton Gorge offers excellent walking trails leading to waterfalls and swimming holes. Another popular stop is Cape Hillsborough National Park, with its rich Aboriginal history and nice beaches. Prosperine is a small town at the turnoff for Airlie Beach. It is an administrative centre and home to the Whitsunday Information Centre, a sugar mill tour and a museum. Backpackers usually head directly to Airlie Beach, which is the lively hub of accommodation and nightlife, and the epicentre of Whitsunday tours.

Mackay

Mackay is a compact and diverse city located at the southern gateway to the Great Barrier Reef and northern Queensland. Surrounded by far-reaching fields of sugarcane, it is the region's sugar processing centre and has a stale reputation as a boring agricultural town of no interest to the traveller. However, it is a unique and well preserved city. The city centre does boast some impressive architecture, with stately heritage buildings and art-deco creations in interesting juxtaposition. It may not have a wide range of sights and attractions, but it is the perfect place to stay and it makes a good base for enjoying the rugged wilderness of the nearby Eungella National Park.

Fishing and swimming are popular at some of Mackay's northern beaches, where tiny townships and resorts dot the coastline. There are around 30 beaches here, and many of them are often deserted. Windsurfing and kite surfing are great here due to the prevailing winds.

Practical Information

Mackay Visitors Information Centre

320 Nebo Road, South Mackay
☎ *(07) 4952 2677 or 1300 130 001*
Website *www.mackayregion.com*
Open *Mon-Fri 8.30am-5pm, Sat-Sun 9am-4pm*

63 Sydney Street, Mackay
☎ *(07) 4951 4803*
Website *www.mackayregion.com*
Open *Mon-Fri 8.30am-5pm, Sat-Sun 9am-4pm*

Queensland National Parks & Wildlife Service

2 Wood Street, Mackay
☎ *(07) 4944 7800*
Website *www.epa.qld.gov.au*
Open *Mon-Fri 8.30am-5pm*

Coming & Going

AIR

You can get direct flights to Mackay from Brisbane, Melbourne, Rockhampton, Sydney and Townsville. Jetstar *(**website** www.jetstar.com)* flies to Brisbane; Qantaslink *(**website** www.qantas.com.au)* flies to Brisbane, Rockhampton and Townsville; Tiger Airways *(**website** www.tigerairways.com.au)* fly to Melbourne and Virgin Blue *(**website** www.virginblue.com.au)* flies to Brisbane and Sydney.

Mackay Airport *(**website** www.mackayports.com/airport/)* is around 5km south of the city centre.

BUS

Greyhound *(☎ 1300 473 946; **website** www.greyhound.com.au)* and Premier Motor Service *(**website** www.premierms.com.au)* buses stop at Mackay Bus Terminal at the corner of Macalister and Victoria Streets.

TRAIN

The train station is on Connors Road in Paget about 5km south of the city centre.

Local Transport

Mackay Transit *(☎ (07) 4957 3330; **website** www.mackaytransit.com.au)* runs local buses but services are infrequent on some routes and they only go to outlying suburbs.

The Mackay Explorer runs a free hourly service every Sunday that takes in the major sights between the City Gates (tourist information centre) and Mackay Marina.

Accommodation

Gecko's Rest

Gecko's Rest has a great location in the centre of town. Some parts of the hostel are well maintained, but a few dorms smell of mould and have peeling paint. They have single beds with good mattresses instead of bunks and all rooms are air-conditioned. The kitchen is large, clean and well equipped with heavy wooden tables in the middle. There is a separate TV lounge and games room, both brightly decorated and convivial. They offer laundry, internet access ($5 per hour) and good showers. They also loan guests a clean towel and cutlery on arrival. Reception are kind and there is a good atmosphere here.

34 Sydney Street, Mackay
(07) 4944 1230
***Website** www.geckosrest.com.au*
***Dorm bed** $22 ($20 VIP); **single room** $35 ($33 VIP); **double/twin room** $50 ($46 VIP)*
***Credit cards** MC, Visa*
***Reception open** 8am-9pm*

Maintenance & cleanliness	★★½
Facilities	★★½
Atmosphere & character	★★★½
Security	★★★½
Overall rating	★★★

Larrikin Lodge

Larrikin Lodge is in a quaint little blue house near the centre of Mackay. It has all air-conditioned dorms and nice clean bathrooms. There is laundry, a small above-ground swimming pool and a homely common room. There are plans to partly renovate the kitchen. The friendly management run the Jungle Johno eco-tours to Eungella National Park almost daily, weather permitting. They also help travellers look for work, so many of the guests here are on a working holiday.

32 Peel Street, Mackay
(07) 4951 3728 or 1800 611 953
***Website** www.larrikinlodge.com.au*
***Dorm bed** $21; **double room** $50; **twin room** $48*
***Credit cards** MC, Visa; 2% credit card surcharge*
***Reception open** 7am-8.30pm*

Maintenance & cleanliness	★★★
Facilities	★★★
Atmosphere & character	★★½
Security	★★★
Overall rating	★★★

Sights

Artspace Mackay

Mackay's art gallery is host to a selection of temporary art exhibitions.

Gordon Street, Mackay
(07) 4968 4444 (Mon-Fri); (07) 4957 1775 (Sat-Sun)
***Admission** free*
***Open** Tue-Sun 10am-5pm*

Eungella National Park

Eungella National Park is about an hour inland from Mackay. It is home to a large subtropical rainforest. The park's highlight is the impressive Finch Hatton Gorge.

At Broken River there is a viewing deck that is an excellent place for spotting platypus. Dusk and dawn are the best times to catch a glimpse of a platypus but it helps if you are both quiet and patient.

Eungella National Park is difficult to reach without a car but there are tours to the park that operate from Mackay, which include the excellent **Jungle Johno Tours** (*(07) 4951 3728; **website** www.larrikinlodge.com.au/jungle-tours*) that are geared to backpackers. Jungle Johno has day tours departing from Mackay for $75-90 that take in the park's main attractions including Finch Hatton Gorge and Broken River and give you the opportunity to see Eungella's unique array of wildlife including guarranteed a platypus sighting.

Proserpine

Proserpine is a busy town serving the region's sugar cane farms and it stands in sharp contrast to energetic Airlie Beach.

There's no backpackers' accommodation here, but it is the main transport hub of the Whitsunday region and many backpackers pass through here en route to Airlie Beach and the Whitsunday Islands.

Practical Information

Whitsunday Information Centre
Bruce Highway, Proserpine
☎ *(07) 4945 3711 or 1800 801 252*
Website *www.tourismwhitsundays.com.au*
Open *Mon-Fri 9am-5pm, Sat-Sun 9am-3pm*

Coming & Going

Proserpine enjoys good transport connections with a busy regional airport, train station and frequent coaches up and down the coast.

Greyhound *(☎ 1300 473 946; **website** www.greyhound.com.au)* and Premier Motor Service *(**website** www.premierms.com.au)* buses pass through here en route to Airlie Beach and Whitsunday Transit *(☎ (07) 4946 1800; **website** www.whitsundaytransit.com.au)* provide good connections between Proserpine and Airlie Beach with many services timed to meet airline and train connections.

Proserpine's Whitsunday Coast Airport is 12km south of Proserpine and is served by both Qantas and Virgin Blue. Whitsunday Transit's buses meet every flight but it is essential to book ahead for the airport bus transfer.

Whitsunday Transit also has transfers between Proserpine train station and Airlie Beach.

Airlie Beach

Beautiful Airlie Beach is a relaxed tropical town with great accommodation, restaurants and nightlife. It is the most popular destination for backpackers between Brisbane and Cairns due to its great ambience and perfect position as launching point to the Whitsunday Islands. This small town packs in a lot and Shute Harbour Road, the high street, is full of hostels, pubs, restaurants and tour operators. Everything revolves around tourism and the Whitsundays, but it somehow retains its charm, and residents are friendly and easygoing.

The huge artificial lagoon at the waterfront is an extremely popular place to relax and sunbathe on your day off from activities. There are some great seaside walking trails as well, including the Bicentennial Walkway that links Cannonvale and Airlie Beach with 3km of pathways and boardwalks taking you past the Lagoon and the Marina. The Saturday morning markets at Airlie Point are full of craft stalls and fresh fruits and vegetables, and are popular with locals and visitors alike.

Airlie Beach has a great vibe and many travellers end up spending an extra couple of days here.

Practical Information

Marine Parks Authority Information Centre
Corner Mandalay Street & Shute Harbour Road, Airlie Beach
☎ *(07) 4946 7022*
Open *Mon-Fri 9am-5pm, Sat 9am-1pm*

Whitsundays Central Reservations Centre
259 Shute Harbour Road, Airlie Beach
☎ *(07) 4946 5299 or 1800 677 119*
Website *www.airliebeach.com*
Open *7.30am-8pm daily*

INTERNET ACCESS

Airliebeach.com Internet Centre
259 Shute Harbour Road, Airlie Beach
☎ *(07) 4946 5299 or 1800 677 119*
Website *www.airliebeach.com*
Open *7.30am-8pm daily*

Beaches
356-362 Shute Harbour Road, Airlie Beach
☎ *(07) 4946 6244 or 1800 636 630*
Website *www.beaches.com.au*
Open *6.30am-8pm daily*

LAUNDRY

Airlie Beach Coin Laundry
Shop 12, Beach Plaza, The Esplanade, Airlie Beach
☎ *(07) 4946 4977*

Coming & Going

Most Greyhound (☎ *1300 473 946;* ***website*** *www.greyhound.com.au)* and Premier Motor Service *(**website** www.premierms.com.au)* buses running between Brisbane and Cairns stop in Airlie Beach dropping off on Shute Harbour Road in the centre of town.

The nearest airport and train station is at Proserpine. Whitsunday Transit (☎ *(07) 4946 1800;* ***website*** *www.whitsundaytransit.com.au)* run buses to Airlie Beach that meet flights and train services. The one-way fare from the Proserpine train station is $8.20 and it costs $15 to get to Airlie Beach from Whitsunday Coast Airport. There's another airport at nearby Hamilton Island; but the ferry transfer costs $51.

Fantasea ferries (☎ *(07) 4946 5111;* ***website*** *www.fantasea.com.au)* run between Shute Harbour and Hamilton Island, Long Island and South Molle Island. The ferry to Hamilton Island costs $41 each way.

Local Transport

Airlie Beach is small enough to walk around but Whitsunday Transit (☎ *(07) 4946 1800;* ***website*** *www.whitsundaytransit.com.au)* operates a local bus service that connects it to the neighbouring towns of Cannonvale and Shute Harbour. Buses run about every half hour and cost $2.05 one-way ($3.85 return) between Airlie Beach and the shopping centre in Cannonvale. The $8.50 all day pass includes unlimited travel on all Whitsunday Transit services including buses to Proserpine.

Accommodation

Airlie Beach YHA

This is a lovely purpose built hostel at the end of the main street. There is a large courtyard with a swimming pool and a barbecue area with covered tables, but the common room is a bit empty. Dormitories are large and airy, with lockers, en suite bathrooms and some have balconies. The huge kitchen is new and kept impeccably clean. They have internet including Wi-Fi at $4 per hour and a travel desk with great deals on Whitsunday trips.

394 Shute Harbour Road, Airlie Beach
☎ *(07) 4946 6312 or 1800 247 251*
Website *www.yha.com.au*
Dorm bed *$27 ($24 HI/YHA);* ***double/twin room*** *$71.50 ($64 HI/YHA)*
Credit cards *MC, Visa*
Reception open *7am-7pm*

Maintenance & cleanliness	★★★
Facilities	★★★
Atmosphere & character	★★★½
Security	★★
Overall rating	★★★

Airlie Waterfront Backpackers

This hostel is in a great location, facing the ocean just off the main street in the town centre. The dorms are mostly single beds in large A-frame wooden rooms. Some have a balcony with ocean views, the others in the back have no windows at all. They are all air-conditioned and clean, though the bathrooms are looking a little tired. They sit above a centre courtyard full of shops and inexpensive restaurants, which opens onto covered street side tables. It is a very laid-back and comfortable place to stay. The travel desk at reception has everything you need.

6 The Esplanade, Airlie Beach
☎ *(07) 4948 1300 or 1800 089 000*
Website *www.airliewaterfront.com*
Dorm bed *$25-30;* ***double/twin room*** *$110-120;* ***triple room*** *$150*
Credit cards *MC, Visa*
Reception open *7am-8pm daily*

Maintenance & cleanliness	★★★
Facilities	★★½
Atmosphere & character	★★★½
Security	★★★½
Overall rating	★★★

Backpackers by the Bay

This is a lovely small hostel in a tranquil bush setting five minutes' walk from the town centre. It has nicely decorated dorms of four beds each. There is a very nice saltwater swimming pool and a small outside bar with wooden tables, lounge chairs and a barbecue. Facilities include internet access, laundry and a pool table and the staff are easygoing and give good advice on Whitsunday tours. There

Queensland

is potential to have fun nights here, as they host events at the bar, but it is much more relaxed than the party hostels in the centre of town.
12 Hermitage Drive, Airlie Beach
(07) 4946 7267 or 1800 646 994
***Website** www.backpackersbythebay.com*
***Dorm bed** $27; **double room** $65*
***Credit cards** MC, Visa*
***Reception open** 7am-7.30pm daily*

Maintenance & cleanliness	★★★½
Facilities	★★★½
Atmosphere & character	★★★★½
Security	★
Overall rating	★★★½

Beaches

Beaches has a very lively bar packed with locals and travellers every night. Its location in the centre of town makes it a good meeting place and a convenient home base; but the dorms are sparse, some have bare kitchenettes and some have air conditioning. The kitchen is good size, well equipped and very clean. There is a big swimming pool, barbecue and pool tables. They have a great location and a good tour desk to book your trips. Internet costs $6 per hour. Reception staff can unfortunately be cold and unorganised.
356 Shute Harbour Road, Airlie Beach
(07) 4946 6244 or 1800 636 630
***Website** www.beaches.com.au*
***Dorm bed** $25; **double room** $80*
***Credit cards** MC, Visa*
***Reception open** 6.30am-8pm daily*

Maintenance & cleanliness	★★★
Facilities	★★★
Atmosphere & character	★★★½
Security	★★★
Overall rating	★★★

Bush Village Backpackers Resort

Consisting of 18 cabins set among lush gardens, this hostel has a quiet and peaceful ambience. The dorms are clean and well maintained and some have newly refurbished bathrooms. Each cabin is self contained with a kitchenette, en suite bathroom and a patio with hammocks. Other facilities

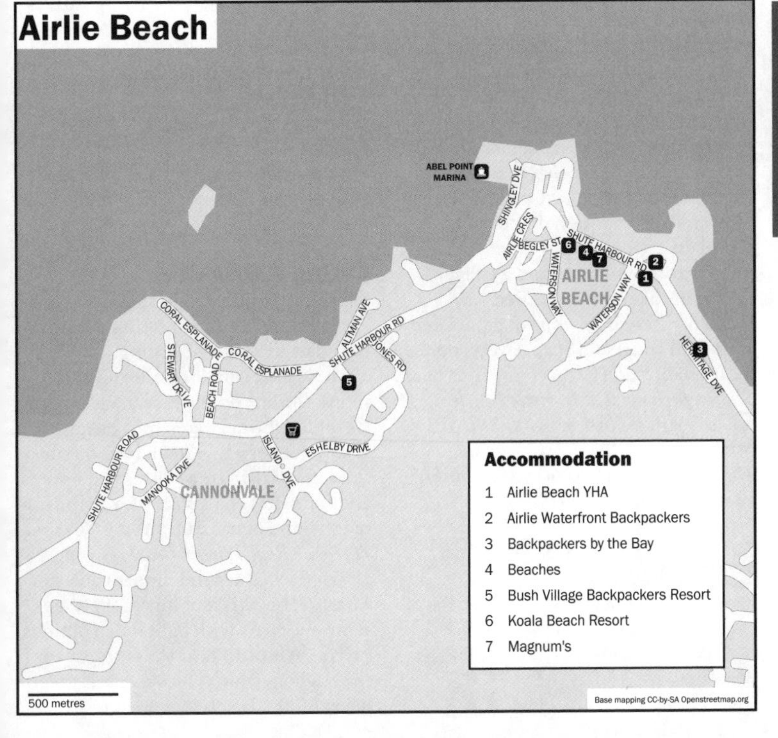

include a swimming pool, spa pool, barbecue and internet access, as well as laundry. It is located just outside of the town centre, but shops and restaurants in Cannonvale are nearby. This hostel used to be known for the kangaroos they used to look after but unfortunately they had to be relocated to protect their health, but wallabies can still be spotted in the area if you are lucky.
2 St Martins Road, Cannonvale
☎ *(07) 4946 6177 or 1800 809 256*
Website *www.bushvillage.com.au*
Dorm bed *$28-32;* ***double/twin room*** *$80-90;* ***studio*** *$100-110; prices include breakfast*
Credit cards *MC, Visa*
Reception open *7am-9pm*

Maintenance & cleanliness	★★★½
Facilities	★★★½
Atmosphere & character	★½
Security	★
Overall rating	★★★

Koala Beach Resort

This place is large, impersonal and party-minded; but since everyone goes elsewhere to party, it seems they try to make their money by booking you into every tour and excursion they can. The dorms are in cabins in a big garden setting and they are spacious but rather dirty and many have a bad odour. The bathrooms have nice new tile and fittings and they each have a kitchenette. However the communal kitchen is just plain awful; it has a couple of old microwaves, hot plates and a fridge that looks like it is never used – or cleaned. There is a swimming pool and volleyball court and they have a good location, but don't expect any frills here.
Shute Harbour Road, Airlie Beach
☎ *(07) 4946 6001 or 1800 800 421*
Website *www.koalaresort.com.au*
Dorm bed *$28 ($26.60 VIP);* ***double room*** *$72 ($68.40 VIP)*
Credit cards *MC Visa*
Reception open *7am-8.30pm daily*

Maintenance & cleanliness	★★½
Facilities	★★★
Atmosphere & character	★★★★
Security	★★
Overall rating	★★★

Magnum's

This is a potentially brilliant hostel with a great location. The accommodation is in large beautifully maintained wooden cabins in tropical gardens with winding pathways. Most dorms are air-conditioned with en suite bathrooms, but the beds are old and poorly maintained. The bathrooms are a hit or miss; some have been renovated, some have not. There is an internet café, a restaurant and a popular bar and nightclub on site that is always buzzing with activity. The tour desk has heaps of advice and they offer free accommodation when you book certain trips. The staff are for the most part friendlier than the other places. It is one of the best places to meet other backpackers, but security can be a problem as doors do not automatically lock and guests sometimes complain of theft.
Shute Harbour Road, Airlie Beach
☎ *(07) 4946 6266 or 1800 624 634*
Website *www.magnums.com.au*
Dorm bed *$17-20;* ***double/twin room*** *$52;* ***triple room*** *$65;* ***camping*** *$18-20 for two people*
Credit cards *MC, Visa*
Reception open *6am-10pm*

Maintenance & cleanliness	★★★
Facilities	★★½
Atmosphere & character	★★★★½
Security	★★
Overall rating	★★★

Eating & Drinking

Shute Harbour Road in the centre of Airlie Beach has many eating options from fast food to fine dining.

There are a couple of fish and chip shops; the one on the Esplanade is popular for lunchtime waterfront eating. A few of the hostels in town have on site restaurants that are a convenient option and sometimes have great deals. The restaurant and bar at **Beaches** *(356-Shute Harbour Road, Airlie Beach)* is almost always packed around dinner time. For a healthy breakfast or lunch, there are some juice bars with light lunch options such as **Wisdom** near the entrance to the Lagoon, which has wraps and great juices.

There is good pizza in Airlie, too. Often, **Beagle Pizza** *(293 Shute Harbour Road, Airlie Beach)* and the pizza restaurant in **Magnum's** *(Shute Harbour Road, Airlie Beach)* compete with **Domino's** *(Shute Harbour Road, Airlie Beach)* by offering huge bargains. Walk through town and check them all out, it only takes a few minutes.

Although it is a party town, the eating options at Airlie Beach shut down early and about the only places open late are McDonalds and KFC next to Magnums hostel.

There is a small supermarket in the centre of town, but for cheaper prices, head to Cannonvale where you'll find **Coles** *(corner Island Drive & Shute Harbour Road, Cannonvale)* and **Woolworths** *(corner Paluma & Shute Harbour Roads, Cannonvale).*

Drinks are expensive even with the deals and discounts offered by hostels. There is a drive-through bottle shop across from the YHA on Shute Harbour Road and a bigger bottle shop in Cannonvale where you can stock up on beer, but many hostels have a no BYO policy. Otherwise, hit happy hour before you go out.

Whitsunday Islands

The Whitsunday Island group offers myriad opportunities for sailing, snorkelling or just cruising around the islands.

The islands are renowned for their lovely beaches, particularly the world famous Whitehaven Beach on Whitsunday Island. The 6km long Whitehaven Beach is the most popular with day-trippers but somehow that doesn't spoil its allure. Make sure you do the 650m walk to the lookout at Hill Inlet.

Many of the islands including Daydream, Hamilton, Hayman and South Molle have upmarket resorts. Although you may feel out of place here, the island resorts provide pockets of civilisation among the wilderness.

Coming & Going

FERRY

Ferries are one of the cheaper options and ideal if you just want to visit one or two of the more popular islands such as Hamilton Island, Long Island or South Molle Island. However you won't get the true Whitsunday sailing experience.

FantaSea *(☎ (07) 4946 5111; **website** www.fantasea.com.au)*, is the main ferry operator in the Whitsundays with frequent shuttle services from Shute Harbour to Daydream Island, Hamilton Island, Long Island, South Molle Island and Whitehaven Beach on Whitsunday Island.

Sailing

Many backpackers opt for a sailing package, which allows you to see a variety of islands and for many people it is the only chance they will ever have of sailing a yacht.

Airlie Beach has a huge range of yachts ranging from modern catamarans and racing maxi yacht to historic tall ships and encompassing everything in between. Two-night sailing excursions start at $269 and go up to around $2000 depending on the boat and the type of onboard accommodation provided, although most backpackers spend between $300 and $450 for a three day/two night sailing trip.

With the exception of day trips on large boats with licensed bars, you can bring your own alcohol but most of the sailing boats prohibit glass, which means you can't enjoy a nice wine aboard the yacht (just beer and cask wine).

You will also need to pay the Great Barrier Reef Marine Park levy and administration charge of $33, which most sailing companies do not include in their prices (although this fee is included in the price of many of the day trips).

Generally the smaller boats offer a more authentic hands-on sailing experience, but the bigger boats are more comfortable and usually cheaper. Most sailing trips have two to three crew and eight to 20 passengers, although some of the larger boats carry over 30 passengers.

Most sailing trips include barbecue meals, free use of snorkelling gear and a visit to Whitehaven Beach.

Companies operating multi-day sailing trips in the Whitsundays include:

Atlantic Clipper

This 34m schooner claims to be the largest boat in the Whitsundays. It has a party reputation and being big it packs more people in, making it a good value option for the budget conscious.
☎ *1800 117 173*
Website *www.atlanticclipper.com.au*
2 days/2 nights *$330*

Australian Tall Ship Cruises

This company has cruises on classic vessels including the *Solway Lass*, a classic square rigged tall ship and the three-masted schooner *Whitsunday Magic*.
Shop 1, 4 The Esplanade Airlie Beach
☎ *(07) 4946 5932 or 1800 355 377*
Website *www.australiantallships.com*
2 days/1 night *$289;* ***3 days/2 nights*** *$429;* ***3 days/3 nights*** *$469-699;* ***6 days/6 nights*** *$859-1249*

Awesome Adventures

Awesome Adventures run good value sailing trips on the *Camira*, a high-speed sailing catamaran. Overnight trips include accommodation on Long Island.
Building 2, Abel Point Marina North, Airlie Beach
Departs *Abel Point Marina*
☎ *(07) 4946 4662 or 1800 293 7663 (1800 AWESOME)*
Website *www.awesomeoz.com*
1 day *$145;* ***3 days/2 nights*** *$249*

Koala Adventures

Koala has a couple of maxi yachts including *Anaconda II* and *the Card*, which have competed in the Sydney-Hobart and Whitbread around the World yacht races.
Shute Harbour Road, Airlie Beach
Departs Abel Point Marina
☎ *(07) 4946 6001 or 1800 800 421*
Website *www.koalaadventures.com*
3 days/2 nights *$429*

Oz Adventure Sailing

This company has a fleet of 25 vessels with a great selection of classic yachts including several tall ships and timber ketches as well as sleek racing yachts including winners of the Sydney-Hobart and Pamelia London-Australia races.
Level 2, 293 Shute Harbour Road, Airlie Beach
Departs *Abel Point Marina*
☎ *(07) 4948 2350*
Website *www.aussiesailing.com.au*
2 days/2 nights *$339-379;* ***3 days/2 nights*** *$339-499*

ProSail Whitsundays

ProSail Whitsundays have several maxi yachts with good value sailing trips around the Whitsundays.
20 Stewart Drive, Cannonvale
☎ *(07) 4946 7533*
Website *www.prosail.com.au*
2 days/1 night *$269;* ***2 days/2 nights*** *$359*

Southern Cross Sailing Adventures

Southern Cross has a fleet of boats that feature ex racing yachts including *Ragamuffin II*, *Southern Cross* and *Maxi Boomerang*.
Shop 1, 4 The Esplanade Airlie Beach
☎ *(07) 4946 4999 or 1800 675 790*
Website *www.soxsail.com.au*
2 days/1 night *$269;* ***2 days/2nights*** *$359;* ***3 days/2 nights*** *$429*

Tongarra Cruises

Tongarra is a spacious catamaran that runs flexible two night sailing trips around the Whitsundays. It is good value and has a reputation as a party boat.
Departs Abel Point Marina
273 Shute Harbour Road, Airlie Beach
☎ *(07) 4946 6952 or 1800 117 173*
Website *www.tongarra.com*
2 days/2 nights *$279*

DAY TRIPS

If your time is limited and you don't mind missing out on the authentic sailing experience, then a launch day trip is a good option for exploring the islands. You may feel like a tourist on these trips but you can pack a lot into one day and most of the trips offer excellent snorkelling opportunities.

Cruise Whitsundays Great Barrier Reef trip

This company operates several day trips including a highly recommended Great

Melbourne Tram Network

metlink

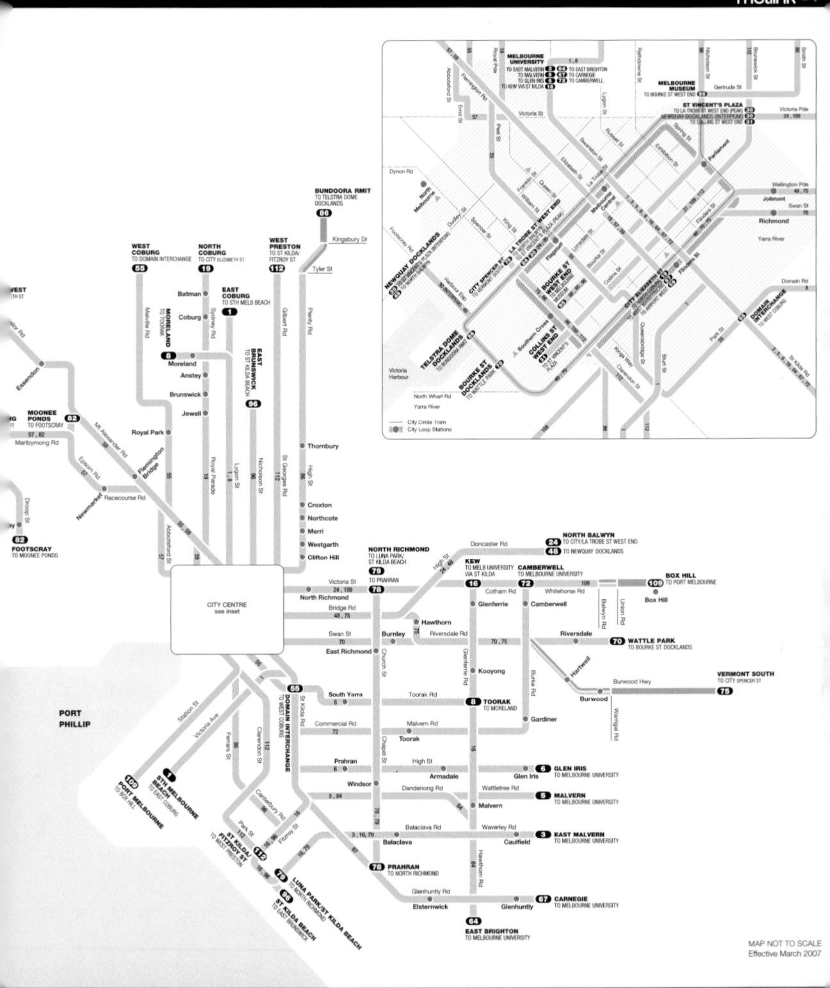

Information

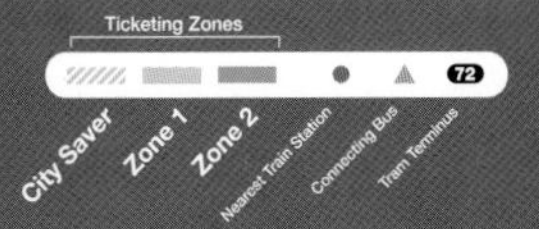

For train, tram and bus information call **131 638 / (TTY) 9619 2727** (6am-10pm daily) or visit **metlinkmelbourne.com.au**

For Yarra Trams customer feedback and lost property call **1800 800 166** (6am-10pm daily) or visit **yarratrams.com.au**

Routes: 1, 3, 5, 6, 8, 16, 19, 24, 30, 31, 48, 55, 57, 59
64, 67, 70, 72, 75, 78, 79, 82, 86, 95, 96, 109, 112

CityRail DayTripper area

N

To CityRail's Newcastle & Central Coast Line and Hunter Line

To CityRail's Blue Mountains Line

Some Southern Highlands services operate directly to and from Central.

Line under construction

Additional station access fee applies at these stations

Hawkesbury River
Sydney Harbour
Botany Bay
City Circle

Cowan
Berowra
Hornsby
Mount Kuring-gai
Mount Colah
Asquith
Waitara
Wahroonga
Warrawee
Turramurra
Pymble
Gordon
Killara
Lindfield
Roseville
Chatswood
Artarmon
St Leonards
Wollstonecraft
Waverton
North Sydney
Milsons Point
Circular Quay
Wynyard
Martin Place
St James
Town Hall
Central
Redfern
Museum
Kings Cross
Edgecliff
Bondi Junction
Normanhurst
Thornleigh
Pennant Hills
Beecroft
Cheltenham
Epping
Macquarie University
Macquarie Park
North Ryde
Eastwood
Denistone
West Ryde
Meadowbank
Rhodes
Concord West
North Strathfield
Carlingford
Telopea
Dundas
Rydalmere
Camellia
Rosehill
Olympic Park
Clyde
Richmond
East Richmond
Clarendon
Windsor
Mulgrave
Vineyard
Riverstone
Schofields
Quakers Hill
Marayong
Blacktown
Emu Plains
Penrith
Kingswood
Werrington
St Marys
Mount Druitt
Rooty Hill
Doonside
Seven Hills
Toongabbie
Pendle Hill
Wentworthville
Westmead
Parramatta
Harris Park
Merrylands
Guildford
Yennora
Granville
Auburn
Lidcombe
Berala
Regents Park
Flemington
Homebush
Strathfield
Burwood
Croydon
Ashfield
Summer Hill
Lewisham
Petersham
Stanmore
Newtown
Macdonaldtown
Erskineville
St Peters
Green Square
Mascot
Domestic Airport
International Airport
Sydenham
Tempe
Wolli Creek
Carramar
Villawood
Leightonfield
Chester Hill
Sefton
Fairfield
Canley Vale
Cabramatta
Warwick Farm
Liverpool
Casula
Glenfield
Birrong
Yagoona
Bankstown
Punchbowl
Wiley Park
Lakemba
Belmore
Campsie
Canterbury
Hurlstone Park
Dulwich Hill
Marrickville
Holsworthy
East Hills
Panania
Revesby
Padstow
Riverwood
Narwee
Beverly Hills
Kingsgrove
Bexley North
Bardwell Park
Turrella
Arncliffe
Banksia
Rockdale
Kogarah
Carlton
Allawah
Hurstville
Penshurst
Mortdale
Oatley
Como
Jannali
Sutherland
Loftus
Engadine
Heathcote
Kirrawee
Gymea
Miranda
Caringbah
Woolooware
Cronulla
Macquarie Fields
Ingleburn
Minto
Leumeah
Campbelltown
Macarthur

Suburban lines

- Eastern Suburbs & Illawarra Line
- Bankstown Line
- Inner West Line
- Cumberland Line
- Airport & East Hills Line
- *Peak hours only*
- South Line
- North Shore and Western Lines
- Northern Line
- Carlingford Line
- Olympic Park Sprint and special event services

Transport interchanges

- Interchange between CityRail services
- Buses (including bus transitways)
- Ferries
- Monorail
- Trams
- Car parks near stations

Stations with wheelchair access

- Wheelchair access (staffed for all train services)
- Wheelchair access (not staffed for all train services)
- Assisted access

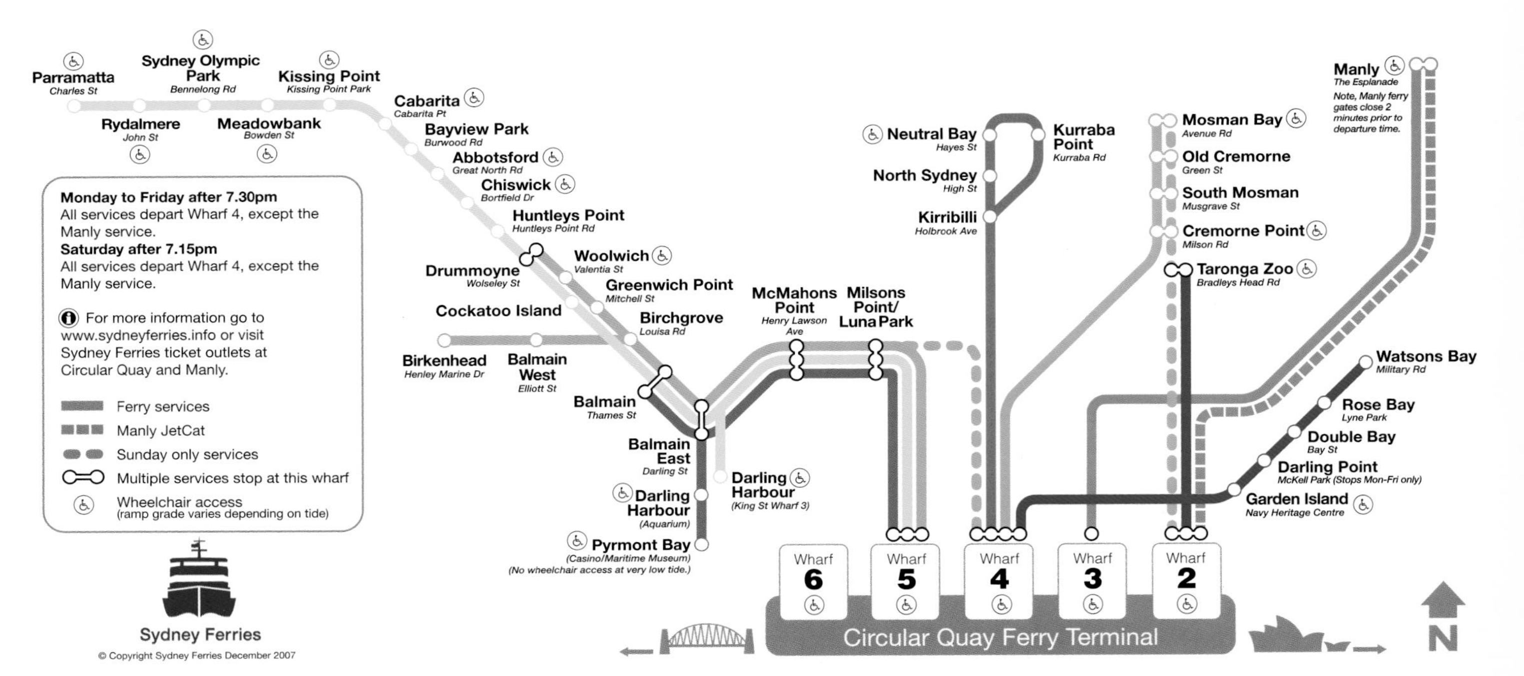
Parramatta
Charles St
Rydalmere
John St
Sydney Olympic Park
Bennelong Rd
Meadowbank
Bowden St
Kissing Point
Kissing Point Park
Cabarita
Cabarita Pt
Bayview Park
Burwood Rd
Abbotsford
Great North Rd
Chiswick
Bortfield Dr
Huntleys Point
Huntleys Point Rd
Drummoyne
Wolseley St
Woolwich
Valentia St
Greenwich Point
Mitchell St
Cockatoo Island
Birchgrove
Louisa Rd
Birkenhead
Henley Marine Dr
Balmain West
Elliott St
Balmain
Thames St
Balmain East
Darling St
Darling Harbour
(Aquarium)
Pyrmont Bay
(Casino/Maritime Museum)
(No wheelchair access at very low tide.)
Darling Harbour
(King St Wharf 3)
McMahons Point
Henry Lawson Ave
Milsons Point/ Luna Park
Neutral Bay
Hayes St
North Sydney
High St
Kirribilli
Holbrook Ave
Kurraba Point
Kurraba Rd
Mosman Bay
Avenue Rd
Old Cremorne
Green St
South Mosman
Musgrave St
Cremorne Point
Milson Rd
Taronga Zoo
Bradleys Head Rd
Manly
The Esplanade
Note, Manly ferry gates close 2 minutes prior to departure time.
Watsons Bay
Military Rd
Rose Bay
Lyne Park
Double Bay
Bay St
Darling Point
McKell Park (Stops Mon-Fri only)
Garden Island
Navy Heritage Centre
Wharf 6
Wharf 5
Wharf 4
Wharf 3
Wharf 2
Circular Quay Ferry Terminal
N
Monday to Friday after 7.30pm
All services depart Wharf 4, except the Manly service.
Saturday after 7.15pm
All services depart Wharf 4, except the Manly service.
For more information go to www.sydneyferries.info or visit Sydney Ferries ticket outlets at Circular Quay and Manly.
Ferry services
Manly JetCat
Sunday only services
Multiple services stop at this wharf
Wheelchair access
(ramp grade varies depending on tide)
Sydney Ferries

Perth Suburban Train Network

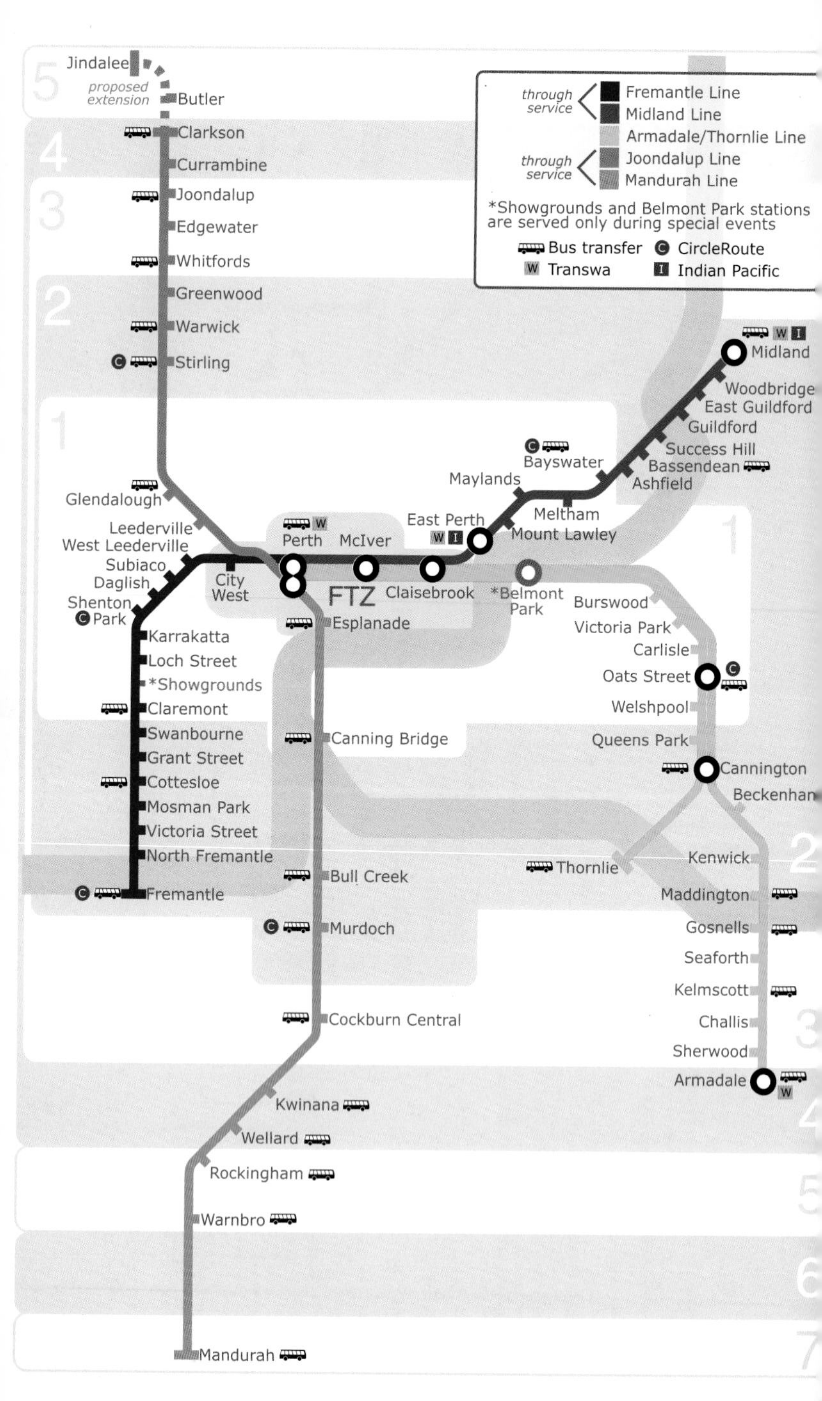

Barrier Reef trip. The reef trip includes a stop at their pontoon on Knuckle Reef with a buffet lunch, an underwater viewing observatory and glass bottom boat trips. There is good snorkelling here, and what better way to get in the water than their own waterslide.
263 Shute Harbour Road, Airlie Beach
Abel Point Marina
☎ *(07) 4946 4662*
Website *www.cruisewhitsundays.com*
Price *$189*

Fantasea Cruises

The Whitsunday's main ferry operator also runs a several day trips including their Reefworld trip and their popular two and three-island day trips.

Reefworld ($209) is Fantasea's floating pontoon at Hardy Reef, which includes underwater observation decks, semi-submersible coral viewing vessels, snorkelling and a buffet lunch.

Fantasea Reefworld & Ragamuffin ($255) is a good value (when compared with the cost of visiting Reefworld on its own) two day trip that combines a day sailing on the maxi yacht Ragamuffin with a day at Reefworld.

Fantasea operates a selection of cruises departing Hamilton Island and Shute Harbour. The more popular options are the two and three island day cruises, both of which include a visit to Whitehaven Beach. The two island cruise ($99; $89 students) goes to Hamilton and Whitsunday Islands and the three island cruise ($130; $99 students) includes Daydream, Hamilton and Whitsunday Islands.

Day trips to the island resorts are also available including the Island Discovery Cruise ($82), a day visiting both Daydream and Hamilton Islands); Daydream Island Resort & Spa Daytripper ($74-81), including lunch at one of two island restaurants and the Hamilton Island Daytripper ($125), which also includes lunch.
Departs Shute Harbour
☎ *(07) 4946 6900*
Website *www.fantasea.com.au*

Ocean Rafting

Ocean Rafting's day trip is on a large high-speed inflatable raft that visits Hook and Whitsunday Islands and includes a guided national park walk and snorkelling on the reef.
Departs Coral Sea Resort, Airlie Beach
☎ *(07) 4946 6848*
Website *www.oceanrafting.com.au*
Price *$103*

Ragamuffin

Ragamuffin is legendary among yacht racing circles as one of the most successful boats in the famous Sydney to Hobart yacht race. This 24m racing yacht now makes one-day sailing trips that either feature snorkelling at Blue Pearl Bay on Hayman Island or a picnic lunch at Whitehaven Beach on Whitsunday Island.
Departs Shute Harbour
☎ *(07) 4946 7777 or 1800 454 777*
Website *www.maxiaction.com.au*
Cost *$142 ($130 students)*

ReefJet

ReefJet's island day trip visits Hook Island, Hayman Island and Whitehaven Beach on Whitsunday Island. They also make a trip to the outer Great Barrier Reef, which gives you up to five hours snorkelling on the reef.
Departs Airlie Beach
☎ *(07) 4946 5366*
Website *www.reefjet.com.au*
Island day trip *$110*

Whitehaven Xpress

Whitehaven Xpress visits Mantaray Bay on Hook Island and includes a barbecue lunch at Whitehaven Beach on Whitsunday Island.
Departs Abel Point Marina
☎ *(07) 4946 7172*
Website *www.whitehavenxpress.com.au*
Price *$133*

Accommodation

Apart from pricey resorts or sleeping on a yacht, camping is the main accommodation option in the islands. The Queensland Parks & Wildlife Service runs 21 campgrounds on the islands, but you'll need to buy a camping permit from the **Marine Parks Authority** office in Airlie Beach *(corner Mandalay Street & Shute Harbour Road, Airlie Beach;* ☎ *(07) 4946*

7022). Camping permits cost $4.50 per night.

Bowen

Bowen is a small seaside town that is popular with travellers on a working holiday due to the fruit-picking work available in the area between March and August. There is not a lot else to see in Bowen besides the beaches, which are good for snorkelling and swimming. The best ones are a short drive north at Horseshoe and Rose Bays. King's Beach is a great spot for kite surfing and windsurfing.

Mullers Lagoon in the centre of town is the home of botanic gardens, hundreds of species of migrating birds, and interesting murals depicting various historical scenes. The surrounding area is renowned for its mangoes, drawing many backpackers to work on the orchards. If you are just driving through town, it is a good idea to stop at one of the fruit stalls or markets and sample some of the fresh produce.

The Baz Luhrmann film, *Australia*, starring Nicole Kidman and Hugh Jackman, was filmed in Bowen to portray Darwin in the 1940s. This was the most excitement Bowen has had in years.

Practical Information

Bowen Visitor Information Centre

Bruce Highway, Mount Gordon
☎ *(07) 4786 4222*
Website *www.bowentourism.com.au*
Open *8.30am-5pm daily*

Coming & Going

Greyhound *(☎ 1300 473 946;* ***website*** *www.greyhound.com.au)* and Premier Motor Service *(****website*** *www.premierms.com.au)* buses stop at Bowen Travel at 40 William Street in the town centre. Bowen is also on the main Brisbane-Cairns train line with the station a couple of km south of the town centre.

Accommodation

Barnacles Backpackers

This hostel is comprised of two houses with a total of 80 beds, mostly catering to travellers on a working holiday. The buildings are old, but well maintained and very clean. The beds have new thick mattresses that the owners are determined to keep bed bug-free. There is a large well stocked kitchen, internet access ($5 per hour), and a good TV lounge with an extensive DVD library. They are a good resource for finding work and offer free transport to jobs. It is absolutely essential that you phone ahead to book in fruit-picking season.

18 Gordon Street, Bowen
☎ *(07) 4786 4400*
Dorm bed *$25 per night, $120-145 per week;* ***double room*** *$50 per night, $320-330 per week*
Credit cards *JCB, MC, Visa*
Reception open *9am-10am & 5pm-6pm daily; phone inquiries 6am-8pm*

Maintenance & cleanliness	★★
Facilities	★★½
Atmosphere & character	★★½
Security	★★★
Overall rating	★★½

Ayr

Ayr is a bustling farming town between Bowen and Townsville at the mouth of the Burdekin river. It doesn't offer many attractions other than fruit picking work, and with a couple of hostels in town set up to provide cheap workers accommodation, it is a comfortable place to call home for a month or three. The town centre is colourful and compact, with lots of shops and restaurants, and a few pubs where workers hang out on weekends. It is quite far away from anything of real interest to the casual traveller or backpacker, although it is popular with divers who come to dive the wreck of the *SS Yongala*.

Practical Information

Burdekin Information Centre

Plantation Park, Bruce Highway, Ayr
☎ *(07) 4783 5988*
Website *www.burdekintourism.com.au*
Open *10am-4pm daily*

Coming & Going

Greyhound *(☎ 1300 473 946;* ***website*** *www.greyhound.com.au)* and Premier

Motor Service *(**website** www.premierms.com.au)* buses stop at Rotary Park on Graham Street. Trains on the Brisbane-Cairns line stop at the new train station on Railway Street.

Accommodation

Ayr Backpackers

Ayr Backpackers is an extension of a family's home, with some tired-looking accommodation out the back. They cater exclusively to long-term working holiday guests. The dorms are self contained with shabby kitchenettes and poorly-maintained bathrooms. There is a swimming pool and common area in the garden. The owners are friendly and helpful with finding work.

54 Wilmington Street, Ayr
☎ *(07) 4783 5837*
***Website** www.ayrbackpackers.com.au*
***Dorm bed** $110 per week, transport to work $7 per day*
***Reception open** 6am-11am & 3.30pm-7.30pm daily; **seasonal opening** Jan & Apr-Dec*

Maintenance & cleanliness	★½
Facilities	★★
Atmosphere & character	★½
Security	★★½
Overall rating	★★

Delta Backpackers

This is a spacious hostel has 115 beds in large dorms mostly for working holiday-makers. It is rather institutional and poorly-maintained and features a huge swimming pool, a bar, laundry, internet access ($4 per hour) and a barbecue, but there are mostly workers staying here, so the atmosphere is lacking. The bathrooms are not the cleanest, but the kitchen is large and well maintained.

139 Queen Street, Ayr
☎ *(07) 4783 3991*
***Dorm bed** $20 per night, $119 per week*
***Reception open** 4.30am-8pm daily; seasonal opening Apr-Dec*

Maintenance & cleanliness	★★
Facilities	★★★½
Atmosphere & character	★★½
Security	★★½
Overall rating	★★½

Diving

SS Yongala Wreck

This 109m passenger ship sank sank off Cape Bowling Green, 35km north-east of Ayr, in 1911 and it is now one of Australia's top dive sites. Several dive companies including **Prodive Townsville** *(☎ (07) 4721 1760; **website** www.prodivetownsville.com.au)* and **Yongala Dive** *(☎ (07) 4783 1519; **website** www.yongaladive.com.au)* operate dive trips out to the *SS Yongala*.

North Queensland

North Queensland offers travellers the convenience of cities like Cairns and Townsville and the seclusion of islands like Hinchinbrook. The area is perfect for nature-lovers, with a wide range of hiking trails, rainforest adventures and idyllic beaches. This section of coastline lies at the doorstop to the Great Barrier Reef and is naturally a haven for divers, with endless diving opportunities including the famed Yongala wreck.

Townsville is a mellow seaside city with a very unique suburb of sorts: Magnetic Island. Part wilderness retreat, part backpacker party spot, Magnetic Island offers a taste of island life which often compels visits to Dunk, Bedarra and Orpheus Islands, and for the die-hard campers and hikers – Hinchinbrook Island, with its famous Thorsborne Trail. Cardwell and Tully are pleasant places to stop a while to work on fruit farms. Mission Beach is a sleepy little town offering sublime beaches and lots of activities, especially diving and water sports. Travelling north, Innisfail, with its interesting architecture and sights, will wake you up again and prepares you for the last big city in Queensland and the best place to plan adventure activities, Cairns.

Townsville

Townsville is a relaxed, tropical, coastal city at the base of red granite Castle Hill. With around 150,000 people, it is the largest city in Queensland north of the Sunshine Coast and it is the most important city in North Queensland with many companies and government departments maintaining their regional offices here.

Despite its importance, Townsville has relatively little tourism compared with Cairns. However it is central to heaps of activities, sights and attractions. Just 8km offshore is Magnetic Island with its fantastic beaches, a few kilometres south of Townsville is the popular Billabong Sanctuary, and just north are nice beaches, great diving, and national parks like Paluma Range National Park.

The city centre has some nice architecture and great nightlife and the Strand, which runs along the shoreline, is filled with cafés offering lovely beach views. The pedestrian Flinders Street Mall in the city centre is currently under complete renovation and will soon re-open as a huge indoor shopping complex. The city has several excellent attractions, including the Reef HQ aquarium, which has a walk-through underwater glass tunnel. Next door to that is a great Cultural Centre where you can learn about Aboriginal culture; and next to that is the Museum of Tropical Queensland, which is a must-see while you are in the area. A walk or drive up to Castle Hill affords beautiful views of Magnetic Island and the city.

Practical Information

Townsville Tourist Information Centre

Flinders Mall, Townsville
☎ *(07) 4778 3555 or 1800 801 902*
Website *www.townsvilleholidays.info*
Open *9am-5pm daily*

70-102 Flinders Street East, Townsville
☎ *(07) 4721 1116 or 1800 801 902*
Website *www.townsvilleholidays.info*
Open *9am-5pm daily*

Marine & National Park Information Centre

Reef HQ, 2/68 Flinders Street, Townsville
☎ *(07) 4721 2399*
Open *Mon-Sat 9am-5pm, Sun 9am-1pm*

INTERNET ACCESS

Internet Lounge

238 Charters Towers Road, Hermit Park
☎ *(07) 4728 4568*
Website *www.internetlounge.com.au*
Open *Mon-Fri 8.30am-5.30pm, Sat 9am-1pmComing & Going*

Coming & Going

AIR

Townsville Airport *(**website** www.townsvilleairport.com.au)* is 5km north of the city centre and has regular flights to Brisbane and Cairns.

BUS

Townsville is an important hub with many travellers stopping here to transfer between the coastal Brisbane-Cairns route and the inland route between Townsville and the Northern Territory. Greyhound *(☎ 1300 473 946; **website** www.greyhound.com.au)* buses arrive at and depart from the Sunferries Breakwater Terminal on Sir Leslie Thiess Drive and Premier Motor Service *(**website** www.premierms.com.au)* buses stop at the Transit Centre on Plume Street in South Townsville.

TRAIN

Trains stop at the new station on Charters Towers Road, which has train departures to Brisbane and Cairns and trains running through the outback to Mount Isa.

Local Transport

Sunbus *(☎ (07) 4725 8482; **website** www.sunbus.com.au)* operates Townsville's local bus service with most routes converging near Flinders Street Mall.

Accommodation

Adventurers Resort

This hostel has the ambience of an old motel. Dorms are just bare cement block boxes with bunk beds and a fridge; the kitchen is massive, but again it is empty feeling. Other facilities include the usual laundry, a barbecue and a big games/TV room with pool tables, couches and air hockey, but it doesn't seem to get much use. The reception area has a shop and

internet access ($5 per hour) and heaps of information on tours. Location is inconvenient, but they offer shuttle buses throughout the day.
79 Palmer Street, South Townsville
☎ *(07) 4721 1522*
Website *www.adventurersresort.com*
Dorm bed *$22 ($20 HI/YHA);* ***single room*** *$40 ($38 HI/YHA);* ***double room*** *$48 ($44 HI/YHA);* ***twin/family room*** *$50 ($46 HI/YHA)*
Credit cards *MC, Visa*
Reception open *8am-8pm daily*

Maintenance & cleanliness	★★½
Facilities	★★½
Atmosphere & character	★★★
Security	★★★
Overall rating	★★½

Globetrotters Hostel

This hostel recently relocated to a more central location, and is now set up in an old motel. It is still undergoing renovations, but what has been done looks promising. The bathrooms need some new fittings and the communal kitchen is tiny and messy. A few of the dorms have kitchenettes and they all have en suite bathrooms. They have a nice big internet café, a nice swimming pool and laundry facilities. There are plans for a new outdoor common area with live music stage. The hostel has free breakfast and guests can get their evening meals at the pub down the street. Hopefully this place will see some intensive maintenance in the near future so it can live up to its potential.
121 Flinders Street, Townsville
☎ *(07) 4771 5000*
Website *www.globetrottersaustralia.com*
Dorm bed *$24;* ***double room*** *$70; prices include breakfast & an evening meal*
Credit cards *MC, Visa*
Reception open *8am-7pm daily*

Maintenance & cleanliness	★½
Facilities	★★½
Atmosphere & character	★★★
Security	★★★
Overall rating	★★½

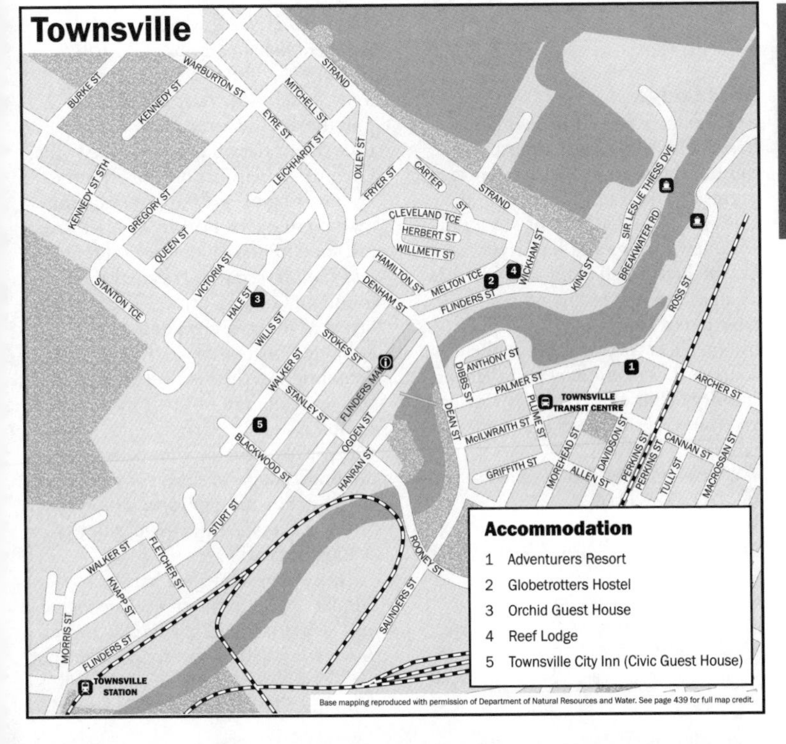

Orchid Guest House

Orchid Guest House is a small, cosy place with a quiet location. The dorms are air conditioned with television, a fridge, and very comfy made-up beds. They are clean and well maintained, painted in pastel blues and greens with nice carpet and flowery duvets. The bathrooms are gorgeously maintained with shiny tiles, great showers and perfect water pressure. The downstairs kitchen is a bit dated, but it is clean and stocks everything you need to cook. They offer free pick-up and a free washing machine with a drying line. The owners of this place couldn't be nicer. It's a great place to relax.

34 Hale Street, Townsville
(07) 4771 6683
***Dorm bed** $25; **single room** $45-$60; **double/twin room** $60-80*
***Credit cards** MC, Visa*
***Reception open** 7am-8pm daily, late check in by prior arrangement*

Maintenance & cleanliness	★★★½
Facilities	★★
Atmosphere & character	★★★½
Security	★★
Overall rating	★★★

Reef Lodge

Reef Lodge is a beautifully maintained hostel with a laid back atmosphere right in the heart of the city centre. The dorms are air-conditioned, comfortable and clean; bathrooms are spotless with new fittings and hairdryers and the kitchen is well equipped. There is a games room/gym and with a pool table plus a couple of cosy TV lounges. Internet access is available in the courtyard ($5 per hour) and there are laundry facilities. Security is very good and the reception staff are wonderfully kind and helpful.

4 Wickham Street, Townsville
(07) 4721 1112
***Website** www.reeflodge.com.au*
***Dorm bed** $21-23; **double/twin room** $54-72*
***Credit cards** MC, Visa*
***Reception open** 8am-8.30pm daily*

Maintenance & cleanliness	★★★★
Facilities	★★★
Atmosphere & character	★★★★½
Security	★★★½
Overall rating	★★★★

Townsville City Inn (Civic Guest House)

Civic Guesthouse is a neat and tidy place west of the city centre. Facilities include the usual TV lounge and kitchen plus an outdoor spa pool.

262 Walker Street, Townsville
(07) 4771 5381 or 1800 646 619
***Website** www.civicguesthouse.com*
***Dorm bed** $22-24; **double room** $50-70; **twin room** $55-75*
***Credit cards** MC, Visa*
***Reception open** 8am-7pm*

Maintenance & cleanliness	★★½
Facilities	★★½
Atmosphere & character	★★½
Security	★
Overall rating	★★½

Eating & Drinking

Townsville has a few great spots for inexpensive dining including **Harold's Seafood** on the Strand *(Shop 5/58 The Strand, North Ward)*, which has excellent fish and chips and **Molly Malone's** *(87-95 Flinders Street, Townsville)* with cheap backpacker pub meals. The Strand has some more upmarket cafés and restaurants, while Gregory Street (just off the Strand to the north) gives way to unpretentious seafood markets, healthy eateries and fast food joints. Thai, Greek, French and Italian restaurants can also be found on Gregory Street. The Flinders Street Mall has a few good spots, although most of the mall is due for demolition in the near future to make way for a modern multi-story shopping complex.

If you're preparing your own food you can find a couple of supermarkets in the city centre including **Coles** *(136 Ogden Street, Townsville)* and **Woolworths** on Walker Street.

There are several good bars in Flinders Street in the city centre including the **Brewery** *(252 Flinders Street, Townsville)*, which is a very popular spot with locals and visitors for nights out drinking. On Palmer Street in South

Townsville you can find cheap pubs, cafés and Italian restaurants.

Sights

Billabong Sanctuary

This wildlife sanctuary is about 20 minutes south of town and features a selection of native animals including kangaroos, wombats and snakes.
Bruce Highway, 17km south of Townsville
☎ *(07) 4778 8344*
Website *www.billabongsanctuary.com.au*
Admission *$28 ($25 HI/YHA, ISIC, Nomads, VIP)*
Open *8am-5pm daily*

Castle Hill

The lookout at the summit of Castle Hill offers great views of Townsville. Some hostels operate trips up here although it is more rewarding to hike up the steep trail to the top.
Walking track from Hillside Crescent, Townsville

Markets

The **Strand Night Craft Market** *(Strand Park, Townsville; open 1st Fri May-Dec 5pm-9.30pm)*on Townsville's beach features entertainment and food. The **Flinders Mall Cotters Market** *(Flinders Mall, Townsville; open Sun 8am-1pm)* claims to be North Queensland's largest arts and craft market.

Museum of Tropical Queensland

The Museum of Tropical Queensland is an excellent new museum, which is situated next door to Reef HQ and focuses on the history and nature of North Queensland.
70-102 Flinders Street, Townsville
☎ *(07) 4726 0606*
Website *www.mtq.qld.gov.au*
Admission *$12*
Open *9.30am-5pm daily (last entry 4pm)*

ReefHQ

ReefHQ includes a huge aquarium that also features a theatre and informative displays about the Reef.
2-68 Flinders Street, Townsville
☎ *(07) 4750 0800*
Website *www.reefhq.com.au*
Admission *$21.50 ($19.35 HI/YHA, VIP)*
Open *9.30am-5pm daily*

Townsville Maritime Museum

Townsville's Maritime Museum features exhibits on the city's port and its maritime history. It is near the Transit Centre in South Townsville.
42-68 Palmer Street, South Townsville
☎ *(07) 4721 5251*
Website *www.townsvillemaritimemuseum.org.au*
Admission *$6*
Open *Mon-Fri 10am-4pm, Sat-Sun noon-4pm*

Magnetic Island

Magnetic Island, or "Maggie", as it is affectionately dubbed by locals, is a very popular backpacker destination that has plenty of fun adventure activities, but manages to retain a retreat-like atmosphere. It is just a 20-minute ferry ride from Townsville and it boasts 23 bays and beaches, extensive hiking trails and a good choice of hostel accommodation. It also has a substantial residential community and quite a few of its 2000 residents commute to work in Townsville by ferry.

Much of the island's lush interior is national park and the surrounding water is part of the Great Barrier Reef World Heritage Area, providing some great diving and snorkelling not far from the shore. The island is home to an impressive range of wildlife including koalas, possums, rock wallabies and various bird species. With an average of 320 sunny days per year, Maggie is a nature-lover's paradise. Nightlife here is not very good, unless you count (and perhaps you should) the monthly full moon parties put on by Base Backpackers.

Coming & Going

Fantasea Cruises and Sunferries both operate a ferry service between Townsville and Magnetic Island.
Sunferries (☎ *(07) 4726 0800; **website** www.sunferries.com.au)* is the more popular of the two ferry companies and the return fare from Townsville costs $26.70. Sunferries depart from

the Breakwater terminal on Sir Leslie Thiess Drive in Townsville and go to Nelly Bay Harbour on Magnetic Island. Sunferries have the fastest boats but they're restricted to passengers only.

Fantasea Cruises (☎ *(07) 4772 5422;* ***website*** *www.fantaseacruisingmagnetic.com.au)* is slower but they are cheaper and are the only boats that take cars. The return fare is $23 and they depart from the terminal on Ross Street in South Townsville, directly across the river from Sunferries' Breakwater terminal. They sail to Nelly Bay on Magnetic Island.

Local Transport

The island is serviced by a bus that runs once or twice an hour, but is not the most punctual or reliable. A good alternative is renting a scooter, Moke or bike to get around, as the towns are just far enough away to warrant transport other than walking.

Magnetic Island Buses (☎ *(07) 4778 5130)* run a route between Picnic Bay and Horseshoe Bay. Buses run at least once an hour and one-way fares range from $1.90 to $3.60, although most fares are either $2.40 or $3.10. The bigger hostels on Magnetic Island also run their own shuttle buses between the hostel and the ferry terminal.

Accommodation

Base Backpackers

This is a great hostel with a beautiful waterfront location. The dorms are set in cabins fronted by wide wooden balconies; some are A-frames, which are too small but have comfortable beds and air conditioning. Girls can opt for a Sanctuary dorm, which is more spacious and comes with towels, a spa kit, and a free drink (worth the extra $4). The double rooms are gorgeous A-frame cabins on the water with great views. The bathrooms are clean, but the shower fittings need replacement, and some of the rooms are quite far away from the shared facilities. There is a very small and dirty "tent kitchen" with a canvas roof and old appliances. There is a dive school on-site with cheap courses. There is also a bar, a beachfront swimming pool, an open common room with pool tables, and an internet café ($6 per hour). Full moon parties are held almost every month and are extremely popular, so book ahead.

1 Nelly Bay Road, Nelly Bay
☎ *(07) 4778 5777 or 1800 24 BASE*
Website *www.stayatbase.com*
Dorm bed *$26-30;* ***bed in a canvas tent*** *$20;* ***double room*** *$95-110;* ***camping*** *$12 per person*
Credit cards *MC, Visa*
Reception open *7.45am-9pm daily*

Maintenance & cleanliness	★★★
Facilities	★★★½
Atmosphere & character	★★★★½
Security	★★★
Overall rating	★★★½

Bungalow Bay Koala Village YHA

This YHA is an excellent hostel. The dorms are in spacious A-frame cabins with new comfortable beds and shiny en suite bathrooms. The kitchen is dirty and old, but there is an onsite restaurant and the bar does great $10 pizzas. The bar/common area gets very lively at night with trivia nights and music, which ensures a fun atmosphere. The hostel also features a wildlife rescue and care centre, where you get the chance to hold a koala and interact with other animals. There is also an internet café, a gorgeous swimming pool, laundry facilities, bike and kayak hire and a tour desk. The staff are some of the most outgoing and friendly around.

40 Horseshoe Bay Road, Horseshoe Bay, Magnetic Island
☎ *(07) 4778 5577*
Website *www.bungalowbay.com*
Dorm bed *$ 27 ($24 HI/YHA);* ***double room*** *$64-80 ($58-72 HI/YHA);* ***camping*** *$12.50-15 per person*
Credit cards *MC, Visa*
Reception open *7.30am-6pm daily (check in at the bar until 11pm)*

Maintenance & cleanliness	★★★½
Facilities	★★★
Atmosphere & character	★★★★½
Security	★★½
Overall rating	★★★½

Forest Haven
This is a lovely and peaceful little hostel tucked away in quiet gardens. The dorms are lacking in maintenance, but they have kitchens and plenty of charm. The shared apartments are nice and a great value. The bathrooms are pretty shabby, but there is a nice swimming pool and covered barbecue area. They offer internet at $4 per hour, laundry facilities and free pick up from the ferry terminal. It is located steps away from shops and Alma Bay and it is a good place to rest your head after partying at Magnums across the road. The family who run this place are welcoming and talkative.
11 Cook Road, Arcadia, Magnetic Island
☎ *(07) 4778 5153 or 1800 665 153*
Website *www.foresthaven.com.au*
Dorm bed *$15-18;* ***double/twin room*** *$40;* ***apartment*** *$70 for two people, $80 for 3 people, $90 for 4 people*
Credit cards *MC, Visa*
Reception open *8.30am-6.30pm*

Maintenance & cleanliness	★★
Facilities	★★★½
Atmosphere & character	★★★★
Security	★★½
Overall rating	★★★

Magnum's
This hostel is a large complex across from Alma Bay. It has a huge bar and a café on site, as well as two large swimming pools. The dorms are air conditioned and have clean en suite bathrooms, but they are not very well maintained and the beds only have one sheet and no pillows. The kitchen is small and messy and there are barely any cooking facilities. They offer internet access ($6 per hour), laundry facilities, and an outside TV lounge and common area. Staff are upbeat and friendly, though a bit disorganised.
7 Marine Parade, Arcadia, Magnetic Island
☎ *(07) 4778 5177 or 1800 663 666*
Website *www.magnums.com.au*
Dorm bed *$18-22;* ***double room*** *$65*
Credit cards *MC, Visa*

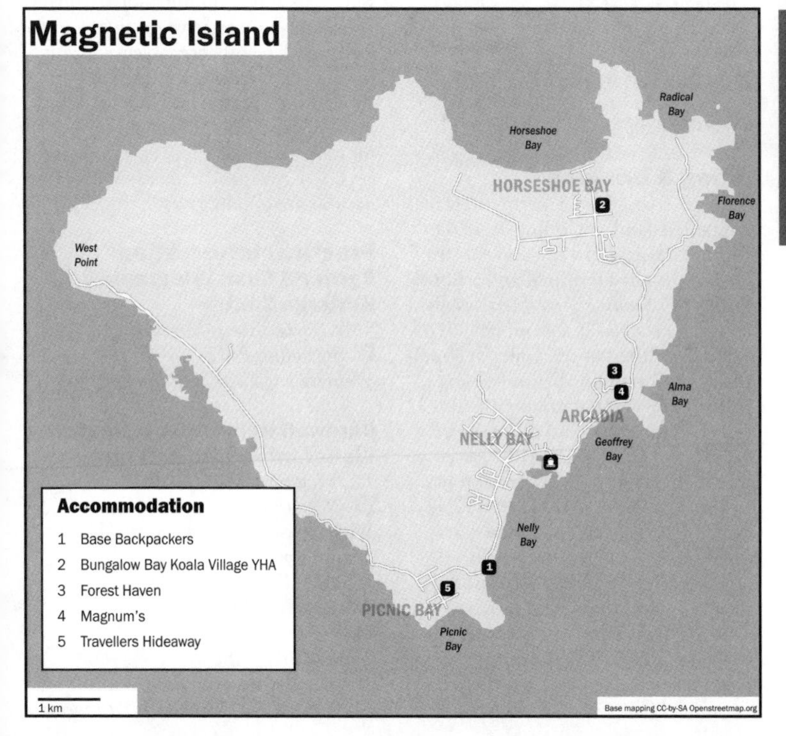

***Reception open** 8.30am-6.30pm*

Maintenance & cleanliness	★★½
Facilities	★★½
Atmosphere & character	★★★½
Security	★★½
Overall rating	★★★

Travellers Hideaway
This hostel has three to four-bed dormitories and a nice swimming pool, but the dorms are very basic and some are quite stuffy. The bathrooms need a renovation and the kitchen is a mess – the whole place just seems a bit tired. Other facilities include internet access, a barbecue, hammocks, a TV lounge and a laundry with old washing machines. It is in Picnic Bay, which is an inconvenient location, now that the ferry arrives at Nelly Bay.
32 Picnic Street, Picnic Bay, Magnetic Island
☎ *(07) 4778 5314 or 1800 000 290*
***Website** www.travellersbackpackers.com*
***Dorm bed** $18-20; **double/twin room** $50*

Maintenance & cleanliness	★★
Facilities	★★★
Atmosphere & character	★★★
Security	★★½
Overall rating	★★½

Eating & Drinking

There are a couple of supermarkets on Magnetic Island, including an **IGA** *(147-153 Sooning Street, Nelly Bay)* in front of the ferry terminal and a **Food-Works** *(55 Sooning Street)* near Nelly Bay. However you'll save money if you grab a few things at the Coles or Woolworths in Townsville before leaving.

Most cafés and restaurants are in Nelly Bay, but the others are scattered and sometimes far apart. Most travellers end up eating in the hostel if it has a restaurant. **Base Café** *(1 Nelly Bay Road, Nelly Bay)* has good food, but it is a bit pricey for a backpackers' hostel; Bungalow Bay YHA has **Swenson's** restaurant *(40 Horseshoe Bay Road, Horseshoe Bay)*, which is also expensive, but has some backpacker specials including great cheap pizzas. There is also a small Chinese takeaway spot in Picnic Bay and a Latin Bar with good beer in Horseshoe Bay. The Island Tavern in Arcadia has a beer garden and very affordable meals.

Cardwell

Cardwell is a seaside town straddling the Bruce Highway at the edge of the Hinchinbrook Channel. It is a quiet place without many attractions of its own but it has a perfect location for visiting the rugged Hinchinbrook Island. Some travellers come here just for that reason, while others come to work on the nearby banana and prawn farms. The hostels here cater mostly to guests on a working holiday.

The other big draw is fishing, and there are boat hire companies and guided fishing tours on offer all through town. Five Mile Swimming Hole is a good place for a dip in the water and is popular with local families who use the barbecue facilities there. There are walking tracks throughout the Edmund Kennedy National Park, as well as some waterfalls and swimming holes. Murray Falls (a 45-minute drive north of Cardwell) are the most accessible waterfalls in the area. Cardwell stretches only about 3km, so it can be a bit boring for many backpackers. If you will be here for more than a day, it is a great idea to get out of town and explore some of the natural surroundings.

Practical Information

Cardwell Bush Telegraph Heritage Centre
53 Victoria Street, Cardwell
☎ *(07) 4066 2412*
***Website** www.cardwelltourism.com*

Cardwell Rainforest & Reef Visitor Information Centre
142 Victoria Street, Cardwell
☎ *(07) 4066 8601*
***Website** www.greatgreenwaytourism.com/rainforestreef.html*

Coming & Going

BUS

Cardwell is on the main bus route between Cairns and Townsville. Greyhound *(☎ 1300 473 946; **website*** *www.greyhound.com.au)* buses stop at the Seaview Cafe at 89 Victoria Street and Premier Motor Service *(**website** www.premierms.com.au)* buses stop on Brasenose Street.

FERRY
Ferries between Cardwell and Hinchinbrook Island are operated by Hinchinbrook Ferries (☎ *(07) 4066 8270 or 1800 682 702; **website** www.hinchinbrookferries.com.au)*. A day return fare costs $125 and they can drop you off at Ramsay Bay at the northern end of the Thorsborne Trail for $85. Transport between the other end of the trail and the mainland costs $46 and is operated by Hinchinbrook Wilderness Safaris (☎ *(07) 4777 8307; **website** www.hinchinbrookwildernesssafaris.com.au)*.

Accommodation
Cardwell Backpackers Hostel
This place caters exclusively to working backpackers and they arrange jobs and provide free transport to and from work. The hostel has a large 12-bed dormitory and several small "cubes" – small two-bed dorms with colourful aluminium walls. The dorms get messy and the kitchen needs to be better maintained; but it has a swimming pool/barbecue area, a nice TV lounge with a pool table, a small bar at reception and a shop. It would be a good place to stay if you are working in the area.

178 Bowen Street, Cardwell
☎ *(07) 4066 8014*
***Website** www.users.bigpond.com/cardwellbackpackers/*
***Dorm bed** $133-140 per week; price includes transport to and from work*
***Credit cards** MC, Visa*
***Reception open** 6am-10pm*

Maintenance & cleanliness	★★
Facilities	★★★½
Atmosphere & character	★★½
Security	★
Overall rating	★★½

Hinchinbrook Hop
This place is actually more of a caravan park, but they have a few small self-contained units with dorm beds. The backpackers' accommodation here is extremely run down and some of the beds are in old smelly caravans with rags as curtains, rusty appliances and mouldy wooden cabinets. Good luck if you get one of the non air-conditioned units. There are also small cabins, but they have not been very well maintained either. The bathrooms are simply appalling. There is a swimming pool, but it looks more like a mosquito breeding ground. There are no other facilities besides a laundry. There are much better places to stay in Cardwell.

186 Victoria Street, Cardwell
☎ *(07) 4066 8671*
***Website** www.users.bigpond.net.au/hinchinbrookhop/*
***Dorm bed** $20*
***Credit cards** MC, Visa*
***Reception open** 6am-8pm daily*

Maintenance & cleanliness	★
Facilities	★½
Atmosphere & character	★
Security	★
Overall rating	★

Kookaburra Holiday Park
This hostel is in a large caravan park with a wide range of accommodation options. The dorms are very dated with paisley laminate flooring and curtains. The beds are plain and the air-conditioning costs $1 for three hours. The bathrooms are very well maintained and clean, though, and they have hairdryers. The kitchen is also clean and well equipped. This hostel caters mostly to workers, and in the off season it is pretty boring here. They have a nice swimming pool and a bar. Guest have free use of bikes, fishing gear, kayaks and tennis rackets.

175 Bruce Highway, Cardwell
☎ *(07) 4066 8648*
***Website** www.kookaburraholidaypark.com.au*
***Dorm bed** $20; **double room** $40*
***Credit cards** MC, Visa*
***Reception open** 8am-6pm daily*

Maintenance & cleanliness	★★½
Facilities	★★★★
Atmosphere & character	★★
Security	★★
Overall rating	★★★

Sights

Historic Cardwell Post Office & Telegraph Station

Cardwell's old post office has been restored and reopened as a museum. The museum features exhibits on local history with displays on the construction of the telegraph and the road and rail lines.
53 Victoria Street, Cardwell
☎ *(07) 4066 2412*
Admission *free*
Open *Tue-Thu 10am-1pm, Sat 9am-noon*

Hinchinbrook Island

Hinchinbrook Island is Australia's largest island national park and it is home to a diverse natural habitat that encompasses mountains, rainforest and the Great Barrier Reef World Heritage Area.

The Thorsborne Trail is the highlight of the island but there are also shorter hiking trails that are ideal if you're just visiting for the day.

Coming & Going

Ferries between Cardwell and Hinchinbrook Island are operated by Hinchinbrook Ferries (☎ *(07) 4066 8270 or 1800 682 702;* ***website*** *www.hinchinbrookferries.com.au)*. A day return fare costs $125 and they can drop you off at Ramsay Bay at the northern end of the Thorsborne Trail for $85.

Transport between the mainland and the George Point end of the trail costs $46 and is operated by Hinchinbrook Wilderness Safaris (☎ *(07) 4777 8307;* ***website*** *www.hinchinbrookwilderness-safaris.com.au)*.

Hiking

Hinchinbrook Island has some great hiking trails and the highlight is the brilliant Thorsborne Trail.

THE THORSBORNE TRAIL

This 32km trail is a fairly difficult track, recommended for experienced hikers. Permits are required to hike the trail and it's best to apply in advance as only a maximum of 40 people are permitted on the trail at any time. Most hikers take at least four days and three nights to complete the trail. Permits are available from the Rainforest and Reef Centre in Cardwell.

You can hike the trail in either direction but the north to south direction is described below:

Ramsay Bay to Little Ramsay Bay *(6.5km, 4½ hours)*
The ferry from Cardwell drops you at Ramsay Bay and the trail starts out by following the beach southward and then going through tall forest and mangrove swamps to Nina Bay where there is a campsite with toilets. From Nina Bay the trail follows the headland to Boulder Bay, where green sea turtles can often be seen and then heads over a ridge to the campsite at Little Ramsay Bay.

Little Ramsay Bay to Zoe Bay *(10.5km, 6 hours)*
The trail follows the coast past Little Ramsay Bay to Banksia Bay and then heads inland through open forest and rainforest. Parts of this section of the track towards the Zoe Bay campsite pass swampy areas and involve several creek crossings.

Zoe Bay to Mulligan Falls *(7.5km, 4½ hours)*
After leaving Zoe Bay the trail follows South Zoe Creek and passes Zoe Falls. It then goes inland and crosses Diamantina Creek shortly before arriving at Mulligan Falls campsite.

Mulligan Falls to George Point *(7.5km, 2½ hours)*
The final leg of the track starts in rainforest but is mostly a beach walk along Mulligan Bay.

Mission Beach

Mission Beach is the perfect spot for a day off from the stress of travel. This sleepy little region encompasses four villages: Bingil Bay, Mission Beach, Wongaling Beach and South Mission Beach, strung along 14km of lush tropical rainforest on the coast. Its long sandy beaches fringed with palms and mangroves are a lovely place to swim or sunbathe, while the centre of Mission Beach town has quite a few dining options as well as some nightlife. There is no shortage of activities in the area, from hiking to snorkelling and trips to Dunk Island and the Great Barrier Reef. You can kayak all the way out to Dunk Island or hop aboard a ferry, which only takes 10 minutes. White water rafting trips are a popular excursion, most of which take place on the Tully River. This is also a great place to organise a sky dive, as the views are spectacular and it is one of the few places where you can land on the beach.

There are some lovely walking trails in Mission Beach, but for the more adventurous, trekking up into the rainforest is also an option. Mission Beach is home to Australia's largest bird, the endangered cassowary, and if you are lucky you may see one on the side of the road. This area is also home to 60% of all Australian butterfly species, and numerous other types of wildlife, such as the white-lipped green tree frog.

Practical Information

Wet Tropics Visitor Information Centre

Porter Promenade, Mission Beach
☎ *(07) 4068 7099*
Website *www.missionbeachtourism.com*
Open *9am-5.30pm daily*

Coming & Going

Greyhound *(☎ 1300 473 946; **website** www.greyhound.com.au)* and Premier Motor Service *(**website** www.premierms.com.au)* buses stop by the Big Cassowary at the Wongaling Shopping Centre near the Mission Beach Resort in Wongaling Beach.

The closest train station is Tully.

Local Transport

For a small town, Mission Beach is spread out over a wide area and it is necessary to either drive or catch a bus to get from one end to the other. Mission Beach Bus Service *(☎ (07) 4068 7400; **website** www.transnorthbus.com/missionbeach.html)* operates a route between Bingil Bay and South Mission Beach. The bus does not operate on Sundays.

Accommodation

Beach Shack

This place doesn't look like much from the outside, but inside it is a real gem. The interior is painted in beachy blues and violets, with personal touches like flowers and art adorning the halls. The air-conditioned dorms are cheerful and impeccably clean. The kitchen is also well maintained and has all the fittings, including a good working oven. It is open and breezy, with a beautiful swimming pool nestled in lush gardens and palm trees, a barbecue area and laundry facilities. The common room/TV lounge is cosy and convivial, and the bathroom has a spa bath. There is also a games room with pool table. It is a five-minute walk from the centre of town, near nice beaches and rainforest. The family who run this hostel are a lovely and gregarious lot who really provide a home away from home. Australia needs more places like this.

86 Porters Promenade, Mission Beach
☎ *(07) 4068 7783 or 1800 333 115*
Website *www.missionbeachshack.com*
Dorm bed *$22;* ***double room*** *$55;* ***twin room*** *$50*
Credit cards *MC, Visa*
Reception open *7.30am-noon & 3pm-7pm daily*

Maintenance & cleanliness	★★★½
Facilities	★★★★
Atmosphere & character	★★★★½
Security	★½
Overall rating	★★★½

Mission Beach Retreat

This small hostel is painted in bright ocean blue and has a mellow atmosphere. It has an excellent location in the centre of town and the dorms are very clean with comfortable beds. The kitchen and bathrooms are ordinary, but kept quite clean. They offer internet access, free pickup from the bus station and have laundry facilities. There is a barbecue area and very nice swimming pool with a small waterfall at the front of the hostel. Management are pleasant and talkative.

49 Porters Promenade, Mission Beach
☎ *(07) 4088 6229 or 1800 001 056*
Website *www.missionbeachretreat.com.au*
Dorm bed *$21;* ***double/twin room*** *$46*
Credit cards *MC, Visa*
Reception open *7.30am-11.30am & 4pm-7pm*

Maintenance & cleanliness	★★★
Facilities	★★★½
Atmosphere & character	★★★
Security	★★
Overall rating	★★★

Sanctuary Retreat

This place is located at the top of a steep hill in dense rainforest; it is a bit difficult to get to, but if you are looking for total seclusion and peace, this is the spot for you. It is more of a retreat, but offers a few twin share rooms at dorm prices. The common room has a bar, internet access and a restaurant, and is built of timber and offers exquisite views of the surrounding rainforest-covered mountains and valleys. The dorms are twin share huts that are clean and relaxing, with boardwalks connecting to other huts. There is a small fully equipped kitchen and bathrooms are spotless. There is also a beautiful swimming pool and services you wouldn't expect at a regular backpackers' place like yoga and massage services. The surrounding area is home to lots of wildlife, including a large number of cassowaries that you have a good chance of spotting.
72 Holt Road, Bingil Bay
☎ *(07) 4088 6064*
Website *www.sanctuaryretreat.com.au*
Dorm bed *$32.50;* ***single room*** *$60.50;* ***double/twin room*** *$65*
Credit cards *MC, Visa*
Reception open *7.30am-8.30pm daily*

Maintenance & cleanliness	★★★★★
Facilities	★★★½
Atmosphere & character	★★★★★
Security	★
Overall rating	★★★★

Scotty's

Scotty's is known around town as the party hostel, even though it is located far from the bars and action of the town centre. It has a fun, happy atmosphere with brightly coloured wooden buildings and large decking in front set around an inviting swimming pool and nice gardens. The air-conditioned dorms are clean, but the bathrooms could do with a sprucing up and the kitchen is small and threadbare, but it does the trick. There is also a laundry, internet access (including Wi-Fi) and a tour desk. The management and staff are good humoured and helpful.
167 Reid Road, Wongaling Beach
☎ *(07) 4068 8676 or 1800 777 012*
Website *www.scottysbeachhouse.com.au*
Dorm bed *$21-26 ($20-25 HI/YHA, ISIC, Nomads, VIP);* ***double room*** *$49-59 ($47-57 HI/YHA, ISIC, Nomads, VIP)*
Credit cards *MC, Visa*
Reception open *7.30am-8.30pm daily*

Maintenance & cleanliness	★★★
Facilities	★★★★
Atmosphere & character	★★★★½
Security	★½
Overall rating	★★★½

Treehouse YHA

The Treehouse is in the rainforest a bit far from the centre of town, giving it a retreat-like ambience. The large wooden building is open and airy with hammocks and nice views, and the main common area has a large deck overlooking a nice swimming pool. The bathrooms are under renovation and should be brand new by the time of publication. Dorm rooms are breezy and clean with nice beds, high ceilings and wood beams. There is no air-conditioning so it can get muggy if there is no breeze coming through the big windows. There is a lounge area, a few steps away from the main building, for anyone who wants to stay up late and make any kind of noise. The Treehouse is a good place to chill out and socialise, but not to party.
13 Frizelle Road, Bingil Bay
☎ *(07) 4068 7137*
Website *www.yha.com.au*
Dorm bed *$23 ($20.50 HI/YHA);* ***double/twin room*** *$55 ($49.50 HI/YHA);* ***camping*** *$13.50 ($12 HI/YHA) per person*

Credit cards *MC, Visa*
Reception open *7.30am-8.30pm daily*

Maintenance & cleanliness	★★★½
Facilities	★★★
Atmosphere & character	★★★★
Security	★
Overall rating	★★★½

Eating & Drinking

There is a good range of places to eat in Mission Beach. Due to the increasing numbers of backpackers coming here, some inexpensive cafes have sprung up and backpacker deals can be found in most restaurants.

There is a supermarket in Wongaling Beach and Mission Beach, but eating out is a good way to mingle with the locals and meet other backpackers. **Coconutz** *(Porters Promenade, Mission Beach)* is a local favourite for its cool ambience, and has a fabulous beer and pizza backpacker special; **Shrubbery Taverna** *(44 Marine Parade, Mission Beach)* is also on the top of many lists, though the views come with a hefty price tag. A beer with a view is a good alternative, though. For breakfast or lunch, try **Gecko Café** *(Porters Promenade, Mission Beach)* in central Mission for its healthy and surprisingly cheap fare. **Scotty's Beach House** *(167 Reid Road, Wongaling Beach)* is hands down the best place to drink cheaply and party, and there is a Thai restaurant opening soon that should have some good deals for backpackers.

Activities

HIKING

There are some good hiking trails around Mission Beach, including the Licuala Walking Track.

Licuala Walking Track

This popular 7.8km walk through the Tam O'Shanter State Forest gives you the opportunity to see the rare cassowary.

REEF TRIPS

Quick Cat Cruises *(☎ (07) 4068 7289; **website** www.quickcatcruises.com.au)* run day trips to the Great Barrier Reef. Cruises cost $160 and give you around 3½ hours on the reef. The price includes lunch, reef tax and pick up from hostels in the Mission Beach area.

SKYDIVING

The beach landing on either Dunk Island or Mission Beach makes this a popular spot for skydiving.

Jump the Beach

☎ 1800 638 005
Website *www.jumpthebeach.com*
9000ft tandem skydive *$210;*
11000ft tandem skydive *$244;*
14000ft tandem skydive *$295; plus compulsory Australian Parachute Federation Student License $25 and $10 fuel levy*

Paul's Parachuting

☎ 1800 005 006
Website *www.paulsparachuting.com.au*
10000ft tandem skydive *$244;*
14000ft tandem skydive *$295; plus compulsory Australian Parachute Federation Student License $25 and fuel levy $10*

WHITE WATER RAFTING

The nearby Tully River has some of Australia's best rafting. See the Tully section on page 240 for more information.

Dunk Island

Dunk Island is easily accessible from Mission Beach. It is a typical tropical island with beautiful white sand beaches and well worth the excursion. The island is home to a National and Marine Park, although the eastern end of the island has a big resort. There are some good walking tracks including the Island Circuit (9.2km, 3hrs return) and Coconut Beach walk (6km, 2km return).

A Great Barrier Reef Marine Park tax ($8) is payable by all visitors to Dunk Island.

Coming & Going

Quick Cat Cruises *(☎ (07) 4068 7289; **website** www.quickcatcruises.com.au)* operates ferries between Mission Beach and Dunk Island. The return fare is $52.

A cheaper option is the Dunk Island Express Water Taxi *(☎ (07) 4068 8310)*, which departs from Point Banfield Parade, Wongaling Beach near Scotty's hostel. They charge $30 for a day return.

Coral Sea Kayaking *(☎ (07) 4068 9154; **website** www.coralseakayaking.com)* is by far the most fun way to get to the island. The $118 trip involves paddling out to the island and includes lunch and snorkelling gear.

Tully

Tully is a modest little town 24km south of Mission Beach that does not have much to entice the casual traveller. It is claimed to be the wettest spot in Australia, with an average of four metres of annual rainfall. An old – and still thriving – sugar mill town, it is surrounded by cane fields and you can take tours of the sugar mill in crushing season (Jun-Nov).

There is a good view of the town and surrounding region including offshore islands from the summit of Mount Tyson or Mount Mackay, both of which have challenging hiking trails. The Misty Mountain Trails is a network of hiking trails that has longer hiking expeditions into the rainforest. White water rafting is the most popular of the area's activities and many travellers come to Tully for the day to go rafting, then go back to Mission Beach to sleep. The only backpackers who stay in Tully are working on the banana farms and hostels here are geared toward travellers on a working holiday.

Practical Information

Tully Visitor & Heritage Centre

Bruce Highway, Tully
☎ *(07) 4068 2288*
***Open** Mon-Fri 8.30am-4.45pm, Sat-Sun 9.30am-4.30pm*

Coming & Going

Tully is on the main train and coach route linking Brisbane and Cairns. Greyhound *(☎ 1300 473 946; **website** www.greyhound.com.au)* and Premier Motor Service *(**website** www.premierms.com.au)* buses stop in Banyan Park, near the Big Gumboot.

Trains stop at the station on the Bruce Highway north of the Visitor Information Centre.

Accommodation

Banana Barracks & Rafters

This place has gone downhill in the past few years, but there are new owners so it should see some improvements. At the moment, rooms are untidy and beds are old; the kitchen is run down and the bathrooms are rather dingy, too. There is a good common area with a big TV and rows of hammock-like seating, but they too are getting ripped and stained. However there is a good swimming pool and beach volleyball court, and a great bar that is popular with locals on the weekends. The dorms in the bungalows out back are much nicer than the accommodation in the main building.

50 Butler Street, Tully
☎ *(07) 4068 0455*
***Website** www.bananabarracks.com*
***Dorm bed** $24-28; **single/double room** $60*
***Credit cards** MC, Visa*
***Reception open** Mon-Fri 8am-6pm, Sat 8am-noon & 3pm-6pm, Sun 8am-11am & 3pm-6pm*

Maintenance & cleanliness	★★
Facilities	★★★
Atmosphere & character	★★★
Security	★★★
Overall rating	★★½

Hotel Tully Backpackers

This hostel is in a nice building in the centre of town with a bar and restaurant. The air-conditioned dorms are tiny and jam-packed with travellers' things and there are clean newly renovated bathrooms. There are plans to renovate the kitchen as well, which is desperately needed. The beds are comfortable and the management is friendly and organised, but it still lacks in atmosphere. There is a bar with pokie machines next door.

5 Butler Street, Tully
☎ *(07) 4068 1044*

***Dorm bed** $20 per night, $100-120 per week*
***Credit cards** Amex, Diners, JCB, MC, Visa*
***Reception open** 10am-10pm daily*

Maintenance & cleanliness	★★★
Facilities	★★★
Atmosphere & character	★★★
Security	★★
Overall rating	★★★

Mount Tyson Hotel

This hostel is above a bar/restaurant in an old hotel. It is severely poorly maintained and has barely any facilities. The kitchen is inadequate and unclean, the common room consists of a couple of old ripped sofas and the bathrooms are simply disgusting. Dorms are also dated, dreary and messy. It is cheap, but be warned that you get what you pay for.
23 Butler Street, Tully
(07) 4068 1088
***Dorm bed** $20 per night, $90 per week; **single room** $110 per week*
***Reception open** 10am-10pm daily*

Maintenance & cleanliness	½
Facilities	½
Atmosphere & character	★★
Security	★
Overall rating	★

The Savoy Backpackers

The Savoy is another workers' hostel, but it is the cleanest one in town. Dorms are spacious with a fresh coat of sky blue paint and clean beds. It is in a well maintained old cane farmer's building, with a cool loft common area. There is a large, clean kitchen; a very cosy TV lounge with big pillows and a big couch lining the walls plus a laundry, a swimming pool and barbecue, and in a refreshing stroke of genius, a boot room for the workers' dirty shoes. Why other places don't do that, we don't know. They also have internet access and free use of body boards (although there's no surf to use them in Tully).
4 Plumb Street, Tully
(07) 4068 2400
***Website** www.thesavoybackpackers.com.au*
***Dorm bed** $20 per night, $120 per week; **double room** $40 per night, $250 per week*
***Credit cards** MC, Visa*
***Reception open** 8am-7pm daily*

Maintenance & cleanliness	★★½
Facilities	★★½
Atmosphere & character	★★★½
Security	★★
Overall rating	★★★

Sights & Activities

Tully Sugar

The Tully Sugar Mill runs tours during the crushing season (Jun-Nov). Tours take around 1½ hours
Book at the visitor information on the Bruce Highway
(07) 4068 2288
***Admission** $12*
***Tours** Mon-Fri 10am, 11am, 1.30pm, Sat-Sun 11am, 1.30pm*

RAFTING

Tully is handy to the Tully River which is the country's best one day rafting experience and also the most popular rafting destination for backpackers. Two companies – R'n'R Rafting and Raging Thunder – offer rafting on the Tully River with transfers from as far a field as Port Douglas, however both Tully and Mission Beach are the cheapest spots to organise your rafting from.

Raging Thunder

(07) 4030 7990
***Website** www.ragingthunder.com.au*
***One day trip** $145 plus $30 park fee*

R'n'R Rafting

1800 079 039
***Website** www.raft.com.au*
***One day trip** $145 plus $25 park fee*

Innisfail

Innisfail is a large town on the banks of the Johnstone River. It is a great place to work in the sugar cane and banana industries for a month or so, and the hostels here are set up for travellers on a working holiday. Travellers may also want to stop here for the area's good white water rafting and fishing. The town centre is a busy little cosmopolitan cluster of shops and cheap restaurants. There is a sizeable Chinese and Italian community here, so there are some good places to eat. It has some interesting architecture as well, with Art Deco façades lining a few of the central streets. Otherwise, it does not offer much in the way of attractions, so if you are not planning on working in the area, you probably won't want to spend too much time here.

Practical Information

Johnstone Shire Council & Information Centre

71 Rankin Street, Innisfail
☎ *(07) 4030 2224*
Website *www.innisfailtourism.com.au*

INTERNET ACCESS

Innisfail Cyber Café

38 Rankin Street
☎ *(07) 4061 8357*
Open *Mon-Thu 8.30am-6.30pm, Fri 8.30am-6pm, Sat 9am-1pm*

Coming & Going

Both buses and trains travelling between Cairns and Townsville stop at Innisfail.

Greyhound *(☎ 1300 473 946; **website** www.greyhound.com.au)* and Premier Motor Service *(**website** www.premierms.com.au)* buses stop opposite King George Park.

The train station is west of the town centre on Station Street.

Accommodation

Codge Lodge

This hostel is in a large tropical blue Queenslander-style house in a good location. For a worker's hostel, and for Innisfail, it is one of the best. It is under new management this year, and has seen improvements to some of its facilities. There are wide verandas to lounge on, a huge swimming pool, several small but clean kitchens and good security. The bathrooms are kept spotlessly clean, and they offer free internet, washing machines and entertainment areas. The rooms are plain with new mattresses, and while some become quite cluttered, they are still not bad for a worker's hostel. It is the best choice for independent travellers in Innisfail.

63 Rankin Street, Innisfail
☎ *(07) 4061 8055*
Website *www.codgelodge.com*
Dorm bed *$25 per night, $140 per week;* ***double room*** *$50 per night, $280-300 per week*
Credit cards *MC, Visa*
Reception open *8am-8pm daily*

Maintenance & cleanliness	★★½
Facilities	★★
Atmosphere & character	★★★½
Security	★★½
Overall rating	★★½

Innisfail Backpackers Retreat

This is a modest workers' hostel in a Queenslander-style building. It has good facilities, but lacks in maintenance. There are two messy kitchens and a good TV lounge with a large TV. Rooms are spacious and air-conditioned and some have TVs and DVD players. There is an outside common area with a pool table that looks run-down and dirty, but the swimming pool is well maintained and very clean. The front door stays open all day and there is no on-site reception or staff. This place caters mostly to travellers on a working holiday.

73 Rankin Street, Innisfail
☎ *(07) 4061 2284*
Dorm bed *$25 per night, $140 per week*

Maintenance & cleanliness	★½
Facilities	★★½
Atmosphere & character	★★
Security	★★
Overall rating	★★

Walkabout Motel & Backpackers

This hostel is set in a huge old motel near the centre of town. It is quite a popular place for workers, despite some maintenance issues, and there seem to be many return guests. The air-conditioned rooms have TVs and kitchenettes, and most have en suite bathrooms. There is also a large

communal kitchen that could be cleaner and they have a common room with a big TV and pool table. Management are friendly and helpful with finding jobs.
20-24 McGowen Drive, Innisfail
(07) 4061 2311
Dorm bed *$25 per night, $140 per week*
Credit cards *Amex, Diners, MC, Visa*
Reception open *6am-9pm daily*

Maintenance & cleanliness	★★
Facilities	★★½
Atmosphere & character	★★
Security	★
Overall rating	★★

Sights
Johnstone River Crocodile Farm
This crocodile-breeding farm has over 1500 crocodiles as well as native animals including emus, kangaroos, wallabies and even two cassowaries.
Flying Fish Point Road, Innisfail
(07) 4061 1121
Website *www.crocfarm.com*
Admission *$18*
Open *8.30am-4.30pm daily; tours begin 9.30am*

Sugar Industry Museum
The Australian Sugar Industry Museum gives you the facts about the history of the industry and how the fields of cane are processed into sugar.
Corner Bruce Highway & Peregrine Street, Mourilyan
(07) 4063 2656
Website *www.sugarmuseum.org.au*
Admission *$5*
Open *Mon-Sat 9am-5pm, Sun 9am-3pm*

Cairns
Cairns is perfectly set up for the hordes of backpackers who descend on the city every year. It has a massive hostel infrastructure and lots of cheap places to eat making it an economical place to spend some time. Although the city does not have a substantial amount of attractions in itself, it does act as the most popular jumping off point to the Great Barrier Reef – an attraction that beats them all, and one which backpackers come here for and take full advantage of. Many travellers set aside several days or weeks to attain their dive certification here, although you can take any of the numerous day trips to the reef and join an introductory dive, which is just as awe-inspiring.

The city has a relaxed ambience, but at night the young and restless backpacker crowd converges on the city centre, and there is no shortage of partying and debauchery well into the morning. Pubs, bars and nightclubs, however casual, still inspire a rowdy scene. It is a good idea to spend a few nights in one of the hostels known for its social aspect, but move to one of the more low-key places if you are planning a trip in the morning and need a good night's sleep. The vast range of hostels makes this easy to do. A good place to refresh in the daytime is the huge swimming lagoon just off the Esplanade.

Practical Information
INFORMATION CENTRES
Cairns Visitor Centre
51 The Esplanade, Cairns
(07) 4051 3588
Website *www.tropicalaustralia.com.au*
Open *8.30am-6.30pm daily*

Queensland Parks & Wildlife Centre
10 McLeod Street, Cairns
(07) 4046 6600
Open *Mon-Fri 8.30am-5pm*

INTERNET ACCESS
Global Gossip – Abbott Street
125 Abbott Street, Cairns
(07) 4031 6411
Website *www.globalgossip.com*
Open *8.30am-11pm daily*

Global Gossip – Shields Street
Shop 9, 7 Shields Street, Cairns
(07) 4051 8485
Website *www.globalgossip.com*

Coming & Going
Cairns is reasonably well connected to all forms of transport. There's a busy international airport as well as regular train, bus and ferry connections.

AIR
Cairns International Airport *(☎ (07) 4052 9744; **website** www.cairnsairport.com)* is about 6km north of the city centre on Captain Cook Highway and handles frequent flights within Australia and is increasingly becoming a popular international gateway with flights from Asia and Papua New Guinea.

Many backpackers either arrive or depart Cairns by air and flights between Cairns and Alice Springs, Darwin and Sydney are often bundled with backpacker bus package deals.

There are buses between the airport and the centre of Cairns, although many hostels also provide a free shuttle service. Alternatively there's an Airport Shuttle *(☎ (07) 4048 8355; **website** www.australiacoach.com)* between the city centre and the airport. A taxi between the airport and the city centre costs around $15 for up to four passengers.

BUS
Both Greyhound *(☎ 1300 473 946; **website** www.greyhound.com.au)* and Premier Motor Service *(**website** www.premierms.com.au)* have buses going south to Sydney and Melbourne and Greyhound also have buses to the Northern Territory. Coral Reef Coaches *(☎ (07) 4031 7577; **website** www.coralreefcoaches.com.au)* have buses to Port Douglas, Cape Tribulation and Cooktown.

Premier buses depart from stop D near Woolworths on Lake Street and the Greyhound terminal is in the Reef Fleet Terminal Area.

TRAIN
The train station is located between Bunda and McLeod Streets, next to the Cairns Central shopping centre. There are five trains a week down the coast to Brisbane as well as daily trains to Kuranda.

HITCHHIKING
It's not too difficult finding a good hitching spot for a lift out of Cairns and there are usually plenty of other backpackers driving in and out of town that may give you a ride. It is easier, however, to put a notice up in the hostels around town asking for a lift or to use a web-based ride sharing service.

The Bruce Highway runs south from Cairns and the Captain Cook Highway heads north. Take bus 1, 1A or 1Z up the Captain Cook Highway for rides north to Port Douglas and Cape Tribulation or bus 1B south to the Bruce Highway for a lift down the coast.

Local Transport
Local buses run by Sunbus *(☎ (07) 4057 7411; **website** www.sunbus.com.au)* operate from the Lake Street Transit Centre in City Place with many routes operating 24-hours. Fares start at $1.80 but longer trips can cost as much as $6.70.

Accommodation
Asylum Backpackers
Asylum is a very run down complex of buildings with depressingly shoddy rooms. Bathrooms are dirty, as are the common areas. The swimming pool in front is not very inviting and the games room in an old shed has dusty furniture and a couple of pool tables. They do offer $3 barbecues, pub crawls, pizza nights, free internet access and a tour desk, but there is still not much of an atmosphere. Staff are mostly unfriendly.

149 Grafton Street, Cairns
☎ (07) 4031 1474 or 1800 065 464
***Website** www.asylumcairns.com*
***Dorm bed** $17; **single room** $34; **double room** $48-53; **twin room** $48*
***Credit cards** Amex, Diners, JCB, MC, Visa*
***Reception open** 6.30am-midnight*

Maintenance & cleanliness	★½
Facilities	★★★½
Atmosphere & character	★★½
Security	★★★
Overall rating	★★½

The Bellview
The Bellview is an old shabby motel with cheap dormitory accommodation in a few rooms. It has a good location on the Esplanade near cheap cafés, but facilities are limited and

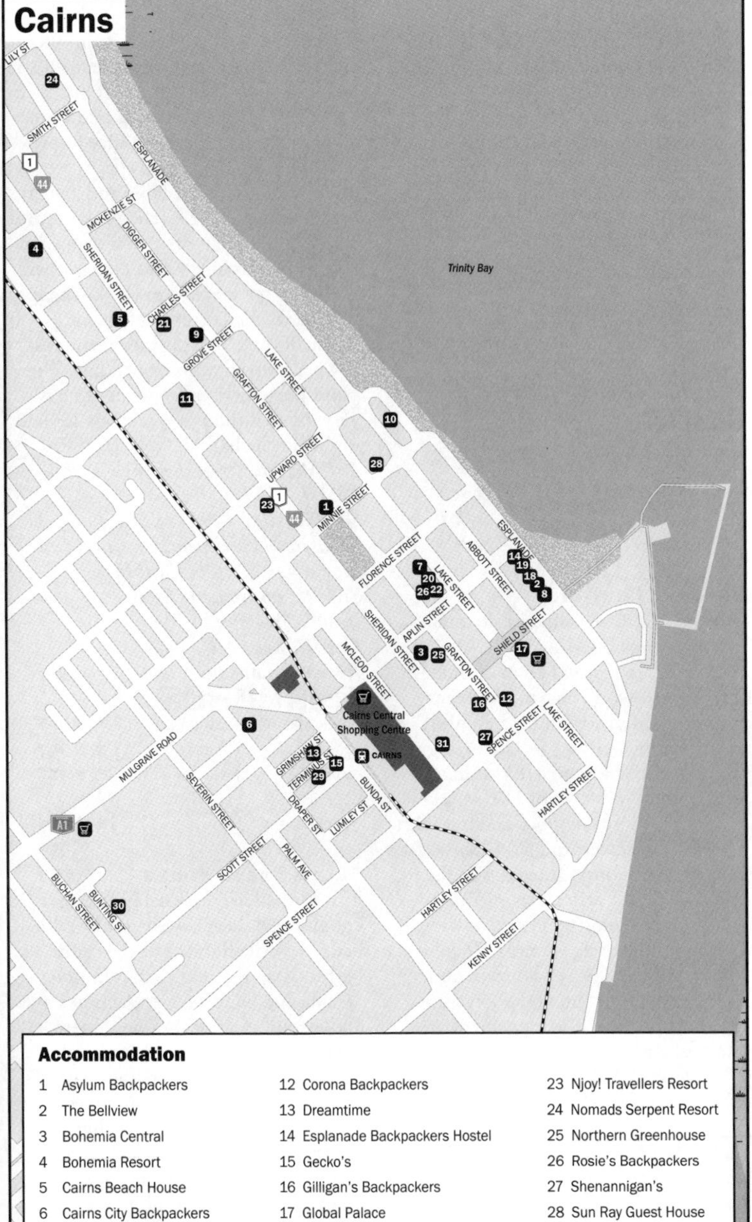

Accommodation

1 Asylum Backpackers
2 The Bellview
3 Bohemia Central
4 Bohemia Resort
5 Cairns Beach House
6 Cairns City Backpackers
7 Cairns Girls Hostel
8 Cairns International Hostel
9 Calypso Inn
10 Caravella's City Backpackers
11 Castaway's Backpackers
12 Corona Backpackers
13 Dreamtime
14 Esplanade Backpackers Hostel
15 Gecko's
16 Gilligan's Backpackers
17 Global Palace
18 H20 Backpackers
19 Hostel 89 (Esplanade Beach Hostel)
20 Inn the City
21 JJ's
22 Koala Beach Resort
23 Njoy! Travellers Resort
24 Nomads Serpent Resort
25 Northern Greenhouse
26 Rosie's Backpackers
27 Shenannigan's
28 Sun Ray Guest House
29 Traveller's Oasis
30 Tropic Days
31 YHA Cairns Central

there is no atmosphere. The dorms are air-conditioned and there is a nice swimming pool, but the common area is very dated and seldom ever used. The kitchen is tiny and useless, there is no internet access and things are not particularly clean. It is an inexpensive option if there is nothing else and the reception staff are very kind.

85-87 The Esplanade, Cairns
1, 2, 2A, 5, 5A, 6, 6A, 7
(07) 4031 4377
***Website** www.bellviewcairns.com.au*
***Dorm bed** $19-22; **double room** $49-65*
***Credit cards** MC, Visa*
***Reception open** 6am-10pm daily*

Maintenance & cleanliness	★½
Facilities	★★½
Atmosphere & character	★★★
Security	★★½
Overall rating	★★½

Bohemia Central

Bohemia Central is in a nicely renovated heritage building in the city centre. It has a good fusion of modern interior, old world charm and breezy tropical gardens, giving it a comfortable ambience. There are theme nights in the garden bar and a TV lounge with a small selection of DVDs. There is a good swimming pool and bar with a projection screen and a 24-hour café on site. Dorms are very simple, but they are all very clean and air-conditioned; some open onto a wide Queenslander-style veranda. There is internet access ($4 per hour), laundry facilities, free pickup and good security. Reception and management are cheerful and friendly.

100 Sheridan Street, Cairns
(07) 4052 1818 or 1800 558 589
***Website** www.bohemiacentral.com.au*
***Dorm bed** $24-25; **single room** $49; **double room** $75; **twin room** $65*
***Credit cards** MC; Visa; $2 credit card surcharge*
***Reception open** 24 hours*

Maintenance & cleanliness	★★★½
Facilities	★★★½
Atmosphere & character	★★★★
Security	★★★★½
Overall rating	★★★★

Bohemia Resort

Bohemia Resort is a bit far from the centre, but they have a frequent shuttle bus into town. The dorms are spacious and clean, with single beds and some with balconies. There is a nice resort size swimming pool and spa, an outdoor bar with a pool table and a great barbecue area. The kitchen is large and clean, but you have to pay a deposit at reception for cutlery and plates. There is also no refrigerator in the kitchen; instead there are small refrigerators in the dorms. There is internet access ($4 per hour) and free breakfast. The atmosphere here most of the time is very quiet, although weekends see late nights in the bar.

231 McLeod Street, Cairns
1N, 5, 5A, 6, 6A
(07) 4041 7290 or 1800 155 353
***Website** www.bohemiaresort.com.au*
***Dorm bed** $23-25; **double room** $65-85; **apartment** $150-250; prices include breakfast*
***Credit cards** MC, Visa*
***Reception open** 6.30am-10pm daily*

Maintenance & cleanliness	★★★½
Facilities	★★★½
Atmosphere & character	★★★
Security	★½
Overall rating	★★★½

Cairns Beach House

This hostel has impeccably clean air-conditioned dorms with comfortable beds, new tile flooring and en suite bathrooms. The large bar/common area has pool tables, a projection screen and a good swimming pool. There is a good atmosphere and every night there are different events in the bar and guests get a free evening meal. The hostel also offers free shuttle buses, an internet café and a tour desk. However the hostel is lacking in security and the reception staff can be a bit careless.

239 Sheridan Street, Cairns
1B, 1C, 1E, 1G, 1H, 1X, 7
(07) 4041 4116 or 1800 229 228
***Website** www.cairnsbeachhouse.com.au*
***Dorm bed** $18-25; **double room** $80; prices include an evening meal*
***Credit cards** Amex, Diners, JCB, MC, UnionPay, Visa*

***Reception open** 7am-10pm daily*

Maintenance & cleanliness	★★★½
Facilities	★★★★
Atmosphere & character	★★★½
Security	★½
Overall rating	★★★½

Cairns City Backpackers

This place offers inexpensive and comfortable accommodation in a good location. Dorms are clean with strings of ivy and flowers painted on the walls; but the communal showers are small, and some are a bit on the dirty side. There are two kitchens that are simple and homely with all the necessary fittings, and there is a small swimming pool and garden barbecue area. The hostel runs partly on solar power and has water and electricity saving facilities. They offer tour and activity advice and free pickup from the airport. It has a quiet atmosphere.

274 Draper Street, Cairns

1, 1A, 1F, 1G, 1H, 1Z, 3, 11, 12, 13

(07) 4051 6160

***Dorm bed** $17-19; **single room** $38; **double room** $40-46; **twin room** $46; **triple room** $66; prices include an evening meal*

***Credit cards** MC, Visa*

***Reception open** 7.30am-noon & 4.30pm-9pm daily*

Maintenance & cleanliness	★★½
Facilities	★★★½
Atmosphere & character	★★½
Security	★★★½
Overall rating	★★★

Cairns Girls Hostel

Cairns Girls Hostel is a female-only hostel in a meticulously maintained old house. The dorms have mostly single beds and are freshly painted in pastel colours with lace curtains, bedside tables and new carpet. The bathrooms are very clean and there are three fully equipped, immaculate kitchens. Beds are comfortable and made up, and they have laundry facilities, a barbecue and great tour advice. Management is extremely pleasant and friendly, and although there is a 10pm curfew, it is a safe and clean choice for girls and it still has a nice atmosphere.

147 Lake Street, Cairns

(07) 4051 2016 or 1800 011 950

***Website** www.cairnsgirlshostel.com.au*

***Dorm bed** $20; **twin room** $48*

***Reception open** 7.30am-9pm daily; **curfew** 10pm*

Maintenance & cleanliness	★★★½
Facilities	★★½
Atmosphere & character	★★½
Security	★★
Overall rating	★★★

Cairns International Hostel

This is the run down sister hostel to Global Palace. It has small dark rooms and old bathrooms. There is an upstairs TV lounge with a pool table and nice ocean view, but it is looking very tired. They offer cheap internet ($3.50 per hour) and a tour desk, but facilities are otherwise limited. The kitchen is substandard and there is not much of an atmosphere.

67 The Esplanade, Cairns

1C, 1D, 1E, 1G, 1H, 1N, 1X, 2, 2A, 5, 5A, 6, 6A, 7

(07) 4031 1545 or 1800 682 647

***Website** www.internationalhostel.com.au*

***Dorm bed** $23-26 ($22-25 VIP); **single room** $34 ($33 VIP); **double room** $52 ($51 VIP); **twin room** $50 ($49 VIP)*

***Credit cards** Amex, Diners, JCB, MC, UnionPay, Visa*

***Reception open** 7am-10pm daily*

Maintenance & cleanliness	★★
Facilities	★★
Atmosphere & character	★★★
Security	★★★½
Overall rating	★★½

Calypso Inn

Calypso is a colourful and fun hostel. It is farther from the centre than some of the others, but has its own bar, good facilities and a great atmosphere. The dorms are simple, spacious, airconditioned and kept very clean. The bathrooms are spotless with good showers. There is a lovely swimming pool and a barbecue area and plenty

of long wooden tables outside where everyone hangs out. They do a cheap buffet barbecue regularly and they have cheap internet access ($3.50 per hour), laundry facilities and a good tour desk.
5-9 Digger Street, Cairns
(07) 4031 0910 or 1800 815 628
***Website** www.calypsobackpackers.com*
***Dorm bed** $24 ($23 VIP); **single room** $38 ($37 VIP); **double/twin room** $54 ($52 VIP); **apartment** $64 ($62 VIP)*
***Credit cards** Amex, MC, Visa*
***Reception open** 7am-10pm daily*

Maintenance & cleanliness	★★★
Facilities	★★★
Atmosphere & character	★★★★
Security	★★★
Overall rating	★★★½

Caravella's City Backpackers
This hostel is in a breezy complex with a wide range of accommodation. Dorms are for the most part very clean and well maintained, with air-conditioning and new tile flooring. There is a central courtyard with a large swimming pool and a spacious kitchen which could use some new appliances but is cleaned regularly. There is also a tour desk and a good café with cheap breakfast and lunch. They offer free evening meals and a frequent shuttle bus into town, as well as free parking. It may be a good place to meet other backpackers, but the strict curfew keeps things quiet at night. Most guests go into town for their free meal and end up staying out to party elsewhere.
149 The Esplanade, Cairns
1C, 1D, 1E, 1G, 1H, 1N, 1X, 2, 2A, 5, 5A, 6, 6A, 7
(07) 4031 5680
***Website** www.caravellahostels.com*
***Dorm bed** $22 ($21 VIP); **double room** $60-70 ($58-68 VIP); prices include an evening meal*
***Credit cards** MC, Visa*
***Reception open** 7.30am-10.30pm daily*

Maintenance & cleanliness	★★★
Facilities	★★★
Atmosphere & character	★★
Security	★★½
Overall rating	★★★

Castaway's Backpackers
Castaway's is a small, quiet hostel with simple dorms and lots of amenities. All rooms are air-conditioned and have single beds instead of bunks. The beds are made up, but the rooms are quite bland otherwise, and you have to pay $1 for three hours of air-con. The kitchen is too small, but has more than enough supplies to cook with. There is a small swimming pool and a pretty veranda. They have laundry facilities and guests get free internet access, free use of bikes, free evening meals, free wine and cheese nights and free shuttle service into town. Reception staff are smiley and nice, and they run a good tour desk.
207 Sheridan Street, Cairns
1B, 1C, 1D, 1E, 1G, 1H, 1X, 7
(07) 4051 1238
***Website** www.castawaysbackpackers.com.au*
***Dorm bed** $24 ($23 VIP); **single room** $40 ($39 VIP); **double/twin room** $54-70 ($52-68 VIP); prices include an evening meal*
***Credit cards** MC, Visa*
***Reception open** 7am-8pm daily*

Maintenance & cleanliness	★★★
Facilities	★★★½
Atmosphere & character	★★★
Security	★
Overall rating	★★★

Corona Backpackers
Corona Backpackers is a small hostel with spacious, tidy dorms painted in bright and cheerful colours. It has a central location and is just upstairs from a great café. There are two small kitchens with ovens, but not much seating. There is no real common area either. However the bathrooms are clean with new tiles and the reception staff are outgoing and friendly. It's a shame that it is lacking in facilities and atmosphere, as it is a clean and inexpensive place in the city centre.
72 Grafton Street, Cairns
(07) 4041 5288
***Dorm bed** $14-18; **double room** $45; prices include an evening meal*
***Credit cards** MC, Visa*
***Reception open** 8am-noon & 4pm-7pm daily*

Maintenance & cleanliness	★★★½
Facilities	★
Atmosphere & character	★★
Security	★★
Overall rating	★★½

Dreamtime

Dreamtime is a small, relaxed hostel with a friendly atmosphere. The dorms are eccentrically decorated with stained glass, bright paint, and artwork adorning the walls. They are all air-conditioned, and some have en suite bathrooms. On site is the new Café Melt, which has a groovy ambience and cheap but good quality food and drinks. The swimming pool is small but clean; same with the kitchen, but the common areas are quite convivial. There are laundry facilities, a tour desk and internet access, including Wi-Fi ($4 for two hours). Management and staff are extremely pleasant and friendly.

4 Terminus Street, Cairns
(07) 4031 6753 or 1800 058 440
***Website** www.dreamtimetravel.com.au*
***Dorm bed** $22-24; **double room** $55-58*
***Credit cards** MC, Visa*
***Reception open** 7.30am-noon & 4pm-8pm daily*

Maintenance & cleanliness	★★★½
Facilities	★★½
Atmosphere & character	★★★★½
Security	★½
Overall rating	★★★½

Esplanade Backpackers Hostel

This hostel has plain dorms due for renovation soon; the bathrooms are also a bit dated. Dorms are air-conditioned and have been updated with new comfortable beds, but some of them are really tiny. It has a large fully-equipped kitchen and a good lounge area that is also being renovated. They offer free evening meals, free pickup service and laundry facilities. Reception staff are very friendly.

93 The Esplanade, Cairns
1C, 1D, 1E, 1G, 1H, 1N, 1X, 2, 2A, 5, 5A, 6, 6A, 7
(07) 4041 0378 or 1800 175 716
***Website** www.esplanadebackpackers.com*
***Dorm bed** $21-25; **double/twin room** $59; prices include an evening meal*
***Credit cards** MC, Visa*
***Reception open** 7am-10pm daily*

Maintenance & cleanliness	★★½
Facilities	★★★
Atmosphere & character	★★★½
Security	★★½
Overall rating	★★★

Gecko's

Gecko's is a large yet quaint hostel next to the train station. The dorms are appealing and well-maintained and bathrooms are spotless. The kitchen isn't much, but it has what you need, and guests get free breakfast as well as a free evening meal. It has a nice swimming pool and barbecue in the back yard, a small TV lounge and internet access ($3 per hour). The hostel is breezy and homely, the beds are new and comfortable, and the double rooms are great value. The price is right and reception staff are kind.

187 Bunda Street, Cairns
(07) 4031 1344 or 1800 011 344
***Website** www.geckosbackpackers.com.au*
***Dorm bed** $21; **single room** $31-35; **double/twin room** $47-50; prices include breakfast & an evening meal*
***Credit cards** MC, Visa*
***Reception open** 7am-noon & 4pm-8pm*

Maintenance & cleanliness	★★★½
Facilities	★★★
Atmosphere & character	★★★★½
Security	★★
Overall rating	★★★½

Gilligan's Backpackers

This is the first place backpackers try to book when coming to Cairns. It has around 500 beds, but is often completely full. Gilligan's is a modern, purpose-built hostel with the ambience of a five star hotel. There are four floors, each with its own kitchen and comfy TV lounge. The air-conditioned dorms are immaculate and have en suite bathrooms. On the ground level, there is a beauty salon, travel agency, a huge bar, restaurant and nightclub plus beach volleyball and a resort size swimming pool with a spa and

waterfall. They also have internet access, a gym and laundry room. On weekends, there is an excellent fruit and vegetable market right next door. Security is great, location is central, and surprisingly for such a big place, the staff are mostly friendly.
57-89 Grafton Street, Cairns
(07) 4041 6566
***Website** www.gilligansbackpackers.com.au*
***Dorm bed** $22-28; **double room** $120*
***Credit cards** Amex, JCB, MC, Visa*
***Reception open** 24 hours*

Maintenance & cleanliness	★★★★★
Facilities	★★★★
Atmosphere & character	★★★★½
Security	★★★★★
Overall rating	★★★★½

Global Palace

Global Palace is a large, modern and stylish hostel with a great ambience. The air-conditioned dorms have single beds, though some of them have badly stained carpets. There is a fully-equipped kitchen and a nice dining area on a wide veranda overlooking the main square in town. There is also a TV lounge with nice black leather couches and a pool table plus a rooftop swimming pool with sun lounges, a barbecue and bamboo furniture. Downstairs there are shops, a massage salon and an inexpensive sushi restaurant. It is right the heart of the city near just about everything and has a convivial atmosphere. Reception staff are for the most part friendly.
City Place, Corner Lake &Shields Streets, Cairns
all Sunbus routes
(07) 4031 7921 or 1800 819 024
***Website** www.globalpalace.com.au*
***Dorm bed** $26-27 ($25-26 VIP); **double room** $56 ($55 VIP); **twin room** $54 ($53 VIP)*
***Credit cards** MC, Visa*
***Reception open** 7am-10pm daily*

Maintenance & cleanliness	★★★½
Facilities	★★★
Atmosphere & character	★★★★
Security	★★
Overall rating	★★★½

H²O Backpackers

At the time of our visit, this hostel had recently changed management and was undergoing extensive renovations. It has a lot of potential and the changes made so far look good. The air-conditioned dorms have all new comfortable beds and clean newly-renovated bathrooms. Facilities include laundry, a full travel booking agency at reception, a very nice common area and a big swimming pool plus a kitchen, which is tattered but should see some improvements by the time of publication. Guests get free evening meals and the helpful staff put on nightly events such as wine and cheese nights.
83 The Esplanade, Cairns
1C, 1D, 1E, 1G, 1H, 1N, 1X, 2, 2A, 5, 5A, 6, 6A, 7
(07) 4031 4411
***Dorm bed** $19-26; **double room** $45-60; price includes an evening meal*
***Credit cards** MC, Visa*
***Reception open** 24 hours*

Maintenance & cleanliness	★★★½
Facilities	★★★½
Atmosphere & character	★★★½
Security	★★★½
Overall rating	★★★½

Hostel 89 (Esplanade Beach Hostel)

This hostel has a great location on the Esplanade right in front of the lagoon. The dorm rooms tend to be a bit too small, but they are being renovated with brand new beds coming in. They are kept very clean, and the double rooms are very nice. The kitchen is nothing special, but is sufficient for cooking the basics. There is a useful tour desk downstairs with some of the friendliest staff around. There is a good common area with internet, TV, books and couches. Things may change in the near future, though as renovations are ongoing in the next year.
89 The Esplanade, Cairns
1C, 1D, 1E, 1G, 1H, 1N, 1X, 2, 2A, 5, 5A, 6, 6A, 7
(07) 4031 7477
***Dorm bed** $23; **double room** $55; **twin room** $45*
***Credit cards** MC, Visa*

Queensland

Reception open *7am-10pm daily*

Maintenance & cleanliness	★★½
Facilities	★★½
Atmosphere & character	★★★★
Security	★★
Overall rating	★★★

Inn the City

This old hostel is a bit rough around the edges, although it has a fair amount of charm. The air-conditioned dorms are spacious with comfortable beds and the kitchen is old but has two ovens and plenty of pots and pans. There is an excellent swimming pool and barbecue area where they host free barbecues, as well as free evening meals. Under the house is a TV lounge with some dusty furniture and a small TV which does not look very inviting, so the atmosphere here is not as convivial as the others.

141 Lake Street, Cairns

(07) 4031 1326

Website *www.inn-the-city.com*

Dorm bed *$20;* ***single room*** *$45-65;* ***double room*** *$50-70; prices include an evening meal*

Credit cards *Amex, Diners, MC, JCB, UnionPay, Visa*

Reception open *7.30am-6pm daily*

Maintenance & cleanliness	★★
Facilities	★★½
Atmosphere & character	★★★
Security	★★½
Overall rating	★★½

JJ's

From the outside this place looks great. Bright orange and green buildings and a good swimming pool set inside a high fence. But the dorms are dirty, dated, and poorly-maintained. They have good new beds, but the rooms are otherwise austere, with old carpet and most have only a fan. The bathrooms have old tiles and some showers need to be replaced. The kitchen is surprisingly good – it is spacious, clean and well equipped. There is no internet access, but they offer free evening meal vouchers and regular shuttle service to town. The atmosphere here is a bit dull relative to the other hostels in Cairns.

11-13 Charles Street, Cairns

1C, 1D, 1E, 1G, 1H, 1N, 1X, 2, 2A, 7

1800 666 336

Website *www.jjsbackpackers.com*

Dorm bed *$23($22 HI/YHA, ISIC, VIP);* ***single room*** *$28 ($27 HI/YHA, ISIC, VIP);* ***double/twin room*** *$52 ($50 HI/YHA, ISIC, VIP); prices include breakfast and an evening meal*

Credit cards *MC, Visa*

Reception open *7am-noon & 4.30pm-7.30pm daily*

Maintenance & cleanliness	★★½
Facilities	★★★
Atmosphere & character	★★½
Security	★½
Overall rating	★★½

Koala Beach Resort

This is one of Australia's better Koala hostels. The air-conditioned dorms have kitchenettes, lounges and good beds, but some of them feel more like motel rooms. Bathrooms are spotless and there is a nice garden swimming pool. The only drawback is the kitchen, as it is dirty and poorly maintained with barely any tableware or cooking supplies - not surprisingly, it is right next to the bar and restaurant. The bar does have a good happy hour, though, and there is a relatively good atmosphere here. They also offer cheap internet ($3 per hour), laundry facilities and a tour desk. Reception staff are friendly.

137-139 Lake Street, Cairns

(07) 4051 4933 or 1800 066 514

Website *www.koalaresort.com.au*

Dorm bed *$28 ($26.60 VIP);* ***double/twin room*** *$72 ($68.40 VIP)*

Credit cards *Amex, Diners, MC, Visa*

Reception open *7am-8pm daily*

Maintenance & cleanliness	★★½
Facilities	★★★
Atmosphere & character	★★★½
Security	★½
Overall rating	★★★

Njoy! Travellers Resort

Njoy! is a small colourful hostel with a cheerful atmosphere. There is a bridge walkway over the swimming pool, connecting reception to the dorms, which are all air conditioned and tidy with good beds. The common area near the pool has lots of heavy wooden tables, a pool table and a barbecue. Things are a bit rough around the edges, but kept clean enough. They offer free shuttle service to and from town, laundry facilities, tour booking, internet access including Wi-Fi (Global Gossip Connect; $4 per hour) and movie nights. It has a convivial atmosphere without being an all-out party hostel.

141 Sheridan Street, Cairns
1C, 1D, 1E, 1G, 1H, 1N, 1X, 2, 2A, 5, 5A, 6, 6A, 7
(07) 4031 1088 or 1800 807 055
***Website** www.njoy.net.au*
***Dorm bed** $22 ($21 VIP); **single room** $38-52 ($37-51 VIP); **double room** $52-62 ($50-60 VIP)*
***Credit cards** Amex, MC, Visa*
***Reception open** 7am-10pm daily*

Maintenance & cleanliness	★★★
Facilities	★★★½
Atmosphere & character	★★★½
Security	★★½
Overall rating	★★★½

Nomads Serpent Resort

Nomads Serpent Resort is a big flash purpose-built hostel that has comfortable accommodation in air-conditioned rooms. The hostel has very good facilities that include a large kitchen and several TV rooms scattered throughout the hostel plus a good bar with pool tables and a nice big swimming pool and beach volleyball court. Everything here is new and very clean. It's a long walk from the city centre but there is a courtesy bus into town every hour.

341 Lake Street, Cairns
1B, 1C, 1D, 1E, 1G, 1H, 1X, 7
(07) 4040 7777 or 1800 737 736
***Website** www.serpenthostel.com*
***Dorm bed** $14-25; **double room** $60-80; **twin room** $60-70; prices include an evening meal*
***Credit cards** Amex, Diners, JCB, MC, UnionPay, Visa*
***Reception open** 7am-10pm daily; 24 hour check in*

Maintenance & cleanliness	★★★★½
Facilities	★★★★
Atmosphere & character	★★★½
Security	★★★★★
Overall rating	★★★★½

Northern Greenhouse

This is a beautifully maintained hostel in a great location. The air-conditioned dorms are perfectly clean and all have sparkling en suite bathrooms. There is a clean fully-equipped kitchen, a large veranda/common area with lots of couches overlooking a nice swimming pool plus a small bar with a great atmosphere. Guests get free breakfast and 30 minutes of free internet access per day and there is a free pickup bus. Although it has a great bar, it is not by any means a party hostel and it has more of a relaxing ambience. Reception staff can be a bit aloof compared with other hostels in town.

117 Grafton Street, Cairns
(07) 4047 7200 or 1800 000 541
***Website** www.friendlygroup.com.au*
***Dorm bed** $25-27; **double room** $95; **family room** $120; prices include breakfast*
***Credit cards** MC, Visa*
***Reception open** 24 hours*

Maintenance & cleanliness	★★★★½
Facilities	★★★★
Atmosphere & character	★★★
Security	★★★★
Overall rating	★★★★

Rosie's Backpackers

Rosie's is a small building in the city centre with chipping paint and old appliances. The dorms are air-conditioned, but are also cramped and messy, and the bathrooms are poorly maintained. The kitchen is untidy but well equipped, and the outside common area is too small; but there is a swimming pool and a garage in the back that has been made into a TV lounge, and they have laundry facilities, pool tables and cheap internet access, as well as almost free (just chip in a few dollars for petrol) organised trips to the Cascades. Reception and management are mellow and friendly.

136 Grafton Street, Cairns

☎ *(07) 4041 0267 or (07) 4041 0249*
Website *www.rosiesbackpackers.com.au*
Dorm bed *$19-22;* ***double room*** *$45-55; prices include breakfast and an evening meal*
Credit cards *MC, Visa*
Reception open *7am-noon & 4.30pm-7.30pm daily*

Maintenance & cleanliness	★★★½
Facilities	★★★
Atmosphere & character	★★★
Security	★★★
Overall rating	★★★

Shenannigan's

Shennanigan's has dormitory accommodation above a great corner pub of the same name. The air-conditioned dorms are well maintained with new beds and the bathrooms are clean. The kitchen is a bit empty but is otherwise well-kept, there is a small TV lounge with new comfy couches and a large upstairs veranda perfect for socialising at night. Guests get free breakfast and 15 minutes of free internet a day. It is a good standard of accommodation with a great atmosphere, although with the bar and location on a busy street, it can get pretty noisy at night.
Corner Spence & Sheridan Streets, Cairns
1, 1A, 1C, 1D, 1E, 1G, 1H, 1X, 7
☎ *(07) 4051 2490*
Website *www.shenanniganscairns.com.au*
Dorm bed *$18-25;* ***double/twin room*** *$49-65;* ***triple room*** *$75-85; prices include breakfast*
Credit cards *MC, Visa*
Reception open *8am-9pm daily*

Maintenance & cleanliness	★★★½
Facilities	★★½
Atmosphere & character	★★★★½
Security	★★
Overall rating	★★★½

Sun Ray Guest House

This old run down house is a last resort. The dorms are dark and dingy, bathrooms are old but relatively clean and the kitchen is poorly maintained and messy. There is a small common area with a few old chairs and a table, but there is really no backpacker atmosphere here. Guests have free use of bikes and free internet access, though. This hostel is popular with Asian backpackers.
4 Minnie Street, Cairns
1C, 1D, 1E, 1G, 1H, 1N, 1X, 2, 2A, 5, 5A, 6, 6A, 7
☎ *(07) 4051 3370*
Dorm bed *$17;* ***double room*** *$45-50*
Credit cards *MC, Visa*
Reception open *7am-7pm daily*

Maintenance & cleanliness	★½
Facilities	★★
Atmosphere & character	★★
Security	★★
Overall rating	★★

Traveller's Oasis

This is a lovely hostel consisting of a few buildings set around a lovely swimming pool and gardens with a nice outdoor common area. What sets this place apart is attention to detail. The air-conditioned dorms have polished wood flooring, light peach and aqua green paint and comfortable single beds made up with flowery duvets. There are accents on the walls and the windows have wooden blinds. The bathrooms are immaculately clean with hairdryers and great shower heads. There are two clean fully-equipped kitchens, laundry facilities, internet access and staff provide fresh towels and plenty of friendly advice on tours and sightseeing. It is an intimate, safe and smiley hostel on a side road just far enough away from the noise of McLeod Street, but close enough to walk everywhere.
8 Scott Street Cairns
☎ *(07) 4052 1377 or 1800 621 353*
Website *www.travoasis.com.au*
Dorm bed *$25;* ***single room*** *$42;* ***double room*** *$59-69;* ***twin room*** *$59*
Credit cards *MC, Visa*
Reception open *7am-noon & 4pm-8pm daily*

Maintenance & cleanliness	★★★★
Facilities	★★★½
Atmosphere & character	★★★★½
Security	★
Overall rating	★★★½

Tropic Days

Like its sister hostel, Travellers Oasis, Tropic Days is a home away from home. It is in an old house, but everything is beautifully maintained. Dorm rooms are cosy with brand new beds, fresh paint and personal touches from the cheerful owners. There are three clean kitchens with free tea and coffee and six single bathrooms with spacious showers and some with hairdryers. There are a couple of lounges with internet access, TV and a DVD library plus a gorgeous swimming pool surrounded by tall palm trees and gardens. It has a quiet atmosphere, but it is still a fun place to stay. They put on an excellent weekly barbecue with kangaroo, emu and crocodile and have free didgeridoo lessons. There is a regular shuttle service into town and they can book tours for you in reception. When you stay here you feel like you are surrounded by family.

26-28 Bunting Street, Cairns
1, 1A, 1C, 1D, 1G, 1E, 1H, 1X, 7
(07) 4041 1521
Website *www.tropicdays.com.au*
Dorm bed *$25;* ***single room*** *$42;* ***double room*** *$59-69;* ***twin room*** *$59;* ***camping*** *$11 per person; prices include an evening meal*
Credit cards *MC, Visa*

Maintenance & cleanliness	★★★½
Facilities	★★★½
Atmosphere & character	★★★★½
Security	★★
Overall rating	★★★½

YHA Cairns Central

This YHA hostel is indeed very central. It occupies a spacious, colourful building in the centre of town and it has a good atmosphere. The dorm rooms are very clean and sleek – although bordering on institutional – and some of them are a bit too small. But almost all of them have spotless en suite bathrooms with new tiles and nice glass showers. The large, fully-equipped kitchen is excellent with indoor and outdoor seating. There is also a cosy movie lounge with couches and a huge screen TV, but most people hang out near the swimming pool, which has two gorgeous spa baths. There are deluxe family rooms available, which are huge and luxurious and perfect for a couple days of spoiling yourself. There is also excellent security, which is rare in Cairns, and the reception staff are for the most part friendly and welcoming. It is not a party hostel, but still has a convivial ambience.

20-24 McLeod Street, Cairns
1 1A 1C 1D 1E 1H 1X
(07) 4051 0772
Website *www.yha.com.au*
Dorm bed *$26-31.50 ($23-28 HI/YHA);* ***double/twin room*** *$67-84.50 ($60-76 HI/YHA);* ***family room*** *$182.50 ($160 HI/YHA)*
Credit cards *JCB, MC, Visa*
Reception open *6.30am-11pm daily*

Maintenance & cleanliness	★★★★
Facilities	★★★★
Atmosphere & character	★★★
Security	★★★★
Overall rating	★★★★

Eating & Drinking

Cairns is one of the best places in Australia to find cheap food and drinks. Most hostels offer free breakfasts or free evening meals, and often both. Pubs often have the best deals, with $5-10 backpacker meals every night. Many hostels supply free meal vouchers to the **Woolshed** *(24 Shields Street, Cairns)*, a famous bar/restaurant where a hearty $10 meal turns into a night of cheap drinks and dancing. **PJ O'Brien's** *(87 Lake Street, Cairns)* also has cheap food, drinks and a good atmosphere. There are fast food joints all over town and the Cairns Central Shopping Centre has a huge food court with cheap places to eat, as well as a **Coles** supermarket. There is a **Woolworths** *(103 Abbott Street, Cairns)* in the city centre. There are also a couple of Night Owl convenience stores for late night snacks and some pizza and sandwich places stay open late for the party crowd as well.

There is a wide range of international dining in Cairns, from modern Australian to Vietnamese. Takeaway Thai and Chinese restaurants are a popular choice for many backpackers and Cairns has some very good sushi places. Try **Café China** in Rydges Plaza *(Spence Street, Cairns)* for excellent noodle dishes. The local tropical fruits are used by juice stands and the best place to sample and buy fresh fruit and vegetables is **Rusty's Markets** next to Gilligan's Hostel. Grafton Street and the Esplanade are loaded with cafés and are the best places to look for cheap breakfast and good coffee.

Sights

Cairns' city centre doesn't have very much in the way of sights and most travellers use it mainly as a base for exploring the Great Barrier Reef and the surrounding region.

Cairns Museum

This small museum with exhibits on local history including Aboriginal and Chinese artifacts and displays on the impact of the railway and origins of the tourism industry.
Corner Lake & Shields Streets, Cairns
all Sunbus routes
(07) 4051 5582
Website *www.cairnsmuseum.org.au*
Admission *$5*
Open *Mon-Sat 10am-4pm*

Cairns Regional Art Gallery

This central gallery has exhibitions of works by local artists and it also hosts a programme of temporary exhibits.
Corner Abbot & Shields Streets, Cairns
(07) 4031 6865
Website *www.cairnsregionalgallery.com.au*
Admission *$5*
Open *Mon-Sat 10am-5pm, Sun 1pm-5pm*

Flecker Botanic Gardens

Cairns' botanic gardens feature a variety of tropical plants and a boardwalk through wetlands. There is also a rainforest boardwalk across the road in Centenary Lakes.
Collins Avenue, Edge Hill
1N, 7
(07) 4044 3398
Admission *free*
Open *Mon-Sat 7.30am-5.30pm, Sat-Sun 8.30am-5.30pm*

Reef Teach

The Reef Teach slide show and lecture provides an entertaining and educational insight into the reef. It is highly recommended if you plan on diving or snorkelling on the Great Barrier Reef
85 Lake Street, Cairns
(07) 4031 7794
Website *www.reefteach.com.au*
Admission *$13*
Show *Mon-Sat 6.30pm*

Royal Flying Doctor Service

Cairns is the Royal Flying Doctors Service regional office for northern Queensland and like most other branches of the RFDS, there is a visitors' centre with a small museum about the service.
1 Junction Street, Edge Hill
5A, 6, 6A, 7
(07) 4053 5687
Website *www.flyingdoctorqueensland.com*
Admission *$5.50*
Open *Mon-Sat 8.30am-5pm; tours depart every half-hour*

Tjapukai Aboriginal Dance Theatre

The Tjapukai Aboriginal Cultural Park at the base of Skyrail is home to the Tjapukai Aboriginal Dance Theatre and there are also exhibits on Aboriginal culture.
Captain Cook Highway, Smithfield
1C, 1E, 1X, 1, 1A, 4, 7
(07) 4042 9999
Website *www.tjapukai.com.au*
Admission *$31 day; $90 evening performace*
Open *9am-5pm daily; evening performance 7.30pm*

Activities

While there may not be too much to see in Cairns, there's certainly plenty to do. Activities include bungee jumping, white water rafting and scuba and skydiving.

BUNGEE JUMPING

AJ Hackett runs a popular bungee site north of Cairns with a 44m jump.
MacGregor Road, Smithfield
(07) 4057 7188 or 1800 622 888

Website *www.ajhackett.com.au*
Bungee jump *$125;* ***bungee jump & Minjin Jungle Swing combo*** *$169;* ***unlimited jump, lunch & Minjin Jungle Swing combo*** *$249;* ***bungee, Tully whitewater rafting, skydive and Fitzroy Island ferry transfers*** *$533*
Open *10am-5pm daily*

DIVE COURSES

There are several companies offering scuba dive courses that include several dives on the reef. These courses give you PADI certification, which is essential for diving on the reef.

Most dive schools run several different courses but the open water courses are the most popular; these courses combine theory and pool dives with a couple of dives on the Great Barrier Reef. Open water PADI courses generally run over four to five days, the cheaper courses involve daily trips out to the reef and the more expensive course include accommodation aboard a boat on the reef.

You can still dive without PADI certification, but this will involve doing an introductory dive as part of a day trip to the reef. An introductory dive is a good way to find out whether diving is for you.

Cairns Dive Centre
121 Abbott Street, Cairns
☎ *(07) 4051 0294 or 1800 642 591*
Website *www.cairnsdive.com.au*
Open water course *$370-59*

Deep Sea Divers Den
319 Draper Street, Cairns
☎ *(07) 4046 7333*
Website *www.divers-den.com*
Open water course *$500-595*

Down Under Dive
287 Draper Street, Cairns
☎ *(07) 4052 8300 or 1800 079 099*
Website *www.downunderdive.com.au*
Open water dive course *$469-584*

Pro Dive
116 Spence Street, Cairns
☎ *(07) 4031 5255*
Website *www.prodive-cairns.com.au*
Open water course *$725*

Tusa Dive
Corner Shield Street & Esplanade, Cairns
☎ *(07) 4031 1028*
Website *www.tusadive.com*
Open water dive course *$595*

REEF TRIPS

Cairns has excellent access to the Great Barrier Reef and there's a huge range of trips available that offer both diving and snorkelling. Most reef trips depart from Marlin Marina.

Cairns Dive Centre
121 Abbott Street, Cairns
☎ *(07) 4051 0294 or 1800 642 591*
Website *www.cairnsdive.com.au*
Snorkelling day trip *$75;* ***diving day trip*** *$120 (includes two dives)*

Compass Cruises
100 Abbott Street, Cairns
☎ *(07) 4051 5777 or 1 800 GO REEF*
Website *www.reeftrip.com*
Snorkelling day trip *$60*

Deep Sea Divers Den
319 Draper Street, Cairns
☎ *(07) 4046 7333*
Website *www.divers-den.com*
Snorkelling day trip *$100;* ***introductory dive day trip*** *$160-225;* ***certified dive day trip*** *$165-160*

Down Under Dive
287 Draper Street, Cairns
☎ *(07) 4052 8300 or 1800 079 099*
Website *www.downunderdive.com.au*
Snorkelling day trip *$95-149*

Passions of Paradise
☎ *(07) 4041 1600*
Website *www.passions.com.au*
Snorkelling day trip *$135*

Tusa Dive
Corner Shield Street & Esplanade, Cairns
☎ *(07) 4031 1028*
Website *www.tusadive.com*
Snorkelling day trip *$145;* ***certified dive day trip*** *$205-225*

JUNGLE SWING

AJ Hackett's bungy jump site is also home to the Minjin Jungle Swing. This

involves being strapped into a harness suspended by stainless steel cables and swinging from 40 metres at 100km/h.
MacGregor Road, Smithfield
☎ *(07) 4057 7188 or 1800 622 888*
Website *www.ajhackett.com.au*
Swing *$69 (per person);* ***bungee jump & Minjin Jungle Swing combo*** *$169;* ***unlimited bungee jump, lunch & Minjin Jungle Swing combo*** *$249*
Open *10am-5pm daily*

SKYDIVING

Cairns is a popular skydiving destination and two companies offer tandem jumps.

Paul's Parachuting

☎ *1800 005 006*
Website *www.paulsparachuting.com.au*
10000ft tandem skydive *$244;* ***14000ft tandem skydive*** *$295; plus compulsory Australian Parachute Federation Student License $25*

Skydive Cairns

☎ *(07) 4031 5466 or 1800 444 568*
Website *www.skydivecairns.com.au*
9000ft tandem skydive *$210;* ***11000ft tandem skydive*** *$244;* ***14000ft tandem skydive*** *$295; plus compulsory Australian Parachute Federation Student License $25*

WHITE WATER RAFTING

Cairns is a good base for rafting the Barron, Johnstone, Russell and Tully Rivers.

The Barron River (grade 3 rapids) is only a 20-minute drive north of Cairns, the Russell River (grade 3-4 rapids) is an hour south of Cairns and the Tully River (grade 3-4 rapids) – Australia's best one-day rafting trip – is over 1½ hour south of Cairns. If you're planning to visit Mission Beach or Tully it is cheaper to raft the Tully River from there.

The remote Johnstone River features World Heritage rainforest but it is only accessible by helicopter and it's a very expensive multi-day camping trip.

All rafting trips include transport from Cairns, Port Douglas, Mission Beach or the Northern Beaches but require payment of an additional rafting levy ($25). The trips may be slightly cheaper if you drive to the rafting destination (Mission Beach and Tully are the cheapest places for rafting on the Tully River).

Foaming Fury

Foaming Fury runs half-day rafting trips on the Barron River and full day trips on the Russell River.
19-21 Barry Street, Cairns
☎ *(07) 4031 3460 or 1800 801 540*
Website *www.foamingfury.com.au*
Barron River half-day trip *$96 plus $25 rafting levy;* ***Russell River full-day trip*** *$130 plus $25 rafting levy*

Raging Thunder

Raging Thunder operate rafting trips on the Barron and Tully Rivers.
☎ *(07) 4030 7990*
Website *www.ragingthunder.com.au*
Barron River half-day trip *$98 plus $25 rafting levy;* ***Tully River full-day trip*** *$155 plus $25 rafting levy*

R'n'R White Water Rafting

R'n'R runs half-day trips on the Barron River and full-day trips on the Tully River. They also run multi-day adventures on the Johnstone River.
Corner Shields & Abbott Streets, Cairns
☎ *(07) 4041 2272*
Website *www.raft.com.au*
Barron River half-day trip *$98 plus $25 rafting levy;* ***Tully River full-day trip*** *$155 plus $25 rafting levy;* ***North Johnstone River*** *$1300 (4 days) plus $100 rafting levy*

Around Cairns

From Cairns, boats travel daily to Green Island, Fitzroy Island and the outer reef where visitors can peer through a diving mask or a glass-bottomed boat at numerous species of coral and marine life.

A short distance northwest of Cairns is Kuranda, a village in the rainforest that makes a great daytrip. Inland from Kuranda is farming country and the Atherton tablelands.

Most travellers head north from Cairns to Cape Tribulation and the Daintree rainforest and stop at Port

Douglas. Cooktown is as far north as most independent travellers go, as roads north of there require 4WD vehicles.

Green Island

This tiny coral cay, just 26km off the coast of Cairns, is a popular spot with daytrippers. The island is a national park and there is very good snorkelling.

It is best visited as a day trip as accommodation on the island is expensive. Part of the resort has facilities for daytrippers.

Coming & Going

Great Adventures (☎ *(07) 4044 9944 or 1800 079 080;* ***website*** *www.greatadventures.com.au)* ferry passengers between Cairns and Green Island. Prices start at $69 return but full day trips cost $109 including lunch and use of resort facilities.

Fitzroy Island

Fitzroy Island is larger than Green Island. It is also a national park that offers good snorkelling. There are also a couple of hiking trails on the island and also some good beaches.

Fitzroy Island is about the same distance from Cairns as Green Island, but it is less crowded, cheaper to get to and a more popular destination among backpackers.

A $5 national park fee is payable by visitors to the island.

Coming & Going

The *Fitzroy Flyer* (☎ *(07) 4030 7907;* ***website*** *www.huntgroup.com.au/Default.aspx?tabid=123)* takes 45 minutes to sail from Cairns to the island. The return trip costs $45.

Activities

Dive Courses

Several Cairns-based dive courses operate from here (see the Cairns Sights & Activities section for more information).

Sea Kayaking

Raging Thunder runs daytrips to Fitzroy Island, which include the ferry trip over and sea kayaking to the more remote parts of the island.

☎ *(07) 4030 7900*
Website *www.ragingthunder.com.au*
Cost *$155*

Kuranda

Getting to Kuranda is half the fun – the Kuranda Scenic Railway and the Skyrail line both offer stunning views from Cairns and up to the forest-covered hills into town and the steep winding road through the rainforest makes for a great drive. It is for this reason that most of the tourist activity is highest at midday when the day trippers are perusing the markets and taking photos.

The small town of Kuranda is relaxed and friendly and it is worth an overnight if you have time to spare. Look out for heightened prices on the day tripper circuit, though. There are a few good wildlife sanctuaries in the area and a large Aboriginal community. The daily markets are the biggest draw card, with fresh produce and crafts on display every morning. Kuranda is not far from the Barron Gorge National Park with its gorgeous waterfalls, which are especially mighty in the wet season.

Coming & Going

BUS

Whitecar Coaches (☎ *(07) 4091 1855;* ***website*** *http://users.qldnet.com.au/~whitecars/)* operate a regular service from Cairns to Atherton, stopping at Kuranda along the way.

CABLE CAR

If you've slept in and missed the train, you can always take the Skyrail cable car (☎ *(07) 4038 1555;* ***website*** *www.skyrail.com.au)* – the world's longest gondola cableway that runs to Kuranda above the rainforest for 7½km from Smithfield, north of Cairns. It is possible to get off at points along the way to explore the rainforest. The Skyrail Rainforest Cableway operates 8.15am-5.15pm daily. As you would expect, this is an expensive transport option at $40 for a one-way, $58 return or $80 returning by train.

TRAIN

The train is the nicest way to travel from Cairns to Kuranda. The Kuranda Scenic Railway (☎ *(07) 4031 3636;* ***website*** *www.kurandascenicrailway.com.au)* operates the historic train and the ride is so popular that most people rate the train trip higher than Kuranda itself, although others find the endless commentary a little irritating. Trains leave Cairns at 8.30am and 9.30am, returning at 2pm and 3.30pm. The train isn't cheap at $40 ($33 students) for a one-way ticket or $59 ($53 students) return.

Accommodation

Kuranda Backpackers Hostel

This is a terrible hostel. It is in an old house that desperately needs to be renovated. The "dorms" are just rows of beds scattered throughout the second floor, many of which are on an old veranda. They do not look very clean. The bathrooms are cleaned, but they also need work and the swimming pool is an unhealthy shade of green. There is one computer with internet access plus a pool table and table tennis in the TV room, which is in a dirty space underneath the house. There few other facilities and the hostel has a very lonely atmosphere.

6 Arara Street, Kuranda
☎ *(07) 4093 7355*
Website *www.kurandabackpackershostel.com*
Dorm bed *$19;* ***single room*** *$46;* ***double room*** *$49*
Credit cards *MC, Visa*
Reception open *9am-noon & 4pm-6.30pm*

TV K L

Maintenance & cleanliness	★½
Facilities	★★½
Atmosphere & character	★★
Security	★★
Overall rating	★★

Sights

Birdworld

This large aviary is home to Australia's largest collection of free flying birds representing almost 80 species.

Heritage Markets, Therwine Street, Kuranda
☎ *(07) 4093 9188*
Website *www.birdworldkuranda.com*
Admission *$15; $38 including admission to the Butterfly Sanctuary and Koala Gardens*
Open *9am-4pm daily*

Butterfly Sanctuary

Just like Birdworld, but with butterflies. There are regular guided tours that depart every 10-15 minutes.

8 Rob Vievers Drive, Kuranda
☎ *(07) 4093 7575*
Website *www.australianbutterflies.com*
Admission *$16; $38 including admission to Birdworld and Koala Gardens*
Open *10am-4pm daily*

Kuranda Koala Gardens

The Kuranda Koala Gardens are similar to Birdworld and the Butterfly Sanctuary, but with koalas.

Rob Vievers Drive, Kuranda
☎ *(07) 4093 9953*
Website *www.koalagardens.com*
Admission *$15, an additional $13 if you want to hold a koala; $38 including admission to Birdworld and the Butterfly Sanctuary*
Open *9am-4pm daily*

Kuranda Markets

The most popular attraction in Kuranda is the Kuranda Markets, which feature arts and crafts as well as clothing stalls.

Corner Therwine & Thooree Streets, Kuranda
Admission *free*
Open *8.30am-3pm daily, but it's best to visit Wed-Sun when the original markets are also open*

Atherton Tablelands

The Atherton Tablelands plateau is about an hour inland from Cairns. It offers a cooler climate and very different scenery to what you would find on the coast and features waterfalls, some great hiking trails and the opportunity to see wildlife including platypus and tree kangaroos.

The major towns on the tablelands include Mareeba, Atherton and Yungaburra.

Coming & Going

Whitecar Coaches (☎ *(07) 4091 1855; **website** http://users.qldnet.com.au/~whitecars/)* operate a regular bus service from Cairns to Atherton.

There are also several tours that operate from Cairns that are a good option for travellers without a car; these include Bandicoot Bike Tours, On the Wallaby and Uncle Brian's. **Bandicoot Bike Tours** (☎ *(07) 4055 0155; **website** www.bandicootbicycles.com)* operates cycling tours on quiet back roads in the Tablelands with day trips costing $99. **On the Wallaby** (☎ *(07) 4091 3552; **website** www.onthewallaby.com)* run excellent tours including a one-day canoe tour ($85), one-day waterfalls tour ($95) or an overnight tour ($165) with accommodation at their hostel in Yungaburra. **Uncle Brian's** (☎ *(07) 4050 0615; **website** www.unclebrian.com.au)* have fun day tours for $109. All three tours get you to the waterfalls and give you the opportunity to see wildlife.

Atherton

Atherton is the main town in the Atherton Tablelands. It is a modest town with just the bare essentials, but cheap prices on food and supplies. The only backpackers who stay here are on working holiday, but it is a good place to look for work, as there is a great hostel, and the surrounding area is absolutely gorgeous.

Queensland

Practical Information

Atherton Tourist Information Centre

Corner Silo Road & Main Street, Atherton
☎ *(07) 4091 4222*
***Website** www.athertontablelands.com.au*
***Open** 9am-5pm daily*

Accommodation

Atherton Travellers Lodge

This is the only hostel in Atherton but luckily it is a good one. It is in a beautifully kept old Queenslander house with wide verandas outside each dorm. The nice dorms have comfortable beds and the long hall has polished wooden floorboards and nice paintings. The bathrooms are clean and spacious and the excellent kitchen has dark paint, recessed lighting and new steel appliances. There is a cosy TV lounge with a huge log fireplace and a great pool table. The only problem is that there are mostly workers staying here, so there is not a big backpacker atmosphere. But it is a quiet, clean place to stay if you are in Atherton.

37 Alice Street, Atherton
☎ *(07) 4091 3552*
***Website** www.athertontravellerslodge.com.au*
***Dorm bed** $25 per night, $150 per week; **single room** $40 per night, $240 per week; **double/twin room** $60 per night, $360 per week*
***Credit cards** Amex, Diners, JCB, MC, UnionPay, Visa*
***Reception open** 9am-10pm daily*

Maintenance & cleanliness	★★★★
Facilities	★★★½
Atmosphere & character	★★★
Security	★★★
Overall rating	★★★½

Mareeba

This town between Kuranda and Atherton produces over 90% of Australia's small coffee crop and is also recognised as the country's premier hot air ballooning spot.

Practical Information

Mareeba Tourist Information Centre

345 Byrnes Street, Mareeba
☎ *(07) 4092 5674*
***Open** 8am-4pm daily*

Sights

Mareeba Heritage Museum

This small museum adjoining the tourist information centre has exhibits relating to local history. Displays include a unique rail ambulance and a working blacksmith shop.

345 Byrnes Street, Mareeba
☎ *(07) 4092 5674*
***Website** www.mareebaheritagecentre.com.au*
***Admission** $5*
***Open** 8am-4pm daily*

Yungaburra

Yungaburra is a quaint little historic village in the heart of the Atherton Tablelands and it is the perfect base for exploring the area. Nearby is the easily accessible curtain fig tree, with its long boardwalk and viewing platforms. Lake Eacham and Lake Tinaroo are great for swimming and fishing, or canoeing. The monthly markets are a popular stop for many local residents, and the Tablelands area is home to the Waterfall Circuit, the Nerada Tea Plantation, and the Mungalli Creek Dairy Farm where you can learn about dairy production and have free samples. This area has a high amount of rare tree kangaroos and is a great spot to see other wildlife, including platypus.

Practical Information

Yungaburra Visitor Information Centre

Cedar Street, Yungaburra
☎ *(07) 4095 2416*
Website *www.yungaburra.com*

Accommodation

On the Wallaby

This brilliant hostel in the heart of the historic village of Yungaburra is wonderfully maintained, with new beds and clean bathrooms with great showers. The kitchen is small but fully equipped and very clean and there is a nice wooden dining table and outside common area where travellers get together every night. The hostel is beautifully maintained and homely and the staff are friendly and welcoming. They organise tours and excursions in the Tablelands region and offer some really great deals. It is definitely worth a few nights stay.

34 Eacham Road, Yungaburra
☎ *(07) 4050 0650*
Website *www.onthewallaby.com*
Dorm bed *$22 ($21 VIP);* ***double room*** *$55 ($53 VIP);* ***camping*** *$10 per person*
Credit cards *MC, Visa*
Reception open *8am-noon & 4pm-8pm*

Maintenance & cleanliness	★★★★
Facilities	★★
Atmosphere & character	★★★★½
Security	★★
Overall rating	★★★½

Port Douglas

About an hour's drive north from Cairns is the quiet town of Port Douglas. Although its foundations are as a resort destination, there are some brilliant budget accommodation options as well. Its location is perfect for access to the reef and the rainforest and it sits next to the beautiful Four Mile Beach, which makes it a good alternative to Cairns if you are looking for something a little more laid-back. Port Douglas town is a short string of shops and restaurants with plenty of alfresco cafés and juice bars. It is quaint and inviting, albeit pricier than Cairns. Tour operators abound here and you have quicker access to the Low Isles of the Great Barrier Reef, Cape Tribulation and the Daintree Rainforest. It is a very popular place to take a dive course, and there are several reputable companies offering four-day PADI certifications.

Practical Information

Port Douglas Tourist Information Centre

23 Macrossan Street, Port Douglas
☎ *(07) 4099 5599*
Website *www.tourismportdouglas.com.au*

Coming & Going

Coral Reef Coaches (☎ *(07) 4098 2600;* ***website*** *www.coralreefcoaches.com.au)* operate buses that run between Port Douglas and Cairns, Cairns Airport, Cape Tribulation, Cooktown and Mossman. Buses depart from the end of Dixie Street.

Accommodation

Dougie's Backpackers

Dougie's is a great place to stay in Port Douglas. It is near the beach and not far from town. The air-conditioned dorms are set in large sturdy cabins in tropical gardens and have a relaxing atmosphere. It is very clean. The kitchen is part of the central common area, which has wide spaces and soft lighting, wooden beams and plenty of games and activities, including an internet room upstairs. There is a jukebox, plush seating and a large TV plus

an outside bar and swimming pool with hammocks and a barbecue area. Management are pleasant and helpful and they offer guests free use of bikes and fishing gear hire, free laundry facilities, free barbecues on Tuesdays and free pickup from Cairns.
111 Davidson Street, Port Douglas
(07) 4099 6047
***Website** www.dougies.com.au*
***Dorm bed** $27 ($26 HI/YHA, VIP or a photo from home) per night, $140 per week; **bed in a stylie (dorm tent)** $23 ($22 HI/YHA, VIP or a photo from home) per night, $125 per week; **double/twin room** $80 ($78 HI/YHA, VIP or a photo from home) per night, $450 per week; **camping** $14 ($13 HI/YHA, VIP or a photo from home) per night, $80 per week*
***Credit cards** MC, Visa*
***Reception open** 7.30am-6.30pm; check in until midnight*

Maintenance & cleanliness	★★★½
Facilities	★★★½
Atmosphere & character	★★★★½
Security	★★½
Overall rating	★★★½

Parrotfish Lodge

This hostel is in a large modern building near the centre of Port Douglas. The air-conditioned dorms are very spacious and clean with comfortable beds and the bathrooms are also very clean. It may seem a bit sterile, but the outdoor common areas give it some character. There are large wooden tables and comfy couches and a large TV set up on both floors and there is a restaurant, bar, kitchen, pool table and internet room downstairs. The huge swimming pool is clean and surrounded by a large deck with a barbecue area. They offer free shuttle service and a tour desk.
37-39 Warner Street, Port Douglas
(07) 4099 5011 or 1800 995 011
***Website** www.parrotfishlodge.com*
***Dorm bed** $25-33; **double/twin room** $85-95*
***Credit cards** MC, Visa*
***Reception open** 7am-9pm daily; check in 24 hours*

Maintenance & cleanliness	★★★
Facilities	★★★
Atmosphere & character	★★★½
Security	★½
Overall rating	★★★

Port O Call Lodge

This YHA hostel is small and a bit tired looking at first, but the dorms are immaculately clean and extremely well maintained. Each is air conditioned and has a spotless en suite bathroom with a hairdryer. Facilities include a TV, fridge and lockers in each room plus a laundry, internet access, bike hire, swimming pool, kitchen and a nice dining area. However the focus is on the bar/café, which has outdoor tables and cheap food. They have a full service tour desk and offer free transport to and from Cairns. It is an eco-friendly place running on solar energy.
7 Craven Close, Port Douglas
(07) 4099 5422 or 1800 892 800
***Website** www.portocall.com.au*
***Dorm bed** $27-32 ($24-28.50 HI/YHA); **double/twin room** $77-110 ($69-99 HI/YHA)*
***Credit cards** MC, Visa*
***Reception open** Mon-Sat 7.30am-7.30pm, Sun 8am-1pm & 4pm-7pm*

Maintenance & cleanliness	★★★½
Facilities	★★★½
Atmosphere & character	★★★½
Security	★★½
Overall rating	★★★½

Sights

Port Douglas Court House Museum

This small museum in Port Douglas's old courthouse has exhibits on local history.
Wharf Street, Port Douglas
(07) 4099 4635
***Website** www.douglas-shire-historical-society.org/court_house_museum.htm*
***Admission** $2*
***Open** Tue, Thu & Sat-Sun 10am-3pm*

Rainforest Habitat

Rainforest Habitat is an enclosed animal park in a rainforest setting, featuring 1600 animals and 180 different species.

Corner Port Douglas Road & Captain Cook Highway, Port Douglas
☎ *(07) 4099 3235*
Website *www.rainforesthabitat.com.au*
Admission *$29*
Open *8am-5.30pm daily (last entry 4.30pm)*

Activities

DIVE COURSES

You can learn to dive in Port Douglas, but it is more expensive than Cairns.

Tech Dive Acadamy

1/18 Macrossan Street, Port Douglas
☎ *(07) 4099 6880*
Website *www.tech-dive-academy.com*
Open *water dive course $750*

REEF TRIPS

Several companies run trips to the outer Barrier Reef from Port Douglas, including:

Quicksilver Dive

Marina Mirage, Port Douglas
☎ *(07) 4099 5050*
Website *www.silverseries.com.au*
Snorkelling day trip *$157;* ***introductory dive trip*** *$219;* ***certified dive trip*** *$209-244*

Wavelength

2/38 Wharf Street, Port Douglas
☎ *(07) 4099 5031*
Website *www.wavelength-reef.com.au*
Snorkelling day trip *$180*

Cape Tribulation

Cape Tribulation is around 30km north of the Daintree River ferry crossing, although the region often referred to as Cape Tribulation (which incorporates nearby localities like Cape Kimberley and Cow Bay) starts just a few kilometres after driving off the ferry.

Cape Trib is a mystifying rainforest hideaway with a spattering of accommodation and places to eat. The winding road north is incredibly scenic, with dense rainforest letting out for quick sights of pristine beaches, coastal mangroves and imposing mountains. The area is home to masses of flora and fauna, including cassowaries, estuarine crocodiles and unique bird species. The Kuku Yalangi are the local Aboriginal people who have inhabited the region for thousands of years and know the area as Kulki, but it became known as Cape Tribulation after Captain Cook's ship ran aground on the offshore reef.

There are several excellent hostels spread far apart from each other. The only place you could really call a village is the area near PK's hostel, where there is a convenience store, restaurant and an information centre where you can book tours. Mason's Shop acts as the local information centre, and you should stop here if you are planning a trip in the area.

Coming & Going

Coral Reef Coaches *(☎ (07) 4098 2600;* ***website*** *www.coralreefcoaches.com.au)* operate buses from Cairns and Port Douglas which stop at all the hostels, except Koala, and continue north to Cooktown.

If you are driving you will need to take the car ferry across the Daintree River, which operates from 6am to midnight and costs $16 return.

Accommodation

Cape Tribulation Beach House

This is the nicest hostel in Cape Trib. The air-conditioned dorms are in lovely A-frame cabins with wheelchair access following a long winding pathway under rainforest canopy to a sandy beach. The dorms and bathrooms are clean and well maintained with good showers. There is a huge bar and bistro with a mellow, social ambience and pool tables and games, next to a lovely swimming pool with deck chairs. The communal kitchen is very small but clean and well equipped. Their tour desk can book any adventure activity in the area. There is also internet access and a laundry. The staff are warm and friendly.

MS 2041, Cape Tribulation QLD 4873
☎ *(07) 4098 0030 or 1800 111 124*
Website *www.capetribbeach.com.au*
Dorm bed *$25;* ***double room*** *$79-89;* ***cabin*** *$139-189*
Credit cards *Amex, Diners, MC, Visa*
Reception open *7.30am-7.30pm daily*

Maintenance & cleanliness	★★★½
Facilities	★★★
Atmosphere & character	★★★½
Security	★½
Overall rating	★★★

Club Daintree Koala Beach Resort

This Koala hostel is undergoing extensive renovations and should be re-opened by the time of publication. It has rows of cabins set in a rainforest clearing next to the beach. The dorms are a bit small and uninteresting, but they are all air-conditioned. The bathrooms are being refitted at the moment, so they should be clean and new by the time of your visit and there is a small outdoor kitchen with plenty of cooking supplies plus a barbecue. The main common areas are centred on the nice small swimming pool and the bar with pool tables and heavy wooden furniture. Guests have free use of bikes and body boards. Reception and management are outgoing and friendly and will pick you up from the bus stop and organise trips to Snapper Island, which is very close to the property.

Cape Kimberly Road, Cape Kimberly
☎ *(07) 4090 7500*
Website *www.koalaresort.com.au*
Dorm bed *$25 ($24 VIP);* ***double room*** *$50;* ***cabin*** *$99-120;* ***camping*** *$10-13*
Credit cards *MC, Visa*
Reception open *8am-9pm daily*

Maintenance & cleanliness	★★½
Facilities	★★★★
Atmosphere & character	★★★½
Security	★
Overall rating	★★★

Crocodylus Village YHA

This place is nicely tucked into dense tropical rainforest, with covered pathways leading to large cabins with canvas roofs. The eight-bed dorms are huge with en suite bathrooms, but the four-bed dorms are a bit cramped. All of them are very clean and air-conditioned. There is a small kitchen and a huge covered lounge area with nice couches and a pool table. There is also a great little bar and restaurant and plenty of seating, so there is often a very good atmosphere at night. There is a swimming pool and a barbecue, and staff organise tours in the area. It is quite secluded, a perfect place to relax after a long day.

Buchanan Creek Road, Cow Bay
☎ *(07) 4098 9166*
Website *www.crocodyluscaapetrib.com*
Dorm bed *$24.50 ($22 HI/YHA);* ***double room*** *$80 ($72 HI/YHA)*
Credit card *MC, Visa*
Reception open *6am-10pm daily*

Maintenance & cleanliness	★★★
Facilities	★★★
Atmosphere & character	★★★★
Security	★½
Overall rating	★★★

PK's Jungle Village

This hostel is conveniently located near shops with a pharmacy and store on-site as well. Dorms here are large and simple, each with eight beds. The large swimming pool is popular with guests during the day and there is a volleyball court and barbecue area nearby. It has a livelier atmosphere than the other hostels in Cape Trib with a good restaurant and bar with ample seating, a pool table, games and music. There is also a small communal kitchen, laundry, internet access and reception can book any tours in the area.

Cape Tribulation Road, Cape Tribulation
☎ *(07) 4098 0040 or 1800 232 333*
Website *www.pksjunglevillage.com.au*
Dorm bed *$23;* ***double room*** *$115;* ***triple room*** *$92-120;* ***camping*** *$15 per person*
Credit cards *Amex, JCB, MC, Visa*
Reception open *7.30am-7.30pm daily*

Maintenance & cleanliness	555
Facilities	5556
Atmosphere & character	5555
Security	55
Overall rating	5556

Sights

Cape Tribulation Environment Centre (the Bat House)

This interpretive centre is run by the Australian Tropical Research

Foundation and has informative displays about the rainforest environment.
Cape Tribulation Road, Cape Tribulation
☎ *(07) 4098 0063*
Website *www.austrop.org.au/bat_house.html*
Admission *$2*
Open *11.30am-3.30pm daily*

Daintree Discovery Centre

The Daintree Discovery Centre has displays about the rainforest and an audio-visual theatre but the main feature is the network of elevated boardwalks, aerial walkway and the 23m-high canopy tower.
Corner Cape Tribulation & Tulip Oak Roads, Cow Bay
☎ *(07) 4098 9171*
Website *www.daintree-rec.com.au*
Admission *$28*
Open *8.30am-5pm daily*

Cooktown

Unless you've got a 4WD, Cooktown is as far north as you can get in Queensland and even getting there without one requires some determination; but this lovely historic coastal town is definitely worth the effort. It is relatively isolated, and has very limited services during parts of the wet season, but its charm and frontier feel make it a popular destination for those seeking an authentic experience. The views of the surrounding countryside, ocean and river are stunning from town and the Grassy Hill Lookout, where there is a small, old lighthouse. The James Cook Museum is an inexpensive and fascinating tribute to Captain Cook, and it has an Aboriginal learning centre and accounts of the Palmer River gold rush.

Cooktown has some great fishing, and if you have a 4WD, taking the Bloomfield Track from Cape Tribulation is the best (read: most adventurous) way to go. This is the world's oldest rainforest, and simply cannot be missed. You can take 4WD tours from Cape Trib, or hire a vehicle for a self-guided trip. On this route, be sure to stop in at the Lion's Den Hotel for some food and a beer with the locals.

Practical Information

Cooktown Visitor Information Centre (Nature's PowerHouse)

Finch Bay Road, Cooktown
☎ *1800 174 895*
Website *www.cook.qld.gov.au*
Open *10am-4pm daily*

Coming & Going

Coral Reef Coaches *(☎ (07) 4098 2600; **website** www.coralreefcoaches.com.au)* run between Cairns and Cooktown. The buses take the scenic Bloomfield Track through the Daintree Rainforest calling in at Cape Tribulation and Port Douglas.

If you're driving, this route is recommended for 4WD vehicles only as it involves several river crossings. There is an alternate inland route if you're driving a regular car.

Accommodation

Pam's Place

Pam's Place is a lovely hostel set among tropical gardens with a saltwater swimming pool and a barbeque area with fireplace. It also features a relaxed TV room, pool table and internet access. There is a small bar on-site plus a clean fully-equipped kitchen. The air-conditioned dorms are small but nicely fitted out with good beds and colourful duvets. The management are kind and friendly, and there is a good relaxed atmosphere here. It is a great place to unwind after exploring the area.
9 Boundary Street, Cooktown
☎ *(07) 4069 5166*
Website *www.cooktownhostel.com*
Dorm bed *$28 ($25 HI/YHA);* ***double room*** *$67 ($60 HI/YHA);* ***twin room*** *$67-100 ($60-90 HI/YHA)*
Credit cards *MC, Visa*
Reception open *7am-11pm daily*

Maintenance & cleanliness	★★★
Facilities	★★★★
Atmosphere & character	★★★½
Security	★★★
Overall rating	★★★½

Sights

James Cook Museum

This museum contains artefacts relating to Captain James Cook including

the original anchor and one of the cannons from the *Endeavour*. It also has exhibits on Cooktown's local history.
Corner Furneaux & Helen Streets, Cooktown
(07) 4069 5386
***Admission** $10*
***Open** 9.30am-4pm daily*

Outback Queensland

This is an expansive landscape extending north from the New South Wales-Queensland border to the Burke and Wills Junction on the edge of the Gulf Country, a distance of some 1,600km.

Undara Volcanic National Park

Located around four hours inland from Cairns, this small national park is best known for its extensive lava tube system, which is one of the world's longest.

The park is also home to a wide variety of wildlife and you'll see plenty of birds and the odd kangaroo or wallaby around the lodge.

Accommodation

Undara Wilderness Lodge

Undara Lodge is an extensive complex with a variety of accommodation including budget options such as camping, permanently erected campotel tents and the Wilderness Lodge with small four-bed dorms in prefabricated buildings arranged around a courtyard. The complex is in a natural setting that abounds with wildlife and it features a swimming pool, Internet access and a bar and restaurant set in old railway carriages. At night there are free activities like slide shows and bush poetry.
Savannah Way, via Mt Surprise
(07) 4097 1411
***Website** www.undara.com.au*
***Dorm bed** in Wilderness Lodge $35; **camping** $20-30 for two people*
***Credit cards** MC, Visa*
***Reception open** 7.30am-7pm daily*

Maintenance & cleanliness	★★★½
Facilities	★★
Atmosphere & character	★★
Security	★
Overall rating	★★

Sights

Lava Tubes

The Undara Lava Tubes *((07) 4097 1411; **website** www.undara.com.au)* were formed by a major volcanic eruption around 190,000 years ago. As the top layer of lava cooled, the magma continued to flow below creating the lava tubes. One of the lava flows is over 160km-long.

Entry to the lava tubes is by guided tour with two-hour ($45), four-hour ($80) and full day tours ($125) departing from Undara Lodge.

Hiking

There are several relatively short hiking trails in the national park. These include the **Atkinsons lookout trail** *(3.8km; 1½ hours)* that goes from the Undara Lava Lodge to a large granite slab that offers views to the Granites and Racecourse Hill.

Kalakani Crater rim walk *(2½ km; 1½ hours)* climbs the saddle of the Kalkani Crater and then follows the rim where you can see the lava plains and volcanic vents.

The **Rosella Plains lookout track** *(12km; 6 hours)* starts out following the original telegraph line and then passes through a granite landscape with rosella bushes. If you're short on time – or energy – it is possible to just do the first section of the track (3km; 2 hours).

Charters Towers

Although Charters Towers is less than two hours inland from Townsville and is not really the true outback, this town is the gateway to the outback and you'll pass through here if you're travelling between Townsville and the Northern Territory.

Gold was discovered here in 1871 making it Queensland's second largest city for a brief period. In its heyday in the 1880s, Charters Towers was home to Australia's first stock market. Although it's now only a shadow of its former self, the wealth generated by the gold rush is evident in the city's grand architecture.

Practical Information

Charters Towers Visitor Information Centre

74 Mosman Street, Charters Towers
☎ *(07) 4752 0314*
Website *www.charterstowers.qld.gov.au*
Open *Mon-Fri 8.30am-5pm*

Coming & Going

Charters Towers lies on the bus and train routes between Townsville and Mount Isa. Trains only pass through here twice a week in each direction. Buses are much a much frequent alternative with daily coaches on the Townsville-Tennant Creek run.

The train station is on Enterprise Road on the eastern edge of Charters Towers and Greyhound *(☎ 1300 473 946; **website** www.greyhound.com.au)* buses stop at the Woolworths service station.

Hughenden

This small town is a pleasant enough place to stop on the long drive between Townsville and Mount Isa. A lot of dinosaur fossils have been found in the region between Hughenden and Mount Isa and a Muttaburrasauras skeleton is on display at the dinosaur centre behind the visitor information centre on Gray Street.

Practical Information

Hughenden Visitor Information Centre

37 Gray Street, Hughenden
☎ *(07) 4741 1021*
Website *www.hughenden.com*
Open *9am-5pm daily*

Coming & Going

Hughenden lies on the bus and train routes between Townsville and Mount Isa. Trains only pass through here twice a week in each direction. Buses are much a much frequent alternative with daily coaches on the Townsville-Tennant Creek run.

The train station is on Resolution Street south of the town centre and Greyhound *(☎ 1300 473 946; **website** www.greyhound.com.au)* buses stop at Hughenden Agencies at 49 Brodie Street.

Accommodation

Grand Hotel Backpackers

The Grand Hotel is an old pub with backpackers' accommodation upstairs. It's an old wooden building with lots of character and it also shows plenty of wear and tear although it is kept clean. It has a small TV lounge and a balcony looking over the dinosaur in the main street.

Corner Gray & Stansfield Streets, Hughenden
☎ *(07) 4741 1588*
Dorm bed *$20;* ***double/twin room*** *$35*
Credit cards *MC, Visa*
Reception open *Mon-Fri 10am-late, Sat-Sun 10am-1am*
K

Maintenance & cleanliness	★½
Facilities	★½
Atmosphere & character	★★★
Security	★
Overall rating	★★

Sights

Flinders Discovery Centre

The Flinders Discovery Centre is a small museum adjoining the visitor information centre that has exhibits on dinosaurs found in the region, including fossils and a life-size replica of the Muttaburrasaurus Langdoni. There is also a display on the sheep shearing industry.

37 Gray Street, Hughenden
☎ *(07) 4741 1021*
Website *www.hughenden.com*
Admission *$3.50*
Open *9am-5pm daily*

Richmond

Lying in the heart of Queensland's dinosaur country, Richmond is a good rest stop with an excellent marine fossil museum.

Practical Information
Kronosaurus Korner Information Centre
93 Goldwing Street (Flinders Highway), Richmond
☎ *(07) 4741 3429*
***Website** www.kronosauruskorner.com.au*
***Open** 8.30am-4.45pm daily*

Coming & Going
Richmond is on the main bus and train route linking Townsville with Mount Isa. Trains only pass through here twice a week in each direction, buses are much a much frequent alternative with daily coaches on the Townsville-Tennant Creek run.

The train station is on Middleton Street in the town centre and Greyhound *(☎ 1300 473 946; **website** www.greyhound.com.au)* buses stop at Richmond Agencies at 54 Goldring Street.

Accommodation
Richmond Van Park
This caravan park has backpackers' accommodation in prefabricated units that feature two-bed dorms with made-up beds. It is a clean and well-maintained place but it is not set up in a manner that is conducive to meeting other travellers so it doesn't score well for atmosphere. Facilities are limited to a small kitchen.
109 Goldwing Street, Richmond
☎ *(07) 4741 3772*
***Dorm bed** $20; **double/twin room** $40; **camping** $11-14 per site*
***Credit cards** MC, Visa*

Maintenance & cleanliness	★★★½
Facilities	★★½
Atmosphere & character	½
Security	★
Overall rating	★★

Sights
Richmond Marine Fossil Museum (Kronosaurus Korner)
This excellent little museum has some of the world's best palaeontology artefacts including the Richmond Pliosaur, which many believe to be the best vertebrate fossil found in Australia. Another highlight is a 100 million year old dinosaur with its fossilised skin still intact.
93 Goldwing Street, Richmond
☎ *(07) 4741 3429*
***Website** www.kronosauruskorner.com.au*
***Admission** $12*
***Open** 8.30am-4.45pm daily*

Mount Isa
Miles from anywhere, Mount Isa is the biggest town on the long road between Townsville and the Northern Territory. It is a busy mining town producing copper, lead, silver and zinc and doesn't hold much to entice the traveller to stay. Most backpackers stop for fuel and food and leave as soon as they can.

Practical Information
Mount Isa Visitor Information Centre
19 Marion Street, Mount Isa
☎ *(07) 4749 1555*
***Website** www.riversleigh.qld.gov.au*
***Open** Mon-Fri 9am-4.30pm, Sat-Sun 9am-noon*

Coming & Going
Mount Isa is on the Barkly Highway, which connects Townsville with the Northern Territory and it lies at the terminus of the train line from Townsville.

Greyhound *(☎ 1300 473 946; **website** www.greyhound.com.au)* buses stop at the Outback at Isa Centre on Marian Street. The train station is located on Station Street in Miles End, west of the city centre.

Accommodation
Traveller's Haven
This hostel has a dated feel with cracked lino floors, old curtains and creaky bunk beds. Although facilities are minimal, it does have a swimming pool in addition to the usual TV lounge, kitchen and Internet access.
Corner Pamela & Spence Streets, Mount Isa
☎ *(07) 4743 0313*
***Website** http://users.bigpond.net.au/travellershaven/*
***Dorm bed** $25; **single room** $40; **double/twin room** $60*

Credit cards *MC, Visa*
Reception open *6am-7pm*

Maintenance & cleanliness	★★
Facilities	★★★½
Atmosphere & character	★
Security	★½
Overall rating	★★

Sights

Mount Isa Underground Hospital & Museum

Following the WWII bombing of Darwin Hospital, a bomb-proof underground hospital was constructed in Mount Isa. The hospital has now been opened as a museum.
Joan Street, Mount Isa
(07) 4749 0281
Admission *$10*
Open *Apr-Sep 10am-2pm daily*

OUTBACK AT ISA

This tourist complex is comprised of the Isa Experience Gallery, the Hard Times Mine and the Riversleigh Fossil Centre. A combined entry ticket for all attractions in the complex costs $55 and combined entry to the Isa Experience Gallery and Riversleigh Fossil Centre is $18.

Hard Times Mine

This mine was never actually an underground mine, but was built specificially for underground mine tours after Mount Isa Mines stopped offering their underground tours. However it is an authentic mine experience as visitors kit themselves out in overalls, boots and a hardhat and descend via the Alimak Cage to the base of the mine where you can see the mine equipement and work the mine drill.
19 Marian Street, Mount Isa
(07) 4749 1555 or 1300 659 660
Website *www.outbackatisa.com.au*
Admission *$45*
Open *8.30am-5pm*

Isa Experience Gallery

This interesting museum has exhibits about Mount Isa with a focus on the mining industry and the city's history.
19 Marian Street, Mount Isa
(07) 4749 1555 or 1300 659 660
Website *www.outbackatisa.com.au*
Admission *$10*
Open *8.30am-5pm daily*

Riversleigh Fossil Centre

The museum focuses on the world heritage Riversleigh fossil sites just north of Mount Isa and features a huge replica fossil studded limestone outcrop, a simulated tropical rainforest recreating the Miocene period of 25 million years ago and many other displays.
19 Marian Street, Mount Isa
(07) 4749 1555 or 1300 659 660
Website *www.outbackatisa.com.au*
Admission *$10*
Open *Mon-Fri 9am-4.30pm, Sat-Sun 9am-noon*

Longreach

This small outback town is considered the major town in central Queensland and it has a couple of impressive attractions considering its diminutive population.

Longreach was the original home of Queensland and Northern Territory Aerial Service (now known as Qantas), and the company was headquartered here until 1930.

Practical Information

Longreach Visitor Information Centre

Corner Duck & Eagle Streets, Longreach
(07) 4658 3555
Website *www.longreach.qld.gov.au*
Open *Mon-Fri 8.30am-5pm, Sat-Sun 9am-noon*

Coming & Going

Greyhound (*1300 473 946;* ***website*** *www.greyhound.com.au*) buses connect Longreach to Brisbane, Mount Isa and Rockhampton and stop at the Outback Travel Centre at 115 Eagle Street.

The train station on Landsborough Highway serves the twice-weekly *Spirit of the Outback* service to Rockhampton.

Accommodation

Royal Hotel

This pub in the town centre offers cheap accommodation in small rooms upstairs. Facilities are a little run down

and are limited to an old TV. It's not really a real hostel and most accommodation is in single and double rooms.
111 Eagle Street, Longreach
☎ *(07) 4658 2118*
Single room *$25-55;* ***double room*** *$40-70*
Reception open *Mon-Thu 10am-11pm, Fri-Sat 10am-2am, Sun 10am-11pm*
TV L

Maintenance & cleanliness	★½
Facilities	★
Atmosphere & character	★★★
Security	★
Overall rating	★½

Sights

Qantas Founders Outback Museum

Aviation buffs and plane spotters will love this museum at Longreach Airport, which is home to the original Qantas hangar as well as a replica of the first Qantas aircraft. The museum is the only place in the world where you can take a tour of a fully equipped Boeing 747.
Hudson Fysh Drive, Longreach Airport
☎ *(07) 4658 3737*
Website *www.qfom.com.au*
Admission *$19 ($10 students); 747 tour $19 ($10 students); ultimate tour including museum admission & all tours including 707, 747 & wing walk $115*
Open *9am-5pm daily*

Stockman's Hall of Fame

Outback Queensland's biggest and best attraction is an outstanding museum dedicated to the pioneers of the early outback. It is well worth the visit – some people even go as far as saying that this museum alone is worth the trip to Longreach.
Landsborough Highway, Longreach
☎ *(07) 4658 2166*
Website *www.outbackheritage.com.au*
Admission *$22.50 ($12 students)*
Open *9am-5pm daily*

Winton

This small town is best known as the place where Banjo Patterson wrote the ballad *Waltzing Matilda*, which was first performed at the North Gregory Hotel on 6 April 1895. Along with Longreach, Winton claims to be the home of Qantas (the airline's first flight was between the two towns).

Practical Information

Winton Tourist Information Centre

50 Elderslie Street, Winton
☎ *(07) 4657 1886 or 1300 665 115*
Website *www.experiencewinton.com.au*
Open *Jan-Feb 8.30am-4pm daily; Mar-Nov 8.30am-5pm daily; Dec 8.30am-4pm daily*

Coming & Going

Greyhound *(☎ 1300 473 946;* ***website*** *www.greyhound.com.au)* buses go to Brisbane, Mount Isa and Rockhampton and stop at Waltzing Matilda Centre on Elderslie Street.

Accommodation

North Gregory Hotel

The North Gregory Hotel is a pub in the town centre with good quality backpackers' accommodation upstairs and more basic accommodation in an annex out the back. The rooms are nice and clean with comfortable beds but the décor looks dated and shared facilities are limited to the bar downstairs.
67 Elderslie Street, Winton
☎ *1800 801 611*
Dorm bed *$22;* ***single room*** *$44;* ***double/twin room*** *$55-65*
Credit cards *Amex, MC, Visa*
Reception open *8am-10pm*

Maintenance & cleanliness	★★★
Facilities	★½
Atmosphere & character	★★
Security	★½
Overall rating	★★½

Sights

Waltzing Matilda Centre

The Waltzing Matilda Centre has displays about the history and lifestyle of Winton including exhibits on Qantas and outback art. However the centre's main focus is the origin of the famous song, *Waltzing Matilda*.
50 Elderslie Street, Winton
☎ *(07) 4657 1886*
Website *www.matildacentre.com.au*
Admission *$19*
Open *9am-5pm daily*

Queensland

South Australia

South Australia is known for its food, wine and festivals but the great beaches and awesome stretches of outback are the main drawcard for backpackers.

South Australia differs from other Australian states in several respects. It was colonised by free settlers without the use of convicts. Many early settlers were religious non-conformists and South Australia has led Australia in social and political reform. It was the first state to grant votes to women, first to appoint an Aboriginal governor and first to appoint a woman governor.

Known as the wine state, South Australia produces more than 70 per cent of Australia's wine, which rivals the world's best. There are more than 50 wineries in the Barossa Valley alone and many visitors make a day trip to the

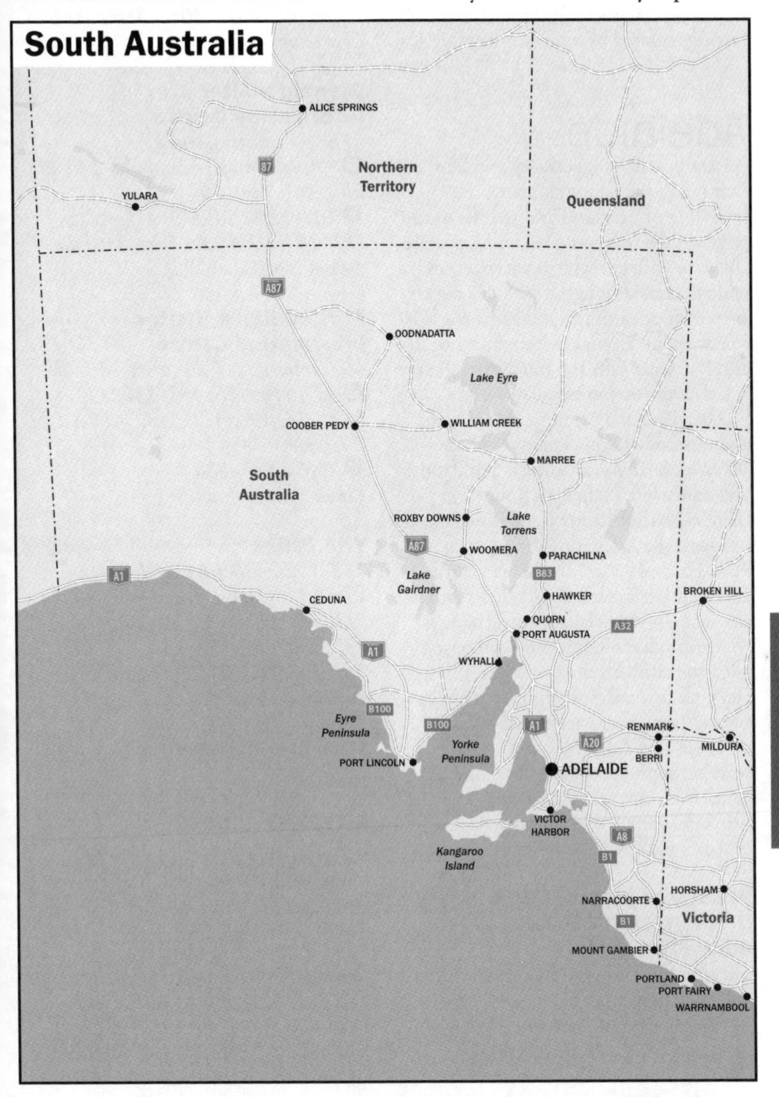

> **Must do in South Australia**
>
> - Visit Adelaide
> - Look for kangaroos on Kangaroo Island
> - Taste wine in the Barossa Valley and Coonawarra wine regions
> - Hike in Wilpena Pound in the Flinders Ranges National Park
> - Sleep in an underground hostel in Coober Pedy

Barossa to take advantage of the free tastings offered by many of the wineries.

Adelaide

Australia's fifth biggest city and South Australia's state-capital is surrounded by 850ha of parkland and thanks to the city founder's master plan it's a very likeable city with gardens, open space and wide roads. Although it's a fairly big city with over one million residents, the logical street layout makes it easily navigable and it doesn't take too much time before it feels like you know the place.

Adelaide has a vibrant cultural scene and it is known for its many festivals. WOMAdelaide is an annual world music and dance festival held in Botanic Park, there's also the bi-annual Adelaide Festival of Ideas, the Adelaide Film Festival, the Feast Festival – a gay and lesbian cultural event, and there's the big and internationally renowned Adelaide Festival of Arts.

Although seldom visited compared with the cities on the east coast, it is a city that is worth spending the time to get to know. Backpackers are drawn to "Awesome Adelaide" and the city's student population gives Adelaide a youthful feel and a lively eating and drinking scene. Adelaide also has some of Australia's best city beaches.

Practical Information

INFORMATION CENTRES

Adelaide Greeters

Local volunteers give free three to four-hour orientations of their city, answering any questions that you may have. Advance bookings are essential.
☎ *(08) 8267 5840*
Website *www.adelaidegreeters.asn.au*
Open *9am-5pm daily*

South Australian Information Centre

18 King William Street, Adelaide
🚌 *F40, 200, 210, 211, 212, 213, 214, 215, 216, 217, T217, 218, T219, 296, 297, 719, 720, 721, T721, 722, T722, 723, 724, 725, 727F* 🚋 *Rundle Mall*
🚆 *Adelaide*
☎ *(08) 8303 2201 or 1300 655 276*
Website *www.southaustralia.com*
Open *Mon-Fri 8.30am-5pm, Sat-Sun 9am-2pm*

Glenelg Visitor Information Centre

Moseley Square, Glenelg
🚋 *Glenelg Mosely Square* 🚌 *190, 260, 264, 265, 600, 601*
☎ *(08) 8294 5833*
Open *Mon-Fri 9am-5pm, Sat-Sun 10am-3pm*

Port Adelaide Visitor Information Centre

66 Commercial Road, Port Adelaide
🚌 *117, 118, 136, 153, 230, 232, 252, 254, 333, 352, 353, 361* 🚆 *Port Adelaide*
☎ *(08) 8447 4788*
Open *9am-5pm daily*

YHA Office

135 Waymouth Street, Adelaide
🚌 *J1, J2, J3, 99C City Loop, 110, 111, 113, 115, 117, 118, 130, 131, 132, 133, 135, 136, 137, 138, 139, 167, 168, 231, 235, 237, 238, 239*
☎ *(08) 8414 3000*
Website *www.yha.com.au*
Open *Mon-Fri 9am-6pm, Sat 10am-1pm*

INTERNET ACCESS

If you're travelling with a notebook computer you're in luck as Adelaide has Australia's best wireless internet access. Free wireless hotspots throughout the city are operated by **Internode** (***website*** *https://hotspot.internode.on.net*) and include hot zones on Rundel Mall, O'Connell Street, Hutt Street; a hotspot at Terminal 1 of Adelaide Airport and at and branches of **Cibo**

Espresso *(**website** www.ciboespresso.com.au).*

You can also access the internet at most hostels.

Coming & Going

Adelaide is well connected by road and rail to the rest of the country and most travellers heading to the outback will pass through the city.

AIR

Adelaide Airport *(**website** www.aal.com.au)* is located between the city centre and West Beach. The airport has frequent flights to most Australian destinations including Alice Springs, Melbourne, Perth and Sydney and also handles some international flights.

Many hostels in Adelaide offer free pick up from the airport but it is best to phone ahead to book first. The Jetbus is the cheapest way to travel between the airport and the city centre. The trip costs just $4.10 ($2.50 off peak) and you can use Adelaide Metro Multitrip and Daytrip tickets on Jetbus services. A more expensive option is the Skylink airport shuttle bus *(☎ (08) 8332 2644; **website** www.skylinkadelaide.com)*, which costs $8 and runs between the airport terminals and the city centre with a stop at the Keswick Rail Terminal.

If you're arriving on a late flight you'll need to take a taxi into town, which will cost around $15.

BUS

The Adelaide Central Bus Station is located at 85 Franklin Street and is close to several backpackers hostels.

Premier Stateliner *(☎ (08) 8415 5555; **website** www.premierstateliner.com.au)*and several other smaller companies run to destinations within South Australia, Firefly *(☎ 1300 730 740; **website** www.fireflyexpress.com.au)* go to Melbourne and Sydney and Greyhound *(☎ 1300 473 946; **website** www.greyhound.com.au)* go to Melbourne, Sydney and across the outback to Alice Springs.

There are quite a few travel agencies in the area around the Adelaide Central Bus Station that sell discounted tickets and travel passes.

TRAIN

Train service is pretty good out of Adelaide with trains to Alice Springs, Broken Hill, Darwin, Melbourne, Perth and Sydney. Trains terminate at the Keswick Interstate Rail Terminal about 2km southwest of the city centre.

Both the *Ghan* to Alice Springs and Darwin and the *Indian Pacific* to Perth are rated as Australia's top train journeys. Although you're really just looking at desert for hours on end, it is a much more comfortable option than the bus. The train is usually more expensive than travelling by bus, but the discounts offered by flashing your HI/YHA or VIP card make this a travel option worth considering. Check the budget travel agents around Franklin Street for the best deal.

HITCHHIKING

Hitching out of Adelaide isn't too bad and you can sometimes get lucky with long rides, especially if you're heading north or west.

If you're heading to Melbourne it is best to wait for a lift on Glen Osmond Road before it joins the South Eastern Freeway. Take bus 100, 230F, 840, T840, 841F, 861, 863, T863 or 864 and get off at the intersection of Cross Road and Glen Osmond Road. The area on Mount Barker Road to the east of the intersection of Cross, Glen Osmond and Portrush Roads is a good spot to try your luck. Use a sign because this road gets a lot of local traffic to the Adelaide Hills.

Main North Road between Elizabeth and Gawler is your best bet for lifts to the fruit picking spots on the Murray River as well as rides to Broken Hill and Sydney. Take the train to Munno Para or Kudla station and walk about five minutes to Main North Road to wait for a lift. This road gets some local traffic to the Barossa Valley and splits into two roads shortly after the turn off for Gawler so you'll need to use a sign indicating either your destination or the road you want to travel along. The Barrier Highway (route 32) goes to Sydney via Broken Hill. The Sturt Highway (route 20) goes via the fruit picking areas near the Murray and Murrumbidgee Rivers and joins up with the Hume Highway near Wagga Wagga where you can continue on to Sydney.

You may be lucky enough to get some really long lifts if you're heading north towards Coober Pedy, Alice Springs and Darwin or west towards Perth. For all directions north and west you'll need to get a lift north along the Princes Highway towards Port Augusta. At Port Augusta the road splits into two, the Eyre Highway (route 1) to Perth and the Stuart Highway (route 87) north to Alice Springs and Darwin. To leave Adelaide in this direction, you'll need to get a northbound lift on the Princes Highway (route 1), also known as Port Wakefield Road. Take buses 222 or 224 past the intersection where the road splits into Main North Road (route 20) and Port Wakefield Road (route 1), bus 222 terminates at this intersection and bus 224 continues along Port Wakefield Road. Get off the bus on Port Wakefield Road and find a safe place to wait for a lift.

Be careful not to confuse the Sturt and Stuart Highways if you're hitching with a sign showing the name of the road you want to travel on.

Local Transport

Adelaide has a good public transport network comprising trains, trams and buses. It is an affordable way to get around particularly if you buy a day pass or take advantage of the free bus and tram services in Glenelg and the city centre.

The different modes of transport use the same ticketing system that is organised by Adelaide Metro *(☎ (08) 8210 1000; **website** www.adelaidemetro.com.au)* who also run an extremely helpful information centre on King William Street near the corner with Currie Street. The Adelaide Metro information centre sells travel passes and has route maps and timetables for all train and bus routes. Pop in to pick up a free copy of The Metro Guide, this handy booklet explains the whole system and has maps of all bus routes. This is especially handy as the bus and train routes are superimposed upon a map showing all the streets in the metropolitan area – it's good enough to use as a street directory.

TRAM

Adelaide has only one tram route, but it's a handy option for travellers as it connects the city centre with the beach at Glenelg. The tram is free between North and South Terrace in the city centre.

TRAIN

The suburban train network is the quickest way to get out to the suburbs. Most backpackers don't use the train to get around Adelaide as it generally doesn't go to the places that backpackers need to go to, but it is a good way to get to the Keswick interstate train station and historic Port Adelaide.

BUS

Like most cities, the bus routes fill the gaps where there are no trains or trams. The bus is a good way to get to the airport and some beaches and there are also routes to the good hitchhiking spots and a service to McLaren Vale.

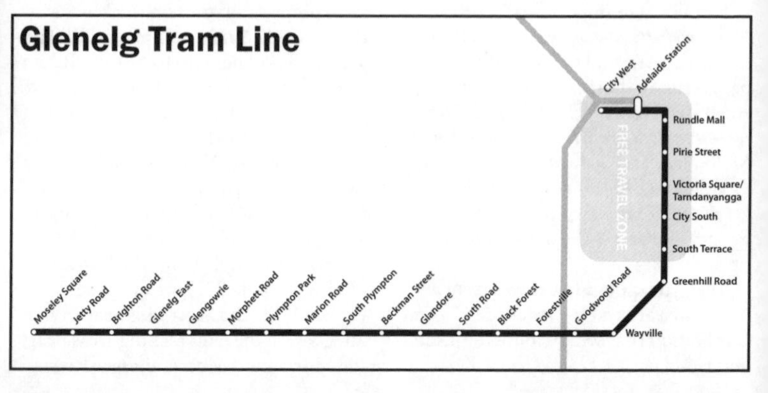

Glenelg Tram Line

Buses are also a good way of getting around in the city centre. With a day pass you should be able to hop on any bus to get a lift around the city although there are also two free bus services for those without a day pass. The free City Loop bus (route 99C) runs around the city centre calling at the Central Bus Station, Victoria Square, Hindmarsh Square, North Terrace and Light Square.

Adelaide's unique O-Bahn is one of the world's longest guided bus ways. Basically these are just regular buses in the city centre (they stop on Grenfell Street between King William and Pulteney Streets) that join a guided track outside the city centre. O-Bahn services run about every five minutes, and are a quick way to get between the city centre and the suburban shopping centre/bus interchange at Tea Tree Plaza.

FARES & TICKETS

The same fare structure applies on buses, trams and trains, and metro-tickets are valid on all modes of transport.

There are three main types of tickets: Singletrip, Daytrip and Multitrip.

A Singletrip ticket is your best option if you're planning on making only one journey during a day or if you're making your return trip within two hours. You're better off with a Daytrip ticket if you are making a return journey on the same day. There are a couple of different Singletrip tickets available depending on the distance you are travelling and whether you are travelling during a peak or off-peak period. Generally a Zone ticket means that you can go anywhere in Adelaide, transferring between buses, trains and the tram taking up to two hours to complete your trip. A two-section ticket is a little cheaper but is restricted to shorter trips of around three kilometres.

Most travellers find the Daytrip ticket the best value. It allows unlimited travel on the tram, trains and buses during an entire day. Daytrip tickets cost $7.70.

Multitrip tickets are a good idea if you're planning on staying in Adelaide for a few days. These tickets are good for ten trips.

You are required to validate your ticket each time you board a bus, tram or train.

All tickets are available at train stations, post offices and convenience stores and only Daytrip and Singletrip tickets can be bought on board buses and trams.

Ticket	Zone	Time	Cost
Singletrip	Zone	All times	$4.10
Singletrip	Zone	Interpeak	$2.50
Singletrip	2-section	All times	$2.40
Singletrip	2-section	Interpeak	$1.60
Multitrip	Zone	All times	$26.90
Multitrip	Zone	Interpeak	$14.80
Multitrip	2-section	All times	$14.60
Multitrip	2-section	Interpeak	$11.30

Accommodation

Adelaide Backpackers Inn

Adelaide Backpackers Inn need a bit of work to bring it up to scratch, but the guests seem happy and the atmosphere is good. Facilities include a TV room, internet access and a decent kitchen, but there isn't a laundry. The guests are served free apple pie every night.

112 Carrington Street, Adelaide

190, 191, 192, 194, 196, 198, 199, 230, 232, 863, T863, 864F

(08) 8223 6635 or 1800 247 725

***Website** www.adelaidebackpackersinn.net.au*

***Dorm bed** $24; price includes breakfast*

***Credit cards** MC, Visa*

***Reception open** 6am-7.30pm daily*

TV K

Maintenance & cleanliness	★★½
Facilities	★½
Atmosphere & character	★★★½
Security	★½
Overall rating	★★½

Adelaide Central YHA

This huge youth hostel has high standards and the building is bright and modern. With 240 beds it might feel impersonal and corporate, but it is clean and well maintained with very good facilities. The spacious common area is bright has good comfortable couches and there is a pool table, table tennis, table football and board games available plus two TV lounges and a

South Australia

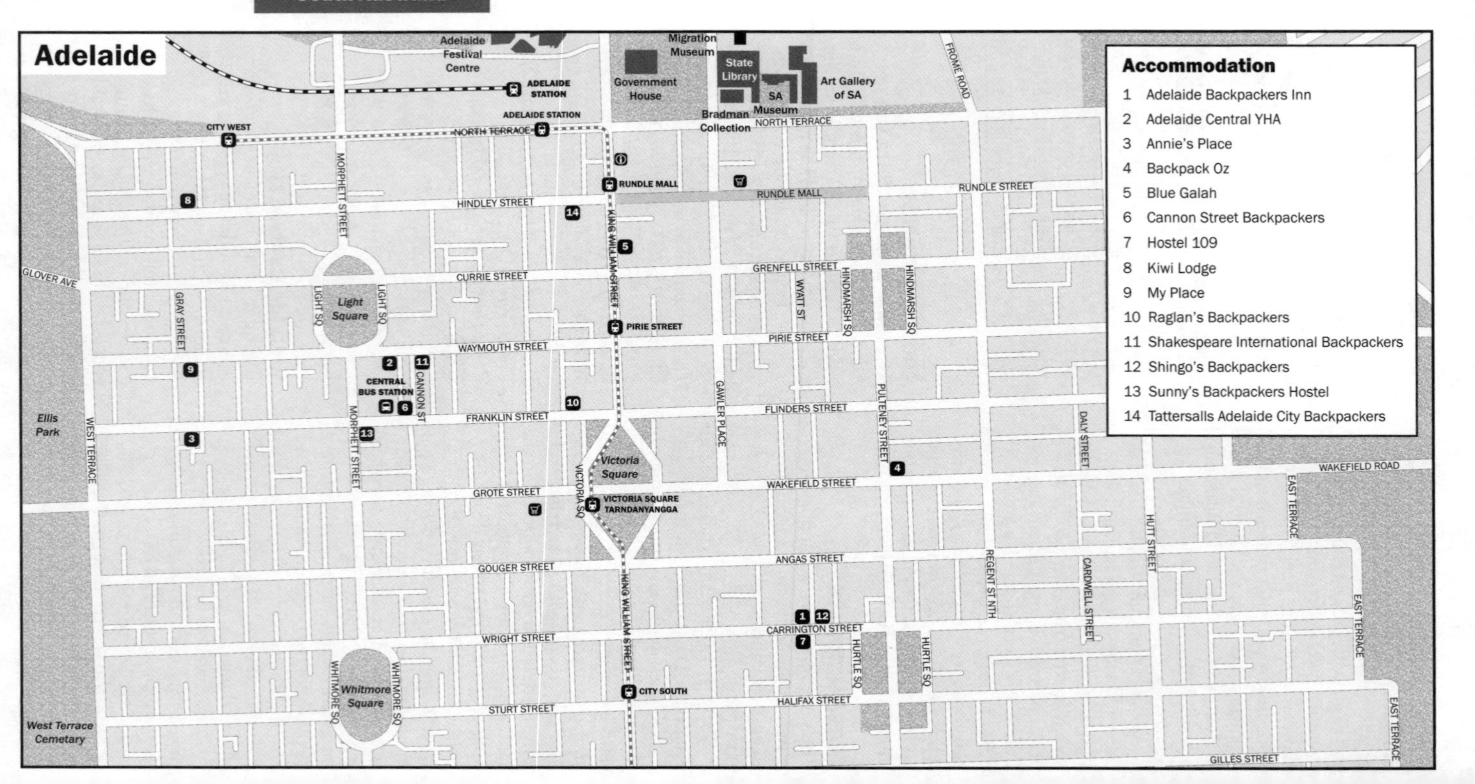
Adelaide
Accommodation
1 Adelaide Backpackers Inn
2 Adelaide Central YHA
3 Annie's Place
4 Backpack Oz
5 Blue Galah
6 Cannon Street Backpackers
7 Hostel 109
8 Kiwi Lodge
9 My Place
10 Raglan's Backpackers
11 Shakespeare International Backpackers
12 Shingo's Backpackers
13 Sunny's Backpackers Hostel
14 Tattersalls Adelaide City Backpackers
Adelaide Festival Centre
ADELAIDE STATION
Government House
Migration Museum
State Library
SA Museum
Art Gallery of SA
Bradman Collection
CITY WEST
ADELAIDE STATION
RUNDLE MALL
PIRIE STREET
VICTORIA SQUARE TARNDANYANGGA
CITY SOUTH
CENTRAL BUS STATION
Light Square
Victoria Square
Whitmore Square
Ellis Park
West Terrace Cemetery
NORTH TERRACE
HINDLEY STREET
RUNDLE MALL
RUNDLE STREET
CURRIE STREET
GRENFELL STREET
WAYMOUTH STREET
PIRIE STREET
FRANKLIN STREET
FLINDERS STREET
GROTE STREET
WAKEFIELD STREET
GOUGER STREET
ANGAS STREET
WRIGHT STREET
CARRINGTON STREET
STURT STREET
HALIFAX STREET
GILLES STREET
KING WILLIAM STREET
MORPHETT STREET
GAWLER PLACE
PULTENEY STREET
HINDMARSH SQ
WYATT ST
REGENT ST NTH
HURTLE SQ
DALY STREET
CARDWELL STREET
HUTT STREET
EAST TERRACE
WAKEFIELD ROAD
FROME ROAD
WEST TERRACE
GLOVER AVE
GRAY STREET
CANNON ST
LIGHT SQ
VICTORIA SQ
WHITMORE SQ

quiet reading room. There is a large kitchen with free tea, coffee and rice and a free pancake breakfast is served every Tuesday and Friday morning.
135 Waymouth Street, Adelaide
J1, J2, J3, 99C City Loop, 110, 111, 113, 115, 117, 118, 130, 131, 132, 133, 135, 136, 137, 138, 139, 167, 168, 231, 235, 237, 238, 239
(08) 8414 3010
***Website** www.yha.com.au*
***Dorm bed** $24-28.50 ($21.50-25.20 HI/YHA); **double/twin room** $75 ($67.50 HI/YHA)*
***Credit cards** Amex, JCB, MC, Visa*
***Reception open** 7am-11pm daily; check-in 24 hours*

Maintenance & cleanliness	★★★★★
Facilities	★★½
Atmosphere & character	★★★½
Security	★★★½
Overall rating	★★★★

Annie's Place

Annie's Place is a charming 140-year-old building with tall ceilings and lots of character. The entrance is impressive with warm colours and a huge chandelier in the hallway gives the hostel a bit of charisma. There are plenty of other kitschy odds and sods around the hostel such as the sculpture in the courtyard and even a porn room (a double room with the walls tastefully covered in nude photos). The eclectic décor works surprisingly well making Annie's Place stand apart from other more sterile hostels. It has the usual facilities such as a good kitchen, laundry and barbecue area but there is no TV lounge as there are televisions in all the rooms instead, which detracts from the otherwise excellent atmosphere. Guests get free breakfast and a free evening meal.
239 Franklin Street, Adelaide
M44, G44, 250, 251, 252, 253, 254
(08) 8212 2668
***Website** www.anniesplace.com.au*
***Dorm bed** $23-25 ($22-24 HI/YHA, VIP); **double/twin room** $65-75; prices include breakfast & an evening meal*
***Credit cards** MC, Visa*
***Reception open** 8am-noon & 4pm-9pm daily*

Maintenance & cleanliness	★★★½
Facilities	★★
Atmosphere & character	★★★½
Security	★
Overall rating	★★★

Backpack Oz

Backpack Oz is a clean and well maintained hostel with a good atmosphere. The dorms have good mattresses plus shelves to hang and arrange your clothes. There is a well equipped kitchen plus internet access (including free Wi-Fi) and a good TV lounge with a selection of videos. The staff cook up a free barbecue meal every Wednesday.
144 Wakefield Street, Adelaide
99C City Loop, 170, 171, 172, 173, 174, 175, 177, 178, 179
(08) 8223 3551 or 1800 633 307
***Website** www.backpackoz.com.au*
***Dorm bed** $22-25; **single room** $50-65; **double/twin room** $60-75; prices include breakfast*
***Credit cards** MC, Visa*
***Reception open** 6am-10pm daily; late check-in by prior arrangement*

Maintenance & cleanliness	★★★½
Facilities	★★½
Atmosphere & character	★★★
Security	★½
Overall rating	★★★

Blue Galah

This centrally located hostel is clean and well-maintained. It has a lively atmosphere and the dorms are air-conditioned and have good quality inner-spring mattresses. The hostel's facilities include a laundry, a good kitchen, internet access and a TV lounge plus a bar.
1st floor, 62 King William Street, Adelaide
Rundle Mall F40, 170, 171, 172, 173, 190, 191, 192, 194, 196, 198, 199, 210, 211, 212, 213, 214, 215, 216, 217, T217, 218, T219, 296, 297
(08) 8231 9295 or 1800 555 322
***Website** www.bluegalah.com.au*
***Dorm bed** $26 ($24 HI/YHA, ISIC, VIP); **single room** $66; **twin room** $66; prices include breakfast*
***Credit cards** MC, Visa*
***Reception open** 7am-11pm daily*

Maintenance & cleanliness	★★★½
Facilities	★★½
Atmosphere & character	★★★
Security	★★
Overall rating	★★★

Cannon Street Backpackers

Cannon Street Backpackers has a lot of space and it feels a bit like they don't really know how to fill it. The hostel is air-conditioned and has all the usual facilities including laundry, internet access (including Wi-Fi), a kitchen and a games room with table tennis and pool tables. The hostel also has a bar. The staff serve free apple pie every night.

11 Cannon Street, Adelaide
99C City Loop, 830F, 840F, T840, 841F
(08) 8410 1218 or 1800 804 133
***Website** www.cannonst.com.au*
***Dorm bed** $19-22; **single room** $52; **double/twin room** $59; prices include breakfast*
***Credit cards** MC, Visa*
***Reception open** Mon-Fri 7am-8.30pm, Sat-Sun 7am-1.30pm & 3.30pm-8.30pm*

Maintenance & cleanliness	★★★
Facilities	★★
Atmosphere & character	★★½
Security	★
Overall rating	★★½

Glenelg Beach Hostel

This big backpackers' hostel is in a clean and well-maintained row of terrace houses with good facilities and a lively atmosphere. It has the usual laundry, kitchen and Internet access, in addition to a pool table, table football and a good TV lounge. In the basement there's a good bar/nightclub, which makes Glenelg Beach Hostel an obvious party place. The dorms are clean and the beds have good quality mattresses.

1-7 Moseley Street, Glenelg
Glenelg Mosely Square 190, 260, 264, 265, 600, 601
(08) 8376 0007 or 1800 066 422
***Website** www.glenelgbeachhostel.com.au*
***Dorm bed** $25; **single room** $50; **double room** $70*
***Credit cards** MC, Visa*
***Reception open** 7am-11pm daily*

Maintenance & cleanliness	★★★★
Facilities	★★½
Atmosphere & character	★★★★½
Security	★½
Overall rating	★★★½

Hostel 109

Hostel 109 is a small, comfortable and perfectly clean hostel with good facilities and bright common areas. The neat and tidy small dormitories have good inner-spring mattresses, the kitchen is equipped with all the necessary utensils and the TV lounge is comfortable. There is a separate work-space with a desk and a couple of computers with free internet access (including Wi-Fi). The hostel's atmosphere is relaxed and mature.

109 Carrington Street, Adelaide
190, 191, 192, 194, 196, 198, 199, 230, 232, 861, 863, T863, 864F
(08) 8223 1771 or 1800 099 318
***Website** www.hostel109.com*
***Dorm bed** $25; **single room** $55; **double room** $70; **twin room** $60*
***Credit cards** MC, Visa*
***Reception open** 8am-noon & 3pm-9pm daily*

Maintenance & cleanliness	★★★★★
Facilities	★★½
Atmosphere & character	★★★★
Security	★★
Overall rating	★★★★

Kiwi Lodge

Kiwi Lodge is a dreary little hostel adjoining an old motel on Hindley Street. The accommodation here is gloomy with old furniture that should have been retired years ago; however it is clean and a few freshly painted walls tell us that the hostel might last a few more years. Most of the usual facilities are here, including a poorly equipped kitchen, a laundry and a crappy old television. There isn't any internet access and character and atmosphere are sadly lacking as well.

262 Hindley Street, Adelaide
City West 99C City Loop

(08) 8231 9524
***Dorm bed** $22; **single room** $55; **double room** $55; **twin room** $60; prices include breakfast*
***Credit cards** MC, Visa*
***Reception open** Mon-Fri 7.30am-10pm, Sat-Sun 8.30am-10pm*
TV K L

Maintenance & cleanliness	★★½
Facilities	★½
Atmosphere & character	★½
Security	★
Overall rating	★★

My Place

My Place is a good hostel with the usual laundry, Internet access, kitchen and TV room. The dorms are air conditioned and equipped with good beds and mattresses and the house is clean and well-maintained. The range of facilities isn't amazing, but it's a comfortable place to stay, and the atmosphere isn't bad. The showers aren't sex segregated, but they have lockable doors so privacy is not a problem.
257 Waymouth Street, Adelaide
J1, J2, J3, 110, 111, 113, 115, 117, 118, 115, 117, 118, 130, 131, 132, 133, 135, 136, 137, 138, 139, 167, 168
(08) 8221 5299
***Website** www.adelaidehostel.com.au*
***Dorm bed** $22 ($22 HI/YHA, VIP)*
***Credit cards** MC, Visa*
***Reception open** 8am-8pm*
TV K L

Maintenance & cleanliness	★★★★
Facilities	★★
Atmosphere & character	★★★
Security	★★½
Overall rating	★★★

Raglan's Backpackers

This is basically a bar that happens to have some accommodation upstairs and it doesn't really feel like a hostel. The bar is well maintained and has pool tables, internet access and a big screen television, but the rooms upstairs aren't as nice, nor have they many facilities. The small kitchen is awful, but the dorms have good bunk beds and there are a few lockers available. The social atmosphere upstairs is not good and the building doesn't have a lot of character, but the bar is just down the stairs.
2 Franklin Street, Adelaide
Pirie Street F40, M44, 174, 175, 177, 178, 179, 181, 182, 222, 224, 225, 226, 228, 229, 291
(08) 8231 4703
***Dorm bed** $18-22; **single room** $50; **double/twin room** $60*
***Credit cards** MC, Visa*
***Reception open** 6am-11pm daily*
TV K

Maintenance & cleanliness	★★½
Facilities	★
Atmosphere & character	★★
Security	★
Overall rating	★★

Shakespeare International Backpackers

This is a nice friendly hostel with a good atmosphere. Facilities include is a laundry, a kitchen, a good TV lounge with a big screen and internet access (including Wi-Fi). The hostel is popular with travellers and is just a short walk to the bus terminal.
123 Waymouth Street, Adelaide
J1, J2, J3, 99C City Loop, 110, 111, 113, 115, 117, 118, 130, 131, 132, 133, 135, 136, 137, 138, 139, 167, 168, 231, 235, 237, 238, 239
(08) 8231 7655 or 1800 556 889
***Website** www.shakeys.com.au*
***Dorm bed** $26 ($24 HI/YHA, ISIC, VIP); **single room** $66; **double/twin room** $66*
***Credit cards** Amex, Diners, MC, Visa*
***Reception open** 6am-10.30pm daily*
TV K L

Maintenance & cleanliness	★★★½
Facilities	★★
Atmosphere & character	★★★★
Security	★½
Overall rating	★★★

Shingo's Backpackers

Shingo's is a fairly small hostel that is popular with Asian travellers. This place is shabby and a bit dirty, but it is a popular place to stay with an excellent laid-back atmosphere. With Adelaide's lowest prices, this hostel is great value if you can put up with the mess.
118 Carrington Street, Adelaide
190, 191, 192, 194, 196, 198, 199, 230, 232, 861, 863, T863, 864F

(08) 8232 3234
Website *www.shingosbackpackers.com.au*
Dorm bed *$16*
Reception open *7am-9pm daily*

Maintenance & cleanliness	★★
Facilities	★★½
Atmosphere & character	★★★★
Security	★
Overall rating	★★

Sunny's Backpackers Hostel

Sunny's is a small 52-bed hostel with a lively atmosphere and the usual facilities. The kitchen is badly maintained and the building feels shabby, but the cleanliness is kept at an acceptable level and the laid-back vibe is a bonus. The TV lounge is OK and there's a sunny barbecue area at the front of the hostel. The manager is helpful and friendly.

139 Franklin Street, Adelaide
99C City Loop, 830F, 840F, T840, 841F
(08) 8231 2430 or 1800 225 725
Website *www.sunnys.com.au*
Dorm bed *$22 ($20 HI/YHA, ISIC, VIP);* ***twin room*** *$55 ($50 HI/YHA, ISIC, VIP); prices include breakfast*
Credit cards *Amex, Diners, JCB, MC, Visa*
Reception open *Mon-Fri 7am-8pm, Sat-Sun 7am-noon & 5pm-8pm*

Maintenance & cleanliness	★★★½
Facilities	★★½
Atmosphere & character	★★★★½
Security	★
Overall rating	★★★½

Tattersalls Adelaide City Backpackers

Tattersalls Backpackers has a brilliant location right in the centre of Adelaide. Unfortunately the hostel is drab and lifeless. However it is relatively clean and it has all the usual hostel facilities including a fully-equipped kitchen, laundry, internet access and a barbecue.

17 Hindley Street, Adelaide
Rundle Mall *F40, M44, 174, 175, 177, 178, 179, 205, 206, 207, 208, 209, 230, 232, 250, 251, 252, 253, 254, 291*
(08) 8231 3225 or 1800 133 355
Dorm bed *$20;* ***double room*** *$64; prices include breakfast*
Credit cards *Amex, Diners, MC, Visa*
Reception open *9am-6pm daily*

Maintenance & cleanliness	★★★½
Facilities	★★½
Atmosphere & character	★★
Security	★
Overall rating	★★

Eating & Drinking

There are plenty of good eateries in Adelaide and you don't have to blow the budget as there is a good choice of cheap and decent-priced places to eat.

Rundle Street is an obvious place for restaurants as it boasts over 50 eating outlets although there are several other streets that offer a more eclectic choice. Gouger Street and Hutt Street have a great range of international restaurants with Asian food more prevalent on Gouger Street and European food on Hutt Street. Melbourne Street in North Adelaide is another good street that is lined with affordable restaurants. If you're staying in Glenelg, then Jetty Road is the local restaurant strip.

Adelaide even has its own budget-priced culinary speciality – the pie floater. You can't leave Adelaide without trying this delicious meat pie floating in pea soup and topped with tomato sauce. It tastes much better than it sounds! You can try a pie floater from the pie carts located either outside the train station on North Terrace or outside the post office near the corner of Franklin and King William Streets. This is a good option for a late-night feed, generally pie carts open from the afternoon through to the wee hours of the morning.

If you're preparing your own food, the **Coles** supermarket *(21-39 Grote Street, Adelaide)* near Victoria Square and **Woolworths** *(80-88 Rundle Mall, Adelaide)* are your best options in the city centre. **Adelaide Central Market** *(corner Gouger & Grote Streets, Adelaide)* is a good place to stock up on fresh food or grab a snack.

Drinking in Adelaide is fun and easy, as the "City of Churches" definitely has more watering holes than churches and the pubs are generally much better than you would find in most other Australian cities.

After numerous research trips to Adelaide, our favourite pub is the **Coopers Ale House**, aka the Earl of Aberdeen *(corner of Carrington & Pulteney Streets, Adelaide)*. It's a traditional pub with great atmosphere and food. But don't limit yourself to our favourite as there are a lot of good pubs in Adelaide.

Other bars include **Cargo Club** *(213 Hindley Street, Adelaide)*, which is a cheap place that's popular with students; the **Botanic Bar** *(310 North Terrace, Adelaide)*, a hip lounge bar that attracts an older crowd and the **Garage** *(163 Waymouth Street, Adelaide)*, which is a good place if you're up for dancing. It has a big dance floor and loud tunes roll through the night.

Sights

Adelaide Botanic Gardens

Adelaide's city centre is completely surrounded by parkland including the beautiful Botanic Gardens at the north east of the city. The gardens make a great picnic spot and also features the Palm House, a huge conservatory that recreates a tropical rainforest.

Botanic Road, Adelaide
99C City Loop, 102, 104, 105, 106, 107X, 281, 283, 521
(08) 8222 9311
Website *www.botanicgardens.sa.gov.au*
Admission *free*
Gardens open *Jan 7.15am-7pm; Feb-Mar 7.15am-6.30pm; Apr 7.15am-6pm; May 7.15am-5.30pm; Jun-Jul 7.15am-5pm; Aug 7.15am-5.30pm; Sep 7.15am-6pm; Oct-Nov 7.15am-6.30pm; Dec 7.15am-7pm;* ***Palm House open*** *10am-4pm daily*

Adelaide Gaol

It seems that every Australian City has a prison turned into a museum and Adelaide is no exception. The gaol was operated as a prison as recently as 1988 and was the scene of 49 hangings.

18 Gaol Road, Thebarton
110, 111, 113, 115, 117, 118, 150, 153, 155, 156, 157, 231
(08) 8231 4062
Website *www.adelaidegaol.org.au*
Admission *$8.50*
Open *Mon-Fri 11am-3.30pm, Sun 11am-3.30pm*

Adelaide Zoo

Adelaide's zoo is home to around 1500 animals including an excellent South-East Asian Rainforest exhibit.

Frome Road, Adelaide
235, 237, 238, 239, 271, 273
(08) 8267 3255
Website *www.adelaidezoo.com.au*
Admission *$20*
Open *9.30am-5pm daily*

Art Gallery of South Australia

The Art Gallery of South Australia has a good collection of Australian and European paintings, although it is not quite up there with the galleries in Canberra or Melbourne.

North Terrace, Adelaide
Adelaide Station *99C City Loop, 241, 242, 245, 248* *Adelaide*
(08) 8207 7000
Website *www.artgallery.sa.gov.au*
Admission *free, charge for special exhibitions*
Open *10am-5pm daily*

The Bradman Collection

This exhibition features a collection of cricketing memorabilia dating from 1929 to 1977. Sir Donald Bradman donated most of the collection to the State Library.

State Library of South Australia, Corner Kintore Avenue & North Terrace, Adelaide
Adelaide Station, Rundle Mall
F40, M44, 99C City Loop, 174, 175, 177, 178, 179, 241, 242, 245, 248, 291 *Adelaide*
(08) 8207 7595 or 1800 182 013
Website *www.bradman.sa.com.au*
Admission *free*
Open *Mon-Thu 9.30am-6pm, Fri 9.30am-10pm, Sat-Sun noon-5pm*

Festival Centre

Adelaide's answer to the Sydney Opera House is the Festival Centre, which is the city's major landmark and occupies a lovely riverside setting.

North Terrace, Adelaide

Adelaide Station, Rundle Mall
99C City Loop, 181, 182, 222, 224, 225, 226, 228, 229, 230, 232, 250, 251, 252, 253, 254 *Adelaide*

Maritime Museum

Adelaide's Maritime Museum features several old ships and a lighthouse as well as the usual nautical exhibits.
126 Lipson Street, Port Adelaide
Port Adelaide *136, 153, 230, 232, 252, 254, 353, 361*
(08) 8207 6255
Website *www.history.sa.gov.au/maritime/maritime.htm*
Admission *$8.50*
Open *10am-5pm daily*

Migration Museum

This is a fascinating museum about people who have migrated and settled in South Australia.
82 Kintore Avenue, Adelaide
Adelaide Station, Rundle Mall
F40, M44, 99C City Loop, 174, 175, 177, 178, 179, 241, 242, 245, 248, 291 *Adelaide*
(08) 8207 7580
Website *www.history.sa.gov.au/migration/migration.htm*
Admission *free*
Open *Mon-Fri 10am-5pm, Sat-Sun 1pm-5pm*

South Australian Museum

Adelaide's big museum features all the usual exhibits – rocks, Aboriginal artefacts, an Egyptian mummy and a whale skeleton.
North Terrace, Adelaide
Adelaide Station, Rundle Mall
F40, M44, 99C City Loop, 174, 175, 177, 178, 179, 241, 242, 245, 248, 291 *Adelaide*
(08) 8207 7500
Website *www.samuseum.sa.gov.au*
Admission *free*
Open *10am-5pm daily*

Adelaide Hills

Only around half an hour from central Adelaide, the Adelaide Hills is a pleasant area full of quaint towns with antique and craft shops, country pubs and day-trippers from Adelaide. It is a nice spot to visit particularly as a detour if you're coming to or from the city, and also as an extension to a day-trip in the Barossa Valley.

Practical Information

Adelaide Hills Visitor Information Centre

41 Main Street, Hahndorf
(08) 8388 1185
Website *www.visitadelaidehills.com.au*
Open *Mon-Fri 9am-5pm, Sat-Sun 10am-4pm*

Birdwood

This small town is best known for its excellent car museum. If you're not into cars, it's still a nice spot to stop for a drink or two.

Sights

National Motor Museum

This museum provides a good overview of Australian motoring history with over 300 cars, motorcycles and commercial vehicles. The National Motor Museum also features relics from South Australia's colonial past and interpretive exhibits in the recently opened Holden Pavillion of Australian Motoring.
Shannon Street, Birdwood
(08) 8568 5006
Website *www.history.sa.gov.au/motor/motor.htm*
Admission *$9 ($7 students)*
Open *9am-5pm daily*

Hahndorf

Probably the most popular destination in the Adelaide Hills, Hahndorf is an easy exit off the South Eastern Freeway if you're driving between Adelaide and Melbourne. The town was settled by German immigrants in 1839 and retains a strong German heritage with German themed pubs and Mettwurst shops.

Sights

The Cedars

The home of Hahndorf painter, Hans Heysen, has been restored featuring

the artist's studio. You can only visit by taking a guided tour of the house.
Heysen Road, Hahndorf
☎ *(08) 8388 7277*
***Admission** $10*
***Open** Tue-Sun 10am-4.30pm*

Hahndorf Academy

The largest regional art gallery in South Australia is noted for its exhibits of work by former Hahndorf resident Hans Heysen and also includes a museum that reveals the contribution that German migrants have made to South Australia while explaining what life was like for the region's first German settlers.
Main Street, Hahndorf
☎ *(08) 8388 7250*
***Admission** free*
***Open** 10am-5pm daily*

Barossa Valley

The Barossa is one of Australia's major wine-producing areas with 45 wineries producing about a quarter of Australia's total vintage.

The valley is easy to explore: just 30km long by 14 km wide. The centre of the Barossa is the area bounded by the valley's three main towns, Angaston, Nurioopta and Tanunda; although it extends further south towards Lyndoch.

Tanunda is the cultural heart of the Barossa and it is perhaps the most centrally located of the towns in the Barossa and is home to some good pubs and camping grounds. Most of the Barossa is situated within easy cycling distance from Tanunda.

North of Tanunda, Nurioopta is the more modern commercial centre of the valley while Angaston, 6km east of Nurioopta, retains a more historic ambience.

Practical Information

Barossa Visitor Information Centre

66 Murray Street, Tanunda
☎ *1800 812 662*
***Website** www.barossa-region.org*
***Open** Mon-Fri 9am-5pm, Sat-Sun 10am-4pm*

Coming & Going

The Barossa Valley is close enough to Adelaide to make an easy day-trip. If you're driving follow the Sturt Highway and take the Nurioopta turn-off. However a car won't be much use if you want to indulge in wine tasting when you get there and you may decide to travel to the Barossa by bus or to take a day tour.

Barossa Valley Coaches *(☎ (08) 8564 3022; **website** www.bvcoach.com)* operates an infrequent bus service connecting Angaston, Lyndoch, Nurioopta and Tanunda with Adelaide. The bus departs from the central bus station at Franklin Street in Adelaide. A one-way ticket costs around $11.90 between Adelaide and Tanunda.

Alternatively, you may choose to take a tour starting in Adelaide. There is a good choice of day tours as well as a few that allow you to stay over at a hostel in the Barossa and rejoin the return leg a day or two later.

Oz Experience buses visit the Barossa Valley on their Adelaide to Alice Springs route.

Another option is the day tour offered by Groovy Grape Getaways *(☎ 1800 66 11 77; **website** www.groovygrape.com.au)*. For $75 Groovy Grape's trips take in a few wineries and include a barbecue lunch. Tours run seven days a week and depart Glenelg at 7.15am with pickups in Adelaide city centre at 7.45am.

Local Transport

Although driving is usually the best way to get around rural areas like the Barossa, it's not a good idea since you're not going to appreciate it without stopping for a drink or three – especially since the local police are extremely vigilant when it comes to drink driving.

A better idea is to rent a bicycle from one of the bicycle rental companies in Tanunda. The valley is small enough to make cycling the most enjoyable way to get around. Bike About *(☎ 0413 525 733; **website** www.bikeabout.com.au)* hire bikes from Novotel Barossa Valley Resort *(Golf Links Road, Rowland Flat)* and Barossa Secrets *(91 Murray Street,*

Tanunda). Bikes cost $18.50 for half a day and $30 for a full day.

Eating & Drinking

Sampling the region's wine is the main reason to visit the Barossa. The best way to do this is to rent a bicycle and cycle from one winery to the next, stopping for a picnic lunch en route. You can pick up picnic supplies at the supermarkets at any of the towns in the valley and many of the wineries have picnic areas where you can enjoy their wine.

If you prefer beer to wine, both Angaston and Tanunda have excellent pubs.

Sights

The main attraction in the Barossa Valley is visiting the many wineries. There are also some nice vantage points to see the local scenery.

Mengler Hill Lookout

Although Mengler Hill Lookout is not a huge must-see attraction, this lookout, located east of Tanunda offers sweeping views of the Barossa Valley. It's a pretty steep hill and a hard ride if you're cycling so you really need your own car to get here however many of the day tours to the Barossa also visit this lookout.
Mengler Hill Road, near Tanunda
Admission free

Fleurieu Peninsula

Situated less than an hour south of Adelaide, the Fleurieu Peninsula encompasses the McLaren Vale vineyards and the seaside resort towns of Cape Jervis and Victor Harbor.

The Fleurieu Peninsula makes either a pleasant detour or a day-trip from Adelaide.

Cape Jervis

Most travellers see Cape Jervis as the departure point for the ferry to Kangaroo Island although the small town is also a popular weekend destination for people from Adelaide.

Coming & Going

Cape Jervis is connected to Adelaide by an infrequent bus. There are only two daily coach services between Adelaide and Cape Jervis that cost $20 each way. They depart Adelaide at 6.45am and 3.45pm and return from Cape Jervis at 9.40am and 8.30pm. This is run by Sealink (☎ *13 13 01; **website** www.sealink.com.au)* and it connects with Sealink's ferry to Kangaroo Island. See the Kangaroo Island section for more information about the ferry between Cape Jervis and Penneshaw.

Accommodation

Cape Jervis Station

Cape Jervis Station offers a wide range of accommodation ranging from 4½ star luxury to backpackers' cabins. Backpackers stay in the Shearer's Quarters, which is a two room stone building with a veranda and a small kitchen. Although there are extensive facilities, these are mostly reserved for guests staying in the more upmarket accommodation. It's about 3km from the town centre.
Main Road, Cape Jervis
☎ *(08) 8598 0288*
***Website** www.capejervisstation.com.au*
***Dorm bed** $20; **camping** $14-17 for two people*
***Credit cards** Amex, JCB, MC, Visa*
***Reception open** 7.30am-9pm daily*

Maintenance & cleanliness	★★
Facilities	★★½
Atmosphere & character	★★½
Security	½
Overall rating	★★½

McLaren Vale

After the Barossa Valley and Coonawarra, this is one of South Australia's main wine producing regions. There are more than 45 wineries in McLaren Vale including Andrew Garret Wines, Hardy's and Wirra Wirra. It is a good place to stop over en route from Adelaide to either Victor Harbor or Kangaroo Island.

Practical Information

McLaren Vale & Fleurieu Visitor Information Centre

Main Road, McLaren Vale
☎ *(08) 8323 9944*
Website *www.mclarenvale.info*
Open *10am-5pm daily*

Coming & Going

With only three daily buses to McLaren Vale from Adelaide and infrequent transportation within the region, driving is the easiest way to get around, but whoever is driving will have to keep off the booze since the police often operate random breath tests in wine tasting regions.

Coming from Adelaide, follow Main South Road until you see signs to McLaren Vale.

Victor Harbor

Victor Harbor is a popular weekend destination for people from Adelaide. It is a nice town with plenty of old colonial architecture and good pubs and fish and chip shops. The main attraction here is whale and penguin watching although there are plenty of other attractions ranging from camel rides on the beach to vintage horse-drawn tram rides across the causeway to Granite Island.

The American spelling of Victor Harbor (and the Adelaide suburb of Outer Harbor) is a result of a spelling mistake made by an early surveyor general of South Australia.

Practical Information

Victor Harbor Visitor Information Centre

Causeway, Esplanade, Victor Harbor
☎ *(08) 8552 5738*
Website *www.tourismvictorharbor.com.au*
Open *9am-5pm daily*

INTERNET ACCESS

There is internet access at the Visitor Information Centre and at the library *(1 Bay Road, Victor Harbor).*

Coming & Going

Premier Stateliner *(☎ (08) 8415 5555; **website** www.premierstateliner.com.au)* runs two daily coach services between Adelaide's central bus station and Victor Harbor.

Every Sunday steam trains run between Victor Harbour, Port Elliot and Goolwa.

Accommodation

Grosvenor Hotel

The Grosvenor Hotel features backpackers' accommodation above a pub. It is a beautiful old building with balconies overlooking the main street and the place is well maintained, but the facilities are fairly basic and comprise a TV lounge and fridge, but no kitchen.
40 Ocean Street, Victor Harbor
☎ *(08) 8552 1011*
Website *www.grosvenorvictor.com.au*
Dorm bed *$35;* ***single room*** *$35;* ***double room*** *$70; prices include breakfast*
Credit cards *Amex, Diners, MC, Visa*
Reception open *8am-5pm daily*

Maintenance & cleanliness	★★★½
Facilities	★½
Atmosphere & character	★★½
Security	★★½
Overall rating	★★½

Sights

Granite Island & Penguin Watching

The main attraction here is the penguin watching every night although the island is also a nice excursion during the day as well. Access is by either a horse-drawn tram ($7 return) or a short walk across the causeway.
Granite Island, Victor Harbor
☎ *(08) 8552 7555*
Website *www.graniteisland.com.au*
Guided penguin spotting walks *$12.50*
Penguin spotting walks depart from the island side of the causeway every night at dusk

South Australian Whale Centre

This is the place to come to find out all about marine mammals and get further information on whale watching.
2 Railway Terrace, Victor Harbor
☎ *(08) 8552 5644*
Website *www.sawhalecentre.com*

***Admission** $7*
***Open** 11am-4.30pm daily*

Kangaroo Island

Kangaroo Island southwest of Adelaide is Australia's third biggest island, after Melville Island and Tasmania. At its closest point the mainland is 16km away and the short sea-ride is definitely worth the trip as Kangaroo Island is a marvellous haven for native flora and fauna, and it's renowned for its unspoilt natural environment. Kangaroos, koalas and other wildlife such as birds are abundant all over the island and there are several wilderness protection areas. The island has approximately 150,000 visitors every year, but with its 4,500km² it is big enough to host them all without getting crowded.

A day trip is a good opportunity to see kangaroos, wallabies, emus, goannas, echidna and koalas in their natural habitat and you can also see sea lions on the beaches, but the ferry is expensive so it's a good idea to spend at least one night on the island so you get more for your money, besides in one day it's impossible to see even half of what the island has to offer.

Kangaroo Island is a wilderness refuge with a fascinating past. It was discovered in 1802 by English sea captain Matthew Flinders, who never travelled without his cat, Trim. Flinders and Trim found Kangaroo Island uninhabited, but stone tools since discovered indicate people lived there about 10,000 years ago. The fate of the original inhabitants remains a mystery.

The main towns on the island are American River, Kingscote and Penneshaw.

Coming & Going

Kangaroo Island is easily accessible by air and sea, but it is an expensive island to get to. It is 30 minutes by air from Adelaide and ferries sail there from Cape Jervis on the Fleurieu Peninsula.

Rex *(☎ 13 17 13; **website** www.rex.com.au)* operate frequent flights between Adelaide and Kangaroo Island. Flights arrive at Kingscote Airport near Cygnet River, about 14km from Kingscote.

Kangaroo Island Sealink *(☎ 13 13 01; **website** www.sealink.com.au)* operates several ferries per day between Cape Jervis and Penneshaw on Kangaroo Island. The return fare is $40 per person and $121 for a car.

Campwild Adventures *(☎ 1800 444 321; **website** www.campwild.com.au)*, operate two and three-day trips departing from Adelaide. Campwild's two-day trip costs $335 and their three-day 4WD trip costs $415.

Surf & Sun Safaris *(☎ 1800 786 386; **website** www.surfnsun.com.au)* run two and three-day 4WD adventures to Kangaroo Island. Two-day trips cost $370 ($340 HI/YHA, VIP) and three-day trips cost $440 ($399 HI/YHA, VIP).

Local Transport

KI Coach Service, operated by Sealink *(☎ 13 13 01; **website** www.sealink.com.au)*, links Penneshaw, American River and Kingscote, the three main towns on Kangaroo Island. Unfortunately there are only two services a day, but they do connect with the ferry. The return fare between Penneshaw and Kingscote is $28.

Renting a car is the best way to explore the island, particularly since the main attractions are away from the towns. Although expensive for a single traveller, renting a car becomes more affordable when the cost is split between several people. Rental car companies on Kangaroo Island include Budget *(☎ (08) 8553 3133; **website** www.budget.com.au)* and Hertz *(☎ (08) 8553 2390; **website** www.hertz.com.au)*.

Kingscote

Kingscote is Kangaroo Island's largest town and also South Australia's oldest European settlement. It has the tourist infrastructure of cafés and restaurants and it's a good base for further island-exploration, but the town itself isn't anything special. After its establishment in 1836 it was suggested that Kingscote could be the state capital of South Australia, but because of the island's insufficient resources Adelaide was considered a better alternative. There are only about 1500 residents in Kingscote, but it is the main centre on the island, and you'll need to come here if you need an ATM or supermarket.

Practical Information

National Parks & Wildlife Office

39 Dauncey Street, Kingscote
☎ *(08) 8553 2381*
Website *www.parks.sa.gov.au*
Open *Mon-Fri 9am-5pm*

Accommodation

Kangaroo Island Central Hostel

Kangaroo Island Central Hostel is in a clean and tidy house with a kitchen, a decent television room and good dorms with made-up beds. There's an outdoor barbecue area and the main common area indoors is a quiet and cosy place with a fireplace and comfy seats. The atmosphere might be a bit dull, although it's not bad either. In addition to the dorms there's a neat cabin available, it feels a bit like a tiny one-room flat and it's geared up with a fridge, microwave and a kettle.
19 Murray Street, Kingscote
☎ *(08) 8553 2787*
Dorm bed *$25;* ***single/double/twin room*** *$60;* ***cabin*** *$65*

Maintenance & cleanliness	★★★★
Facilities	★★½
Atmosphere & character	★★★
Security	★
Overall rating	★★★

Sights

Hope Cottage Museum

This small museum is housed in one of the three original cottages built in 1856. Its exhibits include a collection of farm machinery plus displays relating to local history.
Centenary Avenue, Kingscote
☎ *(08) 8553 2656*
Website *www.nationaltrustsa.org.au/properties/kingscote_hope_cottage.htm*
Admission *$5*
Open *Jan 10am-4pm daily; Feb-Jul 1pm-4pm daily; Aug Sat 1pm-4pm; Sep-Dec 1pm-4pm daily*

Kangaroo Island Marine Centre

This small aquarium is home to a variety of South Australian marine life, but the main attraction is tours to the nearby penguin colony.
The Wharf, Kingscote
☎ *(08) 8553 3112*
Website *www.kimarinecentre.com.au*
Open *Jan 8.15pm; Feb-Mar 9pm; Apr-Oct 7pm; Nov 8pm; Dec 8.15pm*
Tours *Jan 8.45pm, 9.45pm; Feb-Mar 8.30pm, 9.30pm; Apr-Oct 7.30pm, 8.30pm; Nov 8.30pm, 9.30pm; Dec 8.45pm, 9.45pm*

Penneshaw

Penneshaw is the tiny port town where you'll arrive if you take the ferry from Cape Jervis. The main attraction in Penneshaw is the penguin colony where you can watch the little penguin (sometimes called fairy penguins or blue penguins) waddle ashore every night at dusk. There are tours organised from Penneshaw if you want to check it out.

Practical Information

Kangaroo Island Gateway Visitor Information Centre

Howard Drive, Penneshaw
☎ *(08) 8553 1185*
Website *www.tourkangarooisland.com.au*
Open *Mon-Fri 9am-5pm, Sat-Sun 10am-4pm*

Accommodation

Kangaroo Island YHA

The island's only YHA hostel is clean and the nice outdoor area has a great view out to sea. Hammocks are hanging from the trees and the house has a relaxing atmosphere. Facilities include internet access, a TV room, laundry, kitchen and a barbecue. The dorms are usually gender segregated and most of the rooms have en suite bathrooms. The beds have good mattresses.
33 Middle Terrace, Penneshaw
☎ *(08) 8553 1344*
Website *www.yha.com.au*
Dorm bed *$28.50 ($25.50 HI/YHA);* ***double/twin room*** *$100 ($90 HI/YHA)*

***Credit cards** MC, Visa*
***Reception open** 9am-1pm & 5.30pm-7.45pm; late check in by prior arrangement*

Maintenance & cleanliness	★★★½
Facilities	★★
Atmosphere & character	★★★
Security	★★
Overall rating	★★★

Parndana

Parndana is 40km away from Kingscote. The tiny town was established shortly after World War II as returning soldiers and their families almost doubled Kangaroo Island's population.

Sights

Parndana Wildlife Park

The Parndana Wildlife Park is the only attraction in the area but it's a good one. The park features the islands largest collection of birds such as black cockatoos, eagles, kookaburras and curlews, and you might come across kangaroos, koala bears, bettongs, potoroos and other native wildlife.
Playford Highway, Parndana
(08) 8559 6050
***Website** www.parndanawildlifepark.com*
***Admission** $9*
***Open** 9am-5pm daily*

Seal Bay

A large colony of sea lions live at Seal Bay, and this makes it a protected area that is also very popular tourist destination.

If you want to walk out to see the amazing sea lions, you will need to take an organised tour, which costs $13.50.

Flinders Chase National Park

Wildlife is the main reason to visit Kangaroo Island, and Flinders Chase National Park is where you have the best chance of seeing it. The park is situated at the western end of the island with Rocky River as its small commercial centre. Among other creatures, the national park is home to echidnas, kangaroos, koalas, pelicans, platypus and wallabies.

The park also features the natural phenomenon called Remarkable Rocks, which are huge stones bizarrely shaped by nature, sometimes resembling works of modern and abstract sculpture.

The park management organise a number of tours which include beach, cave and light station tours. A 12-month Kangaroo Island Parks Pass is available for $42 and allows access to the park in addition to tours of Seal Bay Beach, Kelly Hill Show Cave and Cape Borda and Cape Willoughby Light stations. An Island Parks Caving Pass is also available for $45, which gives you all the benefits of the Island Parks Pass plus an adventure caving tour.

Entry to the park is $8 per person.

Practical Information

Flinders Chase Visitor Centre

Rocky River, Flinders Chase National Park
(08) 8559 7235
***Website** www.parks.sa.gov.au/flinderschase*
***Open** 9am-5pm daily*

Accommodation

Flinders Chase Farm Accommodation

This remote hostel is a great place to stay if you're looking for a peaceful retreat. Located out in the bush, Flinders Chase Farm offers spotless accommodation in well-kept dorms and all the usual facilities are in place. Although the rural location gives the house some character the atmosphere is really a hit or miss, as it can be perhaps a bit too quiet as there's often lots of space but not many other guests.
West End Highway, Kangaroo Island
(08) 8559 7223
***Dorm bed** $25-35; **double room** $60-100*

Maintenance & cleanliness	★★★★½
Facilities	★★
Atmosphere & character	★★★★
Security	★½
Overall rating	★★★½

Hanson Bay Sanctuary Homestead

Out in the bush and close to koalas in their natural environment, the Hanson Bay Sanctuary Homestead is a secluded place to stay. Cleanliness and maintenance are good, the single dorm beds (no bunks) are made-up and equipped with inner-spring mattresses and there are the usual kitchen and laundry facilities. There's a tiny television in the main common area and the kitchen. The atmosphere is quiet and perhaps a bit dull, as the big place can feel empty.

South Coast Road, Kangaroo Island (5km west from Kelly Hill Caves)
☎ *(08) 8559 7344*
Website *www.hansonbay.com.au*
Dorm bed *$30*

Maintenance & cleanliness	★★★★
Facilities	★★½
Atmosphere & character	★★★
Security	★
Overall rating	★★★

Eyre Peninsula

The Eyre Peninsula has some great surf beaches and good fishing and is a pleasant detour en route between Adelaide and Perth, and when you're driving to the west coast an extra 300km shouldn't make too much difference.

Although rarely visited by backpackers, this region on the edge of the Nullarbor Plain has a lot to offer the travellers including spectacular white sand dunes, wildlife as well as whale watching and exceptional fishing.

Whyalla

South Australia's third-largest city is an industrial town that is not really worth the detour. Whyalla's main attraction is the OneSteel Whyalla Steelworks, which dominates the town.

Practical Information

Whyalla Visitor Information Centre

Lincoln Highway, Whyalla
☎ *(08) 8645 7900 or 1800 088 589*
Website *www.whyalla.com*
Open *Mon-Fri 9am-5pm, Sat 9am-4pm, Sun 10am-4pm*

Sights

OneSteel Whyalla Steelworks

OneSteel Whyalla Steelworks is the city's largest employer and visitors can take tours of the steel-making plant. This is Australia's longest-running steelworks tour. Tours depart from the Tourist Information Centre on Lincoln Highway.

☎ *(08) 8645 7900 or 1800 088 589*
Tours cost *$18*
Tours depart *Mon, Wed, Fri 9.30am*

Whyalla Maritime Museum

This maritime museum features the *HMAS Whyalla*, Australia's largest permanently landlocked ship, which was the first ship to be built at the Whyalla shipyards. The museum has exhibits of the city's ship building industry and the WWII warships that were constructed here.

Lincoln Highway, Whyalla
☎ *(08) 8645 8900*
Website *www.maritime.org/hnsa-whyalla.htm*
Admission *$8*
Ship tours *Jan-Mar 11am, noon, 1pm, 2pm, 3pm; Apr-Oct 10am, 11am, noon, 1pm, 2pm; Nov-Dec 11am, noon, 1pm, 2pm, 3pm*

Port Lincoln

Port Lincoln is a busy fishing port on Boston Bay, the world's second-largest natural harbour.

Commercial fishing is the main industry with a big tuna exporting business that has made the town very wealthy. Port Lincoln is a popular destination for amateur anglers from Adelaide and some backpackers visit for the opportunity to swim with sea lions and tuna.

Practical Information

Port Lincoln Visitor Information Centre

3 Adelaide Place, Port Lincoln
☎ *(08) 8683 3544 or 1300 788 378*
Website *www.visitportlincoln.net*
Open 9am-5pm daily

Coming & Going

AIR

Rex (☎ *13 17 13; **website** www.rex.com.au)* flies to Port Lincoln from Adelaide. The flight takes 45 minutes and is the best option if you're travelling on a Rex backpacker air travel pass. The airport is around 10km north of Port Lincoln.

BUS

Premier Stateliner *(☎ (08) 8682 1288; **website** www.premierstateliner.com.au)* buses go to Adelaide via Whyalla and Port Augusta. Buses stop at 24 Lewis Street.

Sights & Activities

Axel Stenross Maritime Museum

This maritime museum is in the boat building workshop established by the Finnish boat builder, Axel Stenross. It features nautical exhibits with an emphasis on windjammer sailing boats.
97 Lincoln Highway, Port Lincoln
☎ *(08) 8682 2963*
***Admission** $5*
***Open** Tue & Thu 9.30am-4.30pm, Sat 1pm-4.30pm, Sun 9.30am-4.30pm*

Swimming with Sealions & Tuna

Adventure Bay Charters *(☎ 0488 428 862 (0488 I C TUNA); **website** www.adventurebaycharters.com.au)* run unique tours that give you the opportunity to swim with sealions and tuna. The tuna tours involve a 15-minute cruise to a tuna farm where you can feed the tuna from a purpose-built pontoon and also swim with the fish. Don't be fooled by those tiny cans in the supermarket, tuna really are big fish! Tuna tours cost $55.

Sealion tours involve a 1½ hour cruise to Hopkins Island where you can swim with sealions. On the way back the tour stops at the tuna farm where you can swim with the tuna. Sealion tours cost $160.

Both tours depart from the jetty at the Marina Hotel.

Port Kenny & Venus Bay

Port Kenny lies on Venus Bay and the little town that was established at the start of the 19th century gets its economic input from agriculture and tourism. The town is quite dull and there's little to do, but the surrounding waters have some good spots for fishing and Venus Bay is nearby.

However Venus Bay isn't gigantic either, with a population of only around 500 people, but it's a popular base for surfers heading for the beaches. Venus Bay can get crowded during the peak season and there's not much infrastructure in town, just a few eateries, a surf shop and a caravan park. The backpacker accommodation is very good though, a few kilometres away from Port Kenny and Venus Bay at Coodlie Park.

Accommodation

Coodlie Park YHA

This charming hostel is the perfect place if you need a break from the big city as it is a long way from chaotic traffic and huge shopping malls. Coodlie Park has clean rooms with good beds and limited facilities that include a tiny telly, two kitchens (one good and the other not so good) and a barbecue, but the staff are very friendly and they'll ensure you have a good time. The manager also runs a tour agency so there's plenty to do during the day.
Flinders Highway, Port Kenny
☎ *(08) 8687 0411*
***Website** www.yha.com.au*
***Dorm bed** $26-28 ($23-25 HI/YHA); **double room** $87 ($78 HI/YHA); **twin room** $56 ($50 HI/YHA)*
***Credit cards** MC, Visa*
***Reception open** 8am-8pm*
TV K

Maintenance & cleanliness	★★★★
Facilities	★
Atmosphere & character	★★★★½
Security	★
Overall rating	★★★

Ceduna

Ceduna is the last real town before the long boring drive across the Nullarbor Plain to Western Australia. There's not a lot to do in town, although the surrounding area is spectacular. Ceduna is a good place to stock up on supplies before the long journey.

South Australia

Practical Information

Ceduna Gateway Tourist Centre

58 Poynton Street, Ceduna
☎ *(08) 8625 2780 or 1800 639 413*
Website *www.cedunatourism.com.au*
Open *Mon-Fri 9am-5.30pm, Sat-Sun 9am-5pm*

Coming & Going

Most people who visit Ceduna come here because they are driving across the Nullarbor. However you can fly here or take the bus if you really want to visit.

AIR

Rex (☎ *13 17 13;* ***website*** *www.rex.com.au)* flies to Ceduna from Adelaide. The airport is just a couple of kilometres outside town.

BUS

Premier Stateliner (☎ *(08) 8682 1288;* ***website*** *www.premierstateliner.com.au)* buses go to Adelaide via Port Augusta.

Riverland

South Australia's Riverland region doesn't offer as many attractions as the area around the Murray across the border in Victoria, but it is a popular spot for many travellers who come here to pick up fruit picking work.

Renmark

The oldest town in the Riverland region has a lovely riverfront and it is one of the more interesting places in the area. The town is a popular spot for cruises and houseboat rentals and is home to the *PS Industry*, a wood-fired paddle steamer that operates cruises on the river on the first Sunday of each month.

Practical Information

Renmark Paringa Visitor Information Centre

84 Murray Avenue, Renmark
☎ *(08) 8586 6704*
Website *www.riverland.info*
Open *Mon-Fri 9am-5pm, Sat 9am-4pm, Sun 10am-4pm*

Coming & Going

Premier Stateliner (☎ *(08) 8415 5555;* ***website*** *www.premierstateliner.com.au)* coaches run between Adelaide and Renmark. Premier Stateliner buses leave from the tourist information centre at 84 Murray Avenue.

Renmark is on the Sturt Highway, which runs between Adelaide and Sydney, so Greyhound (☎ *1300 473 946;* ***website*** *www.greyhound.com.au)* buses also stop here. Greyhound stops at the Caltex service station at 18th Street and Renmark Avenue.

Accommodation

Renmark International Backpackers

This hostel's bland exterior doesn't do much for this place, but once inside it is a surprisingly good hostel. It is in an old CWA hall and the easiest way to find the place is to look for the prominent CWA sign outside as a small blackboard with the name of the hostel scrawled on it is the only indication that it is now a hostel. The interior of the hostel has been recently renovated with jarrah hardwood floors, brand new dorms (with new bunks) and brand new bathrooms. Shared facilities include the usual kitchen, laundry and TV lounge.

89 Ral Ral Avenue, Renmark
☎ *(08) 8586 4486*
Dorm bed *$25 per night, $130 per week*
TV K L

Maintenance & cleanliness	★★★★
Facilities	★½
Atmosphere & character	★★½
Security	★★
Overall rating	★★★

Berri

Many travellers come to Berri for fruit picking work. The town doesn't have a lot of attractions but it is home to one of Australia's best worker's hostels. The main crops here are grapes and oranges and the town is home to a large fruit juice factory and Australia's largest winery, which produces the cheap cask wine that is so popular with many backpackers.

Practical Information
Berri Library & Information Centre
Kay Avenue, Berri
☎ *(08) 8595 2666*
Open *Mon-Wed 8am-6pm, Thu 8am-8pm, Fri 8am-6pm, Sat 9am-noon*

Berri Visitor Information Centre
Riverview Drive, Berri
☎ *(08) 8582 1922*
Website *www.riverland.info*
Open *Mon-Fri 9am-5.30pm, Sat-Sun 10am-4pm*

Coming & Going
Premier Stateliner (☎ *(08) 8415 5555;* ***website*** *www.premierstateliner.com.au)* coaches stop at Berri on their Adelaide-Renmark run. As Berri is on the Sturt Highway, which runs between Adelaide and Sydney, Greyhound (☎ *1300 473 946;* ***website*** *www.greyhound.com.au)* also operate daily coaches that stop here (but they also run an Adelaide-Sydney service via Broken Hill that doesn't stop in Berri). Coaches stop outside the Visitor Information Centre on Riverview Drive.

Accommodation
Berri Backpackers
Berri Backpackers is a big hostel with lots of facilities and a really good atmosphere. There are extensive garden areas with lots of sculptures plus hammocks, a massage table, meditation room and yoga room an outdoor kitchen and a couple of tree houses (if you're feeling romantic). There is also a beach volleyball court, tennis court, swimming pool and sauna. Some of the buildings are a big old but they are clean and the bathrooms are newly renovated. Inside there is a TV lounge with loads of books and several small kitchens and there's a cosy games room with table tennis and a pool table. Guests have free use of bicycles.
Old Sturt Highway, Berri SA 5343
☎ *(08) 8582 3144*
Website *www.berribackpackers.com.au*
Dorm bed *$25 per night, $140 per week*
Reception open *8am-noon & 4pm-7pm daily*

Maintenance & cleanliness	★★★
Facilities	★★★★★
Atmosphere & character	★★★★★
Security	★
Overall rating	★★★★

Loxton
This charming garden town has more character than other towns in the region and some travellers use Loxton as a base for fruit picking work. The Loxton Historical Village, a small open-air museum, is the main tourist attraction here.

Practical Information
Loxton Visitor Information & Arts Centre
Bookpurnong Terrace, Loxton
☎ *(08) 8584 7919*
Website *www.riverland.info*
Open *Mon-Fri 9am-5pm, Sat 9am-12.30pm, Sun 1pm-4pm*

Coming & Going
Premier Stateliner (☎ *(08) 8415 5555;* ***website*** *www.premierstateliner.com.au)* run a coach service between Adelaide and Loxton.

Accommodation
Harvest Trail Lodge
The Harvest Trail Lodge is a big concrete building with an institutional atmosphere, but it is clean enough and it has a central location near the tourist information centre. The hostel has a big veranda with a pool table, table tennis and a barbecue plus two small kitchens, a TV lounge and air-conditioning throughout the hostel.
Kokoda Terrace, Loxton
☎ *(08) 8584 5646*
Website *www.harvesttrail.com*
Dorm bed *$15-45 (the higher price applies to short stays in peak weekend periods)*
Credit cards *MC, Visa*
Reception open *10am-10pm daily*

Maintenance & cleanliness	★★★½
Facilities	★★
Atmosphere & character	★★½
Security	★★
Overall rating	★★

South Australia

Sights
Loxton Historical Village
This small open-air museum is a historical village with a main street that features more than 30 buildings. The Historical Village has been created to portray life here during the early 20th century.
Riverfront Road, Loxton
☎ *(08) 8584 7194*
Website *www.loxtonhistoricalvillage.com.au*
Admission *$8*
Open *Mon-Fri 10am-4pm, Sat-Sun 10am-5pm*

Barmera
Barmera is a small town on Lake Bonney where some backpackers stay while working on farms in the region.

Practical Information
Barmera Travel & Visitor Information Centre
Barwell Avenue, Barmera
☎ *(08) 8588 2289*

Coming & Going
Premier Stateliner *(☎ (08) 8415 5555; **website** www.premierstateliner.com.au)* coaches stop at Barmera on their Adelaide-Renmark run. As Barmera is on the Sturt Highway, which runs between Adelaide and Sydney, Greyhound *(☎ 1300 473 946; **website** www.greyhound.com.au)* also operate daily buses that stop here. Buses stop at Barmera Travel on Barwell Avenue.

Accommodation
Barmera Backpackers YHA
Barmera Backpackers is a basic hostel near the centre of town. Facilities are limited to a small TV lounge; a small, but fully-equipped, kitchen and a barren outdoor area with a barbecue and a rather sad looking table tennis table. It feels a bit neglected and the bland looking buildings don't do much to create any atmosphere.
6 Bice Street, Barmera
☎ *(08) 8588 3007*
Website *www.yha.com.au*
Dorm bed *$25 per night, $130 per week*
Credit cards *MC, Visa*
Reception open *9am-5pm daily*

Maintenance & cleanliness	★★½
Facilities	★★½
Atmosphere & character	★★
Security	★★
Overall rating	★★½

Kingston-on-Murray
This small village looks run down and it doesn't offer much for visitors, but there is a large vineyard and wetlands conservation complex several kilometres outside town that is worth a visit.

Accommodation
Nomads on Murray
Nomads on Murray would be just another basic workers' hostel in a rundown motel if it were not for the extensive facilities. The hub of the place is a bar with a pool table, TV and lots of board games, but there is also a fully-equipped kitchen, a back deck with a barbecue and a swimming pool. There is also a fleet of old cars that backpackers can use to drive to and from work. It is in the middle of nowhere – 3km from the centre of Kingston-on-Murray and a 10-minute drive to Barmera – but at least it does have a nice position on a hill with views of the Murray River.
Albrecht Road, Kingston-on-Murray
☎ *(08) 8583 0211 or 1800 665 166*
Website *www.nomadsworld.com*
Dorm bed *$23-25 per night, $140-155 per week;* ***double room*** *$55 per night, $320 per week*
Credit cards *MC, Visa*

Maintenance & cleanliness	★★★½
Facilities	★★★
Atmosphere & character	★★★★
Security	★
Overall rating	★★★

Sights
Banrock Station Wine & Wetlands Centre
This wetlands centre is managed by the Banrock Station Winery and features a boardwalk that lets you view the vineyards, wetlands and the region's bird life.

Holmes Road, Kingston-on-Murray
☎ *(08) 8583 0299*
Website *www.banrockstation.com.au*
Admission *$5*
Open *10am-5pm daily*

Limestone Coast

Most people speed through this region while travelling between Adelaide and Melbourne, perhaps stopping for no more than a quick bite. If you're driving along the coastal route between Adelaide and the South Australia/Victoria border you'll pass by the Coorong National Park that is noted for its bird life, particularly pelicans. Closer the to border at the extreme southeast of the state, you'll find Mount Gambier, a pleasant regional city known for its crater lakes; between the two is Robe, a lovely coastal town with a brilliant hostel.

Coorong National Park

This large national park on the coast around mid-way between Adelaide and the Victorian border is known for its lagoons, sand dunes and bird life.

Practical Information

National Park Information Centre
32-34 Princes Highway, Meningie
☎ *(08) 8575 1200*
Website *www.parks.sa.gov.au/coorong/*
Open *Mon, Wed, Fri 9am-5pm*

Coming & Going

Access to the Coorong National Park is via several points on Princes Highway that include Jack's Point, Policeman's Point and Salt Creek. Access from the Princes Highway is normally to bird watching observation points although there is also some access to campgrounds.

Alternatively you can organise tours from Meningie, which is the closest major town. If you're come here for fishing, then Meningie is the best access point for the park. It is also possible to visit the Coorong National Park by taking a cruise from Goolwa on the Fleurieu Peninsula.

Accommodation

There are several camping grounds within the national park. Visit the national parks office on Princes Highway in Meningie for detailed information and to organise camping permits ($5 per car or $3 per person). Camping permits are also available from the Shell service station in Salt Creek.

Mount Gambier

Located in South Australia's southeast corner, Mount Gambier is a major regional centre that is worth a look. The main attractions are the two crater lakes, Blue Lake and Valley Lake, which are both located on an extinct volcano overlooking the city.

Mount Gambier is also a good base for exploring the Coonawarra wine region, which is about 30km north of town.

Practical Information

Lady Nelson Visitor & Discovery Centre
Jubilee Highway East, Mount Gambier
☎ *1800 087 187*
Website *www.mountgambiertourism.com.au*
Open *9am-5pm daily*

Coming & Going

AIR

Rex (☎ *13 17 13;* ***website*** *www.rex.com.au)* flies to Adelaide and Melbourne from Mount Gambier. The airport is 10km north of town on Penola Road (Riddoch Highway).

BUS

Premier Stateliner (☎ *(08) 8415 5555;* ***website*** *www.premierstateliner.com.au)* buses go to Adelaide. V/line (☎ *13 61 96;* ***website*** *www.vline.com.au)* buses go to Melbourne via Warrnambool and Ballarat. Buses stop at the Lady Nelson Visitor & Discovery Centre on Jubilee Highway.

Accommodation

The Jail

The Jail is a unique hostel in an old prison that was built in 1866 and operated for 129 years. It has been restored to its original condition and features tall stone walls topped with razor wire, a big exercise yard and accommodation in former cells. It also has a bar/restaurant with a pool table and free internet access. It is a unique place to stay. Some travellers find the whole prison experience a bit too spooky and others come here for the novelty of staying in a cell, but it was never intended as holiday accommodation so the accommodation is basic and parts of it are a bit shabby.

25 Margaret Street, Mount Gambier
☎ *(08) 8723 0032*
Website *www.jailbackpackers.com*
Dorm bed *$22;* ***single room*** *$33;* ***double/twin room*** *$52; prices include breakfast*
Credit cards *MC, Visa*
Reception open *9am-2pm & 4.30pm-10pm*

Maintenance & cleanliness	★★
Facilities	★½
Atmosphere & character	★★★½
Security	★★
Overall rating	★★

Sights

CAVES

Mount Gambier has a huge network of caves. The Cave Gardens in the city centre is a nice spot for a picnic and from here you can walk down into the cave.

If you want to more fully explore the caves you can take the Engelbrecht Cave Tour (☎ *0418 133 407*), which costs $6 for the 45 minute tour.

CRATER LAKES

Mount Gambier's main attractions are the three crater lakes: Blue Lake, Valley Lake and Leg of Mutton Lake. There is a wildlife park with boardwalks over Valley Lake and walking trails around the dry Leg of Mutton Lake.

Naracoorte Caves National Park

South Australia's only World Heritage area *(****website*** *www.parks.sa.gov.au/naracoorte)* is comprised of several caves that feature fragile stalactite and stalagmite formations. The caves have earned their World Heritage listing because of the extensive collection of fossils that have been unearthed here.

Fossils found in the caves provide a unique glimpse into the past and the Wonambi Fossil Centre inside the park has an excellent display featuring animatronic depictions of the extinct marsupial megafauna that lived here around 200,000 years ago.

One of the caves is home to a colony of the rare southern bentwing bat and infrared video cameras have been set up that allow you to view the bat from the Bat Cave Teleview Centre.

There are various tours of the different caves, each with its own unique features.

An hour-long tour takes you to a large fossil deposit in the Victorian Fossil Cave where you get to experience the cave's World Heritage values.

Alexandra and Cathedral Caves offers a beautiful glimpse of cave decorations.

Tickets for the Alexandra Cave and Wonambi Fossil Centre also include entrance to Wet Cave, which features a self-guided walk that is ideal if you want to explore the cave at your own pace.

With the exception of adventure caving trips (see below) and the Cathedral Cave tour ($15), cave tours cost $12 for one tour, $19.50 for two tours, $27 for three tours and $34.50 for four tours.

Most of the cave tours are fairly tame, focusing mostly on the caves' natural history but there are also some excellent value adventure caving tours that operate in Stick-Tomato, Blackberry and Fox Caves. Adventure caving trips cost $30-55.

Coming & Going

Naracoorte Caves National Park is 10km south of Naracoorte and it is difficult to reach without your own transport.

Oz Experience stops here, but if you're travelling by regular bus you'll need to take a taxi from Naracoorte.

Accommodation

The closest hostel to the national park is Naracoorte Backpackers in Naracoorte, but it is also an easy trip from the Jail in Mount Gambier, a one-hour drive south of the Naracoorte Caves National Park.

There is also a camping site at the park ($21 per car) that is well equipped and features a free laundry.

Naracoorte Backpackers Hostel

This small hostel caters mostly to backpackers working around Naracoorte. It provides basic accommodation with limited facilities that include two kitchens, a TV lounge and a games room with a pool table. Although it's little old, the manager does a good job organising work and he runs bus trips on the weekends.

4 Jones Street, Naracoorte
☎ *(08) 8762 3835*
Dorm bed *$20 per night;* ***double/twin room*** *$44*
TV K

Maintenance & cleanliness	★½
Facilities	★★½
Atmosphere & character	★★★★
Security	★½
Overall rating	★★½

Robe

Robe small fishing port is one of the nicest places on the Limestone Coast. It is a pleasant village with a great hostel, a good beach and some nice bars, cafés and restaurants. There is not a lot to do, but many travellers find that they end up staying longer than they initially planned to.

Practical Information

Robe Visitor Information Centre

Mundy Terrace, Robe
☎ *(08) 87682465*
Website *www.robe.sa.gov.au*

Coming & Going

Premier Stateliner *(☎ (08) 8415 5555;* ***website*** *www.premierstateliner.com.au)* buses stop in Robe en route between Adelaide and Mount Gambier.

Accommodation

Lakeside Manor YHA

Robe's lovely YHA hostel is an old manor house dating from 1884 that overlooks Lake Fellmongery. The beautiful building features polished Baltic pine floors, stained glass windows and lots of antique flourishes. The majestic hallway is the length of two cricket pitches and wide enough to drive a car down and the library has comfortable leather sofas and a large blackwood and mahogany bookcase with leather and gold leaf trimming. Apart from the library, the hostel's amenities include a fully-equipped kitchen, a dining area and television lounge with internet access ($6 per hour). There is also a barbecue area and a garden with pine, cypress, sheoaks and Moreton Bay fig trees. Guests have free use of bikes and surfboards. It is a really nice place to stay and offers a touch of class and old world charm while still providing all the mod cons.

22 Main Road, Robe
☎ *(08) 8768 1995*
Website *www.lakesidemanorbackpackers.com.au*
Dorm bed *$27 ($24 HI/YHA);* ***double room*** *$72.50-100 ($65-90 HI/YHA)*
Credit cards *MC, Visa*
Reception open *8am-noon & 4pm-8pm*
TV K L

Maintenance & cleanliness	★★★★½
Facilities	★★★½
Atmosphere & character	★★★★★
Security	★★½
Overall rating	★★★★

Port Augusta

If you're travelling west or north from Adelaide, you'll pass through Port Augusta. This industrial city lies at a crossroads between Adelaide, Alice Springs and Perth and is the last large town before the outback.

Port Augusta doesn't have a lot to offer the traveller, apart from a convenient place to stock up on supplies before heading into the outback.

The town doesn't have a very good reputation with Adelaide residents, however its attractions are surprisingly interesting and worth visiting if you have time to spare. In general the town's sights reflect Port Augusta's position as gateway to the outback and the Flinders Ranges.

Practical Information

Port Augusta Tourist Information Centre

Wadlata Outback Centre, 41 Flinders Terrace, Port Augusta
☎ *(08) 8641 0793 or 1800 633 060*
Website *www.flinders.outback.on.net*
Open *Mon-Fri 9am-5pm, Sat-Sun 10am-4pm*

Coming & Going

BUS

Premier Stateliner *(☎ (08) 8415 5555; **website** www.premierstateliner.com.au)* and Greyhound *(☎ 1300 473 946; **website** www.greyhound.com.au)* buses go to Adelaide. Premier Stateliner also go to Ceduna, Whyalla, Port Lincoln, Woomera and Roxby Downs and Greyhound heads north to Alice Springs. Buses stop at the coach terminal on McKay Street.

TRAIN

Port Augusta lies at the crossroads of two long-distance rail lines: the *Ghan* (Adelaide to Darwin) and the *Indian Pacific* (Sydney to Perth). The Pitchi Ritchi Railway *(**website** www.prr.org.au)* has trains to Quorn in the foothills of the Flinders Ranges. The train station is on Stirling Road.

Accommodation

There is no longer a hostel in Port Augusta. The closest hostel is in Quorn, just a one-hour drive to the north.

Sights

Arid Lands Botanic Gardens

This unique park north of the town centre showcases a range of plant-life that thrives in desert conditions. The gardens also include a research centre and information centre.
Stuart Highway, Port Augusta
☎ *(08) 8641 1049*
Website *www.australian-aridlands-botanic-garden.org*
Admission *free*
Open *Mon-Fri 9am-5pm, Sat-Sun 10am-4pm*

School of the Air

Children living in remote outback areas learn through this correspondence school that is noted for running classes over the airwaves.
59 Power Crescent, Port Augusta
☎ *(08) 8642 2077*
Admission *$2.50*
Tours *Mon-Fri 10am except school holidays*

Wadlata Outback Centre

The Wadlata Outback Centre adjoins the visitor information centre and is an interesting attraction depicting outback culture with displays on early exploration, geology and Aboriginal culture.
41 Flinders Terrace, Port Augusta
☎ *(08) 8642 4511*
Website *www.wadlata.sa.gov.au*
Admission *$9.95*
Open *Mon-Fri 9am-5.30pm, Sat-Sun 10am-4pm*

Flinders Ranges

This remote mountain range, which encompasses Wilpena Pound and the Flinders Ranges National Park, is one of South Australia's best attractions. The Flinders Ranges start south of Port Augusta, although the big attraction is Wilpena Pound in the north-central Flinders Ranges.

Coming & Going & Local Transport

Although most express buses bypass the Flinders Ranges, backpacker buses such as Adventure Tours, Groovy Grape, Oz Experience, and the Wayward Bus go via this region on their routes connecting Adelaide with Alice Springs. Even if you are travelling on an express bus pass, it's possible to pick up a Premier Stateliner *(☎ (08) 8415 5555; **website** www.premierstateliner.com.au)* bus from Adelaide or Port Augusta as far as Wilpena Pound.

Quorn

Quorn is a quaint town with some interesting old buildings.

The unique heritage streetscapes have been a backdrop for many Australian films during the 1970s and 1980s including *Gallipoli*, *the Shiralee* and *the Sundowners*.

It was once an important railway town to service the *Old Ghan* railway before the route was discontinued in 1980 in favour of the less flood-prone route that more closely follows the Stuart Highway.

This is the first town after the turn-off for Wilpena Pound and is worth a stop.

Practical Information

Flinders Ranges Visitor Information Centre

3 Seventh Street, Quorn
☎ *(08) 8648 6419*
Website *www.flindersranges.com*
Open *9am-5pm daily*

Accommodation

Andu Lodge Backpackers

Andu Lodge is an old house on a residential street close to the centre of Quorn, which makes a good base for exploring the Flinders Ranges. However everything about the hostel feels old and tired and with most furniture and fittings dating at least 30 years, it is crying out for a complete makeover. Facilities include an old TV lounge with uncomfortable scratchy sofas plus a kitchen and dining room with 1950s-style retro furniture. Security is also a weak point – although the building can be locked up at night, guests don't get keys to their rooms.
12 First Street, Quorn
☎ *(08) 8648 6020*
Dorm bed *$25; prices include breakfast*
Reception open *7.30am-9pm*
TV K L

Maintenance & cleanliness	★★
Facilities	★★½
Atmosphere & character	★★
Security	★
Overall rating	★★

Eating & Drinking

There are four pubs in Quorn, although the Transcontinental, aka the Tranny, is by far the most popular with excellent meals at bargain prices.

Sights

Warren Gorge

This small scenic reserve makes a nice daytrip from Quorn or a detour en route between Quorn and Flinders Ranges National Park.

The gorge itself is around 300m long and 100m deep and is one of several small gorges in the area.

The main reason to visit is to spot the endangered yellow footed rock wallaby. You can spot the wallaby from your car as you drive around the reserve, but you'll have better luck if you walk around, as they're easier to find if you are quiet.

Warren Gorge is around a 20-minute drive north of Quorn and there are no entry fees to the reserve. Free camping is available in the reserve.

The Dutchmans Stern

This hill, northwest of Quorn, has a popular hiking trail (10.5km, five hours) that goes up to the ridge offering views to Port Augusta and Wilpena Pound. It is accessible by bicycle from Quorn, making it a popular excursion for travellers staying at the Andu Lodge.

Pichi Richi Railway

Enthusiasts have restored part of the *Old Ghan* railway and now operate a number of steam trains between Quorn and Port Augusta.
☎ *(08) 8658 1109*
Website *www.prr.org.au*
One-way *$45;* ***return*** *$39-71*
Trains run *Apr-Oct Sat-Mon*

Hawker

Heading north, Hawker is the last real town before the national park so you'll need to stop here to buy groceries, fuel, get money from the ATM and buy some snacks for the trip north. There's not much else to do in town, although some people use the town as a base and there are several places where you can organise trips to the national park including scenic flights and camel trekking.

Practical Information

Hawker Visitor Information Centre

Hawker Motors, Corner Cradock & Wilpena Roads, Hawker
☎ *(08) 8648 4022*
Open *8.30am-5.30pm daily*

National Parks & Wildlife Service
60 Elder Street, Hawker
(08) 8648 4244
***Website** www.parks.sa.gov.au*

Wilpena Pound & Flinders Ranges National Park

The Flinders Ranges National Park is home to some of the most spectacular scenery in the outback and it is one of South Australia's most visited national parks. The national park has an extensive network of walking tracks which range from short ten-minute walks to more challenging hikes lasting for several days.

Wilpena Pound is the main centre within the national park and is home to the information centre, camping grounds, motel and general store. Many of the walking tracks within the park originate here. Wilpena Pound is a spectacular natural basin ringed by steep cliffs with some rewarding hiking trails. Perhaps the most popular short hike is the two-hour walk to Wangara Lookout that offers dramatic views. Popular longer walks include Edowie Gorge and St Mary's Peak, each of these is a very long day hike although the two walks can be combined into a longer two or three day trek.

The region is also home to fascinating Aboriginal rock paintings. Ask at the information centre about hiking trails that include rock art. If you're travelling on Adventure Tours or Oz Experience you'll stop at the Yourambulla Caves that contain some of the area's best rock paintings.

If you're going on any walks in the park, remember to take plenty of water, particularly in summer. A litre for every couple of hours is essential.

Admission to the national park costs $7.50 per day for a car or $3 if you're arriving by bus. Alternatively you can buy a two month parks pass for $30 that allows you to visit all South Australian national parks except desert parks and parks on Kangaroo Island.

Practical Information

Wilpena Pound Visitor Information Centre
National Park entrance, Wilpena Pound
(08) 8648 0048
***Website** www.wilpenapound.com.au*
***Open** 8am-6pm daily*

Coming & Going

If you're not driving or travelling on one of the backpackers' buses, then your only transport option is the Premier Stateliner *((08) 8415 5555; **website** www.premierstateliner.com.au)* bus from Adelaide via Port Augusta.

Accommodation

Wilpena Pound Resort

The Wilpena Pound Resort has a wide variety of accommodation ranging from four-star suites to backpacker dorms and camping. The backpackers' accommodation is in motel-style rooms that comprise four single beds (not bunks) along with a TV, fridge, and en suite bathrooms in each unit. The self-contained nature of the accommodation means that backpackers are unlikely to socialise with travellers staying in other units. Backpackers have access to resort facilities that include a bar, restaurant and swimming pool. It is very handy to the most important sights in the Flinders Ranges, but you will need to budget the additional national park entry fees as it is located inside the national park.

Wilpena Pound, Flinders Ranges National Park
(08) 8648 0004 or 1800 805 802
***Website** www.wilpenapound.com.au*
***Dorm bed** $35*
***Credit cards** Amex, Diners, MC, Visa*
***Reception open** 7.30am-7.30pm*

Maintenance & cleanliness	★★★★
Facilities	★★★
Atmosphere & character	★★½
Security	★
Overall rating	★★★

Parachilna

With a population of only eight, Parachilna is barely a blip on most maps, but it has cheap accommodation that is handy for exploring the northern Flinders Ranges plus a great outback pub that does excellent food (your chance to try camel, emu or kangaroo).

Accommodation

Parachilna Overflow

At first glance the Parachilna Overflow looks like a hodgepodge of old wooden huts and pre-fabricated units, like you find on construction sites, but initial impressions can be deceptive as the accommodation is actually quite nice inside and all the rooms are air-conditioned. Facilities are limited to a swimming pool, laundry and an outdoor camp kitchen but most travellers spend most of their time in the pub anyway. A lot of tour companies stop here and if you're travelling with Adventure Tours you also get access to a big common area with a pool table, kitchen and enclosed barbecue area.

Corner High Street & West Terrace, Parachilna

☎ *(08) 8648 4814*

Website *www.prairiehotel.com.au*

Dorm bed *$25-35;* ***single room*** *$35-90;* ***double room*** *$60-120;* ***camping*** *$15 (1 person), $25 (2 people)*

Credit cards *Amex, Diners, MC, Visa*

Reception open *8am-late, check in at pub*

Maintenance & cleanliness	★★★½
Facilities	★★½
Atmosphere & character	★½
Security	★
Overall rating	★★★

Eating & Drinking

The Pararie Hotel, across the road from the Parachilna Overflow, is a classic outback pub that is a surprisingly good place to eat. Their specialty is the "feral grill" with camel, emu and kangaroo. They also have cold beer and very good gelati.

Outback South Australia

South Australia is Australia's driest state and this is most evident when travelling in the outback. For most travellers, the outback is the vast expanse of red sand that you see from the bus window en route to destinations north and west of Port Augusta. In most cases the only places you'll stop are the lonely roadhouses on the highway, although Coober Pedy on the Stuart Highway between Adelaide and Alice Springs is a popular and unique stop over.

If you're travelling on one of the backpackers' buses, you may take the Oodnadatta Track between the Flinders Ranges and Coober Pedy.

The Oodnadatta Track

The 615km Oodnadatta Track is a convenient shortcut between the Flinders Ranges and Central Australia. It also gives you a more genuine outback experience than you would get if you stick to the highway.

The track runs from Marree, 184km north of Parachilna, to Marla, on the Stuart Highway between Coober Pedy and Alice Springs. Many travellers, and several of the backpacker buses, take the track as far as William Creek and then continue on William Creek Road to Coober Pedy.

The Oodnadatta Track follows the path of the old *Ghan* railway and also passes by the 5,300km-long dog fence and the southern edge of Lake Eyre. Some of the small outback communities on the track provide a glimpse of Australia that few tourists ever have the chance to experience. The main towns on the track are Marla, William Creek and Oodnadatta.

Marree is the starting point for both the Oodnadatta and Birdsville Tracks. Normally a sleepy hamlet of around 80 people, it comes alive in July when it hosts the annual Camel Cup. If possible it is worth planning your trip around this event since it is not everyday that you get the opportunity to attend a camel race.

William Creek is Australia's smallest town with a population of only 12, but it is located on the world's largest cattle property. At 32,500km², Anna Creek Station is about the same size as

Belgium. Scenic flights over Lake Eyre depart from here.

If you continue north along the track, you'll come to Oodnadatta; an uninspiring place that was the birthplace of the Royal Flying Doctor Service. There are a few interesting sites here including a small museum.

Despite popular misconceptions, a 4WD vehicle is not necessary to tackle the track and many people head up this way in a regular car, especially during dry weather. However it is an unsealed road so you are prohibited from taking rental cars on it.

Accommodation

MARREE

Marree Drover's Rest Tourist Park

This caravan park has air-conditioned cabins, but not much in the way of other facilities.

Corner Oodnadatta & Birdsville Tracks, Marree

☎ *(08) 8675 8371*

***Dorm bed** $20; **double room** $80*

WILLIAM CREEK

William Creek Hotel

The backpackers' accommodation at the William Creek Hotel consists of prefabricated units with old beds. There aren't any communal facilities other than the pub, which is where most people staying here spend all their time.

Oodnadatta Track, William Creek

☎ *(08) 8670 7880*

***Website** www.williamcreekhotel.net.au*

***Single room** $40-50; **double room** $60-70*

***Credit cards** Amex, MC, Visa*

Maintenance & cleanliness	★½
Facilities	½
Atmosphere & character	★½
Security	★½
Overall rating	★½

OODNADATTA

Pink Roadhouse

The Pink Roadhouse offers very basic accommodation in an old shack behind their shop. Everything here is old and worn and facilities are limited, however it's cheap and the people who work here are a mine of information about travelling along the track.

Oodnadatta Track, Oodnadatta

☎ *(08) 8670 7822*

***Website** www.biziworks.com.au/pink/*

***Dorm bed** $15; **double room** $48;* **camping** *$9.50 for the first person then $5 per each extra person*

Maintenance & cleanliness	½
Facilities	★
Atmosphere & character	★
Security	★
Overall rating	★

Woomera

This modern town between Port Augusta and Coober Pedy is an interesting place with an intriging history. The location of Woomera was top secret for many years and visiting the town was prohibited until 1982.

Woomera was established in 1947 as missile testing site for the British government and over 4,000 missiles were launched from the expansive Woomera Prohibited Area over the following 30 years. Some of the rockets and missiles tested here are on display at the Woomera Missile Park in the town centre.

Although originally a British base, Woomera has played host to a number of military and aerospace organisations including ELDO (European Launcher Development Organisation), NASA and the United States Air Force.

In its heyday Woomera had a population of 6,800 but this has dropped to the 600 that live here today. The town's former importance means it has an excellent infrastructure that is the envy of other towns of a similar size.

Practical Information

Woomera Heritage & Visitor Centre

Dewrang Avenue, Woomera

☎ *(08) 8673 7799*

***Website** www.woomera.com.au*

***Open** 9am-5pm daily*

Sights

Woomera Heritage Centre

The Woomera Heritage Centre is a small museum with fascinating exhibits

about previously classified aspects of Woomera's history.
Dewrang Street, Woomera
☎ *(08) 8673 7042*
***Website** www.woomera.com.au*
***Admission** $3*
***Open** 9am-5pm daily*

Coober Pedy

This outback opal-mining town is unique in that much of it is built underground. Many of Coober Pedy's homes and other facilities such as churches and a backpackers hostel have been built underground to escape the summer heat, which sometimes reaches 50° C.

Coober Pedy is the source of 80% of the world's opals. If you want to buy opals you may get a better deal here than in the big cities, although the shops here do a roaring business with passing tourist coaches so it would be best to avoid the busy times if you want to save money.

There are thousands of abandoned mine shafts around Coober Pedy so in the interests of your safety it is a good idea to avoid wandering around the outskirts of town alone.

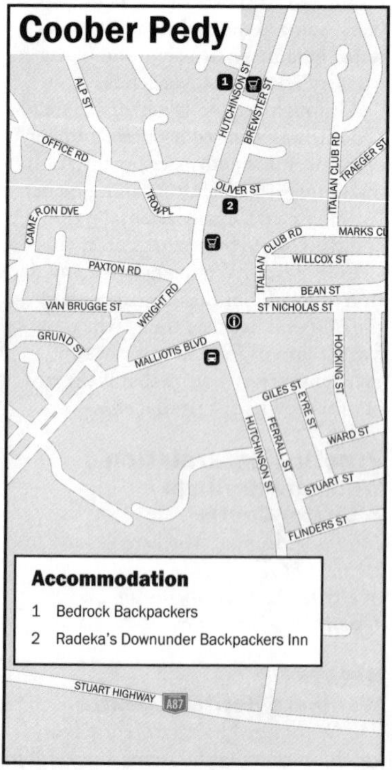

The town's unique setting has been used as the film-set for several movies including Priscilla Queen of the Desert and Mad Max III.

Coober Pedy

Accommodation

1 Bedrock Backpackers
2 Radeka's Downunder Backpackers Inn

Practical Information

Coober Pedy Visitor Information Centre

Hutchison Street, Coober Pedy
☎ *(08) 8672 5298 or 1800 637 076*
***Website** www.opalcapitaloftheworld.com.au*
***Open** Mon-Fri 8.30am-5pm, Sat-Sun 10am-1pm*

Coming & Going

AIR

Rex *(☎ 13 17 13; **website** www.rex.com.au)* flies to Coober Pedy from Adelaide. The flight takes two hours and is a good travel option if you are travelling on a Rex backpacker air travel pass. The airport is around 5km southwest of the town centre.

BUS

Greyhound *(☎ 1300 473 946; **website** www.greyhound.com.au)* stop in Coober Pedy en route from Adelaide to Alice Springs.

TRAIN

The *Ghan* train from Adelaide to Darwin stops at Manguri Station, which is 47km from Coober Pedy. If you are arriving by train you will need to arrange transport between Manguri Station and Coober Pedy before departure from Adelaide or Alice Springs.

Accommodation

Hostels in Coober Pedy have at least some accommodation underground. An underground hostel is basically a series of caves and there are not always doors to the rooms, for this reason there may not be the same level of security or privacy that you would find in a more conventional hostel.

Bedrock Backpackers

Bedrock is an underground hostel in a dugout with individual four-bed dorms but there are no doors to each dorm (just a curtain). Facilities are limited to basic cooking facilities and a small dining room with an old TV. The showers and toilets are in a separate (above ground) building next to the spaceship in the car park. Check in at the Opal Cave shop that faces the hostel car park.

Hutchison Street, Coober Pedy
(08) 8672 5028
Website *www.opalcavecooberpedy.com*
Dorm bed *$20-22*
Credit cards *Amex, JCB, MC, Visa*
Reception open *8am-6pm*

Maintenance & cleanliness	★★
Facilities	½★
Atmosphere & character	★★★
Security	★
Overall rating	★½

Radeka's Downunder Backpackers Inn

Radeka's is a long established underground hostel with lots of accommodation in a deep dug out. The dorm accommodation consists of a 6.5m deep cavern with lots of big dorms separated from the main corridor by curtains, although double and twin rooms have proper doors. Shared facilities include an above ground fully-equipped kitchen and a dining room with a TV plus a bar with a pool table. Like most places in Coober Pedy, the reception doubles as an opal shop.

Corner Hutchison & Oliver Streets, Coober Pedy
(08) 8672 5223 or 1800 633 891
Website *www.radekadownunder.com.au*
Dorm bed *$22 ($21 HI/YHA, VIP);*
double room *$55 ($53 HI/YHA, VIP)*
Credit cards *MC, Visa*
Reception open *8am-9pm daily*

Maintenance & cleanliness	★★★
Facilities	★★
Atmosphere & character	★★★½
Security	★
Overall rating	★★½

Tasmania

Australia's island state provides a totally different experience from the mainland. Forget any notions of arid outback – Tasmania is a land of rugged mountains, rolling green hills and raging rivers.

Tasmania is one of the world's most picturesque islands. About 20% of Tasmania has been designated World Heritage area and another 10% is national park or reserve.

There's more to Tasmania than the great outdoors, the island state has a fascinating convict past and it was one of the first areas in Australia to be settled by Europeans. Although small, the main cities have a more established feel than elsewhere in Australia. The former penal colony at Port Arthur on the Tasman Peninsula is the state's most popular tourist attraction and perhaps your best opportunity to gain an understanding of what life was like during the convict days.

Coming & Going

Most travellers visit Tasmania via Melbourne, which is the departure point for most flights and ferries.

Flying is generally the quickest and cheapest option, but you can take the ferry if you want to take a car over and avoid car rental.

AIR

Although there are some flights from other places like Sydney, the majority of flights to Tasmania depart from Melbourne Airport.

Jetstar *(☎ 13 15 38; **website** www.jetstar.com)* flies to Launceston from Brisbane and Sydney and from Brisbane to Hobart; Qantas *(☎ 13 13 13; **website** www.qantas.com.au)* flies from Melbourne to Devonport, Launceston and Hobart and from Sydney to Hobart; Rex *(☎ 13 17 13; **website** www.rex.com.au)* flies from Melbourne to Burnie; Tiger Airways *(☎ (03) 9335*

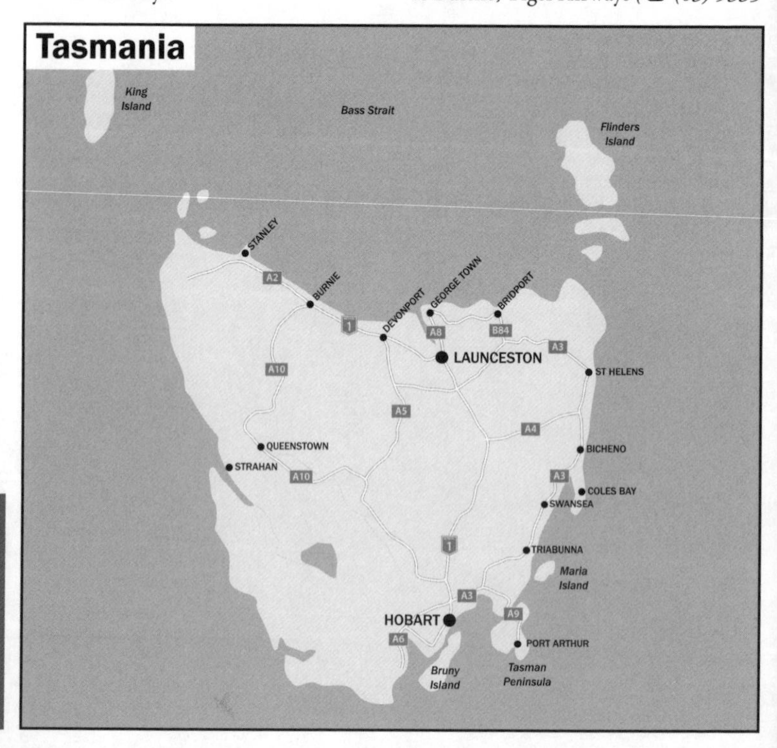

3033; ***website*** *www.tigerairways.com)* and Virgin Blue *(☎ 13 67 89;* ***website*** *www.virginblue.com.au)* fly from Melbourne to Hobart and Launceston.

Many travellers book one-way tickets and fly into one city and out from another.

FERRY

The *Spirit of Tasmania (☎ 1800 634 906;* ***website*** *www.spiritoftasmania.com.au)* sails between Melbourne and Devonport. It departs Melbourne and Devonport most nights and there are also day sailings during peak periods. Fares are $120-198 one-way per person, higher fares apply for cabin accommodation.

You can take a car or campervan across for $72, higher prices apply if your car is wider than two metres.

It is a good idea to book well ahead as ferries can fill up fast, particularly during long weekends and school holidays.

Local Transport

Tasmania is cut-off from mainland Australia, meaning that transport networks have developed separately to the rest of the country. For instance, apart from tourist railways, there are no regular passenger train services and Greyhound do not operate in Tasmania.

Many travellers choose to rent a car to explore Tassie and this gives you the most freedom, but there is a bus network that offers some good value travel passes.

BUS

Tassielink *(☎ 1300 653 633;* ***website*** *www.tassielink.com.au)* and Redline *(☎ (03) 6336 1446 or 1300 360 000;* ***website*** *www.tasredline.com)* are Tasmania's two main coach operators with scheduled services to most major destinations within the state. They also offer several travel passes that are good value, particularly for solo travellers who may not be able to justify the cost of car rental.

Both companies meet the Devonport ferry and run services to Cradle Mountain-Lake St Clair National Park, but Tassielink has the more extensive route network.

Must do in Tasmania

- Spend a few hours in Hobart's Salamanca Place market
- Learn about Australia's convict past at Port Arthur
- Walk to Wine Glass Bay in Freycinet National Park
- Hike the Overland Track between Cradle Mountain and Lake St Claire
- Take a boat trip on Strahan's Macquarie Harbour

Redline Tassie Pass

This pass allows unlimited travel on Redline coaches within the timeframe indicated on the pass.

Pass	Cost
7 day pass	$135
10 day pass	$160
14 day pass	$185
21 day pass	$219

Tassielink Explorer Bus Pass

This pass allows unlimited travel on Tassielink buses within a network that covers most major destinations in Tasmania including the Tasman Peninsula. It even gets you off the beaten track to destinations like national parks and World Heritage areas.

Pass	Cost
7 travel days in a 10 day period	$189
10 travel days in a 15 day period	$225
14 travel days in a 20 day period	$260
21 travel days in a 30 day period	$299

TOURS

There are several companies that operate tours aimed at the backpacker market. You may want to consider these if you want to see a lot and your time is limited although they don't have the flexibility that comes with independent travel. The following companies offer tours of Tasmania:

Adventure Tours

Adventure Tours *(☎ 1300 654 604;* ***website*** *www.adventuretours.com.au)* operate several excellent tours. Three-day tours cost $445-460 and the longer six and seven-day tours cost $825-840.

Bottom Bits Bus
Bottom Bits Bus (☎ *1800 777 103; **website** www.bottombitsbus.com.au)* run day tours from Hobart to Freycinet National Park and Mount Field National Park and from Launceston to Cradle Mountain; these day tours cost $105 ($99 HI/YHA, ISIC, VIP).

Under Down Under
Under Down Under (☎ *(03) 6369 5555 or 1800 064 726; **website** www.underdownunder.com.au)* operate a good selection of tours that range from two to seven days.

DRIVING
Car rental is by far the most popular transport option in Tasmania. It's the most flexible way to get around as you're not tied to bus routes or timetables and it is relatively affordable, particularly if the cost is split among several travellers.

National Parks
Tasmania's wilderness is one of its main attractions with thousands of travellers visiting its national parks each year. Entry fees for Tasmanian national parks are $22 per day for a car and up to eight passengers or $11 per person travelling by bike or public transport.

Most travellers find the Holiday Pass much better value – this allows you to visit national parks throughout the state for up to two months. The Holiday Pass costs $56 for a car and up to eight passengers or $28 per person travelling by bike or public transport.

National Park Passes can be bought at park entry booths, tourist information centres and national park visitor centres.

Hobart National Park Visitor Centre
134 Macquarie Street, Hobart
☎ *(03) 6233 6191*
***Website** www.parks.tas.gov.au*
***Open** Mon-Fri 9am-5pm*

Launceston National Park Visitor Centre
Prospect Offices, Bass Highway, South Launceston
☎ *(03) 6336 5312*
***Website** www.parks.tas.gov.au*
***Open** Mon-Fri 9am-5pm*

Hobart
Tasmania's largest city is perfectly situated at the mouth of the Derwent River with a compact centre and suburbs clinging to the hillside overlooking the wide estuary. The city is well located as a base for exploring the surrounding countryside making it ideal for excursions to the Huon Valley, Port Arthur on the Tasman Peninsula, and nearby towns like Richmond and New Norfolk.

It is the second oldest state capital and it has retained its old colonial architecture more so than any other large Australian city. Battery Point and the downtown area, particularly around Salamanca Place, is full of renovated sandstone buildings which have been converted into pubs, cafés and restaurants which give the city a vibrant air despite the general slow pace of the city. Held here each Saturday, Salamanca Market is a great place to hang around and soak up the atmosphere.

Although Tasmania's main appeal is its wilderness, Hobart does have a few worthwhile sights. There are some interesting museums and it is also possible to take a guided tour of the Cadbury chocolate factory and the Cascade brewery, both of which offer tastings.

Practical Information
Hobart Information Centre
20 Davey Street, Hobart
☎ *(03) 6230 8233*
***Website** www.discovertasmania.com*
***Open** Mon-Fri 8.30am-5.15pm, Sat-Sun 8am-4pm*

INTERNET ACCESS
Free Wi-Fi hotspots are hard to come by in Hobart, but if you're willing to pay $7 per hour or $50 for 10 hours you can log on to one of the Mouse on Mars (☎ *(03) 6231 5421; **website** www.mouseonmars.com.au)* hotspots around town including Adelphi Court YHA, Central City Backpackers, Montgomery's Hotel YHA plus the

Tasmania

Tassielink coach terminal on Brisbane Street and the Retro Café on Salamanca Place.

Alternatively you can use the computers at most hostels and also at the following internet cafés:

Mouse on Mars
112 Liverpool Street, Hobart
☎ *(03) 6231 5421*
Website *www.mouseonmars.com.au*
Open *10am-10pm daily*

The Pelican Loft
35A Elizabeth Street, Hobart
☎ *(03) 6234 2225*
Open *summer Mon-Fri 9am-9pm, Sat 10.30am-6pm; winter Mon-Fri 9am-6pm, Sat 10.30am-4pm*

Coming & Going
AIR
Hobart Airport *(☎ (03) 6216 1600; **website** www.hobartairpt.com.au)* is on the A3 highway about 17km east of the city centre. The Airporter bus service *(☎ 0419 382240; **website** www.redlinecoaches.com.au)* runs regularly between the airport and central Hobart and they can drop you off at your hostel. The 15-minute trip costs $12.80.

BUS
Bus travel is the main form of public transport in Tasmania, and Hobart is well connected to other destinations within the state. Redline *(☎ 0419 382240; **website** www.redlinecoaches.com.au)* buses stop at the Transit Centre at 199 Collins Street and the Tassielink *(☎ 1300 300 520; **website** www.tassielink.com.au)* coach terminal is at 64 Brisbane Street.

HITCHHIKING
Tasmania is Australia's best state for hitching and Hobart is a great city to hitch from.

The Midland Highway (route 1) is the main road through the middle of Tasmania and the quickest route to Devonport and Launceston. The Murchison Highway (route A10) runs from Hobart to Burnie on the north coast via Queenstown. Either of these roads is a good bet if you're heading to the north coast, although the Midland Highway will be a much quicker run. The best hitching spot to catch traffic bound for both these roads is the patch of road just north of Claremont in Hobart's northern suburbs. Use a sign as the spot has traffic bound for both highways. Local buses run from the centre of Hobart to Claremont.

The Tasman Highway (route A3) runs from Hobart up the east coast. If you're heading in this direction, take a bus to Cambridge (near the airport) and try your luck from there.

Local Transport
Hobart Metro *(☎ 13 22 01; **website** www.metrotas.com.au)* runs buses within the Hobart area with most buses terminating near the main post office on Elizabeth Street and also in Macquarie Street and Franklin Square in the city centre.

Single tickets start at $2 and go up to $4.50 depending on the route. Day Rover tickets cost $5-6.

Accommodation
Adelphi Court YHA
This YHA is in an old but well kept building built around a grassy courtyard. Amenities include a TV lounge with a pool table, table tennis and internet access plus kitchen and laundry facilities. It has an institutional feel to it and there isn't much of an atmosphere. It is located in suburban New Town, which is too far from the city centre for most travellers but it has ample parking so people travelling by car may want to consider staying here.
17 Stoke Street, New Town
🚌 *15, 16, 25-42, 100, 105-128*
☎ *(03) 6228 4829*
Website *www.yha.com.au*
Dorm bed *$27 ($24 HI/YHA)*
Credit cards *MC, Visa*
Reception open *7.30am-10.30am & 4pm-9pm*
🚗 TV K L

Maintenance & cleanliness	★★½
Facilities	★★
Atmosphere & character	★★
Security	★
Overall rating	★★

Tasmania

Central City Backpackers

With around 200 beds, Central City Backpackers is one of Tasmania's biggest hostels. It is an older building and parts of the hostel feel a little tired but the common areas are well kept and it has a pretty good atmosphere. Facilities include a fully-equipped kitchen, a good TV lounge, internet access including Wi-Fi ($7 per hour; Mouse on Mars) plus a laundry. It has a very central location in the heart of Hobart city centre.

138 Collins Street, Hobart
☎ *(03) 6224 2404 or 1800 811 507*
Website *www.centralcityhobart.com*
Dorm bed *$23-27 ($22-26 VIP);* ***single room*** *$55 ($54 VIP);* ***double/twin room*** *$69 ($67 VIP)*
Credit cards *MC, Visa*
Reception open *8am-9pm daily*
TV K L

Maintenance & cleanliness	★★★½
Facilities	★★★½
Atmosphere & character	★★★★½
Security	★★
Overall rating	★★★½

Hobart Hostel

Hobart Hostel is a new hostel in an old building close to the Tassielink coach terminal. It has laundry facilities, a fully-equipped kitchen, TV lounge and internet access. The building shows its age and there are old mismatched furnishings in the common areas that make the hostel look a bit shabby but the dorms are clean enough and the en suite double rooms are in a nicer new building.

41 Barrack Street, Hobart
☎ *(03) 6234 6122*
Website *www.hobarthostel.com*
Dorm bed *$21-26;* ***double/twin room*** *$70-80*
Credit cards *MC, Visa*
Reception open *summer 8am-9pm daily; winter 8am-12.30pm & 4.30pm-9pm daily*
TV K L

Maintenance & cleanliness	★★
Facilities	★½
Atmosphere & character	★★★½
Security	★★½
Overall rating	★★½

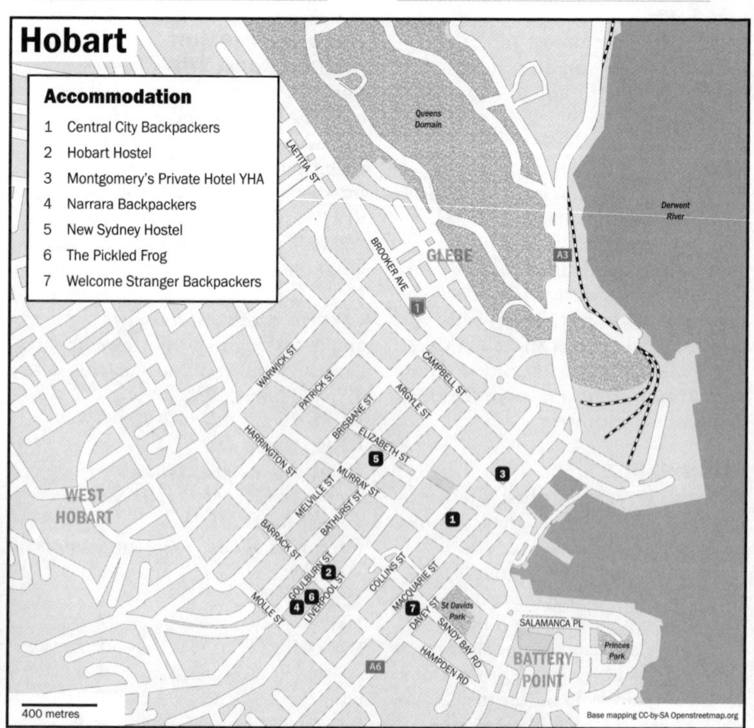

Montgomery's Private Hotel YHA

Montgomery's YHA is a clean and well maintained hostel a short walk to museums and the waterfront. There is a small fully-equipped kitchen and a TV lounge with internet access including Wi-Fi ($7 per hour, $50 10 hours; Mouse on Mars). The accommodation is of a high standard but it doesn't have the atmosphere of smaller hostels.

9 Argyle Street, Hobart
(03) 6231 2660
Website *www.yha.com.au*
Dorm bed *$29 ($26 HI/YHA);* ***single room*** *$90-112.50 ($81-101 HI/YHA);* ***double room*** *$90-112.50 ($81-101 HI/YHA)*
Credit cards *MC, Visa*
Reception open *8am-10pm daily*

Maintenance & cleanliness	★★★½
Facilities	★★
Atmosphere & character	★★½
Security	★★★★
Overall rating	★★★

Narrara Backpackers

Narrara Backpackers is one of Hobart's better hostels. It is relatively clean and well maintained although the building is starting to show its age. Facilities include a fully-equipped kitchen, laundry, a TV lounge and internet access. Accommodation is in clean tidy dorms and it has a good atmosphere.

88 Goulburn Street, Hobart
(03) 6231 3191
Website *www.narrarabackpackers.com*
Dorm bed *$19-23;* ***double/twin room*** *$49-69*
Reception open *8am-10pm daily*

Maintenance & cleanliness	★★★★
Facilities	★½
Atmosphere & character	★★★★½
Security	★★
Overall rating	★★★

New Sydney Hostel

There is clean accommodation in freshly painted rooms above this excellent little pub in the centre of Hobart. Apart from the bar there are limited common areas – just a small lounge with a TV, microwave and kettle – but the bathrooms have been recently renovated and the bar has a great atmosphere.

87 Bathurst Street, Hobart
(03) 6234 4516
Website *www.view.com.au/newsydney/*
Dorm bed *$25*
Credit cards *MC, Visa*
Reception open *Mon noon-10pm, Tue noon-midnight, Wed-Fri 11.30am-midnight, Sat 4pm-midnight, Sun 4pm-9pm*

Maintenance & cleanliness	★★★½
Facilities	★
Atmosphere & character	★★★★
Security	★★
Overall rating	★★★

The Pickled Frog

The Pickled Frog is an older building in the south western end of the city centre. It has a good atmosphere in the common areas, which include a lounge with a big TV, a pool table and a cosy nook for reading. There is also a bar next to the reception area with cheap beer. However furnishings are old and worn and the accommodation upstairs shows its age and could be better maintained.

281 Liverpool Street, Hobart
(03) 6234 7977
Website *www.thepickledfrog.com*
Dorm bed *$23-25 ($22-24 ISIC, VIP);* ***single room*** *$60 ($55 ISIC, VIP);* ***double/twin room*** *$65 ($60 ISIC, VIP)*
Credit cards *MC, Visa*
Reception open *summer 8am-11am daily; winter 8.30am-9.30pm daily*

Maintenance & cleanliness	★★
Facilities	★★½
Atmosphere & character	★★★★
Security	★½
Overall rating	★★½

Welcome Stranger Backpackers

The Welcome Stranger is a pub one block from the top end of Salamanca Place. The bar has loads of pool tables but otherwise is nothing special. Upstairs the accommodation is neat and tidy with clean dormitories and double rooms with TVs and en suite facilities. The hostel's amenities include a kitchen, TV and laundry.

58 Harrington Street, Hobart
☎ *(03) 6223 6655*
***Website** www.welcomestrangerhotel.com.au*
***Dorm bed** $25; **single room** $85; **double/twin room** $99; **bed linen** $2; private room prices include breakfast*
***Credit cards** MC, Visa*
***Reception open** Mon-Fri 9am-4am, Sat 9am-midnight, Sun noon-4am*
TV K L

Maintenance & cleanliness	★★★½
Facilities	★★
Atmosphere & character	★★
Security	★★
Overall rating	★★★½

Eating & Drinking

Tasmania has a reputation for excellent food, but it's noted mainly for quality ingredients like salmon and King Island creams and cheeses rather than its restaurants.

From a budget traveller's perspective, the best value meals are the fish and chip shops around Constitution and Victoria Docks. **Mure's** *(Constitution Dock, Hobart)* is the biggest fish and chip place and is a Hobart landmark with a brilliant location right in the centre of Constitution Dock. It's nice and dry on a rainy day but if the sun is shining one of the other four small fish and chips shops on Constitution Dock may be a better – and cheaper – option. Also recommended is **Fish Frenzy** *(Elizabeth Street Pier, Hobart)*, which is just a short walk away.

Tasmania has Australia's best beer and some of Australia's best pubs are located in the historic area around Salamanca Place. Salamanca Place, and nearby Salamanca Square, also have a good choice of nice restaurants and cafés.

On Saturdays go to Salamanca Market for both the fast food stalls and fresh fruit and picnic food. When the market isn't open your best bet is to head to either the small supermarket on Salamanca Place or the **Woolworths** supermarket *(189 Campbell Street, Hobart)* in the city centre.

Sights

Cadbury Chocolate Factory

This is a popular factory tour where you can see Cadbury chocolate being produced and you also get the chance to sample the finished product. Tours are popular and it's essential to phone to make a booking.

Cadbury Road, Claremont
🚌 *37, 38, 38E, 38T, 40, 40T, X4, X4A, X10*
☎ *(03) 6249 0333 or 1800 627 367*
***Website** www.cadbury.com.au*
***Admission** $5*
***Tours** Mon-Fri 8am-4pm*

Cascade Brewery

The factory tour of Australia's oldest brewery is very popular with backpackers. Like all good brewery tours, there's free beer awaiting you at the end. Tours are popular and it's essential to phone ahead to make a booking.

140 Cascade Road, South Hobart
🚌 *43, 44, 46, 49*
☎ *(03) 6221 8300*
***Website** www.cascadebrewery.com.au*
***Admission** $20*
***Tours** Mon-Fri 9.30am, 10am, 1pm, 1.30pm*

Female Factory Historic Site

This former prison is the female equivalent to Port Arthur and female convicts were kept here between 1828 and 1877.

16 Degraves Street, South Hobart
🚌 *43, 44, 46, 49*
☎ *(03) 6223 1559*
***Website** www.femalefactory.com.au*
***Admission** $10*
***Tours** Mon-Fri 9.30am & 2pm, Sat-Sun 9.30am*

Maritime Museum

This is an interesting museum exploring Tasmania's maritime past with exhibits on whaling and shipwrecks.

Corner Argyle & Davey Streets, Hobart
☎ *(03) 6223 5082*
***Website** www.maritimetas.org*
***Admission** $7*
***Open** 9am-5pm daily*

Mercury Print Museum

Housed in one of Tasmania's oldest buildings, this museum focuses on newspaper publishing and the history of printing.

89 Macquarie Street, Hobart

☎ *(03) 6230 0736*
Website *http://ink.news.com.au/mercury/print_museum/menu.html*
Admission *$2.50*
Open *Mon-Thu 10am-1pm & 2pm-4pm*

Mount Wellington

If you have a car an excursion to the summit of Mount Wellington is a must. The views of the city from here are spectacular and on a clear day you can see half of Tasmania.

Mount Wellington Shuttle Bus Service *(☎ 0408 341 804)* leaves the city centre for Mt Wellington Mon-Fri 9.30am, noon & 2.30pm, Sat-Sun 9.30am, 1.30pm. The return fare is $25.

Alternatively Island Cycle Tours *(☎ 1300 880 334; website www.islandcycletours.com)* run trips to the summit of Mt Wellington with a downhill mountain bike ride back to Hobart. The trip takes around three hours and costs $75.

Tasmanian Museum & Art Gallery

This museum and gallery exhibits modern Australian art and artefacts depicting Tasmania's convict history.
40 Macquarie Street, Hobart
☎ *(03) 6235 0777*
Website *www.tmag.tas.gov.au*
Admission *free*
Open *10am-5pm daily*

Huon Valley

This region, around an hour southwest of Hobart, is a popular spot with backpackers who come here for fruit picking work between Nov and May.

Huonville is the main town in the Huon Valley, but travellers stay in either Cygnet or Geeveston.

Huonville

This small town on the Huon River is the main centre of the Huon Valley. Although there are no hostels in town, backpackers picking fruit in the region and staying in Cygnet or Geeveston often come here to buy groceries and travellers passing through often stop for jet boat rides on the river.

Practical Information

Huonville Visitor Information Centre

Esplanade, Huonville
☎ *(03) 6264 1838*
Website *www.huonjet.com/trips/viscentre1.html*
Open *9am-5pm daily*

National Parks Shop

24 Main Road, Huonville
☎ *(03) 6264 8460*
Website *www.parks.tas.gov.au*
Open *Mon-Fri 9am-4.30pm*

INTERNET ACCESS

Huonville Online Access Centre

23 Wilmot Road, Huonville
☎ *(03) 6264 3441*
Open *Mon-Fri 10am-5pm, Sat-Sun 10am-1pm*

Coming & Going

Tassielink *(☎ 1300 300 520; **website** www.tassielink.com.au)* have several buses a day from Huonville to Geeveston and Hobart.

Activities

Jet Boating

The Huon Jet boat operates jet boat rides from the outside the Huonville Visitor Information Centre, taking take you for a 35-minute spin on the Huon River.
Esplanade, Huonville
☎ *(03) 6264 1838*
Website *www.huonjet.com*
Price *$65*
Open *9am-5pm daily*

Cygnet

This small village, 17km south of Huonville is a pleasant spot to stop if you're touring the region. There is a backpackers' hostel nearby.

Accommodation

Huon Valley Backpackers (Balfes Hill)

This workers' hostel is comprised of several buildings in a rural location on Balfes Hill with views of the Huon Valley. It is quite well equipped compared with workers' hostels elsewhere

in Australia, having a games room with a pool table, table football and table tennis; a TV lounge with old ratty sofas and another lounge next to the kitchen. It is located near Cygnet and is also not too far from Huonville.
4 Sandhill Road, Cradoc
☎ *(03) 6295 1551*
Website *www.huonvalleybackpackers.com*
Dorm bed *$25;* ***double room*** *$60-90*
Reception open *Mon-Sat 9.30am-10.30am & 6pm-8.30pm, Sun 7pm-8pm*

Maintenance & cleanliness	★★½
Facilities	★★
Atmosphere & character	★★★
Security	★
Overall rating	★★½

Geeveston

This village, 22km southwest of Huonville, is a nice place with a couple of good hostels. It makes a good base for visiting the Tahune Forest Reserve.

Practical Information

Geeveston Forest & Heritage Centre

Church Street, Geeveston
☎ *(03) 6297 1836*
Website *www.forestandheritagecentre.com.au*
Open *9am-5pm daily*

INTERNET ACCESS

Geeveston Online Access Centre

School Road, Geeveston
☎ *(03) 6297 0074*
Open *Mon 10am-5pm, Tue noon-6pm, Wed 10am-5pm, Thu noon-6pm, Fri 10am-5pm*

Coming & Going

Tassielink (☎ *1300 300 520;* ***website*** *www.tassielink.com.au*) run buses between several buses a day between Geeveston and Hobart.

Accommodation

Bob's Bunkhouse

Bob's Bunkhouse is a great little hostel a short walk from the centre of Geeveston. It is an old wooden house with a basic kitchen, laundry facilities and a cosy lounge with a fireplace, TV and lots of books and board games. It's not the Ritz but it has a warm welcome and a great atmosphere.
Corner Huon Highway & School Road, Geeveston
☎ *(03) 6297 1069*
Website *www.bobsbunkhousegeeveston-backpackers.com.au*
Dorm bed *$20*

Maintenance & cleanliness	★★
Facilities	★½
Atmosphere & character	★★★★★
Security	★
Overall rating	★★½

Forest House Backpackers

Forest House Backpackers is in an old house close to the town centre. Although relatively basic, it is kept neat and tidy with newly renovated bathrooms. Amenities are limited to a cosy lounge with a fireplace plus a small kitchen.
Arve Road, Geeveston
☎ *(03) 6297 1844*
Dorm bed *$20;* ***double room*** *$50*

Maintenance & cleanliness	★★½
Facilities	★½
Atmosphere & character	★★★
Security	★½
Overall rating	★★½

Tahune Forest Reserve

The Tahune Forest Reserve is a popular destination because of the impressive Tahune Forest Air Walk and it is an easy day trip from Hobart.

Coming & Going

Tahune is about a 70-minute drive south from Hobart. Take the Huon Highway (A6) south to Geeveston before turning off the main road towards the Tahune Forest Reserve.

Sights & Activities

Tahune Forest Air Walk

The Air Walk is 570m long and allows visitors to see the forest from an unusual perspective among the treetops at a height of between 25m and 45m above ground level.

Tahune Forest Reserve, via Geeveston
☎ *(03) 6297 0068*
Website *www.tasforestrytourism.com.au/pages/site_s_tahune.html*
Admission *$22*
Open *9am-5pm daily*

Dover & Far South Tasmania

Dover is the most southern town in Tasmania and it makes a good base for exploring the island's far south. Attractions include sea kayaking and tours of glowworm caves. This region also provides access to the South West National Park.

Coming & Going

Tassielink (☎ *1300 300 520;* ***website*** *www.tassielink.com.au)* run buses between Hobart and Dover.

Accommodation

Far South Wilderness Lodge & Backpackers

Australia's southern-most backpackers' hostel is made up of log cabins on 35 acres of native bush on the waterfront. It has a big common room with a fireplace and TV and also has a bar and a big dining room with a commercial kitchen.

247 Narrows Road, Strathblane
☎ *(03) 6298 1922*
Website *www.farsouthwilderness.com.au*
Dorm bed *$25 first night, then $20 per night;* ***double room*** *$65 first night, then $50 per night*
Credit cards *MC, Visa*
Reception open *8am-11am & 4pm-8pm*

Maintenance & cleanliness	★★★★½
Facilities	★★½
Atmosphere & character	★★★★½
Security	★
Overall rating	★★★½

Richmond

Richmond is a small town with plenty of buildings dating from convict times.

It is a popular destination for day-trippers from Hobart with the usual collection of cafés, craft shops and guesthouses. The main attractions here include Australia's oldest Catholic church, Australia's oldest bridge and the nearby river where you can feed the ducks. Richmond Gaol is the most authentic reminder of the town's convict history.

Coming & Going

Tassielink (☎ *1300 300 520;* ***website*** *www.tassielink.com.au)* run buses between Hobart and Richmond. The Richmond Tourist Bus (☎ *0408 341 804)* is another, more expensive, option with two daily services between Hobart and Richmond.

Sights

Richmond Gaol

Australia's oldest existing colonial gaol is well preserved and offers the only surviving example of female solitary confinement cells in Tasmania as well as an extensive collection of convict relics.

37 Bathurst Street, Richmond
☎ *(03) 6260 2127*
Website *www.parks.tas.gov.au/historic/visguide/richmond_gaol/intro.html*
Admission *$7*
Open *9am-5pm daily*

Port Arthur & the Tasman Peninsula

The notorious convict settlement at Port Arthur is Tasmania's biggest tourist attraction and one of the most educational attractions in the state. Elsewhere on the peninsula are the natural rock formations on the rugged coast and the Tasmanian Devil Park at Taranna midway between Eaglehawk Neck and Port Arthur.

There are other attractions outside the Port Arthur Historic Site that are worth visiting if you've got your own car. You may want to take the turn-off near Eaglehawk Neck and take a look at the natural attractions on the peninsula's rugged coast, which include

Devils Kitchen, Tasman Arch, Tasman Blowhole and Tessellated Pavement. A short walk on the Tasman Trail will take you to Waterfall Bluff; if you continue on this trail you will end up at Fortescue Bay.

Practical Information

Port Arthur Visitor Information Centre

Port Arthur Historic Site, Port Arthur
☎ *(03) 6251 2371*
***Open** 8.30am-dusk*

Coming & Going

Tassielink *(☎ 1300 300 520; **website** www.tassielink.com.au)* run a daily service between Hobart and Port Arthur. The one-way fare is $24.20.

Accommodation

Port Arthur Caravan & Cabin Park

This caravan park has backpackers' accommodation in a charmless concrete block with nine-bed dorms with three-tier bunks beds and plastic-coated mattresses. Backpackers can use the park's facilities that include a spacious kitchen, covered barbecue areas and a laundry. The bathroom facilities are clean but they have coin-operated showers. It is set among bushland 3km outside Port Arthur village.
Garden Point, Port Arthur
☎ *(03) 6250 2340*
***Website** www.portarthurcaravan-cabinpark.com.au*
***Dorm bed** $18*
***Credit cards** MC, Visa*
***Reception open** 8am-8pm daily*

Maintenance & cleanliness	★★★
Facilities	½★
Atmosphere & character	½★
Security	★
Overall rating	★½

Eaglehawk Neck Backpackers

This tiny hostel has only four beds and four camping spots but it is the only real alternative on the Tasman Peninsula to the caravan park at Port Arthur. Facilities are old, dated and very basic but it is clean enough and many travellers like the atmosphere.
94 Old Jetty Road, Eaglehawk Neck
☎ *(03) 6250 3248*
***Website** http://backpackers.eaglehawkneck.com/*
***Dorm bed** $20; **camping** $8 per person*

Maintenance & cleanliness	★★
Facilities	★½
Atmosphere & character	★★★
Security	★
Overall rating	★★

Sights

Tasman National Park

Tasman National Park is easily accessible from Port Arthur. The park's rugged coastline is home to caves and natural features including Devils Kitchen, Tasman Arch and Tasman Blowhole. Seals, penguins, dolphins and whales are among the wildlife that can be seen at the park.
Taranna Field Centre, 5801 Arthur Highway, Taranna
☎ *(03) 6250 3497*
***Website** www.parks.tas.gov.au/natparks/tasman/*
***Admission** $11 per person, $22 for a car and up to eight passengers*

Tasmanian Devil Park

This wildlife park features Tasmanian Devils plus other animals such as kangaroos, wallabies and eagles.
5990 Arthur Highway, Taranna
☎ *(03) 6250 3230*
***Website** www.tasmaniandevilpark.com*
***Admission** $24*
***Open** 9am-5.30pm daily; devil feeding 10am, 11am, 1.30pm, 4.30pm daily; kangaroo & wallaby feeding 2.30pm daily; outdoor bird presentation 11.15am, 3.30pm daily*

Historic Ghost Tour

This a popular walking tour that recounts spooky stories about convict ghosts.
Tours depart from the Port Arthur Visitor's Centre.
☎ *(03) 6251 2371*
***Website** www.portarthur.org.au*
***Tours cost** $20*
***Tours depart** summer 8.45pm, 9pm daily; winter 6.30pm, 8.30pm daily*

Port Arthur Historic Park

This is a must-see attraction that gives you an excellent impression of Australia's convict history. The Port Arthur Historic Park covers a large area and includes ruins of the prison settlement with several restored buildings. Admission to the site includes a guided tour and a cruise around the harbour.
Port Arthur Historic Site, Port Arthur
☎ *1800 659 101*
Website *www.portarthur.org.au*
Admission *$28*
Open *8.30am-dusk daily, most buildings close at 5pm*

East Coast

Moving north from Hobart along the Tasman Highway takes you through many small pleasant seaside towns as well as Freycinet National Park's renowned hiking trail to Wine Glass Bay. The sunny east coast is a popular route for those who are either driving or cycling and it's a preferable route to the Midland Highway.

Triabunna & Maria Island National Park

Maria Island, 15km offshore from Triabunna, is a former penal settlement that has been protected as a national park. The park is also known for its wildlife and many endangered species have been introduced to the island in a bid to build their numbers in a car-free environment.

There are some good hiking trails on the island. The **Fossil Cliffs walk** *(2 hours)* and **Painted Cliffs walk** *(2½ hours)* are popular with day trippers and the challenging **Bishop and Clerk walk** *(4 hours)* offers breathtaking ocean views. The ruins of the penal settlement at Darlington, where the ferry arrives, is also worth exploring.

There are no shops on the island so you'll need to stock up on supplies in Triabunna. A lot of travellers use Triabunna as a base for exploring the island but many stay at the hostels in Bicheno or Swansea before catching the ferry to the island.

The national park fee is $11 per person.

Practical Information

Triabunna Visitor Information Centre

Esplanade, Triabunna
☎ *(03) 6257 4772*
Open *10am-4pm daily*

Coming & Going

TassieLink *(☎ 1300 300 520; **website** www.tassielink.com.au)* stop at Triabunna on their Hobart-Swansea service. Buses stop outside the Shell service station.

Seawings *(☎ 0419 746 668; **website** www.seawingsecotours.com.au)* operate a ferry service between Triabunna and Maria Island on Mondays, Wednesdays, Fridays and Sundays departing Triabunna at 10.30am and 3.15pm and returning at 11.30am and 4pm. The return fare is $50.

Accommodation

There is no longer a hostel in Triabunna so the closest backpackers accommodation is now in Swansea.

Camping and basic dormitory-style accommodation is available on the island. Camping at Darlington on Maria Island costs $4.40 per person and there are free campsites at Encampment Grove and French's Farm, both campsites are a three to four hour hike from Darlington. Dormitory accommodation on the island is in the Old Penitentiary.

Old Penitentiary

The Parks & Wildlife Service runs the Old Penitentiary in Darlington as very basic dormitory accommodation. There are nine rooms, each with six bunk beds. Facilities are limited to a wood-fired heater that can also be used for cooking, plus a barbecue area and an amenities block with hot showers.
Darlington, Maria Island
☎ *(03) 6257 1420*
Dorm bed *$8.80*

Swansea

Overlooking Great Oyster Bay, this historic seaside resort is a pleasant spot to break your journey. There isn't a lot to do in town although there is an interesting bark mill and a small museum. You can sometimes see dolphins in the bay.

Coming & Going

Tassielink (☎ *1300 300 520; **website** www.tassielink.com.au)* run bus services between Hobart and Swansea.

Accommodation

Swansea Backpackers

This modern building next to the Bark Mill Museum is a brand new purpose-built flashpackers hostel that features a bright spacious open-air common area that includes a dining/TV area, a fully-equipped kitchen and an area with a pool table. There is also an outdoor courtyard with barbecue facilities. It is an expensive hostel, but you get what you pay for.

96 Tasman Highway, Swansea
☎ *(03) 6257 8650*
***Website** www.swanseabackpackers.com.au*
***Dorm bed** $34; **double room** $75*
***Credit cards** MC, Visa*
***Reception open** 7.30am-8.30pm daily*

Maintenance & cleanliness	★★★★★
Facilities	★★½
Atmosphere & character	★★★½
Security	★★
Overall rating	★★★½

Sights

Black Wattle Bark Mill & Museum

Australia's only bark crusher was once used to make leather tan from black wattle bark. The adjoining museum details the town's history.

96 Tasman Highway, Swansea
☎ *(03) 6257 8382*
***Admission** $10*
***Open** 9am-5pm daily*

Bicheno

This small town is a popular stop on the east coast. It is conveniently situated as an ideal base for exploring both the Douglas Apsley and Freycinet National Parks.

Penguin spotting tours are the main attraction in Bicheno.

Practical Information

INTERNET ACCESS

Bicheno Online Access Centre

The Oval, Burgess Street, Bicheno
☎ *(03) 6375 1892*
***Open** Tue 10am-1pm, Thu 9am-noon, Fri-Sat 10am-2pm*

Coming & Going

Tassielink (☎ *1300 300 520; **website** www.tassielink.com.au)* buses run between Bicheno and Hobart and Bicheno Coach Service (☎ *(03) 6257 0293)* has buses to Coles Bay.

Accommodation

Bicheno Backpackers Hostel

Bicheno Backpackers is a small hostel near the town centre with a great cosy atmosphere. Common areas include a lounge with a TV plus a fully-equipped kitchen, a laundry and barbecue area. Accommodation is in nice cosy dorms with curtains for each bed and individual bedside lights and there are ocean views from some rooms.

11 Morrison Street, Bicheno
☎ *(03) 6375 1651*
***Website** www.bichenobackpackers.com*
***Dorm bed** $22-24; **double room** $55-65*
***Credit cards** MC, Visa*
***Reception open** 8am-2pm & 4pm-8.30pm daily*

Maintenance & cleanliness	★★★
Facilities	★½
Atmosphere & character	★★★★½
Security	★★
Overall rating	★★★

Seaview Holiday Park

Seaview Holiday Park is a relatively large complex on a residential street with lovely sea views. Accommodation is in neat and tidy bunk rooms and common areas include two fully equipped kitchens plus a beach volleyball court, tennis court and barbecue area. New management have made a big improvement to this hostel but it still doesn't have the cosy atmosphere of Bicheno's other hostel.

29 Banksia Street, Bicheno
☎ *(03) 6375 1247*

Dorm bed *$20-25*
Credit cards *MC, Visa*
Reception open *8am-6pm*

Maintenance & cleanliness	★★½
Facilities	★★½
Atmosphere & character	★½
Security	★
Overall rating	★★

Sights & Activities

Cycling, Kayaking & Surfing

You can rent mountain bikes ($10 1st hour, $5 each additional hour, $35 per day); body boards ($10 1st hour, $5 each additional hour, $35 per day); kayaks ($15 1st hour, $5 each additional hour, $40 per day) and surfboards ($15 1st hour, $5 each additional hour, $40 per day) from **Bicheno Backpackers** *(11 Morrison Street, Bicheno; ☎ (03) 6375 1651; **website** www.bichenobackpackers.com).*

Penguin Tours

Bicheno Penguin Tours *(☎ (03) 6375 1333; **website** www.bichenopenguintours.com.au)* is a unique experience where you are taken in a small group to see little penguins waddle in from the sea at dusk. It's highly recommended as it is a much more intimate experience than penguin viewing centres in Victoria or New Zealand and the number of penguins is relatively high, particularly between July and November. Penguin tours cost $20.

Coles Bay & Freycinet National Park

Coles Bay is the gateway to Freycinet National Park *(☎ (03) 6257 0107; **website** www.parks.tas.gov.au/natparks/freycinet/)*, and is the perfect place to rest after hiking in the park.

Practical Information

National Park Information Centre

Park entrance, Freycinet National Park
☎ *(03) 6256 7000*
Website *www.parks.tas.gov.au/natparks/freycinet/*
Open *9am-6pm daily*

Coming & Going

Bicheno Coach Service *(☎ (03) 6257 0293)* runs between Coles Bay and Bicheno and connect with Tassielink *(☎ 1300 300 520; **website** www.tassielink.com.au)* buses to Hobart at the Coles Bay turn-off on the A3 highway.

Accommodation

Iluka Holiday Centre YHA

Iluka Holiday Centre YHA feels dated with lino floors and old furnishings. Facilities include a barren TV lounge, a fully-equipped kitchen and dining area with a fireplace. It is a clean hostel but it shows its age and it has the ambience of a depressing old folks' home.
The Esplanade, Coles Bay
☎ *(03) 6257 0115*
Website *www.yha.com.au*
Dorm bed *$27 ($24 HI/YHA);* ***double/twin room*** *$67.50 ($60 HI/YHA)*
Credit cards *MC, Visa*
Reception open *8am-6pm daily*

Maintenance & cleanliness	★★½
Facilities	★½
Atmosphere & character	★★
Security	★½
Overall rating	★★

Hiking

The most popular hiking trail in Freycinet National Park is the one-hour walk to the Wine Glass Bay lookout although many backpackers prefer the longer route that continues on to Wine Glass Bay and Hazards Beach (5 hours return).

Douglas Apsley National Park

Being one of Tasmania's less popular national parks means that you don't have to share the wilderness with too many other people. Douglas Apsley National Park is mostly dry eucalypt forest, however it also harbours pockets of rainforest and there are plenty of hiking trails and spots for a swim. The easiest hike is the 10-minute walk to the Apsley Waterhole from the southern car park.

This is a relatively new park with very basic facilities. There is free camping in the park including a campground at the Apsley Waterhole. There is no fresh water in the park so stock up on supplies before you get here.

St Helens

St Helens is both the most northerly and the largest town on the east coast. There isn't really a lot to do here apart from surfing and you'll probably just stop long enough to visit the supermarket and get cash from the ATM.

Practical Information

St Helens Visitor Information Centre

59 Cecilia Street, St Helens
☎ *(03) 6376 1744*
***Open** Mon-Fri 9am-5pm, Sat 9am-noon, Sun 10am-2pm*

INTERNET ACCESS

St Helens Online Access Centre

State Library Building, 61 Cecilia Street, St Helens
☎ *(03) 6376 1116*
***Open** Mon-Fri 9am-5pm, Sat-Sun 10am-noon*

Coming & Going

Tassielink (☎ *1300 300 520; **website** www.tassielink.com.au)* run bus services between Hobart and St Helens and Redline (☎ *1300 3600 000; **website** www.tasredline.com)* have a service to Launceston.

Accommodation

St Helens Backpackers

St Helens Backpackers is a modern brick and wood house close to the town centre. It has very pleasant double/twin rooms upstairs and downstairs there is a nice lounge with high ceilings and there is also a nice deck outside with a barbecue. The hostel doesn't have a TV, which encourages guests to talk to each other creating a good atmosphere.
9 Cecilia Street, St Helens
☎ *(03) 6376 2017*
***Website** www.sthelensbackpackers.com.au*
***Dorm bed** $22; **double room** $55-60*
***Reception open** 8.30am-11am & 4pm-6.30pm daily*

Maintenance & cleanliness	★★★★
Facilities	★½
Atmosphere & character	★★★★
Security	★½
Overall rating	★★★

St Helens YHA

This is a demoralising old house on a quiet residential street with basic facilities that include a lounge with a TV, fireplace and a few books. It is a traditional YHA that manages to make even a small house feel depressing and institutional with its rules (no alcohol and don't even think about enjoying yourselves) and overbearing management.
5 Cameron Street, St Helens
☎ *(03) 6376 1661*
***Website** www.yha.com.au*
***Dorm bed** $25 ($22 HI/YHA); **double room** $60-70 ($47-55 HI/YHA)*
***Reception open** 8am-10am & 5pm-8pm*

Maintenance & cleanliness	★★
Facilities	★★
Atmosphere & character	★
Security	★½
Overall rating	★★

Launceston

Tasmania's second largest city is also one of Australia's oldest.

This pleasant city is built on the banks of the Tamar River and boasts some outstanding natural attractions; particularly the awesome Cataract Gorge, which is only 15 minutes walk from the city centre.

Practical Information

Launceston Visitor Information Centre

Cornwall Square, 12-16 St John Street, Launceston
☎ *(03) 6336 3133*
***Website** www.discoverlaunceston.com*

Launceston National Park Visitor Centre

Prospect Offices, Bass Highway, South Launceston

☎ *(03) 6336 5312*
Website *www.parks.tas.gov.au*
Open *Mon-Fri 9am-5pm*

INTERNET ACCESS

Cyber King Internet Lounge
113 George Street, Launceston
☎ *0417 393 540*
Website *www.cyberking.com.au*
Open *Mon-Fri 8.30am-7.30pm, Sat-Sun 9.30am-6.30pm*

Launceston Online Access Centre
State Library, Civic Square, Launceston
☎ *(03) 6334 9559*
Open *Mon-Wed 9am-6pm, Thu-Fri 9am-7pm, Sat 9am-12.30pm*

There is free Wi-Fi access at the Arthouse hostel so it is a good idea to stay there if you're travelling with your own computer.

Coming & Going

AIR

Launceston Airport *(**website** www.launcestonairport.com.au)* is 20km south of the city centre and has flights to Melbourne, Sydney and Brisbane. JetStar, Qantas and Virgin Blue fly into here.

The Airporter Shuttle Bus *(☎ (03) 6343 6677)* connects with all flights and will pick up and drop off at hostels. The one-way fare to the city centre is $12.

BUS

Buses operate to destinations throughout Tasmania. Tassielink *(☎ 1300 300 520; **website** www.tassielink.com.au)* coaches arrive and depart from the terminal at 101 George Street in the city centre. The Redline *(☎ 1300 360 000; **website** www.tasredline.com)* coach terminal is at 18 Charles Street.

Local Transport

Launceston has a fairly comprehensive bus network with one-way fares ranging from $2-4.50. An all day ticket costs $5-6. The main drawback is that buses stop running at around 7pm. Most things in Launceston are centrally located and it's unlikely that you'll need to use the bus.

Accommodation

Arthouse Backpacker Hostel

The Arthouse is a newly renovated 1888 building in Invermay, just north of Launceston's city centre. The hostel has lovely polished hardwood floors and offers a high standard of accommodation with new beds and clean newly renovated bathrooms. Amenities include a fully-equipped kitchen, and another smaller kitchen upstairs; a nice TV lounge, laundry, free Wi-Fi access and a nice courtyard with a barbecue and herb garden. The Arthouse is the best budget accommodation option in Launceston even though it isn't in the city centre.

20 Lindsay Street, Launceston
🚌 *2, 6, 7, 10*
☎ *(03) 6333 0222*
Website *www.arthousehostel.com.au*
Dorm bed *$23-27;* ***single room*** *$55;* ***double/twin room*** *$65*
Credit cards *MC, Visa*
Reception open *8am-9pm daily*
TV L K

Maintenance & cleanliness	★★★★
Facilities	★★★½
Atmosphere & character	★★★★
Security	★★
Overall rating	★★★½

Backpacker Hub & Bar

This hostel, also known as Andy's Backpackers and Tamar Backpackers, is above a bar/restaurant and gelati shop near the Boag's Brewery. The bar and restaurant on the ground floor are really nice but the accommodation upstairs is very basic with no common areas (apart from the bar) to speak of. Basically it's just accommodation above a pub.

1 Tamar Street, Launceston
🚌 *2, 6, 7, 10*
☎ *(03) 6334 9288*
Website *www.backpackerhub.com.au*
Dorm bed *$23 ($21 VIP);* ***single room*** *$49 ($47 VIP);* ***double room*** *$54 ($51 VIP)*
Credit cards *MC, Visa*
Reception open *9am-midnight/1am*
L

Maintenance & cleanliness	★★
Facilities	★½
Atmosphere & character	★
Security	★★
Overall rating	★½

Irish Murphy's

Irish Murphy's is a great little Irish pub with live music every day. There is accommodation for 35 people upstairs with shared facilities that include a small kitchen and TV lounge. It has an excellent location close to the centre of Launceston.

211 Brisbane Street, Launceston
☎ *(03) 6331 4440*
Website *www.irishmurphys.com.au*
Dorm bed *$21;* ***double room*** *$45*
Credit cards *Amex, MC, Visa*
Reception open *Mon-Thu noon-midnight; Fri-Sun noon-3.30pm*

Maintenance & cleanliness	★★½
Facilities	★
Atmosphere & character	★★★
Security	★½
Overall rating	★★

Launceston Backpackers

Launceston Backpackers is a good hostel in a lovely old building in a relatively quiet location opposite a park but just a short walk to the city centre and a 15-minute walk to the gorge. It features accommodation in big spacious rooms plus a big TV lounge, a huge kitchen and common room with a piano.

103 Canning Street, Launceston
40, 50
☎ *(03) 6334 2327*
Website *www.launcestonbackpackers.com.au*
Dorm bed *$20-21;* ***single room*** *$48;* ***double room*** *$55-65;* ***twin room*** *$52*
Credit cards *MC, Visa*
Reception open *summer 8am-10pm daily; winter 8am-11am & 3pm-10pm daily*

Maintenance & cleanliness	★★★½
Facilities	★½
Atmosphere & character	★★★
Security	★★
Overall rating	★★½

Lloyd's Hotel Backpackers

This hostel consists of rooms above a pub. Accommodation is in small dormitories (mostly two to four beds)

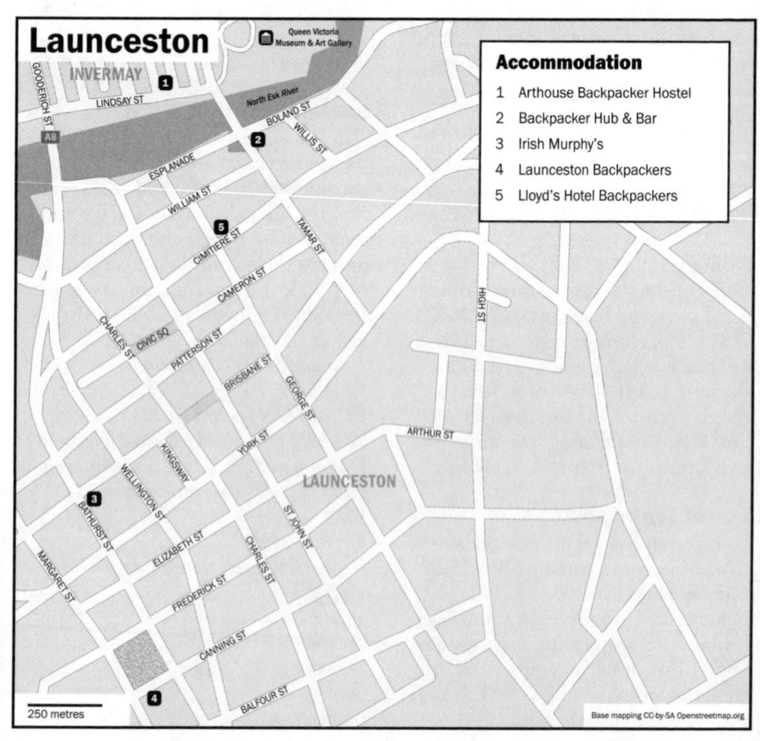

Tasmania

all with en suite facilities. There are quite a lot of common areas compared with other pub/hostels; these include a fully-equipped kitchen, a spacious TV lounge and internet access including Wi-Fi ($1 per 9 minutes; PIE). However it feels a bit dated and it doesn't have the atmosphere of a regular backpackers' hostel.

23 George Street, Launceston
☎ *1300 858 861*
Website *http://www.backpackers-accommodation.com.au/*
Dorm bed *$22;* ***single room*** *$55;* ***double/twin room*** *$70*
Credit cards *MC, Visa*
Reception open *8am-8pm*
TV K L

Maintenance & cleanliness	★★½
Facilities	★★
Atmosphere & character	★★
Security	★★½
Overall rating	★★½

The Mowbray Backpackers

The Mowbray is an old-man's pub in Launceston's northern suburbs with backpackers' accommodation upstairs. The accommodation is relatively clean with basic facilities that include a barren TV lounge but it is overpriced considering the inconvenient suburban location. It is around five minutes by bus to the city centre.

254 Invermay Road, Mowbray
10, 12, 13, 14, 17, 18, 19
☎ *(03) 6326 1633*
Dorm bed *$40;* ***double/twin room*** *$55*
Credit cards *MC, Visa*
Reception open *10am-8pm*
TV

Maintenance & cleanliness	★★★
Facilities	★
Atmosphere & character	★
Security	★★
Overall rating	★★

Eating & Drinking

Launceston is a pretty good place for eating out, particularly when you consider the city's small size.

There are plenty of places around the city centre for a quick bite at lunchtime including the usual selection of fast food places and food courts. **Morty's Food Hall** *(25 Wellington Street, Launceston)* has a good selection of cheap tasty food.

Launceston has some good pubs that serve substantial meals. These include **Irish Murphy's** *(211 Brisbane Street, Launceston)*, an Irish pub with a hostel upstairs and good hearty pub food and the more upmarket **Royal on George** *(90 George Street, Launceston)* – a historic pub with good atmosphere, live music and tasty food. As far as Tasmanian pubs go, **Hotel Tasmania**, aka the Launceston Saloon, *(191 Charles Street, Launceston)* is nothing special – and the Wild West décor is a bit tacky; but it does have very cheap food such as roast of the day for $6.95.

If you're preparing your own food, the cheapest option is the **Coles** *(198 Charles Street, Launceston)* and **Woolworths** *(128 Wellington Street, Launceston)* supermarkets.

Sights

Boags Brewery Tours

The J Boag & Son Brewery offer tours of their historic brewery each weekday. Tours include the entire production process from the brewhouse to the packaging line. There is also a small museum on site with displays about the history of the Boags Brewery. Advance bookings are essential.

39 William Street, Launceston
☎ *(03) 6332 6300*
Website *www.boags.com.au*
Admission *museum free; tours $18-25*
Open *Mon-Fri 8.45am-4.30pm*

Cataract Gorge

Launceston's major attraction is the spectacular Cataract Gorge. The gorge is about a 15-minute walk from the centre of Launceston and there are several lovely walks within the Cataract Gorge Reserve.

The reserve is also home to the Duck Reach Power Station, which was the first hydroelectric power station in the Southern Hemisphere when it was constructed in 1895.

Queen Victoria Museum & Art Galley

Launceston's most important museum has two branches – at Royal Park and

at Inveresk. The Royal Park museum is home to a Chinese temple, decorative arts and an exhibit of metals in Tasmania. The Inveresk museum has an art gallery plus exhibits on migration and railways. There are plans to give the Inveresk museum more of a focus on science and develop the Royal Park museum into a world-class gallery of decorative and fine arts.
Corner Cameron & Wellington Streets, Launceston
☎ *(03) 6323 3777*
Website *www.qvmag.tas.gov.au*
Admission *museum free*
Open *museum 10am-5pm daily*

Around Launceston

The area around Launceston includes the ports of George Town and Bridport. These places can be visited either as a day trip or en route to the east coast.

Bridport

This small seaside town is a relaxing spot to spend a day or two, although there isn't a lot to do here.

Practical Information

INTERNET ACCESS

Bridport Online Access Centre
Behind the library, Main Street, Bridport
☎ *(03) 6356 0258*
Open *Mon 10am-noon & 1pm-4pm, Tue 10am-noon, Wed 10am-noon & 2pm-5pm, Thu 10am-noon, Fri 10am-noon & 1pm-4pm, Sat 10am-noon*

Coming & Going

Stan's Coach Service (☎ *(03) 6356 1662)* runs a twice-daily service to Scottsdale, where it connects with the Redline bus to Launceston.

You can travel by ferry from Bridport to Flinders Island in Bass Strait or Port Welshpool in Victoria. The ferry is operated by Southern Shipping (☎ *(03) 6356 1753;* ***website*** *www.southernshipping.com.au).*

Accommodation

Bridport has an excellent hostel but if you're driving you may want to take advantage of the free camping site at Northeast Park on Ringarooma Road (A3) in Scottsdale, about a 20-minute drive south of Bridport. Maximum stay seven days.

Bridport Seaside Lodge

Bridport Seaside Lodge is a beautiful purpose-built hostel with exposed beams, polished Tasmanian oak floors and huge windows to take in the sea views. The hostel's facilities include a common area that includes a fully-equipped kitchen, a lounge with a TV and a nice front deck with a barbecue. Accommodation is in small, clean and comfortable rooms.
47 Main Street, Bridport
☎ *(03) 6356 1585*
Website *http://www.bridportseasidelodge.com/*
Dorm bed *$22;* ***double/twin room*** *$50-75*
Credit cards *MC, Visa*
🚗 TV K L

Maintenance & cleanliness	★★★½
Facilities	★★
Atmosphere & character	★★★
Security	★½
Overall rating	★★★

George Town

Australia's third oldest settlement doesn't really have a lot to show for all its years of history, but it is a pleasant enough town to visit.

Practical Information

George Town Visitor Information Centre
Main Road, George Town
☎ *(03) 6382 1700*
Website *www.tamarvalley.com.au*
Open *9am-5pm daily*

INTERNET ACCESS

George Town Online Access Centre
Macquarie Street, George Town
☎ *(03) 6382 1356*
Open *Mon-Fri 9am-1pm, Sat-Sun 1pm-8pm*

Coming & Going

Redline (☎ *1300 360 000; **website** www.tasredline.com)* have several buses running each day between Launceston and George Town.

Great Western Tiers

This scenic region south of Devonport is best known for the caves at Mole Creek.

Deloraine

About midway between Devonport and Launceston, Deloraine is a good base for exploring the Great Western Tiers region.

Practical Information

Great Western Tiers Visitor Centre

98-100 Emu Bay Road, Deloraine
☎ *(03) 6362 3471*
***Website** www.greatwesterntiers.net.au*
***Open** 9am-5pm daily*

INTERNET ACCESS

Deloraine Online Access Centre

West Parade, Deloraine
☎ *(03) 6362 3537*
***Open** Mon-Tue 10am-4pm, Wed 10am-7pm, Thu 10am-4pm, Fri 10am-7pm, Sun 1pm-4pm*

Accommodation

There is a YHA in Deloraine, but if you're travelling by campervan you may want to stop at Westbury, 15km west of Deloraine, where there's free camping at the rear of Andy's Hot Bread shop.

Highview Lodge YHA

Deloraine's YHA hostel keeps alive the traditional image of the depressing institutional youth hostel where having fun is frowned upon. There are rules posted all over the hostel and the sign stating that it is a home first suggests that guests take second place. There are no keys to the rooms but the front door is locked at midnight ruling out a late night at the local pub. Although the hostel has quite nice wooden floorboards, the furnishings are old and the whole place feels very dated. Facilities include a cosy TV lounge and a kitchen with lots of pots and pans – although the fridges appear to date from the 1970s. Toilets and showers are outside. The hostel is an old house perched high on a hill overlooking Deloraine with a view of the mountains.

8 Blake Street, Deloraine
☎ *(03) 6362 2996*
***Website** www.yha.com.au*
***Dorm bed** $21.50-24; **double/twin room** $49-54.50*
***Credit cards** MC, Visa*
***Reception open** 8am-10am & 5pm-10pm; **curfew** midnight*

Maintenance & cleanliness	★★
Facilities	★★½
Atmosphere & character	★
Security	★
Overall rating	★★½

Sights

Deloraine Museum & Yarns Artwork in Silk

Deloraine Museum has displays on local history. The museum is accompanied by *Yarns Artwork in Silk*, which is a series of four large silk panels, each depicting the Great Western Tiers in a different season.

98-100 Emu Bay Road, Deloraine
☎ *(03) 6362 3471*
***Admission** $7*
***Open** 9am-5pm daily*

Mole Creek Karst National Park

Around midway between Deloraine and Cradle Mountain, Mole Creek Karst National Park is noted for its spectacular caves.

There are over 200 caves but the two main ones are Marakoopa and King Solomons Caves, which are located 11km apart. The Parks & Wildlife department *(**website** www.parks.tas.gov.au)* operate tours of both these caves.

King Solomons Cave

King Solomons Cave is much smaller than Marakoopa and it has lavish decorative stalagmites and stalactite formations.

☎ *(03) 6363 5182*
***Admission** $15*
***Tours** 10.30am, 11.30am, 12.30pm, 2.30pm, 3.30pm, 4.30pm daily*

Marakoopa Cave

Marakoopa Cave is best known for its glow-worms, boasting Australia's largest glow-worm display.

☎ *(03) 6363 5182*
***Admission** $15*
***Tours** 10am, noon, 1pm, 2pm, 4pm daily*

Devonport

Devonport will be your first taste of Tasmania if you're arriving from Melbourne on the *Spirit of Tasmania*.

This industrial city doesn't really have a lot to offer and isn't typical of the rest of the state but it has a developed infrastructure and it's a good place to organise the rest of your trip. Its close proximity to Cradle Mountain and the Overland Track also means that you get plenty of handy tips from people who have just done the trek.

Practical Information

Devonport Visitor Information Centre

92 Formby Road, Devonport
☎ *(03) 6424 4466*
***Website** www.discovertasmania.com*
***Open** 7.30am-5pm daily*

INTERNET ACCESS

Devonport Online Access Centre

21 Oldaker Street, Devonport
☎ *(03) 6424 9413*
***Open** Mon-Tue 9.30am-5.30pm, Wed 9.30am-6.30pm, Thu-Fri 9.30am-5.30pm, Sat 9.30am-3.30pm*

Coming & Going

AIR

Qantas flies between Devonport and Melbourne. Devonport's small airport is only 10km outside town. A shuttle bus *(☎ 1300 659 878)* runs to the airport from the tourist information centre on Formby Road. The fare is $10 per person but it is better value to catch a taxi ($20) if there are two or more of you.

BUS

Both Tassielink *(☎ 1300 300 520; **website** www.tassielink.com.au)* and Redline *(☎ 1300 360 000; **website** www.tasredline.com)* buses run between Devonport and most destinations in Tasmania. Buses stop at the corner of Best and Edward Streets.

FERRY

The *Spirit of Tasmania (☎ 1800 634 906; **website** www.spiritoftasmania.com.au)* ferry arrives at the ferry terminal in East Devonport. Ferries depart Devonport at 9pm every day.

Local Transport

Merseylink *(☎ 1300 367 590; **website** www.merseylink.com.au)* operates a local bus service with six routes running Mon-Sat. Many backpackers find they need to use the bus, especially if they're staying at the Tasman House or MacWright House YHA hostels, which are a long way from the town centre.

The most useful bus service is route 40, which runs between Latrobe and the city centre via the Formby Road, Tasman House and MacWright House YHA hostels. Buses 20 and 25 also go to the Tasman House hostel.

Fares are $1.90-3.10 for a single journey or $3.80 for a Daytripper ticket.

Accommodation

Devonport has some of the cheapest hostel beds in Australia but unfortunately you get what you pay for.

Alexander Hotel

The Alexander Hotel is a fairly ordinary pub on busy Formby Road with basic accommodation upstairs with dormitory rooms plus a TV lounge and small kitchen. It is expensive for Devonport although it's a better standard of accommodation than most other budget options. At the end of the day it is just rooms above a pub.

78 Formby Road, Devonport
☎ *(03) 6424 1070*
***Dorm bed** $25; **single room** $49; **double room** $59*
***Credit cards** MC, Visa*
***Reception open** Mon 10am-9pm, Tue-Sat 10am-midnight, Sun 10am-9pm*

Maintenance & cleanliness	★★½
Facilities	★½
Atmosphere & character	★★
Security	★½
Overall rating	★★

Formby Road Hostel

This long running hostel is in an old building on Formby Road around 1km from the centre of town. It has a fully-equipped kitchen, laundry, TV lounge and a small courtyard but the standard of accommodation is nothing special.

16 Formby Road, Devonport
40
☎ *(03) 6423 6563*
***Dorm bed** $18*
***Reception open** 4.30pm-9pm daily*

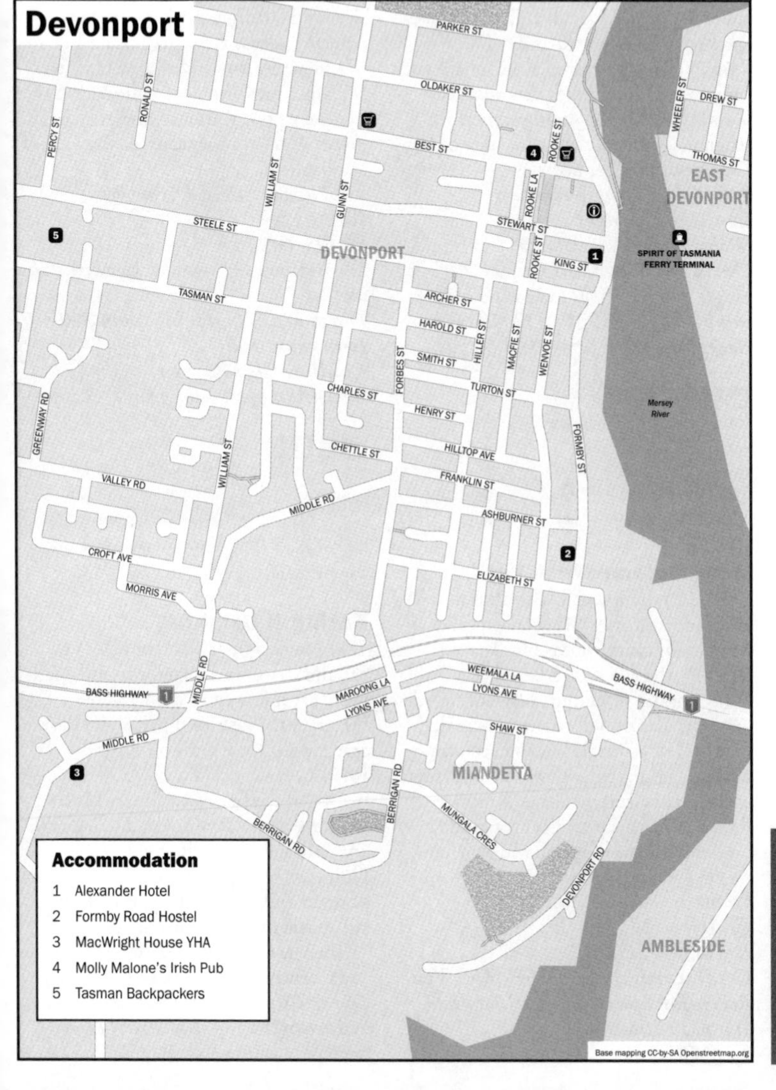

Tasmania

Maintenance & cleanliness	★½
Facilities	★½
Atmosphere & character	★★
Security	★½
Overall rating	★½

MacWright House YHA

This old house is on a quiet residential street far from the centre of Devonport. It is a traditional (an institutional 1960s-style) youth hostel with a depressing feel and old dowdy furnishings. However it is cheap and clean enough and all the basic facilities are there including a small fully-equipped kitchen, a dining area and a TV lounge. The depressing atmosphere and remote location makes this a last resort – and that is really saying something when you consider the dire state of Devonport's other hostels!

115 Middle Road, Devonport
(03) 6424 5696
***Website** www.yha.com.au*
***Dorm bed** $18.50 ($15 HI/YHA); **single room** $25.50 ($22 HI/YHA); **double room** $35.50 ($32 HI/YHA)*
***Reception open** 7am-10am & 5pm-10pm*

Maintenance & cleanliness	★★
Facilities	★½
Atmosphere & character	★
Security	★½
Overall rating	★½

Molly Malone's Irish Pub

This centrally located Irish Pub has cheap dormitory-style accommodation upstairs in clean rooms plus shared facilities that include a laundry, a TV lounge and a small but fully-equipped kitchen. The pub downstairs is really nice and does meals but the accommodation feels dated with old-style carpets and old furniture in the common rooms. It is cheap and central and probably the best option in town.

34 Best Street, Devonport
40
(03) 6424 1898
***Dorm bed** $15-20*
***Credit cards** Amex, Diners, MC, Visa*
***Reception open** Mon-Sat 10am-late, Sun noon-10pm*

Maintenance & cleanliness	★★★½
Facilities	★★
Atmosphere & character	★★
Security	★★
Overall rating	★★★½

Tasman Backpackers

Tasman Backpackers is a large hostel with an institutional atmosphere but the hostel's size means that there is room for more common areas than Devonport's other hostels. Facilities include a cinema, a common room with a pool table, fireplace and television and a fully-equipped kitchen. Internet access is $5 per hour and Wi-Fi access costs $5 a day. However the amenities and accommodation is of a very poor standard and the cheap prices don't compensate for the lack of atmosphere.

114 Tasman Street, Devonport
20, 25, 40
(03) 6423 2335
***Website** www.tasmanbackpackers.com.au*
***Dorm bed** $16; **double room** $40-50; **twin room** $36*
***Credit cards** MC, Visa*
***Reception open** 7am-noon & 3.30pm-10pm*

Maintenance & cleanliness	★½
Facilities	★★½
Atmosphere & character	★½
Security	★★½
Overall rating	★★

Eating & Drinking

There's not a big choice of places to eat and drink in Devonport, although there are a few cafés along Rooke Street, some fast food places on Best Street and a few pubs on Formby Road.

One of the better options is **Molly Malone's** *(34 Best Street, Devonport)*, an Irish pub with filling pub meals and Guinness on tap. It is right in the centre of town and especially convenient if you're staying in the hostel upstairs.

There are a few supermarkets near the town centre including **Coles** *(corner Best & Gunn Streets, Devonport)* and **Woolworths** *(74 Best Street, Devonport)*.

Sights

Penguin Viewing

Every evening at sunset during the nesting season (Oct-Mar) you can watch little penguins return to their burrows from the specially constructed viewing platforms.
Lillico Beach, Devonport

Tiagarra Aboriginal Cultural Centre

Tiagarra is an interesting museum and cultural centre exploring Tasmania's Aboriginal history. It is north of the centre at Devonport Bluff.
Off Bluff Road, Mersey Bluff
☎ *(03) 6424 8250*
***Admission** $4*
***Open** 9am-5pm daily*

North-West Coast

By Tasmanian standards, the north-west coast is densely populated with a string of medium sized towns stretching from Devonport to Stanley. There isn't really a lot to see or do here, but it's a nice coastal drive.

Burnie

The region's major town is of little interest to most travellers but you may have to pass through town to make transport connections.

Practical Information

Burnie Visitor Information Centre

Little Alexander Street, Burnie
☎ *(03) 6434 6111*
***Website** www.discovertasmania.com*
***Open** 8am-5pm daily*

INTERNET ACCESS

Burnie Online Access Centre

2 Spring Street, Burnie
☎ *(03) 6431 9469*
***Open** Mon-Wed 9am-5pm, Fri 9am-8pm, Sat 9.30am-12.30pm*

Sights

Pioneer Village Museum

The Pioneer Village Museum features an indoor recreation of a street scene from the late 19th century.
Civic Centre Plaza, Little Alexander Street, Burnie
☎ *(03) 6430 5746*
***Admission** $6*
***Open** Mon-Fri 9am-5pm*

Wynyard

With flights from Melbourne, this small town is a gateway to Tasmania for some travellers.

There are some nice coastal walks starting in town including the popular and easy 3km walk to Fossil Bluff.

Practical Information

Wynyard Visitor Information Centre

8 Exhibition Link, Wynyard
☎ *(03) 6443 8330*
Open 9am-5pm daily

INTERNET ACCESS

Wynyard Online Access Centre

21 Saunders Street, Wynyard
☎ *(03) 6442 4499*
***Open** Mon-Thu 10am-5pm, Fri 10am-4pm, Sat 7pm-9pm*

Coming & Going

Wynyard-Burnie Airport *(**website** www.burnie.net/html/934_1622.htm)* is less than a kilometre from the centre of Wynyard so you can just walk into town. Rex *(**website** www.rex.com.au)* flies here from Melbourne.

There are buses to other destinations on the northwest coast, with services between Burnie and Wynyard the most frequent. You may need to make transport connections at Burnie or Devonport for destinations further afield.

Stanley

This small town is built around the base of a volcanic rock formation known as The Nut. Most visitors either take the chairlift or climb to the top of The Nut for a rewarding view of the town and surrounding countryside.

Practical Information

Visitor Information Centre

45 Main Road, Stanley
☎ *(03) 6458 1330*

Website *www.stanley.com.au*
Open *Mon-Fri 9am-5pm, Sat-Sun noon-4pm*

Accommodation
Stanley Cabin & Tourist Park
The Stanley Cabin and Tourist Park is a caravan park in the shadow of the Nut that has an old wooden building with hostel-style accommodation. Accommodation is in small two-bed dorms with single beds (not bunks) and shared facilities include a cosy TV lounge plus a small fully-equipped kitchen and a dining area and a sun room with coin-operated internet.
1 Wharf Road, Stanley
☎ *(03) 6458 1266*
Website *http://www.stanleycabinpark.com.au/*
Dorm bed *$24;* ***double room*** *$75-95*
Credit cards *MC, Visa*
Reception open *Mon-Sat 8am-8pm, Sun 9am-6pm*

Maintenance & cleanliness	★★★½
Facilities	★★½
Atmosphere & character	★★
Security	★★½
Overall rating	★★

Western & Central Tasmania
The wild west coast and central region of Tasmania is a popular area for hiking and home to many of Tasmania's better known national parks including a large chunk of Tasmania that has been classified as a World Heritage Area.

Strahan
The nicest town in western Tasmania is situated on Macquarie Harbour. It started out as a transport hub for the penal colony at nearby Sarah Island but later became a major port for the timber and mining industries. Nowadays Strahan is a popular base for travellers exploring the Franklin-Gordon Wild Rivers National Park.

Practical Information
Strahan Visitor Information Centre
The Esplanade, Strahan
☎ *(03) 6471 7622*
Website *www.tasmaniaswestcoast.com.au*
Open *Jan-Feb 10am-9pm daily; Mar-Dec 10am-8pm daily*

Parks & Wildlife Office
The Esplanade, Strahan
☎ *(03) 6471 7122*
Website *www.parks.tas.gov.au*
Open *Mon-Fri 9am-noon & 1pm-5pm*

INTERNET ACCESS
Strahan Online Access Centre
The Esplanade, Strahan
☎ *(03) 6471 7788*
Open *Mon-Tue 1pm-5pm, Wed 10am-1pm, Thu 2pm-5pm daily*

Coming & Going
Tassielink *(☎ 1300 300 520;* ***website*** *www.tassielink.com.au)* has daily buses to Hobart and two buses a week to Launceston.

Accommodation
Strahan Backpackers
Strahan Backpackers is comprised of several cabins with accommodation in small dormitories. It features a common room with a TV and a fully-equipped kitchen plus a courtyard barbecue area. The hostel has a bush setting but is still within walking distance to the town centre. It is not a bad hostel but it is expensive for what you get.
43 Harvey Street, Strahan
☎ *(03) 6471 7255 or 1800 444 442*
Website *www.cosycabins.com.au*
Dorm bed *$35*
Credit cards *MC, Visa*
Reception open *8am-6pm daily*

Maintenance & cleanliness	★★★
Facilities	★★½
Atmosphere & character	★★★
Security	★
Overall rating	★★★½

Eating & Drinking
There are some good places to eat along Strahan's waterfront Esplanade. **Banjo's Bakehouse** *(The Esplanade,*

Strahan) is the cheapest place in town with fresh bread, pies and pastries. The best budget dining option is the **Fish Café on the Wharf** *(41 The Esplanade, Strahan)*, which serves pizza and delicious locally-caught fish and chips.

Hamer's Hotel *(The Esplanade, Strahan)* serves good quality pub meals and is there is a great atmosphere with an open fireplace. It is the only real place to go out at night and it can get busy on Friday and Saturday nights.

Activities

Jet Boating

50 minute jet boat rides go up the King River past Huon forests and under the historic Teepookana Bridge.

☎ *(03) 6225 7016 or 1800 420 155*
***Website** www.puretasmania.com.au*
***Cost** $65*

Macquarie Harbour Cruises

World Heritage Cruises operate boat trips on the harbour that include a visit to Sarah Island.

☎ *(03) 6471 7174*
***Website** www.worldheritagecruises.com.au*
***Full-day cruise** $85-110*

Queenstown

This mining town has a unique Wild West ambience with a few interesting old buildings. The surrounding region has a barren landscape that makes it such a contrast to the rest of Tasmania; this was caused by a combination of mining and extensive deforestation that has created a landscape almost devoid of trees or other vegetation.

Coming & Going

Tassielink *(☎ 1300 300 520; **website** www.tassielink.com.au)* has daily buses to Hobart and two buses a week to Launceston.

Accommodation

Mountain View Holiday Lodge

Mountain View Holiday Lodge provides basic accommodation in en suite rooms that include four single beds, fridge, TV and a kettle. There is also a basic kitchen with an old oven that looks like it has come straight from a museum. It is really a last resort – only stay here if the hostels in Strahan and Tullah are full.

1 Penghana Road, Queenstown
☎ *(03) 6471 1163*
***Dorm bed** $30; **double room** $75*

Maintenance & cleanliness	★½
Facilities	★½
Atmosphere & character	★½
Security	★
Overall rating	★½

Sights

ABT West Coast Wilderness Railway

This restored steam railway runs through pristine wilderness between Queenstown and Strahan crossing 40 bridges and climbing a 1:16 gradient. It is very expensive although it's a great trip.

Driffield Street, Queenstown
☎ *(03) 6471 1700*
***Website** www.westcoastwildernessrailway.com.au*
***One-way fare** $121-195*

Eric Thomas Galley Museum

The Eric Thomas Galley Museum documents the history of life in Queenstown through photographic exhibits.

Corner Sticht & Driffield Streets, Queenstown
☎ *(03) 6471 1483*
***Admission** $4*
***Open** Jan-Mar Mon-Fri 9.30am-6pm, Sat-Sun 12.30pm-6pm; Apr-Sep Mon-Fri 10am-5pm, Sat-Sun 1pm-5pm; Oct-Dec Mon-Fri 9.30am-6pm, Sat-Sun 12.30pm-6pm*

Tullah

This small town on Lake Roseberry has basic facilities but the lakeside location is an idyllic place to spend a night.

Coming & Going

TassieLink *(☎ 1300 300 520; **website** www.tassielink.com.au)* has two buses a week to Launceston and Strahan.

Accommodation

Tullah Lakeside Chalet

This hostel is part of a large complex that includes a motel and apartments.

It has a lovely location right on Lake Rosebery and there are brilliant lake views from the warm and cosy bar. The backpackers' accommodation is in the older part of the complex with basic facilities that include a small kitchen and dining area, but the rooms are clean and have en suite facilities. Although parts of the complex are a bit tired, the beds are comfy, the bar is great and the views are breathtaking.

Farrell Street, Tullah
(03) 6473 4121
Website *www.tullahresort.com.au*
Dorm bed *$25;* ***single room*** *$80-140;* ***double/twin room*** *$80-140*
Credit cards *Amex, DC, MC, Visa*
Reception open *8am-8pm daily*

Maintenance & cleanliness	★★½
Facilities	★½
Atmosphere & character	★★★½
Security	★
Overall rating	★★½

Cradle Mountain-Lake St Clair National Park

Tasmania's most popular national park attracts visitors from around the world. The best way to explore the park is by hiking the Overland Track – a five-day hike from Cradle Mountain to Lake St Clair – however there are many other shorter walks that are also rewarding.

The park is broken into two parts: Lake St Clair, accessible from the south and Cradle Mountain, accessible from Devonport or Launceston in the north. Most visitors to the park visit Cradle Mountain at the northern end of the national park.

Practical Information

Cradle Mountain Visitors Centre

Cradle Mountain, Cradle Mountain-Lake St Clair National Park
(03) 6492 1133
Website *www.parks.tas.gov.au*
Open *8am-5.30pm daily*

Lake St Clair Visitors Centre

Lake St Clair, Cradle Mountain-Lake St Clair National Park
(03) 6289 1172
Website *www.parks.tas.gov.au*
Open *8am-5pm daily*

Coming & Going & Local Transport

The park is one of Tasmania's biggest attractions and it is well served by public transport. Tassielink's *(1300 300 520;* ***website*** *www.tassielink.com.au)* Strahan to Launceston service calls in at the Cradle Mountain Transit Centre at the northern end of the national park and their Strahan to Hobart service stops at Lake St Clair at the southern end of the park.

Accommodation

Cradle Mountain Tourist Park

This large accommodation complex is close to the transit centre where shuttle buses to the national park depart from. The backpackers' accommodation is comprised of several wooden bunkhouses with a common area in each accommodation block that is comprised of a kitchen and dining area with a fireplace. The complex is in a natural setting and includes laundry facilities, a barbecue area and a small shop.

3832 Cradle Mountain Road, Cradle Mountain
(03) 6492 1395
Website *www.yha.com.au*
Dorm bed *$40 ($38 HI/YHA);* ***double room*** *$85 ($80 HI/YHA)*
Credit cards *MC, Visa*
Reception open *8am-6pm*

K L

Maintenance & cleanliness	★★★
Facilities	★½
Atmosphere & character	★★★
Security	★
Overall rating	★★½

Hiking

Day Hikes in Cradle Mountain

There are plenty of day hikes originating at both the northern and southern parts of the national park. These range from easy ten-minute walks to more strenuous treks up Cradle Mountain. The Dove Lake Loop Track (2 hours) is the most popular and is a good introduction to the park. The information centre sells a detailed map of these hiking trails for $4.

Day Hikes in Lake St Clair

There's also a good range of hiking trails in the southern – Lake St Clair – part of the park. These include the Watersmeet walk (1 hour), which is noted for its wildflowers that bloom in springtime. It is possible to continue on along the Platypus Bay track and the Woodland Naturewalk (1½ hours).

The Overland Track

One of Australia's most popular hiking trails is the 80km Overland Track that runs between Cradle Mountain and Lake St Clair. The track is well maintained with eight huts along the route, however it is a very popular trek and the huts are often full, making it essential to bring along a tent and a warm sleeping bag. Public transport is available with pick-ups at either end of the track from both Hobart and Launceston. It is also possible to stay at luxury accommodation en route with hot showers and fully catered meals, but this option is guaranteed to blow your budget.

Franklin-Gordon Wild Rivers National Park

This huge national park in south-west Tasmania has been classified as a World Heritage Area. Much of the Franklin-Gordon Wild Rivers National Park is pure wilderness with virtually no roads and very few hiking trails, making it a difficult place to explore. However there are several short walks that originate from various points along the Lyell Highway (A10) that are very accessible.

Frenchmans Cap track (46km, 4-5 days) is no stroll in the park, this epic hiking trail is one of the most arduous in Australia and it is recommended that you practice on several other overnight hikes before attempting this one. A detailed map and hiking guide is available from Service Tasmania shops (☎ *1300 135 513;* ***website*** *www.servicetasmania.tas.gov.au)* for $9.

It is possible to raft the Franklin River, which rates among the world's best white water rafting trips. However rafting the Franklin is a very expensive activity with rafting trips costing over a thousand dollars. Rafting here is no ordinary day-trip, and rafting expeditions on the Franklin River can last anywhere from five to eleven days and the price does include the seaplane back to Strahan.

South West National Park

Tasmania's largest national park is in the midst of a World Heritage Area.

It's a very difficult national park to visit if you want to attempt the more difficult hiking trails. Often the only way in is by light plane and many hikers arrange for their food supplies to be air-dropped in. The park's isolation makes it a reasonably expensive place to visit.

There are several short walks in South West National Park that are relatively accessible. These shorter walks include the highly recommended Creepy Crawly Nature Trail (2.5km, 20 mins).

More challenging day walks include the Eliza Plateau walk (5-6 hours) and the Lake Judd walk (8 hours). These two walks should only be attempted by experienced hikers.

Overnight walks in the South West National Park include the Mount Anne Circuit, Port Davey Track, South Coast Track and the Western Arthurs Traverse.

Victoria

Victoria is Australia's smallest and most densely populated mainland state. It is slightly smaller than the United Kingdom and all destinations within it are no more than a day's drive from Melbourne.

Melbourne is home to more than seven in every 10 Victorians but there is much more to see than one big city. Other places worth visiting are historic gold mining cities of Ballarat and Bendigo, wildlife in the Grampians National Park and the spectacular coastal drive along the Great Ocean Road.

Must do in Victoria

- Discover hidden bars and cafés in Melbourne's laneways
- Take a Neighbours tour and go to the Neighbours trivia night (only if you're a fan)
- Drive along the Great Ocean Road
- Watch penguins waddle ashore at Phillip Island
- See kangaroos in the Grampians

Melbourne

With lovely parks and gardens, Melbourne stands on the banks of the Yarra River and the shores of Port Phillip Bay. The city is Australia's second largest and home to around four million people.

It is Australia's major events capital – home to such international sporting events as the Australian Formula One Grand Prix, the Australian Tennis Open, the AFL Grand Final and the Melbourne Cup horse race.

Melbourne is a city of diverse and vibrant neighbourhoods. Each of these areas has its own character and personality and combined they make up the cultural patchwork that is Melbourne.

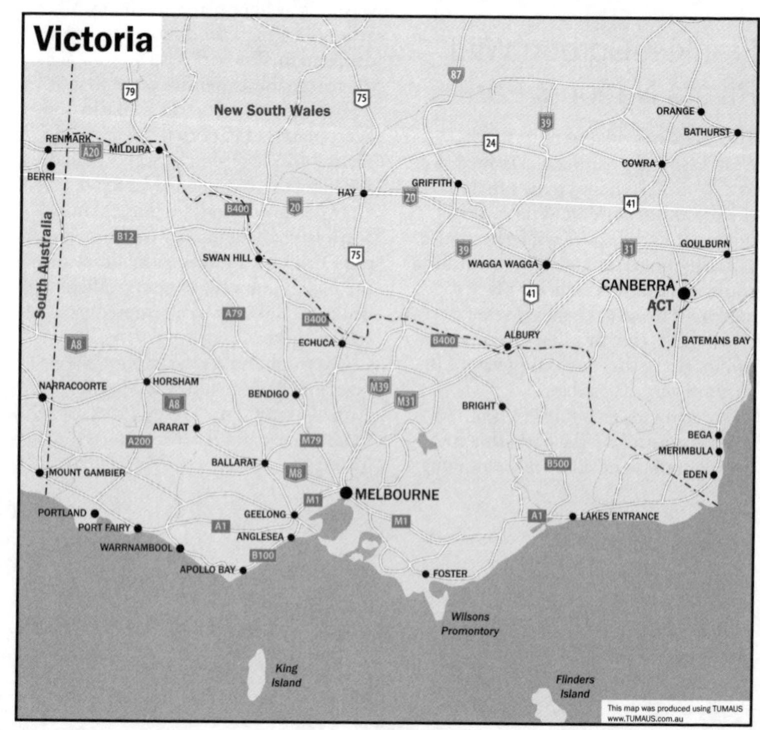

Venture away from the skyscrapers of the city centre and explore the quirky nature of Melbourne's neighbourhoods. Toorak Road and Chapel Street in South Yarra offer the city's best shopping, dining and people watching, Lygon Street, Carlton is Melbourne's slice of Italy, with pizza and pasta restaurants galore or perhaps enjoy authentic and cheap Vietnamese cuisine in one of the many restaurants on Victoria Street, Richmond, known as Melbourne's Little Saigon.

The beachfront neighbourhood of St Kilda is best known for its cake shops and backpacker scene. It has two distinct faces: the 24-hour nightlife of Fitzroy Street and the cafés and delicatessens of Acland Street. St Kilda's landmark is Luna Park with its laughing face and roller coaster rides. St Kilda Beach also features a weekend craft market.

Brunswick Street, Fitzroy, reflects the alternative side of Melbourne. The streets buzz with activity and are crammed with alternative lifestyle shops, second-hand clothing and funky restaurants.

Practical Information

INFORMATION CENTRES & USEFUL ADDRESSES

Melbourne Visitor Information Centre

Federation Square, Corner Flinders Street & St Kilda Road, Melbourne
1, 3, 5, 6, 8, 11, 12, 16, 22, 25, 42, 64, 67, 72, 109 *Flinders Street*
(03) 9658 9658
Website *www.thatsmelbourne.com.au & www.visitvictoria.com*
Open *9am-6pm daily*

EMBASSIES & CONSULATES

British Consulate

17th Floor, 90 Collins Street, Melbourne
11, 12, 42, 109 *Parliament*
(03) 9652 1600
Website *www.uk.emb.gov.au*
Open *Mon-Fri 9am-4.30pm*

Canadian Consulate

Level 50, 101 Collins Street, Melbourne
11, 12, 31, 42, 109, 112 *Flinders Street, Parliament* *313, 315, 316, 605*
(03) 9653 9674
Website *www.canada.org.au*
Open *Mon-Fri 8.30am-5.15pm*

New Zealand Consulate

Suite 2 North, Level 3, 350 Collins Street, Melbourne
11, 12, 19, 31, 42, 57, 59, 68, 109, 112 *Flinders Street*
(03) 9642 1279
Website *www.nzembassy.com/australia*
Open *Mon-Fri 9am-12.30pm & 1.30pm-5pm*

USA Consulate

6th Floor, 553 St Kilda Road, Melbourne
3, 5, 6, 16, 64, 67
(03) 8526 5900
Website *http://usembassy-australia.state.gov/melbourne/*
Open *Mon-Fri 9am-noon*

INTERNET ACCESS

eLounge

Level 1, 9 Elizabeth Street, Melbourne
19, 48, 57, 59, 70, 75 *Flinders Street*
(03) 9629 3188
Website *www.elounge.com.au*

Global Gossip

440 Elizabeth Street, Melbourne.
19, 57, 59, 68 *Melbourne Central*
(03) 9663 0511
Website *www.globalgossip.com*
Open *Mon-Fri 8am-midnight, Sat-Sun 9am-midnight*

Free Wi-Fi hotspots can be found at the QV Centre on Swanston Street *(1, 3, 5, 6, 8, 16, 24, 30, 64, 67, 72 Melbourne Central)* in the courtyard between Three Degrees and Wagamama; at the State Library *(corner LaTrobe & Swanston Streets; 1, 3, 5, 6, 8, 16, 24, 30, 64, 67, 72 Melbourne Central)*, in the food court at the Australia on Collins Centre *(260 Collins Street; 31, 109, 112 Flinders Street)* and at Magnation *(88 Elizabeth Street; 19, 31, 57, 59, 109, 112 Flinders Street)*.

Coming & Going

AIR

Melbourne is served by Avalon and Melbourne airports.

Avalon Airport

Melbourne's newest airport is Avalon (☎ *(03) 5227 9100; **website** www.avalonairport.com.au)*, 55km southwest of the city centre near Geelong. At this stage Avalon only handles JetStar flights to Adelaide, Brisbane and Sydney. Sunbus *(☎ (03) 9689 6888; **website** www.sunbusaustralia.com.au)* run a bus service linking Avalon with Melbourne city with stops at Southern Cross (Spencer Street) and Franklin Street bus stations. The one-way fare is $20.

Melbourne Airport

Melbourne International Airport *(☎ (03) 9297 1600; **website** www.melair.com.au)*, is in Tullamarine 21km north of the city centre. This airport handles all international flights and most domestic flights.

Skybus *(☎ (03) 9335 2811; **website** www.skybus.com.au)* run frequent airport bus services to the Southern Cross coach terminal on Spencer Street in the city centre. The Skybus runs 24 hours with services every 15 minutes during the day and costs $16 one-way. Between 7am and 6pm Skybus provide a complimentary shuttle service between the Spencer Street and Franklin Street coach terminals and to backpackers hostels in the city centre.

A taxi from the airport to the city centre costs between $45 and $50.

BUS

Greyhound *(☎ 1300 473 946; **website** www.greyhound.com.au)* has buses to Adelaide, Brisbane and Sydney; Firefly Express *(☎ 1300 730 740; **website** www.fireflyexpress.com.au)* has buses to Adelaide and Sydney; Premier Motor Service *(☎ 13 34 10; **website** www.premierms.com.au)* buses take the coastal route to Sydney. Destinations in regional Victoria are served by V/line *(☎ 13 61 96; **website** www.vline.com.au)*.

Melbourne has two bus terminals. The Southern Cross Coach Terminal is on Spencer Street next to Southern Cross train station and handles Firefly Express, Premier Motor Service and V/line buses. The Franklin Street Coach Terminal is a few streets north of Melbourne Central Station on Franklin Street, near RMIT University and is the terminus for Greyhound buses.

TRAIN

V/line *(☎ 13 61 96; **website** www.vline.com.au)* operates trains within Victoria with services to Albury, Ararat, Echuca, Shepparton, Swan Hill, Traralgon and Warrnambool. Interstate train services are operated by CountryLink *(☎ 13 22 32; **website** www.countrylink.info)* to Sydney and Great Southern Railway's the *Overland* *(☎ 13 21 47; **website** www.gsr.com.au)* to Adelaide.

All long-distance train services terminates at Southern Cross Station on Spencer Street at the western edge of the city centre.

FERRY

The *Spirit of Tasmania* *(☎ 1800 634 906; **website** www.spiritoftasmania.com.au)* leaves Station Pier in Port Melbourne every night at 9pm for Devonport, Tasmania. Tram 109 runs between Station Pier and the city centre.

HITCHHIKING

It is illegal to hitchhike on roads in Victoria so you will need to be discreet and find a safe spot off the road.

It is pretty easy to get a lift out of Melbourne as just a few roads carry the majority of traffic heading out of the city.

For lifts to Sydney, take a train to Upfield and walk to the Hume Highway. This used to be a great hitching spot but a lot of traffic bypasses this spot now that the Hume Freeway has been extended. Although it is a longer route, it may be easier to get a lift to Sydney via the coastal Princes Highway. Take a train to Traralgon and walk west out of town on the Princes Highway.

If you're heading to Adelaide, Ballarat or the Grampians, take a train to Deer Park, then walk up Station Road to the Western Highway and try your luck there.

Local Transport

Melbourne's public transport system is operated by several companies collectively known as Metlink *(website www.metlinkmelbourne.com.au)* and is comprised of buses, trams and trains.

BUS

Buses take you everywhere that isn't covered by trams or trains, although it is unlikely that you'll need to travel by bus.

One bus you are likely to use is the Melbourne City Tourist Shuttle. This is a free bus that runs every 15 to 20 minutes between 9.30am and 4.30pm stopping at 11 points of interest. Stops include NGV International, Federation Square, Melbourne Museum, Lygon Street, Melbourne University, Queen Victoria Market, Southbank and the Shrine of Remembrance.

TRAM

Most travellers find trams the most useful way to get around the city. They slowly rattle down the major streets and cover most inner city neighbourhoods. Trams are particularly useful for travelling between the city centre, South Melbourne and St Kilda.
The best deal is the free City Circle tram, which runs a circular route around the city centre along Flinders, La Trobe, Spencer and Spring Streets.

TRAIN

Trains are a good way to get to the outer suburbs. The five stations on the underground city loop serve as the core of Melbourne's extensive suburban train network of 232 stations. Taking a train is a handy way to get out to the choice hitchhiking spots on the edge of town, for catching the Phillip Island ferry at Stony Point, for visiting friends or going to job interviews in the suburbs.

FARES

The Metcard ticketing system allows you to transfer between these three modes of transport within a two-hour, daily, weekly or monthly period. The Melbourne area is divided into two fare zones, with virtually everything of interest located within Zone One.

Two-hour tickets are valid for two hours from the next full hour. For instance a ticket purchased or validated at 10.55am expires at 1pm, but if you wait 10 minutes and validate your ticket at 11.05am it will not expire until 2pm. Two-hour tickets are valid until 2am the next morning if validated after 6pm.

A limited range of tickets is available from buses, trams and at the machines at some of the smaller train stations. The full range of tickets is available from major train stations and many convenience stores. Note that some ticket machines only accept coins.

Refer to the following table for ticket prices:

Zones	2 hour	Daily	Weekly
1	$3.50	$6.50	$28
2	$2.70	$4.60	$19.20
1 & 2	$5.50	$10.10	$47.40

The two-hour and daily tickets,are cheaper if you buy a multi-trip ticket that bundles either 10 two-hour tickets or five daily tickets. This is often the best ticket option if you're staying a while in Melbourne, but don't need to use public transport every day. Prices for these tickets are as follows:

Zones	10 X 2 hour	5 X Daily
1	$28	$28
2	$19.20	$19.20
1 & 2	$47.40	$47.20

Another option is the City Saver ticket, which is good for a single trip within the city centre and some inner city neighbourhoods. This ticket costs $2.60 or $20.90 for 10 City Saver tickets.

DRIVING

Melbourne is one of Australia's more challenging cities to drive in as you will be sharing the road with trams,

Whenever a tram stops at a tram stop you must also come to a complete stop and wait until the tram leaves the tram stop before you start moving again, so people can alight safely. This is not necessary at many of the tram stops in the city centre which have a barrier called a Safety Zone or when you are travelling in the opposite direction to the tram.

Hook Turns

A hook turn is a bizarre driving rule unique to Melbourne. At certain intersections in the city centre (where there is a sign indicating Right Turn from Left Lane), a right-hand-turn must be made from the left-hand-side of the road. Although this sounds confusing, it actually makes a lot of sense, as hook turns prevent trams from being held up in traffic.

Instead of turning right from the right lane, you should get into the left lane and cross three-quarters of the intersection and then stop, indicating to turn right, until you have a green light in the direction you are turning. Only when you have a green light should you complete the hook turn.

PHOTO: TIM UDEN

If you're driving in the rain, avoid braking on tram tracks. They can be very slippery.

Citylink & Eastlink

Melbourne has a couple of toll roads that are a quick way to get in and out of the city. The Citylink (☎ *13 26 29; **website** www.citylink.com.au*) tollway runs from Tullamarine Freeway at Bell Street to the Westgate Freeway and also from the city centre to the Monash Freeway up to Toorak Road. The Eastlink (☎ *13 54 65 (13 LINK); **website** www.eastlink.com.au*) tollway runs north-south in the eastern suburbs between Ringwood and Frankston. The electronic payment system ensures that there are no queues at tollbooths and is a convenient system for residents, but for visitors to Melbourne it is much less convenient. Residents using Citylink or Eastlink affix an electronic device to their windscreen called an eTag, which automatically debits the toll from their account.

If you're just visiting Melbourne, it is inconvenient and expensive to buy an eTag and it's a better idea to buy a 24-hour or weekend Citylink pass for $11.55 that allows you to use Citylink for either a 24-hour period during weekdays or all weekend. Passes are available from Citylink offices, Post Offices and from machines inside most Shell service stations around Melbourne. You have until the following morning after driving on Citylink to pay for your Citylink pass. Passes can also be ordered by calling 13 26 29 or online at www.citylink.com.au. There are heavy fines if you do not pay. A one-way pass for travel on Eastlink costs $4.96, you can pay for an Eastlink pass at post offices and Coles Express service stations or by phoning 13 54 65 (13 LINK).

There are alternate routes if you want to avoid the tolls. Going to the airport from the city centre, you can avoid Citylink by getting on the West Gate Freeway at Power Street or Kings Way and heading west and then taking the Western Ring Road north to the Tullamarine Freeway. If you're heading to Gippsland, Phillip Island or the southeastern suburbs, you can get to the Monash Freeway via Toorak Road. You can avoid Eastlink by taking either Springvale or Stud Roads instead.

Accommodation

Many hostels in Melbourne put their prices up during the AFL Grand Final, the Australian Open and the Australian Grand Prix.

CITY CENTRE & NORTH MELBOURNE

The city centre is close to all the action and is handy for transport connections to other parts of Melbourne. A lot of Melbourne's hostels are clustered around Queen Victoria Market, and a few are north of Victoria Street in North Melbourne.

All Nations

From the outside the All Nations looks run down – it is an older building with peeling paint – however it is not too bad inside. The common areas include a TV lounge, a small kitchen, an employment agency and a lounge area. The common areas could be cleaner but the rooms we saw were tidy with nice polished hardwood floors and tall ceilings. It has over 200 beds on three levels and dormitories have four, six and eight beds. It's on the corner of Flinders and Spencer Streets – not the nicest part of town, but it is handy to most attractions and just a short walk to Southern Cross Station and the Crown casino complex.

2 Spencer Street, Melbourne
City Circle, 12, 48, 70, 75, 96, 109, 112 Southern Cross 232, 238
(03) 9620 1022 or 1800 222 238
***Dorm bed** $25-30*
***Credit cards** MC, Visa*
***Reception open** 24 hours*

TV K

Maintenance & cleanliness	★★½
Facilities	★
Atmosphere & character	★★★½
Security	★★½
Overall rating	★★½

The Arthouse

One of the grungier hostels in town, but for the Arthouse's clientele this is actually a selling point. Directly above a popular and long-running music venue, the Arthouse is a punk backpacker's (backpunker?) dream come true. The price of a bed includes free entrance to shows six nights a week, featuring local and touring hardcore, punk, and rock bands. As for the hostel itself – it has a mismatched, thrift-store vibe and a kitchen tagged up with markers, but it was reasonably clean when we checked it out. There's an outdoor deck with a barbecue, and the prices are rock bottom. But really, the Arthouse is meant to appeal to a certain type of music lover; you probably already know who you are. One nice feature: after all those late-night shows, you have until 4pm to check out.

616 Elizabeth Street, Melbourne
19, 57, 59
(03) 9347 3917
***Website** www.thearthouse.com*
***Dorm bed** $18 per night, $105 per week; **single room** $120 per week*

TV K L Bar

Maintenance & cleanliness	★★
Facilities	★★
Atmosphere & character	★★½
Security	★½
Overall rating	★★

Bev & Mick's Backpackers

Long-term stays for backpackers working in Melbourne are the norm in this homely old place above the Red Gum Bar and Café (named for the striking tree-trunk bar). High ceilings and timber floors gives Bev and Mick's a dose of character that some of the newer hostels lack; however, if you are allergic to clutter you might want to consider looking elsewhere. The pub downstairs offers the prospect of a warm welcome after a hard day of work, and Bev & Mick guarantee you'll make "friends for life". Former residents are said to actually hold reunions!

312 Victoria Street, Melbourne
55, 57 546
***Dorm bed** $120 per week; **double room** $280 per week*

TV K Bar

Maintenance & cleanliness	★★½
Facilities	★½
Atmosphere & character	★★★★
Security	★★½
Overall rating	★★½

Hotel Discovery

An airy, wide-open reception area welcomes guests to this huge and slightly impersonal 650-bed hostel, formerly known as Hotel Bakpak. Loads of activities are on offer to keep even the most attention-deficient backpacker entertained: daily walking and biking tours, football matches against other hostels, belly-dancing and combat classes, comedy shows on the roof deck, nightly films in the large-screen cinema room, and more. Some of the four-bed dorms with en suite bathrooms are quite charming, while the larger dorms are rather plain. The Velvet Underground basement bar has a nice, lodge-like feel and is a good place to hang out over a game of pool or table football. Hotel Discovery also has a café, internet access and an

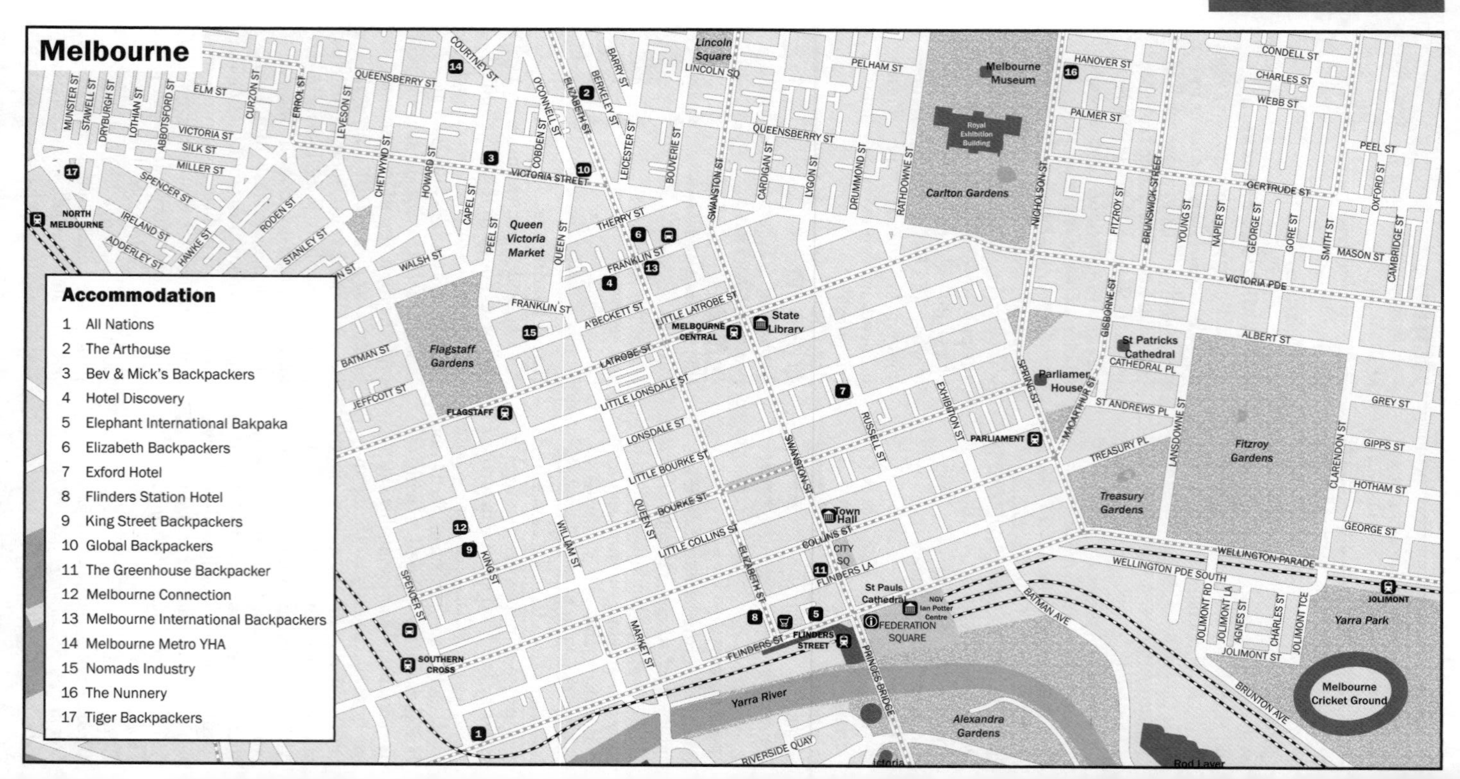

Melbourne
Accommodation
1 All Nations
2 The Arthouse
3 Bev & Mick's Backpackers
4 Hotel Discovery
5 Elephant International Bakpaka
6 Elizabeth Backpackers
7 Exford Hotel
8 Flinders Station Hotel
9 King Street Backpackers
10 Global Backpackers
11 The Greenhouse Backpacker
12 Melbourne Connection
13 Melbourne International Backpackers
14 Melbourne Metro YHA
15 Nomads Industry
16 The Nunnery
17 Tiger Backpackers
Lincoln Square
Melbourne Museum
Royal Exhibition Building
Carlton Gardens
Queen Victoria Market
Flagstaff Gardens
FLAGSTAFF
MELBOURNE CENTRAL
State Library
St Patricks Cathedral
Parliament House
PARLIAMENT
Fitzroy Gardens
Treasury Gardens
Town Hall
CITY SQ
St Pauls Cathedral
NGV Ian Potter Centre
FEDERATION SQUARE
FLINDERS STREET
SOUTHERN CROSS
NORTH MELBOURNE
JOLIMONT
Yarra Park
Melbourne Cricket Ground
Yarra River
Alexandra Gardens
PRINCES BRIDGE
RIVERSIDE QUAY
SWANSTON ST
ELIZABETH ST
QUEEN ST
WILLIAM ST
KING ST
SPENCER ST
MARKET ST
RUSSELL ST
EXHIBITION ST
SPRING ST
FLINDERS ST
FLINDERS LA
COLLINS ST
LITTLE COLLINS ST
BOURKE ST
LITTLE BOURKE ST
LONSDALE ST
LITTLE LONSDALE ST
LATROBE ST
LITTLE LATROBE ST
A'BECKETT ST
FRANKLIN ST
VICTORIA STREET
VICTORIA PDE
NICHOLSON ST
WELLINGTON PARADE
WELLINGTON PDE SOUTH
BATMAN AVE
BRUNTON AVE

employment agency on the ground floor. Free airport pick-up is offered with a three night minimum booking.
167 Franklin Street, Melbourne
19, 57, 59, 68 Melbourne Central
220, 232
(03) 9329 7525
***Website** www.hoteldiscovery.com.au/*
***Dorm bed** $25-$32 ($24-$31 VIP) per night, $154-$175 per week; **double/twin room** $85-$100 ($81-$96 VIP) per night; **family room** $110 ($106 VIP) per night*
***Credit cards** MC, Visa*
***Reception open** 24 hours*

Maintenance & cleanliness	★★★½
Facilities	★★★½
Atmosphere & character	★★★½
Security	★★★★
Overall rating	★★★½

Elephant International Bakpaka

This hostel, formerly the Elephant Backpacker (why the silly spelling change?), is located directly across the street from Flinders Street Station. It's not the loveliest place, with slightly grotty carpeting on the floor and sparse functional rooms. Hallways are brightly painted, and we should note that the hostel was undergoing renovation when we visited, so it may be worth another look in the future. Amenities include a downstairs common area with a TV lounge, kitchen, and internet access. One unfortunate architectural quirk is that the walls of the rooms don't reach the ceiling, making noise and privacy a real concern.
250 Flinders Street, Melbourne
City Circle, 1, 3, 5, 6, 8, 16, 19, 22, 48, 57, 59, 64, 67, 68, 70, 72, 75
Flinders Street 235, 237, 238, 253, 350, 479
(03) 9654 2616
***Dorm bed** $19-$25; **single room** $40; **double/twin room** $60*
***Credit cards** MC, Visa*
***Reception open** 24 hours*

Maintenance & cleanliness	★★
Facilities	★½
Atmosphere & character	½
Security	★★★½
Overall rating	★★

Elizabeth Backpackers

Check in is at a convenience store counter, but Elizabeth Backpackers is nicer than you might expect from that first impression. Facilities are basic, but clean, and there are a few perks, including real spring mattresses on beds and a fridge in every room. Plus, free internet access is provided; there's no actual time limit, but the hostel shares only two computers and guests are supposed to keep to a half an hour at a time. The biggest surprise has to be the TV room, which features a large projection screen and stadium-style seating. It's almost incongruous with the otherwise modest settings. The owners are quite friendly and you can't beat the, er, convenience to the attached grocery and liquor store downstairs. It's located right near the Queen Victoria Market and the Greyhound Bus Terminal.
490-494 Elizabeth Street, Melbourne
19, 57, 59, 68 Melbourne Central
(03) 9663 1685 or 1800 611 897
***Website** www.elizabethhostel.com.au*
***Dorm bed** $23-$31; **single room** $65-$70; **double/twin room** $74-$78*
***Credit cards** MC, Visa (4% credit card surcharge)*
***Reception open** 8am-10pm daily*

Maintenance & cleanliness	★★½
Facilities	★★
Atmosphere & character	★★½
Security	★★★½
Overall rating	★★½

Exford Hotel

The Exford Hotel is set in a well-preserved 1854 Edwardian building right in Melbourne's Chinatown. There's plenty of atmosphere inside and out: nice mouldings and architectural details on the painted brick exterior, and a pressed-metal ceiling and great stained-glass windows in the downstairs pub. The dormitory and common spaces have been kept in good shape as well. Rooms were clean and looked recently painted and furnished. Facilities include a small TV lounge, a nice kitchen, an outdoor deck, and private toilets and showers. The downstairs bar has a pool table and features weekly live music and DJs.

199 Russell Street, Melbourne

1, 3, 5, 6, 8, 16, 22, 64, 67, 72, 86, 96 *200, 201, 203, 207, 250, 241*

(03) 9663 2697

Website *www.exfordhotel.com.au*

Dorm bed *$22-$30 ($21-$29 VIP);* ***double/twin room*** *$64-$74 ($62-$72 VIP)*

Credit cards *Amex, Diners, MC, Visa*

Reception open *11am-5am daily*

Maintenance & cleanliness	★★★
Facilities	★★½
Atmosphere & character	★★★½
Security	★★★★
Overall rating	★★★

Flinders Station Hotel

The Flinders Station Hotel occupies 11 floors of a building in the city centre, right down the street from the train station. An institutional feel prevails, but the Flinders is reasonably clean and well kept. There's a large kitchen and dining area and a couple of TV lounges. The common area includes table tennis, a rarity among Melbourne hostels. Internet access including Wi-Fi is available for a charge. Security features are good, with lockers for every bed and key card access to the building and rooms. The connected bar next door, The Joint, is usually hopping until the wee hours of the morning.

35 Elizabeth Street, Melbourne

City Circle, 11, 12, 19, 31, 42, 48, 57, 59, 68, 70, 75, 109, 112 *Flinders Street* *235, 237, 253, 350*

(03) 9620 5100

Website *www.flindersbp.com.au*

Dorm bed *$23-$27 ($22-$26 VIP);* ***double/twin room*** *$67-$87 ($65-$85 VIP); prices include breakfast*

Credit cards *Amex, Diners, MC, Visa; 3.2% surcharge for Amex & Diners*

Reception open *midnight-3am, 4am-2pm, 3pm-10pm & 11pm-midnight daily*

Maintenance & cleanliness	★★★
Facilities	★★½
Atmosphere & character	★★
Security	★★★★★
Overall rating	★★★

King Street Backpackers

A warm and sunny reception/common area greets guests at King Street Backpackers, and the general feeling persists throughout the hostel. Everything is clean and well-maintained, although the dorms and bathrooms are on the smaller side. Free breakfast is offered daily, as well as a free dinner once a week. Internet access is also provided free of charge for a half-hour daily; there are, however, only two computers available and Wi-Fi and internet access beyond the free time is billed at $3 per hour. King Street Backpackers is extremely convenient to Southern Cross Station and bus terminal, which is 200m down the street. The Skybus Shuttle to Melbourne Airport runs from here, as well as long-distance buses and trains.

197 King Street, Melbourne

(03) 9670 1111 or 1800 671 115

55, 70, 86, 96 *Southern Cross* *216, 219, 684*

Website *www.kingstreetbackpackers.com.au*

Dorm bed *$22-$28;* ***single/twin/double room*** *$78*

Credit cards *MC, Visa*

Reception open *24 hours*

Maintenance & cleanliness	★★★
Facilities	★★
Atmosphere & character	★★★
Security	★★★★
Overall rating	★★★

Global Backpackers

Global Backpackers is in an old building opposite the Queen Victoria Market. It feels a bit retro with magazine pictures stuck to the walls, which look a bit tacky but somehow add to the character. It has a small but fully equipped kitchen, a small rooftop barbecue area and a friendly bar with a big screen to show films.

238 Victoria Street, Melbourne

19, 55, 57, 59, 68 *Melbourne Central* *220, 232, 546*

(03) 9328 3728 or 1800 700 478

Website *www.globalbackpackers.com.au*

Dorm bed *$26;* ***double room*** *$65*

Reception open *Mon-Fri 7am-1pm & 4pm-9pm, Sat-Sun 7am-noon & 4pm-9pm*

Maintenance & cleanliness	★★½
Facilities	★★
Atmosphere & character	★★★½
Security	★½
Overall rating	★★½

The Greenhouse Backpacker

This clean and cheerful hostel occupies the top four floors of a commercial building right in the heart of the city centre, just one block away from Flinders Street Station. The décor won't blow you away, but rooms are well laid-out for privacy and feature quality bedding and nice touches like individual reading lights. There's free breakfast and half an hour of free Internet access daily. A rooftop deck offers a free weekly barbecue as well as a great view of Eureka Tower (and extreme close-ups of some neighboring buildings). The Greenhouse is not the most party-oriented hostel, having no bar, but it does offer free tours and activities every day. And, as mentioned, it's about as central a location as you will find in Melbourne.

228 Flinders Lane, Melbourne
City Circle, 1, 3, 5, 6, 8, 11, 12, 16, 19, 22, 31, 42, 48. 57, 59, 64, 67, 68, 70, 72, 75, 109, 112 *Flinders Street*
235, 237, 238, 253, 350
(03) 9639 6400 or 1800 249 207
***Website** www.friendlygroup.com.au*
***Dorm bed** $30 per night, $182 per week; **single room** $65; **double/twin room** $78 per night, $546 per week; **triple room** $90*
***Credit cards** MC, Visa*
***Reception open** 24 hours*

Maintenance & cleanliness	★★★★
Facilities	★★★
Atmosphere & character	★★½
Security	★★★★★
Overall rating	★★★½

Melbourne Connection

Melbourne Connection is a small, affable hostel right down the road from the Southern Cross bus and train station. There's a cool, relaxed vibe here. Facilities are rather basic, with a little kitchen and dining area, and a pair of TV lounges. Dorms feature real spring mattresses, and there's a locker for each bed. A bit of art on the walls livens things up. There's an alcohol ban throughout the hostel, but Melbourne Connection still manages to maintain a friendly, social atmosphere. Wireless internet access is available for a fee.

205 King Street, Melbourne
55, 70, 86, 96 *Southern Cross*
216, 219, 684
(03) 9642 4464
***Website** www.melbourneconnection.com*
***Dorm bed** $20-29; **double/twin room** $65-85*
***Credit cards** Amex, Diners, JCB, MC, Visa*
***Reception open** 8am-8.30pm daily*

Maintenance & cleanliness	★★★½
Facilities	★½
Atmosphere & character	★★★
Security	★★★
Overall rating	★★★

Melbourne International Backpackers

There is not much in the way of charm at this centrally-located hostel, but it is functional and secure. Local event posters and used car flyers decorate the cramped reception area. Hallways are on the dim and dingy side, and could definitely use new carpeting. The accommodation is in spartan rooms with foam mattresses on the bunks. On the plus side, Melbourne International Backpackers is reasonably clean, has a decent TV lounge and kitchen facilities, and security is very good with lockers for all beds, 24-hour reception, video surveillance, and key card access to the building and rooms. It's located near Melbourne Central shopping centre and Queen Victoria Market. The entrance is on Franklin Street.

450 Elizabeth Street, Melbourne
19, 57, 59, 68 *Melbourne Central*
(03) 9662 4066
***Website** www.mibp.com.au*
***Dorm bed** $23-$27 ($22-$26 VIP); **double/twin room** $67-$74 ($65-$72 VIP)*
***Credit cards** MC, Visa*

Reception open *24 hours*

Maintenance & cleanliness	★★★½
Facilities	★★½
Atmosphere & character	★★
Security	★★★★★
Overall rating	★★★½

Melbourne Metro YHA

Opposite a church on a quiet residential street, the Melbourne Metro YHA is a serene alternative to Melbourne's more party-oriented hostels. You can't quite escape the concrete block, institutional feel of the building itself, but good interior design and attention to detail go a long way towards making the YHA one of Melbourne's finest. A lovely common area is decorated in rope-wrapped columns and a subdued tan and brown colour scheme. Small TV and reading lounges are nice places to hang out, and there's a fantastic indoor/outdoor roof area with stunning views of the city, plus all the solar panels atop the building show the eco-friendly nature of this hostel. The dorms feature real mattresses and individual bedside lamps. Internet access (including Wi-Fi) is available for $4 an hour. The YHA is about 15-minutes walk to the city centre and local shops on Errol Street are a five-minute walk away.

78 Howard Street, North Melbourne
55, 57 *402, 546*
(03) 9329 8599
Website *www.yha.com.au*
Dorm bed *$29-33.50 ($26-$30 HI/YHA);* ***single room*** *$78-89 ($70-$80 HI/YHA);* ***double room*** *$89-$100 ($80-$90 HI/YHA);* ***family room*** *$110-$139 ($99-$125 HI/YHA)*
Credit cards *MC, Visa*
Reception open *24 hours*

Maintenance & cleanliness	★★★★½
Facilities	★★★½
Atmosphere & character	★★★
Security	★★★★½
Overall rating	★★★★

Melbourne Oasis YHA

The Melbourne Oasis YHA has fewer facilities than the larger YHA hostel closer to the city centre, but it is a clean and well-maintained hostel. It has two kitchens, internet access (Global Gossip; $4 per hour) and a small backyard with a herb garden and barbecue. It is on a quiet residential street, north of the city centre near Royal Park.

76 Chapman Street, North Melbourne
55, 57, 59, 68 *402, 479*
(03) 9328 3595
Website *www.yha.com.au*
Dorm bed *$30.50-33.50 ($27-30 HI/YHA);* ***single room*** *$62.50 ($56 HI/YHA);* ***double room*** *$74.50 ($67 HI/YHA);* ***twin room*** *$67 ($60 HI/YHA)*
Credit cards *MC, Visa*
Reception open *7.30am-11pm daily*

Maintenance & cleanliness	★★★★
Facilities	★★
Atmosphere & character	★★½
Security	★★★½
Overall rating	★★★

Nomads Industry

Putting the chic in "industrial chic" and the flash in "flashpackers", Nomads Industry is certainly one of the most stylish hostels in town. Red and black leather sofas, brushed steel accents and other attractive touches dominate the reception area and the attached Industry Bar and Lounge. Dorm rooms are comfortable, if not overly large, and every level features individual toilets and showers – no communal shower blocks here. Kitchen facilities are limited, but this is offset by a free meal every evening. Other features include a rooftop lounge and nightly movies on a big projection screen. Several private rooms are also available and it's no stretch to say Nomads easily doubles as a smart hotel. It's located just a stone's throw away from Queen Victoria market.

198 A'Beckett Street, Melbourne
24, 30, 55, City Circle *Flagstaff*
(03) 9328 4383 or 1800 447 762
Website *www.nomadsindustry.com*
Dorm bed *$28-$36 ($21-$33 Nomads);* ***double/twin room*** *$90-$115 ($85-$105 Nomads)*
Credit cards *MC, Visa*
Reception open *24 hours*

Maintenance & cleanliness	★★★★½
Facilities	★★★
Atmosphere & character	★★★★
Security	★★★★½
Overall rating	★★★★

Tiger Backpackers

Tiger Backpackers is a basic backpackers' hostel above an old pub that offers very good value accommodation and it is popular with backpackers working in Melbourne. For the most part it feels a bit dated but there are some areas that have been renovated and many of the rooms have nice polished floorboards. The small TV lounge has old torn furnishings but the dorm rooms are much nicer and have new bunk beds. There is also free internet access, including wireless, and a big old-style bar on the ground floor with a big screen telly and pool table. It is in West Melbourne about a 20-minute walk into the city centre, which is hardly the best location, although it is right across the street from North Melbourne station with regular trains into the city.

118 Ireland Street, West Melbourne
North Melbourne *401*
(03) 9328 1773
Website *www.tigerbackpackers.com*
Dorm bed *$17*
Credit cards *MC, Visa*

TV

Maintenance & cleanliness	★★½
Facilities	★½
Atmosphere & character	★★★
Security	★★
Overall rating	★★½

Urban Central

This big hostel overlooking a motorway in Southbank offers a high standard of accommodation in spacious rooms with high ceilings. Facilities are what you would expect in a big city hostel and include a TV lounge plus several quiet lounges, a kitchen (with free rice and pasta) and a good bar with pool tables, table football and a big projection screen. The en suite dorms even have bathtubs. Security is excellent with a big locker for every bed and the lockers all have powerpoints so you can recharge your mobile phone and MP3 player while it is secure and locked up. The place feels a bit sterile, but with the right crowd the bar could have a good atmosphere.

334 City Road, Southbank
96, 109, 112 *250, 251, 253*
(03) 9693 3700 or 1800 631 288
Website *www.urbancentral.com.au*
Dorm bed *$25-35;* ***double room*** *$89-99; prices include breakfast*
Credit cards *MC, Visa*
Reception open *24 hours*

TV K L

Maintenance & cleanliness	★★★★★
Facilities	★★★
Atmosphere & character	★½
Security	★★★★★
Overall rating	★★★★

FITZROY & CARLTON

The neighbourhoods northeast of the city centre boast lovely Victorian terrace houses and the ambience ranges from the alternative feel of Brunswick Street in Fitzroy to the Italian restaurants that line Lygon Street in Carlton. The main attractions here include Melbourne Museum and the Royal Exhibition Buildings in Carlton Gardens.

The Nunnery

The Nunnery consists of four grand old Victorian terrace houses that were once used as a nunnery. The buildings are beautiful with hardwood floors, tall ceilings and antique trimmings such as stained glass windows. Facilities include a small fully-equipped kitchen, a laundry and a nice TV lounge with leather sofas and a fireplace. Internet access costs $4 per hour and Wi-Fi is also available ($4 per hour, $15 per day, $50 per week). It has a really nice atmosphere and can be a fun place to stay. The location is good, across the road from Melbourne Museum and the Royal Exhibition Buildings and within walking distance of the city centre, Lygon Street in Carlton and Brunswick Street, Fitzroy.

116 Nicholson Street, Fitzroy
96
(03) 9419 8637 or 1800 032 635
Website *www.nunnery.com.au*
Dorm bed *$28-32;* ***single room***

Victoria

$70-80; ***double room*** *$95-115;* ***twin room*** *$85-115*
Credit cards *MC, Visa*
Reception open *8am-10.30pm daily; late check in with prior arrangement*
TV K L

Maintenance & cleanliness	★★★½
Facilities	★★
Atmosphere & character	★★★★
Security	★★★½
Overall rating	★★★

ST KILDA

This bohemian seaside suburb is popular with backpackers and has plenty of good value hostels. The area has a good beach, great pubs and cafés and a busy weekend market.

Base Backpackers

It's not brand-new anymore, but Base is still sleek and distinctive as ever in its shiny red perspex (the colour, we're told, is officially called "Hot Lips Red"). Base has a futuristic, space-station feel, with announcements being piped over a PA and an architecturally interesting environment with lots of quirky angles and interesting sight lines. Semi-opaque skyways connect different sections of the building and a skylit atrium on the ground floor has a nice indoor/outdoor feel. Shared facilities include a basement kitchen and TV lounge, plus the buzzing Red Eye bar. All rooms have air-conditioning and en suite bathrooms, and there's a girls-only level called "Sanctuary" with hair dryers and Aveda care packs in the rooms. The staff are young and hip and provide helpful "best of" lists to guide travellers to some of Melbourne's more hidden places. That said, there is something of a corporate-chain feel to the hostel, and it is starting to show its years slightly.
17 Carlisle Street, St Kilda
16, 79, 96
(03) 8598 6200 or 1800 24 BASE
Website *www.basebackpackers.com/stkilda.htm*
Dorm bed *$24-$40;* ***double room*** *$99-$140*
Credit cards *Amex, Diners, MC, Visa*
Reception open *24 hours*

Maintenance & cleanliness	★★★★½
Facilities	★★★
Atmosphere & character	★★★½
Security	★★★★★
Overall rating	★★★★

Coffee Palace Backpackers

Palace may not be the most accurate description of this St Kilda standby; it's on the grungy side, but it does have a young and very friendly atmosphere. Coffee Palace is set in a sturdy, old, three-storey building, with a rooftop barbecue area. There's a big, high-ceilinged common room filled with old and mismatched furniture, a bar on site, and a rec room with a pool table. Every evening there are events like barbecues, pool competitions and pub crawls to keep backpackers meeting and mingling. Overall, a fun vibe, but Coffee Palace could do with some sprucing up.
24 Grey Street, St Kilda
16, 96, 112 *600, 922, 923*
(03) 9534 5283 or 1800 654 098
Website *www.coffeepalacebackpackers.com.au/*
Dorm bed *$23-$29;* ***double/twin room*** *$70; price includes breakfast*
Credit cards *MC, Visa*
Reception open *24 hours*
TV K L

Maintenance & cleanliness	★½
Facilities	★★
Atmosphere & character	★★★½
Security	★★½
Overall rating	★★

Cooee on St Kilda

This large 210-bed hostel is a great accommodation option, although its location is not as good as the other St Kilda hostels. It is very clean and well maintained with new fittings and comfortable beds. The bathrooms are squeaky clean – yes, they really squeak! The big ground floor common area has a kitchen, pool table and internet access ($4 per hour) including Wi-Fi and there is also a laundry and a nice courtyard barbecue area. This hostel features a big secure parking area that makes it a top choice if you're driving.
333 St Kilda Road, St Kilda
3, 67

(03) 9537 3777 or 1800 202 500
Website *www.cooeeonstkilda.com*
Dorm bed *$22-36;* ***double/twin room*** *$79-160*
Credit cards *MC, Visa*
Reception open *24 hours*

Maintenance & cleanliness	★★★★★
Facilities	★★★
Atmosphere & character	★★★★
Security	★★★★★
Overall rating	★★★★½

Home Travellers Motel
This motel-style hostel is quite clean despite being in an older building. The common area consists of a kitchen and TV lounge with internet access ($4 per hour) and free Wi-Fi. The accommodation is in former motel rooms that feel dated but the beds are comfortable and the rooms all have en suite bathrooms. It is a better choice than many other hostels in former motels.
32 Carlisle Street, St Kilda
3, 16, 96
(03) 9534 0300 or 1800 008 718
Website *www.hometravellersmotel.com.au*
Dorm bed *$21-28;* ***double/twin room*** *$85*
Credit cards *MC, Visa*
Reception open *24 hours*

Maintenance & cleanliness	556
Facilities	★★
Atmosphere & character	★★½
Security	★★
Overall rating	★★½

Jackson's Manor
Jackson's Manor is a big old house on a quiet residential street close to the centre of St Kilda. It is a lovely old building with quite nice common areas, but other parts of the hostel including many rooms are dirty and poorly maintained. The common areas include a TV lounge with polished hardwood floors and stained glass windows and a kitchen and dining room with a pool table. It caters mostly to long-term guests staying here on their working holiday.

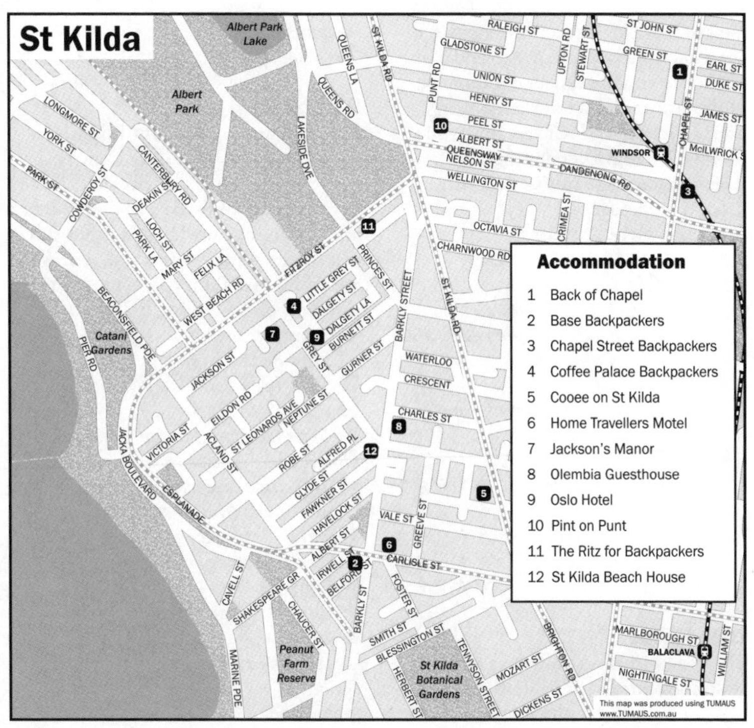

53 Jackson Street, St Kilda
16, 96, 112
(03) 9534 1877
***Dorm bed** $23-25 per night, $135-145 per week; **double/twin room** $60 per night, $320 per week*

Maintenance & cleanliness	★★
Facilities	★
Atmosphere & character	★★★
Security	★★
Overall rating	★★

Olembia Guesthouse

The Olembia Guesthouse feels much more like a charming B&B than a hostel. A leafy, well-tended front yard welcomes guests to this beautiful 1920 Edwardian-style house. The sitting room is filled with antique furniture and has book-lined shelves, a window seat and a fireplace. There is also a small TV/dining lounge and the kitchen facilities are stellar. Everything is very tasteful and casually elegant, with careful attention to detail. Most dorm rooms have only three beds and all but one have a sink in the room. The Olembia is a place that older travellers, couples, or those looking just looking to add a bit of class to their backpacking experience will enjoy. Still, it's not stuffy; there's a very friendly and relaxed air. Be sure to say hello to Alexander the Great, a tabby cat who roams imperiously around the house.
96 Barkly Street, St Kilda
3, 67, 79 246
(03) 9537 1412
***Website** www.olembia.com.au*
***Dorm bed** $28-$30; **single room** $60; **double/twin room** $80*
***Credit cards** MC, Visa*
***Reception open** 8am-1pm & 5pm-7pm daily*

Maintenance & cleanliness	★★★★½
Facilities	★★½
Atmosphere & character	★★★★★
Security	★★
Overall rating	★★★★

Oslo Hotel

The Oslo Hotel isn't much to look at from the outside – it's a drab yellow-and-brown affair with an unkempt front yard, and apart from a startlingly nice common area and pool room at the front of the house, the inside isn't much better. Many of the rooms and facilities exude a ramshackle quality with second-hand furniture; old, gaudy carpeting that doesn't match from hallway to hallway, dim lighting, labyrinthine corridors and stairs. Some rooms are better than others and a few bathrooms have been nicely renovated but the overall impression is still one of dreariness. Internet access is available and there's a courtyard with a barbecue.
38 Grey Street, St Kilda
16, 96, 112 600. 922, 923
(03) 9525 4498 or 1800 501 752
***Website** www.oslohotel.com.au*
***Dorm bed** $16-$25; **single room** $40-$50; **double room** $45-$65*
***Credit cards** Diners, MC, Visa*
***Reception open** summer Mon-Fri 7am-11pm, Sat-Sun 8am-11pm; winter Mon-Fri 9am-11pm, Sat-Sun 8am-11pm*

Maintenance & cleanliness	★
Facilities	★½
Atmosphere & character	½
Security	★★½
Overall rating	★½

Pint on Punt

Pint on Punt is a brilliant English-style pub on St Kilda Junction. The accommodation is fairly basic and the amenities are limited to a small kitchen and TV lounge upstairs. It is basically just some rooms above a pub, but what a pub! Pint on Punt caters mostly to travellers on a working holiday who stay here long-term.
42 Punt Road, Windsor
3, 5, 16, 64, 67 Windsor
(03) 9510 4273
***Website** www.pintonpunt.com.au*
***Dorm bed** $24-25; **twin room** $60; prices include breakfast*
***Credit cards** MC, Visa*
***Reception open** 8am-midnight daily; late check in with prior arrangement*

Maintenance & cleanliness	★★
Facilities	★½
Atmosphere & character	★★★
Security	★★½
Overall rating	★★

The Ritz for Backpackers

The Ritz for Backpackers is located above a traditional British pub and is clean and well-maintained for an older house. Rooms are on the small side, but there are some attractive features on offer, including a free daily pancake breakfast and – even better – free use of bikes. St Kilda's a great place to cruise around on two wheels, with loads of interesting streets and bike trails in Albert Park and along the bay. A comfortable common room with pool table and TV lounge is available for hanging out and there's a fully-equipped kitchen and a small courtyard. Plus, if you're one of the legions of *Neighbours* fanatics, you can't get much closer to the action than the Ritz. The downstairs pub hosts a twice-weekly "Neighbours Night" where fans can meet the stars of the show and see Waiting Room (Dr Karl Kennedy's band) play.

169 Fitzroy Street, St Kilda
16, 96, 112 600, 922, 923
(03) 9525 3501 or 1800 670 364
***Website** www.ritzbackpackers.com*
***Dorm bed** $20-$30; **double/twin room** $60-$80*
***Credit cards** MC, Visa*
***Reception open** 24 hours*

Maintenance & cleanliness	★★★½
Facilities	★★½
Atmosphere & character	★★★
Security	★★★
Overall rating	★★★

St Kilda Beach House (at Hotel Barkly)

Hotel Barkly is a swanky, boutique hotel that also caters to backpackers, with dorm rooms and facilities of an incredibly high standard. The downstairs bar and restaurant is sleek and stylish, with leather furniture and smart décor (and surprisingly backpacker budget-friendly food and drink specials). Springy, hotel carpeting lines the labyrinthine hallways. Dorm rooms feature high-quality bedding, en suite bathrooms, air-conditioning and nice little touches like power points by all the beds. Small common areas and chill-out rooms are located around the hostel. A rooftop bar/nightclub, the Next Level, is sleek and white, with great views over St Kilda and Luna Park. It may not be the ideal place for the party-seeking flip flops-and-singlet crowd but if you're looking for a great deal of style and a bit more urban refinement than your ordinary hostel, you'd be hard-pressed to find something much better.

109 Barkly Street, St Kilda
3, 67, 79 246
03 9525 3371 or 1800 551 271
***Website** www.stkildabeachhouse.com*
***Dorm bed** $23-$32; **double/twin room** $110-$130; **studio apartment** $130-$150*
***Credit cards** MC, Visa*
***Reception open** 24 hours*

Maintenance & cleanliness	★★★★★
Facilities	★★★
Atmosphere & character	★★★★
Security	★★★★½
Overall rating	★★★★

SOUTH MELBOURNE

The area between St Kilda and the city centre is a nice place to stay with easy access to beaches and the city centre.

Bev & Mick's Backpackers

This is a good hostel popular with long-term guests on a working holiday. Facilities include a TV lounge, internet access, a small kitchen and a bar. There's also a small courtyard with a barbecue. It's on the corner of Cecil and Market Streets, across the road from the bustling South Melbourne Market.

115 Cecil Street, South Melbourne
96, 112 253
(03) 9690 2220
***Dorm bed** $19-23; **double/twin room** $58*
***Credit cards** MC, Visa*

Maintenance & cleanliness	★★½
Facilities	★★½
Atmosphere & character	★★★★
Security	★★★
Overall rating	★★★

Gunn Island Hotel

The Gunn Island Hotel consists of a really nice pub with basic accommodation

upstairs. The accommodation definitely takes second-place to the bar and it feels quite dated upstairs although it is kept reasonably clean. Shared facilities include a kitchen, internet access and a TV lounge. It is in a nice neighbourhood with a friendly village feel and is within walking distance to the beach and just a short tram ride to St Kilda or the city centre.
102 Canterbury Road, Middle Park
96
(03) 9690 1882
***Website** www.gunnisland.com.au*
***Dorm bed** $25; **single room** $40; **double/twin room** $60*
***Credit cards** Amex, MC, Visa*
***Reception open** Mon-Fri 10am-6pm; check in at the bar when the reception is closed*

Maintenance & cleanliness	★★★½
Facilities	★½
Atmosphere & character	★★½
Security	★½
Overall rating	★★

SOUTH YARRA & PRAHRAN

Chapel Street, which runs through South Yarra and Prahran, is one of Melbourne's best shopping streets and this area also has good pubs and nightlife. There are several good hostels in this area, mostly around Prahran and in Windsor at the southern (cheaper) end of Chapel Street.

Back of Chapel

This small hostel near Chapel Street in Prahran features a couple of small lounges at the front – one with a big screen TV and the other quieter room with comfy seating and internet access ($4 per hour). There is also a clean (but basic) kitchen and a nice backyard area with a barbecue. The hostel has a great atmosphere and friendly management.
50 Green Street, Prahran
6, 78, 79 Windsor
(03) 9521 5338
***Website** www.backofchapel.com*
***Dorm bed** $22-26; **double room** $65-75; prices include breakfast*
***Credit cards** MC, Visa*
***Reception open** Mon 8am-6pm, Tue-Thu 8am-4pm, Fri 8am-6pm, Sat-Sun 9am-1pm & 3pm-7pm*

Maintenance & cleanliness	★★★
Facilities	★★
Atmosphere & character	★★★★
Security	★★★★
Overall rating	★★★

Chapel Street Backpackers

This is a very clean and well maintained small hostel at the cheaper Windsor end of Chapel Street. Facilities include a small kitchen, TV lounge, internet access and a nice courtyard. Accommodation is of a high standard and most rooms have en suite bathrooms.
22 Chapel Street, Windsor
5, 64, 78, 79 Windsor
(03) 9533 6855
***Website** www.csbackpackers.com.au*
***Dorm bed** $27-28; **double room** $85; **twin room** $70-77*
***Credit cards** Amex, MC, Visa*
***Reception open** 7am-midnight daily*

Maintenance & cleanliness	★★★★½
Facilities	★½
Atmosphere & character	★★★★½
Security	★★★★
Overall rating	★★★★

Lord's Lodge

Lord's Lodge is an old 1870s mansion with hardwood floors and loads of character. It has a small fully-equipped kitchen and a lounge room with a fireplace, TV and internet access (including free Wi-Fi). Double/twin rooms are in bungalows in the small backyard and there's a nice barbecue area and a croquet court in the front yard. It is on busy Punt Road near the corner of Greville Street and it's a short walk to St Kilda Road and the shops and restaurants in the Prahran/South Yarra area.
204 Punt Road, Prahran
6 Prahran 246
(03) 9510 5658
***Website** www.lordslodge.com.au*
***Dorm bed** $21; **single room** $45-50; **double room** $58-68*
***Credit cards** MC, Visa*
***Open** Mon-Sat 8am-noon & 5pm-7pm; Sun 8am-1pm*

Maintenance & cleanliness	★★½
Facilities	★★
Atmosphere & character	★★★★½
Security	★★★★
Overall rating	★★★

St Arnaud Guest House

St Arnaud is an old-style guest house with some dorm rooms for backpackers. It's in an old building in a nice part of town that is furnished with antiques and it feels quite posh, although there are parts of the hostel that certainly are a bit dated. Common areas include a couple of TV lounges, a fully-equipped kitchen, a dining room with internet access ($3 per hour including Wi-Fi) plus a laundry and a small garden with a barbecue.

98-101 Park Street, South Yarra
8
(03) 9866 3992
***Website** www.starnaudguesthouse.com*
***Dorm bed** $29-32; **single room** $60-75; **double room** $76-90; **twin room** $70-90; prices include breakfast*
***Credit cards** Amex, JCB, MC, Visa*
***Reception open** 8am-8pm*
TV K L

Maintenance & cleanliness	★★★
Facilities	★★
Atmosphere & character	★★★½
Security	★★
Overall rating	★★★

Eating & Drinking

Melbourne has a reputation as the best Australian city for eating out, with a good selection of restaurants falling within a backpackers' budget.

Much of Melbourne's culinary scene can be attributed to the city's rich ethnic heritage with different immigrants introducing their cuisine.

Melbourne's Italian restaurant strip is on Lygon Street in Carlton (*200, 201, 203, 207 1, 8*), although Italian food can be found all over the city.

Greek restaurants are clustered along Lonsdale Street (*1, 3, 5, 6, 8, 16, 64, 67, 72 Melbourne Central*) in the city centre, although one would expect a bigger choice of Greek restaurants considering that Melbourne has the world's largest Greek population after Athens and Thessaloniki.

Melbourne's large Greek and Turkish communities serve excellent kebabs and souvlaki. There are many contenders for the city's best souvlaki and kebabs including **Souvlaki Bar** *(163 Russell Street, Melbourne)*, **Souvlaki King** *(311 Brunswick Street, Fitzroy)*, **Lambs Restaurant** *(98 Lygon Street, Carlton)* and **Lamb on Chapel** *(394 Chapel Street, South Yarra)*; although in our opinion Melbourne's best kebabs come from **Hollywood Palace** *(181 Bridge Road, Richmond)*.

Chinese restaurants are in Chinatown on Little Bourke Street (*1, 3, 5, 6, 8, 16, 64, 67, 72*).

Victoria Street in Richmond (*24, 109 North Richmond*) is Melbourne's Little Saigon. This is the best spot for Vietnamese food and definitely worth the tram ride. Bring your own bottle of wine for a cheap night out.

Brunswick Street in Fitzroy (*112*) has an alternative feel and an eclectic mix of affordable bars and restaurants.

Melbourne is known for its many small laneways, many of which are home to small restaurants and cosy cafés. Tiny Degraves Street and Centre Place near Flinders Street Station are particularly good for good value cooked breakfasts with strong coffee and a warm ambience.

You can also find cheap meals at food courts around the city, particularly inside Melbourne Central and the QV centre, which are often full of students from nearby RMIT University.

If you're preparing your own food, then head to the **Queen Victoria Market** *(corner Elizabeth Street & Victoria Parade, Melbourne)*. This is one of the world's largest markets and is particularly good value for meat as well as fruit and vegetables.

The best centrally located supermarket is the **Safeway** *(corner Lonsdale & Swanston Streets, Melbourne)* in the QV Centre, although there are several other supermarkets in the city including several **Coles**, including one near Flinders Street Station *(2 Elizabeth Street, Melbourne)*, one near Southern Cross Station *(201 Spencer Street, Melbourne)* and another near the station entrance inside Melbourne Central shopping centre *(corner LaTrobe & Swanston Streets, Melbourne)*.

If you're staying at one of the hostels in St Kilda, then you'll find both **Coles** *(183 Barkly Street, St Kilda)* and **Safeway** *(Acland Street, St Kilda)* supermarkets on Acland Street. If you're staying at one of the hostels in the Windsor/Prahran/South Yarra area, there are two supermarkets – a Coles *(303 Chapel Street, Prahran)* and a Safeway *(corner Cato & Wattle Streets, Prahran)* – near the corner of Chapel Street and Commercial Road in Prahran.

Like many Australian cities, Melbourne has plenty of places to drink but a lot of them feel plastic and charmless. However there are a few really nice pubs such as the **Pumphouse** *(128 Nicholson Street, Fitzroy)* near Melbourne Museum and the Nunnery and **James Squire Brew Pub** *(115 Russell Street, Melbourne)* and *(439 Docklands Drive, Docklands)*. The **Elephant & Wheelbarrow** is a backpacker favourite with two locations; one in the city centre *(94 Bourke Street, Melbourne)* and another below the Ritz hostel in St Kilda *(169 Fitzroy Street, St Kilda)*, which is a regular venue for Alan Fletcher's (Dr Karl Kennedy from *Neighbours*) band Waiting Room.

Other popular backpackers' bars include **Industry Bar & Lounge** *(198 A'Beckett Street, Melbourne)* at Nomads Industry; the **Joint** *(35 Elizabeth Street, Melbourne)* next to Flinders Station Backpackers and the **Velvet Underground** *(167 Franklin Street, Melbourne)* at Hotel Discovery. If you're staying in Prahran or St Kilda, the **Pint on Punt** *(42 Punt Road, Windsor)* in St Kilda Junction has a great atmosphere and backpacker meals starting at just $6.

Sights

THE CITY CENTRE

The central business district bounded by Flinders, La Trobe, Spencer and Spring Streets is generally called The City. This is where you'll find most of Melbourne's attractions.

Australian/Chinese Museum

This great little museum is in the heart of Chinatown and traces the history of Melbourne's Chinese community, from the gold rushes of the 1850s to the present day. The museum is also home to Dai Loong, one of the world's largest Chinese dragons.

22 Cohen Place, Melbourne
23, 24, 30, 34, 86, 96, City Circle
Parliament
(03) 9662 2888
Website *www.chinesemuseum.com.au*
Admission *$7.50*
Open *10am-5pm daily*

City Museum at Old Treasury

The former state treasury building has been converted into a museum focusing on the story of gold and its role in the development of Victoria.

Spring Street, Melbourne
11, 12, 31, 42, 109, City Circle
Parliament
(03) 9561 2233
Website *www.oldtreasurymuseum.org.au*
Admission *$8.50*
Open *Mon-Fri 9am-5pm, Sat-Sun 10am-4pm*

Federation Square

The Federation Square complex includes part of the National Gallery of Victoria as well as restaurants, cafés, pubs and shops. One of the main features of the buildings in Federation Square is the striking design that utilises sandstone, zinc and glass. The square also features open areas including courtyards and a large central plaza.

Corner Swanston & Flinders Streets, Melbourne
1, 3, 5, 6, 8, 16, 22, 25, 64, 67, 72, City Circle *Flinders Street* *235, 237, 238, 253, 350, 479, 605*
Website *www.federationsquare.com.au*

Flinders Street Station

Flinders Street Station is the hub of Melbourne's suburban rail network and for many years has been Melbourne's major landmark. The clocks on the corner of this ornate station have been the favourite meeting place for generations of Melburnians.

Corner Swanston & Flinders Streets, Melbourne
1, 3, 5, 6, 8, 16, 22, 25, 64, 67, 72, City Circle *Flinders Street*

Immigration Museum

This fascinating museum recalls the journeys of thousands of migrants and their contribution to Australia.

Old Customs House, Corner Flinders & William Streets, Melbourne
48, 55, 70, 75, City Circle
(03) 9927 2700
Website *http://museumvictoria.com.au/ImmigrationMuseum/*
Admission *$6*
Open *10am-5pm daily*

Melbourne Aquarium

Melbourne's impressive new aquarium is home to a variety of Marine Life and features transparent tunnels allowing you to be surrounded by fish in the 2.2 million-litre Oceanarium.

Corner Flinders & King Streets, Melbourne
48, 70, 96, 109, 112, City Circle
(03) 9620 0999
Website *www.melbourneaquarium.com.au*
Admission *$26.50; dive with the sharks $242 (certified divers), $349 (non-divers)*
Open *1-26 Jan 9.30am-9pm daily (last entry 8pm); 27 Jan-31 Dec 9.30am-6pm daily (last entry 5pm)*

Melbourne Museum

Situated behind the Royal Exhibition Buildings, Australia's largest museum contains some excellent exhibits with a good selection on local and natural history. The museum contains a lot of new exhibits and is divided along different themes with Australian history, Aboriginal and Pacific Island culture, science and natural history. The exhibits include a set from the TV show *Neighbours*. The complex also houses an IMAX theatre.

Carlton Gardens, 11 Nicholson Street, Carlton
86, 96 *250, 251, 253, 402*
13 11 02
Website *http://museumvictoria.com.au/MelbourneMuseum/*
Admission *$6*
Open *10am-5pm daily*

NGV – Ian Potter Centre

The National Gallery of Victoria's Ian Potter Centre houses an excellent collection of Australian art ranging from Aboriginal art through to colonial and contemporary art.

Federation Square, Corner Flinders & Swanston Streets, Melbourne
1, 3, 5, 6, 8, 16, 22, 25, 64, 67, 72, City Circle *Flinders Street* *235, 237, 238, 253, 350, 479, 605*
(03) 9208 0222
Website *www.ngv.vic.gov.au*
Admission *free*
Open *Mon-Wed 10am-5pm, Thu 10am-9pm, Fri-Sun 10am-5pm*

Old Melbourne Gaol

Built in 1841, this prison has a history of 104 hangings including that of the infamous Ned Kelly in 1880. Displays include Kelly's armour, his guns and his death mask.

Russell Street, Melbourne
23, 24, 30, 34, City Circle *Melbourne Central* *200, 201, 203, 207, 479*
(03) 9663 7228
Website *www.oldmelbournegaol.com.au*
Admission *$18*
Open *9.30am-5pm daily*

Parliament House

This imposing building served as the home of Australia's parliament from 1901 till 1927 after which time it has been home to the Victorian state parliament. There are guided tours when parliament is not sitting, and you may sit in on parliament when it is in session.

Spring Street, Melbourne
31, 96, 109, 112, City Circle
Parliament
(03) 9651 8568
Website *www.parliament.vic.gov.au*
Admission *free*
Tours *10am, 11am, 12noon, 2pm, 3pm & 3.45pm when parliament is in recess*

Queen Victoria Market

With more than 1100 stalls, the Victoria Market is one of the world's largest. It is a great place to stock up on fresh food at bargain prices, and there is a huge flea market on weekends.

513 Elizabeth Street, Melbourne
19, 55, 57, 59, 68 *Melbourne Central* *220, 232, 546*
(03) 9320 5822

Website *www.qvm.com.au*
Admission *free*
Open *Tue & Thu 6am-2pm, Fri 6am-6pm, Sat 6am-3pm, Sun 9am-4pm*

Rialto Towers

The taller of the two Rialto Towers is Melbourne's tallest office building. There are great views from the observation deck at the top. The best time to visit is just before sunset so you can see the city during the day and night.
525 Collins Street, Melbourne
11, 12, 31, 42, 48, 55, 70, 75, 109, City Circle *Southern Cross*
(03) 9629 8222
Website *www.melbournedeck.com.au*
Admission *$14.50 ($9.90 students)*
Open *10am-10pm daily*

Royal Exhibition Buildings

Built in 1879 for the International Exhibition of 1880, this exhibition centre is an architectural masterpiece; the concrete dome over the main hall was modelled on Brunelleschi's cathedral in Florence. It is one of the world's oldest exhibition pavilions and is Australia's first non-Aboriginal cultural site to be classified as a World Heritage Site. The exterior is more impressive than the interior, partially due to its setting within the Carlton Gardens.
9 Nicholson Street, Carlton
86, 96 *250, 251, 253, 402*
13 11 02
Website *http://museumvictoria.com.au/REB/*
Tours depart *2pm most days, call 13 11 02 for bookings*

SOUTHBANK & SOUTH MELBOURNE

Central Melbourne is expanding across the river into South Melbourne and the heart of all this development is known as Southbank. This new development is growing into a neighbourhood of new inner city apartments, theatres, cafés, restaurants and a casino.

Southbank is home to the Victorian Arts Centre, the Melbourne Exhibition Centre, the huge Crown Casino complex and Southbank Promenade – a pedestrian mall along the river bank which has many sidewalk cafés spilling out from the new shopping complex. It can get quite busy here on weekends and during lunchtime on weekdays when the place is full of office workers.

Eureka Tower

Melbourne's tallest building claims to be the world's tallest residential building. The Q1 in Surfers Paradise also claims this title (Eureka Tower's roof is higher than the Q1, but the Q1 is taller if measured to the top of its spire). The 300m-high (38m taller than the Trump World Tower in New York), 91-storey Eureka Tower has an observation deck on the 88th floor with stunning views of Melbourne, which is the highest public observation point in the southern hemisphere. The Edge is a unique feature of the tower (with an additional $12 admission charge); this is a glass cube that projects three metres outside the building – with you in it – allowing you to see the city through the glass floor.
Riverside Quay, Southbank
3, 5, 6, 8, 16, 25, 55, 64, 67, 72
Flinders Street *216, 219, 220, 250, 251, 253*
(03) 9693 8888
Website *www.eurekaskydeck.com.au*
Admission *$16.50; the Edge $12*
Open *10am-10pm daily*

NGV – International

This branch of the National Gallery of Victoria has exhibits of international art. Its permanent collection includes works by Rembrandt, Rubens and Tintoretto as well as a collection of Egyptian artefacts. It also hosts a world-class programme of temporary exhibits.
180 St Kilda Road, Melbourne
1, 3, 5, 6, 16, 64, 67, 72 *Flinders Street*
(03) 8620 2222
Website *www.ngv.vic.gov.au/ngvinternational/*
Admission *permanent collection free, charge for temporary exhibits*
Open *Mon & Wed-Sun 10am-5pm*

Shrine of Remembrance

If you look south down the middle of Swanston Street, you'll be looking

directly at the Shrine of Remembrance, which was built as a memorial for those who died in the First World War and now stands as a memorial for all the wars in which Australia has played a part. There's a great view of the city from the top.
Kings Domain (off St Kilda Road), Melbourne
3, 5, 6, 8, 16, 25, 64, 67, 72
216, 219, 220
(03) 9654 8415
***Website** www.shrine.org.au*
***Admission** free*
***Open** 10am-5pm daily*

VICTORIAN ARTS CENTRE

The Victorian Arts Centre encompasses: the Melbourne Concert Hall, State Theatre, Playhouse Theatre, Studio Theatre, Westpac Gallery, National Gallery of Victoria, Performing Arts Museum, the Australian Ballet Centre and the Victorian College of the Arts. This extensive collection of facilities for both the visual and performing arts makes it one of the best arts centres in the world. While not as visually stimulating, the Arts Centre's theatres have a greater capacity than the Sydney Opera House. The 115-metre spire on the main theatre building is illuminated at night.
100 St Kilda Road, Southbank
3, 5, 6, 8, 16, 25, 64, 67, 72
Flinders Street D 216, 219, 220
(03) 9281 8000
***Website** www.theartscentre.com.au*

OTHER AREAS

National Sports Museum & MCG Tours

This museum covers Australia's involvement in a wide range of sporting events, with emphasis on Australian Rules Football, cricket and the Olympic Games. The museum is housed in the Melbourne Cricket Ground (MCG), which frequently holds capacity crowds of around 100,000 while hosting cricket matches during the summer and Australian Rules Football in the winter. The MCG was the main venue for the 1956 Olympic Games. A must for sports enthusiasts.
Melbourne Cricket Ground, Jolimont Street, East Melbourne
48, 70, 75 Jolimont 605
(03) 9657 8879
***Website** www.nsm.org.au*
***Admission** $15, $7.50 on event days; **MCG tour** $15; **museum entry & MCG tour** $22*
***Open** 10am-5pm daily (last entry 4pm); tours 10am-3pm non-event days*

Carlton Brewhouse Abbotsford

This is one of the world's busiest breweries producing over 1½ million bottles of beer daily and is the home of Fosters Lager and Victoria Bitter. The brewery offers tours that conclude with a free tasting.
Corner Nelson & South Audley Streets, Abbotsford
24, 109
(03) 9420 6800
***Website** www.visitfostersvenues.com/venues/carlton_brewhouse_abbotsford.asp*
***Admission** $18*
***Tours** Mon-Fri 10am & 2pm, bookings essential*

Luna Park

A huge laughing face greets visitors to this small amusement park at St Kilda Beach. Rides include the Scenic Railway (the world's oldest continuously operating roller coaster) as well as a Ferris wheel and several newer "jaw dropping, eye ball popping, lose your lunch super thrill rides" like the Enterprise, Metropolis and the Pharaoh's Curse.
Lower Esplanade, St Kilda
16, 79, 96 246, 600, 606, 623, 646
1300 888 272
***Website** www.lunapark.com.au*
***Admission** free, rides $7, unlimited ride ticket $35.95*
***Open** 1 Jan-27 Apr Fri 7pm-11pm, Sat 11am-11pm, Sun 11am-6pm; 28 Apr-19 Sep Sat-Sun 11am-6pm; 20 Sep-31 Dec Fri 7pm-11pm, Sat 11am-11pm, Sun 11am-6pm*

Ramsay Street

Neighbours fans may want to visit the street where the TV show is filmed.

Ramsay Street is actually Pin Oak Court in Vermont South, about a 30 to 40-minute drive into the eastern suburbs.
Pin Oak Court, Vermont South
75

If you don't have a car you may want to take one of the tours run by the Backpacker King that includes gossip about the show. The tours are highly recommended, take around three hours and run twice daily Mon-Fri. On weekends there is a back lot tour that takes you into Global Television studios to see the exterior sets from the TV show including the Lassiters complex.
Pick-up from 570 Flinders Street, Melbourne
48, 70, 96, 109, 112 *Southern Cross*
(03) 9534 4755
Website *www.neighbourstour.com*
Tours depart *Mon-Fri 8.45am, 1.45pm; back lot tour Sat-Sun 8.45am*
Tour cost *$40; back lot tour $55*

The Backpacker King also organises *Neighbours* trivia nights where you get to meet the stars of the show.
Elephant & Wheelbarrow, 169 Fitzroy Street, St Kilda
16, 96, 112
(03) 9534 4755 for bookings
Website *www.backpackerking.com.au*
Admission *$40*
Open *Mon 6.30pm, Fri 6pm*

Scienceworks
This museum of science and technology is full of hands-on interactive exhibits. Although it was designed for children, it's a lot of fun for everyone.
2 Booker Street, Spotswood
Spotswood *Scienceworks*
(03) 9392 4800
Website *http://museumvictoria.com.au/Scienceworks/*
Admission *$6; $11 including Planetarium*
Open *10am-4.30pm daily*

St Kilda Beach
This is a great place to catch some rays, or if you're feeling more energetic, go for a swim or rent a bike or a pair of inline skates to cruise the bike path which runs along the beachfront. On Sundays, check out the street market on the Esplanade.
16, 79, 96, 112 *246, 600, 606, 623, 646*

Around Melbourne

There are many attractions within a short drive of Melbourne. In a day, you can visit the Bellarine or Mornington peninsulas with their ocean and bay beaches on either side of Melbourne. Other day trips that you can make from Melbourne include seeing the little penguins at Phillip Island or exploring the Yarra Valley wineries.

Mornington Peninsula

The Mornington Peninsula, southeast of Melbourne, has a variety of beaches – both sheltered swimming beaches and surf beaches – and is a popular weekend getaway for Melburnians. Although part of Melbourne's metropolitan area it maintains a separate identity and a laidback holiday atmosphere.

Sorrento is the most popular town on the Peninsula for backpackers. Apart from being the only town in the area with a hostel, it is also a charming town that's far enough from Melbourne to be considered a separate destination.

Practical Information

Peninsula Visitor Information Centre
Point Nepean Road, Dromana
(03) 5987 3078 or 1800 804 009
Website *www.visitmorningtonpeninsula.org*

Sorrento Information Centre
2 St Aubins Way, Sorrento
(03) 5984 5678

Coming & Going & Local Transport

The Melbourne suburb of Frankston is easily accessible by train from Melbourne. From Frankston you can transfer to buses down the Peninsula or the V/line train to Stony Point.

There are various bus routes on the Mornington Peninsula but bus 788 is the most useful as it runs along the coast for the entire length of the Peninsula from Frankston to Portsea.

Accommodation

Sorrento YHA

This is a small hostel on a quiet residential street that's only a five minute walk to the centre of Sorrento, which is among the nicest towns on the Peninsula. The common areas consist of a small kitchen and dining area with a wood fire and a cosy TV area. It is a clean and well-maintained hostel with a warm friendly atmosphere.

3 Miranda Street, Sorrento
787, 788
(03) 5984 4323
***Website** www.yha.com.au*
***Dorm bed** $35 ($25 HI/YHA); **double room** $90-100 ($75-80 HI/YHA)*
***Credit cards** MC, Visa*
***Reception open** 8.30am-10.30am & 5pm-9pm*

Maintenance & cleanliness	★★★★
Facilities	★
Atmosphere & character	★★★★
Security	★★½
Overall rating	★★★

Dandenong Ranges

The Dandenong Ranges lie at the eastern edge of Melbourne's suburban sprawl. Not to be confused with Dandenong, an the industrial suburb with a similar name, the Dandenongs is a region of natural bush land and a favourite picnic spot for Melburnians.

At the summit of Mount Dandenong is a scenic lookout that many locals claim has the best view of the city, but it is over-rated and not worth the effort – there's a view of the eastern suburbs, but central Melbourne is too far away and often shrouded in smog.

A much better idea is to take a ride on *Puffing Billy*. This is an old steam train that runs from Belgrave to Gembrook through the most scenic parts of the Dandenongs, although it is expensive for a return trip.

Practical Information

Dandenong Ranges & Knox Visitor Information Centre

1211 Burwood Highway, Upper Ferntree Gully
Upper Ferntree Gully
1800 645 505
***Website** www.dandenongrangestourism.com.au*
***Open** 9am-5pm daily*

Coming & Going

Take the train to Belgrave station, then transfer to bus 688, 694 or 698, which will take you along Mount Dandenong Tourist Road, past the area's main attractions. Belgrave station is also the terminus for the Puffing Billy steam railway.

Sights

Puffing Billy Railway

Puffing Billy is a century-old steam train, run by volunteer train enthusiasts, that still runs between Belgrave and Gembrook on its original track. The train takes you through scenic countryside and the trip is a lot of fun. There are between three and six trains a day, although not all of them continue all the way to Gembrook. Trains depart from Belgrave station, which is at the end of the Belgrave line on Melbourne's suburban rail network.

(03) 9754 6800
***Website** www.puffingbilly.com.au*
***Fares** Belgrave-Emerald $19.50 one-way, $33.50 return; Belgrave-Gembrook $30 one-way, $46.50 return*

Yarra Valley

Over the Dandenong Ranges is the Yarra Valley, which is one of Australia's best wine producing regions. If you're in the area pop into some of the wineries to sample the locally produced wines, some of the best include: Fergusson, St Hubert, Domaine Chandon and Yarra Ridge.

Wandin, Silvan and Healesville supply Melbourne with many of its vegetables and there is often work available picking vegetables. Ask around at the market gardens or check the employment listings at the Lilydale Centrelink office.

Practical Information

Yarra Valley Visitor Information Centre

Harker Street, Healesville
☎ *(03) 5962 2600*
Website *www.visityarravalley.com.au*
Open *9am-5pm daily*

Coming & Going

Take the train from any central Melbourne station to Lilydale and then transfer to McKenzies Tourist Service's (☎ *(03) 5962 5088; **website** www.mckenzies.com.au)* bus 685, which goes to Healesville.

Sights & Activities

Healesville Sanctuary

This wildlife sanctuary is home to over 200 species of Australian wildlife including kangaroos, wallabies, wombats, koalas, platypus and Tasmanian devils. A visit is an excellent opportunity to get up close with a wide variety of native Australian animals.

Badger Creek Road, Healesville
🚆 *Lilydale, then* 🚌 *685, 686*
☎ *(03) 5957 2800*
Website *www.zoo.org.au/HealesvilleSanctuary*
Admission *$23*
Open *9am-5pm daily*

Wine tasting

Wine tasting is the main reason most backpackers visit the Yarra Valley. Without your own car and a driver who isn't drinking it can be difficult to get around unless you take a tour. **Backpacker Winery Tours** (☎ *(03) 9877 8333; **website** www.backpackerwinerytours.com.au)* run winery tours for $95 that visit Domaine Chandon, Eyton on Yarra, St Hubert's and Yarra Ridge with pick-ups from hostels in Melbourne.

Hanging Rock

This rock formation, also known as Mount Diogenes, is 70km north of Melbourne via the Calder Highway. It has been made famous by Joan Lindsay's novel *Picnic at Hanging Rock* that Peter Weir later made into a film.

The rock is a popular picnic spot and lots of fun for novice rock climbers, with plenty of crevices to explore and panoramic views from the pinnacles.

The Hanging Rock Recreation Reserve is home to native wildlife such as wallabies, kookaburras and koalas that are usually easy to find sitting high in the gum trees.

On New Year's Day and Australia Day (26 Jan), the Hanging Rock horse races are held at the racecourse within the reserve.

Hanging Rock Recreation Reserve
South Rock Road, Woodend
☎ *1800 244 711*
Website *www.hangingrock.info*
Admission *$8 per car*
Open *9am-5pm daily*

Phillip Island

Less than a two-hour drive from Melbourne, Phillip Island has some fantastic surf beaches and abundance of wildlife; including koalas, kangaroos, wallabies, seals and the little penguins for which Phillip Island is famous.

Practical Information

Phillip Island Information Centre

Phillip Island Road, Newhaven, Phillip Island
☎ *(03) 5956 7447 or 1300 366 422*
Website *www.visitphillipisland.com*
Open *9am-5pm daily*

Coming & Going

If you're not driving, there are a few transport options between Melbourne and the island.

Inter Island Ferries (☎ *(03) 9585 5730; **website** www.interislandferries.com.au)* sail several times a day between Cowes on Phillip Island and Stony Point on the Mornington Peninsula. The one-way fare is $10, but you also need to take a train from Melbourne to Stony Point (change trains at Frankston), which costs an additional $5.50.

V/line (☎ *13 61 96; **website** www.vline.com.au)* run a bus service between Melbourne and Cowes although this service only runs a once a day. The V/line bus departs from Southern Cross Station and the return fare is $20.

There are also several companies that run tours departing from Melbourne.

These include **Autopia Tours** (☎ *1800 000 507; **website** www.autopiatours.com.au*); **Go West** (☎ *1300 736 551; **website** www.gowest.com.au*), which both cost $109 and **Penguin Island Tours** (☎ *(03) 9629 5888; **website** www.penguinislandtour.com.au*) who run tours for $99. The prices for all these tours include admission fees to a wildlife park and the Penguin Parade.

Local Transport

The Duck Truck (☎ *1800 235 998; **website** www.amaroopark.com/ducktruck/*) operates a shuttle bus to the Penguin Parade that picks up from accommodation in Cowes. The return fare is $15.

Accommodation

Amaroo Park YHA

Cowes' YHA hostel is part of a tourist cabin park just a short walk from the centre of town. It is actually quite a good hostel and the backpackers' common areas include a kitchen; a lounge with a fireplace, pool table and internet access and a cosy bar with a great atmosphere. There is also a swimming pool in the complex. The accommodation is split between dorm rooms in an old house, which are clean but show their age; and more expensive dorms in a newer building, which are spotless and very well maintained.

97 Church Street, Cowes
☎ *(03) 5952 2548*
***Website** www.amaroopark.com*
***Dorm bed** $30-35 ($25-30 HI/YHA); **double/twin/family room** $135 ($108 HI/YHA); **camping** $15 per person*
***Credit cards** MC, Visa*
***Reception open** 9am-6pm; check in till 8.30pm*

Maintenance & cleanliness	★★★
Facilities	★★★
Atmosphere & character	★★★★
Security	★★
Overall rating	★★★

Sights & Activities

Koala Conservation Centre

This is a wildlife park dedicated to koalas where you can walk along a boardwalk in the treetops and see koalas up close.

Phillip Island Road, Sunset Strip.
☎ *(03) 5956 8300*
***Website** www.penguins.org.au*
***Admission** $10; 3 Parks Pass including entry to Penguin Parade and Churchill Island $34*

The Nobbies

At the south-western tip of the Phillip Island are a group of rocks called the Nobbies, which are home to a colony of seals that can viewed through coin operated binoculars at the Nobbies kiosk. The **Nobbies Centre** (☎ *(03) 5951 2800; **website** www.nobbies.org.au*) has a café and interactive displays about the region's wildlife.

Penguin Parade

Every night at sunset, little penguins emerge from the sea and make their way across the beach to their home amongst the sand dunes. It's best to come here during the summer when there are more penguins; during winter it can be bitterly cold with winds coming up from Antarctica and very few penguins making the trip to their nesting ground. The Phillip Island Penguin Parade is one of Australia's most popular tourist attractions; a huge grandstand has been built to accommodate the hundreds of spectators, and the beach is floodlit detracting from what would otherwise be an amazing natural attraction. There is also an information centre on the site with displays and a short film about penguins.

Ventnor Road, Summerland Beach
☎ *(03) 5956 8691*
***Website** www.penguins.org.au*
***Admission** $20; 3 Parks Pass including entry to Churchill Island and Koala Conservation Centre $34*
***Open** 10am-11pm daily; arrive 1hr before sunset for penguin parade*

Phillip Island Wildlife Park

There are several wildlife parks around Phillip Island but this one is the closest to Cowes and the most convienent if you're staying in Cowes and don't have a car. It is home to dingoes, emus, koalas and Tasmanian devils and you can hand-feed kangaroos and wallabies.

Phillip Island Road, Cowes
☎ *(03) 5952 2038*
Admission *$15*

Seal Watching Cruises

Although you can see seals through binoculars from the Nobbies, it is a much better experience to take a cruise to the seal colony at Seal Rocks, 2km offshore. **Wildlife Coast Cruises** *(☎ 1300 763 739; **website** www.wildlifecoastcruises.com.au)* run two hour cruises that cost $58 and give you the oppotunity to see thousands of seals up close.

Surfing

Phillip Island has excellent surf beaches along its southern coast. These include Cat Bay, Smiths Beach and Cape Woolamai Surf Beach at the southeastern point of the island.

Island Surfboards & Surf School *(☎ (03) 5952 3443; **website** www.islandsurfboards.com.au)* and **Out There** *(☎ (03) 5956 6450; **website** www.outthere.net.au)* can teach you to surf. Prices start at $50 for a two-hour lesson.

Wildlife Wonderland (the Giant Worm)

This wildlife park features Australian native animals including emus, kangaroos and wombats plus a worm museum. It is on the way to the island and is difficult to reach without a car, but it's an easy detour if you're driving to the island.

Bass Highway, Bass
☎ *(03) 5678 2222*
Website *www.wildlifewonderland.com.au*
Admission *$13.90*
Open *8.30am-6.30pm*

Geelong

Victoria's second city is a thriving commercial and industrial centre and major port, but for most travellers, Geelong is just a place to pass through en route to Torquay and the Great Ocean Road.

It has a pleasant waterfront area but its main attractions are the Wool Museum and the Ford Discovery Centre.

Practical Information

INFORMATION CENTRES

Geelong & Great Ocean Road Visitor Information Centre

Stead Park, Princes Highway, Corio
🚌 *10*
☎ *(03) 5275 5797 or 1800 620 888*
Website *www.visitgeelong.org*
Open *9am-5pm daily*

Geelong Visitor Information Centre

National Wool Museum, corner Moorabool & Brougham Streets, Geelong
🚌 *10, 12, 21, 30, 35, 36, 51, 55*
☎ *(03) 5222 2900 or 1800 620 888*
Website *www.visitgeelong.org*
Open *9am-5pm daily*

Coming & Going

Most people pass through Geelong when driving between Melbourne and the Great Ocean Road.

If you're travelling by public transport, the V/line *(☎ 13 61 96; **website** www.vline.com.au)* train service from Melbourne is the easiest way to get here. Trains run hourly from Southern Cross station in Melbourne and take just over an hour. The one-way fare is $7.20-20.40.

There are also direct bus links between Geelong and Melbourne's two airports. Avalon Airport is only 15 minutes from the centre of Geelong and Avalon Airport Shuttle *(☎ (03) 5278 8788; **website** www.avalonairportshuttle.com.au)* runs between Avalon and Geelong for $17.

Gull *(☎ (03) 5222 4966; **website** www.gull.com.au)* run buses to Melbourne Airport picking up at 45 McKillop Street and Geelong train station. The one-way fare is $25.

Local Transport

The Geelong Transit System is comprised of buses run by Benders Busways *(☎ (03) 5278 5955; **website** www.kefford.com.au/geelong.htm)* and McHarry's *(☎ (03) 5223 2111; **website** www.mcharrys.com.au)*. The $1.80 fare allows you to travel on any Geelong Transit System bus for two to three hours.

There are also some suburban train services run by V/line *(☎ 13 61 96;*

***website** www.vline.com.au)*, although services are infrequent.

Accommodation

Irish Murphys

Irish Murphys is a brilliant Irish pub west of the city centre with backpackers' accommodation upstairs. Although the bar downstairs is really nice, upstairs isn't quite as nice and it feels a bit neglected, although the dorm rooms are clean and comfortable. The common areas are limited to a small kitchen, TV lounge with a pool table and a laundry.

30 Aberdeen Street, Geelong
(03) 5222 2900
***Website** www.irishmurphys.com.au*
***Dorm bed** $20; **single room** $25*
***Credit cards** Amex, Diners, MC, Visa*
TV K L

Maintenance & cleanliness	★★
Facilities	★½
Atmosphere & character	★★★½
Security	★½
Overall rating	★★

National Hotel

The National Hotel is a lively bar right in the heart of Geelong's city centre that has live music and great noodles. The backpackers' accommodation upstairs is pretty basic and shows its age. Shared facilities at this hostel include a small kitchen, TV lounge and wireless internet.

191 Moorabool Street, Geelong
0410 529 935 or (03) 5229 1211
***Website** www.nationalhotel.com.au*
***Dorm bed** $28; **single/double/twin/ triple room** $55*
***Credit cards** MC, Visa*
***Reception open** 9am-late*
TV K

Maintenance & cleanliness	★★
Facilities	★½
Atmosphere & character	★★★
Security	★½
Overall rating	★★

Sights

Ford Discovery Centre

Thousands of Ford cars roll off the production line in Geelong and the Ford Discovery Centre by the waterfront illustrates the history of Ford cars in Australia. It has displays on the production and design process and also features a collection of cars ranging from the Model T to the latest models

Corner Brougham & Gheringhap Streets, Geelong
(03) 5227 8700
***Website** www.forddiscovery.com.au*
***Admission** $7*
***Open** Wed-Mon 10am-5pm daily*

National Wool Museum

Geelong's big attraction is this well designed museum that depicts the history of Australia's wool industry. It also demonstrates the process of shearing, spinning and knitting.

26 Moorabool Street, Geelong
10, 12, 21, 30, 35, 36, 51, 55
(03) 5227 0701
***Website** www.nwm.vic.gov.au*
***Admission** $7.30*
***Open** Mon-Fri 9.30am-5pm, Sat-Sun 1pm-5pm*

Queenscliff & the Bellarine Peninsula

The Bellarine Peninsula near Geelong has a couple of surf beaches on its southern coastline as well as the historic resort town of Queenscliff.

Queenscliff became a fashionable resort in the 19th century when many grand old hotels were built and nowadays it retains an upmarket feel that separates it from coastal resort towns elsewhere in Australia.

Practical Information

Queenscliff Visitor Information Centre

55 Hesse Street, Queenscliff
(03) 5258 4843
***Website** www.queenscliffe.vic.gov.au*
***Open** 9am-5pm daily*

Coming & Going

The Bellarine Peninsula is well connected by public transport from Geelong. McHarry's *((03) 5223 2111; **website** www.mcharrys.com.au)* run buses from Geelong.

Peninsula Searoad Transport *((03) 5258 3244; **website** www.searoad.com.*

au) run ferries every hour (7am-6pm) between Queenscliff and Sorrento on the Mornington Peninsula. The journey takes around half an hour and one-way fares are $9 for a foot passenger or $60-66 for a car with two passengers.

Accommodation

Queenscliff Inn YHA

The Queenscliff Inn is a quiet place, but unlike many other quiet hostels it has loads of atmosphere. It's set in a historic building with lots of charm and it has a classy upmarket ambience. Accommodation is in large, spacious rooms, but some beds are a little squeaky. Facilities include a drawing room with a fireplace, board games and a small television.

59 Hesse Street, Queenscliff
☎ *(03) 5258 3737*
Website *www.yha.com.au*
Dorm bed *$30 ($27 HI/YHA);* ***single room*** *$65 ($58.50 HI/YHA);* ***double/twin room*** *$80 ($72 HI/YHA)*
Credit cards *MC, Visa*
Reception open *8am-10am & 5pm-10pm daily*
TV

Maintenance & cleanliness	★★★
Facilities	★
Atmosphere & character	★★★★
Security	★½
Overall rating	★★½

Sights

Fort Queenscliff

This coastal fortress was constructed in 1882 as part of an elaborate defence network around the Port Phillip Bay heads. Guided tours of the facility take around an hour and allow you to see the fort's lighthouse and military instalments.

1 King Street, Queenscliff
☎ *(03) 5258 1488*
Admission *$6*
Tours *Sat-Sun 1pm, 3pm*

Great Ocean Road

The Great Ocean Road is the most scenic route from Melbourne to Adelaide. It hugs the coastline from Torquay to Peterborough with a brief diversion through the Otway Ranges and connects with the Princes Highway near Warrnambool, which continues onwards toward Adelaide.

Although the entire Great Ocean Road is a scenic drive, the most breathtaking scenery along this route is found around Port Campbell. This includes some spectacular rock formations such as London Bridge and the Twelve Apostles.

Local Transport

If you don't have your own car, V/line *(☎ 13 22 32;* ***website*** *www.vline.com.au)* has a bus service along the Great Ocean Road, and several companies operate tours along this route.

Autopia Tours *(☎ 1800 000 507;* ***website*** *www.autopiatours.com.au)* run day tours from Melbourne that cost $105, and three-day trips that cost $405 and they also include the Great Ocean Road on their popular Adelaide-Melbourne tour.

Go West *(☎ 1300 736 551;* ***website*** *www.gowest.com.au)* run day tours from Melbourne that cost $105.

Otway Discovery *(☎ (03) 9629 5844;* ***website*** *www.otwaydiscovery.com.au)* run a daytrip from Melbourne that visits various spots along the Great Ocean Road, including Bells Beach and the 12 Apostles. This trip costs $95 and for an extra $20 you can jump on and off to stretch your trip over several days.

The Wayward Bus *(☎ 1800 882 823;* ***website*** *www.waywardbus.com.au)* operates a three-day tour between Melbourne and Adelaide taking in the Great Ocean Road en route. This tour costs $395.

Wildlife Tours *(☎ (03) 9534 8868;* ***website*** *www.wildlifetours.com.au)* run one, two and three-day trips from Melbourne that go to the 12 Apostles and most other attractions along the road; one-day tours cost $90, two-day tours cost $160 and the three-day tour costs $195. Wildlife Tours also include the Great Ocean Road on their Adelaide-Melbourne trip.

Oz Experience *(☎ 1300 300 028;* ***website*** *www.ozexperience.com)* also includes the Great Ocean Road on their Melbourne to Adelaide route.

Torquay

Torquay is Australia's surfing capital and it marks the beginning of the Great Ocean Road. Bells Beach, Jan Juc, Point Danger, Point Impossible and Torquay Surf Beach are the main surf beaches.

Each year at Easter, Bells Beach hosts an international surfing championship.

Practical Information

Torquay Visitor Information Centre

Surf City Plaza, Beach Road, Torquay
☎ *(03) 5261 4219*
Open *9am-5pm daily*

Coming & Going

V/line (☎ *13 22 32;* ***website*** *www.vline.com.au)* buses go to Geelong, Melbourne and to Warrnambool along the Great Ocean Road. Buses stop at the corner of Grossmans Road and the Surf Coast Highway.

Accommodation

The Famous Bells Beach Surf Lodge & Backpackers' Palace

This is a good hostel with a handy location and a great laid-back surf atmosphere. It is a clean place with good facilities that include an internet café and a TV lounge although it is the most expensive hostel in this part of Victoria. It was undergoing renovation when we visited so things should improve by the time you visit.

51-53 Surfcoast Highway, Torquay
☎ *(03) 5261 7070*
Website *www.bellsbeachlodge.com.au*
Dorm bed *$40;* ***double room*** *$90; prices include breakfast*
Credit cards *MC, Visa; credit card surcharge*
Reception open *8am-1pm & 4pm-9pm daily*

Maintenance & cleanliness	★★★
Facilities	★½
Atmosphere & character	★★★
Security	★★½
Overall rating	★★½

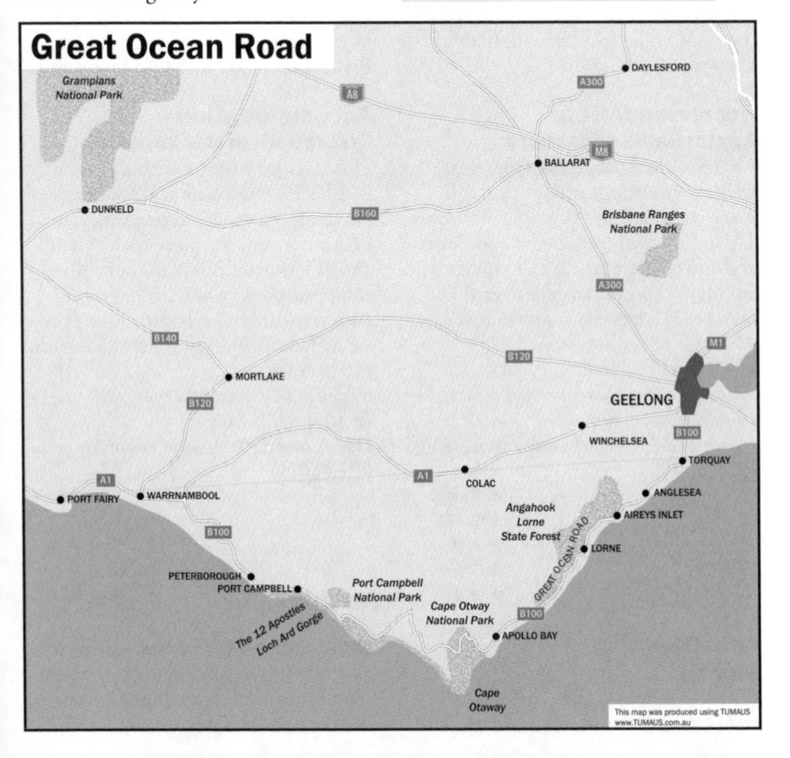

Sights & Activities

Surfing

Although Torquay's beaches are popular with more experienced surfers, it is also possible to learn to surf here. **Go Ride a Wave** (☎ *1300 132 441; **website** www.gorideawave.com.au)* offer three two-hour lessons for $150.

Westcoast Surf School (☎ *(03) 5261 2241; **website** http://westcoast.customer.netspace.net.au/)* charge $50 for a two-hour lesson.

Surfworld

Surfworld is a brilliant museum about surfing and beach culture that delves into everything from physics to surf history.

Surf City Plaza, Beach Road, Torquay
☎ *(03) 5261 4606*
***Website** www.surfworld.org.au*
***Admission** $9*
***Open** 9am-5pm daily*

Anglesea

This small town between Torquay and Lorne has a good beach where you can learn to surf. Anglesea's local golf course is home to a large number of kangaroos.

Accommodation

Anglesea Backpackers

Anglesea Backpackers is a clean and well-maintained hostel. It's a small place with facilities that include a cosy TV lounge with polished wood floors and a fireplace plus a small kitchen and laundry. There is also a backyard barbecue area where you can see rosellas.

40 Noble Street, Anglesea
☎ *(03) 5263 2664*
***Website** http://home.iprimus.com.au/angleseabackpacker*
***Dorm bed** $29-35; **double room** $85-95*

Maintenance & cleanliness	★★★½
Facilities	★½
Atmosphere & character	★★★
Security	★
Overall rating	★★½

Activities

Surfing

Go Ride a Wave (☎ *1300 132 441; **website** www.gorideawave.com.au)* and **Westcoast Surf School** (☎ *(03) 5261 2241; **website** http://westcoast.customer.netspace.net.au/)* can teach you to surf at Anglesea. Go Ride a Wave charge $150 for three lessons and a two-hour lesson with Westcoast costs $50.

Lorne

Lorne is one of the more upmarket resort towns on the Great Ocean Road. Although there isn't really much to see in Lorne, it has a beautiful setting with a very nice beach and some good hiking trails in the surrounding area.

Practical Information

Lorne Visitor Information Centre

144 Mountjoy Parade, Lorne
☎ *(03) 5289 1152*
***Website** www.visitsurfcoast.com*
***Open** 9am-5pm daily*

Coming & Going

V/line (☎ *13 22 32; **website** www.vline.com.au)* buses go to Geelong and Warrnambool along the Great Ocean Road. Buses stop on Mountjoy Parade.

Accommodation

Erskine River Backpackers

This is a lovely hostel with a pleasant laid-back atmosphere and features big shady verandas overlooking the Erskine River. The place is clean and amenities include a small, but fully-equipped kitchen and dining room with retro 1950s-style furniture. It is located above a nice café at the eastern end of town.

6 Mountjoy Parade, Lorne
☎ *(03) 5289 1496*
***Dorm bed** $25; **double room** $60*

Maintenance & cleanliness	★★★
Facilities	★½
Atmosphere & character	★★★★
Security	★½
Overall rating	★★½

Great Ocean Road Backpackers

This is a well-maintained YHA hostel in a beautiful bush setting that is home to wild birds and possums. There are

clean bathrooms, a kitchen and dining room and nice outdoor areas including a balcony and deck.
10 Erskine Avenue, Lorne
☎ *(03) 5289 1809*
Website *www.yha.com.au*
Dorm bed *$23.50-25 ($20 HI/YHA);* ***double/twin room*** *$65-70 ($55 HI/YHA);* ***family room*** *$90-100 ($75 HI/YHA)*
Credit cards *Amex, Diners, MC, Visa*
Reception open *8am-9pm*

Maintenance & cleanliness	★★★½
Facilities	★
Atmosphere & character	★★★½
Security	★
Overall rating	★★½

Activities
Surfing
Go Ride a Wave *(☎ 1300 132 441;* ***website*** *www.gorideawave.com.au)* can teach you to surf at Lorne. Three two-hour lessons cost $150.

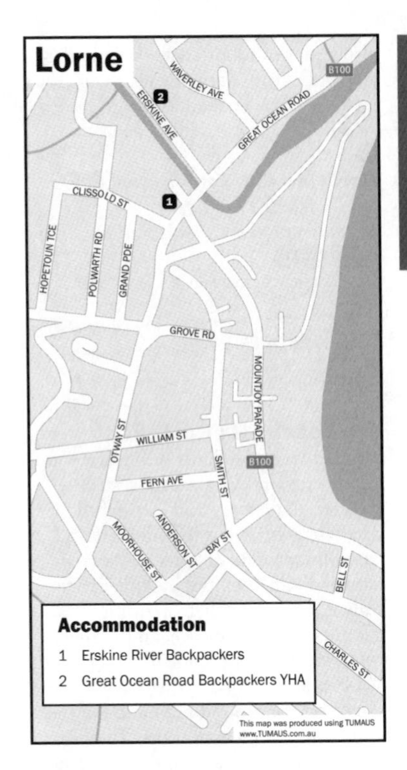

Kennett River
This locality, mid-way between Lorne and Apollo Bay, is home to native wildlife including koalas. The **Kennett River Koala Walk** *(30 minutes)* is about 6km down the Grey River Road, the turn off is not far from the Kennett River Café and Camping Ground. You should be able to spot koalas in the gum trees along the walk and also along the road leading to the trail (just look for the grey fur in the forks between branches).

Apollo Bay
Situated near the Otway National Park, this is another beachside town on the Great Ocean Road with a scenic location. Apollo Bay has a good selection of backpackers' hostels and there is a market on the foreshore every Saturday.

Practical Information
Great Ocean Road Visitor Information Centre
100 Great Ocean Road, Apollo Bay
☎ *(03) 5237 6529*
Website *www.greatoceanroad.org*
Open *9am-5pm daily*

INTERNET ACCESS
There is internet access at Apollo Bay Pharmacy *(121 Great Ocean Road, Apollo Bay)* and the visitor information centre *(100 Great Ocean Road, Apollo Bay).*

Coming & Going
V/line *(☎ 13 22 32;* ***website*** *www.vline.com.au)* buses go to Geelong and Warrnambool along the Great Ocean Road. Buses stop at the Visitor Information Centre on the Great Ocean Road.

Accommodation
Apollo Bay Backpackers
Apollo Bay Backpackers is a small cosy hostel in an old house on a quiet residential street a short walk from the centre of town. Facilities include a common area with a small fully-equipped kitchen; a TV lounge and internet access ($5 per hour). There is

also a nice outdoor area with a barbecue and a front garden where you can feed the birds in the morning.
47 Montrose Street, Apollo Bay
☎ *(03) 5237 7360*
***Dorm bed** $22; **double room** $55; prices include breakfast*
***Reception open** 7.30am-9.30pm daily*

Maintenance & cleanliness	★★½
Facilities	★½
Atmosphere & character	★★★½
Security	★★½
Overall rating	★★½

Eco Beach YHA Hostel
This new purpose-built eco-hostel was architecturally designed to maximise passive solar energy and is tastefully decorated with polished concrete and wood floors, light colours and lots of natural light. Facilities include a nice fully-equipped kitchen, a dining area, a lounge with a fireplace, an internet room ($6 per hour; Global Gossip) with Wi-Fi and a TV lounge with a widescreen on the ground floor and another lounge and kitchen upstairs. There is also a rooftop sundeck and a barbecue area on the balcony. It is one of the best hostels in the country and certainly the best on the Great Ocean Road.
5 Pascoe Street, Apollo Bay
☎ *(03) 5237 7899*
***Website** www.yha.com.au*
***Dorm bed** $30-37 ($27 HI/YHA); **single room** $68.50-72 ($65 HI/YHA); **double room** $83.50-89 ($75 HI/YHA); **family room** $106-109 ($95 HI/YHA)*
***Credit cards** MC, Visa*
***Reception open** 8am-10am & 5pm-10pm daily*

Maintenance & cleanliness	★★★★★
Facilities	★★★
Atmosphere & character	★★★★
Security	★★★
Overall rating	★★★★

Surfside Backpackers
Surfside Backpackers is a small hostel with a homely atmosphere, but the building is a little old and the facilities are a bit dated. Amenities include a small fully-equipped kitchen and a lounge with old sofas, a record player, a coin-operated internet computer ($6 per hour) and big windows with a fantastic view of the beach. There are verandas around the hostel and a nice outdoor barbecue area.
Corner Gambier Street & Great Ocean Road, Apollo Bay
☎ *(03) 5237 7263*
***Dorm bed** $20-22; **double room** $65-85*
***Credit cards** MC, Visa*

Maintenance & cleanliness	★★½
Facilities	★½
Atmosphere & character	★★★½
Security	★½
Overall rating	★★½

Eating & Drinking
There are plenty of cheap places to eat on the Great Ocean Road and **Goossens** *(4 Hardy Street, Apollo Bay)* makes excellent hot chocolate. There are two small supermarkets in Apollo Bay: a **Foodworks** *(4 Hardy Street, Apollo Bay)* and an **IGA** on *(Great Ocean Road, Apollo Bay)*.

Activities
Scenic Flights
There are several companies operating scenic flights of sights on the Great Ocean Road including the Twelve Apostles. Scenic flights operating from Apollo Bay Airport include **12 Apostles Air Adventures** (☎ *(03) 5237 7370; **website** www.tigermothworld.com)* and **12 Apostles Flightseeing** (☎ *1800 538 735; **website** www.apollobayaviation.com.au)*.

Sea Kayaking
Apollo Seal Kayak Tours (☎ *0405 495 909; **website** www.apollobaysurfkayak.com.au)* run two hour sea kayaking tours to the seal colony at the Manengo Marine Sanctuary. Tours cost $55.

Surfing
Apollo Bay Surf School (☎ *0405 495 909; **website** www.apollobaysurfkayak.com.au)* can teach you to surf at Apollo Bay. Lessons cost $45 for 1½ hours.

Otway Ranges

After Apollo Bay, the Great Ocean Road turns inland and crosses the Otway Ranges. This is an area of untouched rainforest with huge towering gum trees and shady ferns. There are hiking trails and campsites in the Otway National Park.

Accommodation

Cape Otway Backpackers

Cape Otway Backpackers is part of the Bimbi Park caravan park and horse riding complex. The backpackers' accommodation consists of bunk beds in two clean and well maintained cabins plus a building with a kitchen, games room with table football and a sheltered barbecue area. It is in a natural bush setting 7km off the Great Ocean Road.

Manna Gum Drive, Cape Otway
☎ *(03) 5237 9246*
***Dorm bed** $20; **double/twin room** $45*
***Credit cards** MC, Visa*
***Reception open** 8am-7pm daily*

Maintenance & cleanliness	★★★
Facilities	★
Atmosphere & character	★★
Security	★
Overall rating	★★

Sights & Activities

Otway Fly

The Otway Fly is the longest and highest tree top canopy walk of its kind. The 25m-high boardwalk lets you walk 600m through the treetops. There is also a 47m-high lookout tower with sweeping views.

Phillips Track, Beech Forest
☎ *(03) 5235 9200 or 1800 300 477*
***Website** www.otwayfly.com*
***Admission** $19.50*
***Open** 9am-5pm daily (last entry 4pm)*

Port Campbell & Port Campbell National Park

From the Otway Ranges to Peterborough, much of the area between the road and the ocean is protected as a national park. Port Campbell National Park is the site of the most spectacular scenery on the Great Ocean Road.

If you're driving, take the time to check out all the scenic spots; particularly the Twelve Apostles, the Bay of Islands, Loch Ard Gorge and London Bridge.

Practical Information

Port Campbell Visitor Information Centre

26 Morris Street, Port Campbell
☎ *(03) 5598 6053*
***Website** www.visit12apostles.com*
Open 9am-5pm daily

Coming & Going

V/line (☎ *13 22 32; **website** www.vline.com.au*) buses go to Geelong and Warrnambool along the Great Ocean Road. Buses stop at the Surf Club on Tregea Street.

Accommodation

The 13th Apostle

The 13th Apostle is a nice purpose-built hostel in the small hamlet of Princetown, 6km east of the 12 Apostles. It is a very clean and well-

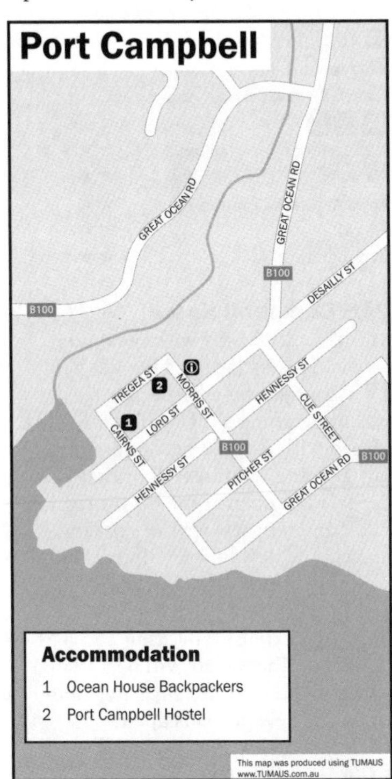

maintained hostel with comfortable beds. There is a common room with a basic kitchen (just a fridge, microwave and a toaster), internet access ($8 per hour) and a TV with lots of DVDs.
Post Office Road, Princetown
☎ *(03) 5598 8062*
***Dorm bed** $28; **double room** $65; prices include breakfast*

Maintenance & cleanliness	★★★★★
Facilities	★☆
Atmosphere & character	★★
Security	★☆
Overall rating	★★★

Ocean House Backpackers

This is a clean and well maintained hostel in a house facing the ocean, but the atmosphere can be a bit dead at times. It features polished hardwood floors and new furnishings and there is a veranda overlooking the sea. It is managed by the Port O'Call Motel *(37 Lord Street, Port Campbell)* and you can check in there when the hostel's reception is unattended.
32 Cairns Street, Port Campbell
☎ *(03) 5598 6206*
***Dorm bed** $27*
***Credit cards** MC, Visa*

Maintenance & cleanliness	★★★★
Facilities	★☆
Atmosphere & character	★★
Security	★☆
Overall rating	★★☆

Port Campbell Hostel

This is a nice hostel with good quality facilities including a big kitchen, a TV lounge and a barbecue area. It was undergoing a big change when we visited with a brand new two-storey hostel being built next door that was expected to open at the beginning of 2009 and will replace the exisiting hostel. The new hostel will have huge common areas with a kitchen, dining and lounge rooms plus outdoor areas including extensive decking and barbecue areas. The review will be updated on the BUG website *(www.bug.co.uk)* when the new hostel is open.
18 Tregea Street, Port Campbell
☎ *(03) 5598 6305*
***Website** www.portcampbellhostel.com.au*
***Dorm bed** $23-25; **double room** $70*
***Credit cards** MC, Visa*
***Reception open** 8am-10am & 5pm-10pm daily*

Maintenance & cleanliness	★★★☆
Facilities	★☆
Atmosphere & character	★★★
Security	★☆
Overall rating	★★☆

Activities

Scenic Flights

There are several companies operating scenic helicopter flights of sights on the Great Ocean Road including the Twelve Apostles. Scenic flights operating from Port Campbell include **12 Apostles Helicopters** *(☎ (03) 5598 6161; **website** www.12ah.com)* and **The Edge Helicopters** *(☎ (03) 5598 8283; **website** www.theedgehelicopters.com).*

Warrnambool

Warrnambool is a major provincial city at the western extremity of the Great Ocean Road. Whales are regularly seen at Logans Beach.

Practical Information

Warrnambool Visitor Information Centre

600 Raglan Parade, Warrnambool
☎ *(03) 5564 7837*
***Website** www.warrnamboolinfo.com.au*
***Open** 9am-5pm daily*

Coming & Going

V/line *(☎ 13 61 96; **website** www.vline.com.au)* operate regular rail services to Geelong and Melbourne and buses to points along the coast as well as Mount Gambier, Ballarat and Melbourne. The train station is located on Merri Street and buses depart from Raglan Parade.

Local Transport

Transit South West *(**website** www.warbus.com.au)* operate a fairly extensive network of local bus routes around Warrnambool.

Accommodation
Warrnambool Beach Backpackers

Everything at Warrnambool Beach Backpackers is new and well maintained. There is a good range of facilities including two kitchens, a laundry, a bar and internet access including Wi-Fi ($10 for 3 hours). Guests get free use of mountain bikes, body boards and fishing gear. It is close to the beach but around a 30 min walk from the town centre.

17 Stanley Street, Warrnambool
(03) 5562 4874
Website *www.beachbackpackers.com.au*
Dorm bed *$23;* ***double room*** *$70*
Credit cards *MC, Visa*
Reception open *7am-noon & 4pm-11pm daily*

Maintenance & cleanliness	★★★½
Facilities	★★½
Atmosphere & character	★★★½
Security	★★
Overall rating	★★★

Sights
Flagstaff Hill Maritime Museum

Flagstaff Hill Maritime Museum comprises a recreated village, restored ships and an exhibition of artefacts recovered from southwest Victoria's many shipwrecks.

Merri Street. Warrnambool
6, 8
(03) 5564 7841
Website *www.flagstaffhill.com*
Admission *$15.95 day entry; Shipwrecked sound and laser show $25.50.*
Open *9am-5pm daily (last entry 4pm)*

Whale Watching

The southern right whale can be seen May-Oct; the best viewing spot is at Logans Beach where a viewing platform has been constructed.

Port Fairy

This historic township is home to around 50 buildings classified by the National Trust and has a great atmosphere; particularly during the annual Port Fairy Folk Festival held on the Labour Day long weekend in March.

Practical Information
Port Fairy Visitor Information Centre

Railway Place, Bank Street, Port Fairy
10
(03) 5568 2682
Website *www.port-fairy.com/vic/*
Open *9am-5pm daily*

Coming & Going

V/line (*13 22 32;* ***website*** *www.vline.com.au*) buses go to Warrnambool, Portland and Mount Gambier in South Australia and Transit South West (***website*** *www.warbus.com.au*) bus route 10 runs between Warrnambool and Port Fairy. Buses stop on Bank Street.

Accommodation
Eumeralla Backpackers

This old school house is a beautiful building with lovely polished hardwood floors and lots of character. It has a small fully-equipped kitchen and a big lounge with a fireplace and a TV and there is a nice barbecue area outside. It's in the tiny village of Yambuk, 18km west of Port Fairy.

High Street, Yambuk (18km west of Port Fairy)
(03) 5568 4204
Dorm bed *$20*

Maintenance & cleanliness	★★★★½
Facilities	★★
Atmosphere & character	★★★★½
Security	★
Overall rating	★★★½

Port Fairy YHA

Port Fairy's youth hostel is in an historic building that was originally built for one of the town's founders. The hostel has a large fully-equipped kitchen; a games room with a pool table; a cosy lounge with a fireplace, a TV and internet access including Wi-Fi ($6 per hour). There is also a small courtyard barbecue area and a backyard with a herb garden.

8 Cox Street, Port Fairy VIC 3284
(03) 5568 2468
Website *www.yha.com.au*
Dorm bed *$26.50-33 ($23-29 HI/YHA);* ***single room*** *$47 ($37 HI/*

*YHA); **double room** $72 ($62 HI/YHA); **twin room** $65 ($55 HI/YHA)*
***Credit cards** MC, Visa*
***Reception open** summer 9am-11am & 5pm-10pm daily; winter 9am-11am & 4pm-9pm daily*

Maintenance & cleanliness	★★★
Facilities	★★½
Atmosphere & character	★★★½
Security	★½
Overall rating	★★★

Portland

Victoria's oldest town was once a busy whaling port but it's now an industrial city that is dominated by a big aluminium smelter. Travellers that are interested in Australian maritime history will no doubt find the place interesting although many travellers bypass Portland altogether.

Practical Information
Portland Visitor Information Centre

Lee Breakwater Road, Portland
☎ *(03) 5523 2671*
***Website** www.visitdiscoverycoast.com*
***Open** 9am-5pm daily*

Coming & Going

V/line (☎ *13 22 32; **website** www.vline.com.au)* buses go to Warrnambool and Mount Gambier in South Australia. Buses stop at Hently Plaza.

Local Transport

There are two bus routes in Portland. Route 1 covers the area north of the town centre and route 2 goes south of the centre.

Sights
Maritime Discovery Centre

This excellent Maritime Discovery Centre has a number of interesting exhibits focusing on local shipwrecks. It also features a huge skeleton of a sperm whale.
Lee Breakwater Road, Portland
☎ *(03) 55232671 or 1800 035567*
***Website** www.visitdiscoverycoast.com*
***Admission** $8, students $5.50*
***Open** 9am-5pm daily*

Goldfields

Victoria was in the midst of gold fever in the mid-1800s and prospectors rushed to the Victorian goldfields. The Goldfields region is home to old gold mining towns and their grand buildings that were financed by the prosperity that gold brought to the area.

Ballarat

In 1851 gold was discovered in Ballarat and within a few years there were thousands of miners trying their luck on the Ballarat goldfields. The city grew on the wealth of the gold rushes and Ballarat is now Victoria's second largest inland city.

Practical Information
Ballarat Visitor Information Centre

39 Sturt Street, Ballarat
☎ *(03) 5332 2694*
***Website** www.visitballarat.com.au*
***Open** 9am-5pm daily*

Coming & Going

Ballarat has good transport connections. V/line (☎ *13 22 32; **website** www.vline.com.au)* have trains to Ararat and Melbourne and V/line buses to other destinations including Bendigo and Geelong. Both trains and buses depart from the train station on Lydiard Street North.

Local Transport

Ballarat's local bus service *(**website** www.davisbuslines.com.au)* has half-hourly departures to most parts of the city with most routes converging near Bridge Street Mall.

Accommodation
Sovereign Hill YHA Lodge

This is a nice hostel done in gold rush period architecture overlooking the Soveriegn Hill outdoor museum, about 3km south of the city centre. Facilities are good and include a big, clean kitchen and landscaped garden barbecue areas. The atmosphere is not as lively as most other hostels.
Magpie Street, Ballarat

☎ *(03) 5333 3409*
***Website** www.yha.com.au*
***Dorm bed** $25 ($22 HI/YHA); **single room** $38 ($34 HI/YHA); **twin room** $58-65 ($50-60 HI/YHA)*
***Credit cards** Amex, Diners, MC, Visa*
***Reception open** 7am-11pm daily*

Maintenance & cleanliness	★★★
Facilities	★★
Atmosphere & character	★★½
Security	★½
Overall rating	★★½

Sights

If you visit most of Ballarat's attractions you may want to consider buying the Ballarat Eureka Pass ($35.50), which allows two days unlimited entry to the Eureka Centre, the Gold Museum and Sovereign Hill plus entry to the Ballarat Fine Art Gallery.

Ballarat Fine Art Gallery

Australia's first provincial art gallery has an impressive collection of early Australian art including collections from the Colonial and Heidelberg Schools. The main exhibit is the original Eureka flag, which was raised during the Eureka Stockade in 1854 and has been displayed here since 1895.
40 Lydiard Street North, Ballarat
☎ *(03) 5331 5622*
***Website** www.balgal.com*
***Admission** $5*
***Open** 9am-5pm daily.*

Eureka Stockade Centre

This museum sits on the site of the Eureka Stockade, which is the closest Australia has come to having a civil war. In 1854 around 800 miners rebelled against the oppressive taxes and police brutality imposed by the British colonial government. On 3 December 1854 government troopers attacked the stockade. The resulting battle lasted only 20 minutes and left 30 miners and five troopers dead.
Stawell Street South, Ballarat
🚌 *8*
☎ *(03) 5333 1854*
***Website** www.eurekaballarat.com*
***Admission** $8*
***Open** 9am-4.30pm daily*

Sovereign Hill

This 1850s gold mining township is Ballarat's main attraction. It is an excellent living history exhibit featuring staff in period costume, and is the best attraction of its kind in Australia. The Sovereign Hill complex incorporates an excellent Gold Museum, which covers Ballarat's history with an emphasis on the impact of the gold rush.
Bradshaw Street, Ballarat
🚌 *2, 9, 10*
☎ *(03) 5331 1944*
***Website** www.sovereignhill.com.au*
***Admission** $35 ($27 students)*
***Open** 10am-5pm daily*

Bendigo

This important provincial city was a major gold mining centre in the 1850s. The city's mineral wealth has resulted in excellent Victorian architecture in the downtown area along Pall Mall.

Practical Information

Bendigo Visitor Information Centre

51-67 Pall Mall, Bendigo
☎ *(03) 5444 4445*
***Website** www.bendigotourism.com*
***Open** 9am-5pm daily*

Coming & Going

Bendigo is 2½ hours north of Melbourne with regular bus and train connections. V/line *(☎ 13 22 32; **website** www.vline.com.au)* buses and trains stop at the station on Railway Plaza at the southern end of Mitchell Street.

Local Transport

Christian's Bus Company *(**website** www.christiansbus.com.au/bendigo.html)* operates a network of 13 bus routes in the Bendigo area. It costs $1.80 for two hours of unlimited travel in the Bendigo area.

Accommodation

Buzza's Backpackers (Bendigo YHA)

Bendigo's YHA is in a house on a quiet street near the city centre. Like many hostels in converted houses, its facilities are minimal and on first impression it

looks a bit basic. However it is clean and it has a warm and cosy atmosphere. Facilities are limited to the standard TV lounge, laundry and kitchen (no oven) and a small barbecue area outside.
33 Creek Street South, Bendigo
☎ *(03) 5443 7680*
Website *www.yha.com.au*
Dorm bed *$25.50 ($22 HI/YHA);* ***double room*** *$61 ($54 HI/YHA)*
Credit cards *MC, Visa*
Reception open *9am-11am & 5pm-10pm daily*
TV K

Maintenance & cleanliness	★★★
Facilities	★★½
Atmosphere & character	★★½
Security	★
Overall rating	★★

Ironbark Bush Cabins

Ironbark Cabins are set among bushland less than a 10-minute drive from Bendigo's city centre. It is comprised mostly of cabins with en suite facilities plus a couple of dormitories and a bush kitchen fitted out with barbecues, a fridge and microwave. The complex also has a horse riding centre ($25 half hour, $35 one hour) and a waterslide ($13 10-rides, $18 all day) although their main business is selling and renting metal detectors to amateur gold prospectors.
Watson Street, Bendigo
☎ *(03) 5448 4140*
Website *www.bwc.com.au/ironbark*
Dorm bed *$22-27.50;* ***double room*** *$61-80*
Reception open *Mon-Sat 8.30am-5pm*
🚗 TV

Maintenance & cleanliness	★★★
Facilities	★★½
Atmosphere & character	★★★
Security	★★½
Overall rating	★★

Sights

Bendigo Art Gallery

Bendigo's art gallery dates from 1887 and features a collection of local and national art.
42 View Street, Bendigo
☎ *(03) 5443 4991*
Website *www.bendigoartgallery.com.au*
Admission *free*
Open *10am-5pm*

Bendigo Joss House

This temple was built in the 1860s by Chinese miners and is regional Victoria's only surviving joss house.
Emu Point, Finn Street, North Bendigo
☎ *(03) 5442 1685*
Admission *$5.00*
Open *Wed & Sat-Sun 11am-4pm*

Bendigo Tramways

Bendigo's talking trams run from the Central Deborah Goldmine along Pall Mall to the Bendigo Joss House stopping at major attractions along the way. They are known as talking trams because of the commentary explaining Bendigo's attractions. They operate hourly on weekends and school holidays.
Terminus Violet Street, Bendigo
☎ *(03) 5443 8070*
Website *www.bendigotramways.com*
Two day ticket *$14*
Trams run *10am-4pm with departures every hour*

Central Deborah Goldmine

Bendigo's last goldmine closed in 1954 and was re-opened for tourists in 1972. The Central Deborah Goldmine has been restored both above and below ground and is a great insight into how gold is mined.
76 Violet Street, Bendigo
☎ *(03) 5443 8322*
Website *www.central-deborah.com*
Mine experience tour *$24;* ***underground adventure tour*** *$68*
Open *9.30am-5pm daily*

Golden Dragon Museum

This museum, run by the Bendigo Chinese Association, has exhibits on Chinese culture in Bendigo from the 1850s to the present day. Exhibits include Sun Loong, the world's longest imperial dragon at more than 100m in length.
5-13 Bridge Street, Bendigo
☎ *(03) 5441 5044*
Website *www.goldendragonmuseum.org*
Admission *$8*
Open *9.30am-5pm daily*

Daylesford-Hepburn Springs

These two former gold mining townships now comprise Australia's spa capital.

Hepburn Springs is the main centre for mineral springs and is home to the historic spa building.

Five kilometres away, Daylesford, the larger of the two townships, is the home to an unusually large number of grand old buildings considering the town's small size. The two townships are surrounded by Hepburn Regional Park that has many hiking trails to mineral springs and disused gold mines. The twin towns make a good stop if you're driving between Ballarat and Bendigo.

Practical Information

Daylesford Visitor Information Centre

98 Vincent Street, Daylesford
☎ *(03) 5321 6123*
***Website** www.visitdaylesford.com.au*
***Open** 9am-5pm daily*

Coming & Going

V/line (☎ *13 22 32; **website** www.vline.com.au*) buses connect Daylesford with Ballarat, Bendigo, Creswick and Woodend. Buses stop on Bridport Street opposite the fire station.

Accommodation

Wildwood YHA

Wildwood YHA is a small hostel in a charming old wooden house. Facilities include a small fully-equipped kitchen and dining area with a fireplace plus a comfortable TV lounge with a well-stocked bookshelf. There is also a nice back deck with a barbecue. It's on the main road about mid-way between the centre of Daylesford and the spa at Hepburn Springs.

42 Main Road, Hepburn Springs
☎ *(03) 5348 4435*
***Website** www.yha.com.au*
***Dorm bed** $27 ($22 HI/YHA); **single room** $40 ($35 HI/YHA); **double/twin room** $64 ($54 HI/YHA)*
***Credit cards** MC, Visa*
***Reception open** 8am-10am & 5pm-10pm daily*

TV K

Maintenance & cleanliness	★★★
Facilities	★★☆ (2½)
Atmosphere & character	★★★★☆ (3½)
Security	★★☆ (1½)
Overall rating	★★★☆ (2½)

Grampians National Park

The Grampians is a rugged area popular with rock climbers and hikers. There is a multitude of hiking trails leading to various mountains, lakes, canyons and rock formations.
This is a great spot for seeing native wildlife in their natural habitat. Kangaroos and koalas are plentiful and the park is covered with colourful wildflowers between August and November.

The Grampians National Park is known as Gariwerd to the local Aboriginal people and is a place of great cultural significance with more than 100 documented rock art sites.

Halls Gap is a small town near the Wonderland Range area of the park, which is a popular base for visitors to the Grampians.

Practical Information

Brambuk National Park & Cultural Centre

This national park information centre also features excellent displays about Aboriginal culture.

Dunkeld Road, Halls Gap
☎ *(03) 5356 4381*
***Website** www.brambuk.com.au*
***Open** 9am-5pm daily*

Halls Gap Visitor Information Centre

Grampians Road, Halls Gap
☎ *(03) 5356 4616 or 1800 065 599*
***Website** www.visitgrampians.com.au*
***Open** 9am-5pm daily*

Coming & Going

The Grampians are difficult to explore properly without your own transport, but there is a daily V/line (☎ *13 22 32; **website** www.vline.com.au*) bus between Halls Gap and Melbourne. Buses stop opposite the newsagency.

Accommodation

BRIMPAEN

Asses Ears Wilderness Lodge

Asses Ears is a sprawling hostel on a 160 ha rural property about a 45-minute drive from Halls Gap. Facilities include an outdoor kitchen with a huge barbecue and a nice common area with a television area and a bar with a piano and pool table. There is also a swimming pool. Accommodation is in tidy cabins with en suite bathrooms. The property has a 1200m-long airstrip where kangaroos often graze early in the morning. It is a great spot to stay for a rural Australian experience.

130 Schmidt Road, Brimpaen
☎ *(03) 5383 9215*
***Website** www.assesearslodge.com.au*
***Dorm bed** $23-25 ($22-24 VIP); **double/twin room** $66 ($64 VIP)*
***Credit cards** MC, Visa*

Maintenance & cleanliness	★★★
Facilities	★★★
Atmosphere & character	★★★½
Security	★
Overall rating	★★★

HALLS GAP

Brambuk Backpackers

Brambuck is a very nice hostel with good facilities including a large well-equipped kitchen and a large deck with a barbecue at the front of the hostel. Accommodation is in clean rooms with en suite bathrooms. It's opposite the Brambuk Cultural Centre, about 3km from the centre of Halls Gap.

Dunkeld Road, Halls Gap
☎ *(03) 5356 4250*
***Website** www.brambuk.com.au*
***Dorm bed** $19-23; **double/twin room** $55*
***Credit cards** MC, Visa*
***Reception open** 9am-11am & 5pm-8pm daily*

Maintenance & cleanliness	★★★½
Facilities	★★
Atmosphere & character	★★★
Security	★★½
Overall rating	★★★

Grampians YHA Eco-Hostel

This is a very nice purpose-built hostel with brand new facilities. It was architecturally designed to be environmentally friendly and it is tastefully decorated and kept very clean. There are two quiet lounge areas, each with a fireplace; a TV lounge; internet access including Wi-Fi ($6 per hour; Global Gossip) and a big fully-equipped kitchen. Guests have free use of bicycles and there's also an herb garden and fresh eggs every day. Security is excellent with lockers in all the dormitories.

Corner Buckler Street & Grampians Road, Halls Gap
☎ *(03) 5356 4544*
***Website** www.yha.com.au*
***Dorm bed** $29 ($26 HI/YHA); **double/twin room** $72.50 ($65 HI/YHA)*
***Credit cards** MC, Visa*
***Reception open** 8am-10am & 5pm-10pm daily*

Maintenance & cleanliness	★★★★★
Facilities	★★½
Atmosphere & character	★★★½
Security	★★½
Overall rating	★★★★

Ned's Beds

Ned's Beds consists of a house with a couple of cabins in the backyard. There are several TV lounges and kitchens, with an espresso machine in the main house and there is also a games room with table tennis, air hockey and internet access. Accommodation is split between rooms in the main house and two self-contained units in the backyard; each with a kitchen, TV lounge and two dorm rooms. The main house feels a bit dated and the standard of accommodation is much better in the units in the backyard.

2 Heath Street, Halls Gap
☎ *(03) 5356 4296*
***Website** www.grampiansbackpackers.com.au*
***Dorm bed** $20-23; **double room** $60*

Maintenance & cleanliness	★★★
Facilities	★½
Atmosphere & character	★★½
Security	★½
Overall rating	★★½

Ned's Other Beds
Ned's Other Beds is a hostel in an old house next door to Tim's Place with cabins out the back for additional accommodation. The main house feels dated but it is kept clean. Facilities include internet access, a small fully-equipped kitchen and a television.
42 Grampians Road, Halls Gap
(03) 5356 4296
***Website** www.grampiansbackpackers.com.au*
***Dorm bed** $23; **double room** $55*

Maintenance & cleanliness	★★½
Facilities	★
Atmosphere & character	★★★
Security	★½
Overall rating	★★

Tim's Place
Tim's Place is a brand new purpose-built hostel. It is very clean and well-maintained and on first impression it looks a bit sterile, but the outdoor common areas have a really nice ambience and Tim gives everyone a warm welcome. Facilities include a fully-equipped kitchen, a quiet indoor lounge plus a nice outdoor TV lounge with a massive plasma screen. Guests have free use of bicycles and there is free internet access including free Wi-Fi
44 Grampians Road, Halls Gap
(03) 5356 4288
***Website** www.timsplace.com.au*
***Dorm bed** $25; **single room** $50; **double/twin room** $65; **triple room** $85*
***Reception open** 7am-11pm daily*

Maintenance & cleanliness	★★★★★
Facilities	★★½
Atmosphere & character	★★★★½
Security	★½
Overall rating	★★★★

Sights & Activities
Brambuk Cultural Centre
The Brambuk Cultural Centre is an excellent place to learn and experience the culture of the Koori communities of southwest Victoria. You can arrange tours of the rock art sites from the centre.
Dunkeld Road, Halls Gap
(03) 5356 4452
***Admission** free*
***Open** 9am-5pm daily*

Rock Climbing & Abseiling
The **Grampians Mountain Adventure Company** (*0427 747 047; **website** www.grampiansadventure.com.au*) runs rock climbing and abseiling trips in the Grampians National Park. Prices start at $60 for an introductory half-day rock climb and abseil. A full day rock climbing and abseiling excursion costs $110.

Zumstein
This camping & picnic area is a good spot for viewing kangaroos and it's very popular with people driving around the park.
Mount Victory Road, Grampians National Park

Hiking
There are some excellent hiking trails around the Grampians. These include popular short walks in the Wonderland Range area near Halls Gap as well as longer overnight hikes.

Beehive Falls
(2.8km, 1-1½ hours)
This easy walk follows a stream to Beehive Falls. It departs from Beehive Falls car park on Roses Gap Road.

Boronia Peak Trail
(6.6km, 2-3 hours)
You can start this trail from either Brambuk Backpackers or Tim's Place. It is a challenging hike to Boronia Peak, where there are nice views of Wonderland Range.

MacKenzie Falls
This is one of the most popular short walks and it can get very crowded at busy times. It is a steep, but short and relatively easy, walk.

Mount Rosea Loop
(12km, 4-5 hours)
This difficult half-day hike starts and finishes at Rosea campground on Mount Victory Road. It offers stunning views from the summit of Mount Rosea.

Wonderland Loop
(9.6km, 5 hours)

The Wonderland Loop is a popular half-day walk that starts and finishes in Halls Gap. It offers brilliant views and visits many of the park's main attractions including Grand Canyon, the Pinnacle, Splitters Falls and Venus Baths. This walk is a good option if you've only got a day to see the park and it is a relatively easy walk for novice hikers.

Murray River

The Murray is one of Australia's longest and most important rivers. It meanders 2,600km from the Snowy Mountains to Encounter Bay in South Australia. The river forms much of the New South Wales/Victorian border and it was once a busy transport route with paddle steamers plying their trade up and down the river.

The area around the Murray is fertile fruit farming country and many backpackers are attracted here by fruit picking work around Echuca and Mildura.

Echuca

In its heyday, Echuca was Australia's largest inland port. Nowadays the historic port area has been restored along with a fleet for paddle steamers. Echuca's heritage makes it the nicest town on the Murray and it is worth visiting if you're in the area.

Although not as popular a fruit picking destination as Mildura, many backpackers come here to pick fruit.

Practical Information
Echuca Visitor Information Centre

2 Heygarth Street, Echuca
☎ *(03) 5480 7555.*
Website *www.echucamoama.com*
Open *9am-5pm daily*

Coming & Going

V/line (☎ *13 22 32;* ***website*** *www.vline.com.au)* has trains to Melbourne and buses to Albury and Mildura. The train station is on Sturt Street in the town centre and V/line buses stop at both the train station and the visitor information centre on Heygarth Street.

CountryLink *(☎ 13 22 32;* ***website*** *www.countrylink.info)* buses stop outside the tourist information centre and go to Wagga Wagga in New South Wales.

Accommodation
Echuca Backpackers

Echuca Backpackers is a workers' hostel in a former school and some of the rooms still have blackboards. It is an established building that shows its age, but it is clean and the smaller dorm rooms upstairs are bright and tidy. Communal rooms include a couple of TV lounges, a fully-equipped kitchen, a laundry and a courtyard with a barbecue.

410-424 High Street, Echuca
☎ *(03) 5480 7866*
Website *www.backpackersechuca.com.au*
Dorm bed *$25 per night; $138 per week;* ***double room*** *$60 per night; $330 per week*
Credit cards *MC, Visa*
Reception open *9am-8pm*

TV K L

Maintenance & cleanliness	★★★
Facilities	★★
Atmosphere & character	★★
Security	★★½
Overall rating	★★½

Echuca Gardens YHA Hostel

Echuca's YHA is a lovely hostel on a quiet residential street about a 10-minute walk from the town centre. It is a small hostel in a 140-year-old cottage, which makes it Australia's second-oldest hostel; but it is much better maintained than many 10-year-old hostels. It is a charming hostel with a cosy atmosphere. Facilities are limited to a small TV lounge with a fireplace, a small kitchen and laundry. It only has 10 beds so it pays to book ahead if you're planning on staying on a weekend. This youth hostel caters exclusively to short term guests (if you're in Echuca to work, then you'll need to stay at the big hostel on High Street).

103 Mitchell Street, Echuca
☎ *(03) 5480 6522*
Website *www.yha.com.au*
Dorm bed *$25-40 ($22.50-36 HI/YHA);* ***double room*** *$60-80 ($54-72 HI/YHA)*
Credit cards *MC, Visa*
Reception open *7.30am-8.30am & 5pm-10pm*
TV K L

Maintenance & cleanliness	★★★★
Facilities	★★★½
Atmosphere & character	★★★★★
Security	★★
Overall rating	★★★½

Sights

Most of Echuca's attractions are centred on the river and the historic port. It's free to wander around the historic streets near the port and several companies, including the Port of Echuca, operate paddle steamer cruises on the Murray.

Historic Port of Echuca

Echuca's historic port features a huge red gum wharf with a multitude of paddle steamers including *PS Adelaide*, the world's oldest wooden hulled paddle steamer; *PS Pevensey* and *PS Alexander Arbuthnot*, the last paddle steamer built during the Murray River's heyday. Apart from the boats, which make regular cruises, the historic port is home to numerous heritage buildings, many that can be seen for free before going through the entrance gates, although you need to pay to see the boats, the Wharf Shed Museum and the wharf.
52 Murray Esplanade, Echuca
☎ *(03) 5482 4248*
Website *www.portofechuca.org.au*
Admission *$12 ($10.50 students); $27.20 ($22 students) including steamer cruise*
Open *9am-5pm daily*

National Holden Motor Museum

This collection of restored Holden cars includes some rare models, but it's only really of interest to enthusiasts.
7-11 Warren Street, Echuca
☎ *(03) 5480 2033*
Website *www.holdenmuseum.com.au*
Admission *$6*
Open *9am-5pm daily*

Pride of the Murray & PS Emmylou

Other paddle steamers include the *PS Emmylou* and *Pride of the Murray*, which run several cruises each day.
57 Murray Esplanade, Echuca
☎ *(03) 5482 5244*
Website *www.emmylou.com.au*
One hour cruise *$17.50-20*
Cruises depart *9.45am, 11am, 12.15pm, 1.30pm, 2.45pm & 4pm*

Swan Hill

Swan Hill is the main town between Echuca and Mildura. There's not much choice of budget accommodation and not many backpackers stay overnight here. However you may want to break your journey here if you're driving a long distance.

Practical Information

Swan Hill Visitor Information Centre

306 Campbell Street, Swan Hill
☎ *(03) 5032 3033 or 1800 625 373*
Website *www.swanhillonline.com*
Open *9am-5pm daily*

Coming & Going

V/line (☎ *13 22 32;* ***website*** *www.vline.com.au)* has trains to Bendigo and Melbourne and buses to Albury, Echuca and Mildura. Both buses and trains leave from the station on Railway Avenue.

Sights

Swan Hill Pioneer Settlement

Australia's first open-air museum is also Swan Hill's leading attraction. This recreated pioneer village showcases life on the Murray between 1830 and 1930. The Pioneer Settlement features heritage streetscapes and cruises on the Murray aboard the *PS Pyap.*
Horseshoe Bend, Swan Hill
☎ *(03) 5032 1093*
Website *www.pioneersettlement.com.au*
Admission *$21.50; including cruise $32.50; including sound and light tour $32.50; including cruise and sound and*

light tour $43
***Open** Tue-Sun 10am-5pm*

Mildura

Lying at the heart of the Sunraysia district, Mildura boasts Victoria's best climate. The sunny climate coupled with irrigation from the Murray makes this one of the best fruit growing, and fruit picking, areas in the Murray region. It is an oasis when compared with the relatively barren land that you pass through en route to Mildura.

Mildura is located at the northwestern corner of Victoria and it is one of the state's most remote cities. It is closer to Broken Hill in outback New South Wales than it is to Melbourne.

Practical Informaton

Mildura Visitors Information & Booking Centre

The Alfred Deakin Centre, 180-190 Deakin Avenue, Mildura
☎ *(03) 5018 8380*
***Website** www.visitmildura.com.au*
***Open** Mon-Fri 9am-5.30pm, Sat-Sun 9am-5pm*

INTERNET ACCESS

Mildura Library

The Alfred Deakin Centre, 180-190 Deakin Avenue, Mildura
☎ *(03) 5023 5011*
***Website** www.mildura.vic.gov.au/library/*
***Open** Mon 1pm-5pm, Tue-Fri 10am-7pm, Sat 10am-2pm, Sun 1pm-5pm*

SHOWERS

Many caravan parks will let you use their shower facilities for a small fee. Alternatively there are public showers in the Fire Station Arcade *(87 Langtree Avenue, Mildura; **open** 8.30am-6pm daily).*

Coming & Going

Although Mildura is remote, by Victorian standards, it is well connected with a surprisingly busy airport plus buses to Adelaide, Sydney and most places in Victoria. The closest train station is in Swan Hill.

AIR

Mildura's airport is southwest of the city centre and has several flights a day to Adelaide, Melbourne and Sydney. Both Rex and Qantas fly here.

BUS

V/line *(☎ 13 22 32; **website** www.vline.com.au)* buses go to Albury, Ballarat, Bendigo, Echuca, Melbourne and Swan Hill. CountryLink *(☎ 13 22 32; **website** www.countrylink.info)* buses go to Hay and Griffith. CountryLink and V/line buses leave from the old train station on 7th Street.

Greyhound *(☎ 1300 473 946; **website** www.greyhound.com.au)* buses stop here en route between Adelaide and Sydney. Greyhound stops at the United service station at the corner of Bentook Avenue and 15th Street.

Local Transport

Sunraysia Bus Lines *(☎ (03) 5023 0274; **website** www.sunbus.net.au)* operate local buses with services as far afield as Merbein and Red Cliffs.

Buses routes 100 and 200 are handy if you're staying at the hostel in Sunnycliffs. Travellers staying closer to the centre of Mildura will find the bus an easy way to get into the city centre and the Centre Plaza shopping centre.

Accommodation

Astra Backpackers

This very clean and well maintained hostel offers the highest standard of backpackers' accommodation in Mildura. Facilities include a fully-equipped kitchen and a dining area with a big TV plus an outdoor area with barbecue and table tennis. It is in a relatively charmless concrete building a short walk from the centre of town.
35 Lemon Avenue, Mildura, VIC 3500
☎ *(03) 5023 8820*
***Website** www.astrabpack.com.au*
***Dorm bed** $25 per night, $140 per week*
***Credit cards** MC, Visa*
♿ TV K L

Maintenance & cleanliness	★★★★★
Facilities	★½
Atmosphere & character	★★★
Security	★★½
Overall rating	★★★½

Juicy Grape Backpackers

This poorly-maintained hostel is neither clean nor charming and travellers reportedly escape the place after their first night. But the atmosphere is quite good among the long-term guests, and some of the veterans apparently find it hard to leave. A guest noted that it's a good place if you're up for saving money, as the house is far away from the town centre and there isn't anywhere near the hostel to spend money. Facilities include an acceptable kitchen, a laundry, a television room, internet access and neat little soccer pitch. The outdoor area is furnished with old but comfy seats.

Calder Highway, Sunnycliffs
100, 200
(03) 5024 2905
***Dorm bed** $20 per night, $140 per week*

Maintenance & cleanliness	★★
Facilities	★½
Atmosphere & character	★★½
Security	★
Overall rating	★★

Mildura Central Backpackers

Mildura Central Backpackers is set in a block of flats with accommodation in self-contained units; each with a TV, kitchen and bathroom. Some travellers like the home-style feel (like living in an apartment), but it also means that there is no central common area for travellers to mix so you end up just hanging out with people in your own unit. It is located south of the city centre on Deakin Avenue, across the road from McDonalds and a short walk from the Centro Mildura shopping centre.

364 Deakin Avenue, Mildura
0408 353 132
***Dorm bed** $25 per night, $140 per week*
***Reception open** 9am-11am & 5pm-7pm daily*

Maintenance & cleanliness	★★★
Facilities	★½
Atmosphere & character	★★
Security	★
Overall rating	★★

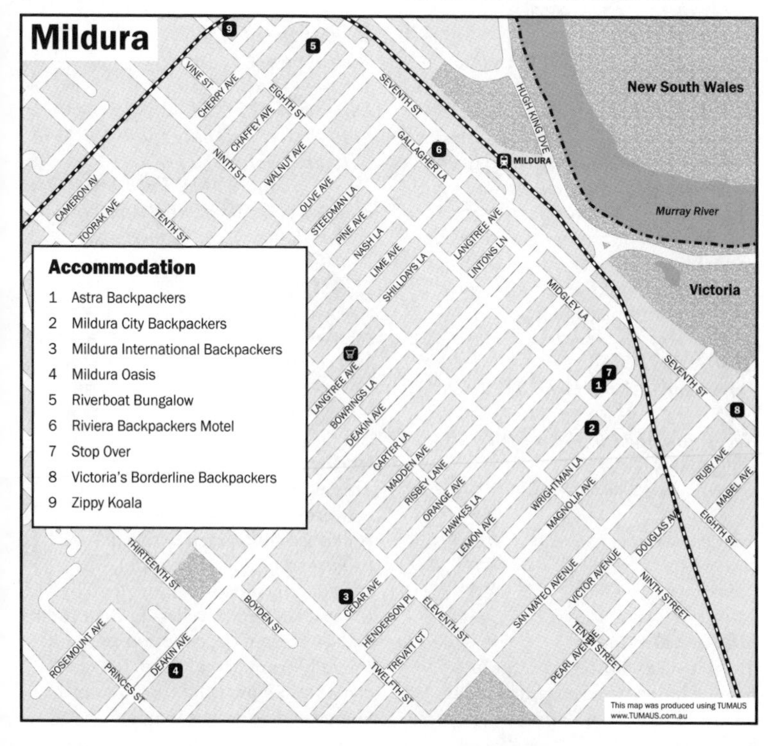

Mildura City Backpackers

This hostel near the centre of Mildura is a big old house with shady verandas at the front of the hostel and an outdoor area with table tennis, TV and a barbecue. There's also a laundry, a small kitchen (no oven) and coin-operated internet computers. It has a good atmosphere but otherwise is nothing special.

50 Lemon Avenue, Mildura
(03) 5022 7922
***Website** www.milduracitybackpackers.com.au*
***Dorm bed** $22 per night, $130 per week*
***Credit cards** MC, Visa*
***Reception open** Mon-Fri 9am-11am & 4pm-6pm, Sat 9am-11am, Sun 4pm-6pm*

Maintenance & cleanliness	★★
Facilities	★★½
Atmosphere & character	★★★★½
Security	★★½
Overall rating	★★

Mildura International Backpackers

This hostel is comprised of a couple of old houses on a quiet residential street near the tourist information centre/swimming pool complex. Facilities include two basic kitchens (no ovens), a TV lounge, laundry and a room with a pool table and coin-operated internet plus an outdoor area with a barbecue and table tennis. The amenities feel a bit tired but with the right crowd it could be a fun place to stay.

5 Cedar Avenue, Mildura
(03) 5021 0133
***Dorm bed** $25 per night, $129 per week*
***Reception open** 6.30pm-8pm*

Maintenance & cleanliness	★★½
Facilities	★★
Atmosphere & character	★★★
Security	★★
Overall rating	★★

Mildura Oasis

This big clean hostel on Deakin Avenue has extensive facilities that include a bar and a swimming pool plus a big kitchen, a big TV lounge with a pool table and free internet access (including Wi-Fi) and a laundry. Accommodation is in four and six-bed dorms and most rooms have en suite facilities. Minimum one week stay.

230-232 Deakin Avenue, Mildura
(03) 5022 8255
***Dorm bed** $140 per week*
***Reception open** 8am-10.30am & 3.30pm-5.30pm daily*

Maintenance & cleanliness	★★★½
Facilities	★★★★
Atmosphere & character	★★½
Security	★★
Overall rating	★★★½

Riverboat Bungalow

The Riverboat Bungalow is an established hostel with a good atmosphere. It is a big old house with polished floorboards, a fully-equipped kitchen, a big TV lounge with a fireplace and free internet access (including Wi-Fi). Accommodation is in relatively spacious four and six-bed dormitories.

27 Chaffey Avenue, Mildura
(03) 5021 5315
***Website** www.hotkey.net.au/~bungalow2/*
***Dorm bed** $25 ($24 VIP) per night, $140 per week; **double room** $50 ($48 VIP) per night, $280 per week*
***Reception open** Mon-Thu 10am-11am & 4.30pm-6.30pm, Fri 10am-11am & 4pm-6.30pm, Sat 9am-10am & 5pm-6pm, Sun 4.30pm-6.30pm*

Maintenance & cleanliness	★★★
Facilities	★★½
Atmosphere & character	★★★½
Security	★★½
Overall rating	★★★

Riviera Backpackers Motel

This old motel near K Mart has been converted into a hostel with self-contained units, each with a TV, fridge and en suite bathroom. The self-contained nature of the motel-style rooms can keep travellers in their rooms and away from the common areas like the fully-equipped kitchen, the covered outdoor area and the upstairs TV lounge and internet room.

157 7th Street, Mildura
☎ *0408 121303*
Dorm bed *$30 per night, $135 per week*
Credit cards *MC, Visa*
Reception open *Mon-Fri 9am-noon & 5.30pm-7pm, Sat 10am-noon*
TV K L

Maintenance & cleanliness	★½
Facilities	★½
Atmosphere & character	★★
Security	★
Overall rating	★½

Stop Over

This clean and well maintained hostel is one of Mildura's best budget accommodation options and it includes a small fully-equipped kitchen, a really nice TV lounge, laundry and a shed-like outdoor area with table tennis and another TV. The only drawback is that the concrete building lacks the atmosphere of some of the older, more established, hostels in Mildura.
29 Lemon Street, Mildura
☎ *(03) 5021 1980*
Website *www.stopover.com.au*
Dorm bed *$20-26 per night, $123-180 per week;* ***double room*** *$45-55 per night, $300-360 per week;* ***twin room*** *$50-60 per night, $320-290 per week*
♿ TV K L

Maintenance & cleanliness	★★★★★
Facilities	★½
Atmosphere & character	★★★
Security	★★★
Overall rating	★★★½

Sunraysia Holiday Park

This is a caravan park on the edge of town consisting of a few cabins with backpackers' dorms. It is close to the airport but 7km from the centre of Mildura. The backpackers' area is comprised of a couple of prefabricated units set around a covered courtyard with a TV, basic kitchen facilities and some cheap plastic furniture. Backpackers have use of caravan park facilities, which include a swimming pool. The remote location and minimal atmosphere are offset by Mildura's cheapest hostel prices.
Corner Sturt Highway & Walnut Avenue, Mildura South
☎ *(03) 5023 1914*
Dorm bed *$12 per night, $70 per week;* ***camping*** *$10 for one person or $14 per site*
Credit cards *MC, Visa*
🚗 TV K 🏊

Maintenance & cleanliness	★★½
Facilities	★½
Atmosphere & character	★½
Security	★
Overall rating	★★

Victoria's Borderline Backpackers

This hostel is one of the worst places to stay in Australia. Piles of dirty plates clutter up the filthy kitchen, the bathroom seems like it has been left to itself for years and the entire house is one big and appalling mess. The Borderline Backpackers has a television and an ugly outdoor barbecue area, but that's far from enough to make this a habitable place.
78 7th Street, Mildura
☎ *(03) 5023 0671*
Website *www.borderlinebackpackers.com*
Dorm bed *$25 per night, $130 per week*
TV K L

Maintenance & cleanliness	★½
Facilities	★
Atmosphere & character	★
Security	★½
Overall rating	★½

Zippy Koala

The Zippy Koala is a small hostel set in two houses on a quiet residential street that's not too far from the town centre. The hostel is clean and well maintained with polished floorboards. Facilities include a fully-equipped kitchen, a TV lounge, laundry and free internet access (including Wi-Fi) and there is also an outdoor area with a volleyball court, table tennis, barbecue and another TV. Guests also get access to the facilities at Riverboat Bungalow.
206 8th Street, Mildura
☎ *0447 967 537 (0447 WORKER)*
Dorm bed *$25 ($24 VIP) per night, $140 per week;* ***double room*** *$50 ($48 VIP) per night, $280 per week*

Victoria

TV K L

Maintenance & cleanliness	★★★½
Facilities	★★★
Atmosphere & character	★★★★
Security	★½
Overall rating	★★★½

Eating & Drinking

Mildura has the usual assortment of fast food places in the city centre, and there is also a McDonalds on Deakin Avenue opposite Mildura Central Backpackers, a few kilometres south of the centre. **Hudaks Bakery Cafe** *(corner 8th Street & Langtree Mall, Mildura)* is an award-winning bakery/café with delicious fresh pastries.

There are a few pubs in town. The **Sandbar** *(45 Langtree Avenue, Mildura)* is a bit nicer than most and has a beer garden and live music. The **Mildura Brewery Pub** *(20 Langtree Avenue, Mildura)* is another good place to drink. The food is a bit overpriced, but it has a good ambience.

Mildura's supermarkets include a **Coles** *(149 Eighth Street, Mildura)* and two **Woolworths**; one in the city centre *(95 Langtree Avenue, Mildura)* and another in the Centre Plaza shopping centre *(corner 15th Street & Deakin Avenue, Mildura)*.

Work

Most work in Mildura involves picking grapes as well as stone fruits like apricots and peaches. The grape-picking season runs from mid-Feb to late Mar and the stone fruit harvest is between late Nov and early Apr.

All backpackers' hostels in Mildura can organise fruit picking work.

Harvest Labour Office

The Harvest Labour Office co-ordinates work on farms around Mildura. It's a good idea to contact them to check the availability of work before coming up to Mildura.

Corner 10th Street & Deakin Avenue, Mildura
100, 400, 500
(03) 5022 1797
Website *www.madec.edu.au/harvest.html*
Open *Mon-Fri 7am-7pm*

High Country

The Victorian High Country was once the stamping ground of the infamous Ned Kelly and fictional characters like the Man From Snowy River.

Heading east from Melbourne, the High Country is the region past the Yarra Valley and over the Great Dividing Range. In winter this area is a popular ski destination with both downhill and cross-country resorts. In summer, snow gives way to horse riding and hiking trails among the twisted snow gums and cool running streams.

Beechworth

This prosperous gold town of the 1880s is a lovely place with tree-lined streets and many relics of the gold rush. It is set amongst the rolling countryside of the Ovens Valley.

Practical Information

Beechworth Visitor Information Centre

Old Shire Hall, Ford Street, Beechworth
(03) 5728 3233 or 1300 366 321
Website *www.beechworth.com*
Open *9am-5pm daily*

Coming & Going

There are daily V/line *(13 22 32; **website** www.vline.com.au)* buses Bright and to Wangaratta, where you can catch a train to Melbourne or Sydney. Buses leave from the corner of Camp and Ford Streets.

Sights

Burke Museum

An excellent museum with exhibits on the gold rush and the exploits of the Kelly gang.

Loch Street, Beechworth
(03) 5728 1420
Website *www.beechworth.com/burkemus/*
Admission *$6.50*
Open *9am-5pm daily*

Bright

Bright used to be a tourist town that was a popular base for skiing, but nowadays most skiers stay on the mountain and it is a quiet town with a nice ambience. It is also a popular destination for paragliding enthusiasts and it makes an ideal base for hiking in the surrounding countryside.

Practical Information

Bright Visitors Information Centre

119 Gavan Street, Bright
(03) 5755 2275 or 1800 500 117
Website
Open 8.30am-5pm daily

Coming & Going

There are daily V/line (*13 22 32; **website** www.vline.com.au*) buses Wangaratta, where you can catch a train to Melbourne or Sydney. Buses depart in front of the Alpine Hotel on Anderson Street.

Accommodation

Bright Hikers Backpackers Hostel

Bright's best hostel enjoys a brilliant location right in the centre of town. It is relatively clean and well maintained with a pretty good atmosphere. The hostel facilities include an internet room with Wi-Fi access and a pool table plus a large common area with a TV lounge and fully-equipped kitchen and a nice balcony overlooking the main street.
4 Ireland Street, Bright
(03) 5750 1244
***Website** www.brighthikers.com.au*
***Dorm bed** $25; **single room** $38; **double/twin room** $52*
***Credit cards** Amex, Diners, JCB, MC, Visa*
***Reception open** 10am-10pm daily*

Maintenance & cleanliness	★★★
Facilities	★★
Atmosphere & character	★★★
Security	★½
Overall rating	★★★½

Outdoor Inn – Bright & Alpine Backpackers

This place is set on eight acres at the edge of town and consists of accommodation in a ramshackle assortment of cabins made of fibre-cement and corrugated iron. Facilities include a barren TV lounge with a wood heater, a bar and a big dining room. The whole place feels very run-down and the common areas are dull and lifeless.
106 Coronation Avenue, Bright
(03) 5755 1154
***Website** www.brightbackpackers.com.au*
***Dorm bed** $20; **double room** $44; **camping** $12-15 per person*

Maintenance & cleanliness	★½
Facilities	★½
Atmosphere & character	★½
Security	★
Overall rating	★½

Eating & Drinking

Food Wine*Friends (*6 Ireland Street, Bright*) does great coffee. Buy groceries from the **IGA** supermarket (*16 Ireland Street, Bright*) just down the road from the Bright Hikers Hostel.

Activities

Paragliding is the main attraction in Bright, but microlight flights are another option.

Microlight flights

Bright Micro Flights (*(03) 5750 1555*) and **Eagle School of Microlighting** (*(03) 5750 1174; **website** www.eagleschool.com.au*) run scenic microlight flights over the countryside surrounding Bright. Prices start at $70 for a 10-minute flight and go up to $200 for a 45-minute flight.

Paragliding

Active Flight (*0428 854 455; **website** www.activeflight.com.au*) and **Alpine Paragliding** (*0428 352 048; **website** www.alpineparagliding.com*) run tandem paragliding flights around Bright. Tandem flights start at $130.

Mansfield

Mansfield is a convenient base for skiing at Mount Buller and it makes a good base for exploring the High Country during the summer.

Practical Information

Mansfield Visitor Information Centre

167 Maroondah Highway, Mansfield
☎ *(03) 5775 7000 or 1800 039 049*
***Website** www.mansfield-mtbuller.com.au*
***Open** Jan to mid-Jun 9am-5pm daily; mid-Jun to Sep 8am-9pm daily; Sep-Dec 9am-5pm*

INTERNET ACCESS

Café Connect

62 High Street, Mansfield
☎ *(03) 5779 1082*

Coming & Going

There are daily V/line *(☎ 13 22 32; **website** www.vline.com.au)* buses to Melbourne and during the ski season buses also go up to Mount Buller.

Accommodation

Mansfield Travellers Lodge

From the street this hostel looks like no more than a small weatherboard house but that's just the reception area and the accommodation is in the much nicer brick buildings at the rear. Facilities include a big common room with a TV, kitchen and table tennis plus a laundry and a barbecue area in the courtyard. It's a clean and comfortable place to stay and it has a great location in the centre of town.

116 High Street, Mansfield
☎ *(03) 5775 1800*
***Website** www.mansfieldtravellodge.com*
***Dorm bed** $25-30; **single room** $85-98; **double room** $90-105*
***Credit cards** MC, Visa*
***Reception open** 8am-9.30pm daily*

Maintenance & cleanliness	★★★½
Facilities	★½
Atmosphere & character	★★★½
Security	★½
Overall rating	★★★

Eating & Drinking

The **Produce Store** *(68 High Street, Mansfield)* does great food and coffee and just down the road there is also tasty food plus cold beer at the **Mansfield Hotel** *(86 High Street, Mansfield)*.

Activities

Camel Treks

High Country Camel Treks organise a variety of camel treks around the surrounding countryside ranging from a simple 10-minute ride to overnight alpine treks lasting up to 4½ days.

Rifle Butts Road, 7km north of Mansfield
☎ *(03) 5775 1591*
***Website** www.calmwaters.com.au/camel/camelhome.htm*
***10 minute ride** $6; **1 hour** $24; **2 hours** $35; **3½ hours** $36; **full day** $104*

Mount Buller

Mount Buller village has a year-round population of 250 but in winter the influx of skiiers and temporary workers swells the population to around 10,000, making it Victoria's largest ski resort.

Coming & Going

During the ski season there are V/line *(☎ 13 22 32; **website** www.vline.com.au)* buses to Mansfield and Melbourne.

Accommodation

Mount Buller YHA Lodge

Mount Buller YHA is an established hostel with a great location right on the Village Square. It has accommodation in mostly six-bed dormitories. Facilities include a fully-equipped kitchen, a cosy lounge with a TV tucked away in the corner and ski storage and a drying room downstairs. It's Australia's most expensive hostel, but it is still the cheapest place to stay on the mountain.

The Avenue, Mount Buller
☎ *(03) 5777 6181*
***Website** www.yha.com.au*
***Dorm bed** $72-80*
***Credit cards** MC, Visa*
***Open** Jun-Sep (ski season); **reception open** 8am-10am & 5pm-10pm*

Maintenance & cleanliness	★★½
Facilities	★½
Atmosphere & character	★★★½
Security	★★½
Overall rating	★★½

Eating & Drinking

Being a ski resort there are a lot of expensive places for après-ski eating and drinking, but travellers on a budget head to the **Foodworks** supermarket *(Athletes Way, Mount Buller)* just off the Village Square.

Gippsland

This region in eastern Victoria includes a beautiful coastline that features the solitude of Ninety Mile Beach, the inland waterways of Lakes Entrance and the Gippsland Lakes and the rugged coastline of Wilsons Promontory National Park.

Foster

This small town is the closest decent-sized town to Wilsons Promontory National Park, which is 30km south of here. Many travellers stay in Foster before and after visiting Wilsons Prom and some people visit as a day trip from here.

Practical Information

Foster Visitor Information Centre

Stockyard Gallery, Main Street, Foster
☎ *(03) 5682 1125*
Website *www.gippslandtourism.com.au*
Open *Thu-Sun 10am-4pm*

Accommodation

Prom Coast Backpackers YHA

Foster's small YHA hostel is a tidy house with polished floorboards close to the town centre. Although small, it has all the necessary facilities including a fully-equipped kitchen and a small TV lounge with internet access. It is a clean and well maintained place with a cosy atmosphere that is a good spot to stay before heading down to explore Wilsons Promontory.
40 Station Road, Foster
☎ *(03) 5682 2171*
Website *www.yha.com.au*
Dorm bed *$30 ($25 HI/YHA);* ***double room*** *$70 ($60 HI/YHA)*
Credit cards *MC, Visa*
TV K L

Maintenance & cleanliness	★★★★
Facilities	★★
Atmosphere & character	★★★★
Security	★
Overall rating	★★★

Wilsons Promontory National Park

Wilsons Promontory is a large national park at the southern most point of the Australian mainland. It has some excellent hiking trails.

Tidal River has the best infrastructure in the park with a big campsite, service station, post office, café and during busy periods, an outdoor cinema.

Practical Information

Tidal River Information Centre

Wilsons Promontory Road, Tidal River
☎ *(03) 5680 9555*
Open *Nov-Easter Sat-Thu 8am-7.30pm, Fri 8am-9.30pm; Easter-Oct 8am-5pm daily*

Coming & Going

It is easiest to visit Wilsons Prom in your own car. If you are relying on public transport you will need to catch a V/line bus from Melbourne to Foster, and then there are limited bus services between Foster and Tidal River with buses leaving Foster on Friday nights and returning on Sunday afternoon.

Accommodation

The closest backpackers accommodation to the park is in nearby Foster, but there are plenty of campsites scattered throughout the park. The main campsite is at Tidal River.

Camping at Tidal River costs $22.50 for up to three people in summer and $18 at other times of the year. Demand is high during Christmas and Easter holidays and long weekends when you will need to book well in advance by a ballot system. Contact the information centre at Tidal River for more information.

Hiking

Wilsons Prom has over 100km of hiking trails, which range from short nature walks to demanding overnight hikes.

SHORT WALKS

Short walks include **Lilly Pilly Gully Nature Walk** *(5km, 2 hours)*, which takes you through eucalyptus and paperbark forest and **Miller's Landing Nature Walk** *(5km, 1½ hours)*, which goes to mangrove swamps at Corner Inlet.

Mount Oberon Nature Walk *(7km, 2-3 hours)* is a popular early morning walk to the summit of Mount Oberon; a great spot to watch the sunrise.

One of the most popular short walks is the **Squeaky Bay Nature Walk** *(5km, 1½ hours)*, which takes you past sand dunes and tea-tree scrub to the dazzling Squeaky Beach.

DAY WALKS

There are several longer day walks in the park including **Oberon Bay Track** *(12.5km, 5 hours)*, which passes Norman Bay Beach and follows the coast to Oberon Bay; **Sealers Cove Track** *(20.5km, 5-6 hours)*, which goes to Sealers Cove on the other side of the Peninsula and **Tongue Point Track** *(5.5km, 2½ hours)*, which goes past two lookouts offering spectacular coastal views.

Maffra

This small town north of Sale has a pretty main street and is a pleasant place to stop over if you're travelling through the region.

Practical Information

Maffra Visitor Information Centre
96 Johnson Street, Maffra
☎ *(03) 5141 1811*
***Website** www.maffra.net.au*
***Open** Mon-Tue & Thu-Sun*

Coming & Going

Premier Motor Service *(☎ 13 34 10; **website** www.premierms.com.au)* buses stop here on the coastal route between Melbourne and Sydney. V/line *(☎ 13 61 96; **website** www.vline.com.au)* has buses to Sale, where the bus meets connecting train services to Melbourne. V/line buses have two stops on Johnson Street; one on the west side of Pearson Street and the other at Lions Club Park.

Accommodation

Cambrai Backpackers

Considering that this is in a part of Australia seldom visited by most backpackers, Maffra's Cambrai Backpackers is a surprisingly good hostel. It is a charming old building with tall ceilings right in the centre of town. It has a great atmosphere and features a brilliant bar with a TV and cosy fireplace plus a kitchen and another TV lounge.
117 Johnson Street, Maffra
☎ *(03) 5147 1600 or 1800 101 113*
***Website** www.southeasthostel.com*
***Dorm bed** $25; **double room** $60*
***Credit cards** Amex, Diners, JCB, MC, Visa*

Maintenance & cleanliness	★★★
Facilities	★★
Atmosphere & character	★★★★½
Security	★½
Overall rating	★★★

Bairnsdale

Bairnsdale doesn't have a lot to offer apart from being the largest town near the Gippsland Lakes. Bairnsdale makes a good base for exploring the lakes and it is big enough to have good supermarkets and camping supplies stores.

Practical Information

Bairnsdale Visitor Information Centre
240 Main Street, Bairnsdale
☎ *(03) 5152 3444 or 1800 637 060*
***Website** www.lakesandwilderness.com.au*
***Open** 9am-5pm daily*

Coming & Going

Premier Motor Service *(☎ 13 34 10; **website** www.premierms.com.au)* buses stop at the BP service station on the Princes Highway on the coastal route between Melbourne and Sydney.

V/line (☎ *13 61 96; **website** www.vline.com.au)* has train services to Melbourne and buses to Canberra and Batemans Bay. The train station is on Macleod Street.

Lakes Entrance

This small resort town is the most popular destination in the Gippsland Lakes and can get very busy in the middle of summer. Lakes Entrance has a fantastic location on the lakes within easy access to ocean beaches.

Practical Information

Lakes Entrance Visitor Information Centre

Corner Marine Parade & Esplanade, Lakes Entrance
☎ *(03) 5155 1966 or 1800 637 060*
***Website** www.lakesandwilderness.com.au*
***Open** 9am-5pm daily*

Coming & Going

Premier Motor Service (☎ *13 34 10; **website** www.premierms.com.au)* buses stop in Lakes Entrance on the coastal route between Melbourne and Sydney.

V/line (☎ *13 61 96; **website** www.vline.com.au)* has buses to Batemans Bay, Canberra and Bairnsdale, where you can connect with trains to Melbourne. Buses stop at the V/line stop next to the post office.

Accommodation

Lakes Main Caravan Park

The backpackers' accommodation at the Lakes Main Caravan Park and Hostel consists of bunk beds in a couple of relatively new cabins. The backpackers' accommodation is nicer than the rest of the caravan park, but it is still a last resort.

7 Willis Street, Lakes Entrance
☎ *(03) 5155 2365*
***Dorm bed** $24-30*
***Credit cards** MC, Visa*
***Reception open** 8am-8.30pm*

Maintenance & cleanliness	★★½
Facilities	★½
Atmosphere & character	★
Security	★
Overall rating	★★

Riviera Backpackers YHA

This functional hostel opposite the waterfront has accommodation in en suite units. There is a kitchen plus a common room with an old TV and internet access. Outside there is a barbecue area and a swimming pool. The beds are new but some bathrooms and the kitchen could be better maintained. The hostel is nothing flash, but it is still the best option in Lakes Entrance.

669 Esplanade, Lakes Entrance
☎ *(03) 5155 2444*
***Website** www.yha.com.au*
***Dorm bed** $21.50-24 ($19-21.60 HI/YHA); **double/twin room** $48-50 ($44-55 HI/YHA)*
***Credit cards** Amex, JCB, MC, Visa*
***Reception open** 8am-10pm*

Maintenance & cleanliness	★★½
Facilities	★★½
Atmosphere & character	★★
Security	★★
Overall rating	★★½

Buchan

This small village north of Lakes Entrance is best known for the Buchan Caves, which feature impressive limestone formations.

Coming & Going

Buchan Bus n' Freight (☎ *(03) 5155 0356; **website** www.buchanbusnfreight.com.au)* operate a daily bus to Lakes Entrance and Bairnsdale. It departs from the Buchan General Store. Buchan Bus n' Freight also run day trips from Lakes Entrance that cost $50.

Accommodation

Buchan Lodge

Buchan Lodge is a good hostel in a big timber building with lots of character. It has a big common area with a fully-equipped kitchen – with lots of utensils and a big selection of herbs and spices – plus a dining/lounge area with a piano and wood heater/fireplace but no TV so people are more likely to talk to each other. There is also an outdoor barbecue area. Accommodation is in

big clean rooms with en suite facilities. It is in a bushland setting but only a five-minute walk to the town centre
9 Saleyard Road, Buchan
☎ *(03) 5155 9421*
Website *www.buchanlodge.com*
Dorm bed *$25; price includes breakfast*

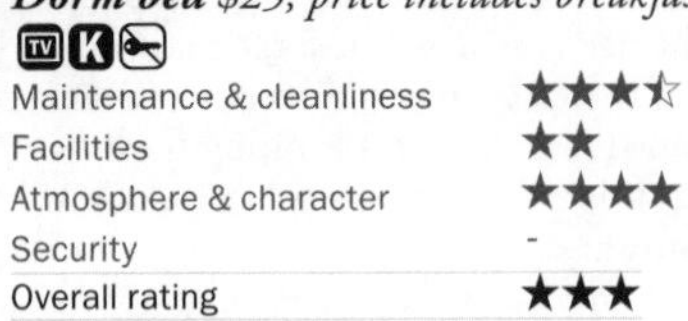

Maintenance & cleanliness	★★★½
Facilities	★★
Atmosphere & character	★★★★
Security	-
Overall rating	★★★

Sights & Activities

Buchan Caves

The Buchan Caves comprise several caves with limestone formations. The most visited is Fairy Cave, which is known for its elaborate stalactites and stalagmites. You can often see kangaroos and lyrebirds in the reserve surrounding the caves.
Caves Road, Buchan
☎ *13 19 63*
Website *www.parkweb.vic.gov.au*
Tours cost *$13*

Western Australia

Australia's biggest state covers a third of the country, is larger than the whole of Western Europe and nearly four times the size of Texas; yet there are only a little over two million people in this enormous state, with three quarters of them living in Perth.

Nowhere do you get a sense of space like in Western Australia. This is the sort of place where you can travel

Must do in Western Australia

- Watch dolphins at Monkey Mia
- Hike in Karijini National Park
- Swim with whalesharks on the Ningaloo Reef
- Watch a film under the stars at Broome's Sun Pictures cinema

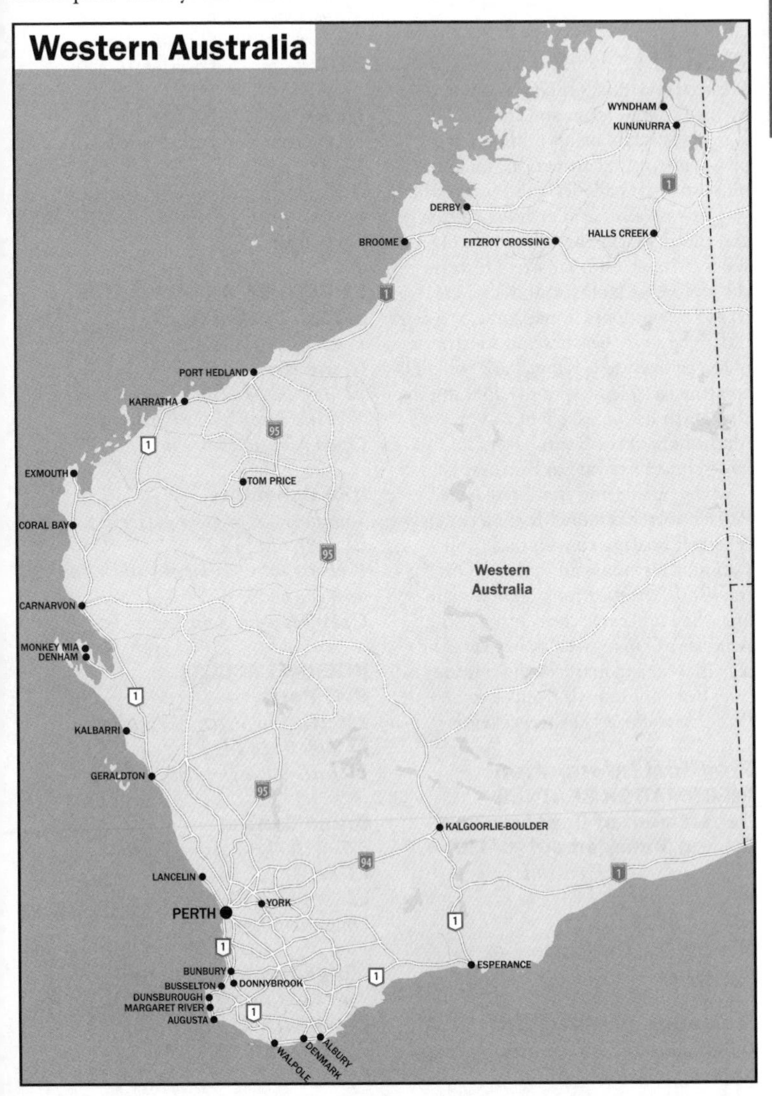

600km and not pass any towns or villages, just a lonely service station – and that's on a major highway.

Travelling such long distances has its rewards. The state has brilliant natural attractions like the stunning Bungle Bungles, teeming marine life of the Ningaloo Reef and gorgeous gorges in Karajini National Park. These are spectacular places that would be overrun with tourists anywhere else, but here it feels like you've got the whole place to yourself.

Perth

Western Australia's capital is flanked by the Indian Ocean and the Darling Range. This city of 1.5 million has plenty of cultural attractions including museums, art galleries and theatres; but very few people visit Perth for culture and the city lacks the urban vibe of other cities of a similar size. However the weather is fantastic and it's a great city to be outdoors. It has some of Australia's best city beaches and southwest of the city centre is Kings Park, which is an attractive picnic spot overlooking the city. Perth has an excellent zoo on the south shore of the Swan River and it is just a short ferry ride to Rottnest Island.

Many people find that Fremantle, Perth's port, has more life than the city centre. It boasts a convict-built police station, courthouse and prison. During the 1980s, the port took on new glamour when it became the centre for the America's Cup regatta. Nowadays, the sea air, weekend markets and outdoor cafés draw the crowds from elsewhere in Perth, particularly at the weekends.

Practical Information

INFORMATION CENTRES

Department of Conservation & Land Management (CALM)
47 Henry Street, Fremantle
Fremantle
(08) 9430 8600
Website *www.calm.wa.gov.au*
Open *Mon-Fri 8am-5pm*

Fremantle Tourist Office
Corner High & William Streets, Kings Square, Fremantle
Orange CAT *Fremantle*
(08) 9431 7878
Website *www.fremantlewesternaustralia.com*
Open *Mon-Fri 9am-5pm, Sat 10am-3pm, Sun noon-3pm*

Western Australia Visitor Centre
Corner Wellington Street & Forrest Place, Perth
Perth
(08) 9483 1111 or 1300 361 351
Website *www.wavisitorcentre.com*
Open *Mon-Thu 8.30am-6pm, Fri 8.30am-7pm, Sat 8.30am-12.30pm*

TransPerth InfoLine
Public transport information.
13 62 13
Website *www.transperth.wa.gov.au*
Open *Mon-Fri 6.30am-10pm, Sat-Sun 7am-10pm*

EMBASSIES & CONSULATES

British Consulate
Level 26, Allendale Square, 77 St Georges Terrace, Perth
(08) 9224 4700
Website *http://bhc.britaus.net/*
Open *Mon-Fri 9am-5pm*

USA Consulate
13th floor, 16 St Georges Terrace, Perth
(08) 9202 1224
Website *http://usembassy-australia.state.gov/perth/*
Open *Mon-Fri 8am-11am*

INTERNET ACCESS

BWT Perth
236 William Street, Northbridge
(08) 9328 1477
Website *www.globalgossip.com*

Grand Central
379 Wellington Street, Perth
Perth
(08) 9421 1123
Open *8am-8pm daily*

Indigo Netcafé & Lodge
256 West Coast Highway, Scarborough
381, 410, 411
(08) 9245 3388
Open *Mon-Sat 8am-9pm, Sun 8am-8pm*

Internet Station
131 William street, Perth
🚉 *Perth*
☎ *(08) 9226 5373*
Website *www.internetstation.com.au*

Coming & Going

Perth is a long way from anywhere and most interstate visitors fly here, however there are also trains to the east coast and buses to most destinations within Western Australia.

AIR

Because of the distance between Perth and the other big cities, flying is the most popular way to get here. Jetstar, Qantas, Skywest, Tiger Airways and Virgin Blue fly into Perth.

Perth Airport *(☎ (08) 9478 8888; **website** www.perthairport.net.au)* is 12km northeast of the city centre. The international and domestic terminals are located several kilometres apart and locals often talk about them as if they're separate airports. The domestic terminal is served by local bus routes 37 and 39 as well as the more expensive Airport City Shuttle and Fremantle Airport Shuttle, which also serve the international terminal.

The Airport City Shuttle *(☎ 1300 666 806; **website** www.perthshuttle.com.au)* is the quickest option into the city centre and charges $20 from the international terminal or $15 from the domestic terminal.

Jandakot Airport, south of the city centre handles some regional flights including flights to Rottnest Island.

BUS

Perth has three bus terminals. Greyhound *(☎ 1300 473 946; **website** www.greyhound.com.au)* buses to Broome and Transwa *(☎ 1300 662 205; **website** www.transwa.wa.gov.au)* buses to destinations in southwestern WA that depart from the East Perth Terminal *(🚉 East Perth)*. Integrity *(☎ (08) 9226 1339; **website** www.integritycoachlines.com.au)* buses to Port Hedland depart from the Wellington Street Bus Station at 554 Wellington Street *(🚉 Perth)*. Southwest Coachlines *(☎ (08) 9324 2333; **website** www.southwestcoachlines.com.au)* operate buses to the southwest including Bunbury, Busselton and Margaret River. Southwest buses depart from the Esplanade Busport on Mounts Bay Road *(🚉 Esplanade)*.

TRAIN

The East Perth Terminal is the terminus for long distance trains. Transwa *(☎ 1300 662 205; **website** www.transwa.wa.gov.au)* has trains to Bunbury and Kalgoorlie and Great Southern Railway operate the Indian Pacific to Sydney with stops at Kalgoorlie, Adelaide and Broken Hill. The East Perth Terminal is part of Transperth's suburban train network with frequent trains to the city centre and Fremantle.

HITCHHIKING

Perth's local buses and trains run a long way from the centre, so it's pretty easy to get to some prime hitchhiking spots.

If you're heading to Bunbury and the Margaret River region, take the train to Mandurah and hitch from there.

If you want a lift to Albany or Esperance take a train to Armadale and then walk to the Albany Highway (route 30).

The Great Eastern Highway (route 94) runs from Perth to Kalgoorlie and across the Nullarbor Plain to Adelaide. Take a train to Midland and then a bus to Mundaring and wait for a lift on the highway just outside town. Use a sign as the road splits soon after Mundaring.

The Brand Highway (route 1) heads north up the west coast to Exmouth, Broome and eventually to Darwin. Take a train to Midland, and then it's a long walk to the better hitching spots on the Brand Highway.

Local Transport

Transperth *(☎ 13 62 13; **website** www.transperth.wa.gov.au)* operates Perth's public transport network, which is comprised of buses, ferries and trains. It is a good value way to get around the city and there's even free transport in the central area.

BUS

Buses form the backbone of Perth's transport system and it is inevitable that you'll ride them at some point or another, particularly if you want to get to the beaches.

Buses are free within the central area, although with regular buses it can be difficult to know which rides are free and which ones you have to pay for. Fortunately there are a couple of frequent bus routes confined to the free central area that are extremely popular with travellers. The Central Area Transit (CAT) buses run three routes – the Red CAT runs an east-west route in the city centre, the Yellow CAT goes between the city centre and East Perth and the more useful Blue CAT connects the hostels in Northbridge with the city centre. The only problem is that the CAT buses stop running shortly after 6pm. There is also an Orange CAT, which runs a loop around Fremantle.

Perth's bus network covers a large area with buses running as far afield as Rockingham and Mandurah.

TRAIN

Perth's rail network consists of five lines. The most useful is the Fremantle line, which runs from the city centre to Fremantle via Cottesloe. Trains run approximately every half hour.

City West, Esplanade, Perth, McIver and Claisebrook stations lie within the Free Transit Zone.

FERRY

Perth has a limited ferry service between Barrack Street Jetty in the city centre and Coode Street and Mends Street Jetties in South Perth. The Barrack Street Jetty to Mends Street Jetty ferry is a popular route for travellers visiting Perth Zoo. Ferries run around every 20 minutes.

FARES

Perth's public transport network is great value, especially considering that there is free transport in the central Free Transit Zone. Even travel outside this zone is good value.

Like many other public transport networks, Perth is divided into different fare zones. Most attractions are in zones one and two; although the transport network extends as far as zone nine. A Perth to Fremantle train trip requires a two-zone ticket, as does a trip between the city centre and the domestic airport terminal.

A one-zone fare is $2.20 and a two-zone fare is $3.40.

If you're planning on using a lot of public transport you may want to invest in a DayRider ticket that allows unlimited travel on Transperth buses, trains and ferries from 9am on weekdays and all day on weekends and public holidays. A DayRider costs $8.10.

Accommodation

BEACHES

Perth has some brilliant beaches and despite the suburban location, they area a great place to stay; particularly if you're visiting Perth during summer.

Ocean Beach Backpackers

This is a good quality big 130-bed hostel. The atmosphere is warm and lively and the hostel's common areas are top notch – the movie room is excellent, the courtyard is a great barbecue spot, the beach is nearby and surf and body boards are available free of charge. The kitchen is well-equipped and very clean for a backpackers' kitchen, and if you're too lazy to make your own eats there's a modern café on the first floor. Bathrooms are acceptable, but the rest of the place is definitely above average, the furnishings feel new and the dormitories are clean and equipped with inner-spring mattresses and en suite bathrooms.

1 Eric Street, Cottesloe
🚌 71, 72, 75, 381 🚆 Grant Street
☎ (08) 9384 5111
***Website** www.obh.com.au/backpackers/*
***Dorm bed** $23 ($22 VIP); **single room** $62; **double room** $67; **triple room** $78*
***Credit cards** MC, Visa*
***Reception open** 24 hours*

Maintenance & cleanliness	★★★½
Facilities	★★½
Atmosphere & character	★★★★
Security	★★½
Overall rating	★★★½

Perth Beach YHA

This is a fairly big hostel, but it still has a good atmosphere. The level of cleanliness and maintenance is just slightly above average, and the extent of the facilities isn't exactly overwhelming. This hostel has the basic facilities including internet access, laundry, kitchen and a television plus a few extras like the swimming pool, nice inner-spring mattresses on the dorm beds and a reception that sells cookies and good coffee. The location isn't bad either – Scarborough Beach is just across the road.

256 West Coast Highway, Scarborough
381, 400, 410, 411
(08) 9245 3388
***Website** www.yha.com.au*
***Dorm bed** $28 ($25.20 HI/YHA); **single room** $41 ($36.90 HI/YHA); **double room** $64 ($57.60 HI/YHA); **twin room** $56 ($50.40 HI/YHA)*
***Credit cards** MC, Visa*
***Reception open** Mon-Thu 8am-8pm, Fri-Sun 8am-7pm*

Maintenance & cleanliness	★★½
Facilities	★★
Atmosphere & character	★★★
Security	★★
Overall rating	★★½

Scarborough Backpackers

The location for this hostel is superb with the beach just a couple of minutes walk away, but it's a dull and rather characterless hostel compared with the other backpackers' accommodation in the area. The hostel is fairly clean and well maintained though and with the swimming pool it's not a bad place. Some of the guests remarked that all common areas except a grey and tedious TV room are closed after 10pm.

190 West Coast Highway, Scarborough
381, 400, 410, 411
(08) 9245 3111
***Website** www.scarboroughbackpackers.com*
***Dorm bed** $30; **double/twin room** $105*
***Credit cards** MC, Visa*

Maintenance & cleanliness	★★★½
Facilities	★★
Atmosphere & character	★★½
Security	★★
Overall rating	★★★

Western Beach Lodge

There's a good friendly atmosphere at this hostel, but the worn-out house and furnishing drags the overall impression down a few steps. There's lots of common space though, and with two TV rooms and a nice seating area in the backyard this is perhaps the most comfortable hostel in the area. The beds are good and all the basic facilities are here including table football and a barbecue. The location is handy to Scarborough Beach, which is just a few minutes' walk away.

6 Westborough Street, Scarborough
400, 408
(08) 9245 1624
***Website** www.westernbeach.com*
***Dorm bed** $24-26; **double room** $60-75*
***Reception open** Mon-Fri 8am-9pm, Sat-Sun 10am-2pm & 4pm-9pm*

Maintenance & cleanliness	★★★
Facilities	★★
Atmosphere & character	★★★½
Security	★★½
Overall rating	★★★

CITY CENTRE & NORTHBRIDGE

The city centre is right in the centre of the action and has excellent transport connections to the rest of the Perth area. Northbridge is a quieter area just north of the central business district and is home to Perth's nightlife scene with plenty of bars, pubs, restaurants and cafés.

12:01 East

This hostel is a few blocks southeast of the city centre, but you'll find that the location is not really a problem as the Red CAT bus stops right outside the door. Cleanliness and maintenance isn't top notch but it's still above average, and the dorms have comfy beds. The atmosphere is relaxed and friendly, and the usual hostel facilities are available including a very good barbecue area in the courtyard. There's a TV lounge in the basement and DVDs can be borrowed from the reception free of charge.

195 Hay Street, Perth
Red CAT, 24, 25, 27, 103, 111, 158

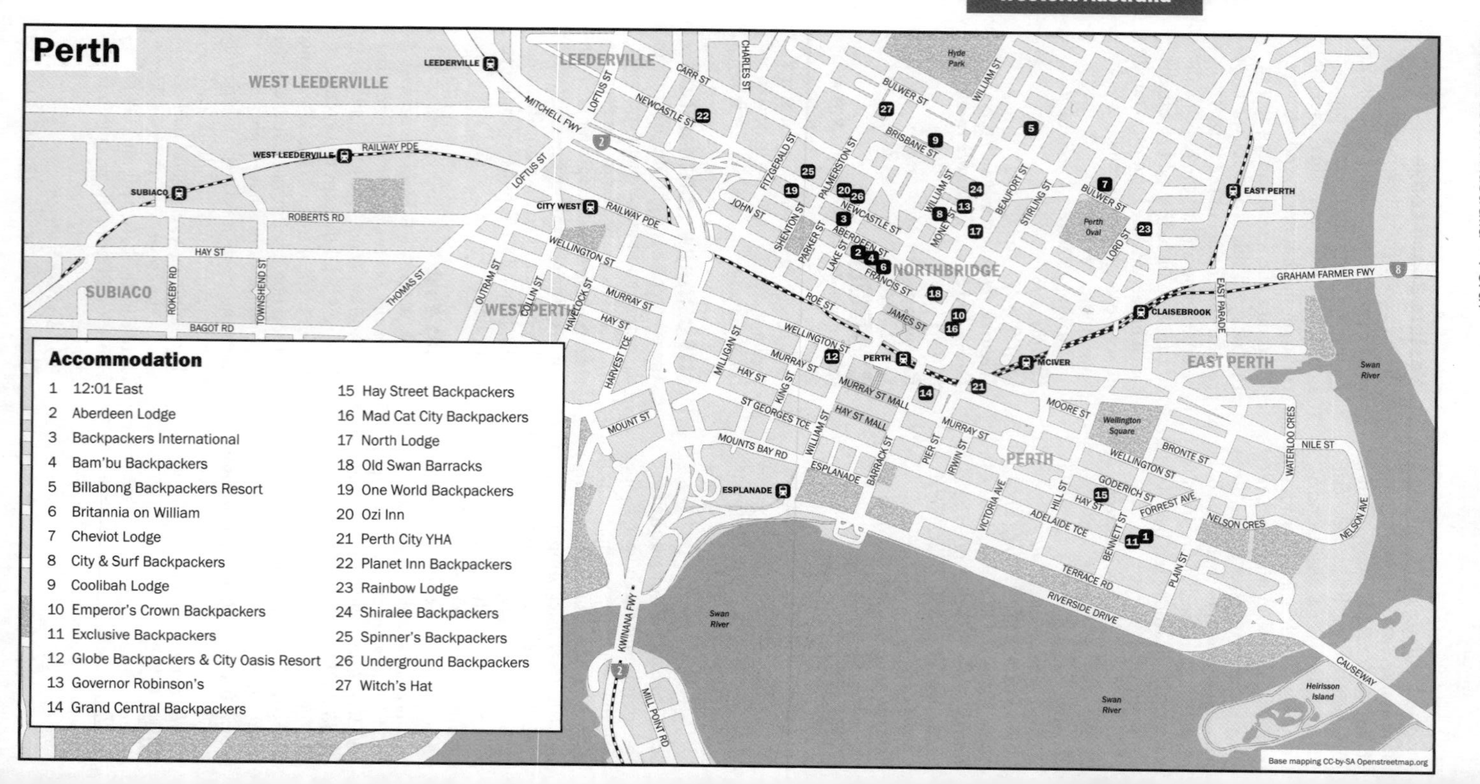
Perth
Accommodation
1 12:01 East
2 Aberdeen Lodge
3 Backpackers International
4 Bam'bu Backpackers
5 Billabong Backpackers Resort
6 Britannia on William
7 Cheviot Lodge
8 City & Surf Backpackers
9 Coolibah Lodge
10 Emperor's Crown Backpackers
11 Exclusive Backpackers
12 Globe Backpackers & City Oasis Resort
13 Governor Robinson's
14 Grand Central Backpackers
15 Hay Street Backpackers
16 Mad Cat City Backpackers
17 North Lodge
18 Old Swan Barracks
19 One World Backpackers
20 Ozi Inn
21 Perth City YHA
22 Planet Inn Backpackers
23 Rainbow Lodge
24 Shiralee Backpackers
25 Spinner's Backpackers
26 Underground Backpackers
27 Witch's Hat
LEEDERVILLE
WEST LEEDERVILLE
SUBIACO
WEST PERTH
NORTHBRIDGE
EAST PERTH
PERTH
Hyde Park
Perth Oval
Wellington Square
Swan River
Heirisson Island
MITCHELL FWY
GRAHAM FARMER FWY
KWINANA FWY
RIVERSIDE DRIVE
CAUSEWAY
LEEDERVILLE
WEST LEEDERVILLE
SUBIACO
CITY WEST
PERTH
MCIVER
CLAISEBROOK
EAST PERTH
ESPLANADE
Base mapping CC-by-SA Openstreetmap.org

(08) 9221 1666
Website *www.1201east.com.au*
Dorm bed *$22 ($21 VIP);* ***double/twin room*** *$60*
Credit cards *MC, Visa*
Reception open *8.30am-11pm daily*

Maintenance & cleanliness	★★★½
Facilities	★★
Atmosphere & character	★★★
Security	★★
Overall rating	★★★

Aberdeen Lodge

This is a small poorly maintained hostel with old furnishings and a dull atmosphere. It has a nice garden area, two TV rooms, a laundry, some board games and a poorly-equipped kitchen. It's not the best place to stay in Perth as it isn't very clean, but its location is convenient as the Blue CAT bus runs close by and the nearby streets are full of cafés and Asian eateries.
79-81 Aberdeen Street, Northbridge
Blue CAT, 15
(08) 9227 6137
Website *www.aberdeenlodgebackpackers.com*
Dorm bed *$20;* ***single room*** *$45;* ***double/twin room*** *$55*
Credit cards *MC, Visa*
Reception open *Mon-Fri 9am-noon & 4.30pm-6.30pm, Sat-Sun 9.15am-noon & 5pm-7pm*

Maintenance & cleanliness	★½
Facilities	★
Atmosphere & character	★★
Security	★★
Overall rating	★½

Backpackers International

This excellent hostel is in an unattractive building that also houses a bar. With 55 beds it is a quite small place and this ensures a personal and homey feel. The common areas are tastefully painted, cleanliness and maintenance are of a high standard and the hostel feels fresh and clean. The excellent TV lounge is comfy and well-equipped with satellite channels, a DVD-player and a big, wide screen telly. The nice small kitchen is clean and geared up with most of what you need to cook and the eating area is a nice place to chat over a few beers. Because there is a bar is in the same building weekend nights can be a bit noisy, but at least you get free earplugs from the hostel management.
110 Aberdeen Street, Northbridge
Blue CAT
(08) 9227 6137
Website *www.backpackersintperth.com*
Dorm bed *$25;* ***double/twin room*** *$54; prices include breakfast*
Credit cards *MC, Visa*
Reception open *8am-11pm; 24 hour check-in with prior arrangement*

Maintenance & cleanliness	★★★★
Facilities	★½
Atmosphere & character	★★★½
Security	★½
Overall rating	★★★

Bam'bu Backpackers

This is one of the coolest places in town. It has loads of character with its plants and Buddha sculptures and the atmosphere is magnificent. The main common area is like a great laid-back bar with tall seats, tasteful decoration, a dark wood bar and a turntable for the DJ. The bathrooms are clean, the kitchen has all the necessary cooking-gear, there's an awesome TV lounge with a big screen and the beds have good quality mattresses. It is a bit pricey compared to other hostels in Perth, but it is good value – you get what you pay for at Bam'bu.
75-77 Aberdeen Street, Northbridge
Blue CAT, 15, 16, 21, 22, 41, 42, 43, 44, 46, 48, 55, 60, 66, 67, 68, 69, 401
(08) 9328 1211
Website *www.bambu.net.au*
Dorm bed *$27-28;* ***single/double/twin room*** *$56; prices include breakfast*
Credit cards *MC, Visa*
Reception open *9am-midnight*

Maintenance & cleanliness	★★★★½
Facilities	★★½
Atmosphere & character	★★★★★
Security	★★
Overall rating	★★★★

Billabong Backpackers Resort

Billabong is a big hostel and its excellent facilities include a good swimming pool, a small gym, a nice barbecue area, a big fully-equipped kitchen and common areas with arcade games, pool tables and table football. Management organise a lot of activities, which ensures that there is a lot going on. With extensive facilities, it is quite a good hostel but it is not too well maintained and the furnishings are a bit shabby.

381 Beaufort Street, Northbridge
21, 22, 66, 67, 68, 69
(08) 9328 7720
***Website** www.billabongresort.com.au*
***Dorm bed** $23-25; **single/double room** $75*
***Credit cards** MC, Visa*
***Reception open** 7am-7pm*

Maintenance & cleanliness	★★★
Facilities	★★★½
Atmosphere & character	★★★
Security	★★★
Overall rating	★★★

Britannia on William

This hostel has cheap and comfortable beds. It is clean enough but the building's decor makes the hostel feel like a grey, dark and boring place. It has extensive common areas, but its dated furnishings match the dullness of the rest of the hostel. It offers the basic kitchen, TV lounge and internet access plus a courtyard barbecue area. Overall Britannia on William is an acceptable alternative if you're on a tight budget, but it's not a place you'll find hard to leave.

253 William Street, Northbridge
Blue CAT, 16, 21, 22, 41, 42, 43, 44, 46, 48, 55, 60, 66, 67, 68, 69, 401
(08) 9227 6000
***Website** www.perthbritannia.com*
***Dorm bed** $22-26 ($20-24 HI/YHA, VIP); single room $39 ($37 HI/YHA, VIP); double/twin room $62 ($58 HI/YHA, VIP)*
***Credit cards** MC, Visa*

Maintenance & cleanliness	★★★
Facilities	★★
Atmosphere & character	★½
Security	★★
Overall rating	★★½

Cheviot Lodge

Cheviot Lodge is a big old house with the cheapest beds in town, but you get what you pay for. The bathrooms and kitchen are really shoddy and the dorms and common areas aren't good either. Nor is it very clean; the bathrooms and the kitchen are right-out filthy. However the backyard barbecue area and the atmosphere aren't too bad.

30 Bulwer Street, East Perth
41, 42, 43, 44, 46, 48, 55
Claisebrook, East Perth
(08) 9227 6817
***Website** www.cheviotlodge.com*
***Dorm bed** $16.50-20; **single room** $38; **double room** $50; **twin room** $45; prices include breakfast*
***Credit cards** MC, Visa*
***Reception open** 8am-noon & 5pm-8pm*

Maintenance & cleanliness	★½
Facilities	★
Atmosphere & character	★★
Security	★½
Overall rating	★½

City & Surf Backpackers

Beds are cheap at City and Surf, and they should be. Dorms, bathrooms, kitchen and common areas are all run-down and shabby, and even the cleanest rooms are below average. Facilities include a dirty kitchen, laundry and a TV room. Besides this there isn't much else to City and Surf, and it's a boring hostel to stay at as it has a depressing atmosphere and no character. The location is the hostel's only strong point: the surrounding streets are calm and peaceful and the restaurants and bars in Lake Street aren't far away.

41 Money Street, Northbridge
Blue CAT, 16, 21, 22, 41, 42, 43, 44, 46, 48, 55, 60, 66, 67, 68, 69, 401
(08) 9227 1234
***Website** www.backpacker.com.au*
***Dorm bed** $20 first night, then $18; **single room** $35; **double room** $55*
***Reception open** 9am-11am & 5pm-7pm*
!acb

Maintenance & cleanliness	★★
Facilities	★
Atmosphere & character	★★½
Security	★½
Overall rating	★★

Coolibah Lodge

The common rooms in this hostel are big, spacious and relaxing and the big windows give the hostel a bright and comfortable mood. The hostel is clean but maintenance a bit below average. Even though this place feels old and out of date it has a good atmosphere and it can get lively at night. The dorm beds have good mattresses, there's a barbecue in the backyard and amenities include usual kitchen, laundry, internet access and a TV room.

194 Brisbane Street, Northbridge
16, 17, 18, 19, 20, 21, 22, 60, 66, 67, 68, 69
(08) 9328 9958 or 1800 280 000
***Website** www.coolibahlodge.com.au*
***Dorm bed** $25 ($24 VIP); **single room** $50 ($48 VIP); **double/twin room** $60 ($58 VIP)*
***Credit cards** MC, Visa*
***Reception open** 8am-10pm daily; 24 hour check in with prior arrangement*

TV K L

Maintenance & cleanliness	★★½
Facilities	★★
Atmosphere & character	★★★
Security	★½
Overall rating	★★½

Emperor's Crown Backpackers

This is a very clean and well maintained hostel. It features an excellent fully-equipped kitchen, a good TV lounge with a big screen, internet access, laundry facilities and a shady barbecue area. The dormitories have good mattresses and are air-conditioned. This is a great place to stay, although some people may feel that it's too sterile.

85 Stirling Street, Perth
15, 16, 21, 22, 60, 66, 67, 68, 69, 401 McIver, Perth
(08) 9227 1400 or 1800 991 553
***Website** www.emperorscrown.com.au*
***Dorm bed** $29; **double/twin room** $80-136*
***Credit cards** Amex, MC, Visa*
***Reception open** 8am-10.30pm daily*

TV K L

Maintenance & cleanliness	★★★★
Facilities	★★½
Atmosphere & character	★★★
Security	★★★
Overall rating	★★★½

Exclusive Backpackers

This is a fresh and clean hostel. The rooms are well maintained, the beds have good mattresses and it's a comfortable place to stay. The atmosphere isn't on fire though, and there aren't many facilities besides the kitchen, laundry and internet access. There isn't much exclusive about Exclusive Backpackers, it's just slightly above average compared with other Perth hostels.

158 Adelaide Terrace, Perth
Red CAT, 32, 33, 35, 36, 37, 38, 39, 72, 75, 106, 150, 160, 170, 176, 177, 179, 210, 211, 212, 282, 283, 288, 293, 296, 298, 299, 709, 730, 731, 787, 788, 799
(08) 9221 9991
***Website** www.exclusivebackpackers.com*
***Dorm bed** $24; **single room** $65; **double room** $65*
***Credit cards** MC, Visa*
***Reception open** 8am-10.30pm*

TV K L

Maintenance & cleanliness	★★★★
Facilities	★½
Atmosphere & character	★★★
Security	★½
Overall rating	★★★

Globe Backpackers & City Oasis Resort

This hostel is a good place to stay. It has free tea & coffee, rice and internet access, a fully-equipped Ikea-furnished kitchen, laundry, a decent TV room, a small swimming pool and a barbecue area with picnic tables. The atmosphere is good and the location – right in the centre of Perth – is excellent. The overall cleanliness and maintenance is fairly good, the dorm has good beds and all guests get their own lockers.

561 Wellington Street, Perth
Blue CAT, Red CAT, Yellow CAT, 8, 10, 12, 28, 81, 84, 85, 91, 92, 95
Perth
(08) 9321 4080
***Website** www.globebackpackers.com.au*
***Dorm bed** $22-28; **single room** $75-90; **double/twin room** $75-90; prices include breakfast*
***Credit cards** MC, Visa*
***Reception open** 24 hours*

TV K L

Maintenance & cleanliness	★★★
Facilities	★★★
Atmosphere & character	★★★
Security	★★
Overall rating	★★★

Governor Robinson's
Perfectly maintained and spotlessly clean, Governor Robinson's clearly stands out from the rest of Perth's hostels. It is a really charming hostel in a beautiful old building with lovely rose bushes outside the entrance. Inside the hostel features polished hardwood floors and classy dark wood furnishings. It is a small hostel so there aren't a lot of facilities, but what they do have is of a very high standard and includes a good kitchen (there's no oven but otherwise it is well equipped), a quiet lounge room and big laundry. It has a quiet yet social atmosphere helped by the lack of a television (to encourage conversation). It is a very likeable hostel and its mood is perhaps more grown-up than some of the more party-oriented places in town.
7 Robinson Avenue, Northbridge
16, 21, 22, 41, 42, 43, 44, 46, 48, 55, 60, 66, 67, 68, 69, 401
(08) 9328 3200
Website *www.govrobinsons.com.au*
Dorm bed *$25;* ***double room*** *$70-80*
Credit cards *Amex, MC, Visa*
Reception open *Mon-Fri 9am-1pm & 4pm-8pm, Sat-Sun 9am-1pm & 4.30pm-7.30pm*
TV K

Maintenance & cleanliness	★★★★★
Facilities	★½
Atmosphere & character	★★★★★
Security	★★½
Overall rating	★★★★

Grand Central Backpackers
Time hasn't been kind to this hostel, which started out as the Grand Central Hotel but now looks and feels worn-out. It isn't very clean, but it has all the basic facilities like a kitchen, TV lounge, internet access and laundry. Unfortunately the hostel's atmosphere is dull and silent and even though the common areas include a pool table and a great TV lounge, it isn't really a place where you will want to spend your evenings.
379 Wellington Street, Perth
Blue CAT, Red CAT, Yellow CAT, 28, 81, 84, 85, 91, 92, 95, 213, 220, 708 *Perth*
(08) 9421 1123
Dorm bed *$19-24;* ***single room*** *$50;* ***double/twin room*** *$60*
Credit cards *MC, Visa*
Reception open *24 hours*
TV K L

Maintenance & cleanliness	★★½
Facilities	★½
Atmosphere & character	★★½
Security	★★
Overall rating	★★

Hay Street Backpackers
This hostel has a nice backyard with a small swimming pool and the overall cleanliness and maintenance is good. Rooms are air-conditioned, the kitchen has most of the necessary cooking gear and TV, internet access and laundry facilities are available. The atmosphere is relaxed and overall this is a good hostel. It is located a few blocks south-east of the centre, but the free Red CAT bus stops nearby so the location is not a problem.
266 Hay Street, Perth
Red CAT, 24, 25, 27, 103, 111, 158
(08) 9221 9880
Website *www.haystbackpackers.com*
Dorm bed *$22;* ***single room*** *$40;* ***double room*** *$60-75*
Credit cards *MC, Visa*
Reception open *Mon-Sat 8.30am-6pm, Sun 9am-5pm*
TV K L

Maintenance & cleanliness	★★★½
Facilities	★★½
Atmosphere & character	★★★
Security	★
Overall rating	★★★

Mad Cat City Backpackers
This hostel really needs a makeover. The decaying house is big, dull and shabby with poorly cleaned rooms. The dirty kitchen is not a nice place for cooking, the common areas don't seem to be taken care of at all and the bathrooms are absolutely horrendous. Mad Cat has free internet access, but that's not nearly enough to earn a recommendation.

55-63 Stirling Street, Northbridge
Blue CAT, 15-22, 38, 41-44, 48, 55, 60, 66-69, 401
(08) 9228 4966
Website *www.madcatbackpackers.com.au*
Dorm bed *$18-25;* ***double/twin room*** *$60*
Credit cards *MC, Visa*
Reception open *8am-midnight*
TV K L

Maintenance & cleanliness	★½
Facilities	★★
Atmosphere & character	★½
Security	★★
Overall rating	★★

North Lodge

This hostel feels like an abandoned hotel and the vibe is hardly exciting. It's a dark, silent and boring place. It is fairly clean, but the maintenance is just acceptable and there's a lack of facilities apart from the usual laundry, a small TV room and basic kitchen facilities.
225 Beaufort Street, Northbridge
16, 21, 22, 60, 66, 67, 68, 69, 401
(08) 9227 7588
Website *www.northlodge-perthwa.com*
Dorm bed *$28;* ***single room*** *$60;* ***double room*** *$60*
Credit cards *MC, Visa*
TV K L

Maintenance & cleanliness	★★½
Facilities	★
Atmosphere & character	★½
Security	★½
Overall rating	★★

Old Swan Barracks

This hostel looks promising as it is in an old military building (hence the name) with a beautiful entrance. However the interior isn't so nice and the common areas are haphazardly slammed together in the huge ex-barracks and it doesn't work very well; it just feels way too spacious and randomly set up. The hostel is clean enough and at the time of writing the dorms were undergoing a major renovation that should improve things by late 2008.
6 Francis Street, Northbridge
Blue CAT, 16, 21, 22, 60, 66, 67, 68, 69, 401
(08) 9428 0000
Website *www.theoldswanbarracks.com*
Dorm bed *$21-26;* ***single room*** *$59;* ***double room*** *$69; prices include breakfast*
Credit cards *MC, Visa*
Reception open *24 hours*
TV K

Maintenance & cleanliness	★★★½
Facilities	★½
Atmosphere & character	★★½
Security	★★½
Overall rating	★★½

One World Backpackers

One World Backpackers is a very clean hostel with friendly staff and a good atmosphere. It has a fully-equipped kitchen with free tea and coffee, a comfortable TV lounge, internet access and lockers for every guest; however the furnishings are old and dated. Overall, One World Backpackers is one of the better hostels in Perth.
162 Aberdeen Street, Northbridge
Blue CAT, 15, 17, 19, 276, 277, 278, 346, 347, 354, 363, 370, 373, 374, 400, 402, 777, 870, 886, 887, 889
(08) 9228 8206 or 1800 188 100
Website *www.oneworldbackpackers.com.au*
Dorm bed *$24-30 ($23-29 HI/YHA, Nomads, VIP);* ***double room*** *$70; prices include breakfast*
Credit cards *MC, Visa*
Reception open *7am-8.30pm; 24 hour check in with prior arrangement*
TV K L

Maintenance & cleanliness	★★★½
Facilities	★★½
Atmosphere & character	★★★★
Security	★★
Overall rating	★★★

Ozi Inn

Ozi's orange minibus advertises this hostel as the friendliest in Perth and it would be a lie to promote this hostel positively in any other way. The standard of cleanliness is appalling, simply because of the filthy kitchen. Apart from internet access and an almost useless kitchen, the hostel is also short on facilities; however the atmosphere can be good and the staff are friendly, but overall this isn't a very good hostel. If you do end up here, make sure your bed is in the main building and not across the street in the non air-conditioned house (called the Dark Side), which is even worse.

282 Newcastle Street, Northbridge
Blue CAT, 15
(08) 9328 1222
***Website** www.oziinn.com*
***Dorm bed** $21-24; price includes breakfast*
***Reception open** 8am-midnight daily*

Maintenance & cleanliness	★½
Facilities	★½
Atmosphere & character	★★
Security	★½
Overall rating	★½

Perth City YHA

Perth City YHA is a big 240-bed hostel in a 1940s art deco building near the train station in the city centre. This is definitely not a party place and it feels corporate and impersonal, appealing to groups and families as well as backpackers. However it's absolutely clean and it has all of the necessary amenities. The hostel is air-conditioned throughout and has good facilities that include a kitchen, TV lounge, reading room, laundry, a café/restaurant and a swimming pool. If you're travelling with your own computer you'll appreciate the Wi-Fi access ($5 for 2 hours) and the excellent security to keep your gear safe.

300 Wellington Street, Perth
Red CAT, Yellow CAT, 28, 81, 84, 85, 91, 92, 95, 213, 220, 708
McIver, Perth
(08) 9427 5100
***Website** www.yha.com.au*
***Dorm bed** $31.50 ($28 HI/YHA); **double/twin room** $85-100 ($75-90 HI/YHA)*
***Credit cards** Diners, JCB, MC, Visa*
***Reception open** 24 hours*

Maintenance & cleanliness	★★★★★
Facilities	★★★
Atmosphere & character	★½
Security	★★★★½
Overall rating	★★★½

Planet Inn Backpackers

Planet Inn Backpackers is a poorly maintained hostel that feels shabby with dark rooms and a gloomy atmosphere. It has the usual facilities including a kitchen, laundry and internet access plus a good TV room, a few board games and a pool table. The backyard dining area is nice and sunny, but overall this isn't the best place to stay.

494 Newcastle Street, West Perth
15
(08) 9227 9969 or 1800 679 969
***Website** www.planetinn.com.au*
***Dorm bed** $19-25; **double/twin room** $64*
***Credit cards** MC, Visa*
***Reception open** 8am-midnight daily*

Maintenance & cleanliness	★★
Facilities	★★
Atmosphere & character	★½
Security	★★½
Overall rating	★★

Rainbow Lodge

This poorly maintained hostel is perhaps the best of Perth's cheapies. It has free internet access (a rarity in this city) and breakfast is included in the low rates. The atmosphere isn't bad and paintings on the walls do a good job at bringing some character to the lodge. All the facilities you would expect are available including a kitchen, laundry and TV room plus table tennis, a pool table, some board games and free use of inline skates. It is relatively clean, but it doesn't feel very clean because of the aged house and shabby furnishings.

133 Summers Street, East Perth
41, 42, 43, 44, 46, 48, 55
Claisebrook, East Perth
(08) 9227 1818
***Website** www.rainbowlodge.com.au*
***Dorm bed** $19-21; **double/twin room** $64; prices include breakfast*
***Reception open** 8am-8pm daily*

Maintenance & cleanliness	★★½
Facilities	★★
Atmosphere & character	★★½
Security	★★
Overall rating	★★½

Shiralee Backpackers

Shiralee Backpackers is a nice popular hostel with a very good atmosphere. It's a fairly big place, but it still has a personal and friendly vibe. The general cleanliness and maintenance is just average, but the common areas are good enough to keep the guests satisfied. The facilities are quite typical; there's a good TV room, laundry, kitchen and a barbecue. Overall – a decent place with good vibes.

107 Brisbane Street, Northbridge
16, 21, 22, 60, 66, 67, 68, 69, 401
(08) 9227 7448
***Website** www.shiralee.com.au*
***Dorm bed** $25-27 ($24-26 VIP); **double/twin room** $66 ($64 VIP)*
***Credit cards** MC, Visa*
***Reception open** 8.30am-1pm & 5pm-10pm; late check in by prior arrangement*

TV K L

Maintenance & cleanliness	★★½
Facilities	★★
Atmosphere & character	★★★½
Security	★
Overall rating	★★½

Spinner's Backpackers

Spinner's is a shabby hostel with little character, but there are comfortable couches in the common areas and it is relatively clean. Facilities include the usual kitchen, TV, laundry and internet access plus a pool table and a selection of board games. Altogether this is just an acceptable hostel, but it's small enough to have a good friendly atmosphere.

342 Newcastle Street, Northbridge
Blue CAT, 15, 17, 19, 276, 277, 278, 346, 347, 354, 363, 370, 373, 374, 400, 402, 777, 870, 886, 887, 889
(08) 9328 9468
***Website** www.spinnersbackpackers.com.au*
***Dorm bed** $25; **twin room** $60*
***Reception open** 24 hours*

TV K L

Maintenance & cleanliness	★★★½
Facilities	★★
Atmosphere & character	★★½
Security	★½
Overall rating	★★½

Underground Backpackers

Underground Backpackers is a big orange building in Northbridge with dorm beds over several floors. The common areas are spacious and include a kitchen, a basement TV lounge with a big screen TV, a bar and a swimming pool. Unfortunately the hostel lacks character and is anonymous and forgettable.

268 Newcastle Street, Northbridge
Blue CAT, 15
(08) 9228 3755
***Website** www.undergroundbackpackers.com.au*
***Dorm bed** $25-28; **single/double/twin room** $65-70*
***Credit cards** Amex, Diners, MC, Visa*
***Reception open** 24 hours*

TV K L

Maintenance & cleanliness	★★★
Facilities	★★★
Atmosphere & character	★★
Security	★★★½
Overall rating	★★★

Witch's Hat

Small witch dolls hang from the ceilings around in this hostel and the bright common areas ensure this place a good score when it comes to atmosphere and character. It's located in a charming building and everything feels clean and well maintained. Like most other Perth hostels, all the typical facilities are available such as a kitchen with free tea and coffee, a comfortable TV lounge, a nice barbecue-equipped backyard and laundry but the Witch's Hat is not like most hostels in Perth – it's one of the best.

148 Palmerston Street, Northbridge
401
(08) 9228 4228 or 1800 818 358
***Website** www.witchs-hat.com*
***Dorm bed** $29; **double room** $76; **twin room** $68; prices include breakfast*
***Credit cards** MC, Visa*
***Reception open** 7am-8pm*

TV K L

Maintenance & cleanliness	★★★★
Facilities	★★½
Atmosphere & character	★★★★½
Security	★★★
Overall rating	★★★½

FREMANTLE

Perth's port is a lively seaside suburb with lots to see and do including several museums, a busy market and some very good pubs. Fremantle has ferries to Rottnest Island and a frequent train service into the city centre.

Australia Backpackers

Australia Backpackers has clean dorms, but the rest of the hostel is poorly maintained and sometimes straight-out dirty. There's a big outdoor area with plants, some of them seem to be dying; a fully-equipped, but dirty, kitchen; new laundry machines; a barbecue and a dull TV room. The atmosphere is pretty much killed by the grey and boring decor. The good location (the Orange CAT bus stops literally two metres outside the front door) seems to be this hostel's only saving grace. This should be your last resort in Fremantle.

4 Beach Street, Fremantle
Orange CAT *Fremantle*
(08) 9433 2055
***Dorm bed** $20-22 ($18-20 HI/YHA, VIP); **double room** $50 ($45 HI/YHA, VIP); **twin room** $45 ($40 HI/YHA, VIP)*
***Credit cards** MC, Visa*
***Reception open** 8am-11pm daily*

TV K L

Maintenance & cleanliness	★★
Facilities	★★
Atmosphere & character	★★
Security	★★½
Overall rating	★★

Backpackers Inn Freo YHA Hostel

The atmosphere is very good at this hostel. It has bright spacious common areas, a good fully-equipped kitchen and a very nice café-like courtyard with sunny seating areas and green surroundings. Although the bathrooms we saw were dirty the general cleanliness and maintenance is OK. All the expected hostel facilities are available plus a gym, a barbecue, a projection-screen cinema, table tennis, table football and board games.

11 Pakenham Street, Fremantle
Orange CAT, 98, 511, 513, 520,

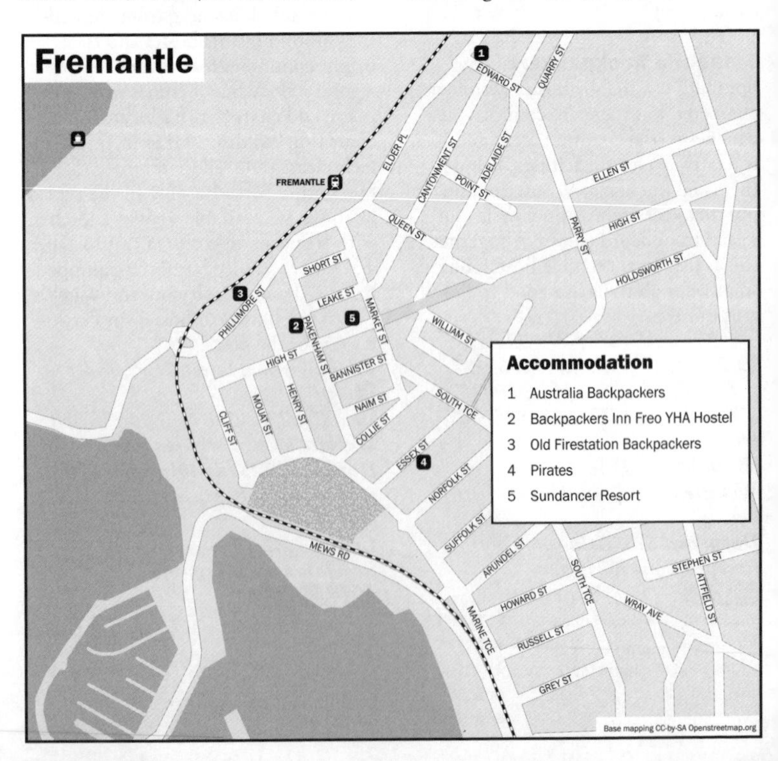

530, 531, 532, 533, 825, 920
Fremantle
(08) 9431 7065
***Website** www.yha.com.au*
***Dorm bed** $24.50-31.50; **single room** $67.50; **double/twin room** $72.50; prices include breakfast*
***Credit cards** Diners, MC, Visa; 3% credit card surcharge*
***Reception open** 8am-8pm*

Maintenance & cleanliness	★★★
Facilities	★★
Atmosphere & character	★★★½
Security	★
Overall rating	★★½

Old Firestation Backpackers

There is a great atmosphere at the Old Firestation, and although cleanliness and maintenance are just OK, this is a good place to stay. There is a women's only area where female travellers can hang out with its own kitchen and TV lounge, but there's no reason for the boys to cry as the main common area is good and has a pool table, comfy couches and a big television. There are lockers for all the beds and there is free internet access. The Old Firestation also houses a restaurant which cooks good affordable meals.
18 Phillimore Street, Fremantle
Orange CAT *Fremantle*
(08) 9430 5454
***Website** www.old-firestation.net*
***Dorm bed** $23-25; **double/twin room** $65*
***Credit cards** Amex, Diners, MC, Visa*
***Reception open** Mon-Sat 8am-9pm, Sun 9am-9pm*

Maintenance & cleanliness	★★★
Facilities	★★
Atmosphere & character	★★★½
Security	★★
Overall rating	★★★

Pirates

This hostel is in a very old building, but they have done a good job at brightening it up with paintings and decorations. Pirates Backpackers has a kitchen, laundry, internet access, pool table and a barbecue. The staff does a good job at arranging activities for the guests and it has a good atmosphere. Overall it's a good place to stay – even though it could be better maintained.
11 Essex Street, Fremantle
Orange CAT, 98, 511, 513, 520, 530, 531, 532, 533, 825, 920
Fremantle
(08) 9335 6635
***Dorm bed** $26-28 ($23-25 VIP)*
***Credit cards** MC, Visa*
***Reception open** 9am-6.30pm*

Maintenance & cleanliness	★★★
Facilities	★½
Atmosphere & character	★★★★
Security	★★
Overall rating	★★½

Sundancer Resort

This old hotel was transformed into a night club before it finally ended up as a hostel – and Sundancer Resort is an excellent hostel. The cool common areas are big and spacious, and are decorated by graffiti, photos and paintings. Internet access is free, the kitchen is geared up with all you need to make your meals and it has two TVs, although the television screens steal a bit too much attention from the main common area. However the atmosphere is laid-back and friendly and it is a good place to stay.
80 High Street, Fremantle
Orange CAT, 98, 511, 513, 520, 530, 531, 532, 533, 825, 920
Fremantle
(08) 9336 6080
***Website** www.sundancer-resort.com.au*
***Dorm bed** $22-24; **single room** $45; **double/twin room** $60*
***Credit cards** MC, Visa*
***Reception open** 24 hours*

Maintenance & cleanliness	★★★
Facilities	★★★
Atmosphere & character	★★★★
Security	★½
Overall rating	★★★

OTHER AREAS

Comfort Hostel

The name is not lying, this is a comfortable place. It is clean and well maintained and it has extensive facilities. In addition to the fully-equipped kitchen, laundry and internet access there is also a spa pool, a barbecue, table football and pool tables. The large air-conditioned dorms have good mattresses and the common rooms are good, although it doesn't feel like a very social hostel. There are free shuttle buses going to the centre of Perth, but Comfort Hostel's suburban location is still a minus – it is far away from anything of interest.

239 Great Eastern Highway, Belmont
36, 40, 296, 299
(08) 9477 4300
***Website** www.comfortbackpackers.com*
***Dorm bed** $20-25 ($18-22 HI/YHA, ISIC, VIP); **double room** $70 ($65 HI/YHA, ISIC, VIP); prices include breakfast*
***Credit cards** Amex, Diners, MC, Visa*
***Reception open** Mon-Fri 7am-1pm, Sat-Sun 7.30am-9pm*

Maintenance & cleanliness	★★★★½
Facilities	★★★
Atmosphere & character	★★★
Security	★★½
Overall rating	★★★½

Perth Hills YHA

This small hostel is 40km from the city centre. It is surrounded by trees and it is an alternative to the city hostels and even though the facilities are very basic this isn't a bad place to stay. It has a good atmosphere and it feels like you're staying at someone's old-fashioned holiday house. With the nearest shops 4km away it might feel a bit far away from civilisation, but there's a pub and an outdoor cinema nearby, and the remote location is really its strongest point. A lake is not too far away and sometimes kangaroos hop around the premises.

Mundaring Weir Road, Mundaring
Midland, then 318
(08) 9295 1809
***Website** www.yha.com.au*
***Dorm bed** $24 ($21 HI/YHA); **single room** $45 ($40 HI/YHA); **twin room** $45 ($40 HI/YHA)*
***Credit cards** MC, Visa*
***Reception open** 8am-10am & 5pm-9pm*

Maintenance & cleanliness	★★★★
Facilities	★½
Atmosphere & character	★★★½
Security	★
Overall rating	★★★

Eating & Drinking

Perth isn't much of a food city and you won't find the eclectic range of ethnic eateries that you'll find in Melbourne, or even Adelaide. However this doesn't mean that you'll starve as there are plenty of affordable places to grab something to eat.

In the city centre there are plenty of food courts catering to office workers on their lunch break including the Metro Food Hall under the Hay Street Mall. Away from the city centre there is a good selection of places to eat in Northbridge, especially around James, Lake and William Streets. If you're staying in Fremantle you'll find plenty of places to eat around the Fremantle Markets and on South Terrace.

Travellers preparing their own food can find a **Woolworths** supermarket in the city centre *(166 Murray Street, Perth)*. This is where most backpackers staying in Northbridge or the city centre buy their groceries. If you're staying in Fremantle you have a better choice with a **Coles** in the Woolstores Shopping Centre *(corner Cantonement & Goldborough Streets, Fremantle)* and also a **Woolworths** *(39 Adelaide Street, Fremantle)*.

Perth has some brilliant beachside pubs that are great places to spend a Sunday session. One of the best is the **Ocean Beach Hotel** *(corner Eric Street & Marine Parade, Cottesloe)* next to Ocean Beach Backpackers. It is right opposite the beach and you can sometimes see whales from the bar. Another good beachside pub is the **Cottesloe Beach Hotel** *(104 Marine Parade, Cottesloe)*, aka the Cott, which is just a five minute walk south from the OBH.

Northbridge has a reputation as Perth's centre of nightlife and although this neighbourhood does have a few bars and clubs it is hardly a happening spot compared with other cities. However Northbridge does have a lot of hostels and there is a good chance you will stay here and want to find somewhere to drink in the neighbourhood. The **Brass Monkey** *(corner James & William Streets, Northbridge)* is one of Northbridge's main drinking spots. It's a huge place with lots of different areas including a beer garden. **The Bog** *(361 Newcastle Street, Northbridge)* is a popular Irish pub that is convenient to many of Northbridge's backpacker hostels. If you're planning a big night out, **The Deen** *(84 Aberdeen Street, Northbridge)* is a great bar to start out at before heading to other clubs. The Deen has six bars, DJs and live music. Monday is backpacker night with happy hour starting at 6pm and a free barbecue around 7.30pm.

Leederville and Subiaco are two suburbs not far from Northbridge and they have some good places to eat and drink. The **Hip-E Club** *(663 Newcastle Street, Leederville)* is one of the most popular backpacker haunts, especially on Thursdays, which is backpacker and student night. There is also a good café scene on Oxford Street in Leederville.

Fremantle is perhaps Perth's best neighbourhood for eating and drinking and it has a particularly good café scene along South Terrace. There are a lot of good pubs around Fremantle including another branch of **the Bog** *(189 High Street, Fremantle)* and **Little Creatures Brewery** *(40 Mews Road, Fremantle)*, which is a microbrewery in an old boat shed near Fremantle's harbour that also does excellent food.

Sights

CITY CENTRE & NORTHBRIDGE

Art Gallery of Western Australia

Australian and international art is exhibited at the state's most important art museum.

Perth Cultural Centre, James Street, Northbridge
Blue CAT *Perth*
(08) 9492 6622
Website *www.artgallery.wa.gov.au*
Admission *free, charge for some temporary exhibits*
Open *10am-5pm daily*

Kings Park

This large city park consists mostly of native bush and is an escape from the city with popular picnic areas and bike paths. There are good views of the city centre from the higher points in the park.

15, 18

Parliament House

You can take a free tour of the Western Australian state parliament building that offers a crash course in Australian politics.

Harvest Terrace, Perth
Red CAT
(08) 9222 7429
Admission *free*
Tours *Mon, Thu 10.30am*

Perth Institute of Contemporary Arts (PICA)

The Perth Institute of Contemporary Arts features exhibits of avant garde and contemporary visual and performing arts.

51 James Street, Northbridge
Blue CAT Train Perth
(08) 9227 6144
Website *www.pica.org.au*
Admission *Gallery free, charge for performances*
Open *Tue-Sun 11am-8pm*

Perth Mint

This impressive building on Hay Street offers a unique insight into how money is made.

310 Hay Street, Perth
Red CAT
(08) 9421 7223 or 1800 098 817
Website *www.perthmint.com.au*
Admission *$15*
Open *Mon-Fri 9am-4pm, Sat-Sun 9am-1pm; gold pours Mon-Fri 10am, 11am, noon, 1pm, 2pm, 3pm, Sat-Sun 10am, 11am, noon*

Scitech Discovery Centre

This hands-on science museum features over 160 interactive exhibits. However, like many science museums, it is geared mostly toward kids.

Corner Railway Parade & Sutherland Street, West Perth
City West
(08) 9481 5789
Website *www.scitech.org.au*
Admission *$14, $10 after 3pm*

***Open** Mon-Fri 9.30am-4pm, Sat-Sun 10am-5pm*

Swan Bells

This impressive 82.5m copper and glass tower in Barrack Square is one of the world's largest musical instruments. It houses a set of 18 bells, which includes 12 bells from St Martin-in-the-Fields in Trafalgar Square, London that date from before the 14th century. The tower features galleries where you can see the bell ringers in action as well as observation decks that boast stunning city views.
Barrack Square, Riverside Drive, Perth
Blue CAT Esplanade Barrack Street Jetty
(08) 9218 8183
***Website** www.swanbells.com.au*
***Admission** $10*
***Open** 10am-5pm daily; bell ringing Mon-Fri 11.30am-12.30pm, Sat-Sun noon-2pm*

Western Australian Cricket Museum

This museum at the WACA Ground is a must for cricket fans.
Nelson Crescent, East Perth
Red CAT, Yellow CAT
(08) 9265 7222
***Admission** $5, tour $10*
***Open** Mon-Fri except match days 10am-3pm; tours Tue-Thu 10am & 1pm*

Western Australian Museum

Western Australia's largest museum features exhibits on natural history including a good selection of stuffed animals and a whale skeleton.
Francis Street, Perth
Blue CAT Perth
(08) 9427 2700
***Website** www.museum.wa.gov.au*
***Admission** free, charge for special exhibits*
***Open** 9.30am-5pm daily*

FREMANTLE

This seaside suburb has long been Perth's port and has hosted the America's Cup yacht race. The area has a hip yet laid-back ambience and is worth at least a day-trip from Perth.

Fremantle Markets

This old market hall has been around since 1897 and is now home to one of Fremantle's most popular attractions with over 150 stalls ranging from fruit and veggies to art and craft.
Corner Henderson Street & South Terrace, Fremantle
Orange CAT, 98, 511, 513, 520, 530, 531, 532, 533, 825, 920 Fremantle
(08) 9335 2515
***Admission** free*
***Open** Fri 9am-9pm, Sat 9am-5pm, Sun 10am-5pm*

Fremantle History Museum

Housed in a former Asylum building, the Fremantle History Museum has exhibits on Western Australia's social history.
1 Finnerty Street, Fremantle
(08) 9430 7966
***Website** www.museum.wa.gov.au*
***Admission** free*
***Open** Mon-Fri 10am-4.30pm, Sat-Sun 10.30am-4.30pm*

Fremantle Prison

The Fremantle Prison was built with convict labour in the 19th century and was operated as a prison until as recently as 1991. It has now been opened to the public and has frequent guided tours.
1 The Terrace, Fremantle
Orange CAT Fremantle
(08) 9336 9200
***Website** www.fremantleprison.com.au*
***Admission** $16.50; night tour $21; tunnel tour $59*
***Open** 10am-5pm daily; tours depart every half hour*

Maritime Museum

The new maritime museum on Victoria Quay features an excellent collection of exhibits including a 90-metre-long submarine.
Forrest Landing, Victoria Quay, Fremantle
Orange CAT Fremantle
(08) 9335 8921
***Website** www.museum.wa.gov.au*
***Admission** $10 museum, $8 submarine*
***Open** 9.30am-5pm daily*

OTHER AREAS

AQWA

AQWA is home to a large variety of marine life and it features several areas that recreate various marine environments. AQWA is Australia's largest aquarium and it also boasts the country's biggest walk-through underwater tunnel.

91 Southside Drive, Hillarys Boat Harbour
Warwick, then 423
(08) 9447 7500
***Website** www.aqwa.com.au*
***Admission** $26*
***Open** 10am-5pm daily*

Perth Zoo

Perth's zoo is home to over 2000 animals representing 280 different species. It has the usual collection of African and native animals and the zoo is also a good spot for a picnic.

20 Labouchere Road, South Perth
35 Mends Street Jetty
(08) 9474 3551
***Website** www.perthzoo.wa.gov.au*
***Admission** $18*
***Open** 9am-5pm daily*

Rottnest Island

Rottnest Island is best known for the island's unique animal, the quokka. The quokka is a small macropod about the size of a large domestic cat, resembling something like a small kangaroo with a rats tail. Early Dutch explorers originally thought the quokka to be rats and named the island "Rat's Nest".

The island is only 11km long and is 19km offshore from Fremantle. The island's eastern coast is built up around the small township of Thompson Bay where most of the shops, restaurants and accommodation can be found.

Practical Information

Rottnest Island Visitors Information Centre

Colebach Avenue, Thompson Bay
(08) 9372 9752
***Website** www.rottnestisland.com*
***Open** Mon-Fri 7am-6.15pm, Sat-Sun 7am-7.30pm*

Coming & Going

There are several ferry companies that ply the waters between Rottnest Island and the mainland.

Oceanic Cruises *((08) 9325 1191; **website** www.oceaniccruises.com.au)* depart from Barrack Street Jetty in Perth and East Street Jetty in Fremantle. Day return fares are $68 from Perth and $54 from Fremantle.

Rottnest Express *((08) 9335 6406; **website** www.rottnestexpress.com.au)* departs from Victoria Quay in Fremantle. Day return tickets cost $53 ($46 HI/YHA, VIP).

Local Transport

Rottnest Island is surprisingly well served by public transport but cycling is the most popular way to get around. Bayseeker operate an hourly bus service around the island. A day ticket is $10 but the last bus stops running around 4.30pm. There is also a free bus service that runs every half hour between the hostel, Thompson Bay and Geordie Bay.

There is even a train between Thompson Bay and Oliver Hill but this is a more expensive tourist service charging $17.40 for the two-hour return trip.

Accommodation

Kingstown Barracks

This hostel is clean and in good shape, but it's a bit dull and there aren't too many facilities available, just the usual kitchen and internet access. The beds are good, lockers are available, and the hostel has some character as it is housed in old military buildings. Kingstown Barracks is a quite forgettable place but its standards are good enough.

Kingstown, Rottnest Island (check in at accommodation office near the ferry terminal)
(08) 9372 9780
***Website** www.rottnestisland.com*
***Dorm bed** $25.20; **twin room** $49.30*
***Credit cards** Amex, Diners, MC, Visa*
*Check in at accommodation office near the ferry terminal; **open** Mon-Fri 7am-6.15pm, Sat-Sun 7am-7.30pm*
TV K

Maintenance & cleanliness	★★★½
Facilities	★
Atmosphere & character	★★½
Security	★½
Overall rating	★★½

Avon Valley

This picturesque region east of Perth is one of Western Australia's first inland regions to be settled. It has some quaint little towns that make a nice daytrip from Perth, which is just a one-hour drive away.

The most visited towns in the valley are Toodyay and York, which are both full of character. There's also the Avon Valley National Park. The 4800 ha park is good for hiking and watching wildlife, and it is possible to camp here as well. The park is open 8am-5pm daily.

Toodyay

This charming town was settled in the late 1830s by farmers searching for cows that had strayed from their farms in the Swan Valley.

Practical Information

Toodyay Visitor Information Centre

7 Piesse Street, Toodyay
☎ *(08) 9574 2435*
Website *www.toodyay.com*
Open *Mon-Sat 9am-5pm, Sun 10am-5pm*

Sights

Connors Mill Museum

This three-storey working flour mill uses 19th century steam-powered machinery.
Stirling Terrace, Toodyay
☎ *(08) 9574 2435*
Admission *$3*
Open *Mon-Sat 9am-5pm, Sun 10am-5pm*

Old Newcastle Gaol

This old prison has a collection of old handcuffs, guns and photographs and exhibits on the outlaws who where once locked up here.
Clinton Street, Toodyay
☎ *(08) 9574 2435*
Admission *$3*
Open *Mon-Fri 10am-3pm, Sat-Sun 10am-4pm*

York

York was Western Australia's first inland settlement and was established in 1831, making it historic by Australian standards. The small town has some charming old buildings, a couple of small museums and some nice restaurants and cafés.

Practical Information

York Tourist Bureau

81 Avon Terrace, York
☎ *(08) 9641 1301*
Website *www.yorktouristbureau.com.au*
Open *9am-5pm daily*

Accommodation

Kookaburra Dream

Kookaburra Dream is a magnificent hostel. The lovely garden courtyard has a nice barbecue area with wooden outdoor furniture and small details like the old windmill add a lot of charm. The furnishings aren't brand new, but they are well maintained and they suit the character of the place. The hostel is clean, the kitchen feels cosy and there is an excellent free breakfast. Although the TV room is nothing flash, it's relaxed and it has comfortable seats. The big clean dorms have wooden bunk-beds with good mattresses, and even though the hostel doesn't have lots of fancy facilities it has a laundry and internet access.
152 Avon Terrace, York
☎ *(08) 9641 2936*
Website *www.yorkbackpackerswa.com*
Dorm bed *$25;* ***single room*** *$45;* ***double/twin room*** *$75; prices include breakfast*
Credit cards *MC, Visa*
Reception open *9.30am-8.30pm daily*

Maintenance & cleanliness	★★★★½
Facilities	★★
Atmosphere & character	★★★★
Security	★½
Overall rating	★★★½

Sights & Activities

Ballooning

Windward Adventures *(☎ (08) 9621 2000; **website** www.windwardballooning.com)* run balloon flights over the Avon Valley.

Residency Museum

This small museum has displays on local history.
Brook Street, York
☎ (08) 9641 1751
***Admission** $4*
***Open** Tue-Thu 1pm-3pm, Sat-Sun 11am-3.30pm*

York Motor Museum

The York Motor Museum has a collection of vintage and classic cars dating back to 1886.
116 Avon Terrace, York
☎ (08) 9641 1288
***Website** www.yorkwa.com.au/Motor.Museum/*
***Admission** $8.50*
***Open** 9.30am-3pm daily*

Southwest WA

The first stop south of the Perth area is Bunbury, the principal city of the southwest. After visiting Bunbury most travellers move onward to the Margaret River region, which lies between Cape Naturaliste and Cape Leeuwin. The land here is honeycombed with limestone caves, some of which are open to the public. The Yallingup Caves near Dunsborough, are particularly impressive.

Western Australia's southwest offers magnificent forests of tall native trees including four species of rare eucalypt that grow in a small area here and nowhere else on earth.

Bunbury

Situated about two hours south of Perth, Bunbury is Western Australia's second largest city. Although it is a reasonably large town with plenty to keep you busy, its main attraction is the dolphins at Koombana Beach. Every day several dolphins swim up to shore and you can watch them in much the same way as at Monkey Mia.

Bunbury also makes a convenient base for exploring the nearby Wellington National Park.

Practical Information

Bunbury Visitor Information Centre

Corner Carmody Place & Haley Street, Bunbury
☎ (08) 9721 7922
***Website** www.visitbunbury.com.au*
***Open** Mon-Sat 9am-5pm, Sun 9.30am-4.30pm*

Coming & Going

Bunbury's proximity to Perth ensures relatively convenient transport connections.

It lies at the southern extremity of Western Australia's rail network with a couple of daily train services to and from Perth. The train station is 3km north of town in Wollaston, and local buses meet with the train to take you into the town centre. One-way fares for the Australind train from Perth are $25.60.

Transwa *(☎ 1300 662 205; **website** www.transwa.wa.gov.au)* coaches terminate at the tourist information centre on Haley Street.

Local Transport

Bunbury City Transit *(**website** www.bct.com.au)* runs Bunbury's local bus network. The most useful bus is the one between the train station and the city centre, which is free when you present your train ticket.

Accommodation

Dolphin Retreat YHA

Bunbury's YHA is a small cosy hostel with clean rooms and comfortable beds. Facilities comprise the usual laundry, internet access and kitchen plus a pool table, table tennis, barbecue and free use of bicycles and body boards. The hostel has a great atmosphere that feels like stepping into someone's home and it seems to be popular among Japanese and Korean travellers on working holidays.
14 Wellington Street, Bunbury

☎ *(08) 9792 4690*
***Website** www.dolphinretreatbunbury.com.au*
***Dorm bed** $24 ($21 HI/YHA); **single room** $40 ($35 HI/YHA); **double/twin room** $60 ($54 HI/YHA)*
***Credit cards** MC, Visa*
***Reception open** 8am-10am & 4pm-9pm daily*

Maintenance & cleanliness	★★★★
Facilities	★★★
Atmosphere & character	★★★★
Security	★★
Overall rating	★★★½

Wander Inn

This popular hostel has clean and fairly well-maintained rooms, a good atmosphere and free homemade cake & coffee every afternoon (the manager does the baking herself). There is a good fully-equipped kitchen, a balcony with a barbecue and a comfortable TV room. It's a good place to stay.
16 Clifton Street, Bunbury
☎ *(08) 9721 3242 or 1800 039 032*
***Website** www.bunburybackpackers.com.au*
***Dorm bed** $25 ($23 HI/YHA, VIP); **single room** $38 ($35 HI/YHA, VIP); **double/twin room** $60 ($56 HI/YHA, VIP); prices include breakfast*
***Credit cards** MC, Visa*
***Reception open** 8am-noon & 4pm-9pm daily*

Maintenance & cleanliness	★★★½
Facilities	★★
Atmosphere & character	★★★½
Security	★½
Overall rating	★★★

Sights

Big Swamp Wildlife Park

Big Swamp Wildlife Park has the usual collection of native wildlife including kangaroos and birds.
Prince Phillip Drive, Bunbury
☎ *(08) 9721 8380*
***Admission** $5.50*
***Open** 10am-5pm daily*

Dolphin Discovery Centre

The Dolphin Discovery Centre features interactive exhibits and a small theatre although the best thing is that you can wade in the water and let the dolphins swim around you.
Koombana Drive, Bunbury
☎ *(08) 9791 3088*
***Website** www.dolphindiscovery.com.au*
***Admission** $7*
***Open** 8am-5pm daily*

Donnybrook

This village has little to interest most visitors but many backpackers visit Donnybrook between November and June to pick fruit on the orchards that surround the town. Donnybrook's main industry is apple growing, which is celebrated with a biennial apple festival.

Practical Information

Donnybrook Visitor Information Centre

Old Railway Station, South West Highway, Donnybrook
☎ *(08) 9731 1720*
***Open** 10am-4pm daily*

Coming & Going

Transwa (☎ *1300 662 205; **website** www.transwa.wa.gov.au)* coaches stop on the South West Highway.

Accommodation

Brook Lodge

Brook Lodge is a good hostel, but it's a place for working travellers and the beds are only sold on a weekly rate. The manager does an impressive job helping out his guests with jobs and he provides free transport to and from work. The hostel has good facilities that include a kitchen, internet access, pool table, table tennis, barbecue, laundry and a bar. There's also a TV room with film characters painted on the walls. It is clean and well maintained.
3 Bridge Street, Donnybrook
☎ *(08) 9731 1520*
***Website** www.brooklodge.com.au*
***Dorm bed** $120-125 per week; **double room** $260 per week*
***Reception open** 10am-10.30am & 5.30pm-9.30pm daily*

Maintenance & cleanliness	★★★★
Facilities	★★½
Atmosphere & character	★★★
Security	★
Overall rating	★★★

Red Rabbit Inn

This hostel is poorly maintained and has little character and few facilities. Facilities are limited to a fully-equipped kitchen plus a bar with a pool table and a barbecue outdoors. The dormitories have fridges and nice mattresses.

58 Southwest Highway, Donnybrook

☎ *(08) 9731 1013*

Dorm bed *$20*

Maintenance & cleanliness	★★★
Facilities	★½
Atmosphere & character	★★½
Security	★
Overall rating	★★½

Busselton

Busselton is a relatively big town of 20,000 people, founded in 1832 by the Bussells, a family of English migrants who arrived in Western Australia to find that all of the good farm land around Perth and Fremantle was taken.

Today Busselton is a popular resort for families from Perth. It boasts good beaches and snorkelling from the 2km-long jetty. It also makes a good base for exploring the wineries of the Margaret River wine region.

Practical Information

Busselton Information Centre

38 Peel Terrace, Busselton

☎ *(08) 9752 1288*

Website *www.downsouth.com.au*

Open *Mon-Fri 8.30am-5pm, Sat 9am-4pm, Sun 10am-3pm*

Coming & Going

Transwa (☎ *1300 662 205;* ***website*** *www.transwa.wa.gov.au)* coaches stop on Peel Terrace.

Accommodation

Busselton Backpackers

Busselton Backpackers has a good atmosphere and a friendly manager who interacts with the guests. The main common area is a combined TV lounge and kitchen. The bathrooms are poorly maintained, but otherwise the hostel is clean and relatively well maintained. There aren't many amenities, but the hostel has a laundry, table tennis and wireless internet. The hostel's good vibe is its strongest point; it has other charms as well: the hostel as its own chickens and travellers sometimes get their eggs for free.

14 Peel Terrace, Busselton

☎ *(08) 9754 2763*

Dorm bed *$25 first night, then $20 per night;* ***double room*** *$45*

Reception open *9am-1pm & 5pm-9pm*

Maintenance & cleanliness	★★½
Facilities	★½
Atmosphere & character	★★★★
Security	★
Overall rating	★★½

Sights

Busselton Jetty

With a length of 2km, this is the longest wooden jetty in the southern hemisphere. There is good snorkelling off the jetty and also a small museum and an underwater observatory.

Busselton Jetty, Busselton

☎ *(08) 9754 3689*

Website *www.busseltonjetty.com.au*

Admission *$2.50;* ***underwater observatory*** *$20*

Open *Jan-Apr 8am-6pm daily; May-Nov 9am-5pm daily; Dec 8am-6pm daily*

Dunsborough

Dunsborough is popular with divers who come here to dive the *Swan* shipwreck. Many travellers visit Sep-Dec when Dunsborough is a popular spot for whale watching. It is also a good base for surfing at Yallingup and exploring the Margaret River wine region.

Practical Information

Dunsborough Yallingup Tourist Bureau

Dunsborough Park Shopping Centre, Seymour Boulevard, Dunsborough

☎ *(08) 9755 3299*
Open *Mon-Fri 9am-5pm, Sat 9am-4pm, Sun 9.30am-4pm*

INTERNET ACCESS
Juice & Bytes
Dunsborough Park Shopping Centre, Dunsborough
☎ *(08) 9756 8358*
Website *www.juiceandbytes.com*
Open *8.30am-6pm daily*

Coming & Going
Transwa (☎ *1300 662 205;* ***website*** *www.transwa.wa.gov.au)* coaches stop on the Seymour Boulevard.

Accommodation
Dunsborough Beach Lodge
This is a nice classy hostel right in the centre of Dunsborough. It is a clean and well maintained hostel with facilities that include laundry, internet access (including Wi-Fi), a fully-equipped kitchen and a sunny balcony with good furnishing and a barbecue. The dormitories are spotless and the bunk-beds have good inner-spring mattresses. Bikes are available for rent and there's a café and restaurant downstairs.
13 Dunn Bay Road, Dunsborough
☎ *(08) 9756 7144*
Website *www.dunsboroughbeachlodge.com.au*
Dorm bed *$25 ($22 HI/YHA, VIP, foreign passport);* ***single room*** *$60 ($50 HI/YHA, VIP, foreign passport);* ***double room*** *$70 ($60 HI/YHA, VIP, foreign passport)*
Credit cards *MC, Visa*
Reception open *8am-8pm*

Maintenance & cleanliness	★★★★½
Facilities	★★
Atmosphere & character	★★★½
Security	★
Overall rating	★★★½

Dunsborough Beachhouse YHA
Dunsborough Beachouse YHA is a good hostel with a brilliant location right on the beach, 3km from the centre of Dunsborough. The hostel has a good atmosphere and facilities include a volleyball court, barbecue, TV lounge, a fully-equipped kitchen, internet access (including Wi-Fi) and a laundry. The sea view is great and it's a nice place to stay.
201-205 Geographe Bay Road, Quindalup
☎ *(08) 9755 3107*
Website *www.dunsboroughbeachouse.com.au*
Dorm bed *$27 ($24 HI/YHA);* ***single room*** *$45 ($40 HI/YHA);* ***double room*** *$66 ($60 HI/YHA);* ***twin room*** *$61 ($55 HI/YHA)*
Credit cards *MC, Visa*
Reception open *8.30am-11am & 3pm-8pm daily*

Maintenance & cleanliness	★★★★
Facilities	★★½
Atmosphere & character	★★★★
Security	★
Overall rating	★★★

Dunsborough Inn
This is a big accommodation complex with dorm beds as well as pricier motel rooms. Facilities include a kitchen with a small TV, laundry, table tennis and a shaded barbecue area with picnic tables. In the motel area there's a good swimming pool and a spa pool. It is clean and well maintained, but Dunsborough Inn hasn't the best atmosphere.
50 Dunn Bay Road, Dunsborough
☎ *(08) 9756 7277 or 1800 819 883*
Website *www.dunsboroughinn.com*
Dorm bed *$25;* ***double room*** *$45-119*
Credit cards *Amex, Diners, MC, Visa*
Reception open *7.30am-7.30pm daily*

Maintenance & cleanliness	★★★½
Facilities	★★½
Atmosphere & character	★★
Security	★
Overall rating	★★½

Activities
Diving
The *Swan* shipwreck is the major attraction for divers to Dunsborough. There are several dive companies in town that organise trips to the wreck and who offer PADI dive courses. These include **Bay Dive & Adventures** *(26 Dunn Bay Road, Dunsborough;* ☎ *(08) 9756 8577)* and

Cape Dive *(222 Naturaliste Terrace, Dunsborough; ☎ (08) 9756 8778;* ***website*** *www.capediveexperience.com).*

Surfing

Dunsborough is close to the excellent surf beaches at Yallingup, about 10km from town. **Yallingup Surf School** (☎ *(08) 9755 2755;* ***website*** *www.yallingupsurfschool.com)* can teach you to surf from $50 for one lesson or $125 for a three-day course.

Sights

Cape Naturaliste Lighthouse

This lighthouse, 13km from Dunsborough, features a small maritime museum and walking trails around the surrounding coastline.

Cape Naturaliste Road, Cape Naturaliste
☎ *(08) 9755 3955*
Admission *$11*
Open *9am-4.30pm daily; tours depart every 30-45 minutes*

Ngilgi Caves

This beautiful cave was discovered in 1899 and was the first cave in Western Australia to be open to the paying public. There are regular tours of the cave that last around 45-60 minutes.

Caves Road, Yallingup
☎ *(08) 9755 2152*
Admission *$18*
Open *9.30am-4.30pm daily*

Margaret River

Margaret River lies at the heart of Western Australia's top winegrowing and gourmet dining region and has easy access to forests and beaches. In earlier days the region surrounding and containing the town was known for hardwood timber and agriculture, but today tourism and wine are the main industries.

Wine is one of the reasons for how the Margaret River region became such a tourist-magnet, and today it produces about 20% of Australia's premium wine. About 90 vineyards have their cellar doors open for wine-tasting and there are over 110 vineyards in the region.

Beautiful beaches are also associated with Margaret River, and there are hundreds of caves within the Leeuwin-Naturaliste National Park - although only four of them are open to visitors.

The town itself has a good selection of cafés and eateries available. There is also good backpackers' accommodation, which definitely makes Margaret River worth a visit.

Practical Information

Margaret River Visitor Information Centre

Corner Bussell Highway & Tunnbridge Street, Margaret River
☎ *(08) 9757 2911*
Website *www.margaretriver.com*
Open *9am-5pm daily*

Coming & Going

There are daily coaches to Perth although it is best to have a car to explore the area around Margaret River. Transwa (☎ *1300 662 205;* ***website*** *www.transwa.wa.gov.au)* coaches stop on Charles West Road near the visitor information centre.

Accommodation

Inne Town Backpackers

Inne Town is a centrally located hostel that is clean and fairly well maintained. It has a very nice balcony and the social atmosphere is good, although the television dominates the main common area and we found the staff rude when we visited. This hostel has the usual kitchen and laundry and also a pool table and barbecue. This is also a good place to arrange activities like touring the wineries and learning to surf.

93 Bussell Highway, Margaret River
☎ *(08) 9757 3698 or 1800 244 115*
Website *www.margaret-river-online.com.au/accom/innetown/*
Dorm bed *$25-27;* ***single room*** *$60;* ***double room*** *$65*
Credit cards *Amex, JCB, MC, Visa*
Reception open *8.30am-11.30pm & 3pm-8pm daily*

Maintenance & cleanliness	★★★★
Facilities	★★½
Atmosphere & character	★★★½
Security	★
Overall rating	★★★

Margaret River Backpackers

This is a brand new purpose-built hostel that is spotlessly clean with top-quality amenities. The hostel's big common areas are excellent and include a fully-equipped kitchen, a good TV lounge with a big flat screen television, internet access and laundry plus a nice barbecue area on the deck. It has an excellent location right in the town centre.

66 Town View Terrace, Margaret River
(08) 9757 9572
Website *www.margaretriverbackpackers.com.au*
Credit cards *MC, Visa*
Reception open *8.30am-11am & 2pm-8pm daily*

Maintenance & cleanliness	★★★★★
Facilities	★★
Atmosphere & character	★★★
Security	★★½
Overall rating	★★★½

Margaret River Lodge YHA

This has the best atmosphere of Margaret River's hostels. The eco-wise YHA is a 15-minute walk from the town centre and this means that there is enough space for a volleyball court, soccer pitch and a swimming pool plus a nice barbecue and outdoor dining area. There is also the usual TV lounge, internet access, laundry and a fully-equipped kitchen and guests can rent bikes and surfboards. It is clean and well maintained hostel.

220 Railway Terrace, Margaret River
(08) 9757 9532
Website *www.mrlodge.com.au*
Dorm bed *$24.50-27.50 ($21-24.50 HI/YHA);* ***double/twin room*** *$63-73 ($56-66 HI/YHA)*
Credit cards *MC, Visa*
Reception open *8.30am-11am & 2pm-8pm daily*

Maintenance & cleanliness	★★★½
Facilities	★★★★
Atmosphere & character	★★★★½
Security	★½
Overall rating	★★★½

Surf Point Resort

This flashpackers hostel is very clean and close to the beach, although it is around 10km from Margaret River town. It is a very clean and well maintained hostel in a stylish modern resort-style building with superior facilities that include a very nice fully-equipped kitchen and a common area with comfortable couches, an excellent TV and a pool table. There's also a swimming pool. Although the social atmosphere isn't too bad, this hostel can feel a bit impersonal and the modern building would hardly be called cosy, even if it is a comfortable place to relax.

Reidle Drive, Gnarabup, Margaret River
(08) 9757 1777 or 1800 071 777
Website *www.surfpoint.com.au*
Dorm bed *$27;* ***double/twin room*** *$86*
Credit cards *MC, Visa*
Reception open *8.30am-8pm daily*

Maintenance & cleanliness	★★★★½
Facilities	★★½
Atmosphere & character	★★★½
Security	★
Overall rating	★★★½

Eating & Drinking

Margaret River is a popular destination for foodies, but it most of the town's eating establishments are quite expensive. Some of the more affordable places include **Goodfella's Cafe** *(97 Bussell Highway, Margaret River)*, which does good pizza and Margaret River's local pub, the **Settler's Tavern** *(114 Bussell Highway, Margaret River)*. There is a **Coles** supermarket at 132-138 Bussell Highway.

Augusta

Augusta is a small town near Cape Leeuwin at the southern extremity of the Margaret River region. It is close to some good beaches and can also be used as a base for exploring the Margaret River wine region.

There's a jewel cave 8km north of the town that allows visitors and the Cape Leeuwin Lighthouse, at the tip of the peninsula where the Southern and Indian Oceans splash into each other, is also an interesting place to visit.

Practical Information

Augusta Visitor Information Centre

75 Blackwood Avenue, Augusta
☎ *(08) 9758 0166*
Open *Mon-Fri 9am-5pm, Sat-Sun 9am-1pm*

INTERNET ACCESS

Augusta Telecentre

65 Allnutt Terrace, Augusta
☎ *(08) 9758 0002*
Website *http://augusta.wa.tc*
Open *Mon-Fri 10am-5pm*

Coming & Going

Transwa (☎ *1300 662 205;* ***website*** *www.transwa.wa.gov.au)* coaches stop on Blackwood Avenue.

Accommodation

Baywatch Manor Resort YHA

This is an excellent hostel with spotless dorms and common areas. It has great outdoor areas, a fully-equipped kitchen, laundry facilities and a nice living room with a log fire. Baywatch Manor is a comfortable place to stay, but it may be a bit too quiet for some. This hostel is equally popular with families and backpackers.

88 Blackwood Avenue, Augusta
☎ *(08) 9758 1290*
Website *www.baywatchmanor.com.au*
Dorm bed *$24 ($21 HI/YHA);* ***double/twin room*** *$60 ($55 HI/YHA)*
Credit cards *MC, Visa*
Reception open *8.30am-11am & 2pm-8pm daily*

Maintenance & cleanliness	★★★★★
Facilities	★★
Atmosphere & character	★★★★
Security	★★
Overall rating	★★★½

Leeuwin House

Leeuwin House is a part of a bigger accommodation complex. The backpackers' accommodation here is affordable and good quality; but it doesn't feel like a hostel at all as there are no facilities beside the kitchen and the tiny television, and the atmosphere here can be non-existent. On a positive note, it is clean and maintained to a high standard and there is a locker for every bed so it is a secure place to stay.

Blackwood Avenue, Augusta
☎ *(08) 9758 1944*
Website *www.augusta-resorts.com.au*
Dorm bed *$24-26*
Credit cards *Amex, Diners, MC, Visa*
Reception open *7.30am-7.30pm daily*

Maintenance & cleanliness	★★★★½
Facilities	★
Atmosphere & character	★★
Security	★★
Overall rating	★★★

Sights

Cape Leeuwin Lighthouse

This lighthouse was built in 1896 and marks Australia's most southwestern point. The view from the top of the lighthouse lets you see Indian and Southern Oceans meet.

Leeuwin Road, Cape Leeuwin, Augusta
Admission *$5;* ***lighthouse tour*** *$12*
Open *9am-4pm daily*

Nannup

This small town in the Blackwood River Valley between Busselton and Pemberton is a quiet and charming place with craft shops and a couple of good cafés. The town has about 600 residents and timber milling and agriculture are the main industries, but it comes to life during the annual Nannup Music Festival held annually over the Labour Day long weekend in March.

Practical Information

Nannup Visitor Information Centre

4 Brockman Street, Nannup
☎ *(08) 9756 1211*
Website *www.nannupwa.com.au*

Coming & Going

Transwa (☎ *1300 662 205;* ***website*** *www.transwa.wa.gov.au)* coaches stop at the visitors information centre on Brockman Street.

Accommodation

Black Cockatoo

This dreamy hostel is absolutely fantastic. An artist has spent hundreds

of hours decorating the house with sculptures, paintings and artsy details that make a stay at the Black Cockatoo a must if you're travelling in this part of the country. The lovely garden is a forest of flowers, plants, herbs, vegetables and fruit trees that are home to birds and frogs. The relaxed and amazingly decorated common area is kept warm with a log fire and it's an excellent place for good conversation as there's no television. The range of facilities isn't fantastic, but there's a laundry and a small kitchen available, as well as board games and a good collection of books. The house is clean and tidy, the dorm beds are cosy and comfortable and there's a marvellously cute caravan that works as a double room. A gorgeous honeymoon suite/cabin is also available.
27 Grange Road, Nannup
☎ *(08) 9756 1035*
Website *www.blackcockatoo.nannup.net*
Dorm bed *$25;* ***double room*** *$50-65*
Credit cards *MC, Visa*
Reception open *8am-9pm daily*

Maintenance & cleanliness	★★★½
Facilities	★
Atmosphere & character	★★★★★
Security	-
Overall rating	★★★

Manjimup

This small town north of Pemberton is a centre for the region's timber industry. Fruit orchards are another industry attracting backpackers who come here to pick apples.

Manjimup's attractions include the Diamond Tree fire lookout; the Four Aces, four gigantic 400-year old trees; and a timber museum. In December the town boasts a cherry festival, which features a cherry spitting contest. The Saturday of this festival is officially known as Cherry Day.

Practical Information

Manjimup Visitor Information Centre

Manjin Park, Giblett Street, Manjimup
☎ *(08) 9771 1831*
Website *www.manjimupwa.com*
Open *9am-5pm daily*

Coming & Going

Transwa *(☎ 1300 662 205;* ***website*** *www.transwa.wa.gov.au)* coaches stop at the corner of Edwards and Rose Streets.

Accommodation

Manjimup Lodge & Backpackers

This is a very clean and well maintained hostel in a modern building. The dormitories have good beds and comfy mattresses, bathrooms and showers are fresh and the kitchen has all the cooking gear you need. The main common area has couches and a big screen telly, and there's darts, a pool table and table tennis. The Lodge also has internet access and laundry and overall it's a good place to stay.
59 Rose Street, Manjimup
☎ *(08) 9771 8077*
Website *www.manjibackpackers.com.au*
Dorm bed *$24.50-28 per night, $112-168 per week;* ***double room*** *$55-65 per night, $298.90-390.60 per week*
Reception open *Mon-Fri 8.30am-5pm, Sat-Sun 9.30am-4pm*

Maintenance & cleanliness	★★★★
Facilities	★★
Atmosphere & character	★★★½
Security	★★
Overall rating	★★★

Sights

Diamond Tree Fire Lookout

The Diamond Tree is a giant tree with a wooden viewing platform 52m above the ground and it was used as a fire lookout between the 1940s and the 1970s. The tree is still occasionally used by officials from the Department of Environment & Conservation, but it is also open to visitors who want to climb up for a look.
South West Highway, Manjimup
☎ *(08) 9771 1831*
Admission *free*

Manjimup Timber & Heritage Park

This museum has displays about the history of the timber industry in southwest WA. Exhibits include historical buildings and an original steam sawmill engine.

Corner Edward & Rose Streets, Manjimup
☎ *(08) 9771 1831*
Admission *free*
Open *summer 8.30am-5.30pm daily; winter 9am-5pm daily*

Pemberton & Gloucester National Park

This small timber town in the heart of tall timber country makes an excellent base for exploring the surrounding area. It is close to both the Beedelup and Warren National Parks, which have some rewarding hiking trails.

Pemberton is just a small village of 800 people and naturally the town centre isn't exactly a wonderland of things to do. Pemberton's attractions are out of town and it really is essential to have your own car. Gloucester National Park is a big attraction to travellers in the area, and the park is famous for its gigantic karri-tree – The Gloucester Tree. The entrance fee to the Gloucester National Park is $10.

Practical Information

Pemberton Visitor Information Centre

Brockman Street, Pemberton
☎ *(08) 9776 1133*
Website *www.pembertontourist.com.au*
Open *9am-5pm daily*

Department of Conservation & Land Management (CALM)

Kennedy Street, Pemberton
☎ *(08) 9776 1207*
Website *www.calm.wa.gov.au*
Open *Mon-Fri 8am-5pm*

Coming & Going

Transwa (☎ *1300 662 205;* ***website*** *www.transwa.wa.gov.au)* coaches stop on Brockman Street.

Accommodation

Pemberton Backpackers YHA

Pemberton Backpackers exists mainly for workers, but there are also dorms and doubles available for travellers passing through. The hostel is in an old building dating from the 1920s and it is relatively clean, although the rooms are drearily furnished and quite charmless. The house has a poorly equipped kitchen, a TV room with a tiny television, good laundry facilities and internet access (including Wi-Fi). The dorms are clean and well-maintained, but the beds are hit or miss as some have good inner-spring mattresses and others are awful plastic coated ones. The atmosphere isn't too good, workers and travellers have their separate common rooms and the mood can be a bit too silent.

7 Brockman Street, Pemberton
☎ *(08) 9776 1105*
Website *www.yha.com.au*
Dorm bed *$26.50 ($24 HI/YHA);* ***double/twin room*** *$65.50 ($59 HI/YHA)*
Credit cards *MC, Visa*
Reception open *8am-11am & 1.30pm-8.30pm daily*
[car] [TV] K L

Maintenance & cleanliness	★★★
Facilities	★
Atmosphere & character	★★
Security	★
Overall rating	★★

Sights

Gloucester Tree

This is the biggest attraction in Pemberton. The staircase built around the tree allows you to climb 61m above the forest. The view is great and it is a fantastic experience.

Burma Road, Pemberton

Dave Evans Bicentennial Tree

At more than 70m this tree is even taller than the Gloucester Tree. It has a platform halfway up for those that aren't adventurous enough to climb all the way.

Warren National Park, 10km south of Pemberton

Walpole & Walpole-Nornalup National Park

This is another popular destination on the tall trees route. Walpole is on the south coast on the way between Pemberton and Denmark, with the

Walpole-Nornalup National Park located 14km out of town.

The park is famous for its tree top walk where you can walk 40m above the forest floor.

Practical Information

Walpole-Nornalup Visitors Centre

South Coast Highway, Walpole
☎ *(08) 9840 1111*
Website *www.walpole.com.au*
Open *Mon-Fri 9am-5pm, Sat-Sun 9am-4pm*

Coming & Going

Transwa (☎ *1300 662 205;* ***website*** *www.transwa.wa.gov.au)* coaches stop at the information bay on the South Coast Highway.

Accommodation

Walpole Lodge

Accommodation here is good value as the house is clean, well-maintained and comfortable. The common room has a great relaxed ambience, the bedrooms are sparkling clean with made-up beds and the bathrooms are very nice. Facilities include a laundry, a good kitchen, internet access, a pool table and a collection of books and board games. There's a big backyard with a barbecue.

Pier Street, Walpole
☎ *(08) 9840 1244*
Website *www.walpolelodge.com.au*
Dorm bed *$22;* ***single room*** *$38;* ***double/twin room*** *$55*
Credit cards *MC, Visa*
Reception open *8am-11.30am & 4pm-8pm daily*

Maintenance & cleanliness	★★★★
Facilities	★★
Atmosphere & character	★★★★
Security	★
Overall rating	★★★

Sights

Valley of the Giants Tree Top Walk

The Tree Top Walk offers a unique perspective where you can look 40m down from up among the trees. This is the main reason to visit the park.

Walpole-Nornalup National Park
☎ *(08) 9840 8263*
Website *www.naturebase.net/content/view/355/1045/*
Admission *$8*
Open *9am-5pm daily (last entry 4.15pm)*

South Coast

The South Coast of Western Australia is home to Albany, the state's oldest city, the seaside city of Esperance and a beautifully untouched coastline.

If you're driving across the country when you get to Norseman, you have the choice of heading to Perth via Kalgoorlie or south via Esperance, Albany and the southwest. Take the southern route - sure you'll miss out on a unique outback mining town, but you'll gain by experiencing the wild southern coast before heading up to Perth through the forested southwest corner of Western Australia.

Albany

Established in 1826, two years before Perth, Albany was the first city in Western Australia to be settled by Europeans. The city has some beautiful old buildings dating from colonial times and has a spectacular location within close range of dense forests and stunning beaches. Once a major centre for the whaling industry, whale watching is now one of Albany's big attractions.

Practical Information

Albany Visitors Information Centre

Old Railway Station, Proudlove Parade, Albany
☎ *(08) 9841 1088*
Website *www.albanytourist.com.au*
Open *9am-5pm daily*

Coming & Going

If you're not driving, bus is the best way to get into town even though the services are fairly infrequent. Transwa (☎ *1300 662 205;* ***website*** *www.transwa.wa.gov.au)* coaches stop at the train station and visitor information centre on Proudlove Parade and run from here to Esperance and Perth via Bunbury, Margaret River and other destinations in the southwest.

Local Transport
Loves Bus Service runs local buses around town. There are a couple of handy routes although Albany is small enough to walk around.

Accommodation
Albany Backpackers
Albany Backpackers has lots of character with murals covering many of the walls. It is a clean and well maintained hostel with good facilities that include the usual kitchen, laundry, internet access, pool table and barbecue plus a cinema-style TV lounge. Like most hostels there is free tea and coffee although here they go a step further and also serve homemade cakes to their guests every day at 6.30pm.

Corner Stirling Terrace & Spencer Street, Albany
☎ *(08) 9842 5255*
***Website** www.albanybackpackers.com.au*
***Dorm bed** $25-26 ($23-24 HI/YHA, VIP); **double/twin room** $60 ($56 HI/YHA, VIP)*
***Credit cards** MC, Visa*
***Reception open** 8am-1pm & 4pm-8pm daily*

TV K L

Maintenance & cleanliness	★★★★
Facilities	★★½
Atmosphere & character	★★★★
Security	★
Overall rating	★★★½

Bayview YHA
Bayview Backpackers YHA is a clean and well maintained youth hostel near the centre of Albany with facilities that include the usual kitchen, TV lounge, internet access, laundry and barbecue.

49 Duke Street, Albany
☎ *(08) 9842 3388*
***Website** www.yha.com.au*
***Dorm bed** $24.50 ($22 HI/YHA); **single room** $51 ($46 HI/YHA); **double/twin room** $58 ($52 HI/YHA)*
***Credit cards** Diners, JCB, MC, Visa*
***Reception open** 8am-11am & 2.30pm-9pm daily*

Car TV K L

Maintenance & cleanliness	★★★½
Facilities	★★
Atmosphere & character	★★★½
Security	★
Overall rating	★★★

Sights
Whaleworld
Albany was home to Australia's last whaling station, which ceased business as recently as 1978. It has now been turned into the country's largest whaling museum. There are two guided tours a day that show you things that aren't on display in the museum.

Frenchmans Bay Road, Albany
☎ *(08) 9844 4021*
***Website** www.whaleworld.org*
***Admission** $20*
***Open** 9am-5pm daily*

Whale Watching
Albany Whale Tours (☎ *0408 451 068; **website** www.albanywhaletours.com.au*) and **Silver Star Cruises** (☎ *0428 429 876; **website** www.whales.com.au*) operate whale watching cruises between (Jun-Oct). Two-hour cruises cost $40-65.

Denmark
Demark is a small town with little to offer other than a good hostel and a bakery with tasty pastries, but there are a few interesting attractions not too far away. The area around Denmark also has a few wineries, whales can be seen as they make their way along the south coast (Jul-Oct), and Denmark's beaches are safe for swimming.

Practical Information
Denmark Information Centre
Corner Bent & Strickland Streets, Denmark
☎ *(08) 9848 2055*
***Website** www.denmarkvisitorcentre.com.au*
***Open** 9am-5pm daily*

Coming & Going
Transwa (☎ *1300 662 205; **website** www.transwa.wa.gov.au*) coaches stop on Strickland Street.

Western Australia

Accommodation

Blue Wren Backpackers

This small hostel has only 20 beds, which ensures a friendly and intimate atmosphere and it is clean and well maintained. The kitchen doesn't have the fanciest equipment, but it's spotless and an easy place to cook. The hostel also has the usual laundry, internet access and barbecue plus a comfortable TV lounge.

17 Price Street, Denmark
☎ *(08) 9848 3300*
Website *www.denmarkbluewren.com.au*
Dorm bed *$23.50 ($21 HI/YHA);* ***double/twin room*** *$58 ($52 HI/YHA)*
Reception open *8am-10am & 4pm-8pm daily*

Maintenance & cleanliness	★★★★½
Facilities	★★
Atmosphere & character	★★★★
Security	★
Overall rating	★★★½

Denmark Budget Accommodation

This hostel has a prime location in the town centre and offers comfortable accommodation in clean rooms. All the rooms have en suite facilities and TVs, which keeps people in their rooms and detracts from the atmosphere.

31 South Coast Highway, Denmark
☎ *(08) 9848 1700*
Website *www.denmarkaccommodation.com.au*
Dorm bed *$25-28;* ***double/twin room*** *$75-80*
Credit cards *MC, Visa*
Reception open *9am-11.30am & 2pm-7pm daily*

Maintenance & cleanliness	★★★★
Facilities	★½
Atmosphere & character	★
Security	★★
Overall rating	★★½

Esperance

Esperance is remote. It is more than 700km from Perth, 500km from Albany and a four-hour drive from Kalgoorlie. Given its location it is surprising that Esperance would be such a popular tourist destination but then maybe it's the beautiful beaches and top diving sites and the fact that in Australia's largest state, a 700km drive isn't considered all that long.

Practical Information

Esperance Visitor Information Centre

Corner Dempster & Kemp Streets, Esperance
☎ *(08) 9071 2330*
Website *www.visitesperance.com*
Open *Mon-Sat 9am-5pm, Sun 10am-4.30pm*

Coming & Going

Although the coach service is infrequent it is the best way to get in and out of Esperance. Transwa *(☎ 1300 662 205;* ***website*** *www.transwa.wa.gov.au)* run coaches to Albany, Kalgoorlie and Perth and stop on Dempster Street.

Accommodation

Blue Waters Lodge YHA

The staff at this YHA hostel are friendly and helpful, the house is clean and there are good bunk beds with real inner-spring mattresses. Facilities include a kitchen, a common room with a television, a laundry, barbecue, internet access and a pool table. The floor in the aging building is very squeaky and the maintenance could be better, but overall it is OK for a night or two.

299 Goldfields Road, Esperance
☎ *(08) 9071 1040*
Website *www.yha.com.au*
Dorm bed *$25 ($22 HI/YHA);* ***single room*** *$38 ($34 HI/YHA);* ***double/twin room*** *$60 ($54 HI/YHA)*
Credit cards *MC, Visa*
Reception open *8am-10am & 4pm-9pm daily*

Maintenance & cleanliness	★★★
Facilities	★★½
Atmosphere & character	★★½
Security	★
Overall rating	★★½

Esperance Backpackers

Esperance Backpackers is a small clean hostel with a nice TV lounge and a

fireplace and internet access. There's also a kitchen and a barbecue area out the back. This hostel organises fishing trips.
14 Emily Street, Esperance
☎ *(08) 9071 4724*
***Dorm bed** $25 ($23.75 VIP); **double/twin room** $60 ($57 VIP)*
***Credit cards** MC, Visa*
***Reception open** 7.30am-11am & 4pm-9pm daily*

Maintenance & cleanliness	★★★½
Facilities	★½
Atmosphere & character	★★★
Security	★½
Overall rating	★★½

Esperance Guest House
This hostel is your best option in Esperance. It's very clean and well maintained and the dormitories have single beds in them, there are no bunks. Facilities include a poorly equipped kitchen, pool table, table tennis, a TV room, laundry and a fairly big book-swap. Guests have free use of bicycles. The dorms are usually gender-segregated and a fairly strict "be quiet at night" policy detracts from the atmosphere, although the hostel feels friendly.
23 Daphne Street, Esperance
☎ *(08) 9071 3396*
***Website** www.esperanceguesthouse.com.au*
***Dorm bed** $25; **single room** $40; **double room** $50; prices include breakfast*
***Credit cards** MC, Visa*
***Reception open** 8am-10pm daily*

Maintenance & cleanliness	★★★★½
Facilities	★★
Atmosphere & character	★★
Security	★
Overall rating	★★★

Goldfields
Many travellers pass through the Western Australian Goldfields while travelling between Perth and Adelaide. Kalgoorlie is the main city in the region and is worth a visit, although most people pass through the area en route to somewhere more interesting.

Norseman
All travellers driving across the Nullarbor will pass through this small town, about halfway between Esperance and Kalgoorlie. Norseman was founded after gold was discovered here at the end of the 18th century, but nowadays its just a sleepy town at the end of the long drive from South Australia. Norseman has an ATM, a grocery store and a telecentre with internet access.

Practical Information
Norseman Tourist Centre
Roberts Street, Norseman
☎ *(08) 9039 1071*
***Website** www.norseman.info*
***Open** 9am-5pm daily*

Coming & Going
Transwa (☎ *1300 662 205; **website** www.transwa.wa.gov.au)* coaches go to Esperance and Kalgoorlie and stop at the roadhouse at the corner of Coolgardie-Esperance Road.

Accommodation
Lodge 101
This small cute hostel feels like staying at a grandmother's house. It's clean and cosy and the old fashioned furnishings give the place a kitschy character. The only common room besides the kitchen is equipped with a telly, the walls decorated by flowers and family pictures. The dorm beds are good and there's a nice outdoor area with a barbecue and another television. The couple that runs the place also lives on the premises; they're sweet and friendly and they will ensure you have a good stay.
101 Prinsep Street, Norseman
☎ *(08) 9039 1541*
***Dorm bed** $22-25; **single room** $45; **twin room** $65*
***Reception open** 8am-10pm daily*

Maintenance & cleanliness	★★★½
Facilities	★★
Atmosphere & character	★★★½
Security	★
Overall rating	★★★

Kalgoorlie

The gold mining town of Kalgoorlie once drew fortune seekers from around the globe to the Golden Mile, the world's richest square mile of gold-bearing earth. Kalgoorlie-Boulder is still a thriving mining town and the first sizable town you come to if you're driving across the Nullarbor Plain.

Kal is an interesting place if you haven't been to an outback mining town before and there are a few grand old buildings along Hannan Street. There are also some good pubs, although there are also some that are worth avoiding.

Despite the rough and ready image there is plenty to see in Kalgoorlie and it is well worth stopping here, particularly if you're just spent the last few days driving from Adelaide. The city's attractions are mostly related to the mining industry and include Hannans North Historic Mining Reserve and the impressive super pit, but Kalgoorlie doesn't have as much to offer as some other outback mining towns such as Broken Hill.

Practical Information

Kalgoorlie Visitor Information Centre

316 Hannan Street, Kalgoorlie
☎ (08) 9091 6671
***Open** 9am-5pm daily*

Coming & Going

Kalgoorlie has plenty of transport options with frequent connections to both Adelaide and Perth.

AIR

Skywest *(☎ 1300 660 088; **website** www.skywest.com.au)* have direct flights from Kalgoorlie to Melbourne and Perth and Qantas *(☎ 13 13 13; **website** www.qantas.com.au)* fly to Perth. The airport is about a five-minute drive from the centre of town and either hostel should be able to pick you up if you have made a reservation.

BUS

Transwa *(☎ 1300 662 205; **website** www.transwa.wa.gov.au)* coaches travel between Kalgoorlie and Esperance and stop at the train station on Forrest Street.

TRAIN

Kalgoorlie is well served by rail. The *Indian Pacific* is one of Australia's greatest rail journeys running between Perth and Sydney with a stop in Kalgoorlie. If you don't have a Great Southern Rail pass, Transwa's daily *Prospector* service to Perth is a cheaper alternative at $76.85 one-way. The train station is on Forrest Street opposite the intersection with Wilson Street.

Local Transport

There is a local bus service that runs between Boulder and Kalgoorlie; this is generally the best way to get around if you don't have access to a car.

Accommodation

Both Kalgoorlie's hostels are situated in the heart of the red light district and are a short walk to supermarkets and the town centre.

Golddust Backpackers Hostel

Golddust is the best hostel in Kalgoorlie, but it's a bit pricey for those without Hostelling International or YHA membership. It is clean and relatively well maintained, although the beds aren't the best. Facilities include two TV rooms, a good kitchen, internet access, a pool table, laundry, a barbecue and a swimming pool. Guests have free use of bicycles.

192 Hay Street, Kalgoorlie
☎ (08) 9091 3737
***Website** www.yha.com.au*
***Dorm bed** $28 ($24 HI/YHA); **single room** $33.50 ($30 HI/YHA); **double/twin room** $52 ($45 HI/YHA)*
***Credit cards** MC, Visa*
***Reception open** Mon-Fri 8am-8pm, Sat-Sun 9am-8pm*

Maintenance & cleanliness	★★★½
Facilities	★★½
Atmosphere & character	★★★
Security	★½
Overall rating	★★★

Kalgoorlie Backpackers

This hostel is not as clean as the other one in town, but it's not dirty either, and the facilities are similar; includ-

ing a kitchen, TV, laundry, pool table, internet access and a swimming pool. Not many travellers stay here as it is often full of mine workers who stay long term, which means that many backpackers feel that it doesn't really have a welcoming atmosphere. However it is OK if you just want a bed for the night.
166 Hay Street, Kalgoorlie
(08) 9091 1482
***Website** www.kalgoorliebackpackers.info*
***Dorm bed** $26*
***Credit cards** MC, Visa*
***Reception open** 7am-10pm daily*

Maintenance & cleanliness	★★★
Facilities	★★
Atmosphere & character	★★
Security	★
Overall rating	★★½

Sights

Mining Hall of Fame

This excellent museum focuses on all aspects of mining encompassing geology, the history of mining and its impact on Kalgoorlie, and modern-day mining techniques. The Mining Hall of Fame sits on an original mine that commenced in 1893 when miners used only a pick and shovel. Gold panning and gold pouring demonstrations take place throughout the day as do underground tours of the mine.
Goldfields Highway, Kalgoorlie
(08) 9091 4074
***Website** www.mininghall.com*
***Tour** $30 (includes surface & underground tours)*
***Open** 9am-4.30pm; gold panning 9.30am, 11.30am, 4pm; gold pouring demonstrations 11.30am, 1.15pm, 3.30pm; underground tours 10am, 12.15pm, 2.30p*

Museum of the Goldfields

This museum provides a good introduction to the city's history and life during the height of the gold rush.
17 Hannan Street, Kalgoorlie
(08) 9021 8533
***Website** www.museum.wa.gov.au*
***Admission** free*
***Open** 10am-4.30pm daily*

Super Pit

The biggest hole in the Southern Hemisphere is worth a look. The massive Super Pit open cut mine can be seen from the lookout in Outram Street in Fimiston near Boulder or from the Golden Mile Loopline.
***Super Pit Lookout** Outram Street, Fimiston; **Golden Mile Loopline** Corner Burt & Hamilton Streets, Boulder*
***Admission** free for the lookout, $12 for a ride on the Golden Mile Loopline*

Turquoise Coast

The Turquoise Coast is a relatively short distance north of Perth. This region includes Nambung National Park, better known for the Pinnacles Desert, as well as the coastal town of Lancelin.

Lancelin

Lancelin is a small town, only 1½ hours north of Perth, which has a great beach and is a brilliant windsurfing spot. Lancelin's sand dunes are another big attraction with sandboarding and 4WD tours.

Accommodation

Lancelin Lodge

This purpose-built hostel is very popular among surfers staying here long-term and it's a great place for everyone else as well. Lancelin Lodge's common areas are excellent and include a spacious fully-equipped kitchen and TV lounge and in the backyard you'll find a barbecue, hammocks and a swimming pool. Guests have free use of bicycles, body boards and snorkelling gear. It is a very clean hostel and the atmosphere is relaxed and friendly.
10 Hopkins Street, Lancelin
(08) 9665 2020
***Website** www.lancelinlodge.com.au*
***Dorm bed** $25 ($22 HI/YHA); **double room** $65 ($60 HI/YHA)*
***Credit cards** MC, Visa*
***Reception open** 8.30am-1pm & 3pm-8.30pm daily*

Maintenance & cleanliness	★★★★
Facilities	★★★½
Atmosphere & character	★★★½
Security	★
Overall rating	★★★½

Activities
Sandboarding & Sand Dune Tours

Desert Storm Adventures (☎ *(08) 9655 2550; **website** www.desertstorm.com.au)* operate tours of the sand dunes in big 4WD buses that include sandboarding on the dunes. The tours cost $45 ($40.50 HI/YHA; $40 students).

Cervantes & Nambung National Park

Nambung National Park is best known for the spectacular Pinnacles Desert and its proximity to Perth makes it a very popular day-trip. The main features of the Pinnacles Desert are the limestone columns, some of which stand up to four metres tall.

If you have a car you can take the scenic drive that takes you past the more impressive areas. If you don't have access to a car, a number of companies run day-trips here from Perth and **Turquoise Coast Enviro Tours** (☎ *(08) 9652 7047; **website** www.thepinnacles.com.au)* runs trips from Cervantes, which is the closest town to the national park. It is here that you'll find accommodation, food and other services.

Practical Information
Pinnacles Visitor Centre

Cadiz Street, Cervantes
☎ *(08) 9652 7700*

Coming & Going

Greyhound (☎ *1300 473 946; **website** www.greyhound.com.au)* coaches stop at the BP roadhouse en route between Broome and Perth.

Accommodation
Pinnacles Beach Backpackers

This brilliant purpose-built hostel has a high standard of facilities, which include a cosy TV lounge, a good kitchen, a barbecue area and a nice restaurant. It is a clean and well maintained hostel and the overall atmosphere is great with photos of crop circles on the walls and sculpted orange trees in the garden.

91 Seville Street, Cervantes
☎ *(08) 9652 7377 or 1800 245 232*
***Website** www.cervanteslodge.com.au*
***Dorm bed** $28; **double room** $80*
***Credit cards** MC, Visa*
***Reception open** 7.30am-8pm daily*

Maintenance & cleanliness	★★★★½
Facilities	★★★
Atmosphere & character	★★★★½
Security	★★½
Overall rating	★★★★

Batavia Coast

The Batavia Coast is where most travellers get to after the first day of driving north from Perth. The main towns here are Geraldton and Kalbarri, although the Hutt River Province is also definitely worth a visit.

Geraldton

Western Australia's third largest city is a busy cray fishing and mining town that doesn't go out of its way to appeal to tourists.

It is a pleasant place with enough attractions to keep you occupied for a day and it is a good spot to stay the night if you're driving up the coast. Geraldton is a departure point for trips to the Houtman Abrolhos Islands and it is also a popular windsurfing destination with internationally renowned windsurfing spots including Coronation Beach, or "Coro".

Many European maritime explorers encountered the nearby Houtman Abrolhos Islands during the 17th and 18th century, but the town of Geraldton wasn't established until 1850.

Practical Information
Geraldton Visitor Information Centre

Corner Bayly Street & Chapman Road, Geraldton
☎ *(08) 9921 3999*

Website *www.geraldtontourist.com.au*
Open *Mon-Fri 8.30am-5pm, Sat 9am-4.30pm, Sun 9.30am-4.30pm*

Coming & Going

Greyhound (☎ *1300 473 946;* ***website*** *www.greyhound.com.au)* stops in Geraldton en route betweeen Perth and Broome and Transwa (☎ *1300 662 205;* ***website*** *www.transwa.wa.gov.au)* coaches go to Kalbarri and Perth. Coaches terminate at the tourist information centre in front of Batavia Backpackers.

Local Transport

Although central Geraldton is small enough to walk around, there is a good network of local bus routes that are a cheap and easy way to get around town.

Route 800, the City Clipper, is a circular route that takes in most of the city centre. Route 800 is a free service, as are any buses that run between Northgate Shopping Centre and Anzac Terrace.

Accommodation

Batavia Backpackers

This hostel is easy to find as it's the large striking building that also houses the tourist information centre. Once you get inside the beauty fades as it could be both cleaner and better maintained. The larger dorms are big with twenty beds and the common areas are shabby. Facilities are rather minimal and are limited to a basic kitchen, laundry, internet access and a TV. The atmosphere isn't very good either – Batavia feels gloomy and empty.

Corner Chapman Road & Bayly Street, Geraldton
☎ *(08) 9964 3001*
Dorm bed *$25;* ***double room*** *$60*
Credit cards *MC, Visa*
Reception open *Mon-Sat 8am-noon & 3pm-8pm, Sun 8am-9.15pm & noon-1pm & 3pm-5.30pm & 7.30pm-8.30pm*

Maintenance & cleanliness	★★★½
Facilities	★★½
Atmosphere & character	★★★½
Security	★★½
Overall rating	★★

Foreshore Backpackers

This place is nothing special, but it's still the best of Geraldton's poor selection of hostels. It is a rambling old house near the beach with limited facilities that include a kitchen and kitschy common areas with a TV, piano, pool table, table tennis and board games. The staff are friendly and the atmosphere isn't too bad even though it feels a bit empty.

172 Marine Terrace, Geraldton
☎ *(08) 9921 3275*
Website *http://foreshorebackpackers.bigpondhosting.com*
Dorm bed *$24;* ***single room*** *$35;* ***double/twin room*** *$55*
Credit cards *MC, Visa*
Reception open *8am-noon & 4pm-8pm daily*

Maintenance & cleanliness	★★★½
Facilities	★★½
Atmosphere & character	★★★½
Security	★★½
Overall rating	★★

Freemasons' Hotel

The bar on the ground floor seems to be the priority at Freemasons Hotel, as it certainly draws more people than the unattractive accommodation upstairs. Dorms and bathrooms are fairly clean, but beside a small dreary TV lounge there are no facilities and the atmosphere is lifeless. For the most part, Freemasons Hotel is not a good place for a backpacker; the only strong point is the central location.

79 Marine Terrace, Geraldton
☎ *(08) 9964 3457*
Website *www.freemasonshotel.com.au*
Dorm bed *$30;* ***double/twin room*** *$80*
Credit cards *Amex, Diners, MC, Visa*
Reception open *11am-8pm daily*

Maintenance & cleanliness	★★★
Facilities	★
Atmosphere & character	★
Security	★
Overall rating	★★

Sights

Museum of Western Australia

The Geraldton branch of the Museum of Western Australia has exhibits

about local history and wildlife with an excellent shipwreck gallery and a cinema that shows an interesting film about the shipwreck and mutiny of the Batavia.
Marine Terrace, Geraldton
☎ *(08) 9921 5080*
***Admission** free*
***Open** 10am-4pm daily*

St Francis Xavier Cathedral

Although nothing special by European standards, this cathedral is particularly impressive for a small Australian town. It was designed by Monsignor Hawes and it is regarded as one of the best historic churches in the country.
Corner Cathedral Avenue & Maitland Street, Geraldton
☎ *(08) 9937 1104*
***Admission** free*
***Tours** Mon 10am, Fri 2pm*

Sydney Memorial

Located on Mount Scott near the city centre, the *HMAS Sydney* Memorial features a dome of 645 silver gulls, each one representing one of the crew that lost their lives when the navy ship sank in 1941.

Hutt River Province

The Hutt River Province *(**website** www.hutt-river-province.com)* bills itself as the second-largest country on the Australian continent. The 7487ha principality is about the same size as Hong Kong and was formed when farmer Leonard Casley seceded from Australia in 1970 after the Western Australian government imposed quotas on wheat production in 1969. Although Queen Elizabeth II has accepted sovereignty, there are Hutt River Province diplomatic representatives in over 30 countries and Hutt River Province passports have been used to travel throughout the world, the principality has never been recognised by Australia as an independent state.

A visit to the Hutt River Province is a unique experience. You are often greeted by Prince Leonard or Princess Shirley, you get a stamp in your passport and the opportunity to buy Hutt River Province stamps (using Hutt River Province currency) and you can even get Hutt River Province citizenship, which comes with a Hutt River passport.

Entry Requirements

Visitors to the Hutt River Province don't need a visa but you can get your passport stamped at the border.

Accommodation

The closest hostel to the Hutt River Province is in Kalbarri, but you can camp for $10 per night.

Kalbarri & Kalbarri National Park

Two Dutch sailors involved in the *Batavia* mutiny on the nearby Houtman Abrolhos Islands were marooned near Kalbarri, making them Australia's earliest European residents. Kalbarri doesn't make a big deal of its history and instead is just a pleasant beach town that is a handy base for exploring nearby Kalbarri National Park.

The national park features impressive gorges and some good hiking trails.

The Rainbow Jungle is another destination that attracts a lot of travellers, and a walk through this parrot breeding centre (just a few kilometres outside the town) can be a lot of fun. Hundreds of animated birds fly around, busy with their daily habits as they sing songs and show off their colours.

During spring, Kalbarri is a popular spot for whale watching and dolphin spotting, and there are also good possibilities for recreational fishing from the beaches at Wittecara Creek and Blue Holes.

Practical Information

Kalbarri Tourist Bureau

Grey Street, Kalbarri
☎ *(08) 9937 1104 or 1800 639 468*
***Website** www.kalbarriwa.info*
***Open** 9am-5pm daily*

Department of Conservation & Land Management (CALM)

Ajana Kalbarri Road, Kalbarri
☎ *(08) 9937 1140*

Website *www.calm.wa.gov.au*
Open *Mon-Fri 8am-5pm*

Coming & Going

Transwa (☎ *1300 662 205;* ***website*** *www.transwa.wa.gov.au)* coaches go to Perth via Geraldton. Coaches depart from the stop on Grey Street.

Accommodation

Kalbarri Backpackers

Kalbarri Backpackers is a relatively clean and well maintained hostel with good facilities that include the usual kitchen, laundry and TV lounge plus a barbecue area and swimming pool. Most dorms have en suite bathrooms. Guests can rent bicycles and snorkelling gear. With around 100 beds it is a relatively large hostel for a small town and it feels a bit impersonal.

52 Mortimer Street, Kalbarri
☎ *(08) 9937 1430*
Website *www.yha.com.au*
Dorm bed *$25 ($23 HI/YHA);* ***double/twin room*** *$65 ($60 HI/YHA)*
Credit cards *MC, Visa*
Reception open *8.30am-1.30pm & 3pm-8pm daily*

Maintenance & cleanliness	★★★½
Facilities	★★½
Atmosphere & character	★★½
Security	★
Overall rating	★★★

Hiking

The park features 80km of gorges and there are some very good hiking trails ranging from the easy **Z Bend** hike *(500m)* that goes to a rock lookout with views to the Murchison River. Longer walks include the **Coastal Trail** *(8km, 3-5 hours)* that takes in coastal views from the cliff tops between Eagle Gorge and Natural Bridge.

Visitors should be very cautious while hiking in the gorge areas and park rangers recommend that you undertake the longer walks in groups of at least five.

Gascoyne Coast

The Gascoyne Coast includes Monkey Mia at Shark Bay, which is famous for its dolphins, and Coral Bay and Exmouth with their easy access to excellent diving and snorkelling on the Ningaloo Reef.

Although remote, a lot of tourists head this way, but for good reason; the beautiful beaches and the unique attractions of the Gascoyne Coast make this a place you shouldn't miss, if you're into diving, surfing or just sunny days at the beach. The marine life is another big plus, and chances are you'll see more than dolphins and dead kangaroos on this stretch of the coast.

Shark Bay & Monkey Mia

Shark Bay is actually a couple of bays encompassed by two narrow peninsulas. The UNESCO World Heritage Site is home to 26 threatened Australian mammal species, almost up to 150 different reptiles and over 230 species of birds. There are many sharks and rays in the water, and the bay is famed for its dolphins that pay daily visits to Monkey Mia.

The main town in the region is Denham, on the western side of the Peron Peninsula. Denham is the main centre for travellers visiting Monkey Mia, 25km away on the other side of the peninsula. Denham is where you'll find most accommodation as well as a supermarket, bakery and a couple of restaurants.

Monkey Mia's main attraction is the dolphins that visit the beach every morning (8am-10am). What makes Monkey Mia special is that the dolphins here are especially tame.

Shark Bay is also known for its dugongs. Around 10,000, or around 10% of the world's dugong population, are estimated to live in Shark Bay.

Facilities at Monkey Mia are fairly basic although it is possible to stay here as the Monkey Mia Dolphin Resort has excellent backpacker accommodation. There's also a small general store but it's expensive and you're better off bringing your food in from Denham.

Entry to Monkey Mia costs $6 per day or $9 per month (national park passes are not valid).

Practical Information

Shark Bay World Heritage Discovery Centre

71 Knight Terrace, Denham
☎ *(08) 9948 1590*
Website *www.sharkbayinterpretivecentre.com.au*
Open *9am-6pm daily*

Department of Conservation & Land Management (CALM)

67 Knight Terrace, Denham
☎ *(08) 9948 1208*
Website *www.calm.wa.gov.au*
Open *Mon-Fri 8am-5pm*

Coming & Going

Greyhound's *(☎ 1300 473 946;* ***website*** *www.greyhound.com.au)* Perth-Broome service stops at the Overlander Roadhouse 150km from Monkey Mia. A shuttle bus meets the bus at Overlander and goes to Denham and Monkey Mia.

Local Transport

There is a limited bus service between Denham and Monkey Mia that leaves Denham at 8am giving you time to play with the dolphins with a return service around midday. The youth hostel in Denham also runs a shuttle bus for their guests.

Accommodation

DENHAM

Bay Lodge YHA

There's a great atmosphere at Bay Lodge YHA and some guests find it hard to leave, overall this is one the better hostels on the Gascoyne Coast. Accommodation is in self-contained units with up to 12 people sharing a kitchen, bathroom and TV lounge. There is also a nice outdoor common area where you can laze about in a hammock by the swimming pool. The hostel operates a free shuttle bus to the dolphins at Monkey Mia.
113 Knight Terrace, Denham
☎ *(08) 9948 1278*
Website *www.yha.com.au*
Dorm bed *$25 ($23 HI/YHA);* ***double room*** *$55*
Credit cards *Amex, MC, Visa*
Reception open *7.30am-10pm daily*

Maintenance & cleanliness	★★★½
Facilities	★★★
Atmosphere & character	★★★
Security	★
Overall rating	★★★

MONKEY MIA

Monkey Mia Dolphin Resort

This resort offers clean and well maintained dormitories for low-budget travellers. The resort has very good facilities that include usual kitchen, laundry, TV and internet access plus a swimming pool, spa pool and a tennis court. There is also a bar that serves food at surprisingly decent prices. Its absolute beachfront location outshines most places in Western Australia and you can walk right up to see the dolphins. Overall this is a very nice place to stay although some travellers may find it too big and impersonal.
Monkey Mia Road, Monkey Mia
☎ *(08) 9948 1320 or 1800 653 611 (0871 711 9836 from the UK)*
Website *www.monkeymia.com.au*
Dorm bed *$25-29 ($22.50-26 HI/YHA);* ***double/twin room*** *$80 ($72 HI/YHA);* ***camping*** *$12 per person*
Credit cards *Amex, Diners, MC, Visa*
Reception open *8am-8pm daily*

Maintenance & cleanliness	★★★★½
Facilities	★★★★
Atmosphere & character	★★½
Security	★★
Overall rating	★★★★

Carnarvon

Carnarvon is a coastal town that is a busy regional centre serving the surrounding farming area and some backpackers find work here.

There isn't a lot to see or do here, but it's an OK stop for an hour or so if you're driving along the coast. The park by the seashore has picnic tables and it is a nice spot for lunch.

Practical Information

Carnarvon Visitors Information Centre

11 Robinson Street, Carnarvon
☎ *(08) 9941 1146*

Website *www.carnarvon.org.au*
Open *Mon-Fri 8.30am-5pm, Sat 8am-noon*

Coming & Going

Greyhound (☎ *1300 473 946;* ***website*** *www.greyhound.com.au)* coaches stop at the Civic Centre (11 Robinson Street, Carnarvon) en route from Perth to Exmouth and Broome.

Accommodation

Carnarvon Backpackers

Carnarvon Backpackers is located right in front of the sea. The old furnishings make this hostel feel a bit shabby, but it has a lot of character. The bathrooms are colourful and the dining areas are a good place to meet other travellers. Facilities here include table football, a TV lounge and trampoline. Bikes are available to rent.

97-99 Olivia Terrace, Carnarvon
☎ *(08) 9941 1095*
Dorm bed *$20 per night, $100 per week;* ***double/twin room*** *$50*
Reception open *9am-10am & 5pm-7pm daily*

Maintenance & cleanliness	★★★½
Facilities	★★
Atmosphere & character	★★★
Security	★
Overall rating	★★★½

Coral Bay

Just 1½ hours south of Exmouth, Coral Bay is a fantastic spot for snorkelling. The Ningaloo Reef at Coral Bay is very close to the shore and it is possible to swim out from the beach.

The small town is also a good spot to see whalesharks. These 12m-long fish are the world's largest. They arrive on the reef in April, but you must travel out past the reef with a licenced operator to snorkel with them.

Each year between October and February, around 200 reef sharks visit an area 1km from the main beach at Coral Bay.

As Coral Bay exists for tourism, food can be quite pricey. Some backpackers solve this problem by stocking up on groceries before they get here.

Coming & Going

Greyhound's *(☎ 1300 473 946;* ***website*** *www.greyhound.com.au)* Perth-Broome service stops at the Minilya Roadhouse, 100km from Coral Bay. A shuttle bus meets the coach at Minilya and goes to Coral Bay and Exmouth. The Coral Bay bus stop is at the Ningaloo Club hostel.

Accommodation

Ningaloo Club

Ningaloo Club at Coral Bay is an outstanding backpackers' hostel with all the amenities you would expect from one of Australia's better hostels. Facilities include a kitchen, barbecue, laundry, TV lounge, internet access and a swimming pool and there is a good bar that's open till midnight. It is just a few minutes' walk from the beach. As this is the only hostel in town, it's advisable to book ahead.

46 Robinson Street, Coral Bay
☎ *(08) 9948 5100*
Website *www.ningalooclub.com*
Dorm bed *$24-26;* ***double/twin room*** *$80-100; twin room $80*
Credit cards *MC, Visa*
Reception open *8am-11pm daily*

Maintenance & cleanliness	★★★★
Facilities	★★★½
Atmosphere & character	★★½
Security	★★★
Overall rating	★★★½

Activities

Swimming with Manta Rays

Manta rays live in the water off Coral Bay year round and Coral Bay Adventures *(☎ (08) 9942 5955;* ***website*** *www.coralbayadventures.com.au)* run half-day boat trips where you can snorkel with manta rays. These trips also give you the opportunity to see dolphins, dugongs and turtles. Trips cost $140.

Swimming with Whalesharks

Growing up to around 12m-long, whalesharks are the world's largest fish and late Mar to mid-Jun they visit the Ningaloo Reef near Coral Bay. **Coral Bay Adventures** *(☎ (08) 9942 5955;* ***website*** *www.coralbayadventures.com.*

au) run full-day snorkelling experiences where you can snorkel with whalesharks and these trips also give you the opportunity to see dolphins, dugongs and turtles. Trips cost $350.

Exmouth

Exmouth is the main destination on the west coast between Monkey Mia and Broome, even though it is just a small town of only 2000 residents. The main attraction here is the excellent diving afforded by easy access to the Ningaloo Reef. It is also a great place to see whales, turtles and whalesharks.

There are several places where you can do a dive course. Expect to pay around $250 for a four-day PADI course.

Practical Information

Exmouth Visitor Information Centre

Murat Road, Exmouth
☎ *(08) 9949 1176 or 1800 287 328*
Website *www.exmouthwa.com.au*
Open *Mon-Fri 9am-5pm, Sat-Sun 10am-4pm*

Department of Conservartion & Land Management (CALM)

Nimitz Street, Exmouth
☎ *(08) 9949 1676*
Website *www.calm.wa.gov.au*
Open *Mon-Fri 8am-5pm*

SHOWERS

There are showers in the tourist information centre on Murat Road.

Coming & Going

Greyhound's *(☎ 1300 473 946; **website** www.greyhound.com.au)* Perth-Broome service stops at the Minilya Roadhouse, 230km from Exmouth. A shuttle bus meets the coach at Minilya and goes to Coral Bay and Exmouth. The Exmouth bus stop is at the Visitor Information Centre on Murat Road.

Accommodation

Blue Reef Backpackers (Exmouth Cape Holiday Park)

This newly renovated resort offers spotless dormitories and bathrooms. Amenities include a big fully-equipped kitchen, a laundry and a nice refreshing swimming pool. In the peak season there is a small outdoor cinema that shows films three times a week. The only downside to this resort is that it's a resort – families, retired couples and backpackers all stay at Cape and this means that it doesn't really have the vibe of a proper backpackers' hostel. There's no party atmosphere, the outdoor movies are all PG-rated and kids are in the pool.

Corner Truscott Crescent & Murat Road, Exmouth
☎ *(08) 9949 1101 or 1800 621 101*
Website *www.aspenparks.com.au*
Dorm bed *$27 ($23.65 HI/YHA, VIP)*
Credit cards *Amex, Diners, MC, Visa*
Reception open *7am-6pm daily*

Maintenance & cleanliness	★★★★★
Facilities	★★★
Atmosphere & character	★★★
Security	★
Overall rating	★★★½

Excape Backpackers YHA (Potshot Resort)

The backpackers' accommodation at the Potshot Hotel complex is nicely air-conditioned with comfortable mattresses on the bunk beds. The hostel has clean bathrooms and a spacious kitchen but the common area in front of the kitchen is furnished with cheap plastic chairs and dominated by television. The bar (the Beer Garden) is the nicest part of the complex and is a good place to meet other travellers and there is also a small swimming pool, although the pool isn't big enough to cope with all the guests during peak season. The complex also has accommodation in motel-style double rooms and pricier hotel rooms.

Corner Murat Road & Payne Street, Exmouth
☎ *(08) 9949 1200*
Website *www.potshotresort.com*
Dorm bed *$24;* ***single/double/twin room*** *$59*
Credit cards *Amex, Diners, MC, Visa*
Reception open *7am-9pm, check in at bar till midnight*

Maintenance & cleanliness	★★½
Facilities	★★½
Atmosphere & character	★★½
Security	★
Overall rating	★★½

Winston's Backpackers
Winston's is a nice relaxed hostel with clean dormitories and green camping areas, but the TV lounge is dire and it's really the only indoor common area. However, there is a pleasant kitchen and barbecue spot outdoors that is a good place to meet other travellers and it is a nice place in the evenings when campers play music from their cars as the sun is going down.
Murat Road, Exmouth
☎ *(08) 9949 2377*
Website *www.exmouthresort.com*
Dorm bed *$27;* ***double/twin room*** *$75;* ***camping*** *$15-20 (1 person), $21-32 (2 people)*
Credit cards *Amex, Diners, MC, Visa*
Reception open *7am-7pm daily*

Maintenance & cleanliness	★★★★
Facilities	★★
Atmosphere & character	★★★
Security	★★
Overall rating	★★★

Activities

Swimming with Whalesharks
Growing up to 12m, whalesharks are the world's largest fish and mid-year (late Mar to late-Jul) they visit the Ningaloo Reef near Exmouth. **Ningaloo Dreaming** *(☎ (08) 9949 4777;* ***website*** *www.ningaloodreaming.com)* run snorkelling trips where you can snorkel with whalesharks. Trips cost $330.

Ningaloo Marine Park & Cape Range National Park

Although smaller and not as well known as the Great Barrier Reef in Queensland, the Ningaloo Reef is much closer to the shore and offers much the same attraction for divers.

The Marine Park stretches for 250km and includes 250 different species of coral and over 500 different types of fish. Diving here is fantastic, and the easy access to the reef makes snorkelling a cheaper and very popular alternative.

Lakeside is the closest snorkelling spot to Exmouth, but Turquoise Bay isn't much further and it is a lot more popular. There are strong currents at Turquoise Bay that you need to swim through to get to the reef so inexperienced swimmers should avoid snorkelling alone.

Cape Range National Park adjoins the marine park and offers an abundance of flora and fauna as well as impressive gorges. The northern entrance to the national park is 40km from Exmouth and most people base themselves in Exmouth and visit as a day trip.

Entry to the park is $10 for a car and eight passengers or $4 per person if you arrive by bus.

Coming & Going

It's best to drive here yourself, particularly if you have a 4WD as this will open up more of the park for you to explore.

If you just want to visit for a day's snorkelling at Turquoise Bay, then you can go on one of the trips that are sometimes organised by the hostels around Exmouth or you can take the **Ningaloo Reef Bus** *(☎ 1800 999 941)*. The bus operates every day Nov-Mar, but only on Mon, Tue, Fri and Sat during Apr-Oct.

The Easyrider bus also makes an excursion to Turquoise Bay and it is well worth the trip if you're travelling this way.

Pilbara

The Pilbara region is often associated with mining towns and is seldom visited by travellers. The main highway passes through the coastal region that includes the towns set up to service the mining region further inland and many travellers who are driving up the coast make a detour inland to see the incredible gorges at Karijini National Park.

Karratha

Karratha is a modern regional centre and home to the state's largest shopping

centre north of Perth. Apart from the excellent infrastructure of shops, accommodation and fuel, there's not a lot to make you want to linger in town.
If you're driving, Karratha is a sensible place to break your journey, especially if you're driving north as there is not another hostel until you get to Broome, which is 830km away.

Practical Information
Karratha Visitor Information Centre
Karratha Road, Karratha
☎ *(08) 9144 4600*
Open *Mon-Fri 8am-5.30pm, Sat-Sun 9am-4pm*

Coming & Going
Greyhound *(☎ 1300 473 946;* ***website*** *www.greyhound.com.au)* coaches stop on Welcome Street near McDonalds and go to Perth and Broome.

Accommodation
Karratha Backpackers
Karratha Backpackers has been around for a while and it really shows its age. An extreme makeover is needed to fix up this run-down hostel. Despite this Karratha Backpackers is usually all booked up – simply because it has the only dormitories in a town with an acute accommodation shortage. The common area seems like a fairly easy place to make new friends, but it is a bit shabby. The owner runs the place in his own way – once in a while he arranges fishing trips or barbecues, sometimes free of charge, sometimes not.
110 Wellard Way, Karratha
☎ *(08) 9144 4904*
Website *www.kisser.net.au/backpackers/*
Dorm bed *$22;* ***double/twin room*** *$55*
Reception open *7am-9pm daily*
🚗 TV K L

Maintenance & cleanliness	★½
Facilities	★½
Atmosphere & character	★★
Security	★★
Overall rating	★½

Port Hedland
Port Hedland is a busy port that serves the mining operations inland. It is an industrial city with little to offer the traveller although it is a good base to organise tours to Karijini National Park

There are two very distinct parts to the city – Port Hedland and South Hedland. Port Hedland is the industrial centre with a busy port. In contrast South Hedland is considered a suburb of Port Hedland and although it is a much quieter and tidier place, the centre of South Hedland actually has more shops and restaurants than Port Hedland.

During the day Port Hedland is an ugly city but at night the whole place lights up like a Christmas tree. At night you can look out to the harbour where you can watch the huge 300m-long ships come into port.

Whale watching trips depart from Port Hedland (Jul-Oct) and you can observe flatback turtles at beaches in the Port Hedland (Oct-Mar).

There are no longer any hostels in Port Hedland so you'll need to sleep in your car or just stay on the bus and keep going.

Practical Information
Port Hedland Visitor Information Centre
13 Wedge Street, Port Hedland
☎*(08) 9173 1711*
Open *8.30am-5pm daily*

Coming & Going
Integrity Coachlines *(☎ 1800 226 339;* ***website*** *www.integritycoachlines.com.au)* take the inland route to Perth and Greyhound *(☎ 1300 473 946;* ***website*** *www.greyhound.com.au)* takes the more interesting coastal route and also goes north to Broome. Buses stop at the information centre *(13 Wedge Street, Port Hedland)* and also at the South Hedland Shopping Centre.

Sights
Port Hedland Shipping Observation Lookout
Port Hedland is a major port with big ships coming into port to load up with iron ore and salt. The lookout in Town Park offers an excellent vantage point to watch the shipping activity.
Town Park, Wedge Street, Port Hedland

Tom Price

Tom Price, like nearby Paraburdoo, is a company town built by Hamersley Iron to house people working on the iron ore mines.

It has a good infrastructure for a small remote place with a good supermarket and even an airport with daily flights to Perth.

Most travellers use Tom Price as a base for exploring the spectacular Karijini National Park, which is 30 minutes outside town.

Practical Information

Tom Price Tourist Bureau

Central Road, Tom Price
☎ *(08) 9188 1112*
Website *www.tompricewa.com.au*
Open *Jan-Apr Mon-Fri 8.30am-2.30pm, Sat 9am-noon; May-Sep Mon-Fri 8.30am-5.30pm, Sat-Sun 9am-noon; Oct-Dec Mon-Fri 8.30am-2.30pm, Sat 9am-noon*

Accommodation

Tom Price Tourist Park

The backpackers' accommodation at this caravan park was set up to cater for backpackers on the Easyrider bus. Accommodation is in prefabricated units that are clean with new furnishings. Other amenities include an outdoor kitchen area and a swimming pool. It is 8km from the town centre.
Mt Nameless Road, Tom Price
☎ *(08) 9189 1515*
Dorm bed *$20*
Credit cards *MC, Visa*

Maintenance & cleanliness	★★½
Facilities	★½
Atmosphere & character	★
Security	★
Overall rating	★★

Karijini National Park

Karijini is becoming one of Western Australia's top attractions and a growing number of travellers are making the detour inland to visit the park. The national park is best known for its gorges, which include waterfalls and several beautiful secluded swimming spots.

Entry to the park is $10 for a car and eight passengers or $4 per person if you arrive by bus.

Practical Information

Karijini National Park Visitors Centre

The national park visitors' centre features excellent exhibits about the park.
Banjima Drive, Karijini National Park
☎ *(08) 9189 8121*
Website *www.calm.wa.gov.au*
Open *9am-4pm daily*

Coming & Going

Tom Price is the closest town to the park and it is a handy place to base yourself, particularly if you're driving.

Greyhound (☎ *1300 473 946;* ***website*** *www.greyhound.com.au)* travels via the coast and the closest spot to Karijini that they stop is Port Hedland. If you're not either on a tour or driving your own car, you'll need to get off the coach in Port Hedland and rent a car.

The Easyrider bus stops at Tom Price and also goes right into the national park on its Exmouth-Broome route. Travellers on Easyrider can either spend half a day in the park or stay in Tom Price and rent a car or book a tour of the park from there.

Hiking

The two main spots in Karijini are Dales Gorge and Junction Pool where the Joffre, Hancock, Red and Weano Gorges converge.

Dales Gorge is the most accessible and also the safer of the two spots and it can easily be visited in half a day.

There are a number of hiking trails in Dales Gorge that include the easy **Gorge Rim walk** *(2km, 2 hours)* which offers breathtaking views into the gorge; the **Fortescue Falls walk** *(800m, 1 hour)* descends the gorge to Fortescue Falls and the swimming spot at Fern Pool. There is also a walking trail to another swimming spot at **Circular Pool** *(800m, 2 hours)* at the other end of the gorge. You can spot a lot of wildlife including goannas and lizards on the **Dales Gorge hike** *(1½km, 3 hours)* that runs along the base of the gorge between Circular Pool and

Fortescue Falls, this is one of the most popular hiking trails in the park since it takes in two lovely swimming spots.

The area around the Joffre, Hancock, Knox, Red and Weano Gorges has more challenging hiking trails.

Easier short walks in this area include the **Joffre Lookout walk** *(100m, 10 minutes)*, which offers views of the waterfalls in the Joffre Gorge. The walk to the **Oxer and Junction Pool Lookouts** *(800m, 30 minutes)* departs from the Weano carpark and offers spectacular views into the gorge. Another good short walk goes to **Knox Lookout** *(300m, 15 minutes)* and is best in the early morning and late afternoon.

Longer walks in this area include **Knox Gorge** *(2km, 3 hours)*, **Joffre Falls** *(3km, 3 hours)*, **Handrail Pool** *(970m, 1½ hours)* and **Hancock Gorge** *(1½km, 3 hours)*.

If you enjoy hiking, there is enough in the park to keep you busy for several days.

Accommodation

Many travellers stay in Tom Price, but you can also camp in the national park for $7.50 per night. The camping sites in the national park are located near Dales, Joffre and Weano Gorges.

Kimberley Region

The Kimberley in Western Australia's far north is a dramatic area of waterfalls, gorges, beaches and rainforest. Despite its remoteness, the Kimberley is growing in popularity as a destination.

Broome

Relaxed Broome serves as the southern gateway to the Kimberley region. It is a nice little town with great hostels, a beautiful beach and an excellent outdoor cinema.

An old pearling port, Broome once supplied eighty per cent of the world's mother-of-pearl shell. In the late 19th century, its fleet of pearling luggers topped 400.

Travellers who visit in Mar-Apr or Aug-Sep may be lucky enough to see a natural phenomenon called "The Staircase to the Moon", an illusion caused by the full moon reflecting on mud flats at extreme low tide. It can be seen from the Roebuck Bay side of Broome during the king tides in those months. Other attractions include Cable Beach, 5km from the town centre.

The centre of Broome is known as Chinatown, even though there is nothing Chinese about it.

Practical Information

Broome Visitor Centre
Short Street, Broome
☎ *(08) 9192 2222*
Website *www.broomevisitorcentre.com.au*
Open *Mon-Fri 8am-5pm, Sat-Sun 9am-1pm*

INTERNET ACCESS

Galactica DMZ internet café *(Shop 4/2 Hamersley Street, Broome; ☎ (08) 9192 5897)*, next to McDonalds, has internet access including wireless for $4.50 per hour with lower prices for heavier use. There is also internet access at all of Broome's hostels.

Coming & Going

Broome is the biggest destination on the west coast between Perth and Darwin and boasts an international airport as well as frequent buses to Perth and Darwin.

AIR

Due to the long distances on the west coast, many travellers fly from Broome to Perth making the trip here relatively painless. The airport is conveniently situated near the town centre with the terminal on McPherson Road just a five-minute walk from the town centre and two of Broome's backpackers' hostels.

BUS

Greyhound *(☎ 1300 473 946;* ***website*** *www.greyhound.com.au)* coaches stop on Broome Road outside the tourist information centre. Coaches go to Darwin and Perth.

Local Transport

Broome's local bus service *(**website** www.broomebus.com.au)* consists of an hourly bus between the town centre and Cable Beach. The town bus serves most of Broome's hostels and major attractions. You'll need to take a taxi if you miss the last bus, which leaves as early as 6.10pm. Fares are $3.50 one-way, $16 for a five-ride ticket and $30 for a 10-ride ticket.

An alternative is to rent a scooter from Broome Broome *(☎ (08) 9192 2210; **website** www.broomebroome.com.au)*. In Western Australia you can ride a 50cc scooter on a car licence and Broome is just the right size to make a scooter the ideal way to get around.

Accommodation

Beaches of Broome

This brand new resort-style flashpackers hostel offers a very high standard of accommodation with spotless dorms and bathrooms. The hostel features extensive outdoor common areas including a sparkling swimming pool with a waterfall at one end. There's a TV in the bar plus a cinema-style DVD room, plus a kitchen and internet access. Beaches of Broome apparently fills up rapidly in the dry season, but unlike Broome's other hostels, it doesn't appear to be a party place as families are just as welcome as backpackers. If you're looking to relax in a resort-like environment at backpacker prices then this may be the hostel for you.

4 Sanctuary Road, Cable Beach
Town Bus
☎ (08) 9192 6665 or 1300 881 031
***Website** www.beachesofbroome.com.au*
***Dorm bed** $24-38; **double room** $100-150; prices include breakfast*
***Credit cards** MC, Visa*

Maintenance & cleanliness	★★★★★
Facilities	★★★½
Atmosphere & character	★★
Security	★★½
Overall rating	★★★★

Broome's Last Resort

What was once a great hostel has been neglected over the past few years and the general opinion among travellers is that it lives up to its name and truly is Broome's Last Resort, however it really isn't so bad when compared with many hostels elsewhere in Australia and there are signs of some work being done to improve things a bit. Although a bit shabby, it has a good atmosphere and the dorms are air-conditioned. Amenities include a kitchen (no oven), laundry, internet access plus a bar and open-air common area with a pool table and a swimming pool surrounded by palm trees. The Last Resort has a handy location and it is less than five minutes walk from the airport, the town centre and the bus station.

2 Bagot Street, Broome
☎ (08) 9193 5000 or 1800 801 918
***Website** www.broomeslastresort.com.au*
***Dorm bed** $18-25 dry season; $15-22 wet season; **double room** $65 dry season; $50 wet season; prices include breakfast*
***Credit cards** MC, Visa*
***Reception open** 7am-11pm daily*

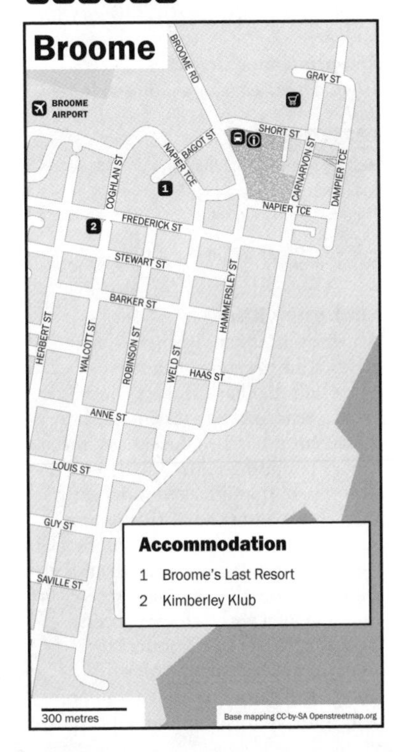

Maintenance & cleanliness	★★½
Facilities	★★★
Atmosphere & character	★★★★
Security	★½
Overall rating	★★★

Cable Beach Backpackers

The blue and orange painted Cable Beach Backpackers definitely feels like a party hostel and it is close to the beach making it a good choice in the dry season. Facilities include a spacious kitchen (no oven), a laundry and a bar with a pool table and huge TV screen plus a swimming pool surrounded by palm trees. Although handy to the beach, it is about 7km to the town centre, but the hostel runs a free shuttle bus into town.

12 Sanctuary Road, Cable Beach
Town Bus
(08) 9193 5511 or 1800 655 011
***Website** www.cablebeachbackpackers.com*
***Dorm bed** $23-27 ($22-26 HI/YHA, VIP); **double room** $70 ($65 HI/YHA, VIP)*
***Credit cards** MC, Visa; $1 credit card surcharge*
***Reception open** dry season 6.30am-10pm daily; wet season 7.30am-10pm daily*

Maintenance & cleanliness	★★½
Facilities	★★★★
Atmosphere & character	★★★★½
Security	★½
Overall rating	★★★½

Kimberley Klub

Way back in the mid-nineties, Kimberley Klub was one of the first purpose-built "flashpackers" hostels. Twelve years on it is starting to show its age but it has also developed into a more established hostel with a great atmosphere that it lacked in its early years. It is comprised of three main buildings; two accommodation blocks separated by a suspended African-style thatch gazebo plus the main reception/common area with internet access, including Wi-Fi ($6 1 hour, $10 2 hours); a kitchen (no oven); a TV lounge and games room with a pool table, table tennis and pool table plus an excellent bar with a huge projection screen TV. There's also a beach volleyball court and an excellent swimming pool. Although relatively compact, there is still room for lush tropical gardens. The rooms are air-conditioned but you have to pay $1 for three hours of air-con so you inevitably wake up in a sweat at 3am when the air-conditioning cuts out. Although not right in the centre of things, Kimberley Klub is still fairly central at about a five-minute walk from the airport terminal, the Broome Boulevard shopping centre and the town centre.

62 Frederick Street, Broome
(08) 9192 3233
***Website** www.kimberleyklub.com*
***Dorm bed** $20-28 ($18-25 HI/YHA); **double/twin room** $60-100 ($50-90 HI/YHA)*
***Credit cards** Amex, MC, Visa*
***Reception open** 6.30am-11pm daily*

Maintenance & cleanliness	★★★½
Facilities	★★★★
Atmosphere & character	★★★★★
Security	★★½
Overall rating	★★★★

Eating & Drinking

There are several affordable food places around Chinatown including the ubiquitous Eagle Boys pizza, McDonalds and Subway plus a few small local outfits like **Shady Lane Café** *(Johnny Chi Lane, Broome)*, which does excellent Barrimundi, chips and salad for $15.

The most central supermarket is the **Coles** in Paspalay Plaza in Chinatown *(corner Carnarvon and Short Streets, Broome)*. There is another branch of Coles near Town Beach and a **Woolworths** in the Broome Boulevard shopping centre *(Frederick Street, Broome)* past Kimberley Klub.

Sights

Broome Bird Observatory

The Broome Bird Observatory is a top destination for birdwatchers and it contains almost half of Australia's bird species. The best time to see shorebirds is two hours before and after high tide.

Crab Creek Road, 25km from Broome
☎ *(08) 9193 5600*
Website *www.birdsaustralia.com.au*
Admission *$5*
Open *dry season 8am-6pm daily; wet season Tue-Sun 8am-6pm*

Broome Historical Society Museum

This small museum has exhibits on the history of Broome with old photographs and displays about the pearling industry.
Lot 271 Saville Street, Broome
☎ *(08) 9192 2075*
Admission *$5*
Open *10am-1pm daily*

Cable Beach

Broome's main attraction is this pristine 22km long beach. There are several companies that offer camel rides along the beach with prices starting at $10 for a 15-minute ride.
Cable Beach Road, 5km from the town centre
🚌 *Town Bus*

Gantheaume Point

The point at the southern extremity of Cable Beach is worth visiting at low tide if you want to search for the 130 million-year-old dinosaur footprints.

Malcolm Douglas Crocodile Farm

This crocodile farm at Cable Beach gives you the opportunity to see some really big crocodiles. It is best to visit for one of the feeding tours.
Cable Beach Road, Cable Beach
🚌 *Town Bus*
☎ *(08) 9192 1489*
Website *www.malcolmdouglas.com.au*
Admission *$25 ($22.50 HI/YHA, ISIC, VIP)*
Open *Apr-Nov Mon-Fri 10am-5pm, Sat-Sun 2pm-5pm; feeding tours Wed-Sun 3pm*

Pearl Luggers

This attraction features exhibits on Broome's pearling history including a couple of restored boats. Rather than walk around at your own pace, visitors are given a tour by a pearl diver.
44 Dampier Terrace, Broome
☎ *(08) 9192 2059*
Website *www.pearlluggers.com.au*
Admission *$18.50*
Tours *Mon-Fri 11am, 2pm; Sat-Sun 11am*

Sun Pictures Outdoor Cinema

The world's oldest outdoor cinema is right in the centre of Chinatown and has a brilliant atmosphere under the stars on a balmy tropical night.
Carnarvon Street, Broome
☎ *(08) 9192 1077*
Website *www.sunpictures.com.au*
Admission *$15*

Derby

There isn't much to make you want to take the turnoff from the main highway to visit this dusty and muddy town. Derby's attractions include a prison built from a boab tree that has a girth of 14.7m and Myall's bore, a 120m-long cattle trough, which is the longest in the southern hemisphere. Derby's 11m tides are the highest in Australia.

Practical Information

Derby Visitors Centre

2 Clarendon Street, Derby
☎ *(08) 9191 1426*
Website *www.derbytourism.com.au*
Open *Jan-Mar Mon-Fri 8.30am-4.30pm, Sat 9am-noon; Apr-May Mon-Fri 8.30am-4.30pm, Sat-Sun 9am-1pm; Jun-Aug Mon-Fri 8.30am-4.30pm, Sat-Sun 9am-4pm; Sep Mon-Fri 8.30am-4.30pm, Sat-Sun 9am-1pm; Oct-Dec Mon-Fri 8.30am-4.30pm, Sat 9am-noon*

Coming & Going

Greyhound (☎ *1300 473 946;* ***website*** *www.greyhound.com.au)* coaches stop outside the visitor information centre on Clarendon Street. Greyhound goes to Broome and Darwin.

Accommodation

Derby Lodge

Derby Lodge is a brand new purpose-built hostel right across the road from the tourist information centre where the Greyhound buses stop. It

is a clean and well maintained hostel with accommodation in nice air-conditioned rooms and good common areas that include a fully-equipped kitchen and a dining area with a big flat screen TV.
15 Clarendon Street, Derby
(08) 9193 2924
***Dorm bed** $30*
***Credit cards** MC, Visa*
***Reception open** 7am-7pm daily*

Maintenance & cleanliness	★★★★★
Facilities	★★½
Atmosphere & character	★★
Security	★★
Overall rating	★★★½

Fitzroy Crossing

Fitzroy Crossing is not much more than a roadhouse, a couple of motels, a pub and a welfare office, but it's a convenient base for exploring the surrounding region that includes Geikie and Windjana Gorges.

Practical Information

Fitzroy Crossing Tourist Information Centre

Forrest Road, Fitzroy Crossing
(08) 9191 5355
***Open** Jan-Mar Mon-Fri 9am-5pm, Sat 9am-1pm; Apr-Sep 8am-5pm daily; Oct-Dec Mon-Fri 9am-5pm, Sat 9am-1pm*

Coming & Going

Greyhound (*1300 473 946; **website** www.greyhound.com.au*) coaches to Broome and Darwin stop outside the visitor information centre and also at Fitzroy Crossing Lodge.

Sights

Geikie Gorge National Park

The best way to explore the gorge is to take one of the cruises on the river, although there are also some good walks along the gorge and elsewhere in the national park. The gorge features some nice picnic and barbecue sites and is home to plenty of freshwater crocodiles. It is worth the visit if you're driving although it's otherwise a bit difficult to get to.
17km northeast of Fitzroy Crossing
(08) 9191 5121
***Cruises cost** $25*
***Cruises depart** Apr-Nov 8am & 3pm daily*
***Park open** Apr-Nov 6.30am-6.30pm daily; entry restricted during wet season (Dec-Mar)*

Halls Creek

The site of Western Australia's first gold rush in 1885, Halls Creek has a bit more to offer than Fitzroy Crossing, but not by much. There's not much reason to stop here except to fill the car with fuel and grab a bite to eat.

Purnululu (Bungle Bungle) National Park

Purnululu National Park is best known for the spectacular Bungle Bungles – a unique mountain range with the appearance of an upside-down egg carton. The Bungle Bungles are best experienced by a scenic flight, although this can get a little too pricey for most backpackers.

You will need a 4WD vehicle to actually explore the national park from the ground and for most people this means an even more expensive 4WD tour. Several companies in Kununurra, including Kununurra Backpackers organise 4WD tours for the Bungle Bungles. If you have access to a 4WD you can get to the trailhead of a number of hiking tracks including hikes to Cathedral Gorge, Echidna Chasm and the longer overnight hike to Piccaninny Gorge.

The park is closed during the wet season (Jan-Mar). The park entry fee is $10 per vehicle.

Kununurra

Kununurra is a fairly modern town, coming into existence in the 1960s to serve as a base for the Ord River irrigation project. The town is now a modern regional centre for the surrounding farming regions and a popular spot with travellers as a base for exploring the Bungle Bungles, Hidden Valley and Lake Argyle.

Mirima (Hidden Valley) National Park is the most accessible of the national parks – you can even walk here from the centre of town. This park offers similar features to the Bungle Bungles for a fraction of the cost. There are several short walks in this park that make it an ideal daytrip from Kununurra.

Created in the 1970s as part of the Ord River Irrigation Project, the massive Lake Argyle is worth a visit. Located 35km south of town, Lake Argyle offers cruises, canoeing and camping.

The surrounding area is very fertile and there is plenty of work on farms (Jun-Nov) and you may be able to arrange some of this through the local hostels.

Avoid swimming around here, the rivers and lakes in this region are home to saltwater crocodiles.

Practical Information

Kununurra Visitors Information Centre

Coolibah Drive, Kununurra
☎ *(08) 9168 1177*
Website *www.kununurratourism.com*
Open *Mon-Fri 9am-4pm, Sat 9am-noon*

Department of Conservation & Land Management (CALM)

Messmate Way, Kununurra
☎ *(08) 9168 2000*
Open *8am-5pm daily*

INTERNET ACCESS

The excellent Boab Bookshop Café has internet access, provided by Global Gossip so you can use your credit here, including a Wi-Fi hotspot.

Coming & Going

Kununurra is surprisingly well connected for a remote small town. Greyhound (*☎ 1300 473 946; **website** www.greyhound.com.au)* coaches to Broome and Darwin stop at the BP service station on Messmate Way.

The airport 5km north of town has direct flights on Air North (*☎ 1800 627 474; **website** www.airnorth.com.au)* to Broome, Darwin and Perth and on Skywest (*☎ 1300 660 088; **website** www.skywest.com.au)* to Broome and Perth.

Accommodation

Kimberley Court Backpackers

Kimberley Court is a centrally located hostel that has a wide range of accommodation ranging from dormitories to spacious double rooms. All the rooms are air-conditioned with en suite bathrooms. The hostel's facilities include internet access at the reception, a kitchen and an outdoor TV and barbecue area with a swimming pool. It caters mostly to travellers working in Kununurra.

2 Riverfig Avenue, Kununurra
☎ *(08) 9168 1411*
Website *www.kimberleycourt.com.au*
Dorm bed *$21-22 per night, $130-140 per week;* ***double/twin room*** *$99-149 per night*
Reception open *8am-1pm & 4pm-8pm daily*

Maintenance & cleanliness	★★
Facilities	★★★
Atmosphere & character	★★
Security	★★
Overall rating	★★½

Kimberley Croc Backpackers YHA

This is an excellent hostel with a great atmosphere and a good range of facilities that include a big kitchen with lots of utensils, but no oven; a good TV lounge; internet access, including Wi-Fi ($5 per hour); an open-air games room with another TV plus air hockey and table football plus a swimming pool and a lush garden. There is a good mix of both travellers staying long term while working in Kununurra and short term guests staying a night or two while travelling through the Kimberley. Most travellers staying just one or two nights stay in the nice new building and longer term guests stay in the older building. Accommodation in both buildings is of a high standard but the bathrooms are better in the newer building.

120 Konkerberry Drive, Kununarra
☎ *(08) 9168 2702*
Website *www.kimberleycroc.com.au*

***Dorm bed** $22 ($20 HI/YHA)*
***Credit cards** MC, Visa*
***Reception open** 6am-6pm; late check in with prior arrangement*

Maintenance & cleanliness	★★★★
Facilities	★★★
Atmosphere & character	★★★★
Security	★★½
Overall rating	★★★½

Kununurra Backpackers Adventure Centre

Kununurra Backpackers Adventure Centre is comprised of three houses that feel a bit dated and need a bit of work. It has good facilities including a nice outdoor area with an open-air TV lounge, a barbecue and swimming pool. Accommodation is in small air-conditioned dorms, but the standard isn't as good as other places in town.

24 Nutwood Crescent, Kununurra
(08) 9169 1998 or 1800 641 998
***Website** www.adventure.kimberley.net.au*
***Dorm bed** $21-23 ($20-22 HI/YHA, VIP); **double/twin room** $54 ($52 HI/YHA, VIP)*
***Credit cards** MC, Visa*
***Reception open** 7am-7pm daily*

Maintenance & cleanliness	★★
Facilities	★★½
Atmosphere & character	★★
Security	★½
Overall rating	★★

Sights

Kellys Knob

Kellys Knob offers an excellent vantage point with views of Kununurra and the surrounding area. Both hostels will drop you off near the summit so you only need to walk back down the hill.

Mirima (Hidden Valley) National Park

This small national park is only 2km from the centre of Kununurra and it offers similar features to the Bungle Bungles. Most travellers visit the park early in the morning before it gets too hot. It is a small park and two to three hours is sufficient time even if you walk every trail in the park.

Hidden Valley Road, Kununurra
***Website** www.naturebase.net*
***Admission** $10 per vehicle, free if you walk to the park*

Map Credits

Maps are created by BUG Travel Publishing Pty Ltd using data and base maps supplied by the following organisations: Department of Lands (NSW); Department of Infrastructure, Planning and Environment (NT); Department of Natural Resources & Water (QLD); Openstreetmap.org (ACT, NSW, QLD, TAS & WA); RAA (SA & NT) and TUMAS (VIC).

Full map acknowledgements are as follows:

The following map uses base mapping reproduced with permission of the Department of Lands; Panorama Avenue, Bathurst NSW 2795 (website www.lands.nsw.gov.au): Byron Bay (NSW).

The following maps use base mapping reproduced with permission of the Department of Infrastructure, Planning and Environment; Darwin NT 0801 (website www.ipe.nt.gov.au): Alice Springs (NT) and Katherine (NT).

The following maps use base mapping reproduced with permission of Department of Natural Resources and Water, Brisbane QLD 4000 (website www.nrm.qld.gov.au): Bundaberg (QLD), Hervey Bay (QLD) and Townsville (QLD).

Based on or contains data provided by the State of Queensland (Department of Natural Resources and Water) 2008. In consideration of the State permitting use of this data you acknowledge and agree that the State gives no warranty in relation to the data (including accuracy, reliability, completeness, currency or suitability) and accepts no liability (including without limitation, liability in negligence) for any loss, damage or costs (including consequential damage) relating to any use of the data. Data must not be used for direct marketing or be used in breach of the privacy laws.

The following maps use base mapping reproduced with permission of the Royal Automobile Association of SA, Adelaide (website www.raa.com.au): Adelaide (SA), Coober Pedy (SA) and Darwin (NT).

The following maps were produced using TUMAUS (website www.TUMAUS.com.au): Great Ocean Road (VIC), Lorne (VIC), Melbourne (VIC), Mildura (VIC), Port Campbell (VIC) and St Kilda (VIC).

The following maps are produced under a CC-by-SA 2.0 licence using data and base maps from the Openstreetmap.org project: Canberra (ACT), Bondi (NSW), Sydney (NSW), Coogee (NSW), Darlinghurst, Woolloomooloo & Kings Cross (NSW), Glebe (NSW), Manly (NSW), Newcastle (NSW), Port Macquarie (NSW), Coffs Harbour (NSW), Brisbane (QLD), Surfers Paradise (QLD), Maroochydore (QLD), Airlie Beach (QLD), Magnetic Island (QLD), Cairns (QLD), Hobart (TAS), Launceston (TAS), Devonport (TAS), Perth (WA), Fremantle (WA) and Broome (WA).

More information on the Openstreetmap.org CC-by-SA 2.0 licence can be found here: http://creativecommons.org/licenses/by-sa/2.0/. More information on the Openstreetmap project can be found at www.openstreetmap.org .

The Glenelg Tram Line (SA) map is created by BUG Travel Publishing Pty Ltd.

The Australia map and individual state maps are based on data and base maps supplied by TUMAUS with additional information supplied by various tourist offices.

The Melbourne Tram Network map in the colour map section is © State of Victoria, 2008

The Sydney Rail Network map in the colour map section is reproduced with permission of RailCorp.

The Sydney Ferries Network map in the colour map section is © Copyright Sydney Ferries December 2007

The Perth Rail Network map in the colour map section is CC-by-SA David Arthur/Wikipedia

Index

WATERPROOF, DURABLE
TEAR-RESISTANT MAPS
EXPLORE
AUSTRALIA
AUSTRALIA
ROAD MAP

WATERPROOF, DURABLE
TEAR-RESISTANT MAPS
EXPLORE
AUSTRALIA
MELBOURNE
ROAD MAP

WATERPROOF, DURABLE
TEAR-RESISTANT MAPS
EXPLORE
AUSTRALIA
SYDNEY
ROAD MAP

Holiday Map
EXPLORE
AUSTRALIA
VICTORIA'S
Great
Ocean Road

Holiday Map
EXPLORE
AUSTRALIA
NEW SOUTH WALES
North Coast

WATERPROOF, DURABLE
TEAR-RESISTANT MAPS
EXPLORE
AUSTRALIA
QUEENSLAND
ROAD MAP

EXPLORE
AUSTRALIA
Melbourne
CITY & SURROUNDS
POCKET MAP GUIDE

EXPLORE
AUSTRALIA
Sydney
CITY & SURROUNDS
POCKET MAP GUIDE